Red Hat Linux

THIRD EDITION

David Pitts, Bill Ball

SAMS

Red Hat Linux Unleashed, Third Edition

International Standard Book Number: 0-672-31410-x

Library of Congress Catalog Card Number: 98-89271

Printed in the United States of America

First Printing: December, 1998

00 99 7 6 5

Trademarks

All terms mentioned in this book that are known to be trademarks or service marks have been appropriately capitalized. Sams Publishing cannot attest to the accuracy of this information. Use of a term in this book should not be regarded as affecting the validity of any trademark or service mark. UNIX is a registered trademark of The Open Group.

Warning and Disclaimer

Every effort has been made to make this book as complete and as accurate as possible, but no warranty or fitness is implied. The information provided is on an "as is" basis. The authors and the publisher shall have neither liability or responsibility to any person or entity with respect to any loss or damages arising from the information contained in this book.

Executive Editor
Jeff Koch

Acquisitions Editor
Jane Brownlow

Development Editors
Mark Cierzniak
Tom Dinse

Project Editor
Kevin Laseau

Copy Editors
Malinda McCain
Kris Simmons

Indexer
Christine Nelsen
Johnna Vanhoose

Proofreader
Benjamin Berg

Interior Design
Gary Adair

Cover Design
Aren Howell

Technical Editors
Eric Richardson
Steve Shah
Nalneesh Gaur
Matt Coffey

Layout Technicians
Ayanna Lacey
Heather Hiatt Miller
Amy Parker

Contents at a Glance

Table of Contents

PART IV AUTOMATION, PROGRAMMING, AND SYSTEM MODIFICATION 561

About the Lead Authors

David Pitts is a senior consultant with BEST Consulting, one of the premier consulting firms west of the Mississippi, with over 1,400 highly trained consultants. Currently on assignment with The Boeing Company, David is an author, system administrator, programmer, instructor, and Web developer. David can be reached at dpitts@mk.net. He lives in Everett, Washington, with the love of his life, Dana. Everett, he explains, is like living on a postcard, with the Puget Sound ten minutes to the west and the year-round snow-capped Cascade Mountains to the east. David's favorite quote comes from Saint Francis of Assisi, "Preach the Gospel, and, if necessary, use words."

Bill Ball, author of *Sams Teach Yourself Linux in 24 Hours* and Que's *Using Linux*, is a technical writer, editor, and magazine journalist. A reformed Macophile, he broke down and bought a PC after using Apple computers for nearly 10 years. Instead of joining the Dark Side, he started using Linux! He has published more than a dozen articles in magazines such as *Computer Shopper* and *MacTech Magazine* and first started editing books for Que in 1986. He is forever grateful to Dale Puckett for lessons in how to use casts and code tight loops in 6800 assembler—and to William Boatman for lessons in how to cast and throw tight loops on the stream. An avid fly fisherman, Bill builds bamboo fly rods and fishes on the nearby Potomac River. He lives in the Shirlington area of Arlington County, Virginia.

About the Contributing Authors

Chris Byers is currently a consultant for a major credit card company. As a consultant and former disaster recovery specialist, he has many years of experience in the wide world of UNIX. He lives in South Jersey with his wife, his son (plus another child on the way), and their cat, Amelia. He can be reached at southst@voicenet.com.

David B. Horvath, CCP, is a Senior Consultant in the Philadelphia, Pennsylvania, area. He has been a consultant for over 14 years and is also a part-time Adjunct Professor at local colleges, teaching topics that include C Programming, UNIX, and Database Techniques. He is currently pursuing an M.S. degree in Dynamics of Organization at the University of Pennsylvania (should receive the degree on December 22, 1998). David has provided seminars and workshops to professional societies and corporations on an international basis. He is the author of *UNIX for the Mainframer* (Prentice-Hall/PTR) and contributing author to *UNIX Unleashed Second Edition: System Administration Edition* and *Internet Edition* volumes (with cover credit), *Red Hat Linux Unleashed, Second Edition*, and *Using UNIX Second Edition* (Que). He has also written numerous magazine articles. When not at the keyboard, he can be found working in the garden or soaking in the hot tub. He has been married for over 11 years and has several dogs and cats. David can be reached at unx3@cobs.com for questions related to this book. No Spam please!

Tim Parker is a consultant and technical writer based in Ottawa, Canada. He is Technical Editor for *SCO World Magazine* and Contributing Editor for *UNIX Review*, *Advanced Systems Magazine*, and *Canadian Computer Reseller*. He has written more than 800 feature articles and two dozen books, including *Linux Unleashed, Third Edition*.

Steve Shah is a systems/network administrator at the Center for Environmental Research and Technology at the University of California, Riverside. In a parallel life he does research in the area of network bandwidth control algorithms and is hoping he can contribute his thesis back into Linux. Sadly, this leaves little time for his better half and personal cheerleader, Heidi, but he is adamant about rectifying the situation as soon as he gets his master's degree next year. Steve is also a contributing author of *Unix Unleashed, System Administrator's Edition* and *Red Hat Linux Unleashed, Second Edition*.

Jack Tackett, Jr., is the Manager of System Operations for Nortel's Information Network, based in Research Triangle Park, North Carolina. He oversees the daily administration of over 50 Linux servers for customers across North America. Jack has developed software on both UNIX and Windows platforms and has ported software from one system to the other. He has also been a system administrator for a variety of operating systems, from Unisys mainframes to UNIX and Windows NT. Jack's books include the best-selling *Special Edition Using Linux* (1st, 2nd, 3rd, and 4th editions) as well as *Using Visual C++* and *The Visual C++ Construction Kit*.

Sriranga Veeraraghavan has been working at Cisco Systems, Inc., in the area of Network Management since 1996. He enjoys developing software in C/C++, Java, Perl, and Shell on Linux and Solaris. He has contributed to several UNIX and Linux books. He takes pleasure in listening to classical music, reading classical literature, mountain biking, and playing Marathon on the home network with his brother, Srivathsa. Sriranga earned a bachelor's degree in Engineering from the University of California at Berkeley in 1997 and is currently working toward a master's degree at Stanford University. He can be reached at ranga@soda.berkeley.edu.

Daniel J. Wilson is a Senior Principal Consultant with Oracle Corporation and works out of the Indianapolis, Indiana, practice. His background includes UNIX systems administration and Oracle database administration in both SMP and clustered environments. He has extensive experience in UNIX systems and Oracle database performance tuning and troubleshooting. He has programmed in C, C++, COBOL, and SQL. Daniel graduated from Ball State University in Muncie, Indiana, in 1984. He currently resides just outside of Indianapolis with his wife Angela and their two children, Timothy and Emily. Many thanks to Linda Billingsley at PRC and to Ron James at Hewlett-Packard for providing the best support ever!

About the Technical Editors

Eric C Richardson (eric@rconsult.com) is a professional Webmaster with nine years Internet experience and over two decades of work with computers under his belt. He has worked as a college instructor, writer, consultant, and author in the Internet field. He currently oversees the Web sites and related extranet for Nabisco Incorporated. He is a member of the World Organization of Webmasters and is a member of their national accreditation board. He enjoys spending time with his wife Stacie and their daughter, Katie. He has written or co-authored eight books on the Internet and has worked as editor on nearly a dozen.

Nalneesh Gaur works for TimeBridge Technologies as a systems engineer. His current work involves UNIX/Windows NT integration, Web design, and Internet/intranet security.

Dedication

This book is dedicated to TM3 and Associates. Thanks, guys (non-gender)!! – David

To my lovely fiancée Cathy and our 22-pound Felis catus, Nat (don't worry, you're a family member, not an emergency food resource!) – Bill

Acknowledgments

To Sylvia Baldwin, Darren Church, Teri Federigi, Jim Farris, Dave Fisher, Dave Hawkins, Rick Jacobson, Don Jantz, Gary Jordan, Bob Jarosky, Susan Lim, Cindy McMillan, Mary Nazarenus, Ed Perez, Bob Poirrier, Lara Ringness, Mike Teutschman, Daynard Schmidt, and Vaughn Blumenthal, so long and thanks for all the fish! To my wife and best friend, I cannot adequately express in words the depths of my love for you. – David Pitts

Thanks are due to the following people at Macmillan: Theresa Ball, Lynette Quinn, Jeff Koch, and Jane Brownlow. My development editor, Mark Cierzniak, will be sorely missed (good luck in your new job, Mark!). Thanks are also due to the kind people at Red Hat Software, Inc.: Ed Bailey for tech help and Melissa London for software. Also, a big vote of thanks to The XFree86 Project, Inc.—these folks and their supporters provide a great graphical interface to the best operating system in the world. – Bill Ball

Tell Us What You Think!

As the reader of this book, *you* are our most important critic and commentator. We value your opinion and want to know what we're doing right, what we could do better, what areas you'd like to see us publish in, and any other words of wisdom you're willing to pass our way.

As the Executive Editor for the Operating Systems team at Macmillan Computer Publishing, I welcome your comments. You can fax, email, or write me directly to let me know what you did or didn't like about this book—as well as what we can do to make our books stronger.

Please note that I cannot help you with technical problems related to the topic of this book, and that due to the high volume of mail I receive, I might not be able to reply to every message.

When you write, please be sure to include this book's title and author as well as your name and phone or fax number. I will carefully review your comments and share them with the author and editors who worked on the book.

Fax: 317-581-4663

Email: `opsys@mcp.com`

Mail: Jeff Koch
Operating Systems
Macmillan Computer Publishing
201 West 103rd Street
Indianapolis, IN 46290 USA

Introduction

I don't know how many times I have been asked what Red Hat is. When I say that it is a distribution of Linux, people tend to know what I am talking about. (At least the people I hang around with do!) The follow-up question is usually something like, "Okay, if it is a distribution of Linux, why should I use it, and not Linux itself?" This introduction should start to answer that question. Red Hat also answers the question on its Web page (`http://www.redhat.com`), which is summarized in this introduction.

Linux is a full-fledged operating system. It provides full multitasking in a multiuser environment. It gives a high quality of software for a cost far lower than other commercial versions of UNIX. Red Hat has opted to take Linux a step further.

Red Hat Software is a computer software development company that sells products and provides services related to Linux. Red Hat's mission is to "provide professional tools to computing professionals." Red Hat provides these professional tools by doing the following:

- Building tools, which Red Hat releases as freely redistributable software available for unrestricted download off of thousands of sites on the Internet
- Publishing books and software applications
- Manufacturing shrink-wrapped software, versions of the Linux OS, making Linux accessible to the broadest possible range of computer users
- Providing technical support

Red Hat's customer-oriented business focus forces it to recognize that the primary benefits of the Linux OS are not any of the particular advanced and reliable features for which it is famous. The primary benefit is the availability of complete source code and its "freely distributable" GPL license. This gives any user the ability to modify the technology to his or her needs and to contribute to the on-going development of the technology to the benefit of all the users, providing benefits such as security and reliability that commercially restricted, binary-only operating systems simply cannot match.

Linux, like UNIX itself, is a very modular operating system. The skills required to select, compile, link, and install the various components that are needed for a complete Linux OS are beyond the experience of most people who might want to use Linux. The various Linux distributions go a long way towards solving this for the average Linux user, but most don't address the problem of how to upgrade your Linux system once you get it successfully installed. Most users found it easier to delete their whole Linux system and reinstall from scratch when they needed to upgrade.

The Red Hat distribution makes Linux easier to install and maintain by providing the user with advanced package management, graphical (point and click!) system installation and control, and system administration tools.

Probably the best feature of Linux, the GNU utilities in general, and Red Hat Linux in particular is that they are distributable under the terms of the GNU Public License (GPL). This feature has allowed research institutions, universities, commercial enterprises, and hackers to develop and use Red Hat Linux and related technologies cooperatively without fear that their work would someday be controlled and restricted by a commercial vendor.

The huge development effort and wide distribution of the Linux OS will ensure that it takes its place as a real, viable, and significant alternative to commercially restricted operating systems. The open development model, availability of source, and lack of license restrictions are features of the Linux OS that commercial OS developers simply cannot offer. Software development groups that need this model include groups from government-affiliated research organizations, to academic research and teaching projects, to commercial software application developers.

The recent rapid increase in new applications becoming available for Linux and the rapidly growing user base of these technologies are causing even the largest computer industry organizations to take Linux seriously. Even Datapro (a McGraw-Hill Company) in its recent 1996 survey of the UNIX industry concluded that, "Programmers are taking a hard look at the viability of Linux on production platforms now that Linux costs less than Microsoft and has the added benefits of UNIX, such as great performance, inherent power tool sets, and communication capabilities."

It was said once that over half of the Web servers used around the world are run on Red Hat Linux. Although I cannot deny or substantiate this claim, it does show how rapidly Red Hat is taking on the commercial operating systems and succeeding. With the purchase of this book, you are taking the first step necessary to take back control of your computing system from the corporate giants. There is an exciting future for Linux, and we are glad that you are now a part of it!

Conventions Used in this Book

The following conventions are used in this book:

- Code lines, commands, statements, variables, and any text you type or see on the screen appears in a `computer` typeface.
- Placeholders in syntax descriptions appear in an *`italic computer`* typeface. Replace the placeholder with the actual filename, parameter, or whatever element it represents.

- *Italics* highlight technical terms when they first appear in the text and are being defined.
- A special icon ➥ is used before a line of code that is really a continuation of the preceding line. Sometimes a line of code is too long to fit as a single line in the book, given the book's limited width. If you see ➥ before a line of code, remember that you should interpret that "line" as part of the line immediately before it.

Introduction and Installation of Red Hat Linux

PART I

IN THIS PART

CHAPTER

Introduction to Red Hat Linux and UNIX

by David Pitts

In This Chapter

UNIX (not to be confused, as Dilbert's boss once did, with a eunuch) is one of the most popular operating systems in the world. UNIX is a trademark of The Open Group, but was originally developed by Ken Thompson, Dennis Ritchie, and others at AT&T. UNIX is a *real* operating system. A real operating system has, as a minimum, two qualifications: More than one person can access the computer at the same time and, while doing so, each person can run multiple applications, making it a *multiuser* and *multitasking* operating system. UNIX was originally designed to be such a multitasking system back in the 1970s, running on mainframes and minicomputers.

With UNIX, each user logs in using a login name. Optionally (and highly recommended), the user must also supply a password. The password ensures that the person logging on with the user login name is really who she claims to be. Users don't just log in to any no-name computer, either. Each computer has a "personality," if you will, which, at a minimum, is a hostname (mine is Lolly). If the computer is attached to a network, it has several other identifying items, including, but not limited to, a domain name and an IP address.

UNIX will run on just about every platform made. Many vendors purchased the source code and have developed their own versions. The various vendors (IBM, Hewlett-Packard, Sun, and so on) have added special touches over the years, but they are not the only ones to further modify UNIX. When UNIX was first developed, the source code was given out freely to colleges and universities. Two schools, the University of California at Berkeley and the Massachusetts Institute of Technology, have been on the front edge of development since the beginning.

As you can imagine, with this wide-ranging distribution, UNIX development went haywire. People all over the globe began to develop tools for UNIX. Unfortunately, there was no coordination to guide all the development, resulting in a lot of differentiation between the various versions of UNIX. Finally, standards started to appear. For UNIX, many of the standards fall under the IEEE POSIX.1 standard.

The downside of UNIX is that it is big. It is also expensive, especially for a PC version. This is where Linux comes in. Linux, as explained in a little more detail later in this chapter, was designed to be small, fast, and inexpensive. So far, the designers have succeeded.

Linux was originally created by Linus Torvalds of the University of Helsinki in Finland. Linus based Linux on a small PC-based implementation of UNIX called *minix*. Near the end of 1991, Linux was first made public. In November of that same year, version 0.10 was released. A month later, in December, version 0.11 was released. Linus made the source code freely available and encouraged others to develop it further. They did. Linux continues to be developed today by a world-wide team, led by Linus, over the Internet.

The current stable version of Linux is version 2.0. Linux uses no code from AT&T or any other proprietary source. Much of the software developed for Linux is developed by the Free Software Foundation's GNU project. Linux, therefore, is very inexpensive; as a matter of fact, it is free (but not cheap).

Advantages of Linux

So, why would you choose Linux over UNIX? As already mentioned, Linux is free. Like UNIX, it is very powerful and is a real operating system. Also, it is fairly small compared to other UNIX operating systems. Many UNIX operating systems require 500MB or more, whereas Linux can be run on as little as 150MB of space and can run on as little as 2MB of RAM. Realistically, though, you will want to have room for development tools, data, and so on, which can take up 250MB or more, and your RAM should be 12–16MB (although the more, the merrier!). Here's what you get in exchange for that valuable space:

- Full multitasking—Multiple tasks can be accomplished, and multiple devices can be accessed at the same time.
- Virtual memory—Linux can use a portion of your hard drive as virtual memory, which increases the efficiency of your system by keeping active processes in RAM and placing less frequently used or inactive portions of memory on disk. Virtual memory also utilizes all your system's memory and doesn't allow memory segmentation to occur.
- The X Window System—The X Window System is a graphics system for UNIX machines. This powerful interface supports many applications and is the standard interface for the industry.
- Built-in networking support—Linux uses standard TCP/IP protocols, including Network File System (NFS) and Network Information Service (NIS, formerly known as YP). By connecting your system with an ethernet card or over a modem to another system, you can access the Internet.
- Shared libraries—Each application, instead of keeping its own copy of software, shares a common library of subroutines it can call at runtime. This saves a lot of hard drive space on your system.
- Compatibility with the IEEE POSIX.1 standard—Because of this compatibility, Linux supports many of the standards set forth for all UNIX systems.
- Nonproprietary source code—The Linux kernel uses no code from AT&T or any other proprietary source. Other organizations, such as commercial companies, the GNU project, hackers, and programmers from all over the world have developed software for Linux.

- Lower cost than most other UNIX systems and UNIX clones—If you have the patience and the time, you can freely download Linux off the Internet. Many books also come with a free copy (this book includes it on CD-ROM).
- GNU software support—Linux can run a wide range of free software available through the GNU project. This software includes everything from application development (GNU C and GNU C++) to system administration (`gawk`, `groff`, and so on) and even games (for example, GNU Chess, GnuGo, NetHack).

At this point, the question is usually asked, "Okay, if Linux is so great, what is this Red Hat version, and why should I get it?" Well, I am glad you asked. Here are several reasons to use Red Hat Linux:

- It is based on Linux 2.0*x*—The current version of Red Hat (v. 5.2) is based on version 2.0*x* of the Linux kernel. This means it comes at the same low cost as Linux—free! Anyone can use FTP to download Red Hat from the Internet and install it on his system. (This also means that the entire list of Linux's attributes applies to the Red Hat version.)
- Red Hat Package Manager is included—For the same low cost (free), you get Red Hat Package Manager (RPM). This means that after you load Red Hat, you'll never have to load it again. The RPM is a sophisticated tool that includes intelligent file-handling across package upgrades, shared file-handling, documentation searching support, and package installation via FTP. You can install, uninstall, query, verify, and upgrade individual RPM packages.
- Good, clean copies—Red Hat has a commitment to providing, as the company puts it, "pristine sources." The RPM source packages include clean, untouched sources, as well as patches and a control file, which define the building and packaging process. This enables you to work with other members of the Linux development community easily and effectively by clearly separating and documenting the code that comes from the Linux development community from any modifications required by Red Hat.
- Disk Druid—Disk Druid, new for version 5 of Red Hat, is Red Hat's disk management utility. In particular, Disk Druid enables you to add and delete partitions through a GUI interface.
- Security—Red Hat leads the industry in providing the most up-to-date security features. In addition, the company strives to provide the latest versions of software, and succeeds.
- Documentation—Red Hat provides more than 250 pages of installation and configuration information that can be downloaded via FTP or viewed from the Red Hat

site. Complete coverage of the Control Panel tools, including the network, user/group, and printer tools, is included.

- Standards—Red Hat tracks both UNIX and Linux standards. Red Hat conforms to the Linux filesystem standard (FSSTND).
- Testing—Red Hat depends on the open development model Linus started with. Thousands of people working around the world are testing applications and providing solutions for today's business and personal needs.

As you can see, Red Hat goes beyond the normal Linux system by providing tools, documentation, and standardization.

Copyright and Warranty

Red Hat Linux is copyrighted under the GNU General Public License. This section doesn't include the entire license, but it does highlight a few items. Basically, the license provides three things:

1. The original author retains the copyright.
2. Others can do with the software what they wish, including modifying it, basing other programs on it, and redistributing or reselling it. The software can even be sold for a profit. The source code must accompany the program as well.
3. The copyright cannot be restricted down the line. This means that if you sell a product for one dollar, the person you sold it to can change it in any way (or not even change it at all) and sell it to a second person for $10—or give it away at no charge to a thousand people.

Why have such unique licensing? The original authors of Linux software didn't intend to make money from the software. It was intended to be freely available to everyone, without warranty. That is correct; there is no warranty. Does this mean you are left out in the cold when you have problems? Of course it doesn't. Numerous resources, including this book, newsgroups, and the Web, are available to assist you. What the no-warranty provision does do, though, is provide the programmers the ability to release software at no cost without the fear of liability. Granted, this lack of liability is a two-edged sword, but it is the simplest method for providing freely available software.

Where to Get Red Hat Linux

Try looking on the CD-ROM that came with this book—Red Hat Linux is there. You can also get Red Hat from the Internet by pointing your browser to `http://www.redhat.com/products/software.html`, where not only will you find Red

Hat for each of the three supported platforms (Intel, Alpha, and SPARC), but also upgrades, updates, answers to frequently asked questions, mailing lists, and much, much more. You can call Red Hat at (888) RED-HAT1 and order products, as well.

Because you already have a copy of Red Hat Linux (from the CD-ROM in the back of this book), you might just need a location where you can get updates, tips, how-to's, and errata. The most timely source for this information is on the Web. Just point the old Netscape browser to `www.redhat.com/support/docs` and find a plethora of information.

System Requirements

Red Hat keeps a listing of the system requirements and supported hardware for the three platforms—Intel, Alpha, and SPARC—on which Linux will run. These lists are presented in this section. As with anything, these lists change. If the particular hardware you have is not listed, check Red Hat's Web page (`http://www.redhat.com/support/docs/hardware.html`) to see if it has been listed there.

System Requirements—Intel

According to Red Hat, these are the system requirements for running Red Hat Linux on an Intel platform:

- Intel 386 or greater, through Pentium Pro and Pentium II
- 40MB of hard drive space in character mode, or 100MB with X Window
- 8MB of memory (although 16 or more is recommended)
- Most video cards supported
- CD-ROM drive
- 3.5-inch disk drive
- SCSI or IDE CD-ROM drive

Plug and Play hardware is not, at the time of this writing, wholly supported. (There is some level of PnP support with the `isapnp` software.) Most Plug and Play hardware has jumpers or BIOS settings that turn off the Plug and Play support. If you turn off this support, the equipment should work with Red Hat Linux. Some Plug and Play support equipment (such as the SoundBlaster 16 PnP) doesn't have a way of physically turning off the Plug and Play option. For these pieces of hardware to work with Linux, some sort of workaround must be performed.

System Requirements—SPARC

Red Hat Linux/SPARC is known to function on the following hardware:

- sun4c architecture machines (IPC, SS1, and so on)
- sun4m architecture machines (Classic, SS5, SS10, and so on)
- bwtwo, cg3, cg6, TCX frame buffers (24 bit on the TCX)
- cg14 frame buffer (in cg3 mode)
- SCSI and ethernet on all of the preceding
- Type 4 and type 5 keyboards and mice
- External SCSI drives
- CD-ROM drives (external and internal)
- SCSI/Ether SBUS expansion cards
- Any original Sun monitor for the listed frame buffers

System Requirements—Alpha

Red Hat Linux/Alpha supports a variety of hardware based on the Alpha processor and the PCI bus. Platforms on which this release is known to work include the following:

- AlphaPC64 (Cabriolet, Aspen Telluride)
- AxpPCI33 (No name)
- EB64+ (Aspen Alpine)
- EB66 (NekoTech Mach 1)
- EB66+
- Jensen (DEC PC 150, 2000 model 300, Cullean)
- Universal Desktop Box (UDB, sometimes called Multia)
- AlphaStation 200, 250, 255, 400 (Avanti machines)
- EB164 (Aspen Avalanche, Timberline, Summit, Microway Screamer)
- Platform 2000 machines from Kinetics
- PC164 machines (Durango)
- Alcor type machines (AlphaStation 500, 600, Maverick, Brett)
- Alpha-XL
- Alpha-XLT (XL 300, XL 366)
- Mikasa-type machines (neither AlphaServer 1000 nor 1000A is supported)

All of the preceding platforms except the Jensen include an NCR 810 SCSI controller, although BusLogic PCI SCSI controllers (other than the FlashPoint), the Adaptec AHA-2940 SCSI controller, and Qlogic 1020 ISP controllers are also supported. The Jensen design uses an AHA-1740 SCSI controller and is supported.

NE2000, DE422, and DE4x5 (PCI) ethernet cards are supported. This includes the UDB's internal Ethernet hardware. Token ring support is also included in the kernels.

The X Window System should work on any machine with an S3-based video card except the Jensen machines. A server is available from `ftp://ftp.azstarnet.com/pub/linux/axp/jensen` for S3 cards. TGA servers (which work on the UDB, for example) are available on your Red Hat Linux/Alpha CD-ROM in the X11 directory. Most of the cards from Orchid and Number 9 will work. Most Diamond Stealth cards are also supported. Digital TGA cards (based on the DC21030 chip) are supported in 8-bit mode, and an X server for Mach64 cards is also provided.

The list of supported hardware is not a list set in stone—new device drivers are constantly being revised. To find the most up-to-date listing of supported hardware, check Red Hat's hardware URL: `http://www.redhat.com/support/docs/hardware.html`.

Summary

UNIX, as a real operating system, is a viable solution to many of the business needs of today. It has been estimated that more than half of the Web servers currently on the Internet are actually Red Hat Linux systems running Apache. Although I cannot confirm or deny that number, I do know that Red Hat Linux, with its support infrastructure, its multiplatform usability, and its reliability, is the choice of many system administrators trying to work on real-world problems and come up with real-world solutions. To quote Mike Kropinack of MK Computer Associates (`http://www.mk.net`), "Linux is an awesome system, be it Red Hat, Slackware, or whatever. I'd choose it over Microsoft or Novell any day because in over two years of using it, I've never seen it crash in any of our production servers."

Installation of Your Red Hat System

by David Pitts

In This Chapter

One of the obvious differences between Red Hat Linux and other versions of Linux is the ease with which Red Hat can be installed. The process is quite straightforward and automated by the Red Hat installation program. The installation program can handle many system configurations and problems nicely, so most problems are taken care of for you.

Before looking at the methods used to install the operating system, you should understand the hardware on which the operating system will be installed. After examining the hardware, the rest of this chapter guides you, step by step, through the installation process, breaking it down to show some of the differences among the four basic methods of installation. This chapter briefly presents the installation of LILO (Linux Loader), but leaves many of those details to Chapter 3, "LILO."

Be Prepared, Be Very Prepared

Understanding the hardware is essential for a successful installation of Red Hat Linux, so take a moment now to familiarize yourself with your hardware. Be prepared to answer the following questions:

1. How many hard drives do you have?
2. What size is each hard drive?
3. If you have more than one hard drive, which is the primary one?
4. How much RAM do you have?
5. If you have a CD-ROM, what type of interface do you have? If it is not a SCSI or an IDE CD-ROM, who made it and what model is it?
6. Do you have a SCSI adapter? If so, who made it and what model is it?
7. What type of mouse do you have?
8. How many buttons are on the mouse?
9. If you have a serial mouse, what COM port is it connected to?
10. What is the make and model of your video card? How much video RAM do you have?
11. What kind of monitor do you have (make and model)?
12. What is the allowable range of horizontal and vertical refresh rates for your monitor?
13. Will you be connecting to a network? If so, what will the following be?
    a. Your IP address
    b. Your netmask

c. Your gateway address
d. Your Domain Name Server's IP address
e. Your domain name
f. Your hostname (I would suggest a hostname even if you were not connected to a network, because it helps give your computer some personality.)
g. Your type of network card

14. Will you be running other operating systems on the same machine?
15. If so, which ones? OS/2? Windows 95? Windows NT?

NOTE

If you are running OS/2, you must create your disk partitions with the OS/2 partitioning software; otherwise, OS/2 might not recognize the disk partitions. During the installation, do not create any new partitions, but do use the Linux `fdisk` to set the proper partition types for your Linux partitions.

16. Will you be using LILO?

After you have answered these questions, the rest of the installation is fairly easy. The entire process is menu-driven, which means you don't have to remember all the configuration information you have to remember for other Linuxes you might want to install.

Installing Red Hat Linux

The installation or upgrade of Red Hat Linux can be done through any of several methods. Depending on which method you use, you need either one or two formatted, high-density (1.44MB), 3.5-inch disks.

Installing from a PCM-CIA CD-ROM or via a PCM-CIA network adapter, installing via FTP, or installing from a hard drive or from an SMB shared drive require a supplemental disk. For all of these installations, you also need a startup disk.

Creating the Startup and Supplemental Disks

Before you make the startup and supplemental disks, label the disks so you will know which is which. The process for making the two disks differs in only one way: When the program asks for the filename, you enter `boot.img` for the startup disk and `supp.img` for the supplemental disk. To create the floppy disks under MS-DOS, you need to use the following commands (assuming your CD-ROM is drive D):

```
d:
cd \images
\dosutils\rawrite.exe
```

`rawrite` asks for the filename of the disk image. Enter **`boot.img`**. Insert a floppy disk into drive A. You are asked for a disk to write to. Enter **`a:`** and label the disk **`Red Hat boot disk`**. Run `rawrite` again, enter **`supp.img`**, insert another disk, and type **`a:`**. Label this disk **`Red Hat supplemental disk`**.

To create the disks under Linux, you can use the `dd` utility. Mount the Red Hat Linux CD-ROM, insert a floppy disk in the drive (do not mount it), and change directories (`cd`) to the images directory on the CD-ROM. Use this command to create the startup disk:

```
dd if=boot.img of=/dev/fd0 bs=1440k
```

To make the supplemental disk, use the following command:

```
dd if=supp.img of=/dev/fd0 bs=1440k
```

Installing Without Using a Startup Disk

If you have MS-DOS on your computer, you can install without using a startup disk. The Red Hat installation program can be started by using these commands:

```
d:
cd \dosutils
autoboot.bat
```

Virtual Consoles

Red Hat's installation goes beyond just a simple sequence of dialog boxes. In fact, while installing, you can look at different diagnostic messages during the installation process. You can actually switch among five different virtual consoles, which can be helpful if you encounter problems during installation. Table 2.1 shows the five consoles, the key sequence to switch to each console, and the purpose of that particular console.

TABLE 2.1 VIRTUAL CONSOLE INFORMATION

Console	*Keystroke*	*Purpose*
1	Alt+F1	Installation dialog
2	Alt+F2	Shell prompt
3	Alt+F3	Install log (messages from the install program)

Console	*Keystroke*	*Purpose*
4	Alt+F4	System log (messages from the kernel and other system programs)
5	Alt+F5	Other messages

Most of the installation time will be spent in console 1, working through the dialog boxes.

Dialog Boxes

The dialog boxes consist of a simple question or statement. From this information, you choose one or more responses. To choose these responses, it is necessary to navigate the boxes. In most dialog boxes, you'll find a cursor or highlight you can move by using the arrow keys. You can also use the Tab key to go to the next section and the Alt+Tab key combination to back up to the previous section. The bottom of each dialog box indicates which movement keys are valid for that particular box.

In addition to moving the cursor, you need to make selections. You'll be selecting two things: a button, such as an OK button, and an item from a list. If you're selecting a button, use the spacebar to "push" the button. Of course, a second push of the button resets it to its original setting. To select a single item, you can press the Enter key. To select one or more items from a list, use the spacebar. Again, a second push of the spacebar deselects a selected item.

Press the F12 button to accept the current values and proceed to the next dialog. In most cases, this is the same as clicking the OK button.

CAUTION

Do not press random keys during installation. Unpredictable results might occur if you do.

Step-by-Step Installation

This next section takes a step-by-step look at the installation process.

Starting

If you do not choose to use the autoboot program and you start the installation directly off the CD-ROM, you have to start with the startup disk.

Insert the startup disk you created into the A drive and restart the computer. At the `boot:` prompt, press Enter to continue.

You can load the Red Hat Linux installation program and begin the installation process from the `boot:` prompt. In most cases, the best way to get started is to simply press the Enter key.

You can pass a number of parameters to the Linux kernel at startup time. These do not include parameters for devices such as CD-ROM drives or ethernet cards.

Certain hardware configurations sometimes have trouble with the automatic hardware detection during the installation. Although this is unusual, it does happen occasionally. If you experience problems during the installation, restart the installation using the Expert mode.

Expert Mode

The default method of installing Red Hat Linux uses autoprobing to automatically detect the hardware in your system. Although most systems can be autoprobed without difficulties, there can be problems in certain cases. You can overcome these problems by using Expert mode.

To start the installation using Expert mode, type **`expert`** and press Enter at the `boot:` prompt.

While in Expert mode, you have complete control over the installation process. You are also able to enter optional module parameters while in Expert mode.

NOTE

This chapter does not cover Expert mode installation.

Rescue Mode

The Red Hat installation program has undergone changes that enable you to create a custom startup disk for your specific system. This new startup disk is customized according to your system's hardware configuration. This will ensure that you will always be able to start your system, even if LILO has been overwritten by another operating system.

You may also create a startup disk after the installation process completes. To do this, consult the mkbootdisk man page. Note that the mkbootdisk package must be installed to create a startup disk after the installation.

Your startup disk is the first disk in a two-part rescue disk set. The second disk required for rescue mode must be created from the rescue.img image file, located in the images directory of the Red Hat Linux CD. To create the second disk, insert a blank floppy disk in your system's floppy drive, and type

```
dd if=rescue.img of=/dev/fd0 bs=72k
```

You can then start in Rescue mode by booting from your startup disk and typing **rescue** at the boot: prompt. Insert the disk created from rescue.img when you're prompted to do so.

Kickstart Mode

Red Hat provides a method for unattended installation of a system, using a text configuration file. To enter the kickstart mode, type **linux ks** at the boot: prompt and press Enter.

Kickstart mode works with both NFS and CD-ROM installations. New options for the kickstart file include the capability to use a wider variety of networking options, including bootp, DHCP, and static IPs.

The installation program looks in the following places for the config files:

- On the broadcast server from bootp
- On the bootp server if no other server name is broadcast
- On the startup floppy disk if you type **linux ks** and press Enter

The bootp server gives the file it looks for. If a directory is given, kickstart looks for a file in that directory with the IP of the client as the filename followed by -kickstart (for example, 172.13.128.44-kickstart). If the floppy drive argument is given, it looks for a file named ks on that floppy disk.

Kernel Parameter Options

Some kernel parameters can be specified on the command line and thus passed to the running kernel. This does not include options to modules such as ethernet cards or devices such as CD-ROM drives.

To pass an option to the kernel, use the following format:

```
linux <options>
```

If you want a different installation mode, enter it after the option(s). For example, to install on a system with 128MB of RAM, using Expert mode, type the following:

```
linux mem=128M expert
```

To pass options to modules, you need to use the Expert mode to disable PCI autoprobing. When the installation asks for the device type to which you need to pass an option or parameter, it gives you a place to type those in at that time.

Watch the startup information to ensure that the kernel detects your hardware. If it doesn't properly detect your hardware, you might need to restart and add some options at the `boot:` prompt. The following is an example:

```
boot: linux hdc=cdrom
```

If you need to enter any extra parameters here, write them down—you will need them later in the installation.

The Installation Program

After the installation program starts, it greets you with `Welcome to Red Hat Linux!` Press Enter to go to the next screen.

Next, it asks you what language you prefer to use during the installation process. The default is English, but other options include Czech, Finnish, German, Norwegian, Romanian, Serbian, and Turkish. (I don't know what happened to French or Redneck, which were a part of version 5.1.) Use the arrow keys to highlight your choice and press the Tab key to move to the OK button. Press Enter to continue using that selection.

The next dialog asks which keyboard configuration you have (see Figure 2.1). Use the Tab key to select the correct one and then press Enter.

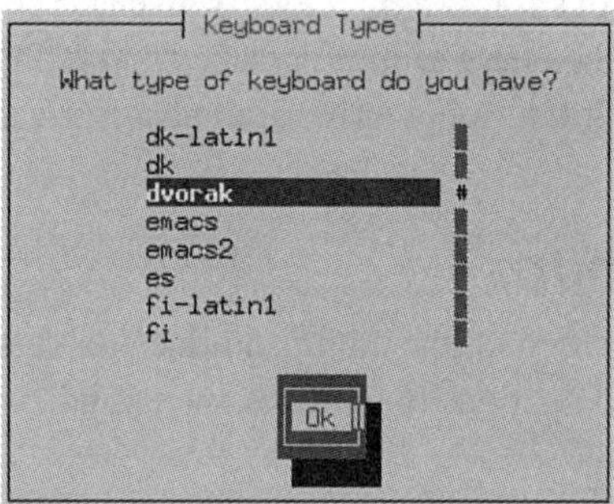

FIGURE 2.1
The Keyboard Type dialog.

The next dialog asks which type of installation you want to use (see Figure 2.2).

FIGURE 2.2
The Installation Method dialog.

Most likely you will choose CD-ROM because that is what is included with this book. Before looking at the installation process for a CD-ROM, look at the other ways of installing Red Hat.

Selecting an Installation Method

There are five basic methods of installing Red Hat Linux. The following is a summary of the methods:

- Local CD-ROM—If you have a supported CD-ROM, a Red Hat Linux CD, and a startup disk, you can install Red Hat Linux with your CD-ROM.
- FTP—For an FTP install, you must have a startup disk and a supplemental disk. You need to have a valid nameserver configured or the IP address of the FTP server you will be using. You also need the path to the root of the Red Hat Linux directory on the FTP site.
- Hard drive—To install Red Hat Linux from a hard drive, you need the same startup and supplemental disks used by the FTP install. You must first create a Red Hat directory called RedHat at the top level of your directory tree. Everything you install should be placed in that directory. First, copy the base subdirectory; then copy the packages you want to install to another subdirectory, called RPMS. You can use available space on an existing DOS partition or a Linux partition that is not required in the install procedure (for example, a partition that would be used for data storage on the installed system).

  If you are using a DOS filesystem, you might not be able to use the full Linux filenames for the RPM (Red Hat Package Manager) packages. The installation process does not care what the filesystem looks like, but it is a good idea to keep track of them so that you will know what you are installing.
- NFS—If you want to install over a network, you need to mount the Red Hat Linux CD-ROM on a machine that supports ISO-9660 filesystems with Rock Ridge

extensions. The machine must also support NFS. Export the CD-ROM filesystem via NFS. You should either have nameservices configured or know the NFS server's IP address and the path to the exported CD-ROM.

- SMB Image—If you want to install over a network from a disk shared by a Windows system (or a Linux system running the Samba SMB connectivity suite), select this option. This is similar to installing from a hard drive—except, in this case, the hard drive is on another system.

The rest of the installation procedures presented here are for a CD-ROM installation. As you can tell from the previous descriptions, using other methods is not much different. As a matter of fact, the installation is the same; the difference is just a matter of the origin of the installation. For example, if you are installing from a shared volume on a Windows 95 or Windows NT server, you have to supply the name of the server, the name of the shared volume, and the account name and password for the volume.

CD-ROM Installation

When you select `Local CDROM`, you are told to insert your Red Hat CD into your CD drive now. Do this if you have not already done so, and click OK.

The installation continues to the "second stage" of the installation process.

> **NOTE**
>
> The installation process uses autoprobing to determine the type of CD-ROM you have. If you have problems with the CD-ROM at this point, refer to the `boot:` prompt information earlier in the chapter.

New or Upgrade

The next question the installation program asks is whether you are installing a new system or upgrading a system that already contains Red Hat Linux 2.0 or greater. In our example, we are installing a new system, so highlight Install and press Enter.

There are three classes of installation: Workstation, Server, and Custom. Here we are installing the Workstation class. As we go along, I'll point out the differences between the Workstation class and the Server class.

SCSI Adapters?

The system scans for any (SCSI) adapters. On most systems, the autoprobe will detect if you have any.

Because this is a new installation, the installation program assumes you do not have your Linux partitions set up yet. It does, however, give the following warning:

CAUTION

All the Linux partitions on your hard drive(s) will be erased. This means that all your previous Linux installations will be destroyed. If you do not want to lose all your Linux partitions, select "Cancel" now, and perform a "Custom" install.

This warning should be heeded, as it will indeed write over any previously installed Linux partitions. You should only get this warning if the system sees Linux partitions already present on your system.

CAUTION

If you install as a Server class, *all* of your partitions will be overwritten. This means you lose whatever else is on the disks—including other operating systems.

If you do have a Linux partition and you did not choose Custom, the system assumes you want to use the same partitions for the new system and begins to overwrite what is already there. It loads 336MB of data into your Linux partition.

NOTE

This means you can install more than one version of Linux on your system, but you must custom install any after the first.

Depending on the speed of your CD-ROM (and the system as a whole), this package install could take anywhere from 5 to 10 minutes. (On a Pentium Pro with a 12x CD-ROM, it takes 6 minutes).

If you are performing a new install (and you did not previously have a Linux partition), or if you chose Custom installation, you are next asked which tool you want to use for setting up your disk(s).

Two tools that come with Red Hat Linux can be used to set up Linux partitions. First is the old standby, `fdisk`; second, the new tool, Disk Druid. Both are acceptable methods for configuring your partitions, but Disk Druid is easier, so we are going to use it.

Disk Druid

Disk Druid is a new tool that started shipping with Red Hat version 5. It is a graphical interface that enables you to configure your hard disk partitions.

Three sections are associated with Disk Druid. Each is explained in detail here.

The Current Disk Partitions Section

Each line in the Current Disk Partitions section represents a disk partition. Note the scrollbar to the right.

> **NOTE**
>
> In Europe they call these "elevators," not scrollbars.

The scrollbar indicates additional items that cannot all be displayed at one time. Use the up- and down-arrow keys to look for any additional partitions. Each line (partition) has five fields:

Mount Point	Indicates where the partitions will be mounted after the Red Hat Linux system is up and running. (At least one partition must have a mount point of "\" before you can move past the Disk Druid screen in the installation process.) Also, swap space does not get a mount point.
Device	The device name of the partition.
Requested	The minimum size requested when the partition was defined.
Actual	The actual amount of space allocated to that partition.
Type	Shows the partition's type.

Drive Summaries

This section shows the hard disk(s) on the system. Just like the Current Disk Partitions section, this section has a scrollbar in case more than a couple of drives are attached to this computer. Each line contains six fields:

Drive	Shows the hard disk's device name.
Geom [C/H/S]	Shows the hard drive's geometry. The geometry consists of three numbers representing the number of cylinders, heads, and sectors as reported by the hard drive.
Total	Shows how much space is on the entire hard drive.
Used	Shows how much space is currently defined to a partition.
Free	Shows how much space is currently available on the hard drive (how much is unallocated).
[######]	A bar graph presenting a visual representation of the space currently used on the hard disk. The more pound signs between the brackets, the less free space is available.

Disk Druid's Buttons

The third section of Disk Druid is the buttons. It has five buttons across the bottom of the screen and six references to F keys:

Add	Used to request a new partition. When selected, a dialog appears containing fields that must be filled in.
Edit	Used to modify the attributes of the partition currently highlighted in the Current Disk Partitions section. Selecting the Edit button opens a dialog containing fields that can be edited.
Delete	Use this button to delete the partition currently highlighted in the Current Disk Partitions section. Selecting Delete causes a confirmation box to appear.
OK	When selected, any changes made are written to disk. At this time, you can confirm that you want the changes written to disk. This information is also passed to the installation program for later filesystem creation.
Back	This is the abort button. If you select the Back button, Disk Druid exits without making changes and you are returned to the previous window, where you can select `fdisk` or Disk Druid to start over.

Function keys	As mentioned earlier, Disk Druid also has six handy function keys. Four of them map directly to the buttons just described (Add, Edit, Delete, and OK). Two are different and are explained next.
F2-Add NFS	The F2 function key opens a dialog in which you can define a read-only NFS served filesystem.
F5-Reset	This function does just what you think it does (no, it does not reset your computer—that is Alt+Ctl+Del). F5 resets the partitions to the way they were before you started editing them in this section.

Adding a Partition

To add a new partition, select the Add button and press Enter. A dialog opens, containing the following fields:

Mount Point	Highlight this field and enter the partition's mount point.
Size	Enter the size (in megabytes) of the partition. The default of 1 can be removed with the backspace so that you can enter a new number.
Growable?	This checkbox indicates whether the size you entered in the previous field is to be considered the partition's exact size or its minimum size. Press the spacebar to check and uncheck this box. When it's checked, the partition will grow to fill all available space on the hard disk.
Type	This field contains a list of partition types. Select the appropriate type by using the up- and down-arrow keys.
Allowable Drives	This field contains a list of the hard disks installed on your system, with a checkbox for each disk. If a box is checked, this partition can be created on that hard disk. If a box is not checked, the partition will never be created on that hard disk.
OK	Select this button and press the spacebar when you finish the settings for this particular partition, and you're ready to create it.
Cancel	If you select this button, the partition you just defined will not be created.

NOTE

At a minimum, you must define at least two filesystems, one for Linux native and one for Linux swap space. The recommendation, however, is for six filesystems. One is swap space and the other five are /, /usr, /var, /home, and /usr/local.

`fdisk`

For you old-timers out there, here are some pointers for `fdisk`. Again, Disk Druid is the recommended (and safer) way of partitioning the disks.

CAUTION

This is the most volatile step of the entire procedure. If you mess up here, you could delete your entire hard drive. I highly recommend, therefore, that you make a backup of your current system before proceeding with the disk partitioning.

Here are some commands and a walk-through of using `fdisk`:

`m`	Provides a listing of the available commands
`p`	Provides a listing of the current partition information
`n`	Adds a new partition
`t`	Sets or changes the partition type
`l`	Provides a listing of the different partition types and their ID numbers
`w`	Saves your information and quits `fdisk`

You want to use `p` to check the current partition information, but first you need to add your root partition. Use `n` to create a new partition and then select either `e` or `p` for extended or primary partition. Most likely you want to create a primary partition. You are asked what partition number should be assigned to it, at which cylinder the partition should start (you will be given a range—just choose the lowest number), and the size of the partition. For example, for a 500MB partition, enter **`+500M`** for the size when asked.

Formatting Swap Space

After you have defined the partitions, the installation program continues. The next thing it asks you is the device to be used for swap space. A checkbox is available to have the computer check for bad blocks during format—this is a wise thing to do.

To create your swap partition, use `n` for a new partition. Choose either primary or extended; you most likely need primary. Give the partition a number and tell it where the first cylinder should be. Last, tell `fdisk` how big you want your swap partition. Now you need to change the partition type to Linux swap. Enter `t` to change the type and enter the partition number of your swap partition. Enter **82** for the hex code for the Linux swap partition.

Now you have created your Linux and Linux swap partitions, and it is time to add any additional partitions you might need (for example, Windows 95). Use `n` again to create a new partition, and enter all the information just as before. However, after you enter the size of the partition, you must change the partition type. Enter **`l`** to get a listing of the hex codes for the different partition types. Find the type of partition you need and use **`t`** to change the partition type. Keep repeating this procedure until all your partitions are created. You can create up to four primary partitions; then you must start putting extended partitions into each primary partition.

After your partitions are created, the installation program looks for Linux swap partitions and asks to initialize them. Choose the swap partitions you want to initialize, check the Check for Bad Blocks During Format box, and click OK. This formats the partition and makes it active so that Linux can use it.

Formatting Partitions

After the swap space has been formatted, you are asked which partitions you would like formatted. I strongly suggest that you format all system partitions (/, /usr, and /var if they exist). You do not need to format /home or /usr/local if they have been configured during a previous install. Again, checking for bad blocks is a good thing.

A Comment on Swap Space

You will want to create your swap partition; give some thought to the size of this partition. The swap partition is used for swapping the unused information in your RAM to disk to make room for more information. You should have at least 16MB total between your RAM and swap space. If you are running X Window, you should have at least 32MB between them.

The problem with using the generic formula is that it doesn't take into consideration what the user might be doing. A formula for determining the amount of swapping you need is given in the next paragraph. Note that if you run out of swap space, your system will thrash about, trying to move memory pages into and out of the swap space, which will take your system to its knees.

For a better estimate of how much RAM you need, figure out the size of all the programs you would run at one time. To this number, add 8MB to cover the OS. If the total is less than 32MB, use a 32MB swap space; otherwise, use the actual value.

You should always configure some swap space, regardless of how much RAM you have. Even a small amount of swap space will have good results on a system with a lot of RAM. For example, on my system, I have 64MB of RAM, which is more than enough for all the programs I run, but I have 32MB of swap space for programs I am running but am not actively using.

Components to Install

The next dialog asks which components you wish to install.

> **NOTE**
>
> If you want to install everything, just go to the bottom of the list and select Everything. "Everything" takes up about 665MB of total disk space. Keep in mind, though, that this includes almost 200MB of documentation (remember how many languages we can install in...).

When you have told the program which packages you want installed and have worked out all the dependencies, a window pops up telling you a complete log of your installation will be in `/tmp/install.log` after you restart your system.

With a simple OK, the system formats your partitions and loads the packages you selected. Depending on the speed of your CD-ROM (and to a limited extent, your hard drive) and how many packages you requested, this could take 10 minutes or longer.

Configuring Your Hardware

This section covers the final part of the installation: hardware configuration.

Choosing a Mouse

The system again autoprobes, this time for your mouse. If it finds one, it tells you what it found. In almost all cases, it will find your mouse. When you click OK, a configuration box opens, asking what type of mouse you have. Unless you are 100% certain of something else, I suggest you go with what the autoprobe found. The other option you have here is whether you want to emulate three buttons on your two-button mouse.

NOTE

Push down both buttons to emulate the third mouse button.

Configuring the X Window System

The next window that comes up asks you about the X Window server you want to run. Autoprobe identifies your graphics card and loads the card driver. It then asks you about your monitor.

Be sure to select a monitor that exactly matches your model. If your model isn't listed, choose Custom and fill in the values listed in your monitor's manual.

CAUTION

Choosing the wrong monitor frequencies can—to use the vernacular—fry your monitor, so make sure you have the correct settings.

Xconfigurator is the program that configures your monitor. These settings can be changed at any time by rerunning Xconfigurator.

If you chose the generic VGA card, you are asked whether you want to probe for settings using `X - probeonly`. Choose not to probe; after a moment, you should move on to the next section of the installation.

CAUTION

On some systems, the probe locks up the system. This means you have to restart the system and start over.

If you do probe and there are errors, you will be asked some specifics about your video card, amount of memory, and clockchip. You'll then be asked to select video modes.

Configuring the Network

The next question is whether you want to configure LAN (not dial-up) networking for your system.

If you will be installing this machine onto a local area network and you want to set up networking now, you should choose the Yes button. If not, choose No. You can always configure the networking later.

If you chose Yes, you are asked what network card driver to try. Scroll down the selection bar until you see one that matches your card.

Setting the Time Zone

You are next asked to set up your system's time zone. The first selection area asks whether your computer's BIOS clock is set to GMT. The next area asks what time zone you are in. Scroll to the zone that best matches your time zone, and then select OK to continue.

Selecting Services to Start Automatically

The next section of the installation goes through the services or daemons to start when the system restarts. The dialog for this section of the install contains a long scrollable list of checkboxes. Pressing F1 will give help on the item currently selected. You can change these services later with the `ntsysv` command.

Configuring Your Printer

You are next asked if you want to configure a printer. Selecting YES brings up a dialog asking where the printer is, with three selections available:

Local	A printer connected directly to the computer.
Remote lpd	A printer connected to your LAN, with which you can communicate via `lpd`.
LAN Manager	Use this if you print to the network printer via a LAN manager or SMB print server.

Root's Password

Root is the all-powerful administrative account. This account has no limitations; therefore, the password for this account must be kept secured. You are asked to enter a password twice. The password must be six to eight characters long. As you type in this new password, notice that nothing is shown on the screen. This is a security feature. You do enter the password into the system twice to make sure you typed it correctly.

Creating a Startup Disk

A custom startup disk provides a way of starting your Linux system without depending on the normal bootloader. This is useful if you don't want to install Lila on your system, another operating system removes Lila, or Lila doesn't work with your hardware configuration. A custom startup disk can also be used with the Red Hat Rescue image, making recovery from severe system failures much easier.

NOTE

Creating a startup disk is very much recommended at this stage in the game.

If you say Yes, you are asked to insert a blank floppy disk into the first drive (/dev/fd0). After you have inserted the blank disk, the system creates a startup disk.

Selecting Startup Options

The next screen (and one of the last, finally) presents you with possible locations of the startup loader. A comment here is necessary to ensure that you do not overwrite the correct one. The choices are the Master Boot Record and the First Sector of Boot Partitions.

The Master Boot Record is the boot record for the entire system. Replacing this will cause LILO to start every time the system starts.

The First Sector of Boot Partitions can be used if you have another bootloader on your system. If these loaders are already in the Master Boot Record of the primary drive, you probably do not want to replace them.

Bootloader

A few systems need to pass special options to the kernel at startup time for the system to function properly. If you need to pass startup options to the kernel, enter them at the next screen. "When in doubt, leave it out."

The second part of bootloader states it can start other operating systems that are on your system. If you have Windows 95 or 98, bootloader recognizes this and gives it a DOS startup label.

Done

Installation is now complete. You need to remove the disk and press Return to restart. You are now ready to log in to your Red Hat Linux system.

The Red Hat Package Manager

If you want to add packages to your Linux system in the future or upgrade current packages, you can use the Red Hat Package Manager (RPM). RPM technology is a very easy way to manage package installs and uninstalls. It keeps track of what is installed and any dependencies that are not met, and then it notifies you of them. You can also access a graphical interface to RPM through the control panel while running X Window.

Using RPM

The basic use of the `rpm` command to install a package is the following:

```
rpm -I packagename.rpm
```

To uninstall a package, you use the following:

```
rpm -u packagename.rpm
```

Many other options are available for RPM, but these two are the most common.

Packages for use with RPM are available at `ftp://ftp.redhat.com/pub/redhat/current/i386/RedHat/RPMS/` or any mirrors of this site.

Summary

The Red Hat Linux installation is the simplest and most straightforward installation available. After going through this chapter and following the step-by-step installation, you should now have a running Linux system. Keeping your system updated with the latest versions of utilities and libraries will ensure compatibility with most new applications being developed for Linux and keep your system operating efficiently.

If you do have problems, you'll find HOW-TOs and FAQs on the CD-ROM that comes with this book. Most of them are in HTML format, so you can view them straight from the CD-ROM by using a Web browser. Also, the Red Hat Web site (`http://www.redhat.com`) contains installation documentation and errata sheets for Red Hat Linux.

LILO

by Bill Ball

In This Chapter

Booting Linux requires you to install a program to load the kernel into your computer. Which program you use depends on the computer you're using: You'll use LILO for Intel-compatible PCs, MILO for Digital Equipment Corp. Alpha PCs, or SILO for SPARC-compatible workstations. Because the CD-ROM included with this book contains Red Hat Intel/Linux, this chapter focuses on LILO, which—according to its author, Werner Almesberger—stands for *Linux Loader*.

This chapter will help you if you chose not to install LILO when you first installed Red Hat Linux or if you need help in properly starting Linux with certain kernel options. You've probably already decided how you want to start Linux on your computer, but you should know there are other ways to fire up your system.

Instead of using LILO, you can start Linux from DOS with `LOADLIN.EXE`, which is included on your CD-ROM under the `Dosutils` directory. I'll discuss `LOADLIN.EXE` later in this chapter in the section "Using `LOADLIN.EXE` to Boot Linux."

You can also use your computer as a diskless workstation by booting Linux over a network. A discussion on this subject is beyond the scope of this chapter, but you'll find the details on how to do this in Robert Nemkin's Diskless-HOWTO, under the `/usr/doc/HOWTO/mini` directory after you install Linux.

Yet another approach is to use a commercial boot loader, such as V Communications, Inc.'s System Commander, which can come in handy if you need to run other operating systems such as OS/2, Solaris, or Windows NT on your computer.

LILO has capabilities similar to commercial solutions, but it's free. For now, I'll assume that you're going to use LILO to boot in one of three traditional ways. You can use LILO to start Linux

- From the Master Boot Record (MBR) of your hard drive
- From the superblock of your root Linux partition on your hard drive
- From a floppy disk

In the following section, I'll show you a list of LILO's configuration parameters and its command-line arguments, and I'll point out some special features.

Installing and Configuring LILO

Although LILO is easy to install by using the `lilo` command (located under the `/sbin` directory), you should first take the time to read its documentation, which you'll find under `/usr/doc`. Along with the documentation, you'll also find a shell script called `QuickInst`, which can be used to replace an existing LILO installation or for a first-time install. LILO's documentation contains details of its features and provides important tips and workarounds for special problems, such as installing boot loaders on very large capacity hard drives or booting from other operating systems.

> **WARNING**
>
> Before trying anything with LILO, you should have an emergency boot disk. Having a system that won't boot is not much fun, and if you don't have a boot disk, you might think there is no possible way to get back in and change things. Spending a few minutes to make yourself a boot disk can save you a big headache down the road. Whatever happens, don't panic! If you need to rescue your system, see Chapter 6, "System Startup and Shutdown," for details.

If you don't install LILO during your Red Hat install or decide not to use the `QuickInst` script, you can install LILO in two basic steps:

1. Configure `/etc/lilo.conf`.
2. Run `/sbin/lilo` to install LILO and make it active.

This discussion describes modifying an existing `lilo.conf` file. Before making any changes, do yourself a favor and create a backup of the file either in the same directory or on a separate disk. Several files important to LILO are created during an initial install:

- `/sbin/lilo`—A map installer; see `man lilo` for more information.
- `/boot/boot.b`—A boot loader.
- `/boot/map`—A boot map, which contains the location of the kernel.
- `/etc/lilo.conf`—LILO's configuration file.

Configuring LILO

Under Linux, your hard drives are abstracted to device files under the `/dev` directory. If you have one or more IDE drives, your first hard drive is referred to as `/dev/hda` and your second hard drive is `/dev/hdb`. SCSI drives are referred to as `/dev/sda` and `/dev/sdb`. When you installed Linux, you most likely partitioned your hard drive. The first partition on your first drive would be `/dev/hda1` or `/dev/sda1`, your second partition would be `/dev/hda2` or `/dev/sda2`, and so on.

Before configuring `LILO`, you should know which partitions have what operating system on them. You should also know where you want to install LILO. In almost all cases, you will want to put LILO on the MBR. You shouldn't do this, however, if you run OS/2.

OS/2's boot loader should go on the MBR, and LILO should then be installed on the superblock of the root partition.

Before installing LILO, you should know where your Linux partition is, and if you have other operating systems, you must know where they are located. For example, your Linux partition might be at `/dev/hda1`, and your Windows 95 partition might be at `/dev/hda2`.

If Linux is the only operating system on your computer or if you have Windows 95 or Windows NT, you will want to install LILO as the MBR of the boot drive. If you have OS/2 also, you will want to install LILO on the root partition of your hard drive and use OS/2's boot loader on the MBR.

NOTE

Red Hat Linux installs LILO at the end of an initial Linux installation or upgrade. Right before the LILO installation process, you'll have the chance to create a boot disk—do it! Even if you don't use the disk, you'll benefit from having a little insurance in case things ever go awry. If you don't install LILO, you'll definitely need the disk.

You will usually want to install LILO after you have partitioned your hard drives and after you have installed either Linux or other operating systems.

Armed with your information, you are now ready to edit LILO's configuration file, `/etc/lilo.conf`.

Editing `lilo.conf`

Editing `lilo.conf` is easy. Make sure you're logged in as root, and load the file into your favorite editor, making sure to save your changes and to save the file as ASCII text. You'll edit `lilo.conf` for a number of reasons:

- You are testing a new kernel and want to be able to boot the same Linux partition with more than one kernel. This is done by using multiple entries of the "image =" section of `lilo.conf`. You may have multiple kernels installed on your Linux partition and can boot to a different kernel by typing its name (specified in the "label =" section).
- You want to add password protection to a partition.
- You have a hardware setup that requires you to specify special options, such as booting a remote file system.

- Your kernel is called something other than /vmlinuz or is in a nonstandard place, such as /etc.

Listing 3.1 shows a sample lilo.conf file.

NOTE

Need more information about configuring LILO? Although you'll find a lot of detailed technical information under the /usr/doc/lilo directory, don't overlook Cameron Spitzer's LILO mini-HOWTO under the /usr/doc/HOWTO directory. You'll find additional troubleshooting tips on how to configure your lilo.conf file.

LISTING 3.19 A SAMPLE LILO.CONF

```
# Start LILO global section
Boot = /dev/hda
Prompt
Vga = normal
Ramdisk = 0
# End LILO global section
image = /vmlinuz
  root = /dev/hda3
  label = linux
  read-only  # Non-UMSDOS filesystems should be mounted read-only for
checking
other = /dev/hda1
  label = dos
  table = /dev/hda
```

You can add the parameters listed in Table 3.1 to your /etc/lilo.conf file. They could also be given at the boot prompt, but it is much simpler for them to reside in your /etc/lilo.conf file. Note that only 13 of LILO's 23 options are listed here. See LILO's documentation for details.

TABLE 3.1 /ETC/LILO.CONF CONFIGURATION PARAMETERS

Parameter	*Description*
boot=<*boot_device*>	Tells the kernel the name of the device that contains the boot sector. If boot is omitted, the boot sector is read from the device currently mounted as root.
linear	Generates linear sector addresses instead of sector/head/cylinder addresses, which can be troublesome, especially when used with the compact option. See LILO's documentation for details.

continues

TABLE 3.1 CONTINUED

Parameter	*Description*
`install=<boot_sector>`	Installs the specified file as the new boot sector. If `install` is omitted, `/etc/lilo/boot.b` is used as the default.
`message=<message_file>`	You can use this to display the file's text and customize the boot prompt, with a maximum message of up to 65,535 bytes. Rerun `/sbin/lilo` if you change this file.
`verbose=<level>`	Turns on progress reporting. Higher numbers give more verbose output, and the numbers can range from `1` to `5`. This also has `-v` and `-q` options; see LILO's documentation for details.
`backup=<backup_file>`	Copies the original boot sector to `<backup_file>` (which can also be a device, such as `/dev/null`) instead of to `/etc/lilo/boot.<number>`.
`force-backup<backup_file>`	Similar to `backup`, this option overwrites the current backup, copy, but `backup` is ignored if `force-backup` is used.
`prompt`	Requires you to type a boot prompt entry.
`timeout=<tsecs>`	Sets a timeout (in tenths of a second) for keyboard input, which is handy if you want to boot right away or wait for longer than the default five seconds. Tip: To make LILO wait indefinitely for your keystrokes, use a value of `0`.
`serial=<parameters>`	Allows input from the designated serial line and the PC's keyboard to LILO. A break on the serial line mimics a Shift-key press from the console. For security, password-protect all your boot images when using this option. The parameter string has the syntax `<port>,<bps><parity><bits>`, as in `/dev/ttyS1,8N1`. The components `<bps>`, `<parity>`, and `<bits>` can be omitted. If one of these components is omitted, all of the following components have to be omitted as well. Additionally, the comma has to be omitted if only the port number is specified. See LILO's documentation for details.
`ignore-table`	Ignore corrupt partition tables.
`password=<password>`	Use this to password-protect your boot images. If you use this option but do not have `lilo.conf` set to root read-only permission (-rw———), LILO issues a warning—the password is not encrypted!
`unsafe`	This keyword is placed after a definition for a partition. The key word tells LILO not to attempt to read the MBR or that disk's partition table entry. You can declare all of the partitions in your system as a log of all existing partitions and then place the `unsafe` keyword entry to prevent LILO from reading it.

After making your changes to `lilo.conf`, make sure to run `/sbin/lilo`. You should also *always* run `/sbin/lilo` after installing a new kernel.

LILO Boot Prompt Options

The following sample list of options can be passed to LILO at the boot prompt to enable special features of your system or to pass options to the Linux kernel to enable a proper boot. Knowing any needed options for your system is especially handy during the Red Hat Linux installation process because you'll be asked for any special options if you choose to install LILO at that time.

Although you'll normally type **`linux`** or **`dos`** at the `LILO:` prompt, you can also try one or two of the following options. For a more up-to-date list of kernel messages or options, read Paul Gortmaker's BootPrompt-HOWTO under the `/usr/doc/HOWTO` directory.

NOTE

If you can't remember the exact labels you've specified in `lilo.conf` for the `LILO:` prompt, press the Tab key to have LILO print a list of available kernels. If this doesn't work, you can also try pressing the Alt or Shift keys before the LILO: prompt appears.

- `rescue`—Boots Linux into single-user mode to allow system fixes (see Chapter 2, "X Window," for details).
- `single`—Similar to `rescue`, but attempts to boot from your hard drive.
- `root=`*`<device>`*—Similar to the `/etc/lilo.conf` entry, this option allows you to boot from a CD-ROM or other storage device.
- `vga=`*`<mode>`*—Enables you to change the resolution of your console; try the `ask` mode.

Using LOADLIN.EXE to Boot Linux

`LOADLIN.EXE` is a program that uses the DOS MBR to boot Linux. This handy program by Hans Lermen also passes along kernel options. `LOADLIN.EXE` is very helpful when you must boot from DOS to properly initialize modems or sound cards to make them work under Linux.

You need to do two things before using `LOADLIN.EXE`:

1. Copy `LOADLIN.EXE` to a DOS partition (for example, `C:\LOADLIN`).
2. Put a copy of your kernel image (`/vmlinuz`) on your DOS partition.

For example, to boot Linux, type the following from the DOS command line:

```
loadlin c:\vmlinuz root=/dev/hda3 ro
```

Make sure you insert your root partition in the command line. The `ro` stands for read-only. When you are first booting a Linux partition, it should be mounted as read-only to prevent data loss.

If you have a UMSDOS file system, you can type

```
loadlin c:\vmlinuz root=/dev/hda1 rw
```

The `rw` stands for read/write. Starting a UMSDOS file system this way is safe. Again, make sure you substitute your own partition. `LOADLIN.EXE` accepts a number of options; see its documentation in the `LOADLIN.TGZ` file under the `Dosutils` directory on the book's CD-ROM.

How to Uninstall LILO

You can uninstall LILO by using the `lilo -u` command, or you can disable it by using `fdisk` under either Linux or MS-DOS to make another partition active.

If LILO has been installed as the MBR, you can restore the original MBR by booting under MS-DOS and using the commands `SYS c:` or `FDISK /MBR`.

Troubleshooting LILO

You shouldn't have any problems with LILO, but if you do, you'll get one of 70 different warnings or error messages. I can't list all of them here, but Table 3.2 lists six of the most probable LILO: prompt or initial errors.

TABLE 3.2 LILO PROMPT ERRORS

Prompt	*Description*
L<nn>	Where nn represents one of 16 disk-error codes.
LI	The second-stage boot loader loaded, but could not run.
LIL	The descriptor table could not be read.
LIL?	The second-stage boot loader loaded at an incorrect address.
LIL-	LILO found a corrupt descriptor table.
LILO	LILO ran successfully.

Disk error codes can indicate problems such as an open floppy door, a drive timeout, a controller error, a media problem, a BIOS error, or even transient read problems (which can be overcome by rebooting). Overall, some common problems with LILO include

- Not rerunning /sbin/lilo following a kernel change
- Incorrect use of /sbin/lilo in creating a new boot map
- Installing and booting Linux from very large (2 GB+) partition
- Installing another or inferior operating system (such as Win95) after installing Linux and LILO
- Errors in `/etc/lilo.conf` after manual edits
- A corrupted MBR
- Installation of LILO in a Linux swap partition (which should be impossible!)
- A missing Linux kernel image (error in `/etc/lilo.conf`)
- Installing Linux on and booting from a DOS partition and then defragmenting the DOS partition
- Passing incorrect kernel messages at the LILO: prompt

If you run into trouble, definitely peruse Almesberger's README file, found under the `/usr/doc/lilo` directory. Take his advice: "Don't panic!" With a little forethought, detection, and perseverance, you should be able to avoid or overcome problems.

Summary

This chapter covers the basics of configuring, installing, and using LILO and introduces you to the `LOADLIN.EXE` boot utility. Hopefully, you've seen that using LILO can give you additional flexibility in the number of operating systems installed on your PC and that Linux can be used along with these other systems. Don't forget to read LILO's documentation, as you'll not only learn about how operating systems boot from your hard drive, but also how you can customize the Linux boot prompt.

CHAPTER

The X Window System

by Bill Ball

In This Chapter

Setting Up Your XFree86 System

The X Window System is the foundation of the graphical interface for Linux. Although you can use Linux without using X, you'll be less productive and will miss out on a lot of useful programs. The X Window System used with most Linux distributions, including Red Hat's, is the collection of programs from The XFree86 Project, Inc. (see the note in this chapter on "The Future of X").

You can also buy a commercial version of the X Window System from vendors such as XiGraphics (`http://www.xig.com`) or Metro Link, Inc. (`http://www.metrolink.com`). These distributions range in price from $39 to $150. However, you'll find the XFree86 distribution, which is free, on the CD-ROM included with this book, and this chapter focuses on configuring and using XFree86's version of X.

If you installed X11 when you first installed Red Hat Linux, you'll find that most of the X Window System resides under the /usr/X11R6 directory. If you have an older version of X11 installed, you can use Red Hat's glint tool to upgrade X. First, insert your Red Hat CD-ROM and mount it like this:

```
# mount /mnt/cdrom
```

Next, start X11, and then from the command line of a terminal window, start `glint` like this:

```
# su -c glint
```

When the glint window appears, click the Available button, wait for the Available Packages window to appear, and then go to the X11 folder to select and install the software.

If you did not install X, you can use Red Hat's rpm command to install the software. Mount your Red Hat CD-ROM and navigate to the RedHat/RPMS/i386 directory. At the command line of your console, use the `rpm` command:

```
# rpm -i XFree*rpm
```

This command installs the XFree86 software. After the software is installed, you'll find a series of directories under the /usr/X11R6 tree, including

/usr/X11R6/bin—Where most X11 clients are stored

/usr/X11R6/include—Programming header files and directories of bitmaps and pixmaps

/usr/X11R6/lib—X11 software libraries needed by X clients and programmers

/usr/X11R6/man—X manual pages

Depending on the software installed, these directories can take up 40 to 400 megabytes of hard drive space, and even more if you install a lot of X window managers, programming libraries, or other software. For details about XFree86, its configuration file XF86Config, and various X servers, read the README.Config document found in the /usr/X11R6/lib/X11/doc directory.

The Future of X

At the time of this writing, the latest version of X11—X11R6.4—is no longer under fee-based licensing restrictions. This is good news. The Open Group (TOG), a consortium of nearly 200 companies (whose membership includes Apple and Microsoft), decided on January 30, 1998, that X11R6.4 would no longer be available to anyone for profit without payment of an annual licensing fee. The fee schedule started at $7,500 for "non-Project" members distributing up to 50,000 units and reached upward to $65,500 for unlimited distribution rights. To be eligible for slightly lower distribution fees, a person or company could become an X Project Team member at a cost of $30,000 and had to sign a contract with a nondisclosure agreement, or NDA clause.

For many members of the Open Source community and programmers dedicated to distributing software under the GNU General Public License, this was a great fear (ever since the MIT Consortium disbanded) quickly realized. However, response was rapid, and the XFree86 Project returned fire 90 days later in a news release on April 7, 1998:

"The XFree86 Project will continue its development based on the freely available X11R6.3 SI [sample implementation] and, where appropriate, attempt to implement future developments to the X11 standards independently of TOG."

Fortunately, TOG changed its mind in early September 1998 and reverted X11R6.4's license to one the same as X11R6.3. What would have happened otherwise?

Basically, development of X would have split into two forks. Although many companies, programmers, and users felt it was a bad time for a rift to occur, especially in light of the massive growth of the Linux user base, the effect might not have been noticed for some time. Many TOG members, such as Hewlett Packard and Digital Equipment Corporation, still only distribute X11R5, a much older version. And although one may have had to pay a licensing fee to distribute X11 library or server binaries, no restrictions were placed on distributing patches to the source so people can build their own X distribution, and no fees were associated with distributing source to X clients that might use X11R6.4 libraries.

continues

The good news was that the XFree86 Project stepped up to the plate and, with the blessing of Linus Torvalds, committed to providing future free distributions of X. The Xfree86 Project rightfully deserves the support of the worldwide Linux community. For details about TOG's X11 licensing and fees for other software, such as Motif, see `http://www.opengroup.org`. For the latest version of X11, and to pledge support for The XFree86 Project, see `http://www.xfree86.org`.

Configuring Your XFree86 System

The largest hurdle most new X users face after installing XFree86 is coming up with a working XF86Config file. If you already have a working setup, chances are your old XF86Config will work. But if you're starting from scratch, one of the first things you should do after installing X is to read as much of the documentation as possible. Although the daring and brave will launch right into configuring X11, even experienced users will benefit from reading about the latest XFree86 developments and checking the XFree86 documentation for tips about their specific hardware.

You'll find just about everything you need under the /usr/X11R6/lib/X11/doc directory. Table 4.1 contains the details of this directory for XFree86 3.3.2. Also check the *XFree86-HOWTO* under the /usr/doc/HOWTO directory—it contains valuable tips on configuring your X software.

TABLE 4.1 XFREE86 DOCUMENTATION

File	*Description*
AccelCards	A list of tested accelerated graphics cards
BUILD	How to compile the XFree86 X distribution from source
COPYRIGHT	Copyright statement
Devices	An old file of contributed XF86Config Device sections
Monitors	An old file of contributed XF86Config Monitor sections
QuickStart.doc	A quick-start guide to setting up XFree86
README	General information about the current XFree86 release
README.Config	Detailed, step-by-step guide to configuring XFree86
README.DECtga	Information for DEC 21030 users
README.DGA	How to program for the XFree86 DGA interface
README.LinkKit	Specific information on how to build XFree86 from scratch
README.Linux	Good information for Linux users about installing and using XFree86

File	Description
README.MGA	Information about the Matrox Millennium and Mystigue video cards
README.Mach32	Information about the Mach32 XFree86 X server
README.Mach64	Release notes about the Mach64 XFree86 X server
README.NV1	Notes for NVidia NV1, SGS-Thomson STG2000, and Rival128 video cards
README.Oak	Notes for Oak Technologies Inc. chipset users
README.P9000	Release notes for the P9000 XFree86 X server
README.S3	Notes for S3 chipset users
README.S3V	Notes for S3 ViRGE, ViRGE/DX, ViRGE/GX, ViRGE/MX, and ViRGE/VX users
README.Sis	Notes for Sis chipset users
README.Video7	A readme file about the Video7 drivers
README.W32	Notes for W32 and ET6000 chipset users
README.WstDig	Notes for Western Digital chipset users
README.agx	Information about the AGX XFree86 X server
README.apm	Notes about the Alliance Promotion chipset
README.ark	Notes for ARK Logic chipset users
README.ati	Information about XFree86's ATI Adapters video drivers
README.chips	Notes about Chips and Technologies chipsets
README.cirrus	Information about XFree86 support for Cirrus Logic chipset
README.clkprog	Programming info about external video clock setting programs
README.mouse	Details about XFree86's X11 mouse support
README.trident	Notes for Trident chipset users
README.tseng	Notes for Tseng chipset users
RELNOTES	The definitive release notes for XFree86
ServersOnly	How your directories should look when building XFree86 X servers
VGADriver.Doc	A HOWTO on adding an SVGA or VGA drive to XFree86
VideoModes.doc	Eric S. Raymond's comprehensive treatise on building XF86Config modelines
xinput	General info on input device (such as joystick) support in XFree86

If you're new to X11, first read the man pages for X and XFree86 for an overview of X. Before you begin to configure X, also read the QuickStart.doc text. You'll need to know some technical details about your computer and your computer's video card and monitor. Following is some of the information that will help:

- The type, make, name, or model of video card installed in your computer
- How much video RAM (not system RAM) is installed for your card
- The type of clockchip used by your video card chipset
- The type of mouse you use (PS/2 or serial, for example)
- The type, make, name, or model of monitor attached to your computer
- The vertical and horizontal refresh rates for your monitor (such as 55–100 vertical, 30–60 horizontal)
- The type of keyboard you use

Armed with this information, you then have to choose the method or tool to configure XFree86 and generate a correct XF86Config file for your system. You can use Red Hat's graphical X11 setup tool, called Xconfigurator, or XFree86's text-mode tool, xf86config, or you can manually build your own XF86Config file. Both the `Xconfigurator` and `xf86config` programs will run from the command line of your console or from the command line of a terminal window.

`Xconfigurator` has the advantage of providing a graphical interface; `xf86config` asks a series of questions in a text-mode screen. If you're lucky, your computer's hardware will exactly match the configuration generated by these programs. Problems can arise if the settings don't work, if you've entered incorrect information, or if your video chipset is not fully supported by the XFree86 servers.

In general, video hardware several years old will fare much better than "bleeding-edge" video cards, because software contributors have had a chance to work with the video chipsets. Laptop users can also run into special problems, and it can be disheartening to buy the latest laptop, only to find that the embedded video system will not work with X—it pays to research! (Of course, I don't even follow my own advice and usually buy a new laptop without checking first!)

Desktop users have the option of installing a new, supported video card, of course. Laptop users should definitely check the Linux laptop user site at

`http://www.cs.utexas.edu/users/kharker/linux-laptop`

If you find you cannot get correct settings, or if your chipset is not supported, you can also buy a commercial X distribution from one of the vendors mentioned in the introduction. Finally, your last resort is to whine at, plead with, cajole, or bribe a knowledgeable programmer to build a server for you from the XFree86 sources (but this rarely works).

The XF86Config File

Without a doubt, the most important configuration file for XFree86 is the XF86Config file. This file is used to properly feed font, keyboard, mouse, video chipset, monitor capabilities, and color depth setting information to your selected X11 display server. XF86Config is a single text file, consisting of several sections:

- Files—Tells the X server where colors, fonts, or specific software modules are located
- Module—Tells the X server what special modules should be loaded
- ServerFlags—On/off flags to allow or deny special actions, such as core dumps, keyboard server shutdown, video-mode switching, video tuning, and mouse and keyboard configuration
- Keyboard—Tells the X server what keyboard to expect and settings to use
- Pointer—Tells the X server what pointer to use and how buttons are handled
- Xinput—A special section for devices such as graphics pads or styluses
- Monitor—Specific details and settings for your monitor, such as name, horizontal sync, vertical sync ranges, and modelines (one for each video resolution, such as 640×480, 800×600, 1024×768)
- Device—Details about your video chipset, such as RAM or clockchips
- Screen—What X server to use, the color depth (such as 8-, 16-, 24- or 32-bits per pixel), screen size (such as 640×480, 800×600, or 1024×768), the size of the virtual screen

CAUTION

Do not use an XF86Config from someone who does not have the same graphics card and monitor as you. Incorrect settings can cause you to harm your monitor. Do not use monitor settings outside your monitor's specifications. You have been warned! On the other hand, if you do come up with a good XF86Config, document it and share it with others. Read postings on `comp.os.linux.x` and check the Linux laptop users Web pages for hints, tips, tricks, and places to share your information.

Before you begin, make sure you read the README.Config file.

Using Xconfigurator

Red Hat's Xconfigurator generates an XF86Config file after it probes your system and asks you several questions. You must run this program as the root operator. Start Xconfigurator from the command line of your console or an X11 terminal window like this:

```
# su -c Xconfigurator
```

The screen clears, and a dialog appears, as shown in Figure 4.1.

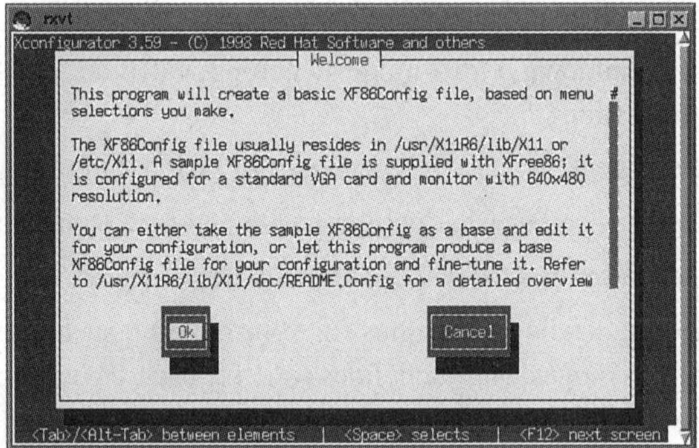

FIGURE 4.1
Red Hat's Xconfigurator generates the required XF86Config file for XFree86.

Use the Tab key to navigate to different buttons on the screen, and then press the Enter key when the OK button is highlighted. Xconfigurator first checks to see if a symbolic link from /usr/X11R6/lib/X11/XF86Config exists to the /etc/X11/XF86Config. If the link exists, Xconfigurator then probes your video card and reports with a dialog, as shown in Figure 4.2.

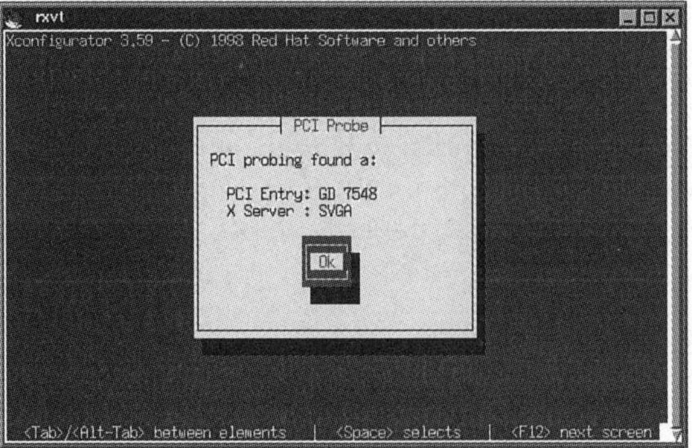

FIGURE 4.2
Xconfigurator reports on your video card with a small dialog.

After you click the OK button, you are presented with a dialog asking for the type of monitor attached to your computer (see Figure 4.3). Nearly 200 monitors are listed in the Xconfigurator's database; desktop users will probably find their model listed. Scroll down the list until your model is highlighted, and click the OK button. Unfortunately, laptop users have to select the Custom monitor at the top of the list. If you have a desktop computer and your monitor is not listed, check the Monitors file under the /usr/X11R6/lib/X11/doc directory—you might find yours there, along with the supported horizontal and vertical frequencies.

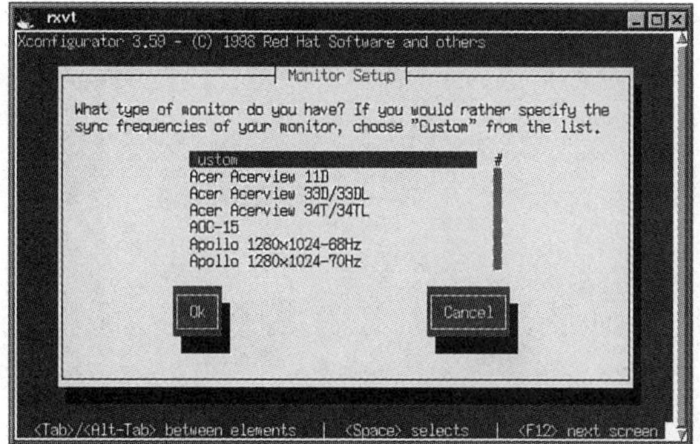

FIGURE 4.3
Xconfigurator has nearly 200 monitors in its model database.

If you don't find your monitor listed, or if you're using a laptop, don't panic. Select the Custom monitor and click the OK button. Xconfigurator then presents an introductory dialog. When you click the OK button, you're presented a list of monitor resolutions and frequencies, as shown in Figure 4.4.

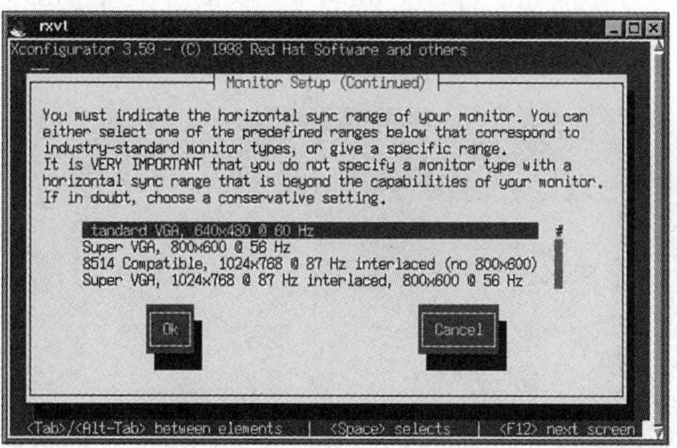

FIGURE 4.4
Xconfigurator allows custom monitor settings.

At this point, using Xconfigurator might be somewhat confusing. Although the program says a horizontal frequency is being selected, you are asked to select a video resolution and monitor frequency. The best bet is to pick a resolution you know is supported by your monitor and click the OK button. If you're not sure the correct information for your monitor will be inserted into your XF86Config file (which Xconfigurator will create after you've finished entering all the information), make sure to edit and change the inserted horizontal frequency settings.

The next dialog, shown in Figure 4.5, asks for the vertical frequency range of your monitor. Although the dialog says you can enter a custom range, you have to pick the range closest to your monitor's and then edit your XF86Config file after Xconfigurator is done.

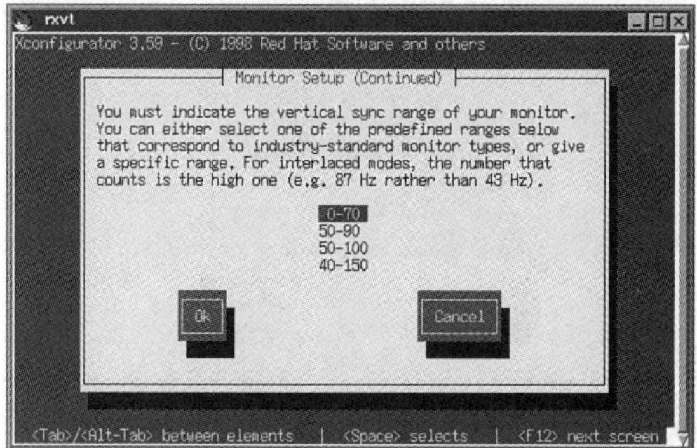

FIGURE 4.5
Xconfigurator offers four vertical frequency monitor settings.

Select your frequency range and click the OK button. The next dialog asks if you want Xconfigurator to probe your video card for resolution (such as 640×480, 800×600, or 1024×768) and color depth (such as 8-, 16-, or 24-bit color). Although the safest approach is not to probe, especially if you have a laptop or unsupported monitor, some users with supported video cards and monitors will benefit by this automatic configuration. Select either the Don't Probe or Probe button (as shown in Figure 4.6).

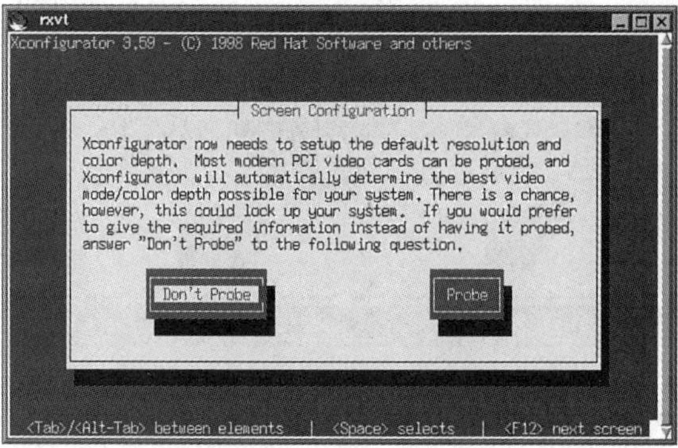

FIGURE 4.6
If you choose Probe, Xconfigurator automatically probes your video for the best resolution and color depth settings.

The next dialog, shown in Figure 4.7, asks for the amount of video memory installed in your computer's motherboard or video card. In general, the more video memory you have, the higher resolution or color depth supported by your computer. If you have upgradable video memory, you may benefit by adding more memory (depending on your monitor and support by the XFree86 server for your video chipset).

Interestingly, no matter what memory value you select, Xconfigurator inserts the value but leaves it commented out in the final XF86Config file. This means you'll have to edit XF86Config manually to use your selected memory setting. If you have more than 8MB of memory, you'll need to edit your final XF86Config file to correct the setting (and you've got one heck of a video system installed). Select the currently installed amount of memory, and click the OK button.

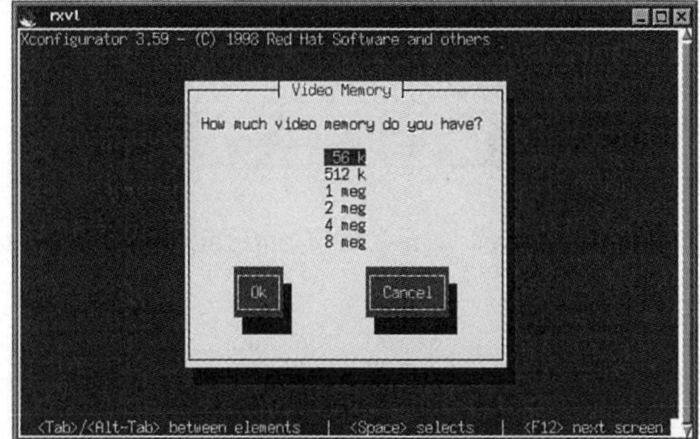

FIGURE 4.7
Xconfigurator offers six video memory configurations.

Xconfigurator next asks for the type of clockchip in your video subsystem (see Figure 4.8). If you're not sure whether your video card uses clockchip settings, select No Clockchip Setting. If you're sure about the type of clockchip used (by checking your video card or computer documentation), select one of the 12 clockchips listed and click the OK button.

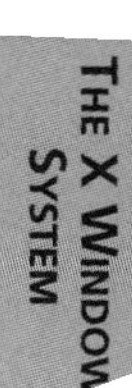

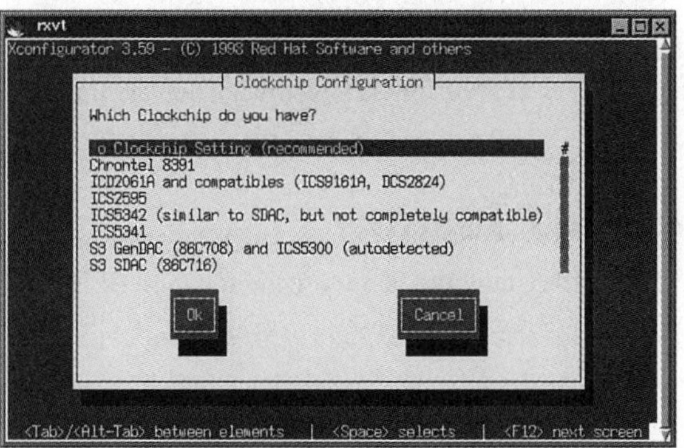

FIGURE 4.8
Xconfigurator lists 12 clockchips.

The next dialog (shown in Figure 4.9) asks for the desired video resolutions and color depths. Select different settings by navigating with your Tab and cursor keys and pressing the Spacebar. Do not select video resolutions greater than allowed by your monitor unless you want to use virtual resolutions (where your display becomes a movable window on a large display). When you're finished, click the OK button.

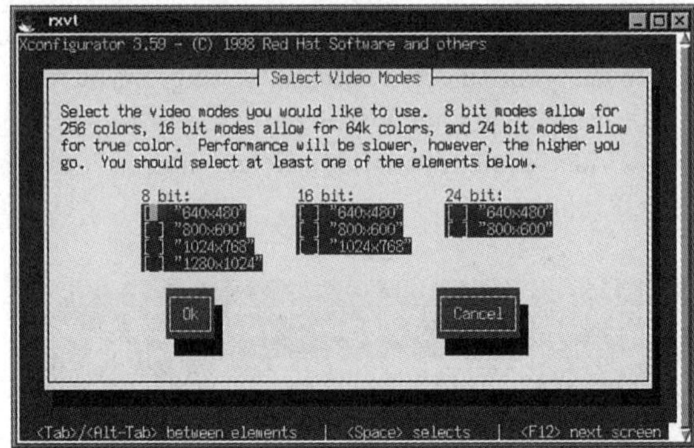

FIGURE 4.9
Xconfigurator configures a combination of video resolutions and color depths.

Xconfigurator then creates and saves your XF86Config file, saving it under the /etc/X11 directory.

Examining the XF86Config File

Before you try to start an X11 session using your new XF86Config settings, open the file in your favorite text editor, making sure to disable line wrapping, and check the settings. Doing this is essential, especially for laptop users, to check the created settings, enable or disable some X server options, enter the correct amount of video memory, and fine-tune monitor settings. For example, open the file (as the root operator) with the pico text editor like this:

```
# su -c "pico -w /etc/X11/XF86Config"
```

The next sections describe several of the more important parts of the XF86Config file you've generated. For an overview of the XF86Config file, see the XF86Config man page.

XF86Config Files Section

The Files section in Listing 4.1 tells the X server the location of the color name database and system fonts.

LISTING 4.1 XF86CONFIG'S FILES SECTION

```
Section "Files"

# The location of the RGB database. Note, this is the name of the
# file minus the extension (such as ".txt" or ".db"). There is normally
# no need to change the default.


    RgbPath      "/usr/X11R6/lib/X11/rgb"

# Multiple FontPath entries are allowed (they are concatenated together)


    FontPath     "/usr/X11R6/lib/X11/fonts/misc/"
    FontPath     "/usr/X11R6/lib/X11/fonts/Type1/"
    FontPath     "/usr/X11R6/lib/X11/fonts/Speedo/"
    FontPath     "/usr/X11R6/lib/X11/fonts/75dpi/"
    FontPath     "/usr/X11R6/lib/X11/fonts/100dpi/"

EndSection
```

XF86Config ServerFlags Section

Several parts of the ServerFlags section, shown in Listing 4.2, can be used to configure special actions allowed by your XFree86 X server. Enable a particular action by removing the pound sign (#) in front of the specific flag. Most users will not disable the DontZap feature because it provides a quick way to exit an X session. The DontZoom feature may be disabled if you use X in only one video resolution, such as 800×600 pixels.

LISTING 4.2 XF86CONFIG'S SERVER FLAGS SECTION

```
# **********************************************************************
# Server flags section.
# **********************************************************************

Section "ServerFlags"

    # Uncomment this to cause a core dump at the spot where a signal is
    # received. This may leave the console in an unusable state, but may
    # provide a better stack trace in the core dump to aid in debugging
    #NoTrapSignals

    # Uncomment this to disable the <Crtl><Alt><BS> server abort sequence
    # This allows clients to receive this key event.
    #DontZap
```

continues

LISTING 4.2 CONTINUED

```
    # Uncomment this to disable the <Crtl><Alt><KP_+>/<KP_-> mode
switching
    # sequences. This allows clients to receive these key events.
    #DontZoom

EndSection
```

XF86Config Keyboard Section

The Keyboard section in Listing 4.3 tells the X server what type of keyboard to expect and what settings to use, such as language type, key character layout, and manufacturer.

LISTING 4.3 XF86CONFIG'S KEYBOARD SECTION

```
# **********************************************************************
# Keyboard section
# **********************************************************************

Section "Keyboard"

    Protocol    "Standard"

    # when using XQUEUE, comment out the above line, and uncomment the
    # following line
    #Protocol   "Xqueue"

    AutoRepeat  500 5

    # Let the server do the NumLock processing. This should only be
    # required when using pre-R6 clients
    #ServerNumLock

    # Specify which keyboard LEDs can be user-controlled (eg, with xset(1))
    #Xleds      1 2 3

    #To set the LeftAlt to Meta, RightAlt key to ModeShift,
    #RightCtl key to Compose, and ScrollLock key to ModeLock:

    LeftAlt        Meta
    RightAlt        Meta
   ScrollLock      Compose
   RightCtl        Control

# To disable the XKEYBOARD extension, uncomment XkbDisable.

#    XkbDisable
```

```
# To customise the XKB settings to suit your keyboard, modify the
# lines below (which are the defaults). For example, for a non-U.S.
# keyboard, you will probably want to use:
#    XkbModel    "pc102"
# If you have a US Microsoft Natural keyboard, you can use:
#    XkbModel    "microsoft"
#
# Then to change the language, change the Layout setting.
# For example, a german layout can be obtained with:
#    XkbLayout   "de"
# or:
#    XkbLayout   "de"
#    XkbVariant  "nodeadkeys"
#
# If you'd like to switch the positions of your capslock and
# control keys, use:
#    XkbOptions  "ctrl:swapcaps"

# These are the default XKB settings for XFree86
#    XkbRules    "xfree86"
#    XkbModel    "pc101"
#    XkbLayout   "us"
#    XkbVariant  ""
#    XkbOptions  ""

   XkbKeycodes     "xfree86"
   XkbTypes        "default"
   XkbCompat       "default"
   XkbSymbols      "us(pc101)"
   XkbGeometry     "pc"
   XkbRules        "xfree86"
   XkbModel        "pc101"
    XkbLayout       "us"
EndSection
```

XF86Config Pointer Section

The Pointer Section in Listing 4.4 tells the X server what pointer, or mouse, to use and how the buttons are handled. Note that Listing 4.4 shows a configuration for a PS/2 mouse. Other Protocol settings are Auto for a serial mouse and BusMouse for a bus mouse. The Device entry, `/dev/mouse`, is a symbolic link to the actual device (such as `/dev/ttyS0` for a serial mouse).

Two-button mouse users will definitely want to enable a three-button emulator, in which a simultaneous depressing of both buttons simulates the middle (or Button 2) press. One common use of Button 2 is to paste text or graphics. For more information about configuring a mouse, see the file README.mouse under the /usr/X11R6/lib/X11/doc directory.

LISTING 4.4 XF86CONFIG'S POINTER SECTION

```
# **********************************************************************
# Pointer section
# **********************************************************************

Section "Pointer"
    Protocol    "PS/2"
    Device      "/dev/mouse"

# When using XQUEUE, comment out the above two lines, and uncomment
# the following line.

#    Protocol  "Xqueue"

# Baudrate and SampleRate are only for some Logitech mice

#    BaudRate  9600
#    SampleRate 150

# Emulate3Buttons is an option for 2-button Microsoft mice
# Emulate3Timeout is the timeout in milliseconds (default is 50ms)

    Emulate3Buttons
    Emulate3Timeout    50

# ChordMiddle is an option for some 3-button Logitech mice

#    ChordMiddle

EndSection
```

XF86Config Monitor Section

The first several parts of the XF86Config file are easy to understand, but many XFree86 users whose initial XF86Config file does not work will want to pay specific attention to the Monitor section (shown in Listing 4.5), the Device section (Listing 4.6), and the Screen section (Listing 4.7). The Monitor section contains specific details and settings for your monitor, such as your monitor's name, its horizontal and vertical sync ranges, and critical modelines (one for each video resolution—for example, 640×480, 800×600, 1024×768). Understanding the modeline is key to fine-tuning your X11 display.

For the best details, see the files VideoModes.doc and README.Config under the /usr/X11R6/lib/X11/doc directory before fine-tuning modelines in your XF86Config file. Another good tutorial is the *XFree86-Video-Timings-HOWTO* under the /usr/doc/HOWTO directory.

The basic parts of a modeline are ten different values representing (from left to right):

- A label of the screen resolution, such as 800×600
- A video frequency in mHz
- The number of visible dots per line on your display
- The Start Horizontal Retrace value (number of pulses before video sync pulse starts)
- The End Horizontal Retrace value (end of sync pulse)
- The total number of visible and invisible dots on your display
- The Vertical Display End value (number of visible lines of dots on your display)
- The Start Vertical Retrace value (number of lines before the sync pulse starts)
- The End Vertical Retrace value (number of lines at the end of the sync pulse)
- The Vertical Total value (total number of visible and invisible line on your display)

LISTING 4.5 THE XF86CONFIG MONITOR SECTION

```
# **********************************************************************
# Monitor section
# **********************************************************************

# Any number of monitor sections may be present

Section "Monitor"

    Identifier  "My Monitor"
    VendorName  "Unknown"
    ModelName   "Unknown"

# HorizSync is in kHz unless units are specified.
# HorizSync may be a comma separated list of discrete values, or a
# comma separated list of ranges of values.
# NOTE: THE VALUES HERE ARE EXAMPLES ONLY. REFER TO YOUR MONITOR'S
# USER MANUAL FOR THE CORRECT NUMBERS.

    HorizSync   31.5 - 35.1

# VertRefresh is in Hz unless units are specified.
# VertRefresh may be a comma separated list of discrete values, or a
# comma separated list of ranges of values.
# NOTE: THE VALUES HERE ARE EXAMPLES ONLY. REFER TO YOUR MONITOR'S
# USER MANUAL FOR THE CORRECT NUMBERS.

    VertRefresh 40-150
```

continues

LISTING 4.5 CONTINUED

```
# Modes can be specified in two formats. A compact one-line format, or
# a multi-line format.

# These two are equivalent

#    ModeLine "1024x768i" 45 1024 1048 1208 1264 768 776 784 817 Interlace

#    Mode "1024x768i"
#        DotClock 45
#        Htimings     1024 1048 1208 1264
#        Vtimings     768 776 784 817
#        Flags        "Interlace"
#    EndMode


# This is a set of standard mode timings. Modes that are out of monitor
# spec are automatically deleted by the server (provided the HorizSync
# and VertRefresh lines are correct), so there's no immediate need to
# delete mode timings (unless particular mode timings don't work on your
# monitor). With these modes, the best standard mode that your monitor
# and video card can support for a given resolution is automatically
# used.

# 640x400 @ 70 Hz, 31.5 kHz hsync
Modeline "640x400"     25.175 640  664  760  800   400  409  411  450
# 640x480 @ 60 Hz, 31.5 kHz hsync
Modeline "640x480"     25.175 640  664  760  800   480  491  493  525
# 800x600 @ 56 Hz, 35.15 kHz hsync
ModeLine "800x600"     36     800  824  896 1024   600  601  603  625
# 1024x768 @ 87 Hz interlaced, 35.5 kHz hsync
#Modeline "1024x768"    44.9  1024 1048 1208 1264   768  776  784  817
Interlace

# 640x480 @ 72 Hz, 36.5 kHz hsync
Modeline "640x480"     31.5   640  680  720  864   480  488  491  521
# 800x600 @ 60 Hz, 37.8 kHz hsync
Modeline "800x600"     40     800  840  968 1056   600  601  605  628
+hsync +vsync

# 800x600 @ 72 Hz, 48.0 kHz hsync
Modeline "800x600"     50     800  856  976 1040   600  637  643  666
+hsync +vsync
# 1024x768 @ 60 Hz, 48.4 kHz hsync
Modeline "1024x768"    65    1024 1032 1176 1344   768  771  777  806 -
hsync -vsync

# 1024x768 @ 70 Hz, 56.5 kHz hsync
Modeline "1024x768"    75    1024 1048 1184 1328   768  771  777  806 -
```

```
hsync -vsync
# 1280x1024 @ 87 Hz interlaced, 51 kHz hsync
#Modeline "1280x1024"   80    1280 1296 1512 1568  1024 1025 1037 1165
Interlace

# 1024x768 @ 76 Hz, 62.5 kHz hsync
Modeline "1024x768"    85    1024 1032 1152 1360   768  784  787  823
# 1280x1024 @ 61 Hz, 64.2 kHz hsync
Modeline "1280x1024"  110    1280 1328 1512 1712  1024 1025 1028 1054

# 1280x1024 @ 74 Hz, 78.85 kHz hsync
Modeline "1280x1024"  135    1280 1312 1456 1712  1024 1027 1030 1064

# 1280x1024 @ 76 Hz, 81.13 kHz hsync
Modeline "1280x1024"  135    1280 1312 1416 1664  1024 1027 1030 1064

# Low-res Doublescan modes
# If your chipset does not support doublescan, you get a 'squashed'
# resolution like 320x400.

# 320x200 @ 70 Hz, 31.5 kHz hsync, 8:5 aspect ratio
Modeline "320x200"     12.588 320  336  384  400   200  204  205  225
Doublescan
# 320x240 @ 60 Hz, 31.5 kHz hsync, 4:3 aspect ratio
Modeline "320x240"     12.588 320  336  384  400   240  245  246  262
Doublescan
# 320x240 @ 72 Hz, 36.5 kHz hsync
Modeline "320x240"     15.750 320  336  384  400   240  244  246  262
Doublescan
# 400x300 @ 56 Hz, 35.2 kHz hsync, 4:3 aspect ratio
ModeLine "400x300"     18     400  416  448  512   300  301  602  312
Doublescan
# 400x300 @ 60 Hz, 37.8 kHz hsync
Modeline "400x300"     20     400  416  480  528   300  301  303  314
Doublescan
# 400x300 @ 72 Hz, 48.0 kHz hsync
Modeline "400x300"     25     400  424  488  520   300  319  322  333
Doublescan
# 480x300 @ 56 Hz, 35.2 kHz hsync, 8:5 aspect ratio
ModeLine "480x300"     21.656 480  496  536  616   300  301  302  312
Doublescan
# 480x300 @ 60 Hz, 37.8 kHz hsync
Modeline "480x300"     23.890 480  496  576  632   300  301  303  314
Doublescan
# 480x300 @ 63 Hz, 39.6 kHz hsync
Modeline "480x300"     25     480  496  576  632   300  301  303  314
Doublescan
# 480x300 @ 72 Hz, 48.0 kHz hsync
Modeline "480x300"     29.952 480  504  584  624   300  319  322  333
Doublescan

EndSection
```

XF86Config Device Section

The Device section in Listing 4.6 contains details about your video chipset, such as RAM or clockchips. Note that even though you told Xconfigurator you have 2MB of video ram, Xconfigurator commented out your choice with a pound sign (#). To properly configure for X, you need to remove the pound sign in front of the VideoRam setting in this part of the XF86Config file.

This section of your XF86Config file is critical—the device definition is used to tell the X server exactly what type of video chipset and options to support. (Your XF86Config will definitely look different from this one.) For a list of device Identifiers and options, see the README file under the /usr/X11R6/lib/X11/doc directory corresponding with your chipset.

LISTING 4.6 THE XF86CONFIG DEVICE SECTION

```
# **********************************************************************
# Graphics device section
# **********************************************************************

# Any number of graphics device sections may be present

Section "Device"
    Identifier        "Generic VGA"
    VendorName        "Unknown"
    BoardName "Unknown"
    Chipset   "generic"

#     VideoRam 256

#     Clocks   25.2 28.3

EndSection

# Device configured by Xconfigurator:

Section "Device"
    Identifier   "GD 7548"
    VendorName   "Unknown"
    BoardName    "Unknown"
    #VideoRam    2048
# Use Option "no_bitblt" if you have graphics problems. If that fails
# try Option "noaccel".
# Refer to /usr/X11R6/lib/doc/README.cirrus.
# To allow linear addressing, uncomment the Option line and the
# address that the card maps the framebuffer to.
    # Insert Clocks lines here if appropriate
EndSection
```

XF86Config Screen Section

The XF86Config Screen section in Listing 4.7 tells what X server to use, the color depth (such as 8-, 16-, 24- or 32-bits per pixel), the screen size (such as 640×480, 800×600, or 1024×768), and the size of the virtual screen. This particular listing shows you have the option to use the `startx` command's -bpp option to have 16- or 32-bit color X sessions. The `startx` command is an easy way to start an X session if you're working on a single computer. There are other ways to start X (see the section about "Using xdm" later on). If your video card and monitor support these features, you can start a 16-bit X session like this:

```
# startx -- -bpp 16
```

The Screen section contains directions for your chosen X server (the XF86_SVGA or other color server, the 4-bit or 16-color XF86_VGA16 server, or the monochrome server, XF86_Mono) on what resolutions and virtual screen size to support.

For example, according to the configuration in Listing 4.7, if you're using the 8-bit or 256-color mode of the XF86_SVGA server, you have the choice of a 640×480 display (with an 800×600 virtual screen) or an 800×600 display. You can toggle resolutions during your X session by holding down the Ctrl+Alt keys and depressing the plus (+) or minus (-) key on your keypad. Laptop users need to use the NumLock key before switching resolutions.

However, if you start your X session with the -bpp 32 option, note that your choice of video resolution is limited to 640×480. Remember that Listing 4.7 was generated from our Xconfigurator session, so your XF86Config file will be different.

LISTING 4.7 THE XF86CONFIG SCREEN SECTION

```
# **********************************************************************
# Screen sections
# **********************************************************************

# The Colour SVGA server

Section "Screen"
    Driver      "svga"
    # Use Device "Generic VGA" for Standard VGA 320x200x256
    #Device      "Generic VGA"
    Device      "GD 7548"
    Monitor     "My Monitor"
    Subsection "Display"
        Depth       8
        # Omit the Modes line for the "Generic VGA" device
```

continues

LISTING 4.7 CONTINUED

```
        Modes       "640x480" "800x600"
        ViewPort    0 0
        # Use Virtual 320 200 for Generic VGA
        Virtual     800 600
    EndSubsection
    Subsection "Display"
        Depth       16
        Modes       "640x480" "800x600"
        ViewPort    0 0
        Virtual     800 600
    EndSubsection
    Subsection "Display"
        Depth       32
        Modes       "640x480"
        ViewPort    0 0
        Virtual     800 600
    EndSubsection
EndSection

# The 16-color VGA server

Section "Screen"
    Driver      "vga16"
    Device      "Generic VGA"
    Monitor     "My Monitor"
    Subsection "Display"
        Modes       "640x480" "800x600"
        ViewPort    0 0
        Virtual     800 600
    EndSubsection
EndSection

# The Mono server

Section "Screen"
    Driver      "vga2"
    Device      "Generic VGA"
    Monitor     "My Monitor"
    Subsection "Display"
        Modes       "640x480" "800x600"
        ViewPort    0 0
        Virtual     800 600
    EndSubsection
EndSection

# The accelerated servers (S3, Mach32, Mach8, 8514, P9000, AGX, W32, Mach64
# I128, and S3V)
Section "Screen"
```

```
    Driver      "accel"
    Device      "GD 7548"
    Monitor     "My Monitor"
    Subsection "Display"
        Depth       8
        Modes       "640x480" "800x600"
        ViewPort    0 0
        Virtual     800 600
    EndSubsection
    Subsection "Display"
        Depth       16
        Modes       "640x480" "800x600"
        ViewPort    0 0
        Virtual     800 600
    EndSubsection
    Subsection "Display"
        Depth       32
        Modes       "640x480" "800x600"
        ViewPort    0 0
        Virtual     800 600
    EndSubsection
EndSection
```

Using xf86config

An alternative way to create an XF86Config for your X session is to use the `xf86config` command, found under the /usr/X11R6/bin directory. This command is not a Red Hat tool, but part of the XFree86 distribution, and works from the command line of your console or an X11 terminal window. Start the command like this:

```
# xf86config
```

Press the Return key twice (after reading two introductory screens) to get to the mouse configuration screen, which looks like this:

```
First specify a mouse protocol type. Choose one from the following list:

 1.  Microsoft compatible (2-button protocol)
 2.  Mouse Systems (3-button protocol)
 3.  Bus Mouse
 4.  PS/2 Mouse
 5.  Logitech Mouse (serial, old type, Logitech protocol)
 6.  Logitech MouseMan (Microsoft compatible)
 7.  MM Series
 8.  MM HitTablet
 9.  Microsoft IntelliMouse
```

```
If you have a two-button mouse, it is most likely of type 1,
and if you have a three-button mouse, it can probably support
both protocol 1 and 2. There are two main varieties of the
latter type: mice with a switch to select the protocol, and mice
that default to 1 and require a button to be held at boot-time to
select protocol 2. Some mice can be convinced to do 2 by sending
a special sequence to the serial port (see the ClearDTR/ClearRTS options).

Enter a protocol number:
```

As you can see, you have a choice of nine different pointers. Enter a number corresponding with your pointer, and press the Enter key. Next you're asked whether you want three-button emulation.

```
If your mouse has only two buttons, it is recommended that you enable
Emulate3Buttons.

Please answer the following question with either 'y' or 'n'.
Do you want to enable Emulate3Buttons?
```

Press the y key if desired, followed by the Enter key. Next you're asked for the Linux device corresponding with your pointer. For Red Hat users, this is `/dev/mouse`.

```
Now give the full device name that the mouse is connected to, for example
/dev/tty00. Just pressing enter will use the default, /dev/mouse.

Mouse device:
```

If you have a different pointer, enter its device name from the /dev directory and press Enter. The next screen asks if you want to use XFree86's XKeyboard extension.

```
Beginning with XFree86 3.1.2D, you can use the new X11R6.1 XKEYBOARD
extension to manage the keyboard layout. If you answer 'n' to the
following
question, the server will use the old method, and you have to adjust
your keyboard layout with xmodmap.

Please answer the following question with either 'y' or 'n'.
Do you want to use XKB?
```

For most users, this is a good idea; unless you have a specialized keyboard or want to customize your keyboard's characters by using the xmodmap client, answer with a **y** and press the Enter key. The `xf86config` command follows up with a series of dialogs, asking about your choice of keyboards.

```
List of preconfigured keymaps:

  1  Standard 101-key, US encoding
  2  Microsoft Natural, US encoding
  3  KeyTronic FlexPro, US encoding
  4  Standard 101-key, US encoding with ISO9995-3 extensions
```

```
  5  Standard 101-key, German encoding
  6  Standard 101-key, French encoding
  7  Standard 101-key, Thai encoding
  8  Standard 101-key, Swiss/German encoding
  9  Standard 101-key, Swiss/French encoding
 10  None of the above

Enter a number to choose the keymap. 10

 You did not select one of the preconfigured keymaps. We will now try to
compose a suitable XKB setting. This setting is untested.
Please select one of the following standard keyboards. Use DEFAULT if
nothing really fits (101-key, tune manually)

  1  Standard 101-key keyboard
  2  Standard 102-key keyboard
  3  101-key with ALT_R = Multi_key
  4  102-key with ALT_R = Multi_key
  5  Microsoft Natural keyboard
  6  KeyTronic FlexPro keyboard
  7  DEFAULT

Enter a number to choose the keyboard.  2
Please choose one of the following countries. Use DEFAULT if nothing
really fits (US encoding, tune manually)
Press enter to continue, or ctrl-c to abort.

  1  Belgium
  2  Bulgaria
  3  Canada
  4  Czechoslovakia
  5  Denmark
  6  Finland
  7  France
  8  Germany
  9  Italy
 10  Norway
 11  Poland
 12  Portugal
 13  Russia
 14  Spain
 15  Sweden
 16  Thailand
 17  Switzerland/French layout
 18  Switzerland/German layout

Enter a number to choose the country.
Press enter for the next page

 19  United Kingdom
 20  USA
 21  DEFAULT
```

```
Enter a number to choose the country.
Press enter for the next page 20
```

After you choose a keyboard, xf86config presents a short introductory screen before asking for your monitor's specifics. Press the Enter key, and you'll see:

```
You must indicate the horizontal sync range of your monitor. You can
either
select one of the predefined ranges below that correspond to industry-
standard monitor types, or give a specific range.

It is VERY IMPORTANT that you do not specify a monitor type with a
horizontal
sync range that is beyond the capabilities of your monitor. If in doubt,
choose a conservative setting.

    hsync in kHz; monitor type with characteristic modes
 1  31.5; Standard VGA, 640x480 @ 60 Hz
 2  31.5 - 35.1; Super VGA, 800x600 @ 56 Hz
 3  31.5, 35.5; 8514 Compatible, 1024x768 @ 87 Hz interlaced (no 800x600)
 4  31.5, 35.15, 35.5; Super VGA, 1024x768 @ 87 Hz interlaced, 800x600 @
    ➥56 Hz
 5  31.5 - 37.9; Extended Super VGA, 800x600 @ 60 Hz, 640x480 @ 72 Hz
 6  31.5 - 48.5; Non-Interlaced SVGA, 1024x768 @ 60 Hz, 800x600 @ 72 Hz
 7  31.5 - 57.0; High Frequency SVGA, 1024x768 @ 70 Hz
 8  31.5 - 64.3; Monitor that can do 1280x1024 @ 60 Hz
 9  31.5 - 79.0; Monitor that can do 1280x1024 @ 74 Hz
10  31.5 - 82.0; Monitor that can do 1280x1024 @ 76 Hz
11  Enter your own horizontal sync range

Enter your choice (1-11):
```

Enter a number corresponding to your monitor's characteristics. If you prefer, enter the number 11 to give a specific horizontal sync range. You then see:

```
Please enter the horizontal sync range of your monitor, in the format used
in the table of monitor types above. You can either specify one or more
continuous ranges (e.g. 15-25, 30-50), or one or more fixed sync
frequencies.

Horizontal sync range: 31.5-37.9
```

Press the Enter key, and you'll then be asked to enter the vertical range.

```
You must indicate the vertical sync range of your monitor. You can either
select one of the predefined ranges below that correspond to industry-
standard monitor types, or give a specific range. For interlaced modes,
the number that counts is the high one (e.g. 87 Hz rather than 43 Hz).

 1  50-70
 2  50-90
 3  50-100
```

```
 4  40-150
 5  Enter your own vertical sync range

Enter your choice:
```

If you prefer to enter your own range, choose **5** and press the Enter key. Now you'll see:

```
Vertical sync range:
```

Enter your monitor's vertical range, such as **50-70**, and press the Enter key. You'll now be asked to enter three lines of description for your monitor. Enter a description, the manufacturer, and the model of your monitor. You can also just press the Enter key, as this information is not critical.

```
You must now enter a few identification/description strings, namely an
identifier, a vendor name, and a model name. Just pressing enter will fill
in default names.

The strings are free-form, spaces are allowed.
Enter an identifier for your monitor definition:
Enter the vendor name of your monitor:
Enter the model name of your monitor:
```

After you enter the model name and press the Enter key, xf86config presents an intro dialog to video card selection and asks if you want to look at the card database.

```
Now we must configure video card specific settings. At this point you can
choose to make a selection out of a database of video card definitions.
Because there can be variation in Ramdacs and clock generators even
between cards of the same model, it is not sensible to blindly copy
the settings (e.g. a Device section). For this reason, after you make a
selection, you will still be asked about the components of the card, with
the settings from the chosen database entry presented as a strong hint.

The database entries include information about the chipset, what server to
run, the Ramdac and ClockChip, and comments that will be included in the
Device section. However, a lot of definitions only hint about what server
to run (based on the chipset the card uses) and are untested.

If you can't find your card in the database, there's nothing to worry
about. You should only choose a database entry that is exactly the same
model as your card; choosing one that looks similar is just a bad idea
(e.g. a GemStone Snail 64 may be as different from a GemStone Snail 64+ in
terms of hardware as can be).

Do you want to look at the card database?  y
```

You'll see the following list of the first 18 video cards in XFree86's card database (located in the file Cards, under the /usr/X11R6/lib/X11 directory):

```
 0  2 the Max MAXColor S3 Trio64V+                       S3 Trio64V+
 1  928Movie                                             S3 928
 2  AGX (generic)                                        AGX-014/15/16
 3  ALG-5434(E)                                          CL-GD5434
 4  ASUS 3Dexplorer                                      RIVA128
 5  ASUS PCI-AV264CT                                     ATI-Mach64
 6  ASUS PCI-V264CT                                      ATI-Mach64
 7  ASUS Video Magic PCI V864                            S3 864
 8  ASUS Video Magic PCI VT64                            S3 Trio64
 9  AT25                                                 Alliance AT3D
10  AT3D                                                 Alliance AT3D
11  ATI 3D Pro Turbo                                     ATI-Mach64
12  ATI 3D Xpression                                     ATI-Mach64
13  ATI 3D Xpression+ PC2TV                              ATI-Mach64
14  ATI 8514 Ultra (no VGA)                              ATI-Mach8
15  ATI All-in-Wonder                                    ATI-Mach64
16  ATI Graphics Pro Turbo                               ATI-Mach64
17  ATI Graphics Pro Turbo 1600                          ATI-Mach64

Enter a number to choose the corresponding card definition.
Press enter for the next page, q to continue configuration.
```

Your choices are to enter a number corresponding to your card (or a card recommended as a close choice by the README file for your card under the /usr/X11R6/lib/X11/doc directory), to press the Enter key to page to the next screen, or to press q to continue the configuration. Note that if you press q, xf86config will use "Unknown" for your graphics device. On the other hand, if you pick a specific card, xf86config will report with an identifier, chipset, and selected server appropriate for your chipset, (after choosing entry 97 in the database).

```
Your selected card definition:

Identifier: Cirrus Logic GD754x (laptop)
Chipset:    CL-GD7541/42/43/48
Server:     XF86_SVGA
Do NOT probe clocks or use any Clocks line.

Press enter to continue, or ctrl-c to abort.
```

Press the Enter key, and you're asked to select the type of server:

```
Now you must determine which server to run. Refer to the manpages and
other
documentation. The following servers are available (they may not all be
installed on your system):

 1  The XF86_Mono server. This a monochrome server that should work on any
    VGA-compatible card, in 640x480 (more on some SVGA chipsets).
 2  The XF86_VGA16 server. This is a 16-color VGA server that should work
    on any VGA-compatible card.
```

```
3  The XF86_SVGA server. This is a 256 color SVGA server that supports
   a number of SVGA chipsets. On some chipsets it is accelerated or
   supports higher color depths.
4  The accelerated servers. These include XF86_S3, XF86_Mach32,
   XF86_Mach8,XF86_8514, XF86_P9000, XF86_AGX, XF86_W32, XF86_Mach64,
   XF86_I128 and XF86_S3V.

These four server types correspond to the four different "Screen" sections
in XF86Config (vga2, vga16, svga, accel).

 5  Choose the server from the card definition, XF86_SVGA.

Which one of these screen types do you intend to run by default (1-5)?
```

Unless you specifically want your X sessions to use black and white or the 16-color server, XF86_VGA16, choose the default server preselected by xf86config by entering **5** and pressing the Enter key. Next you're asked whether you want xf86config to create a symbolic link called X under the /usr/X11R6/bin directory. Don't!

```
The server to run is selected by changing the symbolic link 'X'. For
example,'rm /usr/X11R6/bin/X; ln -s /usr/X11R6/bin/XF86_SVGA
/usr/X11R6/bin/X' selects the SVGA server.

Please answer the following question with either 'y' or 'n'.
Do you want me to set the symbolic link?
```

NOTE

Because of a recent security update to XFree86, the symbolic link X should point to the Xwrapper client, found in the /usr/X11R6/bin directory. These files should look like:

```
# ls -l /usr/X11R6/bin/X
lrwxrwxrwx   1 root     root          8 Jul 26 15:37 /usr/X11/bin/X -> Xwrapper
# ls -l /usr/X11R6/bin/Xwrapper
-rws--x--x   1 root     root       4272 Jun  8 23:09 /usr/X11R6/bin/Xwrapper
```

If you don't find X as this link, log in as the root operator and use the `ln` command to create the link like this:

```
# ln -s /usr/X11R6/bin/Xwrapper /usr/X11R6/bin/X
```

Type **n**, and press the Enter key. You're now asked to enter the amount of video memory installed in your graphics card.

```
Now you must give information about your video card. This will be used for
the "Device" section of your video card in XF86Config.

You must indicate how much video memory you have. It is probably a good
```

```
idea to use the same approximate amount as that detected by the server you
intend to use. If you encounter problems that are due to the used server
not supporting the amount of memory you have (e.g. ATI Mach64 is limited
to 1024K with the SVGA server), specify the maximum amount supported by
the server.

How much video memory do you have on your video card:

 1  256K
 2  512K
 3  1024K
 4  2048K
 5  4096K
 6  Other

Enter your choice:
```

Enter a number corresponding to the amount of memory, or enter **6**, press the Enter key, and then enter the amount of memory, in kilobytes, supported by your card. Note that like Xconfigurator, the xf86config command generates an XF86Config file with the video RAM setting commented out. You'll have to edit the file after you're done to ensure your video RAM setting is used.

You're now asked to enter information as you did for your monitor, but about your video card this time.

```
You must now enter a few identification/description strings, namely an
identifier, a vendor name, and a model name. Just pressing enter will fill
in default names (possibly from a card definition).

Your card definition is Cirrus Logic GD754x (laptop).

The strings are free-form, spaces are allowed.
Enter an identifier for your video card definition:
You can simply press enter here if you have a generic card, or want to
describe your card with one string.
Enter the vendor name of your video card:
Enter the model (board) name of your video card:
```

Again, it's not necessary to fill out this information. After pressing the Enter key, you're asked about your video's RAMDAC setting.

```
The RAMDAC setting only applies to the S3, AGX, W32 servers, and some
drivers in the SVGA servers. Some RAMDACs are auto-detected by the server.
The detection of a RAMDAC is forced by using a Ramdac "identifier" line in
the Device section. The identifiers are shown at the right of the
following
table of RAMDAC types:
```

```
 1  AT&T 20C490 (S3 and AGX servers, ARK driver)              att20c490
 2  AT&T 20C498/21C498/22C498 (S3, autodetected)              att20c498
 3  AT&T 20C409/20C499 (S3, autodetected)                     att20c409
 4  AT&T 20C505 (S3)                                          att20c505
 5  BrookTree BT481 (AGX)                                     bt481
 6  BrookTree BT482 (AGX)                                     bt482
 7  BrookTree BT485/9485 (S3)                                 bt485
 8  Sierra SC15025 (S3, AGX)                                  sc15025
 9  S3 GenDAC (86C708) (autodetected)                         s3gendac
10  S3 SDAC (86C716) (autodetected)                           s3_sdac
11  STG-1700 (S3, autodetected)                               stg1700
12  STG-1703 (S3, autodetected)                               stg1703

Enter a number to choose the corresponding RAMDAC.
Press enter for the next page, q to quit without selection of a RAMDAC.
```

Press **q**, followed by the Enter key if this section does not apply to you. Next, you're asked about your video's clockchip settings, like this:

```
A Clockchip line in the Device section forces the detection of a
programmable clock device. With a clockchip enabled, any required
clock can be programmed without requiring probing of clocks or a
Clocks line. Most cards don't have a programmable clock chip.
Choose from the following list:

 1  Chrontel 8391                                             ch8391
 2  ICD2061A and compatibles (ICS9161A, DCS2824)              icd2061a
 3  ICS2595                                                   ics2595
 4  ICS5342 (similar to SDAC, but not completely compatible)  ics5342
 5  ICS5341                                                   ics5341
 6  S3 GenDAC (86C708) and ICS5300 (autodetected)             s3gendac
 7  S3 SDAC (86C716)                                          s3_sdac
 8  STG 1703 (autodetected)                                   stg1703
 9  Sierra SC11412                                            sc11412
10  TI 3025 (autodetected)                                    ti3025
11  TI 3026 (autodetected)                                    ti3026
12  IBM RGB 51x/52x (autodetected)                            ibm_rgb5xx

Just press enter if you don't want a Clockchip setting.
What Clockchip setting do you want (1-12)?
```

If your video card uses a clockchip (see your card's README file under the /usr/X11R6/lib/X11/doc directory), select the appropriate setting, followed by the Enter key—or just the Enter key if you don't need or want a clockchip setting in your XF86Config's Device section. The xf86config command then asks if you'd like to probe your video card for clockchip settings. Note that our earlier choice of the Cirrus Logic chipset said to NOT probe the clocks (because a clockchip is not used).

HANDY COMMAND-LINE DIAGNOSTICS

Probing your video card for clockchip settings is one way to fine-tune your XF86Config file. Another handy way to diagnose your XF86Config settings before you start your first X session is to use a tip detailed by Eric S. Raymond in his *XFree86-HOWTO* (found under the /usr/doc/HOWTO directory). This method saves the output of the chosen X server, such as XF86_SVGA, while it reads your XF86Config. You can save the output to a file such as myX11.txt with a command line like this: **`X > myX11.txt 2>&1`**. If you jump into your X session, kill the session by holding down the Alt+Ctrl keys and pressing the Backspace key. You can then read the X server's output with the more-or-less command of **`less myX11.txt`** so you can check to see if everything is okay. This command is handy because the output normally scrolls by on your screen too fast to read.

```
For most configurations, a Clocks line is useful since it prevents the
slow and nasty sounding clock probing at server start-up. Probed clocks
are displayed at server startup, along with other server and hardware
configuration info. You can save this information in a file by running
'X -probeonly 2>output_file'. Be warned that clock probing is inherently
imprecise; some clocks may be slightly too high (varies per run).

At this point I can run X -probeonly, and try to extract the clock
information from the output. It is recommended that you do this yourself
and add a clocks line (note that the list of clocks may be split over
multiple Clocks lines) to your Device section afterwards. Be aware that a
clocks line is not appropriate for drivers that have a fixed set of clocks
and don't probe by default (e.g. Cirrus). Also, for the P9000 server you
must simply specify clocks line that matches the modes you want to use.
For the S3 server with a programmable clock chip you need a 'ClockChip'
line and no Clocks line.

You must be root to be able to run X -probeonly now.

The card definition says to NOT probe clocks.
Do you want me to run 'X -probeonly' now?
```

Enter a **`y`** or an **`n`**, and press the Enter key. The xf86config command now asks about your desired screen resolution and color depths. It is unnecessary to make any changes, as the X server will not accept a display size or color depth out of range for your video card, but you should generate a "cleaner" XF86Config file by changing the modes or settings to match the capabilities for your video and monitor. For example, settings of 1024×768 or greater at 16-, 24-, or 32-bits per pixel don't make sense if your display and video card cannot support the settings.

```
For each depth, a list of modes (resolutions) is defined. The default
resolution that the server will start up with will be the first listed
mode that can be supported by the monitor and card.
Currently it is set to:

"640x480" "800x600" "1024x768" "1280x1024" for 8bpp
"640x480" "800x600" "1024x768" for 16bpp
"640x480" "800x600" for 24bpp
"640x480" "800x600" for 32bpp

Note that 16, 24 and 32bpp are only supported on a few configurations.
Modes that cannot be supported due to monitor or clock constraints will
be automatically skipped by the server.

 1  Change the modes for 8pp (256 colors)
 2  Change the modes for 16bpp (32K/64K colors)
 3  Change the modes for 24bpp (24-bit color, packed pixel)
 4  Change the modes for 32bpp (24-bit color)
 5  The modes are OK, continue.

Enter your choice:
```

If you choose to change some of the settings, you're asked to choose specific resolutions for each color depth and whether or not you'd like a virtual screen size larger than your display (such as an 800×600 virtual screen when using a 640×480 display). Change the settings for each mode by pressing a key 1 through 4, or press 5 to accept the defaults, and then press the Enter key to continue. The xf86config command asks if you want to save the generated XF86Config file in the current directory. Enter a **y** and press the Enter key, and you're done.

```
I am going to write the XF86Config file now. Make sure you don't
accidentally overwrite a previously configured one.

Do you want it written to the current directory as 'XF86Config'? y
File has been written. Take a look at it before running 'startx'. Note
that the XF86Config file must be in one of the directories searched by the
server (e.g. /usr/X11R6/lib/X11) in order to be used. Within the server
press ctrl, alt and '+' simultaneously to cycle video resolutions.
Pressing ctrl, alt and backspace simultaneously immediately exits the
server (use if the monitor doesn't sync for a particular mode).

For further configuration, refer to /usr/X11R6/lib/X11/doc/README.Config.
```

The XF86Config file may be located in several different places in your system:

/etc/XF86Config

/etc/X11/XF86Config

/usr/X11R6/lib/X11/XF86Config

/root/XF86Config (but only if you use X as root)

Finally, if you don't want to use Xconfigurator or xf86config to generate an XF86Config file, you can create your own. You'll find a template file, called XF86Config.eg, under the /usr/X11R6/lib/X11 directory. Copy this file to your directory and edit it in your favorite text editor, inserting specifications for your system and X server.

The .xinitrc File

When you use the `startx` command to initiate an X session on your computer, details about which window manager to use or other X clients to start can be found in a file called .xinitrc in your home directory. A template file called xintrc is installed in the /etc/X11/xinit directory. You can copy this file to your home directory with the filename .xinitrc and modify it to suit your needs.

Although the default xinitrc file contains shell script logic to load in system resources or set different environment variables, you can define a simpler version from scratch, such as the one in Listing 4.8, which can be used to start 12 different X window managers. (For more information about various X window managers, including ones included on the CD-ROM in this book, see Chapter 5, "Window Managers.")

LISTING 4.8 SAMPLE .XINITRC FILE

```
# Sample .xinitrc file
#
# This .xinitrc file has configuration support for the following X11
# window managers: AnotherLevel, fvwm, fvmw2, KDE, twm, mlvwm, AfterStep
#                  WindowMaker, wm2, wmx, mwm, GNOME
#
# Use AnotherLevel's configuration of the fvwm2 window manager
fvwm2 -cmd 'FvwmM4 -debug /etc/X11/AnotherLevel/fvwm2rc.m4'
#
# Use fvwm2
# fvwm2
#
# Use fvwm
# fvwm
#
# Use the K Desktop Environment
# startkde
#
# Use twm - note: needs an X terminal started
# twm
# exec xterm &
#
# Use the mlvwm (Macintosh-like) window manager
# mlvwm
#
```

```
# Use AfterStep
# afterstep
#
# Use WindowMaker
# exec wmaker
#
# Use the wm2 window manager
# wm2
#
# Use the wmx window manager
# wmx
#
# Use Motif's or LessTif's mwm
# mwm
#
# Use GNOME
#panel &
#background-properties --init &
#keyboard-properties --init &
#mouse-properties --init &
#fvwm2 -f .fvwm2rc.gnome
```

Note that the sample .xinitrc file in Listing 4.8 is currently set to use Red Hat's AnotherLevel configuration of the fvwm2 window manager. To use a different window manager (if installed on your system), add or remove the appropriate pound sign in the file.

Using Red Hat's wmconfig Command

Each X window manager in Listing 4.8 has its own set of configuration files. Some use a single default system-wide file, and others require numerous files and a complex series of support files for different code modules. To make the job of configuring your window manager easier, Red Hat Linux includes the `wmconfig`, or window-manager configuration command.

The `wmconfig` command, found under the /usr/X11R6/bin directory, creates resource files for use in your home directory for (at the time of this writing) seven X window managers. The resource files are built according to entries in different program files under the /etc/X11/wmconfig directory. This directory contains 106 entries for different commands and X clients. For example, here's the entry for emacs:

```
emacs name "emacs"
emacs description "emacs Editor"
emacs exec "emacs &"
emacs group Utilities
```

The entry shows the program's name, its description, the command line to start the client, and under what menu the program will be found. Unfortunately, it's hard to determine how the different programs are grouped just by looking at the contents of the wmconfig directory; however, if you use wmconfig's --output= with the debug option, you get a tree-like list of how the programs are grouped, along with the names of the main menus that will be built.

To build a configuration file for the fvwm2 window manager, use wmconfig, along with its --output option:

```
# wmconfig --output=fvwm > .fvwm2rc
```

This command line creates a new .fvwm2rc file, so make a copy of your original files before using wmconfig. If you'd like to create your own set of custom configurations, create a .wmconfig directory in your home directory and copy the configuration files from the /etc/X11/wmconfig directory like this:

```
# mkdir .wmconfig ; cp /etc/X11/wmconfig/* .wmconfig
```

You can then edit and create window manager resource files from your .wmconfig directory instead of using the system-wide defaults.

The Personal X Resource File

Most default settings for the various X clients will be found in individual files under the /usr/X11R6/lib/X11/app-defaults directory. For example:

```
# ls /usr/X11R6/lib/X11/app-defaults
Beforelight     Pixmap          XFontSel        XRn              Xloadimage
Bitmap          RXvt            XGammon         XSm              Xmag
Bitmap-color    Seyon           XGetfile        XSysinfo         Xman
Chooser         Seyon-color     XLoad           XSysinfo-color   XmdAirport
Clock-color     Viewres         XLock           XTerm            XmdAnimate
Editres         X3270           XLogo           XTerm-color      XmdDraw
Editres-color   XBanner         XLogo-color     XbmBrowser       XmdFilemanager
Fig             XBanner.org     XMailbox        Xditview         XmdI18nInput
Fig-color       XCalc           XMdb            Xditview-chrtr   XmdPeriodic
Fileview        XCalc-color     XMixer          Xedit            XmdSampler2_0
GV              XCalc.org       XOsview         Xfd              XmdSetDate
GXditview       XClipboard      XPaint          Xfm              XmdTodo
KTerm           XClock          XPat            Xgc              Xmessage
Mwm             XConsole        XPlaycd         Xgopher          Xmh
NXTerm          XDbx            XPlaymidi       Xgopher-color    Xvidtune
```

These are text files each client uses for default window size, color, or other options. As a trivial example, edit the xplaycd client's resource file, XPlaycd, and change the line containing

```
!*reverseVideo:  off
```

to have the client use a reverse-video window. Do this by removing the exclamation point (!) and changing the word "off" to "on":

```
*reverseVideo:  on
```

Save the file and run the program from the command line of an X terminal window like this:

```
# xplaycd &
```

The before and after xplaycd windows are shown in Figure 4.10.

FIGURE 4.10
The xplaycd client's display and other features can be customized through its resource file.

Changes like these will affect all users on your system if you make the change to a client's file in the app-defaults directory. To avoid system-wide changes, create a file called .Xresources in your home directory with an entry for your application and specific settings. The format of this file is detailed in the X man page, but you can easily change defaults by specifying the client name, followed by the client's resource and a value. For example, to change how xplaycd displays (using our previous example), create this entry in your .Xresources file:

```
xplaycd*reverseVideo: on
```

Save the file, and then use the xrdb, or X resource database utility, to merge the values into your current X session:

```
# xrdb -merge .Xresources
```

If you create numerous settings and customized resources for clients during your X sessions and use the sample Listing 4.8, insert the xrdb line into the beginning of the .xinitrc file (the system-wide xinitrc file merges in these settings by default).

Using xdm

You can also use the xdm, or X display manager, to start X11, but in general, if you use xdm, Linux boots right into an X login screen. You can try `xdm` from the command line as the root operator by using the -nodaemon option like this:

```
# xdm -nodaemon
```

The display clears, and you see an xdm login display similar to the one in Figure 4.11. You can then log in to X or use the Ctrl+Alt+F1 keys to go back to your console display and kill the daemon with a Ctrl+C. If you'd like to customize this login screen, see the documentation for the `xbanner` command under the /usr/doc/xbanner directory. If you don't want to use `xbanner`, you'll have to edit the file Xsetup_0 under the /usr/X11R6/lib/X11/xdm directory and remove this line:

```
/usr/X11R6/bin/xbanner
```

After you have a working XF86Config, you might want to start Linux directly to X. To do this, you need to change an entry in the Red Hat Linux initialization table file, /etc/inittab. Look for this line:

```
id:3:initdefault
```

and change it to:

```
id:5:initdefault
```

Be careful—editing inittab is dangerous, and any errors could render your system unbootable. Make sure you have an emergency boot disk on hand, and make a backup copy of the inittab file first. Also note that this might not work with other distributions of Linux. You have been warned!

After you make this change, restart your system by using this shutdown command:

```
# shutdown -r now
```

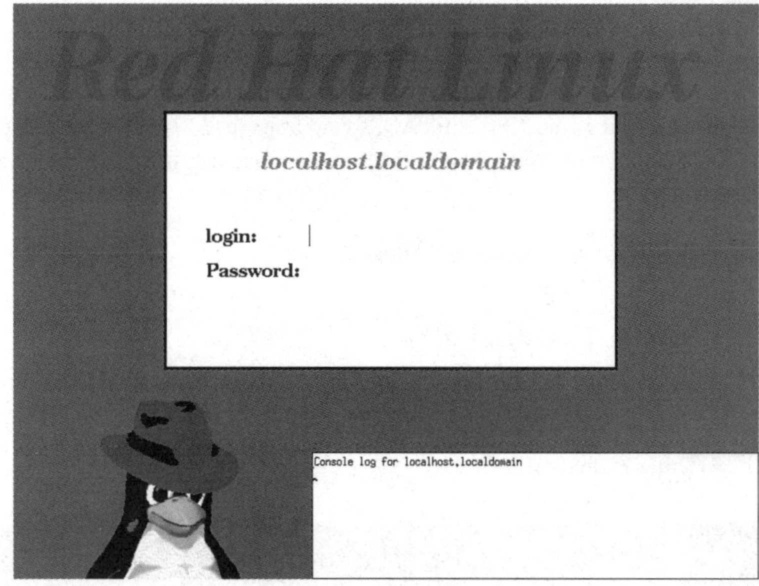

FIGURE 4.11
You can customize the Red Hat Linux xdm login screen for X11 by editing the xbanner program's X resources.

Compiling Programs for X

Red Hat Linux users enjoy the convenience of software installation and maintenance through the `rpm` or `glint` commands, but not all X11 clients are packaged for distribution in binary form. The good news is that most X programmers have simplified the process of building and installing X clients through the use of the Imakefile files. To build most X clients, first download and then decompress the file like this:

```
# tar xvzf newXprogram.tgz
```

Then change to the newly created program directory and use the xmkmf to build the client's Makefile:

```
# xmkmf
```

Building and installing the new X client can then be as easy as

```
# make install
```

The xmkmf shell script runs the `imake` command with a set of arguments, typically -DUseInstalled. For details about xmkmf and imake, see their man pages.

Troubleshooting XFree86

One of the best sources for troubleshooting installation or other problems when using XFree86's X11 is the XFree86 FAQ, found at `http://www.xfree86.org`. The FAQ contains seven sections and includes information covering such difficulties as

- Configuration problems
- Keyboard and mouse problems
- Display problems
- Problems using fonts
- Problems using configurations using symbolic links to X (Xwrapper)
- Chipset support fixes
- Other known problems

NOTE

If you cannot find the answer you need in the X manual pages, the FAQ, or other documentation, try lurking for a while on the `comp.os.linux.x` Usenet newsgroup. Or post a question, clearly stating your distribution and version of Linux, along with the version of XFree86 you've installed.

NOTE

If your Internet Service Provider (ISP) doesn't have `comp.os.linux.x`, or if you don't feel like using a Usenet newsreader to look for answers about Linux and X11, point your favorite web browser to `http://www.dejanews.com`.

Compiling Sources for XFree86

Most of the details about building a new server from the XFree86 source tree are contained in the file README.LinkKit under the /usr/X11R6/lib/X11 directory. You can also build a new XFree86 distribution by downloading the latest sources from `http://www.xfree86.org` or by using `rpm` or `glint` from the SRPMS directory of your book's CD-ROM.

Summary

This chapter has covered the basic installation and configuration of the XFree86 X11 distribution for Red Hat Linux. If you're a new user, you've found out how to correctly configure and install X with fewer problems; if you're an experienced user, we hope you've discovered some new features (such as Xwrapper or wmconfig) that will make your X sessions more productive and enjoyable.

Window Managers

by Bill Ball

In This Chapter

Introduction to X11 Window Managers

This chapter covers a variety of window managers for the X Window System. As you learned in Chapter 4, "The X Window System," X11 provides the base platform for a graphical interface, or window manager, you can use with Linux. You'll find a wealth of different programs for X included on this book's CD-ROM, including many of the programs discussed in this chapter: window managers from the XFree86 distribution, several from Red Hat Software, Inc. (such as a GNOME-enabled fvwm2), the commercial Common Desktop Environment (CDE), and the newer K Desktop Environment (KDE).

What is a Window Manager?

Using Linux and the XFree86 distribution of X11 means freedom of choice—the choice of an operating system and the choice of how you'd like your computer's desktop or root window in X to look. Although a window manager is nothing more than an X11 client, you'll find that using a window manager is virtually necessary if you want to run different programs, drag windows around the display, use icons, create virtual desktops, resize windows, or customize how your X sessions work. Of course, you can run X without a window manager, but you'll lose a lot of functionality.

NOTE

Want to try X without a window manager? Make a copy of your .xinitrc file in your home directory (or see listing 4.8 in Chapter 4) and, using your favorite text editor, create a new one with just one line:

```
exec xterm
```

When you restart X, you'll get an xterm window, as shown in Figure 5.1—but you won't be able to move or resize it. To quit your X session, either type the word **exit** at the command line of the xterm terminal window or use the Ctrl+Alt+Backspace key combination to kill your X session. Without a window manager to provide support for movable windows, you're pretty much stuck with a static xterm screen. Now do you see why window managers are so much fun (and necessary)?

FIGURE 5.1
You can run X11 without a window manager, but is it worth it?

Red Hat Linux comes with several window managers for X. Some window managers are part of the XFree86 X11 distribution, while others are provided by Red Hat for your use. We'll concentrate on the XFree86 window managers first. Then we'll move on to Red Hat's, introduce you to KDE, and wrap up with CDE.

The twm Window Manager

The twm, or Tab window manager (shown in Figure 5.2), comes with the XFree86 X Window distribution. Installed under the /usr/X11R6/bin directory, this window manager provides the basics of window management for X, such as:

- Custom keyboard commands
- Custom mouse commands
- Icon dock
- Icons
- Resizable windows
- Window titles

You'll find twm's system-wide configuration file, system.twmrc, under the /etc/X11/twm directory. This file contains default definitions you can change and use for yourself. Copy system.twmrc to your home directory as .twmrc to make your changes. You can use twm by inserting the following lines in your .xinitrc file:

```
twm
exec xterm &
```

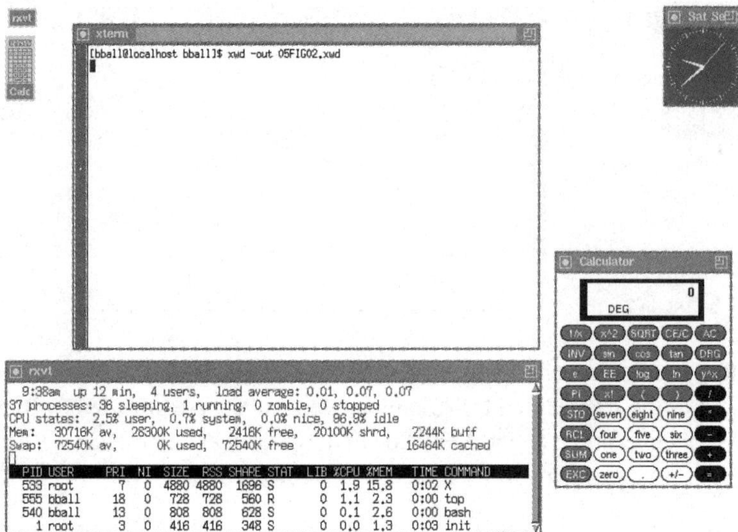

FIGURE 5.2
The twm, or Tab window manager for X provides basic window operations for your X sessions.

You'll need to start an xterm right after starting twm. Why? Because twm's default start-up file, which defines twm's root menu (accessed by pressing the left mouse button in a blank area of the desktop) does not include a menu item definition for a terminal. A much better approach is to open your copy of .twmrc in your favorite text editor, such as `pico`, and insert a menu definition to start a terminal:

```
# pico -w .twmrc
```

Look for the section defining the root menu:

```
menu "defops"
{
"Twm"   f.title
"Iconify"       f.iconify
"Resize"        f.resize
"Move"          f.move
"Raise"         f.raise
"Lower"         f.lower
""              f.nop
"Focus"         f.focus
"Unfocus"       f.unfocus
"Show Iconmgr"  f.showiconmgr
"Hide Iconmgr"  f.hideiconmgr
""              f.nop
"Kill"          f.destroy
"Delete"        f.delete
""              f.nop
```

```
"Restart"       f.restart
"Exit"          f.quit
}
```

Insert a menu item for xterm (or your favorite X11 terminal client) like this:

```
{
"Twm"   f.title
"Iconify"       f.iconify
"Resize"        f.resize
"Move"          f.move
"Raise"         f.raise
"Lower"         f.lower
"------------"  f.nop
"Focus"         f.focus
"Unfocus"       f.unfocus
"Show Iconmgr"  f.showiconmgr
"Hide Iconmgr"  f.hideiconmgr
"------------"  f.nop
"xterm Window"  !"/usr/X11R6/bin/xterm &"
"------------"  f.nop
"Kill"          f.destroy
"Delete"        f.delete
"------------"  f.nop
"Restart"       f.restart
"Exit"          f.quit
}
```

This section of .twmrc contains root menu labels, followed by an appropriate command for the twm window manager. For example, to "kill" a window, you press your left mouse button on the desktop, drag down to select the Kill menu item, and then press your mouse button over the top of a desired window—twm then removes the selected window.

Notice that we've spiffed up the blank areas in the new menu definition with hyphens for a bit more readability. After making your changes, save the new .twmrc file. If you're running twm, press your left mouse button and drag down to select the Restart menu item, which restarts twm, using the newly defined menu. This is how you can customize not only twm, but also other window managers discussed in this chapter.

The fvwm Window Manager

Bob Nation's fvwm window manager (shown in Figure 5.3) is a descendant of the twm window manager but has several advantages, such as using less memory, supporting fancier window decorations, and providing virtual desktops or off-screen displays.

Virtual desktops are especially handy if you don't want to litter your display with icons or overlapping windows. You can also group your windows by function, such as using one desktop for web browsing, another for word processing, and perhaps a third for drawing graphics.

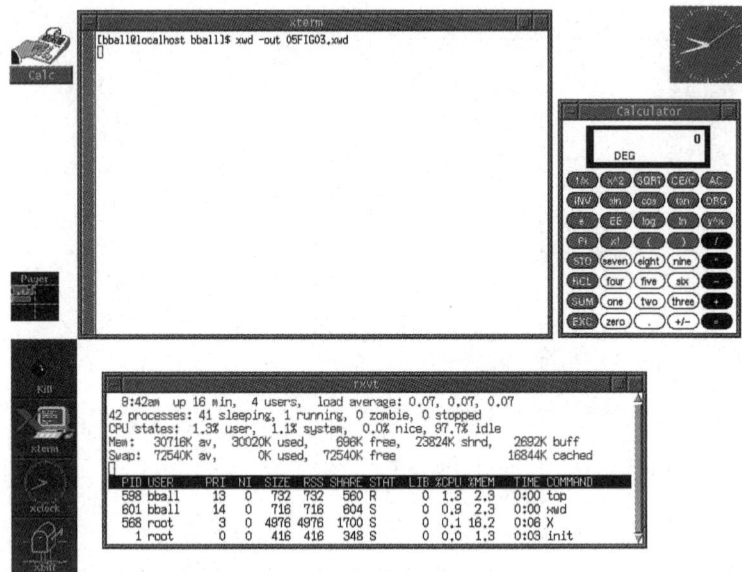

FIGURE 5.3
The fvwm window manager is an improvement over the X11's twm window manager.

Like twm's startup file, you'll find fvwm's default file under the /etc/X11/fvwm directory with the name system.fvwmrc. Copy this file to your home directory with the .fvwmrc, and make changes to customize it for your use. fvwm's startup file contains sections for customizing window colors and style, menus, and the number of virtual desktops. Look for the desktop section, which looks like this:

```
# Set up the virtual desktop and pager
#set the desk top size in units of physical screen size
DeskTopSize 2x2

# and the reduction scale used for the panner/pager
DeskTopScale 32
```

fvwm's default startup file defines four different virtual desktops. You can move to a different desktop by pressing your left mouse button on the appropriate square in the desktop pager's window. By changing the DeskTopSize value, you can either reduce or increase the number of virtual desktops. For example, to add another two desktops, use a setting like this

```
DeskTopSize 2x3
```

When you restart fvwm, you'll see that an additional two desktops have been added to the fvwm pager window. Use fvwm for your X sessions by inserting the word fvwm in your .xinitrc file.

The fvwm2 Window Manager

The fvwm2 window manager (see Figure 5.4), also by Bob Nation, has a lot of improvements over fvwm, such as a configurable taskbar, 3D window frames, buttons, and scrollbars and the capability for extensive customization. Customized configurations of this window manager have been the basis of several complex and popular X desktops provided with Red Hat Linux in the last several Red Hat distributions. Indeed, one of the latest fvwm2 incarnations uses many features of the GNOME software libraries (see "The GNOME X Environment," later in the chapter).

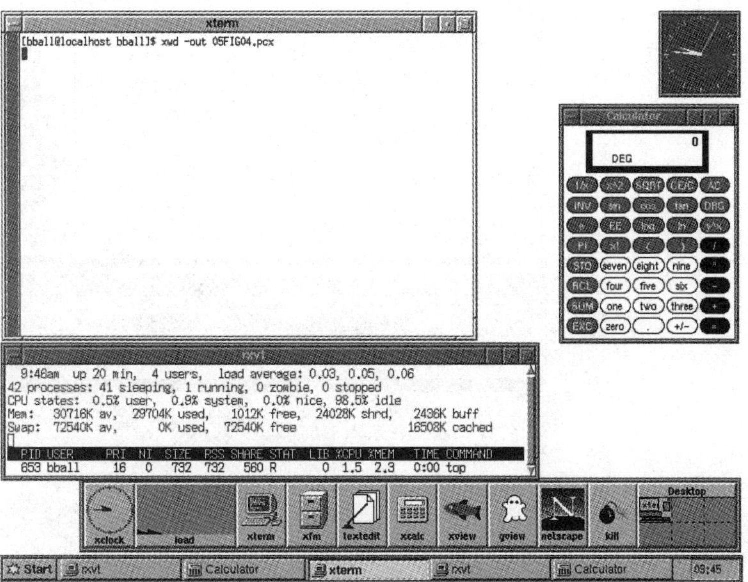

FIGURE 5.4
The fvwm2 window manager provides many sophisticated window controls.

This window manager's default startup file is found under the /etc/X11/fvwm2 directory as system.fvwm2rc. Copy this file to your home directory as .fvwm2rc and make changes to customize your X sessions. To use fvwm2, insert its name in your .xinitrc file.

Features of the AfterStep Window Manager

The AfterStep window manager (see Figure 5.5) is yet another descendant of the fvwm window manager. This X window manager's interface is somewhat similar to the NEXTSTEP interface and incorporates a wharf (floating window) for application buttons, a root menu, and distinctive icons. You might also like its default window-handling animation (displayed after you press the minimize or zoom buttons on windows).

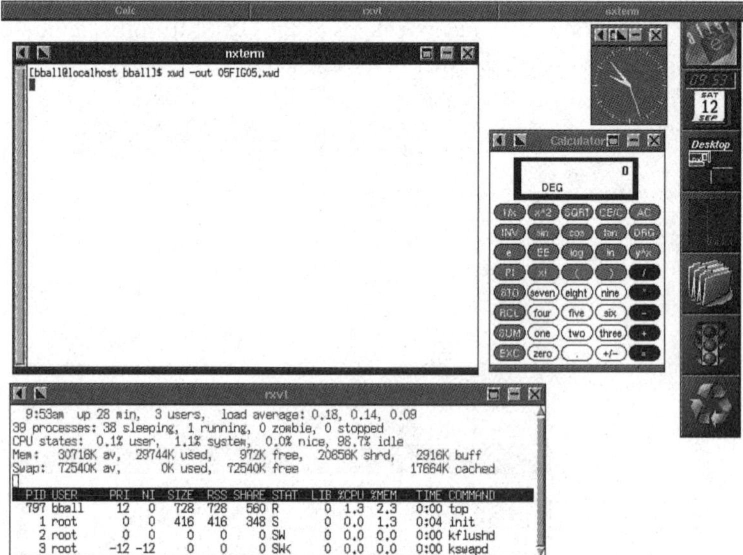

FIGURE 5.5
The AfterStep window manager for X offers a sophisticated X client window and extensive menus.

Important Files

Unlike other window managers included with Red Hat Linux, AfterStep's default, system-wide configuration files are found under the /usr/share/afterstep directory. This directory of configuration files also contains AfterStep's documentation. You can read this documentation, which is Andrew Sullivan's `AfterStep FAQ`, with your favorite web browser, such as lynx, like this:

```
# lynx /usr/share/afterstep/doc/afterstep.html
```

To use AfterStep for your X11 sessions, specify its name, **`afterstep`**, in the .xinitrc file in your home directory, and start X. If you select the AfterStepDoc menu item on

AfterStep's root menu during an X11 session (accessed by clicking your left mouse button, or mouse button 1, on an empty area of the desktop), AfterStep uses the Netscape Navigator web browser to display the FAQ.

When you run AfterStep for the first time, it creates local configuration files under the GNUstep directory in your home directory. The default wharf contains buttons for (starting at the top) getting help, displaying the time and date, virtual desktop control, display of the current system load, launching clients, logging out, and restarting.

Configuring AfterStep

You can control many features of AfterStep, such as background pictures, color schemes, or handling of windows, through menu items on AfterStep's root menu. You can change the look of your desktop, its color scheme, or its handling of windows. For details about other ways to configure AfterStep, read its FAQ or browse to `http://www.afterstep.org`.

Features of the fvwm2 AnotherLevel Configuration

Red Hat Linux's current default X11 window manager is the AnotherLevel configuration of the fvwm2 window manager (see Figure 5.6.). AnotherLevel provides many window decorations, such as close, zoom, and minimize buttons; 3D scrollbars; support modules for virtual desktops; a task bar with Start menu; and even an AfterStep wharf.

Important Files

AnotherLevel's default configuration files are found under the /etc/X11/AnotherLevel directory. Unlike other window managers which use a single configuration file, AnotherLevel uses fvwm2's `-cmd` configuration option to load in a series of configuration files (although you could just use a single system.fvwm2rc or .fvwm2rc file). Most of AnotherLevel's fancy window decorations, menus, and specialized features (such as audio) are built and processed through this mechanism. To use AnotherLevel for your X sessions, your .xinitrc file should have an entry like this:

```
fvwm2 -cmd 'FvwmM4 -debug /etc/X11/AnotherLevel/fvwm2rc.m4'
```

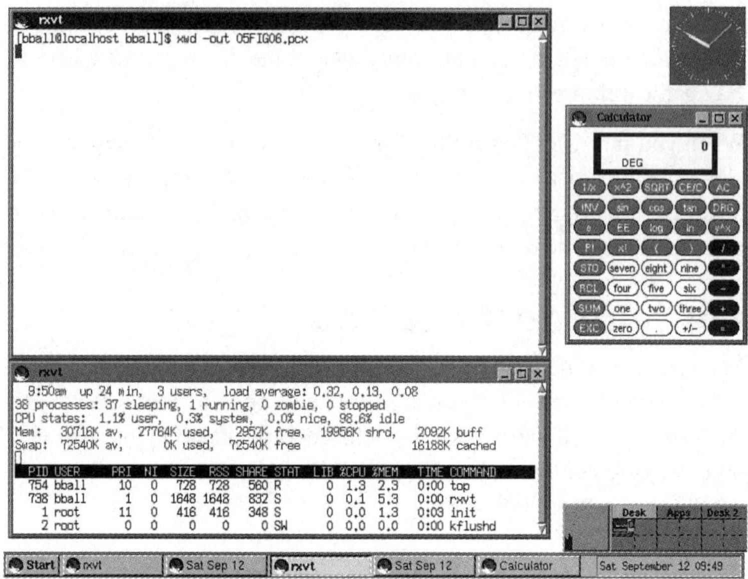

FIGURE 5.6
The AnotherLevel configuration of the fvwm2 window manager uses a number of complex script files under the /etc/X11/AnotherLevel directory.

Configuring AnotherLevel

Although one way to configure AnotherLevel is to edit its startup scripts under the /etc/X11/AnotherLevel directory, you can also build and configure your interface and then choose Preferences, Save Desktop to new.xinitrc. AnotherLevel creates a file called new.xinitrc in your home directory containing the names of all running applications, along with window settings such as size, color, and placement. Here is an example listing of this file:

```
rclock -bg red -fg yellow -update 1 -geometry 80x80-3+3 &
xmessage -title Calendar -file - -geometry 163x142+627+86 &
rvplayer /tmp/M035F9413D0150E3E.rmm -geometry 348x309+520+199 &
rxvt -fg black -bg white -geometry 80x24+5+5 &
applix -wp -geometry 581x416+6+6 &
rxvt -fg black -bg white -geometry 80x11+5+373 &
```

In this example, the rclock, xmessage, rvplayer, applix, and two rxvt terminals were in use when the settings were saved. Each of these lines is a command line that can be modified and used either in your .xinitrc file or in AnotherLevel's fvwm2rc.init file under the /etc/X11/AnotherLevel directory.

Keyboard Controls

Many window managers support keyboard control of the display, the windows, or the X11 pointer. Table 5.1 details the default keyboard controls for AnotherLevel. In some instances, such as moving or resizing a window, the window must be active or highlighted (do this by clicking on the window's title bar).

TABLE 5.1 COMMON ANOTHERLEVEL KEYBOARD COMMANDS.

Command	*Keyboard Command*
Delete current window	Ctrl+Shift+Alt+Backspace
Destroy current window	Ctrl+Shift+Alt+Keypad
Display Window list(menu)	Alt+Esc
Display desktop preferences menu	Ctrl+Shift+Alt+p
Display window operations menu	Ctrl+Shift+Alt+w
Lower window to bottom	Ctrl+Alt+Return
Make next window active	Alt+Tab
Make previous window active	Shift+Alt+Tab
Maximize window horizontally	Ctrl+Shift+right_cursor
Maximize window vertically	Ctrl+Shift+up_cursor
Minimize (iconify) window	Ctrl+Shift+down_cursor
Move to first virtual desktop	Ctrl+Shift+Alt+Home
Move to last virtual desktop	Ctrl+Shift+Alt+End
Move window	Ctrl+Shift+F7
Next desktop down	Ctrl+Shift+Alt+down_cursor
Next desktop to left	Ctrl+Shift+Alt+left_cursor
Next desktop to right	Ctrl+Shift+Alt+right_cursor
Next desktop up	Ctrl+Shift+Alt+up_cursor
Pointer down 100 pixels	Ctrl+Alt+F10
Pointer down 5 pixels	Ctrl+Shift+F10
Pointer left 100 pixels	Ctrl+Alt+F9
Pointer left 5 pixels	Ctrl+Shift+F9
Pointer right 100 pixels	Ctrl+Alt+F12
Pointer right 5 pixels	Ctrl+Shift+F12
Pointer up 100 pixels	Ctrl+Alt+F11
Pointer up 5 pixels	Ctrl+Shift+F11
Raise window to top	Ctrl+Alt+Return
Resize window	Ctrl+Shift+F8

NOTE

To be able to use your keyboard properly during your X11 sessions, make sure you've configured X with the correct keyboard setting for your computer. See Chapter 4 for details about the XF86Config file.

The GNOME X Environment

This section covers GNOME, the GNU Network Object Model Environment, which is supported by and is being developed by programmers from Red Hat Software, Inc., and others around the world. GNOME has received an increasing interest because it is distributed under the GNU GPL, unlike the underlying graphics software libraries, Qt, for KDE. Arguments about licensing constraints aside, GNOME is an important part of the future of the graphical X desktop for Linux for a number of reasons:

- The software is fully Open Source, and commercial software may be built upon the software without purchasing a software license.
- Contributions, changes, and modifications may be made without control by a central source, and there are no licensing restrictions on making and distributing changes.
- The software supports multiple operating systems and external programming languages.
- The software works with any GNOME-aware X11 window manager.

What is GNOME?

GNOME is a set of software libraries and X11 clients built to support an X11 desktop environment. Unlike KDE, GNOME can be used with any GNOME-aware window manager or any window manager that will support its panel component and client features, such as drag-and-drop desktop actions. GNOME is initialized and runs before you start your window manager.

GNOME Installation Components

GNOME consists of a number of software components and, for Red Hat Linux, is distributed in a series of RPM files. You can install GNOME using the `glint` control-panel X11 client or through the `rpm` command. The current distribution of GNOME at the time of this writing consists of the following files:

gnome-admin-0.20-1	GNOME-aware system administration clients
gnome-core-0.20-2	Basic required GNOME applets (programs) and libraries
gnome-core-devel-0.20-2	Software libraries for the GNOME panel
gnome-games-0.20-1	Half a dozen GNOME games
gnome-games-devel-0.20-1	Minimal game development libraries
gnome-graphics-0.20-1	GNOME graphics clients, such as Electric Eyes
gnome-guile-0.20-1	GNOME `gnomeg`, a `guile` interpreter used with GNOME
gnome-guile-devel-0.20-1	Programming support files for GNOME `guile` developers
gnome-libs-0.20-1	Basic GNOME libraries that must be installed
gnome-libs-devel-0.20-1	GNOME programming and development libraries
gnome-media-0.20-1	GNOME-aware multimedia clients
gnome-objc-0.20-1	Support libraries for GNOME Objective C clients
gnome-objc-devel-0.20-1	Programming libraries for GNOME Objective C clients
gnome-rh5.1-release-notes-1.0-5	Release information (/usr/share/gnome/help)
gnome-utils-0.20-1	GNOME clients, such as an editor, calculator, and other clients

If you'd like to get the latest software libraries, GNOME distribution, and the GNOME FAQ or download the newest GNOME applications, you can find them at `http://www.gnome.org`.

Configuring X11 to Use GNOME

The GNOME distribution of X11 clients and software libraries does not include a window manager. GNOME libraries and clients, such as the panel application, are designed to work with your favorite X11 window manager. For example, to use GNOME for your X session with the fvwm2 window manager, your .xinitrc should contain the following entries:

```
panel &
background-properties --init &
keyboard-properties --init &
mouse-properties --init &
exec fvwm2 -f .fvwm2rc.gnome
```

These entries start the GNOME panel (a taskbar client from which to access root menus, configure your desktop, or launch X11 clients), along with desktop, keyboard, and mouse control software. Finally, the fvwm2 window manager is launched, using a Red Hat-supplied configuration file. Figure 5.7 shows what your X11 desktop might look like with several clients running.

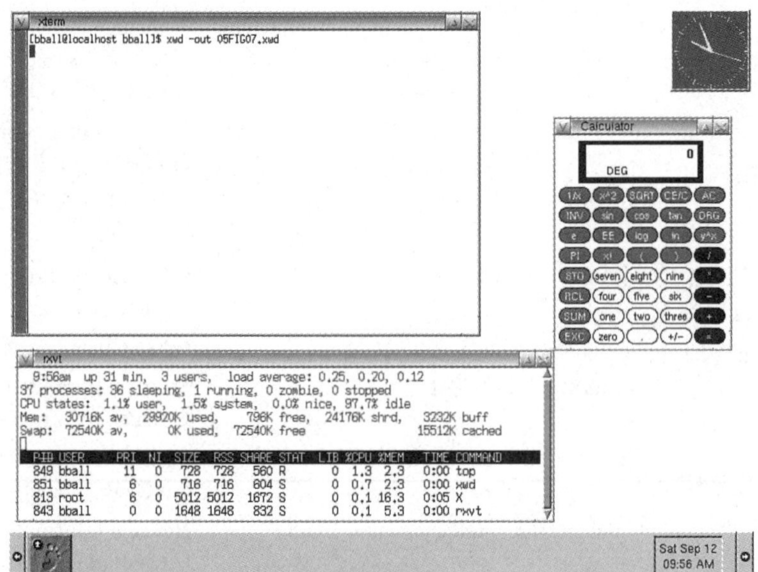

FIGURE 5.7
The fvmw2 X11 desktop using the GNOME environment has a taskbar and other features.

Using GNOME Clients and Tools

The most obvious and first GNOME client you'll see is the panel client, which offers a taskbar at the bottom of your X desktop. From the root menu of the taskbar (displayed by pressing the left mouse button, or mouse button 1 on the GNOME button), you can launch a variety of other GNOME clients:

Configuration utilities	Wallpaper or screen saver settings, mouse handling, keyboard configuration
Electronic Mail	The Balsa mail client
Games	Such as mahjongg, yahtzee, mines

Graphics	Electric Eyes, a graphics editor
Help	To get help on Linux and GNOME
Internet Relay Chat	The Yagirc client
Multimedia	To play music CDs

Because many of the GNOME clients are installed in the Linux file system in the normal places (such as the /bin, /usr/bin, or /usr/X11R6/bin directories), you can also start them from the command line of an X11 terminal window. You'll quickly recognize a GNOME client, because each client should follow the GNOME style guide. This guide stipulates that each program should have supporting documentation and each client should have a File and Help menu, with an Exit menu item on the File menu and an About menu item on the Help menu (see Figure 5.8).

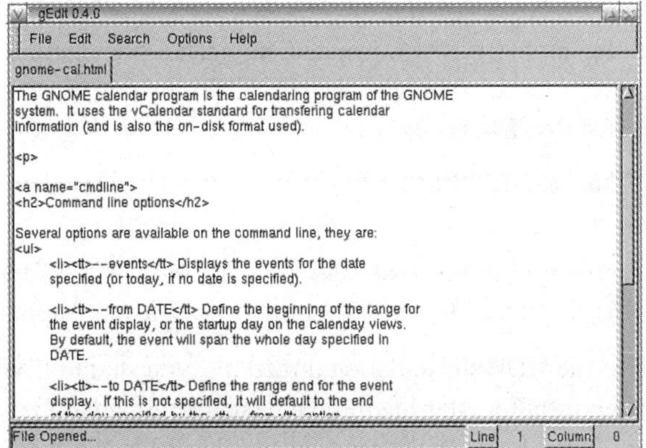

FIGURE 5.8
GNOME clients, such as the `gedit` *editor, generally have a consistent interface with a standard menu bar.*

Downloading and Installing the K Desktop Environment

One of the newest X11 window managers for Linux is the K Desktop Environment, or KDE. This distribution, like CDE, includes a variety of software libraries and X11 clients. A complete graphical interface for X11, KDE supports many of the features you'd expect in a modern desktop environment, including drag-and-drop operations, session management, menu and dialog configuration of the desktop, and automatic launching of network access programs such as browsers or FTP clients. In fact, the current version, according to the KDE folks, consists of nearly 800,000 lines of programming code.

Building and Installing from Source Files

KDE can be downloaded in source form from `http://www.kde.org`. For a complete distribution, you'll need all the source files, along with the Qt X11 graphics library files from Troll Tech at `http://www.troll.no/dl`. This process will definitely consume more than several hours of your time, especially if you attempt to build and download the entire current KDE distribution. One place to find the source code for your version of Red Hat Linux is
`ftp://ftp.kde.org/pub/kde/stable/1.0/contrib/distribution/rpm`.

A much better approach is to download and install precompiled binaries, but if you insist on starting from scratch, you can save time by only downloading and building these RPM files (for Red Hat Linux 5.1):

kdebase-1.0-2rh51.src.rpm	KDE's window manager and other base clients
kdelibs-1.0-2rh51.src.rpm	Shared software libraries
kdesupport-1.0-2rh51.src.rpm	Software support libraries

According to the KDE's installation directions, you should first download the Qt software and then install it (starting directions can be found at `http://www.troll.no/platforms/linux.html`). Following this, build and install the KDE support libraries, followed by the shared software libraries and then the base software. One of the best places to look for information on installing KDE is in its FAQ, at
`http://www.kde.org/faq/kdefaq.html`.

Downloading and Installing Red Hat RPM files

You can save a lot of time by downloading prebuilt binaries for your distribution of Red Hat Linux. After downloading the Red Hat RPM files, install KDE by using the `rpm` command and its `-i` (install) command-line option and the names of the KDE files, like this:

```
# rpm -i kde*rpm
```

In addition to the base, libs, and support files, the full distribution includes these files:

kdeadmin-1.0-2rh51.i386.rpm	Two administration clients
kdegames-1.0-2rh51.i386.rpm	A number of games, such as Tetris, solitaire, mahjongg, and Asteroids

kdegraphics-1.0-2rh51.i386.rpm	Graphic drawing and previewing clients
kdemultimedia-1.0-2rh51.i386.rpm	A music CD player and sound mixer
kdenetwork-1.0-2rh51.i386.rpm	A Usenet news reader, email client, and others
kdeutils-1.0-2rh51.i386.rpm	Clients such as an editor and calculator

KDE's components are installed in the /opt/kde directory. To launch and use KDE clients, you'll need to add the /opt/kde/bin directory to your $PATH environment variable. You should also define the $QTDIR to point to the /usr/local/qt directory and have the /usr/local/qt/lib and /opt/kde/lib directories added to your shell's $LD_LIBRARY_PATH. If you use the `bash` shell, all this can be done by editing the file profile under the /etc directory.

Features of the KDE Desktop

To use KDE as your desktop during X11 sessions, insert the command `startkde` in the .xinitrc file in your home directory, and then start X11 (see Figure 5.9).

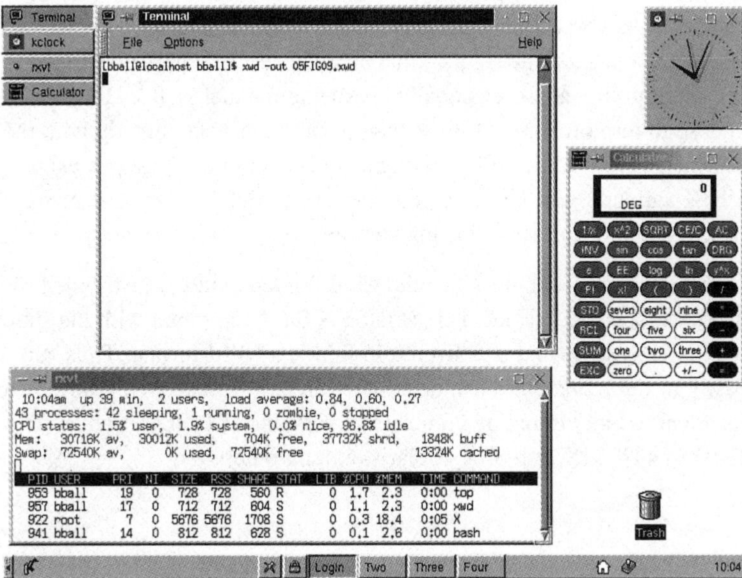

FIGURE 5.9
The KDE is one of the most popular of the newer desktop environments for the X Window System and Linux.

Features of the Common Desktop Environment

In 1993, several major software and hardware vendors joined together in an effort to eliminate many of the arbitrary and confusing discrepancies among the various versions of UNIX. These ranged from the monumental, such as key programming interfaces that made support of several UNIX versions difficult for software developers, to less complicated but no less bothersome or expensive issues, such as unnecessary variations in file locations, formats, and naming conventions. Regardless of how "big" these differences were, the vendors recognized that some standardization would have to take place if UNIX were to continue to withstand the tough competition provided by Microsoft's NT, which was finally becoming a serious competitor to UNIX in the server arena.

As a solution to the problem of inconsistent user interfaces, the Common Desktop Environment (CDE) was presented in 1995 by Hewlett-Packard, Novell, IBM, and SunSoft (the software division of Sun Microsystems). The CDE not only addresses the problem of inconsistencies among versions of UNIX and among OEM versions of X Window, but also greatly increases the accessibility of UNIX to nontechnical users accustomed to environments such as Windows and Macintosh. The CDE presents the same "look and feel" on all supported platforms and also provides base applications—such as a networked workgroup calendar, a printer manager, context-sensitive help, and file and application managers—that enable users to completely avoid the often intimidating shell prompt and occasionally confusing manual pages. However, a power user can choose to turn off some of these features and interface directly with the shell and command-line tools while still enjoying a consistent interface when using more than one UNIX variant. The CDE is so consistent in UNIX versions that many vendors even distribute much of the same documentation.

In this chapter, I will introduce the CDE implementation distributed by Red Hat Software and developed by TriTeal. This version is fully compliant with the standard developed by the major vendors and is delivered in Red Hat RPM format. Thus, any Red Hat user can easily install it and enjoy the benefits of an easy-to-use GUI interface that is virtually identical to that offered by commercial versions of UNIX, such as IBM's AIX, Hewlett-Packard's HP/UX, and Sun's Solaris, among others.

Installing Red Hat's CDE and Library Fixes Using RPM

The Red Hat Package Manager (RPM) makes it easy to install any application delivered in the proper format; however, the TriTeal CDE is even simpler than most because the installation media supplied by Red Hat Software comes with a shell script that installs the packages for you. This script is located in the top-level directory on the CDE CD-ROM and is named `install-cde`.

CAUTION

Red Hat's TriTeal CDE was designed to install cleanly with Red Hat Linux 4.2. Since then, changes have been made to the standard libraries included with Red Hat Linux. If you have Red Hat Linux 5.0 or newer, you'll need to go to Red Hat's web site and download two RPM files that MUST be installed AFTER you install CDE on a 5.0 or newer system.

They are located at: `ftp://ftp.redhat.com/pub/redhat/updates/cde/1.2/rpms`.

These files are:

```
TEDlibc5fix-4.2-00.i386.rpm
ld.so-1.9.5-5.i386.rpm
```

Download and install them AFTER installing but BEFORE running CDE. Use the `rpm` command, along with its `-i` (install) command-line option like this:

```
# rpm -i *.rpm
```

Details about this fix are on Red Hat's site at `http://www.redhat.com/support/docs/cde/cde-1.2-errata.html`.

One reason for the shell script is that the CDE requires several other packages before it will operate properly. Another reason is to enable users to easily alter the base installation directory. The RPM is fully capable of addressing both issues, but because a significant part of the CDE's target market is the beginner or nontechnical user, the shell script is provided to quietly handle the dependencies and interactively prompt the user for installation options. A script with the same name and interface is also supplied with other versions of the CDE, so its inclusion further provides consistency with other platforms and vendors.

The packages required by the CDE are typical of standard Red Hat installations. The required set includes the following:

- `pdksh`, which contains the public domain version of the Korn shell
- `libg++` and `gcc`, which provide the GNU compiler and standard C++ libraries
- Several packages for the support of login security, such as `crack` and `pam`
- `portmap`, which is needed for the CDE's network features

Because these packages are all included on the CDE media, these dependencies are not an issue. The default root directory for the CDE software is /usr/dt, so it is important for the workstation to have the required disk space, about 40MB, available in the appropriate partition. However, because the shell script asks the user if another directory should be used, a problem should not result if the required free space is only available in another partition.

CAUTION

The CDE packages configure the system to automatically start the CDE login manager after a system restart. Because the login manager runs under X Window, it is important that X Window be configured correctly before the CDE is installed.

Getting Started with the CDE

After the installation script is run, the system should be restarted. The CDE login manager starts in the last part of the initialization process. If you are watching the system as it initializes, you will see the normal console prompt, but don't bother trying to log in. The login manager will appear shortly, depending on how long it takes X Window to initialize on your system.

Logging in to the CDE

The login manager (`dtlogin`) screen is based on an older X Window application called `xdm`. With `dtlogin`, users are logged directly into X Window, not only without having to run a shell script such as `startx`, but also with a default environment that can be configured in advance by the system administrator to suit the local environment. Much of this configurability is derived from `xdm`, but like much of the CDE, `dtlogin` adds a lot of new features. From the user's perspective, the login process is simple: Type in the username and press Enter. Then enter the password and press Enter again. `dtlogin` also enables users to select the type of session they want to start. These sessions can be specified by the administrator, but the default setup will probably suit most users' needs:

- Regular—The full-featured CDE session.
- FVWM-95-2—The `fvwm` window manager with the familiar Linux 95 style menu.
- FVWM—A minimally configured `fvwm` environment.
- Fail-safe—A single X terminal, with no window manager. This session is designed for addressing configuration problems.

These options, as well as `dtlogin`'s appearance, can be extensively modified. See the `dtlogin(1X)` manual page and the CDE documentation for details and examples.

In addition to the Fail-safe session, the Linux virtual terminal feature is still available. To change from the CDE to a virtual console, press Ctrl+Alt and F1+F6. To return, press Alt+F7.

When a regular session is started from the `dtlogin` screen, the CDE session manager (Xsession) takes over. Xsession executes the programs necessary to start the required desktop session, depending on the workstation and the user's individual configuration options. By modifying the scripts and configuration files processed by Xsession, a user or system administrator can customize CDE's appearance and specify what applications start at login and are available for use during the session. I will cover these options later in the chapter in the section "Customizing Your Session."

After the session is started, the user interacts with the Front Panel, Workspace Manager, Application Manager, and other CDE tools.

The Desktop Environment

When the desktop is finished loading, the first thing a new CDE user probably notices is the Front Panel, which is shown in Figure 5.10. Whereas the Motif and Open Look window managers offer only menus and the FVWM offers menus and simple icons, CDE provides a Front Panel with pop-up and breakaway icon panels, a virtual screen manager, a trash bin similar to that of the Macintosh, and predefined buttons for operations such as logging out, locking the screen, reading mail, and launching several desktop tools.

After a close inspection of the Front Panel, a new user sees that the CDE offers a lot more than a program launch pad, because it supplies its own set of desktop applications and context-sensitive help.

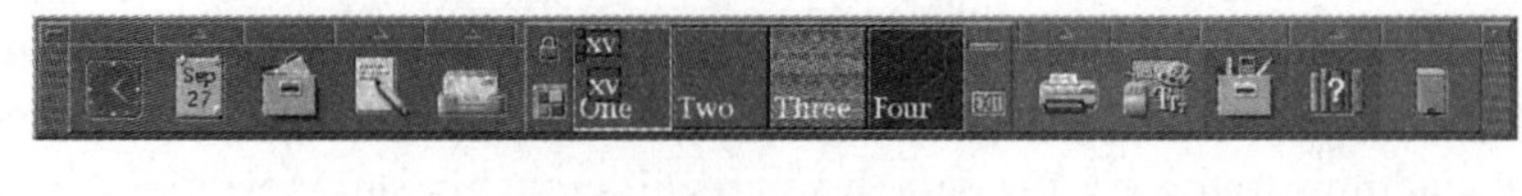

FIGURE 5.10
The CDE Front Panel provides menus and X client access.

On the far left side of the default panel, the CDE supplies an analog clock, which displays the system time, and a calendar, with an icon that displays the current date. The calendar is actually a sophisticated scheduling application that provides an appointment manager capable of notifying the user of appointments via sound, blinking video, pop-up windows, and email. The calendar also provides a To Do list manager and a wide variety of calendar views that should satisfy most users, but the real power of the desktop Calendar Manager lies in its network options. By taking advantage of the desktop's networking capabilities, it allows users to share their schedules with any other user of the CDE, regardless of whether they are using the same workstation and without having to copy or share any files. These sharing capabilities are completely configured from the application—no additional administrative work is required.

The next icon on the Front Panel is for the File Manager. This should look familiar to any Macintosh, Windows 95, or `xfm` user. Files can be viewed as icons or names and can be moved, copied, or deleted with the mouse. As with other file managers, files are moved when they are dragged with the mouse, copied when they are dragged with Shift or Ctrl pressed, and deleted when they are dragged to the Trash icon, which is located in the Control Panel. (All desktop applications share this Trash icon.)

The CDE also supports file associations, much like the Macintosh and Windows operating systems. These associations are governed by desktop actions, which are defined through the Application Manager and can be used in the File Manager. (I'll cover actions in more detail later in the chapter in the section "Customizing Your Session.") These actions enable a user to double-click a file and run the proper application, depending on how that type of file has been defined. The default set of actions provided with the CDE is already very powerful. For example, when a `tar` archive is double-clicked, a window pops up with a table of contents for the archive (a right-click provides an option to actually extract the contents), compressed files are decompressed, and text files are already associated with the desktop GUI editor (but can be reassociated with your favorite editor, such as `vi` or `xemacs`).

The next two icons launch the Text Editor and the Mailer, which are two more desktop tools supplied with the CDE. The Text Editor resembles most GUI text editors, with the addition of the CDE's ever-present help system and some nice little extras, such as word wrap and an integrated spell-checker. The Mailer uses the same spell-checker and offers a lot of other features, such as excellent mail folder features and the capability to create mail templates.

Above the Editor icon is a small arrow that produces a subpanel when clicked (see Figure 5.11). Subpanels are one of the more advanced features of the CDE and provide an easy method for users to customize their environment. Subpanels can be "torn off" and placed anywhere on the desktop, effectively extending the Front Panel and eliminating the need for the root menu. I'll cover how subpanels can be created in the "Customizing Your Session" and "Advanced Front Panel Customization" sections of this chapter.

FIGURE 5.11
A sample CDE subpanel.

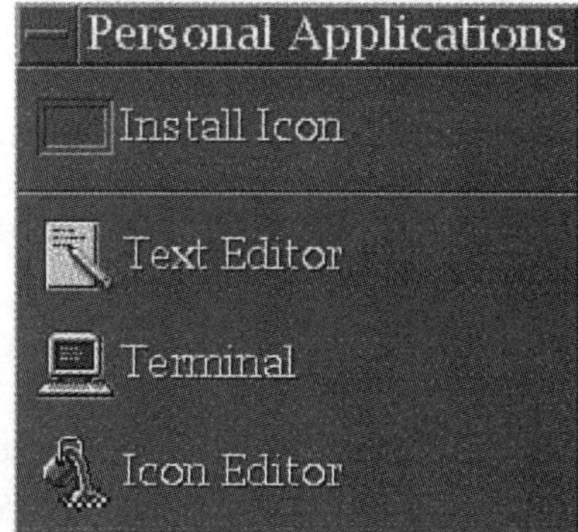

The subpanel located over the Text Editor has an icon for starting a Desktop Terminal (`dtterm`). This terminal very closely resembles an `Xterm` but has menus for operations such as changing the font size and cutting and pasting text, making it easier for new users to perform otherwise advanced operations at the shell prompt.

In the middle of the Front Panel, you see the Graphical Workspace Manager (GWM) and some smaller icons that are installed by default. The lock control locks the screen, the exit control logs you out, the green light indicates when the CDE is busy saving a configuration or launching a new application, and the fourth control brings up a separate Workspace Manager window.

The Workspace Manager has a virtual screen manager provided by TriTeal. TriTeal's version of the CDE has some features above and beyond those offered by the CDE. Although the CDE-specified desktop has buttons corresponding to virtual screens (the number of virtual screens defaults to four but can be easily altered; see the "Customizing Your Session" section), the Workspace Manager presents a graphic representation of each screen and its contents and allows windows to be manipulated from within the screen manager.

TIP

Another useful Workspace Manager tool is the application list. To display it, click the Workspace background (also referred to as the *root window*). This activates the root menu. Select the Application list. If you click an application name in this list, it appears in front. If the application is running in another virtual workspace, it also appears in front and you are brought to that virtual screen.

Immediately to the right of the screen manager is the Printer Control, where you can view printers and manage documents. You can also drag documents to the Printer Control to be processed if the appropriate action has been configured for the application that created it.

The next three icons represent the heart of the CDE: the Style Manager and Application Manager, covered in the "Customizing Your Session" section, and the Help Viewer, explained in detail in "The Help Viewer" section.

Customizing Your Session

Although the default CDE session offers a lot, chances are you will want to customize your environment. When it comes to configuration options, the architects of the CDE stayed with the true UNIX spirit by supplying many different ways to accomplish the same thing. Most configuration preferences can be altered to suit a user's taste with a few simple clicks of the mouse; just about any aspect of the CDE can be managed through its configuration files at an individual user level, that is, without altering the entire system. This allows power users to tailor their environment as much as they want, and still gives less skilled users a very comfortable environment.

In addition, site administrators can easily tailor the desktop to suit their organization's needs by setting up configuration defaults in a shared system area (usually /etc/dt). Files in this area can not only make the necessary applications available; they can also define what users can and cannot alter on their desktops.

The Style Manager

The Style Manager is one of the most convenient features of the CDE. Most X Window environments require changes to be made through the X resource configuration files—too complicated for the average user. Others provide limited configurability through menus and dialog boxes, such as modifying color schemes and basic window behavior, but still leave a bit to be desired when compared to user-friendly systems such as

Windows and Macintosh. The CDE's Style Manager goes a long way toward addressing this issue.

The Style Manager, shown in Figure 5.12, is launched from the Front Panel by clicking the icon that resembles an artist's palette.

FIGURE 5.12
The Style Manager.

With the Style Manager, you can configure various attributes of the CDE by using the following options:

- Color—A color palette manager, which comes with more than 30 palettes already defined. Because the CDE is based on the Motif window manager, color can be changed dynamically; therefore, you can view color changes as you select them. In addition, you can add, delete, or modify palettes. Instead of specifying colors for each display attribute (such as active window, inactive window, and so on), you can adjust the palette with a set of slide controls that affect all aspects of the color scheme as one.
- Font—Enables you to set the default font size for all applications.
- Backdrop—With this option, you can select a bitmap background from the 26 bitmaps that come with the desktop. For each virtual screen, you can choose an individual background to help you keep track of which screen is active.
- Keyboard—Offers the options to choose whether keys will repeat when held and to enable a "click" sound for each keypress.
- Mouse—The CDE offers a surprisingly complete set of options for the mouse. You can switch buttons for left- or right-handedness, adjust the click speed, and set the acceleration and threshold.
- Beep—Allows you to adjust the volume, tone, and length of the default "beep," usually intended as an alert or notifier of an error.
- Screen—Offers you the option of setting the screen to automatically go blank after a specified period of inactivity. In addition, you can configure a screen saver that is activated after a similar interval. The screen saver has all the familiar `xlock` options, such as fireworks, fractals, and Conway's "game of life." The screen saver can also be activated from the Front Panel lock control.

- Window—Enables you to select window behavior, such as whether to activate a window by placing the mouse over it or by clicking it.
- Startup—The CDE's startup options are sometimes the source of confusion for new users. This option enables you to select a "home session" or to specify that the state of the desktop when you last logged out should be restored.

TIP

The CDE cannot restore applications that were started from a command-line session—only those that were started from a desktop application or menu.

The Front Panel

You can customize the Front Panel either from the desktop or by editing configuration files. This section covers the methods available from the desktop. In the section "Advanced Front Panel Customization," I will go over some of the configuration file settings.

The Workspace Manager

Unlike other versions of the CDE, TriTeal places a virtual window manager (called the Workspace Manager) on the front of the toolbar. From this manager, windows can be moved between virtual workspaces by clicking and dragging with the mouse. However, in the Workspace Manager, windows cannot be dragged from the active workspace the way they can in `olvwm`.

You can configure the Workspace Manager by right-clicking it and selecting the Properties menu entry. From the Properties dialog, you can remove the Workspace Manager from the Front Panel. This replaces it with the default for all CDE versions—buttons that select each virtual workspace. Other options include the number of virtual workspaces and how they are displayed within the Front Panel or its separate display window.

Subpanels

The initial Front Panel configuration supplies three subpanels: Help, Personal Printers, and Personal Applications. Adding panels is easy, as is adding additional icons to subpanels.

To add a panel, right-click the icons over which the new panel will be added and select the Add Subpanel option. A new panel is created, with two selections already defined: the icon that was already on the Front Panel and an Install Icon selection.

For example, add a subpanel above the Mail control. First, right-click (or left-click if your mouse is in left-handed mode) the Mail icon immediately left of the virtual screen manager. A small menu appears with three selections, the middle one being Add Subpanel. Select it by pointing the mouse at it and releasing the button. An upward arrow will appear above the Mail icon. When you click this arrow, the subpanel pops up with the title Mail.

To display the use of the Install Icon control, start the Application Manager by clicking the File Drawer icon next to the Style Manager icon. The Application Manager window is shown in Figure 5.13.

FIGURE 5.13
The Application Manager.

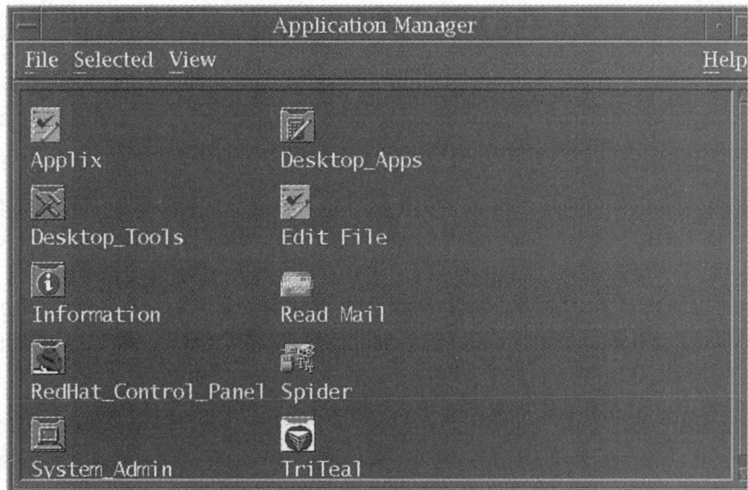

With the new Mail subpanel still extended, drag the Information icon to the Install Icon control on the subpanel. The icon is added to the subpanel. When the new icon is clicked, the Information view of the Application Manager appears on the desktop.

To delete this new icon, click it and select Delete. To delete the new subpanel, click the Mail icon and select Delete Subpanel.

TIP

This is only the beginning of what is available via menus and the right mouse button. Don't be afraid to explore the Front Panel by yourself. If you are worried about making an irreversible change to the desktop, set up a home session (described in "The Style Manager" section) before you experiment. If you make a change that is too much to reverse, log out and log in again. When you have a configuration you like, save your home session again.

Advanced Customizations

Beyond the simple menu selections and drag and drop are customizations that require editing some configuration files and scripts.

Shell and Login Setup

Experienced users might be confused the first time they use the shell after logging into the CDE. Unless some adjustments have already been made, their `.profile` or `.login` scripts are not read. When a user logs into the CDE, the file `.dtprofile` is read instead.

Rather than force users to modify their environments, the CDE designers added a configuration parameter, `DTSOURCEPROFILE`, to the `.dtprofile`. If this variable is set to `true`, `dtlogin` will read the appropriate file, depending on the user's shell. The CDE is built upon `ksh`, so `dtlogin` expects `sh` or `ksh` syntax in `.dtprofile`. It will, however, accept `csh` syntax in `.login`. The default `.dtprofile` contains notes on how users can set up their environments to work well in and out of the desktop.

Another important setting in `.dtprofile` is session logging. Output generated by applications started within the desktop doesn't automatically go to the console as it does in most X Window environments—it is normally discarded. If viewing this output is necessary, direct it to a file (or the console) by setting the `dtstart_sessionlogfile` variable to a valid filename in `.dtprofile`. The default `.dtprofile` has comments explaining how to do this.

Logically, because `.dtprofile` is read in at login, you can make other adjustments to it to suit your needs, such as setting environment variables needed for applications and modifying the search path. Because some changes might be necessary only within X Window, this provides a good mechanism for users who want to keep their non-GUI environment lean.

If you have no `.dtprofile` in your home directory ($HOME), the system uses the default version stored in $CDEROOT/config/sys.dtprofile ($CDEROOT is the base directory of the CDE installation, usually /usr/dt) and copies it into your directory for the next time.

In the event that an administrator wants to make changes to the environment for an entire workstation, regardless of user, the system files listed can be copied into another directory, /etc/dt/config, and modified.

X Resources

Users who want to add personal X resources can simply create an `.Xdefaults` file in their home directory. For system administrators who want to set resources for entire systems, there is a shared file, `sys.resources`, you can modify and place in /etc/dt/config/C/.

Advanced Front Panel Customization

The Front Panel is controlled by a series of configuration files that are loaded dynamically each time the desktop is started. This dynamic loading process enables users to change their panel configuration without having root access to the system. Also, administrators can override default behavior and tailor the desktop to their needs without changing the default configuration files and without making things more difficult for advanced users.

The format of the Front Panel configuration files is described in detail in the `dtfpfile(4X)` manual page. (If this manual page is not available on your system, install the `TEDman` package from the CDE media.) I will cover enough of this file format to make some basic changes.

Configuration files are read from the *action database search path*, which consists of these locations, in this order:

- $HOME/.dt/types/
- /etc/dt/appconfig/types/C/
- /usr/dt/appconfig/types/C/

In the last two locations, C is the *language* directory. Another industry standard is the notion of *locales*. A locale is a set of display conventions and language files that make it possible to use an application effectively in different parts of the world. For example, one locale might display dates using the format MM/DD/YY, while another uses DD/MM/YY. Locales are part of the ISO standards for computing. Set the locale for the CDE with the `LANG` environment variable and by installing the proper locale support files. Support is included for Western Europe, Japanese, traditional Chinese, simplified Chinese, and Korean.

The generic C locale is the default and is generally the one used in the United States.

The order of the search path is important because, in the event that two files specify the same name for two controls, the description that is read first is the one that is used. This enables a system administrator to override the CDE's behavior by placing control descriptions in the system location and enables users to override the administrator's control by placing their own definitions in their home directories.

TIP

All the changes you perform in this section will occur in the first location, the user's home directory. Any or all of the changes can be performed in either of the other two locations and will then affect all users on that system—this is how to integrate an application suite such as Applix or the Cygnus development tools into a company- or department-wide system. However, modifying the third directory, /usr/dt, is generally discouraged: an upgrade to a new version of CDE would remove the changes because a newer version of the configuration files would most likely be copied into the system.

For this reason, make any modifications to the default CDE configuration for an entire workstation or organization in the /etc/dt directory tree.

The Front Panel is divided into five component types—panel, box, control, subpanel, and switch. The panel is the outermost container—the Front Panel itself. For this component, you need to set behavior such as whether a single- or double-click activates controls and whether the Front Panel has a minimize button or default window menu.

A panel contains one or more boxes. A box contains one or more controls. The default configuration contains one box, which is adequate for most Front Panel setups.

A third container type is the subpanel, with which you are already familiar. In a configuration context, a subpanel contains controls, similar to a box.

Another container type, the switch, is the middle panel in the Front Panel. It contains the virtual screen manager and the four small controls that immediately surround it.

A control is an icon such as the Mail and Calendar icons discussed earlier in the chapter in the section "The Desktop Environment."

Let's go through the steps of removing a control from the default configuration of the Front Panel. Suppose you decide to delete the Mail control because you don't use the CDE mail reader.

The Mail control is a *built-in* control, which means it comes in the default configuration and must be explicitly removed with a `DELETE` directive rather than simply left out of the configuration.

The first step is to create a new .fp file in your Front Panel configuration directory, which is $HOME/.dt/types. Almost all desktop modifications are made from the types branch of the directory tree:

```
# cd $HOME/.dt/types
# cp /usr/dt/appconfig/types/(LANGUAGE)/dtwm.fp ./mymail.fp
# chmod +w mymail.fp
```

Next, edit mymail.fp, using a text editor. Remove all the lines in the file except the following, which start at approximately line 94:

```
CONTROL Mail
{
  TYPE                    icon
  CONTAINER_NAME          Top
  CONTAINER_TYPE          BOX
  POSITION_HINTS          5
  ICON                    DtMail
  LABEL                   Mail
  ALTERNATE_ICON          DtMnew
  MONITOR_TYPE            mail
  DROP_ACTION             Dtmail
  PUSH_ACTION             Dtmail
  PUSH_RECALL             true
  CLIENT_NAME             dtmail
  HELP_TOPIC              FPOnItemMail
  HELP_VOLUME             FPanel
}
```

This is the default description for the Mail control. As you can see, a lot of configuration options are available for a control (see the `dtfpfile(4X)` manual page for a complete description). To remove this control, you need to specify its name, its type, and the fact that you want it deleted in a file that will be read prior to /usr/dt/appconfig/types/C/dtwm.fp. You can actually cut the entry down to the following and place in it mymail.fp:

```
CONTROL Mail
{
  CONTAINER_NAME          Top
  CONTAINER_TYPE          BOX
  DELETE                  True
}
```

Save the file and restart the Workspace Manager, either by logging out and in again or by selecting Restart Workspace Manager from the root menu. As the CDE reinitializes, it processes the `DELETE` directive in your home directory and omits the Mail control.

The Front Panel looks a little strange now, so rather than omit the Mail icon completely, replace it with your preferred mail reader (you'll use `elm` for the sake of this exercise). Before you can add this to the Front Panel, you have to detour to the Application Manager and create a new action.

Creating New Actions

The CDE supplies a tool, Create Action, that is intended for—logically enough—creating actions. After an action is defined, it can be installed as an icon on the desktop, the Front Panel, or a subpanel. (Or all of them, if you wish.)

The Create Action tool is located in the Desktop_Apps section of the Application Manager. To start the tool, launch the Application Manager from the Front Panel, double-click the Desktop_Apps icon, and then double-click the Create Action icon.

> **TIP**
>
> If you don't use `elm` to read mail but want to complete this exercise, you can either replace `elm` with the name of your mail reader or complete the exercise and answer No when `elm` asks you whether it should create folders. Running `elm` like this has no permanent effect on your configuration. If you use an X Window–based mail reader, select a window type of Graphical.

In the Create Action dialog box shown in Figure 5.14, you simply need to specify an action name; use Read Mail in the top text box and `elm` for the command to run. Also, select a window type of Terminal (Auto-Close). After these fields are filled in, select File, Save.

Now you have an icon called Read Mail in the root directory of Application Manager. If you want to, you can move this icon to another part of the directory tree. You also now have a desktop configuration file named $HOME/.dt/types/Read_Mail.dt that is read in as part of the Front Panel initialization process, creating an action `Read_Mail` that can be specified in `CONTROL` definitions.

Creating Controls

With this new action, you can now create a completely new control:

```
CONTROL MyOwnMail
{
  TYPE                    icon
  CONTAINER_NAME          Top
  CONTAINER_TYPE          BOX
  POSITION_HINTS          5
  ICON                    DtMail
  LABEL                   Mail
  ALTERNATE_ICON          DtMnew
  MONITOR_TYPE            mail
  PUSH_ACTION             Dtmail
  PUSH_RECALL             true
}
```

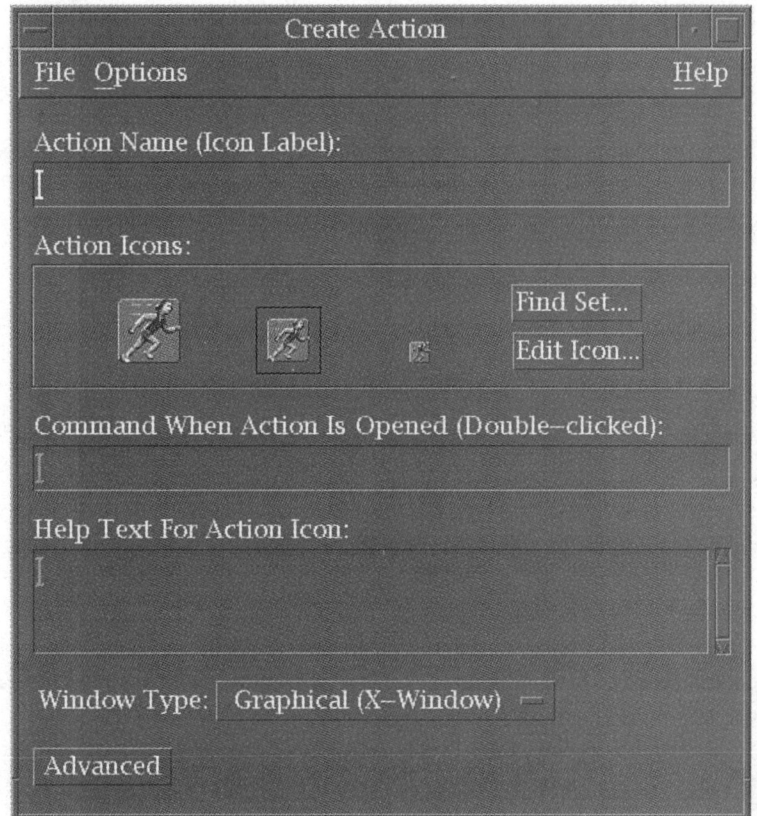

FIGURE 5.14
The Create Action dialog.

Place this in a file named myownmail.fp in the $HOME/.dt/types directory and restart the Workspace Manager. The Mail icon has returned and will launch `elm` in a `dtterm` window if clicked. When `elm` exits, the window closes because you selected an Auto-Close terminal in the Create Action dialog earlier.

This configuration contains a few fewer lines than the original Mail control. You removed the `HELP_TOPIC` and `HELP_VOLUME` directives because they are solely concerned with the help topics included for the desktop mail tool. You also removed the `DROP_ACTION` because `elm` is not prepared to handle drag-and-drop operations. However, you did retain the `MONITOR_TYPE` and `ALTERNATE_ICONS` directives because they will work together to notify you when new mail has arrived by changing the Front Panel icon. See the manual pages `dtfpfile(4)` and `dtdtfile(4)` for more details on component options.

Modifying Controls

Now that you have successfully created a new control, you can do it the easy way. Creating a completely new MyOwnMail control is not necessary.

Move myownmail.fp to mymail.fp. (You need to actually move the file because if myownmail.fp still exists at the end of the exercise, you'll have two Mail icons.)

Modify the file so it reads this way:

```
CONTROL Mail
{
  TYPE                    icon
  CONTAINER_NAME          Top
  CONTAINER_TYPE          BOX
  POSITION_HINTS          5
  ICON                    DtMail
  LABEL                   Mail
  ALTERNATE_ICON          DtMnew
  MONITOR_TYPE            mail
  PUSH_ACTION             Dtmail
  PUSH_RECALL             true
}
```

When the desktop is restarted, the Front Panel remains the same. Because you specified a control name of Mail in your personal configuration, which is read in first, it overrode the default Mail control.

Creating and Modifying Subpanels

Earlier you used the mouse to create new subpanels and add icons to them. When you make changes this way, they are added to the fp_dynamic subdirectory of $HOME/.dt/types. Do not edit these files by hand to make changes and additions to subpanels.

Creating Subpanels

A SUBPANEL definition looks very much like that of a CONTROL:

```
SUBPANEL Games
{
  CONTAINER_NAME          Date
  TITLE                   Games
}
```

This creates a subpanel named Games and places it above the Calendar control because the control name for Calendar is Date in the default configuration. The new panel has a single control for the calendar, which is created automatically by the Workspace Manager.

Now create an action called `Spider`, using the Create Action tool in the Application Manager. Then create a file in $HOME/.dt/types named Spider.fp that contains the following (a quick way would be to copy mymail.fp and edit it):

```
CONTROL Spider
{
  CONTAINER_NAME          Games
  CONTAINER_TYPE          SUBPANEL
  LABEL                   Spider
  ICON                    redhat_folder
  PUSH_ACTION             Spider
  PUSH_RECALL             true
}
```

When the desktop is restarted, a Red Hat icon appears in the Games subpanel. When you click it, the solitaire application Spider starts.

Modifying Subpanels

Like default controls, default subpanels can be modified.

To remove the Install Icon control, add

```
CONTROL_INSTALL False
```

To add a control to a subpanel, specify the subpanel as the container. For example, the following, when placed in an .fp file in the $HOME/.dt/types directory, adds a handy manual page control to the Help subpanel:

```
CONTROL Dtmanpageview
{
   TYPE file
   CONTAINER_TYPE          SUBPANEL
   CONTAINER_NAME          HelpSubpanel
   POSITION_HINTS          last
   ICON Dthover
   FILE_NAME       /usr/dt/appconfig/appmanager/C/Desktop_Apps/Dtmanpageview
   HELP_STRING  The Man Page Viewer (Dtmanpageview) action displays a
➥ man page in a Quick Help viewer window.
}
```

The Install Icon tool inserts this into a file when the Man Page viewer icon is dragged into the file. The two important directives are `CONTAINER_TYPE` and `CONTAINER_NAME`, which specify the container type, a `SUBPANEL`, and its name.

The Install Icon control is probably the best mechanism to use because it avoids errors and installs nice extras, such as the help information shown in the preceding example.

Subpanel Behavior

When you click controls on subpanels, their default behavior is to close. You can override this, but to do so, you must modify the default PANEL definition.

Create a file named main.fp file in $HOME/.dt/types. To main.fp, copy the default PANEL definition found in /usr/dt/appconfig/types/C/dtwm.fp (it starts at approximately line 18).

```
 PANEL FrontPanel
{
  DISPLAY_HANDLES         True
  DISPLAY_MENU            True
  DISPLAY_MINIMIZE        True
  CONTROL_BEHAVIOR        single_click
  DISPLAY_CONTROL_LABELS  False
  HELP_TOPIC              FPOnItemFrontPanel
  HELP_VOLUME             FPanel
}
```

Add the following directive:

```
SUBPANEL_UNPOST           False
```

This is a good example of how to take advantage of the way the Front Panel is dynamically constructed every time the CDE is initialized. A site administrator can add this modification, also, to the /etc/dt/appconfig/types/C area.

Restoring a Session When Something Goes Wrong

The Workspace Manager always saves a backup of the last session when it saves a new one. If something goes wrong, this backup session can be activated to restore a login to working order.

Log in as the user with either the Fail-safe or CommandLine Login, or by switching to one of the virtual terminals.

Change to the $HOME/.dt/sessions directory. The old session is in the current.old directory. Copy it to the current directory—for example,

```
cd current.old; find . | cpio -pdmv ../current
```

Executing Applications and Commands at Login

When users log in to the desktop for the first time, the script sys.session in /usr/dt/config/*language*/ is executed. It starts up a few desktop applications, including the Help Viewer.

Like most files that accompany the default CDE package, this copy of sys.session shouldn't be modified. Instead, users should place a new copy in /etc/dt/config/*language*/ and modify it there. After users logs out for the first time, they will have either a home or last session for the desktop to restore, so this script will not run again.

You might want to execute commands when you log in that cannot be set up via the CDE, such as daemon processes, or perhaps an application such as xv or xsetroot for placing an alternative root window background. To do so, place a script named sessionetc in the directory named $HOME/.dt/sessions.

For example, the following script would place the file companylogo.jpg as the background at login:

```
#!/bin/sh
xv -root -rmode 5 -maxpect -quit $HOME/images/companylogo.jpg
```

NOTE

Backgrounds set by xv are only visible when NoBackdrop is selected in the CDE Style Manager.

sessionetc is executed as a shell script. Therefore, either xv must be in the user's search path, or the path must be fully qualified. In addition, the user must ensure that the path to the image is correct and that the script has the executable bit for owner set. Also, any programs run by sessionetc should either execute and exit in a timely manner or become background, because the script is run in serial with the rest of the login process. Any programs remaining in the foreground for a long time will result in a delayed login.

Executing Commands at Logout

A similar script, sessionexit, can be placed in the same directory with commands to be executed on logout, such as cleaning up a temporary directory or backing up some files. As with sessionetc, the proper path must be available for any programs that are run, and the programs that are run should either exit quickly or be placed in the background.

The Help Viewer

The CDE help facility is a welcome sight to the new UNIX user. It provides fully indexed hyperlinks to topics about all desktop applications and the desktop itself. It also provides context-sensitive help from all applications.

Using the Help Viewer

The Help Viewer is effectively a replacement for "treeware" (paper documentation). Help is divided into volumes, such as one for the File Manager, one for the Front Panel, and another for the Help Viewer itself. This, combined with the Viewer's powerful search system, provides users with the ability to rapidly access exactly the information they need.

The top portion of the window always displays a table of contents for the volume currently in use (see Figure 5.15). The bottom portion displays the help document for the current topic. On the right are navigation buttons for bringing up an index or a history window, for backtracking to previously visited topics, and for jumping directly to the top-level topic in the currently selected volume.

The index is one of the more powerful features included in the Help Viewer. Help volumes are selected in a simple dialog box and can be displayed as tiered indexes or searched. From the index window, the desired help topic can be displayed.

The history window provides rapid access to the help topics visited in the current help session. It also organizes topics into volumes.

Context-Sensitive Help

All CDE controls have a Help option. Place the mouse over the Style Manager control, right-click with the mouse, and select the Help option.

The Help Viewer not only springs to life, but it displays a topic relevant to the control that has focus. This also happens inside any CDE application—try it from the Text Editor or Application Manager.

The control labeled On Item Help produces similar behavior as the F1 key if the control has focus. (When a control has focus, it is framed with a box.)

Adding Help to Icons

Modify the control you created earlier in Spider.fp to read as follows (you are adding a `HELP_STRING` configuration property):

```
CONTROL Spider
{
  CONTAINER_NAME          Games
  CONTAINER_TYPE          SUBPANEL
  LABEL                   Spider
  ICON                    redhat_folder
```

```
PUSH_ACTION          Spider
PUSH_RECALL          true
 HELP_STRING  Linux: What to drive.

}
```

FIGURE 5.15
A help window.

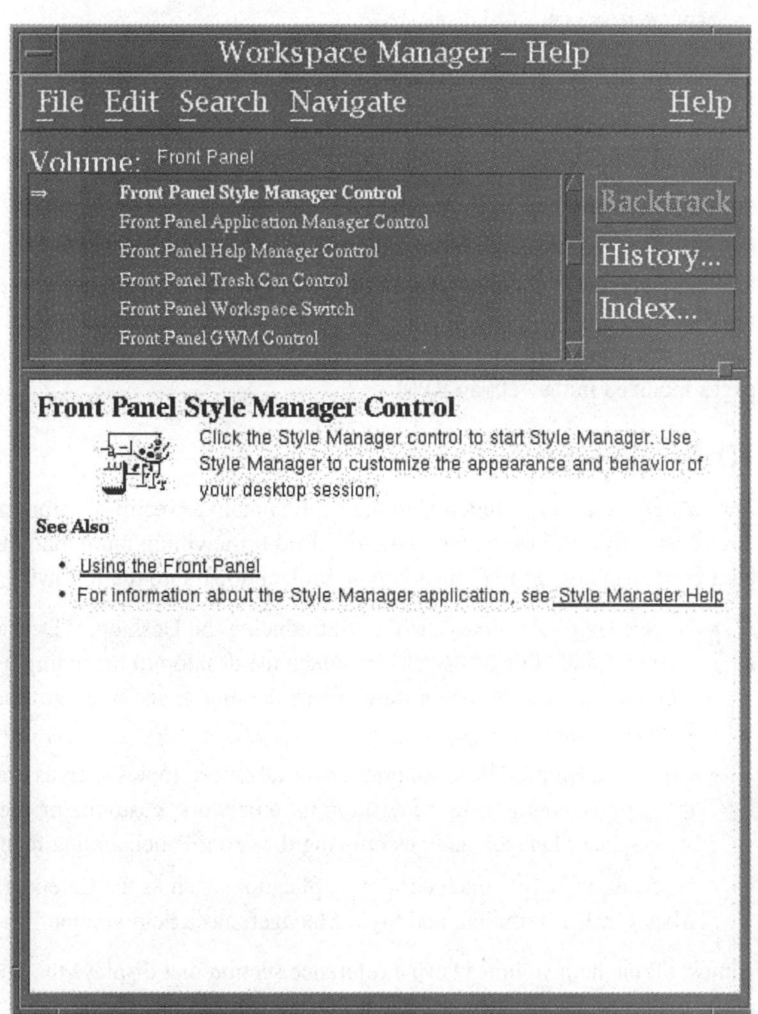

Restart the desktop, go to the Spider control, and bring up the menu by right-clicking it. Select the Help option. The Help Viewer appears, displaying the text you supplied in the control definition.

The Help Viewer can also be passed directives on what topic to bring up in an existing help file. If you take another look at the `FrontPanel` definition in the main.fp file you created earlier, you can see an example:

```
 PANEL FrontPanel
{
  DISPLAY_HANDLES         True
  DISPLAY_MENU            True
  DISPLAY_MINIMIZE        True
  CONTROL_BEHAVIOR        single_click
  DISPLAY_CONTROL_LABELS  False
  HELP_TOPIC              FPOnItemFrontPanel
  HELP_VOLUME             FPanel
SUBPANEL_UNPOST           False
}
```

The two help directives, `HELP_TOPIC` and `HELP_VOLUME`, tell the desktop the name of the topic and the file that contains it in $CDEROOT/appconfig/help/C. This is good to know when you are modifying default icons. Again, for more information, see the manual pages included in the `TEDman` RPM.

Help Topics

The 18 help volumes included with the CDE contain a wealth of information useful for novice and advanced users, removing the need for anything more than the most basic hard-copy manuals. The volumes can be broken down into the following categories:

- Novice Help—Volumes such as "Introducing the Desktop," "Desktop Help System," and "File Manager" introduce the desktop to beginning users. They include basic topics such as how to use the mouse and more advanced operations such as managing files.
- Advanced Help—These volumes cover advanced topics such as creating and deleting actions, configuring the desktop for a network, customizing the Graphical Workspace Manager, and customizing the Front Panel, among many others.
- Application Help—Each desktop application, such as the Calendar, Application Manager, DT Terminal, and Style Manager, has a help volume.

Almost all the help volumes have a reference section that displays the volume's contents in the format of a keyword and topic index, so you can quickly navigate within a topic without using the index window.

Summary

For many different types of window managers, or for pointers to the latest version of your favorite window manager, see `http://www.PLiG.org/xwinman`. You'll find lots of links to additional window themes, icons, and graphics you can use with your X11 desktop.

This chapter presents an overview of various window managers for X11, including the TriTeal Network Desktop for Linux, distributed by Red Hat Software. CDE is one of the many mainstream commercial products available for Linux. This availability is yet another positive sign that Linux is finally receiving the acceptance it deserves in the commercial arena.

Configuring Services

PART II

IN THIS PART

CHAPTER

System Startup and Shutdown

by Bill Ball

IN THIS CHAPTER

This chapter explains how to start the Red Hat Linux system and how to properly shut it down. It also covers system crashes and what to do if your system won't boot.

Also, this chapter presents some tips on how to customize your system and how to avoid problems with system crashes.

The Boot Process

In Chapter 2, "Installation of Your Red Hat System," you learned how to install Linux, and in Chapter 3, "LILO," you found out how to install and use different loaders for different computers. A number of ways exist to start Linux with different computers, and a number of different ways exist to load in the Linux kernel. Intel Linux users will most likely use LILO, `LOADLIN`, `SYSLINUX`, or the commercial alternative, System Commander. SPARC users will use SILO, and Alpha users will probably use MILO. You'll find the basic steps outlined in your *Red Hat Linux Users Guide* or through Red Hat at `http://www.redhat.com/linux-info`.

I'm assuming most readers will install Red Hat Linux/Intel, so here's a little background on how the Red Hat Linux startup process is different from that of other UNIX operating systems, such as BSD.

PCs start by looking at the first sector of the first cylinder of the boot drive and then trying to load and execute code found there (which is how LILO works, as explained in Chapter 3). This is also the case with other (but not all) hardware systems and versions of UNIX. You should be able to set the order in which your PC looks for the boot drive, usually through a BIOS change in a setup menu you can invoke when you first turn on your machine. Setting the order can be handy if you never use a boot floppy disk; for example, laptop users with an external floppy drive can speed up the boot process by directing the computer to look first at the internal hard drive or CD-ROM.

You can also start Linux over a network and run a diskless Linux box. For more information on how to do this, see Robert Nemkin's *Diskless Linux Mini HOWTO*, under /usr/doc/HOWTO/mini. Although Linux shares many similar traits with both System V and BSD UNIX, in the case of booting and starting the system, Linux is closer to the former. This means Linux uses the `init` command and a similar directory structure of associated scripts to start running the system and loading processes.

According to the Red Hat folks, this approach is becoming the standard in the "Linux world" because it is "easier to use and more powerful and flexible." You'll see why it is even easier for Red Hat Linux users when you learn about the `linuxconf` client later in this chapter in the section "`Linuxconf` and Managing Your Services."

The Initialization Process and Startup Scripts

This section describes how Linux starts and details the functions of the startup scripts used to prepare your system for use. An important concept to note is the use of various runlevels or system states of Linux.

System states grew from the need to separate how the system ran according to the forms of maintenance being performed on a system. This is similar to performing a software or hardware upgrade on older PCs, which generally requires a reboot or shutdown and restart of the computer. These days, however, this practice is partially obviated through new software and hardware technologies: "hot-swappable" hardware and software, which means you can change hard drives, PC cards, or associated software on-the-fly—while the system is running.

You'll find a description of various runlevels in the /etc/inittab file, or initialization table. Although Linux differs from other versions of UNIX in several of the levels, Red Hat Intel/Linux mainly uses the following (as listed in /etc/inittab):

```
#   The runlevels used by RHS are:
#   0 - halt (Do NOT set initdefault to this)
#   1 - Single user mode
#   2 - Multiuser, without NFS (The same as 3, if you do not have
networking)
#   3 - Full multiuser mode
#   4 - unused
#   5 - X11
#   6 - reboot (Do NOT set initdefault to this)
```

You'll usually find a line just below this listing that looks like

```
id:3:initdefault:
```

This line, which specifies runlevel 3 and uses the initdefault keyword, tells Linux to go to runlevel 3 (the Full multiuser mode) after loading the kernel (see the inittab man page for other keywords). The next section describes these runlevels, including the first startup script in the initialization table, `/etc/rc.d/rc.sysinit`, or the system initialization script, which is run once at boot time by the `init` command. It also covers the `/etc/rc.d` directory structure and what some of these scripts do.

`init` and `/etc/inittab`

The `init` man page states, "`init` is the father of all processes." Its primary role is to create processes from a script stored in `/etc/inittab`. Much of how Linux starts its processes after loading the kernel comes from another version of UNIX, System V. In fact, the Linux `init` command is compatible with the System V `init` command, and the startup scripts model that approach. Although `init` starts as "the last step of the kernel booting," it is the first command that initializes and configures your system for use. `init` works by parsing `/etc/inittab` and running scripts in `/etc/rc.d` according to either a default or desired runlevel. Each script can start or stop a service, such as a networking, mail, news, or Web service.

Here's a listing of the /etc/rc.d directory:

```
init.d/
rc*
rc.local*
rc.news*
rc.sysinit*
rc0.d/
rc1.d/
rc2.d/
rc3.d/
rc4.d/
rc5.d/
rc6.d/
```

Under the init.d directory, you'll find a number of scripts used to start and stop services. I won't go into the details about each, but you should be able to guess at the function of some of them by their names. Here's a list of scripts:

```
amd.init*
cron.init*
functions*
gpm*
halt*
httpd.init*
inet*
keytable*
killall*
lpd.init*
mars_nwe.init*
named.init*
network*
news*
nfs*
nfsfs*
pcmcia*
portmap.init*
random*
sendmail.init*
single*
skeleton*
```

```
smb*
syslog*
yppasswd.init*
ypserv.init*
```

/etc/inittab and System States

One of the most important scripts in `/etc/inittab` is `rc.sysinit`, the system initialization script. When `init` parses `/etc/inittab`, `rc.sysinit` is the first script found and executed. This differs slightly from other versions of UNIX, which might include the system initialization commands directly in the `/etc/inittab` file.

However, much like other versions of UNIX, the Red Hat Linux `sysinit` script performs some or all of the following functions:

- Sets some initial `$PATH` variables
- Configures networking
- Starts up swapping for virtual memory
- Sets the system hostname
- Checks root filesystems for possible repairs
- Checks root filesystem quotas
- Turns on user and group quotas for root filesystems
- Remounts the root filesystem read/write
- Clears the mounted filesystems table, `/etc/mtab`
- Enters the root filesystem into `mtab`
- Readies the system for loading modules
- Finds module dependencies
- Checks filesystems for possible repairs
- Mounts all other filesystems
- Cleans out several /etc files: /etc/mtab, /etc/fastboot, /etc/nologin
- Deletes UUCP lock files
- Deletes stale subsystem files
- Deletes stale pid files
- Sets the system clock
- Turns on swapping
- Initializes the serial ports
- Loads modules

Whew! That's a lot of work just for the first startup script, but it's only the first step in a number of steps needed to start your system. So far, you've seen that after the Linux kernel is loaded, the `init` command is run. After the `rc.sysinit` is run by `init`, `init` runs `rc.local`. If you look at the Red Hat Linux `rc.local` script, you'll see that it gets the operating system name and architecture of your computer and puts it into a file called /etc/issue, which is later used for display at the login prompt.

NOTE

The purpose of `rc.local` is not to provide a place to put system-specific initializations, although some people do. In BSD UNIX, `rc.local` is generally used for controlling network services. Linux has not always used the same initialization scripts or approach to starting up. You might find differences between distributions, such as Red Hat Linux, Slackware, SuSe, or others. For Red Hat Linux, use one of the graphical interface tools, such as `tksysv`, `ntsysv`, or `linuxconf` to control your system's services. Although you can do it manually by copying a skeleton script from the init.d directory and setting up the proper symbolic links, you'll find most of your needs met by the proper Red Hat tool.

The next task of `init` is to run the scripts for each runlevel. If you look at the listing of the `rc.d` directory, you'll see the various `rcX.d` directories, where *X* is a number from 0 through 6. But if you look at the files under one of these directories, you'll find that each is merely a link to a script under the `init.d`, with an associated name for a particular service. For example, under the `rc3.d` directory, you'll find

```
lrwxrwxrwx   1 root   root   17 Apr 10 09:11 S10network ->
../init.d/network*
lrwxrwxrwx   1 root   root   16 Apr 10 09:18 S30syslog -> ../init.d/syslog*
lrwxrwxrwx   1 root   root   19 Apr 10 09:22 S40cron ->
../init.d/cron.init*
lrwxrwxrwx   1 root   root   22 Apr 10 09:17 S40portmap ->
../init.d/portmap.init*
lrwxrwxrwx   1 root   root   16 Apr 10 09:16 S45pcmcia -> ../init.d/pcmcia*
lrwxrwxrwx   1 root   root   14 Apr 10 09:04 S50inet -> ../init.d/inet*
lrwxrwxrwx   1 root   root   20 Apr 10 09:06 S55named.init ->
../init.d/named.init*
lrwxrwxrwx   1 root   root   18 Jul 15 11:56 S60lpd.init ->
../init.d/lpd.init*
lrwxrwxrwx   1 root   root   13 Apr 10 09:16 S60nfs -> ../init.d/nfs*
lrwxrwxrwx   1 root   root   15 Apr 10 09:11 S70nfsfs -> ../init.d/nfsfs*
lrwxrwxrwx   1 root   root   18 Apr 10 09:11 S75keytable ->
../init.d/keytable*
lrwxrwxrwx   1 root   root   23 Apr 10 09:18 S80sendmail ->
../init.d/sendmail.init*
```

```
lrwxrwxrwx  1 root   root   13 Apr 10 09:10 S85gpm -> ../init.d/gpm*
lrwxrwxrwx  1 root   root   11 Apr 10 09:11 S99local -> ../rc.local*
```

Note the *S* in the front of each name, meaning to start a process or service. Now, if you look at the files under `rc0.d`, you'll see

```
lrwxrwxrwx  1 root   root    18 Apr 10 09:06 K08amd ->../init.d/amd.init*
lrwxrwxrwx  1 root   root    20 Apr 10 09:06 K10named.init ->
../init.d/named.init*
lrwxrwxrwx  1 root   root    15 Apr 10 09:11 K10nfsfs -> ../init.d/nfsfs*
lrwxrwxrwx  1 root   root    13 Apr 10 09:10 K15gpm -> ../init.d/gpm*
lrwxrwxrwx  1 root   root    13 Apr 10 09:16 K20nfs -> ../init.d/nfs*
lrwxrwxrwx  1 root   root    20 Apr 10 09:06 K25httpd ->
../init.d/httpd.init*
lrwxrwxrwx  1 root   root    21 Apr 10 09:11 K25news ->
/etc/rc.d/init.d/news*
lrwxrwxrwx  1 root   root    23 Apr 10 09:18 K30sendmail ->
../init.d/sendmail.init*
lrwxrwxrwx  1 root   root    23 Apr 10 09:14 K32mars_nwe ->
../init.d/mars_nwe.init*
lrwxrwxrwx  1 root   root    23 Apr 10 09:24 K33yppasswd ->
../init.d/yppasswd.init*
lrwxrwxrwx  1 root   root    21 Apr 10 09:24 K35ypserv ->
../init.d/ypserv.init*
lrwxrwxrwx  1 root   root    14 Apr 10 09:04 K50inet -> ../init.d/inet*
lrwxrwxrwx  1 root   root    16 Apr 10 09:16 K52pcmcia ->
../init.d/pcmcia*
lrwxrwxrwx  1 root   root    19 Apr 10 09:22 K60cron ->
../init.d/cron.init*
lrwxrwxrwx  1 root   root    18 Jul 15 11:56 K60lpd.init ->
../init.d/lpd.init*
lrwxrwxrwx  1 root   root    22 Apr 10 09:17 K65portmap ->
../init.d/portmap.init*
lrwxrwxrwx  1 root   root    16 Apr 10 09:18 K70syslog ->
../init.d/syslog*
lrwxrwxrwx  1 root   root    16 Apr 10 09:11 K80random ->
../init.d/random*
lrwxrwxrwx  1 root   root    17 Apr 10 09:11 K99killall ->
../init.d/killall*
lrwxrwxrwx  1 root   root    14 Apr 10 09:11 S00halt -> ../init.d/halt*
```

Notice the *K* in front of each name, meaning to kill a process or service. If you look under each of the `rcX.d` directories, you'll see what services or processes are started or stopped in each runlevel. The symbolic links are numbered to run in the proper order and to start or stop services that might be interdependent (for example, it wouldn't make sense to unmount a filesystem before it stopped network file-sharing). Later in this chapter we'll come back to some of the `rc.sysinit` tasks, because some of the error-checking done when starting up can help pinpoint problems with your system. For now, however, the following section explains the runlevels and what basically happens in each.

Runlevel 0: `/etc/rc.d/rc0.d`

As you can see from the previous directory listing, this runlevel starts the shutdown sequence. Each script is run in the order listed. Some of the tasks run include

- Killing all processes
- Turning off virtual memory file swapping
- Unmounting swap and mounted filesystems

As shown in this section and discussed later in this chapter, some important things are done during a shutdown involving your computer, its services, and its filesystems. Although Linux is a robust operating system with system-checking safeguards, executing a proper shutdown is essential to maintaining the integrity of your computer's hard drive as well as any Linux volumes or partitions.

Runlevel 1: `/etc/rc.d/rc1.d`

Runlevel 1 is the single-user mode, or administrative state, traditionally used by system administrators, or sysadmins, while performing software maintenance. No one else can log in during this mode, and networking is turned off, although necessary filesystems are mounted (others can be mounted manually at the command-line prompt but then must be specifically unmounted before rebooting).

Runlevel 2: `/etc/rc.d/rc2.d`

Runlevel 2 is the multiuser state. Networking is enabled, although NFS is disabled.

Runlevel 3: `/etc/rc.d/rc3.d`

Runlevel 3 is the default runlevel, which is specified as the first line in `/etc/inittab`. Remote file-sharing is enabled, along with all other desired services.

Runlevel 4: `/etc/rc.d/rc4.d`

The runlevel 4 directory is empty. As in other versions of UNIX, if you want to define your own runlevel, here's where you can add the appropriate links, with directions to selectively start or stop processes.

Runlevel 5: `/etc/rc.d/rc5.d`

Runlevel 5 is much the same as the default, with the exception of `named`, the Internet domain nameserver. This is also the runlevel entered when X11 is run under Linux. If you configure the X Window System to use the xdm chooser, your Red Hat Linux system will boot to this runlevel (see Chapter 4, "X Window," for details).

Runlevel 6: /etc/rc.d/rc6.d

Runlevel 6 is the reboot runlevel. The contents of this directory contain links similar to those in runlevel 0, but logic in the halt script under `init.d` determines whether the system is being shut down or rebooted.

Keeping track of which process is started or stopped in which runlevel can be difficult. In the next section, you'll see one more reason why using Red Hat Linux can make your system administration tasks easier.

Linuxconf and Managing Your Services

One of the great things about Red Hat Linux is the number of tools included in the distribution to help you manage your system. One important tool is Jacque Gelinas's `linuxconf`, which can be called from a command line in a terminal window while you're running X, from the command line of your console screen, or through your favorite Web browser. You should use `linuxconf` for a number of reasons:

- `Linuxconf` provides a comprehensive graphic interface for administering your Red Hat system.
- You can save different system configurations, allowing you—for example—to set up your computer as a desktop machine or Internet server at different times with a single command line.
- `Linuxconf` replaces and maintains a number of user, file, and network utilities (such as `usercfg`, `fstool`, and `cabaret`); the program is used as a configuration tool and a service activation tool.
- `Linuxconf` has the capability to use modules to add new features or capabilities.
- The program features built-in help for many services or actions.
- `Linuxconf` allows system maintenance over a network, enabling more efficient management of in-house or remote computers and networks.

`Linuxconf` is found under the /bin directory and weighs in at nearly 800,000 characters. The program, written with more than 80,000 lines of C++ code, also comes with a support directory, /usr/lib/linuxconf, containing more than 6MB of data, Help files in several languages, and code modules.

After you log in as the root operator, start the `linuxconf` program from the command line with:

```
# linuxconf &
```

and press the Enter key. The program's main window appears, as shown in Figure 6.1.

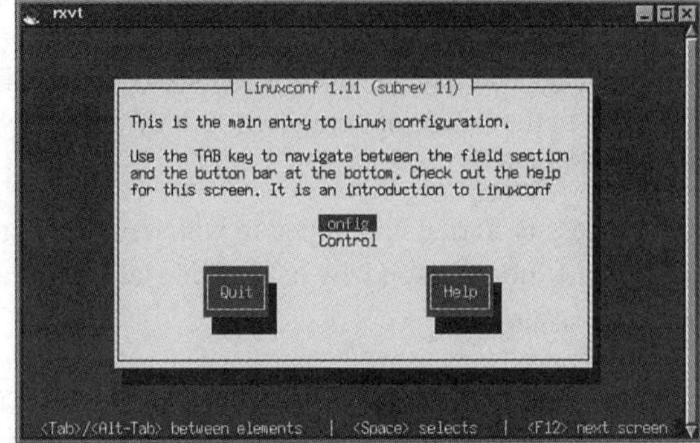

FIGURE 6.1
The `linuxconf` client represents a new generation of graphical Linux administration tools.

The program (which started life as a configuration tool for the XFree86 X11 distribution) responds to keyboard commands just like Red Hat's Linux installation tool and other graphics utilities. Navigate around the program's dialog by pressing the Tab key, and then use the Enter key when the cursor is on a desired button or item in a list.

To perform system configuration, press the up or down arrows to highlight the word Config in `linuxconf`'s main dialog, and press the Enter key. `Linuxconf`'s configuration selections appear, as shown in Figure 6.2.

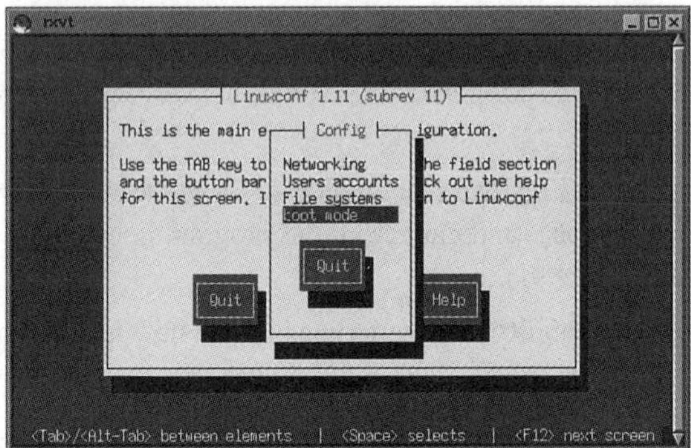

FIGURE 6.2
The `linuxconf` configuration dialog offers a variety of routes to setting up your system.

On the other hand, if you'd like to activate various services, check your system's integrity, or perform other actions, select the Control item from `linuxconf`'s main dialog (see Figure 6.1) and press the Enter key. `Linuxconf`'s control dialog appears, as shown in Figure 6.3.

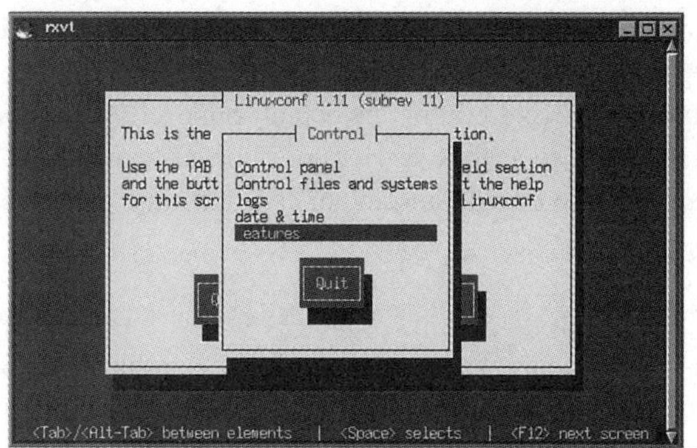

FIGURE 6.3
The `linuxconf` control dialog offers a variety of routes to starting or stopping services for your system.

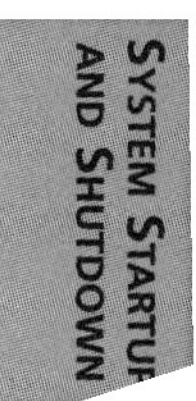

`Linuxconf` can be used not only interactively, but also from the command line. The following new Linux commands will be found under the /bin directory after you install `linuxconf` (part of Red Hat Linux since version 5.1):

- fixperm—A utility to check system file permissions
- lpdconfig—A print-spooling configuration utility
- netconf—A TCP/IP services configuration utility
- userconf—User configuration (to add or delete users)
- xconf—X11 configuration utility (see Chapter 4, "X Window," for details)

Each program is a symbolic link to—you guessed it—`linuxconf`. For example, to delete the user *cloobie* from the command line, use `linuxconf`'s symbolic link `userconf`, like this:

```
# userconf -deluser cloobie
```

The `linuxconf` command will also help you properly start and stop services under Linux while the system is running. Although you can selectively "kill" processes with

```
# kill -9 pid
```

where `pid` is the number of the running process, this is a crude, ineffective, and potentially harmful way to stop processes. However, based on the information you have learned so far, you can also use the following approach—for example, to stop the Web server, `httpd`:

```
# /etc/rc.d/init.d/httpd.init stop
```

Both of these are manual approaches, but the Red Hat folks have taken great pains to make system administration easier, so why not take advantage of menu convenience? When you use `linuxconf`, you can see at one glance which processes are going to be enabled or disabled.

After navigating through the `linuxconf` dialogs and lists, you simply select a service to start or a service to stop. Using `linuxconf` sure beats doing everything by hand, but be careful—making changes by hand-editing the default runlevel for `/etc/inittab` or indiscriminately using `linuxconf` to change services or runlevels can put your system into an unusable state. If you run into trouble, reset your computer and enter the following at the LILO prompt:

```
LILO boot: linux single
```

Booting into single-user mode might allow you to fix any problems (a similar approach to another operating system's "safe mode"). When you boot into single-user mode, you go directly into a root operator command line—handy for enabling a quick fix or performing other system administration tasks.

You should also know that `linuxconf` is a work in progress: not every item in the program is documented or has an associated Help menu or complete Help text. For some additional details about `linuxconf`, tips on using modules, or other errata, see Jonathan Marsden's FAQ at:

```
http://www.xc.org/jonathan/linuxconf-rh51-faq.html
```

Shutting Down the Linux System

By now you've learned not only how Linux starts, but also a little bit about how it shuts down. If you look at the scripts in runlevel 0, you'll find a number of services being shut down, followed by the killing of all active processes, and—finally—the halt script in `inet.d` executing the shutdown.

The halt script is used to either halt or reboot your system, depending on how it is called. But what happens during a shutdown? If you're familiar with other operating systems (such as DOS), you remember that all you had to do was close any active application and then turn off the computer. Although Linux is easy to use, shutting down your computer is not as simple as turning it off. (You can try this if you wish, but you do so at your own risk.) A number of processes must take place before you or Linux turns off your computer. The following sections take a look at some of the commands involved.

`shutdown`

Although many people use Linux as single users on a single computer, many of us use computers on either a distributed or shared network. If you've ever been working under a tight deadline in a networked environment, you know the dreadful experience of seeing a "System is going down in 5 minutes!" message from the system administrator. You might also know the frustration of working on a system on which the system administrator is trying to perform maintenance, suffering seemingly random downtimes or frozen tasks.

Luckily for most users, maintenance jobs are performed during off hours, when most people are home with their loved ones or fast asleep in bed. Unluckily for sysadmins, this is the perfect time for system administration or backups, and one of the top reasons for the `alt.sysadmin.recovery` newsgroup.

The primary command to stop Linux is the `shutdown` command. Like most UNIX commands, `shutdown` has a number of options. A man page for the `shutdown` command is included with Red Hat Linux, but you can find its command-line syntax because it displays a small Help message if you use an illegal option. Thanks to the programmer, here it is:

```
Usage:    shutdown [-krhfnc] [-t secs] time [warning message]
                -k:      don't really shutdown, only warn.
                -r:      reboot after shutdown.
                -h:      halt after shutdown.
                -f:      do a 'fast' reboot.
                -n:      do not go through "init" but go down real fast.
                -c:      cancel a running shutdown.
                -t secs: delay between warning and kill signal.
** the "time" argument is mandatory! (try "now") **
```

To properly shutdown your system immediately, use

```
# shutdown -h now
```

If you want to wait for a while, use the **`-t`** option. If you want to restart your computer, use

```
# shutdown -r now
```

NOTE

You'll find two curious text strings embedded in the shutdown program:

```
"You don't exist. Go away."
"Well hello Mr. Tyler - going DOWN?"
```

Both are found by executing:

```
# strings /sbin/shutdown
```

Hint: To find out about `"You don't exist. Go away,"` see Ian Jackson's *Linux Frequently Asked Questions with Answers*. You should be able to find a copy under the /usr/doc directory or at ftp://sunsite.unc.edu/pub/Linux/docs/HOWTO.

You can also use `linuxconf` to shut down your computer. If you're logged in as the root operator, enter the following from the command line of your console or an X11 terminal window:

```
# linuxconf -shutdown
```

`Linuxconf` presents a shutdown dialog, as shown in Figure 6.4. To restart your system, press the Tab key until you highlight the Accept button, and then press the Enter key. You can also enter a time delay or halt your system immediately.

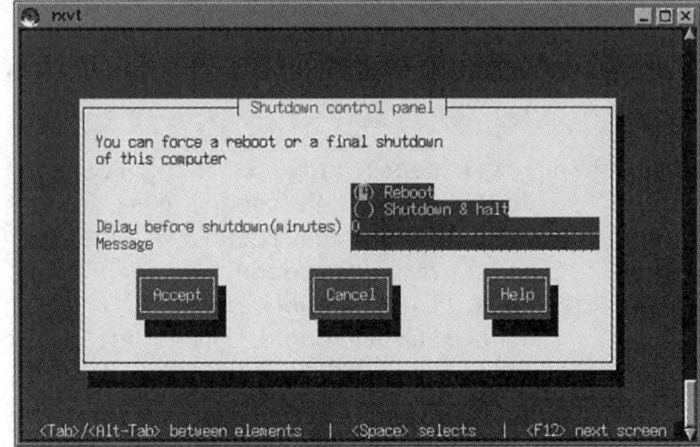

FIGURE 6.4
The `linuxconf` command will perform a reboot or shutdown of your system.

halt and reboot

Two other commands will also stop or restart your system: the `halt` and `reboot` commands. `reboot` is a symbolic link to `halt`, which notifies the kernel of a shutdown or reboot. Although you should always use `shutdown` to restart your system, you can use the "Vulcan neck pinch," `ctrlaltdel`.

If you use the keyboard form of this command, you'll find that Linux uses the following command:

```
# shutdown -t3 -r now
```

Restarting your computer with the shutdown command calls the `sync` command, which updates the inodes (structure representations) of each of your files. If you exit Linux without updating this information, Linux could lose track of your files on disk, and that spells disaster!

NOTE

The only time you'll want to risk shutting down Linux through a hard reset or the power-off switch on your computer is if you can't quickly kill a destructive process, such as an accidental `rm -fr /*`.

By now you should know that exiting Linux properly can help you avoid problems with your system. But what happens if something goes wrong? In the next section you'll learn about preventive measures, how to maintain your filesystem, and how to recover and overcome problems.

When the System Crashes

The best time to deal with a system crash is before the crash happens. This means being prepared with a good backup plan, good backups, emergency boot disks, or copies of important files. These issues are covered in this section, along with tips and hints for maintaining your filesystem integrity and system security.

First, here are some Do's and Don'ts to avoid problems:

- Don't use Linux as the root user.
- Do make a backup after a clean install and setup.
- Do create a set of emergency boot disks with your current kernel.
- Don't just turn off your computer when you finish.
- Do use the `shutdown` command.
- Do consider using an uninterruptible power supply.
- Don't disable `e2fsck` in /etc/rc.d/rc.sysinit.
- Do use `fsck` or `badblocks` to check floppy disks.
- Don't run `fsck` on mounted filesystems.
- Do make backups of important files on floppy disks.
- Don't worry about fragmentation of your Linux partitions.
- Do use your filesystem tools.
- Don't fill your hard drive with unnecessary programs.
- Do consider using flash RAM.
- Do read Lars Wirzenius's *Linux System Administrators' Guide 0.5*.

Running as Root

Don't use Linux as root all of the time. Although you might be tempted, some very good reasons exist for not doing this. First, even though you might have aliased the `rm` command to `rm -i` in your `.bashrc` file, a simple `# rm -fr /*` will wipe out not only your Linux system but also any DOS or Windows partitions mounted under `/mnt`. Instead, create a user for yourself and use the `su` command when you need to do things as the root operator. If you have programs that need to run SUID root, see Phil Hughes's article, "Safely Running Programs as `root`," in the May 1997 issue of *Linux Journal*.

NOTE

If you'd like to install a more flexible superuser command than `su`, try the `sudo` command. This program can be used to selectively extend superstatus to designated users for certain commands. For more information, navigate to http://www.courtesan.com/courtesan/products/sudo.

Creating a Boot Disk

One of the first things you should do following a clean install and setup is to make a boot disk, using the current Linux kernel on your computer. You should always have a working copy in case you make a mistake when recompiling the kernel. Here's one quick, traditional way to not only make a copy of your current kernel, but also create an emergency boot disk. First, make sure your kernel points to your root device. You can check this on a recently built kernel with

```
# rdev zImage
```

Next, format a disk in your floppy drive by using `fdformat` (assuming a 1.44MB drive A:):

```
# fdformat /dev/fd0H1440
```

Next, copy your kernel to the disk with

```
# dd if=zImage of=/dev/fd0
```

Now, assuming your computer is set to look at the floppy drive first, try restarting with your boot disk with

```
# shutdown -r now
```

You should also have a backup set of emergency boot disks that include not just the kernel but also a minimal filesystem to get you started on the road to recovery. Some excellent guides, scripts, and software are available to help you do this (see "For More Information," at the end of this chapter).

Generally, the approach is to create two disks, one containing a kernel and the other containing a compressed filesystem with a minimal directory of files, including file utilities. Because you're a Red Hat Linux user, you'll want to use the `mkbootdisk` command to create your boot disk.

First, boot Linux and log in as the root operator. From the command line of your console or an X11 terminal window, use `mkbootdisk` with its `-device` option, followed by the device name of your floppy drive and the name of your Linux kernel, like this:

```
# mkbootdisk -device /dev/fd0 2.0.34-1
```

Insert a blank floppy disk and press the Enter key to make your boot disk.

NOTE

According to the Red Hat folks, you can find out the name of your kernel by using the `uname` command, followed by its –r option: `uname -r`. For more information about the `mkbootdisk` command, see its man page.

Ackpht! Argggh! I've Deleted My Document!

If you accidentally delete a text file, don't panic. Here's a handy tip, called "Desperate person's text file undelete," from Paul Anderson's *The Linux Tips HOWTO*, courtesy of Michael Hamilton.

Assuming you remember some of the text, know which partition the file was on, and have a spare partition with some room, you should be able to recover a good portion of the file. Hamilton's approach uses the `egrep` and `strings` commands. For example, if you lose a 100-line file with the phrase "Xena," followed by "Lawless," and have room on your DOS partition, use:

```
# egrep -100 'Xena.+Lawless' /dev/hda3 > /mnt/dos/lucy
```

Then you can look for the text with

```
# strings /mnt/dos/lucy ¦ less
```

This approach to file recovery uses the egrep command to search for a string of text directly on your Linux partition. (Remember, everything under Linux is a file, right?) Each 100 lines of text before and after any match are saved into the designated file. Note, however, that this technique won't help you recover or undelete a binary file.

NOTE

If you need to recover binary files or want to explore other methods of file recovery, read Aaron Crane's *Linux Ext2fs Undelete mini-HOWTO*, found under the /usr/doc/HOWTO/mini directory. You'll read about several interesting techniques, including how to create a temporary Linux filesystem in your computer's memory to help provide recovery storage.

Your File Toolbox

You should also learn about and know how to use some of the file tools included with Red Hat Linux. While `e2fsck` is run automatically from the `rc.sysinit` script, it can be helpful in diagnosing and fixing problems. Other commands, such as `dumpe2fs` and `debugfs`, provide detailed technical information concerning your Linux filesystem, while still others, such as `badblocks`, can be helpful if you have a non-IDE hard drive.

Here's a list of just some of the programs available:

e2fsck

Most Linux users choose to use the second extended filesystem, and with good reason: `e2fs` is robust, efficient, speedy, and relatively impervious to fragmentation. This command has a plethora of options aimed at helping you check and repair your filesystem. For safety's sake, unmount the partition and then try

```
# e2fsck -p /dev/hda3
```

to automatically repair the partition /dev/hda3.

badblocks

The `badblocks` command searches a device for bad blocks and also has a number of options. Beware of the `-w` option, as it is a "write-mode" test and will destroy data on a partition.

fsck

The `fsck` command, a front-end program for other filesystem commands such as `e2fsck`, checks and repairs Linux filesystems. Be sure to read its man page, as the `-P` option can be harmful.

dump and restore

The `dump` command can be used for filesystem backup, as it searches your files that need to be backed up. `dump` can also do remote backups. The companion program is `restore`, which also works across networks.

dumpe2fs

The `dumpe2fs` command dumps your filesystem information. You'll get the inode count, block count, block size, last mount, and write time. Running `dumpe2fs` on a 450MB partition generates a 26,000-character report. An interesting part of the report is the mount and maximum mount count, which determines when `e2fsck` is run on a partition when Linux starts.

tune2fs

If you just have to mess with your system's performance, you can use the `tune2fs` command to adjust its tunable parameters—but only if you have an `ext2` filesystem. Use this command to adjust when `e2fsck` is run on your partition, but don't do it when the partition is mounted.

mke2fs

Linux hackers will be familiar with the `mke2fs` program, which creates a Linux second extended filesystem on a partition. And you might need it, too, if you want to create compressed filesystems on emergency disks or if you install a new hard drive.

debugfs

`debugfs` is an `ext2` filesystem debugger, with 34 built-in commands. If you call it with

```
# debugfs /dev/hda3
```

you can examine your filesystem in read-only mode.

Each of these utilities can help you maintain, diagnose, and repair a filesystem. But what if you can't boot? Read on.

Red Hat to the Rescue! When the System Won't Boot

A Linux system might not boot for any of a number of reasons. If you recall the earlier example of making a boot disk, you know that the `rdev` command is used to set the root device. Building a new kernel and then trying to use LILO or `LOADLIN` to load the new kernel won't work unless you've done this. You'll also have problems if you've rebuilt the kernel and hard-coded in the wrong root device.

I told you earlier that you'll appreciate being a Red Hat user. Here's another good reason: You get a set of emergency boot disks with your Red Hat distribution. If your system won't boot, here's how you might be able to recover your system:

First, ALWAYS make a set of emergency boot disks. Use the mkbootdisk command (as described above) to create a boot disk with your Linux kernel. Then use the `dd` command to create a second disk containing the rescue.img file from this book's CD-ROM. Use the `mount` command to mount the CD-ROM like this:

```
# mount /mnt/cdrom
```

Log in as the root operator, insert a blank floppy disk in your computer (label it "rescue"), and then create the rescue disk, using `dd` to copy the rescue.img file:

```
# dd if=/mnt/cdrom/images/rescue.img of=/dev/fd0 bs=1440k
```

Boot Linux from your Red Hat Linux boot disk. Next, at the `boot:` prompt, type **`rescue`**, which loads a kernel from the disk. Follow the prompts and, when asked, eject the boot disk and insert the second "rescue" disk. You'll end up with a # bash shell prompt.

Under the /bin directory, you'll find a minimal set of programs. The idea is to at least get you to the point where you can try to check your existing partitions and possibly mount your drive. For example, if you have a Linux partition on /dev/hda3, you can try to first create a mount point by using the `mkdir` command, and then use `mt` to mount your partition like this:

```
# mkdir /mnt/linux
# mount -t ext2 /dev/hda3 /mnt/linux
```

Your Linux partition will be found under /mnt/linux, and you can then attempt a fix.

If you've installed Red Hat Linux and for some reason your system won't boot, and you don't have your Red Hat boot disks, you can also try booting directly from your Red Hat Linux CD-ROM (you might have to change your BIOS settings to alter the boot device sequence from your hard drive or floppy drive).

You can also try to reboot your computer to DOS, change the directory to the CD-ROM and then `DOSUTILS`, and then type **`AUTOBOOT`**, which will execute the `AUTOBOOT.BAT` batch file and put you into the Red Hat installation process.

For More Information

For more information about the new `linuxconf` tool, navigate to:

`http://www.solucorp.qc.ca/linuxconf`

To subscribe to the `linuxconf` mailing list, put the following text into the body of an email message addressed to linuxconf-request@solucorp.qc.ca:

`subscribe linuxconf`

For information regarding the Linux boot process, a host of handy tips on building boot disks, pointers to bootdisk packages, and a number of helpful scripts, see Tom Fawcett and Graham Chapman's *Linux Bootdisk HOWTO* under /usr/doc/HOWTO or at `http://unsite.unc.edu/mdw/linux.html`.

You should also look for the following rescue packages and other helpful utilities at `http://sunsite.unc.edu/pub/Linux/system/recovery`:

- Scott Burkett's Bootkit
- Oleg Kibirev's CatRescue
- Thomas Heiling's Rescue Shell Scripts
- Karel Kubat's SAR—Search and Rescue
- Tom Fawcett's YARD

Read the man pages for the following commands on your Red Hat Linux system:

- `badblocks`
- `debugfs`
- `dump`
- `dumpe2fs`
- `e2fsck`
- `fsck`
- `fstab`
- `halt`
- `hdparm`
- `init`
- `inittab`

- `mke2fs`
- `mount`
- `rdev`
- `restore`
- `shutdown`
- `swapon`
- `tune2fs`

If you ever lose or destroy your copies of the Red Hat Linux boot disks, you can get replacements at `http://www.redhat.com/mirrors.html`.

For details on how 4.4BSD boots, see Tabbed Section 1 of the *4.4BSD System Manager's Manual*. For details about other UNIX boot processes, see *UNIX Unleashed: System Administrator's Edition*.

For loads of tips on maintaining your system and background information about various Linux filesystems, see Lars Wirzenius's *Linux System Administrators' Guide 0.5*. You'll find a copy at ftp://sunsite.unc.edu/pub/Linux/docs/LDP or under the /usr/doc/LDP/sag directory.

If you're interested in a Linux filesystem defragmenter, check out Stephen Tweedie and Alexei Vovenko's defragmenter, Which you'll find at `http://sunsite.unc.edu/pub/Linux/system/filesystems/defrag-0.70.tar.gz`.

Summary

This chapter has covered a number of topics related to starting and shutting down Linux, including the following:

- How Linux boots
- How Linux starts
- What runlevels are and when to use them
- How to start and stop processes properly
- How to use `linuxconf`
- How to properly shut down your Linux system
- How to properly restart your Linux system
- The do's and don'ts of maintaining your system
- How to create a root disk and copy of your kernel
- How to possibly undelete a file
- How to possibly recover and remount a Linux partition

SMTP and POP

by Chris Byers

In This Chapter

Electronic mail (email) is arguably the most used application of any data network such as the Internet. (Yes, even more so than the World Wide Web.) Early in the Internet's life, many standards were proposed for email between systems. These standards changed often, and the corresponding software changes were significant.

During this time of rapid change in email protocols, a package emerged as a standard for mail transfer—`sendmail`. `sendmail`, written by Eric Allman of U.C. Berkeley, was an unusual program for its time because it thought of the email problem in a different light. Instead of rejecting email from different networks using so-called incorrect protocols, `sendmail` massaged the message and fixed it so the message could be passed on to its destination. The side effect of this level of configurability has been complexity. Several books have been written on the subject (the authoritative texts have reached over 1000 pages); however, for most administrators, these are overkill.

One of the key features of `sendmail` that differentiated it from other mail transfer agents (MTAs) during the 1980s was the separation of mail routing, mail delivery, and mail readers. `sendmail` performed mail routing functions only, leaving delivery to local agents the administrator could select. This also meant users could select their preferred mail readers as long as the readers could read the format of the messages written by the delivery software.

With the advent of larger, heterogeneous networks, the need for mail readers that worked on network clients and connected to designated mail servers to send and receive mail gave way to the Post Office Protocol (POP). POP mail readers have since flourished, with client software available for every imaginable platform and server software for not only various implementations of UNIX (including Linux) but for other less robust operating systems as well.

This chapter covers the most recent work on `sendmail`; its underlying protocol, SMTP; and the `qpopper` package, which implements POP support for Linux.

SMTP and `sendmail`

The Simple Mail Transfer Protocol (SMTP) is the established standard way of transferring mail over the Internet. The `sendmail` program provides the services needed to support SMTP connections for Linux.

This section covers the details you need to understand the `sendmail` package, install it, and configure it. Before getting into the details, however, I'll take a moment to discuss the SMTP protocol in better detail and how the Domain Name Service (DNS) interacts with email across the Internet. (See Chapter 17, "TCP/IP Network Management," for details on DNS configuration).

Armed with a better understanding of the protocols, you can take on understanding sendmail itself, beginning with the various tasks sendmail performs (such as mail routing and header rewriting) as well as its corresponding configuration files.

CAUTION

As with any large software package, sendmail has its share of bugs. Although the bugs that cause sendmail to fail or crash the system have been almost completely eliminated, security holes that provide root access are still found from time to time.

When using any software that provides network connectivity, you *must* keep track of security announcements from the Computer Emergency Response Team (CERT) by either visiting its Web page at http://www.cert.org, joining its mailing list, or reading its moderated newsgroup comp.security.announce.

Internet Mail Protocols

To understand the jobs sendmail performs, you need to know a little about Internet protocols. Protocols are agreed-upon standards that software and hardware use to communicate.

Protocols are usually layered, with higher levels using the lower ones as building blocks. For example, the Internet Protocol (IP) sends packets of data back and forth without building an end-to-end connection such as that used by SMTP and other higher-level protocols. The Transmission Control Protocol (TCP), which is built on top of IP, provides for connection-oriented services such as those used by Telnet and the Simple Mail Transfer Protocol (SMTP). Together, TCP/IP provide the basic network services for the Internet. Higher-level protocols such as the File Transfer Protocol (FTP) and SMTP are built on top of TCP/IP. The advantage of such layering is that programs that implement the SMTP or FTP protocols don't have to know anything about transporting packets on the network and making connections to other hosts. They can use the services provided by TCP/IP for that job.

SMTP defines how programs exchange email on the Internet. It doesn't matter whether the program exchanging the email is sendmail running on an HP workstation or an SMTP client written for an Apple Macintosh. As long as both programs implement the SMTP protocol correctly, they can exchange mail.

The following example of the SMTP protocol in action might help demystify it a little. The user betty at gonzo.gov is sending mail to joe at whizzer.com.

```
$ /usr/sbin/sendmail -v joe@whizzer.com < letter
joe@whizzer.com... Connecting to whizzer.com via tcp...
Trying 123.45.67.1...  connected.
220-whizzer.com SMTP ready at Mon, 6 Jun 1997 18:56:22 -0500
220 ESMTP spoken here
>>> HELO gonzo.gov
250 whizzer.com Hello gonzo.gov [123.45.67.2], pleased to meet you
>>> MAIL From:<betty@gonzo.gov>
250 <betty@gonzo.gov>... Sender ok
>>> RCPT To:<joe@whizzer.com>
250 <joe@whizzer.com>... Recipient ok
>>> DATA
354 Enter mail, end with "." on a line by itself
>>> .
250 SAA08680 Message accepted for delivery
>>> QUIT
221 whizzer.com closing connection
joe@whizzer.com... Sent
$
```

The first line shows one way to invoke `sendmail` directly rather than letting your favorite Mail User Agent (MUA) such as Elm, Pine, or Mutt do it for you. The `-v` option tells `sendmail` to be verbose and shows you the SMTP dialog. The other lines show an SMTP client and server carrying on a conversation. Lines prefaced with `>>>` indicate the client (or sender) on `gonzo.gov`, and the lines that immediately follow are the replies of the server (or receiver) on `whizzer.com`. The first line beginning with `220` is the SMTP server announcing itself after the initial connection, giving its hostname and the date and time, and the second line informs the client that this server understands the Extended SMTP protocol (ESMTP), in case the client wants to use it. Numbers such as `220` are reply codes the SMTP client uses to communicate with the SMTP server. The text following the reply codes is only for human consumption.

Although this dialog might still look a little mysterious, it will soon be very familiar if you take the time to read RFC 821. Running `sendmail` with its `-v` option also helps you understand how an SMTP dialog works.

The Domain Name System and Email

Names like `whizzer.com` are convenient for humans, but computers insist on using numeric IP addresses like `123.45.67.1`. The DNS provides this hostname to IP address translation and other important information.

In the old days (when most of us walked several miles to school through deep snow), only a few thousand hosts were on the Internet. All hosts were registered with the Network Information Center (NIC), which distributed a host table listing the hostnames and IP addresses of all the hosts on the Internet. Those simple times are gone forever. No one really knows how many hosts are connected to the Internet now, but they number in the millions, and an administrative entity such as the NIC can't keep their names straight. Thus was born the DNS.

The DNS distributes authority for naming and numbering hosts to autonomous administrative domains. For example, a company called `whizzer.com` can maintain all the information about the hosts in its own domain. When the host `a.whizzer.com` wants to send mail or Telnet to the host `b.whizzer.com`, it sends an inquiry over the network to the `whizzer.com` nameserver, which might run on a host named `ns.whizzer.com`. The `ns.whizzer.com` nameserver replies to `a.whizzer.com` with the IP address of `b.whizzer.com` (and possibly other information), and the mail is sent or the Telnet connection made. Because `ns.whizzer.com` is authoritative for the `whizzer.com` domain, it can answer any inquiries about `whizzer.com` hosts regardless of where they originate; the authority for naming hosts in this domain has been delegated.

Now, what if someone on `a.whizzer.com` wants to send mail to `joe@gonzo.gov`? `Ns.whizzer.com` has no information about hosts in the `gonzo.gov` domain, but it knows how to find this information. When a nameserver receives a request for a host in a domain for which it has no information, it asks the root nameservers for the names and IP addresses of servers authoritative for that domain—in this case, `gonzo.gov`. The root nameserver gives the `ns.whizzer.com` nameserver the names and IP addresses of hosts running nameservers with authority for `gonzo.gov`. The `ns.whizzer.com` nameserver inquires of them and forwards the reply to `a.whizzer.com`.

From the preceding description, you can see that the DNS is a large, distributed database containing mappings between hostnames and IP addresses, but it contains other information as well. When a program such as `sendmail` delivers mail, it must translate the recipient's hostname into an IP address. This bit of DNS data is known as an A (Address) record, and it is the most fundamental data about a host. A second piece of host data is the Mail eXchanger (MX) record. An MX record for a host such as `a.whizzer.com` lists one or more hosts willing to receive mail for it.

What's the point? Why shouldn't `a.whizzer.com` simply receive its own mail and be done with the process? Isn't a postmaster's life complicated enough without having to worry about mail exchangers? Well, although it's true that the postmaster's life is often overly complicated, MX records serve useful purposes:

- Hosts not on the Internet (for example, UUCP-only hosts) can designate an Internet host to receive their mail and so appear to have Internet addresses. This use of MX records allows non-Internet hosts to appear to be on the Internet (but only to receive email).

- Hosts can be off the Internet for extended times for unpredictable reasons. Thanks to MX records, even if your host is off the Internet, its mail can queue on other hosts until your host returns. The other hosts can be either onsite (that is, in your domain) or offsite, or both.
- MX records hide information and allow you more flexibility to reconfigure your local network. If all your correspondents know your email address is `joe@whizzer.com`, it doesn't matter whether the host that receives mail for `whizzer.com` is named `zippy.whizzer.com` or `pinhead.whizzer.com`. It also doesn't matter if you decide to change the name to `white-whale.whizzer.com`; your correspondents will never know the difference.

For the full details on configuring DNS for Linux, see Chapter 17.

Mail Delivery and MX Records

When an SMTP client delivers mail to a host, it must do more than translate the hostname into an IP address. First, the client asks for MX records. If any exist, it sorts them according to the priority given in the record. For example, `whizzer.com` might have MX records listing the hosts `mailhub.whizzer.com`, `walrus.whizzer.com`, and `mailer.gonzo.gov` as the hosts willing to receive mail for it (and the "host" `whizzer.com` might not exist except as an MX record, meaning that no IP address might be available for it). Although any of these hosts will accept mail for `whizzer.com`, the MX priorities specify which host the SMTP client should try first, and properly behaved SMTP clients will do so. In this case, the system administrator has set up a primary mail relay `mailhub.whizzer.com` and an onsite backup `walrus.whizzer.com` and has arranged with the system administrator at `mailer.gonzo.gov` for an offsite backup. The administrators have set the MX priorities so SMTP clients will try the primary mail relay first, the onsite backup second, and the offsite backup third. This setup takes care of problems with the vendor who doesn't ship your parts on time and the wayward backhoe operator who severs the fiber optic cable that provides your site's Internet connection.

After collecting and sorting the MX records, the SMTP client gathers the IP addresses for the MX hosts and attempts delivery to them in order of MX preference. You should keep this fact in mind when debugging mail problems. Just because a letter is addressed to `joe@whizzer.com` doesn't necessarily mean a host named `whizzer.com` exists. Even if such a host does exist, it might not be the host that is supposed to receive the mail.

Header and Envelope Addresses

The distinction between header and envelope addresses is important, because mail routers can process them differently. An example will help explain the difference between the two.

Suppose you have a paper memo you want to send to your colleagues Mary and Bill at the Gonzo Corporation and Ted and Ben at the Whizzer company. You give a copy of the memo to your trusty mail clerk Alphonse, who notes the multiple recipients. Because he's a clever fellow who wants to save your company 32 cents, Alphonse makes two copies of the memo and puts each in an envelope addressed to the respective companies (instead of sending a copy to each recipient). On the cover of the `Gonzo` envelope, he writes "Mary and Bill," and on the cover of the `Whizzer` envelope, he writes "Ted and Ben." When Alphonse's counterparts at `Gonzo` and `Whizzer` receive the envelopes, they make copies of the memo and send them to Mary, Bill, Ted, and Ben, without inspecting the addresses in the memo itself. As far as the `Gonzo` and `Whizzer` mail clerks are concerned, the memo itself might be addressed to the pope; they care only about the envelope addresses.

SMTP clients and servers work in much the same way. Suppose `joe@gonzo.gov` sends mail to his colleagues `betty@zippy.gov` and `fred@whizzer.com`. The recipient list in the letter's headers might look like this:

```
To: betty@zippy.gov, fred@whizzer.com
```

The SMTP client at `gonzo.gov` connects to the `whizzer.com` mailer to deliver Fred's copy. When it's ready to list the recipients (the envelope address), what should it say? If it gives both recipients as they are listed in the preceding To: line (the header address), Betty will get two copies of the letter because the `whizzer.com` mailer will forward a copy to `zippy.gov`. The same problem occurs if the `gonzo.gov` SMTP client connects to `zippy.gov` and lists both Betty and Fred as recipients. The `zippy.gov` mailer will forward a second copy of Fred's letter.

The solution is the same one Alphonse and the other mail clerks used. The `gonzo.gov` SMTP client puts around the letter an envelope containing only the names of the recipients on each host. The complete recipient list is still in the letter's headers, but they are inside the envelope, and the SMTP servers at `gonzo.gov` and `whizzer.com` don't look at them. In this example, the envelope for the `whizzer.com` mailer lists only `fred`, and the envelope for `zippy.gov` lists only `betty`.

Aliases illustrate another reason header and envelope addresses differ. Suppose you send mail to the alias `homeboys`, which includes the names `alphonse`, `joe`, `betty`, and `george`. In your letter, you write **`To: homeboys`**; however, `sendmail` expands the alias and constructs an envelope that includes all the recipients. Depending on whether the names are also aliases, perhaps on other hosts, the original message might be put into as many as four different envelopes and delivered to four different hosts. In each case, the envelope contains only the name of the recipients, but the original message contains the alias `homeboys` (expanded to `homeboys@`*`your.host.domain`* so replies will work).

A final example shows another way in which envelope addresses might differ from header addresses. With `sendmail`, you can specify recipients on the command line. Suppose you have a file named `letter` that looks like this:

```
$ cat letter
To: null recipient <>
Subject: header and envelope addresses

testing
```

You send this letter with the following command (substituting your own login name for *`yourlogin`*):

```
$ /usr/sbin/sendmail yourlogin < letter
```

Because your address was on the envelope, you will receive the letter even though your login name doesn't appear in the letter's headers. Unless told otherwise (with the `-t` flag), `sendmail` constructs envelope addresses from the recipients you specify on the command line, and a correspondence doesn't necessarily exist between the header addresses and the envelope addresses.

sendmail's Jobs

To better understand how to set up `sendmail`, you need to know what jobs it does and how these jobs fit into the scheme of MUAs, MTAs, mail routers, final delivery agents, and SMTP clients and servers. `sendmail` can act as a mail router, an SMTP client, and an SMTP server; however, it does not do final delivery of mail.

sendmail as Mail Router

`sendmail` is primarily a mail router, meaning it takes a letter, inspects the recipient addresses, and decides the best way to send it. How does `sendmail` perform this task?

`sendmail` determines some of the information it needs on its own, such as the current time and the name of the host on which it's running, but most of its brains are supplied by you, the postmaster, in the form of a configuration file, `sendmail.cf`. This somewhat cryptic file tells `sendmail` exactly how you want various kinds of mail handled. `sendmail.cf` is extremely flexible and powerful, and at first glance seemingly inscrutable; however, one of the strengths of V.8 `sendmail` is its set of modular configuration file building blocks. Most sites can easily construct their configuration files from these modules, and many examples are included. Writing a configuration file from scratch is a daunting task, so you should avoid it if you can.

sendmail as MTA: Client (Sender) and Server (Receiver) SMTP

As mentioned before, sendmail can function as an MTA because it understands the SMTP protocol (V.8 sendmail also understands ESMTP). SMTP is a connection-oriented protocol, so a client and a server (also known as a sender and a receiver) always exist. The SMTP client delivers a letter to an SMTP server, which listens continuously on its computer's SMTP port. sendmail can be an SMTP client or an SMTP server. When run by an MUA, it becomes an SMTP client and speaks client-side SMTP to an SMTP server (not necessarily another sendmail program). When your system starts in daemon mode, it runs as a server, continuously listening on the SMTP port for incoming mail.

sendmail is not a Final Delivery Agent

One thing sendmail doesn't do is final delivery. sendmail's author wisely chose to leave this task to other programs. sendmail is a big, complicated program that runs with superuser privileges—an almost guaranteed recipe for security problems, and quite a few have occurred in sendmail's past. The additional complexity of final mail delivery is the last thing sendmail needs.

sendmail's Auxiliary Files

sendmail depends on a number of auxiliary files to do its job. Most important are the aliases file and the configuration file, sendmail.cf. The statistics file, sendmail.st, can be created or not, depending on whether you want the statistics. sendmail.hf, which is the SMTP help file, should be installed if you intend to run sendmail as an SMTP server (most sites do). That's all that needs to be said about sendmail.st and sendmail.hf. (Other auxiliary files are covered in the Sendmail Installation and Operating Guide, or SIOG for short.) The aliases and sendmail.cf files, on the other hand, are important enough to be covered in their own sections.

The Aliases File

sendmail always checks recipient addresses for aliases, which are alternative names for recipients. For example, each Internet site is required to have a valid address postmaster to whom mail problems can be reported. Most sites don't have an actual account of that name but divert the postmaster's mail to the person or persons responsible for email administration. For example, at the mythical site gonzo.gov, the users joe and betty are jointly responsible for email administration, and the aliases file has the following entry:

```
postmaster: joe, betty
```

This line tells `sendmail` that mail to `postmaster` should instead be delivered to the login names `joe` and `betty`. In fact, these names could also be aliases:

```
postmaster: firstshiftops, secondshiftops, thirdshiftops
firstshiftops: joe, betty
secondshiftops: lou, emma
thirdshiftops: ben, mark, clara
```

In all these examples, the alias names are on the left side of the colon, and the aliases for those names are on the right side. `sendmail` repeatedly evaluates aliases until they resolve to a real user or a remote address. In the preceding example, to resolve the alias `postmaster`, `sendmail` first expands it into the list of recipients—`firstshiftops`, `secondshiftops`, and `thirdshiftops`—and then expands each of these aliases into the final list—`joe`, `betty`, `lou`, `emma`, `ben`, `mark`, and `clara`.

Although the right side of an alias can refer to a remote host, the left side cannot. The alias `joe: joe@whizzer.com` is legal, but `joe@gonzo.gov: joe@whizzer.com` is not.

Reading Aliases from a File: The `:include:` Directive

Aliases can be used to create mailing lists. (In the example shown in the preceding section, the alias `postmaster` is, in effect, a mailing list for the local postmasters.) For big or frequently changing lists, you can use the `:include:` alias form to direct `sendmail` to read the list members from a file. If the aliases file contains the line

```
homeboys: :include:/home/alphonse/homeboys.aliases
```

and the file /home/alphonse/homeboys.aliases contains

```
alphonse
joe
betty
george
```

the effect is the same as the alias

```
homeboys: alphonse, joe, betty, george
```

This directive is handy for mailing lists that are automatically generated, change frequently, or are managed by users other than the postmaster. If you find a user is asking for frequent changes to a mail alias, you might want to put it under her control.

Mail to Programs

Thealiases file aliases file also can be used to send the contents of email to a program. For example, many mailing lists are set up so you can get information about the list or subscribe to it by sending a letter to a special address, `list-request`. The letter usually contains a single word in its body, such as `help` or `subscribe`, which causes a program to mail an information file to the sender. Suppose the gonzo mailing list has such an address, called gonzo-request:

```
gonzo-request: ¦/usr/local/lib/auto-gonzo-reply
```

In this form of alias, the pipe symbol (¦) tells sendmail to use the program mailer, which is usually defined as /bin/sh (see "The M Operator: Mailer Definitions" later in this chapter). sendmail feeds the message to the standard input of /usr/local/lib/auto-gonzo-reply, and if it exits normally, sendmail considers the letter to be delivered.

Mail to Files

You can also create an alias that causes sendmail to send mail to files. An example is the alias nobody, which is common on systems running the Network File System (NFS):

```
nobody: /dev/null
```

Aliases that specify files cause sendmail to append its message to the named file. Because the special file /dev/null is the UNIX bit-bucket, this alias simply throws mail away.

Setting Up sendmail

The easiest way to show you how to set up sendmail is to use a concrete example.

First, you must either obtain the source and compile sendmail or install the included sendmail RPM package. Next, choose a sendmail.cf file that closely models your site's requirements and tinker with it as necessary. Then test sendmail and its configuration file. Finally, install sendmail.cf and other auxiliary files.

The preceding are the basic steps, but depending on where you install sendmail, you might also have to modify a file in the directory /etc/init.d on HPUX or /etc/rc.d on most other SVR4s (such as Solaris and SunOS) so sendmail will be started correctly when the system starts. In addition, if your system doesn't already have one, you must create an aliases file, often named /usr/lib/aliases or /etc/aliases, depending on your operating system (the location of the aliases file is given in sendmail.cf, so you can put it wherever you want). You might also have to make changes to your system's DNS database, but that information is not covered here (see Chapter 17).

Obtaining the Source

Red Hat Linux ships with sendmail 8.8.7. Unfortunately, this isn't the latest version, and sendmail 8.8.7 has a serious security flaw that was recently published in comp.security.announce. If you are concerned with security (and you should be), you will want to download the latest version of sendmail and compile it yourself.

The more secure `sendmail` version 8.8.8 is on the *Red Hat Linux Unleashed* CD-ROM. This was the most recent version available as the CD-ROM for this book went to press, and it is the version documented in the O'Reilly book *sendmail*, 2nd Ed. (ISBN 1-56592-222-0). This version of sendmail is also available from the site at `http://www.sendmail.org` or via FTP at `ftp://ftp.sendmail.org`.

Note that the exact names of the files to download differ depending on the most current version of V.8 `sendmail`, in this case version 8.9.1. Also, because the files are compressed, you must give FTP the `binary` command before transferring them. Note, too, that you should include your complete email address as the password—for example, `mylogin@gonzo.gov`.

Unpacking the Source and Compiling `sendmail`

Now that you have the source, you need to unpack it. (If you're using the version from the CD-ROM and the `sendmail` RPM package files, these steps are not necessary.) Because it's a compressed `tar` image, you must first decompress it and then extract the individual files from the `tar` archive.

Now you're almost ready to compile `sendmail`, but first read the following files, which contain the latest news pertinent to the specific release of `sendmail` you've downloaded:

FAQ

RELEASE_NOTES

KNOWNBUGS

READ_ME

Also take note that the *Sendmail Installation and Operation Guide* (SIOG) is in the doc/op subdirectory.

Now run `cd` and `ls` to see what files are in the source directory:

```
[root@gonzo src]# cd sendmail-8.9.1/src
[root@gonzo src]# ls
Makefile       collect.c     macro.c        parseaddr.c    srvrsmtp.c
Makefiles      conf.c        mailq.0        pathnames.h    stab.c
READ_ME        conf.h        mailq.1        queue.c        stats.c
TRACEFLAGS     convtime.c    mailstats.h    readcf.c       sysexits.c
alias.c        daemon.c      main.c         recipient.c    sysexits.h
aliases        deliver.c     makesendmail   safefile.c     trace.c
aliases.0      domain.c      map.c          savemail.c     udb.c
aliases.5      envelope.c    mci.c          sendmail.0     useful.h
arpadate.c     err.c         mime.c         sendmail.8     usersmtp.c
cdefs.h        headers.c     newaliases.0   sendmail.h     util.c
clock.c        ldap_map.h    newaliases.1   sendmail.hf    version.c
```

Thankfully, Eric Allman and the `sendmail` crew have done a fantastic job of making the installation process very straightforward. To compile your new version of `sendmail`, simply run

```
[root@gonzo src]# makesendmail
```

and watch it run.

CAUTION

Before installing the new `sendmail` configuration, be sure to make a backup of any files you are going to replace, especially the old `sendmail` daemon you have. In the event the new `sendmail` doesn't work for you, you will need to restore the old versions while you troubleshoot the new version.

To install the new version of sendmail, first stop the currently running daemon with the following command:

```
[root@gonzo src]# /etc/rc.d/init.d/sendmail stop
```

Then simply copy the new binary to its proper place:

```
[root@gonzo src]# cp obj.Linux*/sendmail /usr/sbin/sendmail
```

It is also a good idea to copy the new man pages over:

```
[root@gonzo src]# cp aliases.0 /usr/man/man5/aliases.5
[root@gonzo src]# cp mailq.0 /usr/man/man1/mailq.1
[root@gonzo src]# cp newaliases.0 /usr/man/man1/newaliases.1
[root@gonzo src]# cp sendmail.0 /usr/man/man8/sendmail.8
```

With everything in place, you can restart the new daemon with the following:

```
[root@gonzo src]# /etc/rc.d/init.d/sendmail start
```

`sendmail.cf`: The Configuration File

The `sendmail.cf` file provides `sendmail` with its brains, and because it's so important, this section covers it in fairly excruciating detail. Don't worry if you don't understand everything in this section the first time through. It will make more sense upon rereading and after you've had a chance to play with some configuration files of your own.

`sendmail`'s power lies in its flexibility, which comes from its configuration file, `sendmail.cf`. `sendmail.cf` statements comprise a cryptic programming language that at first glance doesn't inspire much confidence (but C language code probably didn't, either, the first time you saw it). However, learning the `sendmail.cf` language isn't very hard, and you won't have to learn the nitty-gritty details unless you plan to write a `sendmail.cf` from scratch—a bad idea at best. You do need to learn enough to understand and adapt the V.8 `sendmail` configuration file templates to your site's needs.

General Form of the Configuration File

Each line of the configuration file begins with a single command character that tells the function and syntax of that line. Lines beginning with a # are comments, and blank lines are ignored. Lines beginning with a space or tab are continuations of the preceding line, although you should usually avoid continuations.

Table 7.1 shows the command characters and their functions. This table is split into three parts, corresponding to the three main functions of a configuration file, which are covered later in the section "A Functional Description of the Configuration File."

TABLE 7.1 `sendmail.cf` COMMAND CHARACTERS

Command Character	*Command Syntax and Example*	*Function*
#	# comments are ignored	A comment line. Always use lots of comments.
	`# Standard RFC822 parsing`	
D	*DX string*	Defines a macro X to have the string value *string*.
	`DMmailhub.gonzo.gov`	
C	CX *word1*, *word2*, and so on	Defines a class *X* as *word1*, *word2*, and so on.
	`Cwlocalhost myuucpname`	
F	FX/*path*/*to*/*a*/*file*	Defines a class X by reading it from a file.
	`Fw/etc/mail/host_aliases`	
H	H?*mailerflag*?*name*:*template*	Defines a mail header.
	`H?F?From: $q`	
O	OX *option arguments*	Sets option X. Most command-line options can be set in `sendmail.cf`.
	`OL9` # sets the log level to 9.	
P	Pclass=*nn*	Sets mail delivery precedence based on the class of the mail.

Command Character	Command Syntax and Example	Function
	`Pjunk=-100`	
V	`V`*n*	Tells V.8 `sendmail` the version level of the configuration file.
	`V3`	
K	`K`*name* class arguments	Defines a key file (database map).
	`Kuucphosts dbm /etc/mail/uucphsts`	
M	`M`*name*`,`*field_1*`=`*value_1*`,...`	Defines a mailer.
	`Mprog,P=/bin/sh,F=lsD,A=sh -c $u`	
S	`S`*nn*	Begins a new rule set.
	`S22`	
R	`R`*lhs rhs comment*	Defines a matching/rewriting rule.
	`R$+ $:$>22 call ruleset 22`	

A Functional Description of the Configuration File

A configuration file does three things. First, it sets the environment for `sendmail` by telling it what options you want set and the locations of the files and databases it uses.

Second, a configuration file defines the characteristics of the mailers (delivery agents or MTAs) `sendmail` uses after it decides where to route a letter. All configuration files must define local and program mailers to handle delivery to users on the local host, most also define one or more SMTP mailers, and sites that must handle UUCP mail define UUCP mailers.

Third, a configuration file specifies rulesets that rewrite sender and recipient addresses and select mailers. All rulesets are user-defined, but some have special meaning to `sendmail`. Ruleset 0, for example, is used to select a mailer. Rulesets 0, 1, 2, 3, and 4 all have special meaning to `sendmail` and are processed in a particular order (see the section "The `S` and `R` Operators: Rulesets and Rewriting Rules" later in this chapter).

The following sections cover the operators in more detail, in the order in which they appear in Table 7.1.

The D Operator: Macros

Macros are like shell variables. After you define a macro's value, you can refer to it later in the configuration file and its value will be substituted for the macro. For example, a configuration file might have many lines that mention the hypothetical mail hub, `mailer.gonzo.gov`. Rather than type that name over and over, you can define a macro `R` (for relay mailer) as follows:

```
DRmailer.gonzo.gov
```

When `sendmail` encounters a `$R` in `sendmail.cf`, it substitutes the string `mailer.gonzo.gov`.

Macro names are always single characters. Quite a few macros are defined by `sendmail` and shouldn't be redefined except to work around broken software. `sendmail` uses lowercase letters for its predefined macros. Uppercase letters can be used freely. V.8 `sendmail`'s predefined macros are fully documented in section 5.1.2 of the SIOG.

The C and F Operators: Classes

Classes are similar to macros but are used for different purposes in rewriting rules (see "The `S` and `R` Operators: Rulesets and Rewriting Rules" later in this chapter). As with macros, classes are named by single characters. Lowercase letters are reserved for `sendmail` and uppercase letters for user-defined classes. A class contains one or more words. For example, you could define a class `H` containing all the hosts in the local domain as follows:

```
CH larry moe curly
```

For convenience, large classes can be continued on subsequent lines. The following definition of the class `H` is the same as the preceding one:

```
CH larry
CH moe
CH curly
```

You can also define a class by reading its words from a file:

```
CF/usr/local/lib/localhosts
```

If the file /usr/local/lib/localhosts contains the words `larry`, `moe`, and `curly`, one per line, this definition is equivalent to the preceding two.

Why use macros and classes? The best reason is that they centralize information in the configuration file. In the preceding example, if you decide to change the name of the mail hub from `mailer.gonzo.gov` to `mailhub.gonzo.gov`, you have to change only the definition of the `$R` macro remedy for the configuration file to work as before. If the name mailer.gonzo.gov is scattered throughout the file, you might forget to change it in some places. Also, if important information is centralized, you can comment it extensively in a single place. Because configuration files tend to be obscure at best, a liberal dose of comments is a good antidote to that sinking feeling you get when, six months later, you wonder why you made a change.

The H Operator: Header Definitions

You probably won't want to change the header definitions given in the V.8 sendmail configuration files, because they already follow accepted standards. Here are some sample headers:

```
H?D?Date: $a
H?F?Resent-From; $q
H?F?From: $q
H?x?Full-Name: $x
```

Note that header definitions can use macros, which are expanded when inserted into a letter. For example, the $x macro used in the preceding Full-Name: header definition expands to the full name of the sender.

The optional ?*mailerflag*? construct tells sendmail to insert a header only if the chosen mailer has that mailer flag set (see "The M Operator: Mailer Definitions" later in this chapter).

Suppose the definition of your local mailer has a flag Q, and sendmail selects that mailer to deliver a letter. If your configuration file contains a header definition like the following one, sendmail inserts that header into letters delivered through the local mailer, substituting the value of the macro $F:

```
H?Q?X-Fruit-of-the-day: $F
```

Why would you use the ?mailerflag? feature? Different protocols can require different mail headers. Because they also need different mailers, you can define appropriate mailer flags for each in the mailer definition and use the ?*mailerflag*? construct in the header definition to tell sendmail whether to insert the header.

The O Operator: Setting Options

sendmail has many options that change its operation or tell it the location of files it uses. Most of them can be given either on the command line or in the configuration file. For example, you can specify the location of the aliases file in either place. To specify the aliases file on the command line, you use the -o option:

```
$ /usr/sbin/sendmail -oA/etc/aliases [other arguments...]
```

To do the same thing in the configuration file, you include a line like this:

```
OA/etc/aliases
```

Either use is equivalent, but options such as the location of the aliases file rarely change, and most people set them in `sendmail.cf`. The V.8 `sendmail` options are fully described in the SIOG.

The P Operator: Mail Precedence

Users can include mail headers indicating the relative importance of their mail, and `sendmail` can use those headers to decide the priority of competing letters. Precedences for V.8 `sendmail` are given as follows:

```
Pspecial-delivery=100
Pfirst-class=0
Plist=-30
Pbulk=-60
Pjunk=-100
```

If users who run large mailing lists include the header `Precedence: bulk` in their letters, `sendmail` gives them a lower priority than letters with the header `Precedence: first-class`.

The V Operator: sendmail.cf Version Levels

As V.8 `sendmail` evolves, its author adds new features. The `V` operator lets V.8 `sendmail` know what features it should expect to find in your configuration file. Older versions of `sendmail` don't understand this command. The SIOG explains the configuration file version levels in detail.

> **NOTE**
>
> The configuration file version level does not correspond to the `sendmail` version level. V.8 `sendmail` understands versions 1 through 5 of configuration files, and no such thing as a version 8 configuration file exists.

The K Operator: Key Files

`sendmail` has always used keyed databases—for example, the aliases databases. Given the key `postmaster`, `sendmail` looks up the data associated with that key and returns the names of the accounts to which the postmaster's mail should be delivered. V.8 `sendmail` extends this concept to arbitrary databases, including NIS maps (Sun's Network Information Service, formerly known as Yellow Pages or YP; see Chapter 17 for details).

The `K` operator tells `sendmail` the location of the database, its class, and how to access it. V.8 `sendmail` supports the following classes of user-defined databases: `dbm`, `btree`, `hash`, and `NIS`. The default used when compiling under Linux is the `dbm` format. See the SIOG for the lowdown on key files.

The `M` Operator: Mailer Definitions

Mailers are either MTAs or final delivery agents. Recall that the aliases file enables you to send mail to a login name (which might be aliased to a remote user), a program, or a file. A special mailer can be defined for each purpose, and even though the SMTP MTA is built in, it must have a mailer definition to tailor `sendmail`'s SMTP operations.

Mailer definitions are important because all recipient addresses must resolve to a mailer in ruleset 0. Resolving to a mailer is just another name for `sendmail`'s main function, mail routing. For example, resolving to the local mailer routes the letter to a local user via the final delivery agent defined in that mailer (such as /bin/mail), and resolving to the SMTP mailer routes the letter to another host via `sendmail`'s built-in SMTP transport, as defined in the SMTP mailer.

A concrete example of a mailer definition will make this information clearer. Because `sendmail` requires a local mailer definition, look at the following:

```
Mlocal, P=/bin/mail, F=lsDFMfSn, S=10, R=20, A=mail -d $u
```

All mailer definitions begin with the `M` operator and the name of the mailer—in this case, `local`. Other fields follow, separated by commas. Each field consists of a field name and its value, separated by an equals sign (=). The allowable fields are explained in section 5.1.4 of the SIOG.

In the preceding local mailer definition, the `P=` equivalence gives the pathname of the program to run to deliver the mail, /bin/mail. The `F=` field gives the `sendmail` flags for the local mailer (see also "The `H` Operator: Header Definitions" earlier in the chapter.) These flags are not passed to the command mentioned in the `P=` field but are used by `sendmail` to modify its operation, depending on the mailer it chooses. For example, `sendmail` usually drops its superuser status before invoking mailers, but you can use the `S` mailer flag to tell `sendmail` to retain this status for certain mailers.

The `S=` and `R=` fields specify rulesets for `sendmail` to use in rewriting sender and recipient addresses. Because you can give different `R=` and `S=` flags for each mailer you define, you can rewrite addresses differently for each mailer. For example, if one of your UUCP neighbors runs obsolete software that doesn't understand domain addressing, you might declare a special mailer just for that site and write mailer-specific rulesets to convert addresses into a form its mailer can understand.

The S= and R= fields can also specify different rulesets to rewrite the envelope and header addresses (see “Header and Envelope Addresses” earlier in this chapter). A specification such as S=21/31 tells sendmail to use ruleset 21 to rewrite sender envelope addresses and ruleset 31 to rewrite sender header addresses. This capability comes in handy for mailers that require addresses to be presented differently in the envelope than in the headers.

The A= field gives the argument vector (command line) for the program that will be run—in this case, /bin/mail. In this example, sendmail runs the command as mail -d $u, expanding the $u macro to the name of the user to whom the mail should be delivered:

```
/bin/mail -d joe
```

You could type this same command to your shell at a command prompt.

You might want to use many other mailer flags to tune mailers—for example, to limit the maximum message size on a per-mailer basis. These flags are all documented in section 5.1.4 of the SIOG.

The S and R Operators: Rulesets and Rewriting Rules

A configuration file is composed of a series of rulesets, which are somewhat like subroutines in a program. Rulesets are used to detect bad addresses, to rewrite addresses into forms remote mailers can understand, and to route mail to one of sendmail’s internal mailers (see the section “The M Operator: Mailer Definitions” earlier in this chapter).

sendmail passes addresses to rulesets according to a built-in order. Rulesets also can call other rulesets not in the built-in order. The built-in order varies, depending on whether the address being handled is a sender or receiver address and what mailer has been chosen to deliver the letter.

Rulesets are announced by the S command, which is followed by a number to identify the ruleset. sendmail collects subsequent R (rule) lines until it finds another S operator or the end of the configuration file. The following example defines ruleset 11:

```
# Ruleset 11
S11
R$+         $: $>22 $1      call ruleset 22
```

This ruleset doesn’t do much that is useful. The important point to note is that sendmail collects ruleset number 11, which is composed of a single rule.

sendmail's Built-in Ruleset Processing Rules

sendmail uses a three-track approach to processing addresses: one to choose a delivery agent, another to process sender addresses, and another for receiver addresses.

All addresses are first sent through ruleset 3 for preprocessing into a canonical form that makes them easy for other rulesets to handle. Regardless of the complexity of the address, ruleset 3's job is to decide the next host to which a letter should be sent. Ruleset 3 tries to locate that host in the address and mark it within angle brackets. In the simplest case, an address like joe@gonzo.gov becomes joe<@gonzo.gov>.

Ruleset 0 then determines the correct delivery agent (mailer) to use for each recipient. For example, a letter from betty@whizzer.com to joe@gonzo.gov (an Internet site) and pinhead!zippy (an old-style UUCP site) requires two different mailers: an SMTP mailer for gonzo.gov and an old-style UUCP mailer for pinhead. Mailer selection determines later processing of sender and recipient addresses, because the rulesets given in the S= and R= mailer flags vary from mailer to mailer.

Addresses sent through ruleset 0 must resolve to a mailer. This means when an address matches the lhs, the rhs gives a triple of mailer, user, and host. The following line shows the syntax for a rule that resolves to a mailer:

```
Rlhs        $#mailer $@host $:user   your comment here...
```

The mailer is the name of one of the mailers you've defined in an M command—for example, smtp. The host and user are usually positional macros taken from the lhs match (see "The Right-Hand Side (rhs) of Rules" later in the chapter).

After sendmail selects a mailer in ruleset 0, it processes sender addresses through ruleset 1 (often empty) and then sends them to the ruleset given in the S= flag for that mailer.

Similarly, sendmail sends recipient addresses through ruleset 2 (also often empty) and then to the ruleset mentioned in the R= mailer flag.

Finally, sendmail post-processes all addresses in ruleset 4, which (among other things) removes the angle brackets inserted by ruleset 3.

Why do mailers have different S= and R= flags? Consider the previous example of the letter sent to joe@gonzo.gov and pinhead!zippy. If betty@whizzer.com sends the mail, her address must appear in a different form to each recipient. For Joe, it should be a domain address, betty@whizzer.com. For Zippy, because pinhead expects old-style UUCP addresses, the return address should be whizzer!betty. Joe's address must also be rewritten for the pinhead UUCP mailer, and Joe's copy must include an address for Zippy that his mailer can handle.

Processing Rules Within Rulesets

`sendmail` passes an address to a ruleset and then processes it through each rule line by line. If the `lhs` of a rule matches the address, it is rewritten by the `rhs`. If it doesn't match, `sendmail` continues to the next rule until it reaches the end of the ruleset. At the end of the ruleset, `sendmail` returns the rewritten address to the calling ruleset or to the next ruleset in its built-in execution sequence.

If an address matches the `lhs` and is rewritten by the `rhs`, the rule is tried again—an implicit loop (but see the "`$:` and `$@`: Altering a Ruleset's Evaluation" section for exceptions).

As shown in Table 7.1, each rewriting rule is introduced by the `R` command and has three fields—the left-hand side (`lhs`, or matching side), the right-hand side (`rhs`, or rewriting side,) and an optional comment, which must be separated from one another by tab characters:

```
Rlhs        rhs         comment
```

`Parsing`: Turning Addresses into Tokens

`sendmail` parses addresses and the `lhs` of rules into tokens and then matches the address and the `lhs`, token by token. The macro `$o` contains the characters `sendmail` uses to separate an address into tokens. It's often defined like this:

```
# address delimiter characters
Do.:%@!^/[]
```

All the characters in `$o` are both token separators and tokens. `sendmail` takes an address such as `rae@rainbow.org` and breaks it into tokens according to the characters in the `o` macro, like this:

```
"rae"     "@"     "rainbow"     "."     "org"
```

sendmail also parses the `lhs` of rewriting rules into tokens so they can be compared one by one with the input address to see whether they match. For example, the `lhs` `$-@rainbow.org` gets parsed as follows:

```
"$-"     "@"     "rainbow"     "."     "org"
```

(Don't worry about the `$-` just yet. It's a pattern-matching operator, similar to a shell wildcard, that matches any single token and is covered later in the section "The Left-Hand Side [`lhs`] of Rules.") Now you can put the two together to show how `sendmail` decides whether an address matches the `lhs` of a rule:

```
"rae"     "@"     "rainbow"     "."     "org"
"$-"      "@"     "rainbow"     "."     "org"
```

In this case, each token from the address matches a constant string (for example, `rainbow`) or a pattern-matching operator (`$-`), so the address matches and `sendmail` will use the `rhs` to rewrite the address.

Consider the effect (usually bad) of changing the value of `$o`. As shown previously, `sendmail` breaks the address `rae@rainbow.org` into five tokens. However, if the `@` character were not in `$o`, the address would be parsed quite differently, into only three tokens:

```
"rae@rainbow"      "."      "org"
```

You can see that changing `$o` has a drastic effect on `sendmail`'s address parsing, and you should leave it alone until you know what you're doing. Even then, you probably won't want to change it, because the V.8 `sendmail` configuration files already have it correctly defined for standard RFC 822 and RFC 976 address interpretation.

The Left-Hand Side (`lhs`) of Rules

The `lhs` is a pattern against which `sendmail` matches the input address. The `lhs` can contain ordinary text or any of the pattern-matching operators shown in Table 7.2.

TABLE 7.2 `lhs` PATTERN-MATCHING OPERATORS

Operator	*Function*
`$-`	Match exactly one token.
`$+`	Match one or more tokens.
`$*`	Match zero or more tokens.
`$@`	Match the null input (used to call the error mailer).

The values of macros and classes are matched in the `lhs` with the operators shown in Table 7.3.

TABLE 7.3 `lhs` MACRO AND CLASS-MATCHING OPERATORS

Operator	*Function*
`$X`	Match the value of macro X.
`$=C`	Match any word in class C.
`$~C`	Match if token is not in class C.

The pattern-matching operators and macro- and class-matching operators are necessary because most rules must match many different input addresses. For example, a rule might need to match all addresses that end with gonzo.gov and begin with one or more of anything.

The Right-Hand Side (rhs) of Rules

The rhs of a rewriting rule tells sendmail how to rewrite an address that matches the lhs. The rhs can include text, macros, and positional references to matches in the lhs. When a pattern-matching operator from Table 7.2 matches the input, sendmail assigns it to a numeric macro $n, corresponding to the position it matches in the lhs. For example, suppose the address joe@pc1.gonzo.gov is passed to the following rule:

```
R$+ @ $+        $: $1 < @ $2 >            focus on domain
```

In this example, joe matches $+ (one or more of anything), so sendmail assigns the string joe to $1. The @ in the address matches the @ in the lhs, but constant strings are not assigned to positional macros. The tokens in the string pc1.gonzo.gov match the second $+ and are assigned to $2. The address is rewritten as $1<@$2>, or joe<@pc1.gonzo.gov>.

$: and $@: Altering a Ruleset's Evaluation

Consider the following rule:

```
R$*   $: $1 < @ $j > add local domain
```

After rewriting an address in the rhs, sendmail tries to match the rewritten address with the lhs of the current rule. Because $* matches zero or more of anything, what prevents sendmail from going into an infinite loop on this rule? After all, no matter how the rhs rewrites the address, it will always match $*.

The $: preface to the rhs comes to the rescue; it tells sendmail to evaluate the rule only once.

Sometimes you might want a ruleset to terminate immediately and return the address to the calling ruleset or the next ruleset in sendmail's built-in sequence. Prefacing a rule's rhs with $@ causes sendmail to exit the ruleset immediately after rewriting the address in the rhs.

$>: Calling Another Ruleset

A ruleset preface>can pass an address to another ruleset by using the $> preface to the rhs. Consider the following rule:

```
R$*         $: $>66 $1            call ruleset 66
```

The lhs $* matches zero or more of anything, so sendmail always does the rhs. As you learned in the preceding section, the $: prevents the rule from being evaluated more than once. The `$>66 $1` calls ruleset 66 with `$1` as its input address. Because the `$1` matches whatever was in the `lhs`, this rule simply passes the entirety of the current input address to ruleset 66. Whatever ruleset 66 returns is passed to the next rule in the ruleset.

Testing Rules and Rulesets: The `-bt`, `-d`, and `-C` Options

Debugging `sendmail.cf` can be a tricky business. Fortunately, `sendmail` provides several ways to test rulesets before you install them.

NOTE

The examples in this section assume that you have a working `sendmail`. If your system does not, try running these examples again after you have installed V.8 `sendmail`.

The `-bt` option tells `sendmail` to enter its rule-testing mode:

```
$ /usr/sbin/sendmail -bt
ADDRESS TEST MODE (ruleset 3 NOT automatically invoked)
Enter <ruleset> <address>
>
```

NOTE

Notice the warning `ruleset 3 NOT automatically invoked`. Older versions of `sendmail` ran ruleset 3 automatically when in address test mode, which made sense because `sendmail` sends all addresses through ruleset 3 anyway. V.8 `sendmail` does not, but invoking ruleset 3 manually is a good idea because later rulesets expect the address to be in canonical form.

The > prompt means `sendmail` is waiting for you to enter one or more ruleset numbers, separated by commas, and an address. Try your login name with rulesets 3 and 0. The result should look something like this:

```
> 3,0 joe
rewrite: ruleset  3   input: joe
rewrite: ruleset  3 returns: joe
rewrite: ruleset  0   input: joe
rewrite: ruleset  3   input: joe
rewrite: ruleset  3 returns: joe
rewrite: ruleset  6   input: joe
```

```
rewrite: ruleset  6 returns: joe
rewrite: ruleset  0 returns: $# local $: joe
>
```

The output shows how sendmail processes the input address joe in each ruleset. Each line of output is identified with the number of the ruleset processing it, the input address, and the address that the ruleset returns. The > is a second prompt indicating that sendmail is waiting for another line of input. When you're done testing, just press Ctrl+D.

Indentation and blank lines better show the flow of processing in this example:

```
rewrite: ruleset  3   input: joe
rewrite: ruleset  3 returns: joe

rewrite: ruleset  0   input: joe

     rewrite: ruleset  3   input: joe
     rewrite: ruleset  3 returns: joe

     rewrite: ruleset  6   input: joe
     rewrite: ruleset  6 returns: joe

rewrite: ruleset  0 returns: $# local $: joe
```

The rulesets called were 3 and 0, in that order. Ruleset 3 was processed and returned the value joe, and then sendmail called ruleset 0. Ruleset 0 called ruleset 3 again and then ruleset 6, an example of how a ruleset can call another one by using $>. Neither ruleset 3 nor ruleset 6 rewrote the input address. Finally, ruleset 0 resolved to a mailer, as it must.

Often you need more detail than -bt provides—usually just before you tear out a large handful of hair because you don't understand why an address doesn't match the lhs of a rule. You can remain hirsute, because sendmail has verbose debugging built into most of its code.

You use the -d option to turn on sendmail's verbose debugging. This option is followed by a numeric code that tells which section of debugging code to turn on and at what level. The following example shows how to run sendmail in one of its debugging modes and the output it produces:

```
$ /usr/sbin/sendmail -bt -d21.12
ADDRESS TEST MODE (ruleset 3 NOT automatically invoked)
Enter <ruleset> <address>
> 3,0 joe
rewrite: ruleset  3   input: joe
--trying rule: $* < > $*
-- rule fails
--trying rule: $* < $* < $* < $+ > $* > $* > $*
-- rule fails
[etc.]
```

The `-d21.12` in the preceding example tells `sendmail` to turn on level 12 debugging in section 21 of its code. The same command with the option `-d21.36` gives more verbose output (debug level 36 instead of 12).

NOTE

You can combine one or more debugging specifications separated by commas, as in `-d21.12,14.2`, which turns on level 12 debugging in section 21 and level 2 debugging in section 14. You can also give a range of debugging sections, as in `-d1-10.35`, which turns on debugging in sections 1 through 10 at level 35. The specification `-d0-91.104` turns on all sections of V.8 `sendmail`'s debugging code at the highest levels and produces thousands of lines of output for a single address.

The `-d` option is not limited for use with `sendmail`'s address testing mode (`-bt`); you can also use it to see how `sendmail` processes rulesets while sending a letter, as the following example shows:

```
$ /usr/sbin/sendmail -d21.36 joe@gonzo.gov < /tmp/letter
[lots and lots of output...]
```

Unfortunately, the SIOG doesn't tell you which numbers correspond to which sections of code. Instead, the author suggests that keeping such documentation current is a lot of work (which it is) and that you should look at the code itself to discover the correct debugging formulas.

The function `tTd()` is the one to look for. For example, suppose you want to turn on debugging in `sendmail`'s address-parsing code. The source file parseaddr.c contains most of this code, and the following command finds the allowable debugging levels:

```
$ egrep tTd parseaddr.c
        if (tTd(20, 1))
[...]
        if (tTd(24, 4))
        if (tTd(22, 11))
[etc.]
```

The `egrep` output shows that debugging specifications such as `-d20.1`, `-d24.4`, and `-d22.11` (and others) will make sense to `sendmail`.

If perusing thousands of lines of C code doesn't appeal to you, the O'Reilly book *sendmail*, 2nd Ed., documents the debugging flags for `sendmail`.

The `-C` option enables you to test new configuration files before you install them, which is always a good idea. If you want to test a different file, use `-C/path/to/the/file`. You can combine it with the `-bt` and `-d` flags. For example, a common invocation for testing new configuration files is

```
/usr/sbin/sendmail -Ctest.cf -bt -d21.12
```

CAUTION

For security, `sendmail` drops its superuser permissions when you use the `-C` option. You should perform final testing of configuration files as the superuser to ensure your testing is compatible with `sendmail`'s normal operating mode.

Testing sendmail and sendmail.cf

Before installing a new or modified `sendmail.cf`, you must test it thoroughly. Even small, apparently innocuous changes can lead to disaster, and people get really irate when you mess up the mail system.

The first step in testing is to create a list of addresses you know should work at your site. For example, at `gonzo.gov`, an Internet site without UUCP connections, the following addresses must work:

```
joe
joe@pc1.gonzo.gov
joe@gonzo.gov
```

If `gonzo.gov` has a UUCP link, those addresses must also be tested. Other addresses to consider include the various kinds of aliases (for example, `postmaster`, an `:include:` list, an alias that mails to a file, and one that mails to a program), nonlocal addresses, source-routed addresses, and so on. If you want to be thorough, you can create a test address for each legal address format in RFC 822.

Now that you have your list of test addresses, you can use the `-C` and `-bt` options to see what happens. At a minimum, you should run the addresses through rulesets 3 and 0 to make sure they are routed to the correct mailer. An easy way to do so is to create a file containing the ruleset invocations and test addresses and then run `sendmail` on it. For example, if the file `addr.test` contains the lines

```
3,0 joe
3,0 joe@pc1.gonzo.gov
3,0 joe@gonzo.gov
```

you can test your configuration file test.cf by typing

```
$ /usr/sbin/sendmail -Ctest.cf -bt < addr.test
rewrite: ruleset  3   input: joe
rewrite: ruleset  3 returns: joe
[etc.]
```

You also might want to follow one or more addresses through the complete rewriting process. For example, if an address resolves to the `smtp` mailer and that mailer specifies `R=21`, you can test recipient address rewriting by using `3,2,21,4` *`test_address`*.

If the `sendmail.cf` appears to work correctly so far, you're ready to move on to sending some real letters. You can do so by using a command like the following:

```
$ /usr/sbin/sendmail -v -oQ/tmp -Ctest.cf recipient < /dev/null
```

The `-v` option tells `sendmail` to be verbose so you can see what's happening. Depending on whether the delivery is local or remote, you can see something as simple as `joe... Sent` or an entire SMTP dialog.

The `-oQ/tmp` tells `sendmail` to use /tmp as its queue directory. Using this option is necessary because `sendmail` drops its superuser permissions when run with the `-C` option and can't write queue files into the normal mail queue directory. Because you are using the `-C` and `-oQ` options, `sendmail` also includes the following warning headers in the letter to help alert the recipient of possible mail forgery:

```
X-Authentication-Warning: gonzo.gov: Processed from queue /tmp
X-Authentication-Warning: gonzo.gov: Processed by joe with -C srvr.cf
```

`sendmail` also inserts the header `Apparently-to: joe` because, although you specified a recipient on the command line, none was listed in the body of the letter. In this case, the letter's body was taken from the empty file /dev/null, so no `To:` header was available. If you do your testing as the superuser, you can skip the `-oQ` argument and `sendmail` won't insert the warning headers. You can avoid the `Apparently-to:` header by creating a file like

```
To: recipient

testing
```

and using it as input instead of /dev/null.

The recipient should be you, so you can inspect the headers of the letter for correctness. In particular, return address lines must include an FQDN for SMTP mail. That is, a header such as `From: joe@gonzo` is incorrect because it doesn't include the domain part of the name, but a header such as `From: joe@gonzo.gov` is fine.

You should repeat this testing for the same variety of addresses you used in the first tests. You might have to create special aliases that point to you for some of the testing.

The amount of testing you do depends on the complexity of your site and the amount of experience you have, but a beginning system administrator should test very thoroughly, even for apparently simple installations.

POP

As much as you might love Linux, the reality is that you must contend with other operating systems out there. Even worse, many of them aren't even UNIX based. Although the Linux community has forgiven the users of "other" operating systems, there is still a long way to go before complete assimilation happens. In the meantime, the best thing that can happen is to use tools to tie the two worlds together.

The following sections cover the integration of the most-used application of any network: electronic mail (or email for short). Because UNIX and "other" operating systems have a very different view of how email should be handled, the Post Office Protocol (POP) was created. This protocol abstracts the details of email to a system-independent level so anyone who writes a POP client can communicate with a POP server.

Configuring a POP Server

The POP server you will configure on the sample systems is the freely available `qpopper` program. This package was originally written at Berkeley but is now maintained by the Eudora division of Qualcomm (`http://www.eudora.com/freeware`). If you also need client software for non-UNIX systems, check out the Eudora Light email package also available from Qualcomm. Like `qpopper`, Eudora Light is available for free. (The Professional version does cost money, however.)

Red Hat has prepared an RPM of the `qpopper` package, which is available on the CD-ROM (`qpopper-2.3-1.i386.rpm`), or you can fetch it from Red Hat's Web site at

`ftp://ftp.redhat.com/pub/contrib/i386/qpopper-2.52-1.i386.rpm.`

To install it from the CD-ROM, simply run

```
rpm -i qpopper-2.3-1.i386.rpm
```

This way, you can install two programs (found in /usr/sbin/): `in.qpopper` and `popauth`. `in.qpopper` is the actual server program you will set up to run from `inetd`. `popauth` is used to configure clients that use APOP authentication.

Configuring `in.qpopper`

Most of `in.qpopper`'s (from this point on called just `qpopper`) options are configured at compile time; therefore, you don't have much of a say in how things are done unless you want to compile the package yourself. If you are interested in pursuing that route, you can fetch the complete package from Qualcomm's site at `http://www.eudora.com/freeware/servers.html`.

The default configuration items are fine for most sites. These defaults are as follows:

- Refusal to retrieve mail for anyone whose UID is below 10 (for example, root)
- Bulletin support in `/var/spool/mail/bulletins`
- Most recently posted bulletin sent to new users
- Verbose logging to `syslog`
- APOP authentication uses /etc/pop.auth (see the section on `popauth` for details)

To allow `qpopper` to start from `inetd`, edit the /etc/inetd.conf file and add the following line:

```
pop-3    stream    tcp    nowait    root    /usr/sbin/tcpd in.qpopper
```

Don't forget to send the HUP signal to `inetd`. You can do so by issuing the following command:

```
kill -1 `cat /var/run/inetd.pid`
```

Now you're ready to test the connection. At a command prompt, enter

```
telnet popserver 110
```

where `popserver` is the name of the machine running the `qpopper` program.

You should get a response similar to the following:

```
+OK QPOP (version 2.3) at mtx.domain.com starting.
<14508.877059136@mtx.domain.com>
```

This result means the POP server has responded and is awaiting an instruction. (Typically, this job is transparently done by the client mail reader.) If you want to test the authentication service, try to log in as yourself and see whether the service registers your current email box. For example, to log in as `sshah` with the password `mars1031`, you enter

```
user sshah
+OK Password required for sshah
pass mars1031
+OK sshah has 5 messages (98031 octets).
quit
+OK Pop server at mtx.domain.com signing off.
```

The first line, `user sshah`, tells the POP server that the user for whom it will be checking mail is `sshah`. The response from the server is an acknowledgment that the user sshah exists and that a password is required to access the mailbox. You can then type **pass mars1031**, where mars1031 is the password for the sshah user. The server acknowledges the correct password by responding with a statement indicating that five messages are currently in user sshah's mail queue. Because you don't want to actually read the mail this way, enter **quit** to terminate the session. The server sends a sign-off message and drops the connection.

Although the stock configuration of qpopper is ideal for most sites, you might want to adjust a few command-line parameters. To use a command-line parameter, simply edit your inetd.conf file so the line invoking the in.qpopper program ends with the parameter you want to pass. For example, if you want to pass -T 10 to the server, your inetd.conf entry would look like this:

```
pop-3     stream     tcp      nowait     root     /usr/sbin/tcpd in.qpopper
-T 10
```

Don't forget to send the HUP signal to the inetd program by using the following command:

```
kill -1 `cat /var/run/inetd.pid`
```

The following parameters are available in in.qpopper:

Parameter	*Description*
-d	Enables the debugging messages to be sent to SYSLOG.
-t *<tracefile>*	Redirects the debugging information to be sent to *<tracefile>*, where *<tracefile>* is a log file on your system.
-s	Enables statistical information about each connection to be logged to SYSLOG.
-T *<timeout>*	Changes the timeout period for connections to *<timeout>* seconds. You might need to set this parameter to a higher value if your clients are connecting through slow connections (for example, PPP links).
-b *<bulldir>*	Specifies what directory to use to hold the bulletins. The default directory is /var/spool/mail/bulletins.

Using popauth

By default, the POP server sends all passwords in *cleartext* (not encrypted). If you are security conscious, using cleartext obviously is a bad idea, and a tighter control is needed on authentication. APOP support comes in at this point. APOP is a more security-minded way of authenticating users, because the passwords are sent over the network already encrypted. qpopper supports APOP and keeps its APOP database in the /etc/pop.auth database. Because this database is kept in a binary format, you need to manipulate it by using the popauth program.

When you installed qpopper, the /etc/pop.auth database was not created. Before you can begin using popauth, you need to initialize the database by using the following command:

```
popauth -init
```

This command sets up the database and prepares it for further manipulation. popauth accepts the following three parameters to list, delete, and add users to its database:

Parameter	*Description*
-list	Displays the existing users in the database by their login names.
-delete *<name>*	Removes user *<name>* from the database, where *<name>* is that user's login.
-user *<name>*	Adds the user *<name>* to the database, where *<name>* is the user's login. When the parameter is invoked, you are prompted to enter the user's password twice (the second time to verify you typed it in correctly) to enable the entry.

For example, to add the user sshah to the database, you use the following:

```
[root@mtx /root]# popauth -user sshah
Changing POP password for sshah.
New password: scrubber
Retype new password: scrubber
```

To see that sshah was in fact added, you type

```
[root@mtx /root]# popauth -list
sshah
```

If you need to remove the user sshah, use the -delete option like this:

```
[root@mtx /root]# popauth -delete sshah
```

Warning: You will not be prompted for confirmation when deleting users from this database.

Managing Bulletins

Occasionally, you might need to send mail to all your users to alert them about changes to the system. (For example, you might send this message: **The servers will be**

offline on Sunday for maintenance.) If most of your users use POP to read their mail, using bulletins will be much easier on your system.

A *bulletin* is a message that is sent to all users as they log in to read their mail. It isn't delivered to the users' server mail queues unless they have elected to keep their mail on the server instead of downloading it. Using bulletins for announcements instead of sending out mail reduces the load on your mail server because it doesn't have to perform delivery to all your user's mail queues. Even better, this approach doesn't waste space on your server, because the message is directly downloaded to the readers' machines.

To create a bulletin, simply create a new file in the /var/spool/mail/bulletins directory (or directory of your choice if you use the `-b` option on `in.qpopper`). The filename should begin with a number, followed by a period and then any arbitrary string. Consider this example:

```
1.welcome_to_our_pop_server
```

This bulletin could be the first one on your system. Each new bulletin must follow the numbering pattern in sequence. So the next bulletin, for example, could be titled

```
2.notice_of_downtime
```

Inside each file must be the necessary email header information so the client POP readers know how to handle the message. A minimal header consists of only a `From` line; however, the users will receive mail that appears to come from no one, with no subject, and no return address. Hence, better mail headers contain not only the `From` line, but also lines for the `From:`, `Date:`, `Subject:`, and `Reply-To:` headers.

The following is a sample message:

```
From sshah@domain.com Tue Sep 16 20:31:15 1997
From:    sshah@domain.com (Steve Shah)
Date:    Tue, 16 Sep 1997 20:31:15 -0700
Subject:    New compute server
    Reply-To: sysadmins@domain.com

Hello Everyone,

For your information, we have finally set up the new dual processor
compute server.
(The old single processor server was getting lonely. ;) If you have any
questions
or problems, feel free to send me mail or call me at x9433.
-Your Systems Group
```

After the file is in place, you do not need to alert the server. The server automatically sees the file and sends it to all users as they log in to read their mail.

The POP3 Protocol

The latest version of POP is POP3. POP2 was originally published as RFC 918 in October 1984 and was superceded by RFC 937 in February 1985.

POP3 was originally published as RFCs 1081 and 1082 in November 1988. RFC 1081 was superceded by RFC 1225 in May 1991. In June 1993, RFC 1460 superceded RFC 1225, and in November 1994, RFC 1725 made the standards track and obsoleted RFC 1460.

Summary

In this chapter, you have learned how to install, set up, and configure the `sendmail` and `qpopper` programs. The key things to remember about this process are the following:

- An MTA is a Mail Transfer Agent (what actually routes and delivers mail), and an MUA is a Mail User Agent (what the user uses to access mail after it has been delivered). `sendmail` is an MTA *only*.
- The Simple Mail Transfer Protocol (SMTP) is the actual protocol used to transfer mail. `sendmail` is a program that uses this protocol to communicate with other mail servers. Other mail servers don't need to run `sendmail`, but they do need to communicate via SMTP.
- `sendmail` does NOT deliver mail once it has reached the destination system. A special program local to the system, such as `/bin/mail` or `/usr/bin/procmail`, is used to perform the delivery functions.
- The aliases file can either remap email addresses to other usernames, redirect mail to files, or pass email messages on to another program for processing.
- `sendmail` is a large program with a past history of security problems. Hence, be sure to keep up with the security bulletins.
- Whenever a new version of `sendmail` is released, download it from `ftp.sendmail.org` and install it.
- The Post Office Protocol (POP) is a protocol for allowing client machines to connect to a mail server and transfer mail. POP is not responsible for delivering mail to other users or systems.
- Although POP isn't nearly as large or complex as `sendmail`, it does have the potential to contain security problems as well. Watch for security announcements and upgrade accordingly.
- Bulletins are a handy way to distribute mail to all of your POP mail users at once without having to make copies for everyone.

- `popauth` is the means by which the POP protocol accepts passwords in an encrypted format.

Telling you all you must know about SMTP and POP in a single chapter is not possible, but as Yogi Berra (or maybe Casey Stengel) once said, "You could look it up," and you should. However, this chapter gives you a good basis for understanding the theory behind SMTP, V.8 `sendmail`, and `qpopper`.

FTP

by Bill Ball

In This Chapter

CHAPTER

Using the File Transfer Protocol (FTP) is a popular way to transfer files from machine to machine across a network. Clients and servers have been written for all the popular platforms, thereby often making FTP the most convenient way of performing file transfers.

You can configure FTP servers in one of two ways. The first is as a private user-only site, which is the default configuration for the FTP server; I will cover this configuration here. A private FTP server allows only users on the system to be able to connect via FTP and access their files. You can place access controls on these users so that certain users can be explicitly denied or granted access.

The other kind of FTP server is anonymous. An anonymous FTP server allows anyone on the network to connect to it and transfer files without having an account. Due to the potential security risks involved with this setup, you should take precautions to allow access only to certain directories on the system.

CAUTION

Configuring an anonymous FTP server always poses a security risk. Because server software is inherently complex, it can have bugs allowing unauthorized users access to your system. The authors of the FTP server you will configure in this chapter have gone to great lengths to avoid this possibility; however, no one can ever be 100% sure.

If you decide to establish an anonymous FTP server, be sure to keep a careful eye on security announcements from CERT (`http://www.cert.org`) and update the server software whenever security issues arise.

Depending on which packages you chose to install during the installation, you might already have the FTP server software installed. To determine whether you have the server software installed, check for the /usr/sbin/in.ftpd file. If it is there, you have the necessary software. If you don't, read the next section to learn how to install it.

Getting and Installing the FTP Server

Red Hat Linux uses the freely available `wu-ftpd` server. It comes as an RPM (Red Hat Package Manager) and is offered as an installation option during initial setup. If you decide you want to run an FTP server but did not install the RPM, fetch `wu-ftpd-2.4.2b17-2.i386.rpm` from the CD-ROM or check `http://www.redhat.com` for the latest edition.

To install the RPM, simply log in as root and run the following:

```
[root@denon /root]# rpm -i wu-ftpd-2.4.2b17-2.i386.rpm
```

If you plan to offer an anonymously accessible site, be sure to install the `anonftp-2.5-1.i386.rpm` from the CD-ROM as well. As always, you can check for the latest version at `http://www.redhat.com`.

To install the anonymous FTP file, log in as root and run the following:

```
[root@denon /root]# rpm -i anonftp-2.5-1.i386.rpm
```

Now you have a working anonymous FTP server. (Of course, you should also have an active Internet network connection and a valid host and domain name for a truly public server. See Chapter 11, "The Domain Name Service," for details about DNS, along with related networking chapters in this book.)

NOTE

Although the `anonftp` package contains the files necessary to set up anonymous FTP service and the `wu-ftpd rpm` file contains the FTP daemon, you'll find the ftp client program in the `ftp rpm` package. Install all three RPMs for complete service.

Although you can find the latest version of `wuftpd` at http://wuarchive.wustl.edu/packages/wuarchive-ftpd, you should periodically check Red Hat's web site for rpm updates to Linux FTP software, especially if you allow public access to your computer over the Internet. Many newer versions of Red Hat's Linux networking or communications software contain security fixes or other enhancements designed to protect your computers from intruders.

To test whether the installation worked, simply use the FTP client and connect to your machine. For the sample FTP server, `denon`, you would respond to the following:

```
[root@denon /root]# ftp denon
Connected to denon.domain.com.
220 denon.domain.com FTP server (Version wu-2.4.2-academ[BETA-12](1)
➥Wed Mar 5 12:37:21 EST 1997) ready.
Name (denon:root): anonymous
331 Guest login ok, send your complete e-mail address as password.
Password: sshah@domain.com                [This is not echoed on the screen]
230 Guest login ok, access restrictions apply.
Remote system type is UNIX.
Using binary mode to transfer files.
ftp>
```

FTP

To quit the FTP client software, simply enter **bye** at the ftp> prompt. If you want to test the private FTP server, rerun the FTP client but use your login instead of the anonymous login. Here's an example:

```
[root@denon /root]# ftp denon
Connected to denon.domain.com
220 denon.domain.com FTP server (Version wu-2.4.2-academ[BETA-12](1)
➥Wed Mar 5 12:37:21 EST 1997) ready.
Name (denon:root): sshah
331 Password required for sshah.
Password: mars1031                [This is not echoed on the screen]
230 User sshah logged in.
Remote system type is UNIX.
Using binary mode to transfer files.
ftp>
```

How the FTP Server Works

FTP service is controlled from the `/etc/inetd.conf` file and is automatically invoked whenever someone connects to the FTP port. (Ports are logical associations from a network connection to a specific service. For example, port 21 associates to FTP, port 23 associates to Telnet, and so on.) When a connection is detected, the FTP daemon (`/usr/sbin/in.ftpd`) is invoked and the session begins. In the `/etc/inetd.conf` file, the default Red Hat distribution contains the necessary line for this step to occur.

After the server is initiated, the client needs to provide a username and corresponding password. Two special usernames—`anonymous` and `ftp`—have been set aside for the purpose of allowing access to the public files. Any other access requires the user to have an account on the server.

If a user accesses the server using her account, an additional check is performed to ensure that the user has a valid shell. A user who doesn't have a valid shell is denied access into the system. This check is useful if you want to allow users limited access to a server (for example, POP mail) but do not want them logging in via Telnet or FTP. For a shell to be valid, it must be listed in the `/etc/shells` file. If you decide to install a new shell, be sure to add it to your `/etc/shells` listing so people using that shell can connect to the system via FTP.

Users accessing the FTP server are placed in their home directories when they first log in. At that point, they can change to any directories on the system to which they have permission. Anonymous users, on the other hand, have several restrictions placed on them.

Anonymous users are placed in the home directory for the FTP users. By default, this directory is set to /home/ftp by the `anonftp` RPM package. After the users get there, the FTP server executes a `chroot` system call, effectively changing the program's root directory to the FTP users' directory. Access to any other directories in the system, which includes the /bin, /etc, and /lib directories, is denied. This change in the root directory has the side effect of the server not being able to see `/etc/passwd`, `/etc/group`, and other necessary binaries such as `/bin/ls`. To make up for this change, the `anonftp` RPM package creates bin, etc, and lib directories under `/home/ftp`, where necessary libraries and programs are placed (such as `ls`) and where the server software can access them even after the `chroot` system call has been made.

For security reasons, files placed under the /home/ftp directory have their permissions set such that only the server can see them. (This is done automatically during `anonftp`'s install.) Any other directories created under /home/ftp should be set up so they are world readable. Most anonymous ftp sites place such files under the pub subdirectory.

Configuring Your FTP Server

Although the default configuration of the FTP server is reasonably secure, you can fine-tune access rights by editing the following files:

- `/etc/ftpaccess`
- `/etc/ftpconversions`
- `/etc/ftphosts`
- `/var/log/xferlog`

With all these files, you can have very fine control of who can connect to your server when and from where, as well as an audit trail of what they do after they connect. The `/etc/ftpaccess` file is the most significant of these because it contains the most configuration options; however, misconfiguring any of the others can lead to denied service.

TIP

When editing any of the files in the /etc directory (FTP related or not), comment the file liberally. Keeping an edit history at the end of the file—listing who last edited the file, when they did it, and what they changed—is a good way to track down problems as well as problem makers.

Controlling Access—The `/etc/ftpaccess` File

The `/etc/ftpaccess` file is the primary means of controlling who and how many users can access your server. Each line in the file controls either defines an attribute or sets its value.

The following commands control access:

- `class`
- `autogroup`
- `deny`
- `guestgroup`
- `limit`
- `loginfails`
- `private`

The following commands control what information the server tells clients:

- `banner`
- `email`
- `message`
- `readme`

These commands control logging capabilities:

- `log commands`
- `log transfers`

The following are miscellaneous commands:

- `alias`
- `cdpath`
- `compress`
- `tar`
- `shutdown`

Permissions controls are set by the following commands:

- `chmod`
- `delete`
- `overwrite`

- `rename`
- `umask`
- `passwd-check`
- `path-filter`
- `upload`

Controlling User Access

The ability to control who may and may not enter your site is a critical component in fine-tuning your anonymous FTP server. The following commands define the criteria used to determine in which group each user should be placed.

class

The `class` command defines a class of users who can access your FTP server. You can define as many classes as you want. Each `class` line comes in the form

```
class <classname> <typelist> <addrglob> [<addrglob> ...]
```

where *<classname>* is the name of the class you are defining, *<typelist>* is the type of user you are allowing into the class, and *<addrglob>* is the range of IP addresses allowed access to that class.

The *<typelist>* is a comma-delimited list in which each entry has one of three values: anonymous, guest, or real. Anonymous users are, of course, any users who connect to the server as user `anonymous` or `ftp` and want to access only publicly available files. Guest users are special because they do not have accounts on the system per se, but they do have special access to key parts of the guest group. (See the description of the `guestgroup` command later in this chapter for additional details.) Real users must have accounts on the FTP server and are authenticated accordingly.

<addrglob> takes the form of a regular expression where `*` implies all sites. Several *<addrglob>*s can be associated with a particular class.

The line

```
class anonclass anonymous *
```

defines the class `anonclass`, which contains only anonymous users. They can originate their connections from anywhere on the network.

On the other hand, the line

```
class localclass real 192.168.42.*
```

allows only real users with accounts on the FTP server access to their accounts via FTP if they are coming from the local area network.

autogroup

The autogroup command is used to control access to anonymous users more tightly by automatically assigning them a certain group permission when they log in. The format of the autogroup line is

```
autogroup <groupname> <class> [<class> ...]
```

where <*groupname*> is the name of the group to which you want the anonymous users set and <*class*> is the name of a class defined by using the class command. You can have multiple <*class*> entries for an autogroup. Only the anonymous users referenced in <*class*> will be affected by autogroup.

Remember that the group to which you are giving the users permission must be in the /etc/group file.

deny

The deny command enables you to explicitly deny service to certain hosts based on their names, their IP addresses, or whether their hostnames can be reverse-resolved via DNS. The format of the deny command is

```
deny <addrglob> <message_file>
```

where <*addrglob*> is a regular expression containing the addresses that are to be denied and <*message_file*> is the filename containing a message that should be displayed to the hosts when they connect.

The following is a sample deny line:

```
deny evilhacker.domain.com /home/ftp/.message.no.evil.hackers
```

This line displays the contents of the file /home/ftp/.message.no.evil.hackers to anyone trying to connect via FTP from evilhacker.domain.com. To deny users access based on whether their IP addresses can be reverse-resolved to their hostnames, use the string !nameserved for the <*addrglob*> entry.

guestgroup

The guestgroup command is useful when you have real users but want them to have only restrictive FTP privileges. The format of the command is

```
guestgroup <groupname> [<groupname> ...]
```

where <*groupname*> is the name of the group (as taken from /etc/group) that you want restricted.

When a user's group is restricted, the user is treated much like an anonymous visitor; hence, the same setups needed for anonymous visitors must be performed in this user's account. The user's password entry is also a little different in the directory field.

The field for the user's home directory is broken up by the `/./` characters. Prior to the split characters is the effective root directory, and after the split characters is the user's relative home directory. For example, consider the following password entry:

```
user1:encrypted password:500:128:User 1:/ftp/./user1:/bin/ftponly
```

Here, /ftp is the user's new relative root directory (bin, etc, and lib directories would need to be created under /ftp for the `ls` command and other necessary libraries), and /ftp/user1 is the user's home directory.

limit

The `limit` command enables you to control the number of users who log in to the system via FTP by class and time of day. This capability is especially useful if you have a popular archive but the system needs to be available to your users during business hours. The format of the `limit` command is

```
limit <class> <n> <times> <message_file>
```

where `<class>` is the class to limit, `<n>` is the maximum number of people allowed in that class, `<times>` is the time during which the limit is in effect, and `<message_file>` is the file that should be displayed to the client when the maximum limit is reached.

The format of the `<times>` parameter is somewhat complex. The parameter is in the form of a comma-delimited string, where each option is for a separate day. The days Sunday through Saturday take the form `Su`, `Mo`, `Tu`, `We`, `Th`, `Fr`, and `Sa`, respectively, and all the weekdays can be referenced as `Wk`. Time should be kept in military format without a colon separating the hours and minutes. A range is specified by the dash character.

For example, to limit the class `anonfolks` to 10 from Monday through Thursday, all day, and Friday from midnight to 5 p.m., you would use the following `limit` line:

```
limit anonfolks 10 MoTuWeTh,Fr0000-1700 /home/ftp/.message.too_many
```

In this case, if the limit is hit, the contents of the file `/home/ftp/.message.too_many` are displayed to the connecting user.

loginfails

The `loginfails` command enables you to set the number of failed login attempts clients can make before being disconnected. By default, this number is five; however, you can set it by using the command

```
loginfails <n>
```

FTP

where *<n>* is the number of attempts. For example, the following line disconnects a user from the FTP server after three failed attempts:

```
loginfails 3
```

private

You might find it convenient to be able to share files with other users via FTP without having to place the file in a 100% public place or having to give these users a real account on the server. The clients use the `SITE GROUP` and `SITE GPASS` commands so they can change to privileged groups that require passwords.

For your FTP server to support this capability, you need to set the `private` flag, using the command

```
private <switch>
```

where *<switch>* is either the string `YES` to turn it on or `NO` to turn it off.

Because you need to require passwords for these special groups, you need to use the `/etc/ftpgroups` file. The format of an access group in `/etc/ftpgroups` is

access_group_name:*encrypted_password*:*real_group*

where *access_group_name* is the name that the client uses to reference the special group, *encrypted_password* is the password users need to supply (via `SITE GPASS`) to access the group, and *real_group* is the actual group referenced in the `/etc/group` file.

TIP

To create the *encrypted_password* entry, use the UNIX `crypt` function. To make generating the encrypted password easier, use the following Perl script:

```
#!/usr/bin/perl
print "Enter password to encrypt: ";
chop ($password=<STDIN>);
print "The encrypted password is: ",crypt($password,$password);
```

Controlling Banner Messages

It is often useful to provide messages to FTP users when they connect to your site or specify a special action. These commands enable you to specify these instances as well as the corresponding messages. Using them is a great way to make your site self-documenting.

banner

The `banner` command enables you to display a sign onscreen before the client has to provide a login and password combination. This is an important opportunity to display your server's security policies, where to upload software, and directions to anonymous users about how to log in or where to find software. The format of this command is

```
banner <path>
```

where `<path>` is the full pathname of the file you want to display. Consider this example:

```
banner /home/ftp/.banner
```

email

The `email` command enables you to specify the site maintainer's email address. Some error messages or information requests provide the information given in this line on demand. The default value in the `/etc/ftpaccess` file is `root@localhost`.

The format of the `email` command is

```
email <address>
```

where `<address>` is the full email address of the site maintainer.

Creating an email alias "FTP" that forwards to the system administrators is generally good practice. Providing this kind of information in the sign-on banner is also a good idea so users know whom to contact if they cannot log in to the system.

message

The `message` command enables you to set up special messages to be sent to the clients when they either log in or change to a certain directory. You can specify multiple messages. The format of this command is

```
message <path> <when> {<class> ...}
```

where `<path>` is the full pathname to the file to be displayed, `<when>` is the condition under which to display the message, and `<class>` is a list of classes to which this message command applies.

The `<when>` parameter should take one of two forms: either `LOGIN` or `CWD=<dir>`. If it is `LOGIN`, the message is displayed upon a successful login. If the parameter is set to `CWD=<dir>`, the message is displayed when clients enter the `<dir>` directory.

The `<class>` parameter is optional. You can list multiple classes for a certain message. This capability is useful, for example, if you want only certain messages going to anonymous users.

The message file itself (specified by <*path*>) can contain special flags that the FTP server substitutes with the appropriate information at runtime. These options are as follows:

Option	*Description*
%T	Local time
%F	Free space in the partition where <*dir*> is located
%C	Current working directory
%E	Site maintainer's email address (specified by the `email` command)
%R	Client hostname
%L	Server hostname
%U	Username provided at login time
%M	Maximum number of users allowed in the specified class
%N	Current number of users in specified class

Remember that when messages are triggered by an anonymous user, the message path needs to be relative to the anonymous FTP directory.

A sample message command is

```
message ./.toomany_anon LOGIN anonfolks
```

where the file `./.toomany_anon` contains

```
Sorry %R, but there are already %N users out of a maximum of %M users in
➥your class.  Please try again in a few minutes.
The FTP Administrator (%E)
```

If, for example, the limit of 25 users is reached at this site, the client sees a message similar to the following:

```
Sorry, technics.domain.com, but there are already 25 out of a maximum
➥of 25 users in your class. Please try again in a few minutes.
The FTP Administrator (ftp@domain.com)
```

readme

The `readme` command enables you to specify the conditions under which clients are notified that a certain file in their current directory was last modified. This command can take the form

```
readme <path> <when> <class>
```

where <*path*> is the name of the file about which you want to alert the clients (for example, `README`), <*when*> is similar to the <*when*> in the `message` command, and <*class*> is the classes for which this command applies. The <*when*> and <*class*> parameters are optional.

Remember that when you're specifying a path for anonymous users, the file must be relative to the anonymous FTP directory.

Controlling Logging

As with any complex network service, security quickly becomes an issue. To contend with possible threats, tracking connections made along with the corresponding commands is a necessity. The following commands enable you to determine how much, if any, logging should be done by the server software.

log commands

Often for security purposes, you might want to log the actions of your FTP users, which you can do by using the `log commands` option. Each command invoked by the clients is sent to your log file. The format of the command is

```
log commands <typelist>
```

where *<typelist>* is a comma-separated list specifying which kinds of users should be logged. The three kinds of users recognized are anonymous, guest, and real. (See the description of the `class` command earlier in this chapter for each user type's description.) For example, to log all the actions taken by anonymous and guest users, you specify the following:

```
log commands anonymous,guest
```

log transfers

If you want to log only file transfers made by clients instead of logging their entire sessions with the `log commands` statement, you should use `log transfers`. The format of this command is

```
log transfers <typelist> <directions>
```

where *<typelist>* is a comma-separated list specifying which kinds of users should be logged (anonymous, guest, or real), and *<directions>* is a comma-separated list specifying which direction the transfer must take to be logged. The two directions you can choose to log are `inbound` and `outbound`.

For example, to log all anonymous transfers that are both `inbound` and `outbound`, you would use the following:

```
log transfers anonymous inbound,outbound
```

The resulting logs are stored in `/var/log/xferlog`. See the section on this file for additional information.

Miscellaneous Server Commands

The following set of commands provides some miscellaneous configuration items. Each command adds a good deal of flexibility to the server, making it that much more useful to you as its administrator.

alias

The alias command enables you to define directory aliases for your FTP clients. These aliases are activated when the clients use the cd command and specify an alias. This capability is useful to provide shortcuts to often-requested files. The format of the command is

```
alias <string> <dir>
```

where *<string>* is the alias and *<dir>* is the actual directory to which the users should be transferred. The following is an example of this command:

```
alias orb_discography /pub/music/ambient/orb_discography
```

Hence, if clients connect and use the command cd orb_discography, they are automatically moved to the /pub/music/ambient/orb_discography directory, regardless of their current locations.

cdpath

Similar to the UNIX PATH environment variable, the cdpath command enables you to establish a list of paths to check whenever clients invoke the cd command. The format of the cdpath command is

```
cdpath <dir>
```

where *<dir>* is the directory on the server to be checked whenever clients use the cd command. Remember to use directories relative to the FTP home directory for your anonymous users. An example of the cdpath command is

```
cdpath /pub/music
cdpath /pub/coffee
```

If clients enter the command cd instant, the server examines the directories in the following order:

1. ./instant
2. Aliases called instant (See the description of alias for more information.)
3. /pub/music/instant
4. /pub/coffee/instant

compress

The wu-ftpd server (the FTP server I have currently installed) offers a special compress feature that enables the server to compress or decompress a file before transmission. With this capability, a client who might not have the necessary software to decompress a file can still fetch it in a usable form. (For example, a file on your server is compressed using gzip, and a Windows client machine needs to get it but does not have the DOS version of gzip available.)

The format of the compress command is

```
compress <switch> <classglob>
```

where *<switch>* is either the string YES to turn on this feature or NO to turn off this feature. *<classglob>* is a comma-separated list of classes to which this compress option applies.

There is, of course, a catch to using this command. You need to configure the /etc/ftpconversions file so the server knows which programs to use for certain file extensions. The default configuration supports compression by either /bin/compress or /bin/gzip.

Read the section on /etc/ftpconversions for details.

tar

Almost identical to the compress option, tar specifies whether the server will tar and untar files for a client on demand. The format of this command is

```
tar <switch> <classglob>
```

where *<switch>* is either the string YES to turn on this feature or NO to turn off this feature. The *<classglob>* option is a comma-separated list of classes the tar command specifies.

Like the compress command, this feature is controlled by the /etc/ftpconversions file. See the section on /etc/ftpconversions for details.

shutdown

The shutdown command tells the server to check for a particular file periodically to see whether the server will be shut down. By default, the RPMs you installed invoke the FTP server whenever there is a request for a connection; therefore, you don't really need this option if you plan to continue using it that way. On the other hand, if you intend to change the system so the server software is constantly running in the background, you might want to use the shutdown option to perform clean shutdowns and to notify users accessing the site.

The format of the shutdown command is

```
shutdown <path>
```

where <*path*> is the full path of the file to check for shutdown information. When that file does become available, it is parsed out and the information gained from it dictates the behavior of the shutdown process as well as the ftpshut program (discussed later in the chapter in the section on ftpshut). While there isn't any standard place for keeping this file, you might find it handy to keep in /etc/ftpshutdown where it will be obvious along with the other FTP configuration files. Make sure the file is readable by root.

The format of the file is

```
<year> <month> <day> <hour> <minute> <deny_offset> <disconnect_offset>
<text>
```

where <*year*> is any year after 1970; <*month*> is from 0 to 11 to represent January to December, respectively; <*day*> is from 0 to 30; <*hour*> is from 0 to 23; and <*minute*> is from 0 to 59. The <deny_offset> parameter specifies the time at which the server should stop accepting new connections in the form HHMM, where HH is the hour in military format and MM is the minute. <*disconnect_offset*> is the time at which existing connections are dropped; it is also in the form HHMM.

The <*text*> parameter is a free-form text block displayed to users to alert them of the impending shutdown. The text can follow the format of the message command (see the description of this command earlier in the chapter) and can have the following special character sequences available:

Option	*Description*
%s	The time the system will shut down
%r	The time new connections will be denied
%d	The time current connections will be dropped

Controlling Permissions

Along with controlling logins and maintaining logs, you will need to keep the permissions of the files placed in the archive under tight control. The following commands enable you to specify what permissions should be set under certain conditions.

chmod

The chmod command determines whether a client has the permission to change permissions on the server's files, using the client's chmod command. The format of this command is

```
chmod <switch> <typelist>
```

where <*switch*> is either YES to turn on the feature or NO to turn off the feature. <*typelist*> is the comma-separated list of user types affected by this command. The user types available are anonymous, guest, and real.

delete

The delete command tells the server whether client connections can delete files residing on the server via FTP. The format of the command is

```
delete <switch> <typelist>
```

where <*switch*> is either YES to turn on the feature or NO to turn off the feature. <*typelist*> is the comma-separated list of user types affected by this command. The user types available are anonymous, guest, and real.

overwrite

To control whether FTP clients can upload files and replace existing files on the server, you use the overwrite command. The format of this command is

```
overwrite <switch> <typelist>
```

where <*switch*> is either YES to turn on the feature or NO to turn off the feature. <*typelist*> is the comma-separated list of user types affected by this command. The user types available are anonymous, guest, and real.

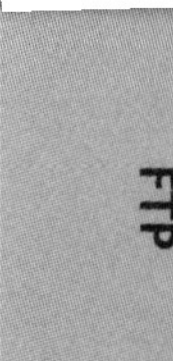

rename

Client FTP software has the option of sending a rename request to the server to rename files. The rename command determines whether this request is acceptable. The format of this command is

```
rename <switch> <typelist>
```

where <*switch*> is either YES to turn on the feature or NO to turn off the feature. <*typelist*> is the comma-separated list of user types affected by this command. The user types available are anonymous, guest, and real.

umask

The umask command determines whether clients can change their default permissions in a fashion similar to the umask shell command. The format of the umask command is

```
umask <switch> <typelist>
```

where <*switch*> is either YES to turn on the feature or NO to turn off the feature. <*typelist*> is the comma-separated list of user types affected by this command. The user types available are anonymous, guest, and real.

passwd-check

Providing a valid email address as a password is considered good manners when connecting to an anonymous FTP site. The `passwd-check` command lets you determine how strict you want to be with what string is submitted as an anonymous user's email address. The format of the command is

```
passwd-check <strictness> <enforcement>
```

where *<strictness>* is one of three possible strings: `none`, `trivial`, or `rfc822`, and *<enforcement>* is one of two possible strings: `warn` or `enforce`.

Selecting `none` for *<strictness>* performs no check at all for the password. `trivial` is slightly more demanding by requiring that at least an `@` (at) symbol appear in the password. `rfc822` is the most strict, requiring the email address to comply with the RFC 822 "Message Header Standard" (for example, `sshah@domain.com`).

Using `warn` as the *<enforcement>* warns the users if they fail to comply with the strictness requirement but allows them to connect with your server anyway. `enforce`, on the other hand, denies the users connections until they use acceptable passwords.

path-filter

If you allow users to upload files to your server via FTP, you might want to dictate what are acceptable filenames (for example, control characters in filenames are not acceptable). You can enforce this restriction by using the `path-filter` command. The format of this command is

```
path-filter <typelist> <mesg> <allowed-regexp> <denied-regexp>
```

where *<typelist>* is a comma-separated list of users this command affects; the user types available are anonymous, guest, and real. *<mesg>* is filename of the message that should be displayed if the file does not meet this criteria. *<allowed-regexp>* is the regular expression the filename must meet to be allowed in. *<denied-regexp>* is the regular expression that, if met, causes the file to be explicitly denied; *<denied-regexp>* is an optional parameter.

For example, the line

```
path-filter anonymous,guest /ftp/.badfilename UL* gif$
```

displays the file `/ftp/.badfilename` to anonymous or guest users if they upload a file that doesn't begin with the string `UL` or that ends with the string `gif`.

upload

You can use the upload command, along with path-filter, to control files placed onto your server. The upload command specifies what permissions the client has to place files in certain directories as well as what permissions the files will take on after they are placed there. The format of this command is

```
upload <directory> <dirglob> <switch> <owner> <group> <mode> <mkdir>
```

where <*directory*> is the directory that is affected by this command, <*dirglob*> is the regular expression used to determine whether a subdirectory under <*directory*> is a valid place to make an upload, and <*switch*> is either YES or NO, thereby establishing that an upload either can or cannot occur there. The <*owner*>, <*group*>, and <*mode*> parameters establish the file's owner, group, and permissions after the file is placed on the server. Finally, you can specify the <*mkdir*> option as either dirs or nodirs, which means the client is or is not able to create subdirectories under the specified directory.

Here is a sample entry:

```
upload /home/ftp * no
upload /home/ftp /incoming yes ftp ftp 0400 nodirs
```

This example specifies that the only location a file can be placed in is the /home/ftp/incoming directory (/incoming to the anonymous client). After the file is placed in this directory, its owner becomes ftp, group ftp, and the permission is 0400. The nodirs option at the end of the second line prevents the anonymous client from creating subdirectories under /incoming.

FTP

TIP

Setting uploads to read-only is a good idea so the /incoming directory doesn't become a trading ground for questionable material—for example, illegal software.

Converting Files On-the-Fly—The /etc/ftpconversions File

The format of the /etc/ftpconversions file is

```
<1>:<2>:<3>:<4>:<5>:<6>:<7>:<8>
```

where <1> is the strip prefix, <2> is the strip postfix, <3> is an add-on prefix, <4> is an add-on postfix, <5> is the external command to invoke to perform the conversion, <6> is the type of file, <7> is the option information used for logging, and <8> is a description of the action.

Confused? Don't be. Each of these options is actually quite simple. In the following sections, I describe them one at a time.

The Strip Prefix

The strip prefix is the string at the beginning of a filename that should be removed when the file is fetched. For example, if you want a special action taken on files beginning with discography., where that prefix is removed after the action, you would specify `.discography` for this option. When the clients specify filenames, they should not include the strip prefix. That is, if a file is called discography.orb and a client issues the command `get orb`, the server performs the optional command on the file and then transfers the results back to the client.

The Strip Postfix

The strip postfix is the string at the end of the filename that should be removed when the file is fetched. The strip postfix is typically used to remove the trailing .gz from a gzipped file that is being decompressed before being transferred back to the client.

The Add-on Prefix

An add-on prefix is the string inserted before the filename when a file is transferred either to or from the server. For example, you might want to insert the string `uppercase.` to all files being pulled from the server that are being converted to uppercase.

The Add-on Postfix

An add-on postfix is the string appended to a filename after an operation on it is complete. This type of postfix is commonly used when the client issues the command `get largefile.gz`, where the actual filename is only largefile; in this case, the server compresses the file using `gzip` and then performs the transfer.

The External Command

The key component of each line is the external command. This entry specifies the program to be run when a file is transferred to or from the server. As the file is transferred, it is filtered through the program where downloads (files sent to the client) need to be sent to the standard out, and uploads (files sent to the server) will be coming from the standard in. For example, if you want to provide decompression with `gzip` for files being downloaded, the entry would look like the following:

```
gzip -dc %s
```

The %s in the line tells the server to substitute the filename being requested by the user.

The Type of File

The type of file field for /etc/ftpconversions is a list of possible kinds of files that can be acted on, with type names separated by the pipe symbol (¦). The three file types recognized are T_REG, T_ASCII, and T_DIR, which represent regular files, ASCII files, and directories, respectively. An example of this entry is T_REG¦T_ASCII.

Options

The options field of /etc/ftpconversions is similar to the type of file field in that it is composed of a list of names separated by the pipe symbol (¦). The three types of options supported are O_COMPRESS, O_UNCOMPRESS, and O_TAR, which specify whether the command compresses files, decompresses files, or uses the tar command. An example entry is O_COMPRESS¦O_TAR, which says the file is both compressed and tarred.

The Description

The last parameter of /etc/ftpconversions, the description of the conversion, is a free-form entry in which you can describe what kind of conversion is done.

Example of an /etc/ftpconversions Entry

The following is a sample entry that compresses files using gzip on demand. This would allow someone who wants to get the file orb_discography.tar to instead request the file orb_discrography.tar.gz and have the server compress the file by using gzip before sending it to him. The configuration line that does this is as follows:

```
: : :.gz:/bin/gzip -9 -c %s:T_REG:O_COMPRESS:GZIP
```

The first two parameters are not necessary because you don't want to remove anything from the filename before sending it to the requester. The third parameter is empty because you don't want to add any strings to the beginning of the filename before sending it. The fourth parameter, though, does have the string .gz, which will result in the file having the .gz suffix added before being sent. The fifth parameter is the actual command used to compress the file, where the -9 option tells gzip to compress the file as much as it can, -c results in the compressed file's being sent to the standard output, and %s is replaced by the server with the filename being requested (for example, orb_discography.tar). T_REG in the sixth parameter tells the server to treat the file being handled as a normal file rather than an ASCII file or directory. The second-to-last parameter, O_COMPRESS, tells the server that the action being taken is file compression and, finally, the last parameter is simply a comment for the administrator so she can determine at a glance the action being taken.

A bit daunting, isn't it? Don't worry, examine the sample `/etc/ftpconversions` file that came with the `wu-ftpd` RPM package to see additional examples of using `tar` and `gzip`. In fact, most sites never need to add to this file because it covers the most popular conversion requests made.

Configuring Host Access—The /etc/ftphosts File

The `/etc/ftphosts` file establishes rules on a per-user basis, defining whether users are allowed to log in from certain hosts or are denied access when they try to log in from other hosts.

Each line in the file can be one of two commands:

```
allow <username> <addrglob>
```

or

```
deny <username> <addrglob>
```

where the `allow` command allows the user specified in *<username>* to connect via FTP from the explicitly listed addresses in *<addrglob>*. You can list multiple addresses.

The `deny` command explicitly denies the specified user *<username>* from the sites listed in *<addrglob>*. You can list multiple sites.

The FTP Log File—/var/log/xferlog

Although `/var/log/xferlog` isn't a configuration file, it is important, nonetheless, because all the logs generated by the FTP server are stored in this file. Each line of the log consists of the following:

current-time	The current time in `DDD MMM dd hh:mm:ss YYYY` format, where `DDD` is the day of the week, `MMM` is the month, `dd` is the day of the month, `hh:mm:ss` is the time in military format, and `YYYY` is the year.
transfer-time	The total time in seconds spent transferring the file.
remote-host	The hostname of the client that initiated the transfer.
file-size	The size of the file that was transferred.
filename	The name of the file that was transferred.
transfer-type	The type of transfer done, where `a` is an ASCII transfer and `b` is a binary transfer.

special-action-flag	A list of actions taken on the file by the server, where `C` means the file was compressed, `U` means the file was uncompressed, `T` means the file was tarred, and `-` means no action was taken.
direction	A flag indicating whether the file was outgoing or incoming, represented by `o` or `i`, respectively.
access-mode	The type of user who performed the action, where `a` is anonymous, `g` is a guest, and `r` is a real user.
username	The local username if the user was of type `real`.
service-name	The name of the service being invoked (most often FTP).
authentication-method	The type of authentication used; `0` means no authentication was done (anonymous user) and `1` means the user was validated with RFC 931 Authentication Server Protocol.
authenticated-user-id	The username by which this transfer was authenticated.

FTP Administrative Tools

Several tools are available to help you administer your FTP server. These tools were automatically installed as part of the `wu-ftp` package when the `wu-ftpd` RPM was installed. These utilities help you see the current status of the server and control its shutdown procedure:

- `ftpshut`
- `ftpwho`
- `ftpcount`

ftpshut

The `ftpshut` command helps make shutting down the FTP server easier. This capability, of course, applies only if you are running the server all the time instead of leaving it to be invoked from inetd as needed. The format of `ftpshut` is

```
ftpshut -l <login-minutes> -d <drop-minutes> <time> <warning message>
```

where *<login-minutes>* is the number of minutes before the server shutdown that the server will begin refusing new FTP transactions. *<drop-minutes>* is the number of minutes before the server shutdown that the server will begin dropping existing connections. The default value for *<login-minutes>* is 10, and the default for *<drop-minutes>* is 5.

<time> is the time at which the server will be shut down. You can specify this time in one of three ways. The first is to specify the time in military format without the colon (for example, **0312** to indicate 3:12 a.m.). The second is to specify the number of minutes to wait before shutting down. The format of this method is +*<min>*, where *<min>* is the number of minutes to wait (for example, **+60** causes the server to shut down in 60 minutes). The last option is the most drastic; if you specify the string **now**, the server shuts down immediately.

<warning message> is the message displayed on all FTP clients that the server will be shut down. See the description of the `shutdown` command for the `/etc/ftpaccess` file earlier in this chapter for details on the formatting available for the warning message.

ftpwho

`ftpwho` displays all the active users on the system connected through FTP. The output of the command is in the format of the `/bin/ps` command. The format of this command is

<pid> <tty> <stat> <time> <connection details>

where *<pid>* is the process ID of the FTP daemon handling the transfer; *<tty>* is always a question mark (`?`) because the connection is coming from FTP, not Telnet; *<stat>* is the status of that particular instance of the daemon, where `S` means it's sleeping, `Z` means it has crashed (gone "zombie"), and `R` means it's the currently running process. *<time>* indicates how much actual CPU time that instance of the FTP has taken and, finally, *<connection details>* tells where the connection is coming from, who the user is, and that user's current function.

The following is an example of output from `ftpwho`:

```
Service class all:
10448  ?  S  0:00 ftpd: vestax.domain.com: anonymous/sshah@domain.com:
➥IDLE
10501  ?  S  0:00 ftpd: toybox.domain.com: heidi: RETR mklinux-ALL.sit.bin
   -    2 users ( -1 maximum)
```

Here you can see that two users are logged in (an unlimited number of users are allowed to connect). The first user is an anonymous user who claims to be `sshah@domain.com` and is currently not performing any functions. The second user, who has the username `heidi`, is currently retrieving the file `mklinux-ALL.sit.bin`.

ftpcount

`ftpcount`, which is a simplified version of `ftpwho`, shows only the total count of users logged in to the system and the maximum number of users allowed. A sample output from `ftpcount` shows the following:

```
Service class all                   -   2 users ( -1 maximum)
```

Summary

You might think the proliferation of the World Wide Web would make FTP servers extinct; however, the last few years have shown us that quite the opposite is true. People are still deploying FTP sites in full force because of the ease with which they can be established and maintained. No cute HTML to do, no extra work—just put the file in the right place for download and let people get it.

This chapter covers a lot of detail on configuring the `wu-ftpd` server. The key points to remember when working with the FTP server are as follows:

- Keep a good watch on security announcements related to FTP servers, especially the `wu-ftpd` server.
- Monitor your logs for suspicious activity.
- Test your configuration carefully. With the large number of options available, you want to be sure it behaves the way you intended.
- When setting up file owners and permissions, be sure the permissions are correct.
- Use a lot of messages to help make your server self-documenting to outside users.

CHAPTER 9

Apache Server

by Jack Tackett, Jr.

IN THIS CHAPTER

This chapter guides you through the installation and configuration of the Apache Web server using Red Hat's RPM system. Red Hat includes the current version of Apache with its overall Linux product. However, if the latest version of Red Hat Linux is a few months old, you can find a more recent version of Apache in the `/pub/contrib` area of Red Hat's FTP server. For information about the latest version of Apache, such as what bug fixes and new features have been added, visit the Apache group's Web site, `http://www.apache.org`, or the Apache Week Web site at `http://www.apacheweek.org`.

The current version of Red Hat Linux, version 5.1, includes Apache version 1.2.6. The latest stable release of Apache available at the time of this printing is 1.3.2, which is available from `http://www.apache.org`. Version 1.2.6 is available in RPM format on Red Hat's FTP server.

There is a lag between the release of new and beta versions of Apache and its corresponding RPM packages. Installing Apache from source code is possible on Red Hat Linux but is beyond the scope of this chapter because the installer must either alter the directory structure of the workstation or imitate the directory structure of a previous Apache RPM.

Server Installation

You can find the Apache RPM either on the Red Hat Linux installation media or on the Red Hat FTP server. You can install it as you do any other RPM with the command-line `rpm` tool or with `glint`, the X Window package management utility. To install the package using `rpm`, execute

```
rpm -i latest_apache.rpm
```

where *`latest_apache.rpm`* is the name of the latest Apache RPM.

If Apache has already been installed on your system, then you might want to upgrade to the newer version. To upgrade the package using `rpm`, execute

```
rpm -U latest_apache.rpm
```

The Apache RPM installs files in the following directories:

- `/etc/httpd/conf`—This directory contains all the Apache configuration files, which include `access.conf`, `httpd.conf`, and `srm.conf`.
- `/etc/rc.d/`—The tree under this directory contains the system startup scripts. The Apache RPM installs a complete set for the Web server. These scripts, which you can use to start and stop the server from the command line, will also automatically start and stop the server when the workstation is halted, started, or rebooted.

- /home/httpd—The RPM installs the default server icons and CGI scripts in this location.
- /usr/doc and /usr/man—The RPM contains manual pages and readme files, which are placed in these directories. As is the case for most RPM packages, the readme and other related documentation is placed in a directory under /usr/doc that is named for the server version.
- /usr/sbin—The executable programs are placed in this directory.

NOTE

If you are upgrading to a newer version of Apache, then RPM will not write over your current configuration files. RPM moves your current files and appends the extension .rpmnew to the file; for example, srm.conf becomes srm.conf.rpmnew.

Runtime Server Configuration Settings

Apache reads its configuration settings from three files: access.conf, httpd.conf, and srm.conf. Primarily, this organization was developed to maintain backward compatibility with the NCSA server, but the reasoning behind it makes good sense. The configuration files reside in the conf subdirectory of the server distribution. The backup copies of the configuration files—access.conf-dist, httpd.conf-dist, and srm.conf-dist—are included in the software distribution.

NOTE

The newest version of Apache uses different configuration files but maintains backward compatibility with the NCSA files.

You perform runtime configuration of your server with *configuration directives*, which are commands that set some option. You use them to tell the server about various options that you want to enable, such as the location of files important to the server configuration and operation. Configuration directives follow this syntax:

```
directive option option...
```

You specify one directive per line. Some directives only set a value such as a filename; others let you specify various options. Some special directives, called *sections*, look like HTML tags. Section directives are surrounded by angle brackets, such as `<directive>`. Sections usually enclose a group of directives that apply only to the directory specified in the section:

```
<Directory somedir/in/your/tree>
  directive option option
  directive option option
</directive>
```

All sections are closed with a matching section tag that looks like `</directive>`. You will see some of these constructs in the `conf/access.conf` and in your `conf/httpd.conf` files. Note that section tags, like any other directives, are specified one per line.

TIP

To help maintain your server's configuration, you should place server-wide configurations in `httpd.conf`. You should place directory-specific configurations in `access.conf` and server-wide resource configurations in `srm.conf`.

Editing `httpd.conf`

`httpd.conf` contains configuration directives that control how the server runs, where its logfiles are found, the user ID (UID) it runs under, the port that it listens to, and so on. You need to edit some of the default configuration values to settings that make sense for your site. I kept most of the defaults in my `httpd.conf` with the exception of the following:

`ServerAdmin` — The `ServerAdmin` directive should be set to the address of the Webmaster managing the server. It should be a valid email address or alias, such as *webmaster@your.domain*. Setting this value to a valid address is important because this address will be returned to a visitor when a problem occurs (see Figure 9.1).

`User` and `Group` — The `User` and `Group` directives set the UID and group ID (GID) that the server will use to process requests. I kept these settings as the defaults: `nobody` and `nogroup`. Verify that the names `nobody` and `nogroup` exist in your `/etc/passwd` and `/etc/group` files, respectively. (They are provided by Red Hat Linux, so they should already be defined.) If you want to use a different UID or GID, go ahead; however, be aware that the server will run with the permissions you define here. The permissions for the specified UID and GID should be limited because, in case of a security hole, whether on the server or (more likely) on your own CGI programs, those programs will run with the assigned UID. If the server runs as `root` or some other privileged user, someone can exploit the security holes and do nasty things to your site. Instead of specifying the `User` and `Group` directives using names, you can specify them using the UID and GID numbers. If you use numbers, be sure that the numbers you specify correspond to the user and group you want and that they are preceded by the pound (#) symbol.

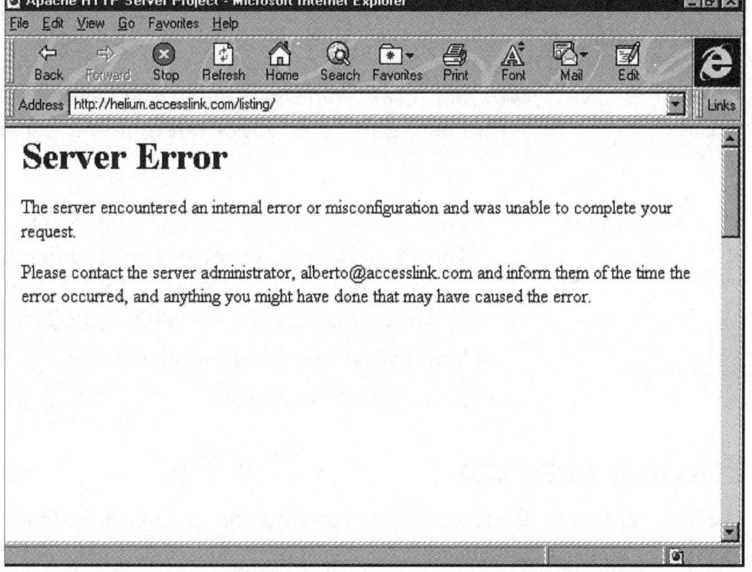

FIGURE 9.1
One of the error messages the server returns if an error occurs. Note that the `ServerAdmin` *was set to* `alberto@accesslink.com`.

Here's how these directives look if specified by name:

```
User nobody
Group nogroup
```

Here's the same specification by UID and GID:

```
User #-1
Group #-1
```

`ServerName` The `ServerName` directive sets the hostname the server will return. Set it to a fully qualified domain name (`fqdn`). If this value is not set, the server will figure out the name by itself and set it to its canonical name. However, you might want the server to return a friendlier address such as `www.your.domain`. Whatever you do, `ServerName` should be a real Domain Name System (DNS) name for your network. If you are administering your own DNS, remember to add a `CNAME` alias for your host. If someone else manages the DNS for you, ask that person to set this name for you.

Your `ServerName` entry should look like this:

```
ServerName servername.your.domain
```

TIP

If you want to install a Web server for test purposes on a standalone machine, you can do so by specifying a `ServerName` of `localhost`. You can then access the server as `http://www.localhost` from the standalone machine. This approach can be useful for trying new configurations or Internet Web servers.

`ServerRoot` This directive sets the absolute path to your server directory. This directive tells the server where to find all the resources and configuration files. Many of these resources are specified in the configuration files relative to the `ServerRoot` directory.

Your `ServerRoot` directive should read

```
ServerRoot /etc/httpd
```

Editing `srm.conf`

The `srm.conf` file is the resource configuration file. It controls settings related to the location of your Web document tree, the CGI program directories, and other resource configuration issues that affect your Web site. I kept most of the defaults in my `srm.conf` file. The most important directives on this configuration file are as follow:

`DocumentRoot` Set this directive to the absolute path of your document tree. Your document tree is the top directory from which Apache will serve files. By default, it is set to `/home/httpd/html`.

`UserDir` This directive defines the directory relative to a local user's home directory where that user will put public HTML documents. It's relative because each user will have his or her own HTML directory. The default setting for this directive is `public_html`, so each user will be able to create a directory called public_html under his or her home directory, and HTML documents placed in that directory will be available as http://servername/~*username*, where *username* is the username of the particular user.

Allowing individual users to put Web content on your server poses several important security considerations. If you are operating a Web server on the Internet rather than on a private network, you should read the WWW Security FAQ by Lincoln Stein. You can find a copy at http://www.genome.wi.mit.edu/WWW/faqs/www-security-faq.html.

A copy of the boilerplate conf/srm.conf file is included at the end of this chapter in Listing 9.3.

Editing access.conf

access.conf is the global *access control file*; it configures the type of access users have to your site and the documents you make available, as well as security issues defining the extent to which users can alter the security settings you might have defined. The default configuration provides unrestricted access to documents in your DocumentRoot. I kept all the defaults in my access.conf file.

If you want to provide a more restrictive site, you might want to verify that all <Directory *path*> sections match the directories they list in your installation. The directory sections specify a set of options, usually involving security issues, on a per-directory basis. In particular, you might want to remove the Indexes option that follows the Options directive on the section that looks like this:

```
<Directory /home/httpd/cgi-bin>
Options Indexes FollowSymLinks
</Directory>
```

Actually, the example given here is a very bad one because it turns on two options for the cgi-bin directory that no decent system administrator would ever allow. The Indexes option allows for server-generated directory listings. You probably don't want anyone peeking at the contents of your cgi-bin directories. The FollowSymLinks directive allows the Web server to follow symbolic links to other directories. This directive is a potential security problem because it could allow the server to "escape" from the server directories and could potentially allow users to access files that you do not want them to see.

Options that you implement on your global configuration files can be overridden with an .htaccess file. .htaccess files allow you to set server directives on a per-directory basis. This capability is particularly useful for user directories, where the user does not have access to the main server configuration files. You can disable all .htaccess overrides by setting the directive `AllowOverride` to `None`, as follows. This directive is by default set to allow all overrides:

```
AllowOverride None
```

Configuring an inetd Server

Normally, Apache runs in standalone mode or daemon mode. How it is run by the system depends on how it is configured by the `ServerType` directive in `conf/httpd.conf`.

A *standalone server* offers superior performance over `inetd`-run servers because usually a server process is ready to serve a request. When run under `inetd` (the Internet daemon), a new server is started every time a request is received on the HTTP port. A considerable amount of overhead is involved in starting a new server process with each new request.

The default setting for `ServerType` is `standalone`; unless you have an extremely light traffic site, you should stick with this setting. `inetd` servers are good for information you want to make available but for which you don't want to dedicate a computer.

TIP

An `inetd` server is great for testing configuration settings because the server rereads all its settings every time it receives a request. On a standalone server, you need to restart the server manually before it sees any changes you made to the configuration files.

To run a server from `inetd`, you need to modify `conf/httpd.conf` once more and change the `ServerType` directive from `standalone` to `inetd`, as follows:

```
ServerType inetd
```

The `Port` directive has no effect on an `inetd` server. A standalone server uses this configuration information to learn which port it should be listening to. Because `inetd` does the binding between the port and the software, this setting has no effect on an `inetd` configuration.

Configuring inetd

`inetd` is the "Internet superserver." It gets started when the machine boots by `/etc/rc`. After it is launched, `inetd` listens for connections on Internet socket ports. When it finds a connection, it starts the program responsible for managing that port. When the request is served and the program exits, `inetd` continues to listen for additional requests on that port.

To make Apache work from `inetd`, you need to edit `/etc/inetd.conf` and `/etc/services`. Configuring an `inetd` server requires a bit more system configuration than a standalone server.

First, you need to edit your `/etc/services` file. The `/etc/services` database contains information about all known services available on the Internet. Each service is represented by a single line listing the following information:

Official service name
Port number
Protocol name
Aliases by which the service is known

Each entry is separated by a tab or spaces. An entry describing `httpd` looks like this:

```
http portnumber/tcp httpd httpd
```

NOTE

TCP/IP ports range from 0 to 65,535; however, the first 1,024 ports are reserved. A reserved port is controlled and assigned by the IANA and, on most systems, can be used only by system (or root) processes or by programs executed by privileged users. (The IANA is the Internet Assigned Numbers Authority. More details about the IANA and reserved ports are available at `http://www.sockets.com/services.htm#WellKnownPorts`.) If you want to run the server at port 80 (the default for `httpd`), the superuser must start `httpd`.

Set *`portnumber`* to the port number on which you want to run the server. Typically, this port will be port 80 for a standalone server. `inetd` servers run better at port 8080, so your entry will look like this:

```
http 8080/tcp httpd httpd
```

If you are running NetInfo, you can type this line into a temporary file, such as `/tmp/services` and then run

```
niload services . < /tmp/services
```

Next, you need to edit `/etc/inetd.conf` to configure `inetd` to listen for `httpd` requests. Each line in `inetd.conf` contains the following information:

Service name

Socket type

Protocol

Wait/no wait

User the server program will run as

Server program

Server program arguments

My completed entry looks like this:

```
httpd  stream  tcp  nowait nobody  /sbin/
httpd httpd -f /etc/httpd/conf/httpd.conf
```

CAUTION

The preceding example starts the server as `nobody`. Typically, you will want a standalone server to be started by the root user so that the server can bind to port 80, the standard HTTP port, and be able to change the UID and GID of its children processes. When the standalone server starts, it forks children processes. These children processes run with a UID of `nobody` and a GID of `nogroup` unless you specified a different setting with the `User` and `Group` directives. The children processes handle the HTTP requests. The main process, owned by `root`, has as its duty the creation and destruction of its children processes. This makes the standard, standalone server secure.

If you specify the root UID in this example with the intention of running the `inetd` server on port 80, the process handling the request is owned by `root`. This setup can create security problems; unlike a standalone server, the `inetd` server doesn't fork any children processes, so it handles requests with the UID and GID of the process owner.

After adding the `httpd` entry to `/etc/inetd.conf`, you need to restart `inetd`. You can easily do so by finding out the `inetd` process number by using `ps` and sending it a `HANGUP` signal:

```
# kill -HUP InetdProcessID
```

Replace the *`InetdProcessID`* with the process number listed by the `ps` command. If the PID listed is 86, you type `kill -HUP 86`.

`inetd` then restarts, rereading the configuration file that instructs it to listen for a request for port 8080.

Running the Web Server for the First Time

Before you can run the server for the first time, you need to create an HTML document. The standard Apache distribution includes such a file, but I have created another file that is more useful, and I am sure that you'll use it time and time again. Using your favorite text editor, create a file called `index.html` inside the `htdocs` directory with this content:

```
<HTML>
<HEAD>
<TITLE>Red Hat Linux Unleashed</TITLE>
</HEAD>
<BODY BGCOLOR="#ffffff" LINK="#000080" VLINK="#000080">
<H1><CENTER>Red Hat Linux Unleashed </CENTER></H1>
<H2><CENTER>Congratulations! Your Apache server was successfully
installed.</CENTER></H2>

<H3>Here are some interesting sites that host information about
the Apache server: </H3>

<UL>
<LI>The official homepage for the
<A HREF="http://www.apache.org">Apache Group</A>

<LI>The official homepage for
<A HREF="http://www.us.apache-ssl.com">Community Connexion</A>
developers of Stronghold: Apache-SSL-US (A Netscape compatible
SSL server based on Apache)

<LI>The official homepage for
<A HREF="http://www.algroup.co.uk/Apache-SSL">Apache-SSL</A>
(A Netscape compatible SSL server based on Apache - only available
to users outside of the United States).

<LI><A HREF="http://www.zyzzyva.com/server/module_registry/">
Apache Module Registry</A>, the place where you can find information
about 3<SUP>rd</SUP> party Apache modules and other development stuff.

<LI><A HREF="http://www.apacheweek.com">The Apache Week Home</A>,
here you will find an essential weekly guide dedicated to Apache server
➥information.

<LI><A HREF="http://www.ukweb.com">UK Web's Apache Support Center</A>

<LI><A HREF="http://www.fastcgi.com">The FastCGI Website</A>
</UL>

<P>
```

```
<STRONG>Deja News a very handy USENET news search engine:</STRONG>
<FORM ACTION="http://search.dejanews.com/dnquery.xp" METHOD=POST>

<P>
<CENTER>
<STRONG>Quick Search For:</STRONG> <INPUT NAME="query" VALUE="Apache"
➥SIZE="37">
<INPUT TYPE="submit" VALUE="Search!"><INPUT NAME="defaultOp"
➥VALUE="AND" TYPE="hidden">
<INPUT NAME="svcclass" VALUE="dncurrent" TYPE="hidden">
<INPUT NAME="maxhits" VALUE="20" TYPE="hidden">
</CENTER>
</FORM>

</BODY>
</HTML>
```

Put this file in your `htdocs` directory. At this point, you are ready to test the server.

Starting a Standalone Server

If you are running a standalone server, you need to start `httpd` manually. You do so by entering the following line:

```
# /sbin/httpd -f /etc/httpd/conf/httpd.conf
```

Note that I started the standalone server from the root account, indicated by the pound sign (#) at the beginning of the line. You need to start standalone servers by `root` so that two important events occur:

- If your standalone server uses the default HTTP port (port 80), only the superuser can bind to Internet ports that are lower than 1025.
- Only processes owned by `root` can change their UID and GID as specified by the `User` and `Group` directives. If you start the server under another UID, it will run with the permissions of the user starting the process.

Starting an `inetd` Server

As you probably guessed, you don't need to start an `inetd` server. `inetd` starts `httpd` every time a request is received in the port assigned to the server. `inetd` servers make good development platforms because configuration settings are reread every time you send a request.

Starting and Stopping the Server

The Apache server, `httpd`, has a few command-line options you can use to set some defaults specifying where `httpd` will read its configuration directives. The Apache `httpd` executable understands the following options:

```
httpd [-d ServerRoot] [-f ConfigurationFile] [-x] [-v] [-?]
```

The `-d` option overrides the location of the *`ServerRoot`* directory. It sets the initial value of the *`ServerRoot`* variable (the directory where the Apache server is installed) to whatever path you specify. This default is usually read from the `ServerRoot` directive in `httpd.conf`.

The `-f` flag specifies the location of the main configuration file, `conf/httpd.conf`. It reads and executes the configuration commands found in *`ConfigurationFile`* on startup. If the *`ConfigurationFile`* is not an absolute path (it doesn't begin with a `/`), its location is assumed to be relative to the path specified in the *`ServerRoot`* directive in `httpd.conf`. By default, this value is set to *`ServerRoot`*`/conf/httpd.conf`.

The `-x` option is used by the developers of Apache as a debugging aid and should not be used under normal server operation. It runs a single server process that does not create any children.

The `-v` option prints the development version of the Apache server and terminates the process.

The `-?` option prints the following usage information for the server:

```
Usage: httpd [-d directory] [-f file] [-v]
-d directory : specify an alternate initial ServerRoot
-f file : specify an alternate ServerConfigFile
```

The `/etc/rc.d` httpd Scripts

Red Hat Linux uses scripts in the `/etc/rc.d` directory to control the startup and shutdown of various services, including the Apache Web server. The main script installed for the Apache Web server is `/etc/rc.d/init.d/httpd` and is shown in Listing 9.1. You can use the following options to control the Web server:

NOTE

`/etc/rc.d/init.d/httpd` is a shell script and is not the same as the Apache server located in `/usr/sbin`. That is, `/usr/sbin/httpd` is the program executable file, and `/etc/rc.d/init.d/httpd` is a shell script that helps control that program.

`start`	The system uses this option to start the Web server during bootup. You, as `root`, can also use this script to start the server.
`stop`	The system uses this option to stop the server gracefully. You should use this script rather than use the `kill` command to stop the server.
`reload`	You can use this option to send the `HUP` signal to the `httpd` server to have it reread the configuration files after modification.
`restart`	This option is a convenient way to stop and then immediately start the Web server.
`status`	This option indicates whether the server is running, and if it is, it provides the various PIDs for each instance of the server.

For example, to check on the current status, use the following command:

```
/etc/rc.d/init.d/httpd status
```

which prints

```
httpd (pid 8643 8642 6510 6102 6101 6100 6099 6323 6322 6098 6097 6096
6095 362 6094 6093) is running...
```

This indicates the Web server is running; in fact, this indicates there are 16 servers currently running.

TIP

Use the `reload` option if you are making many changes to the various server configuration files. This saves time when stopping and starting the server by having the system simply reread the configuration files—without you remembering the PID for the Web server. If you do need to know the PID, the `status` command can provide that information. Also, the system keeps the PID (and many other PIDs) in a file located in `/var/run`.

LISTING 9.1 `/etc/rc.d/init.d/http`

```
#!/bin/sh
#
# Startup script for the Apache Web Server
#
# chkconfig: 345 85 15
# description: Apache is a World Wide Web server. It is used to serve \
#              HTML files and CGI.
# processname: httpd
# pidfile: /var/run/httpd.pid
# config: /etc/httpd/conf/access.conf
```

```
# config: /etc/httpd/conf/httpd.conf
# config: /etc/httpd/conf/srm.conf

# Source function library.
. /etc/rc.d/init.d/functions

# See how we were called.
case "$1" in
  start)
        echo -n "Starting httpd: "
        daemon httpd
        echo
        touch /var/lock/subsys/httpd
        ;;
  stop)
        echo -n "Shutting down http: "
        [ -f /var/run/httpd.pid ] && {
            kill `cat /var/run/httpd.pid`
            echo -n httpd
        }
        echo
        rm -f /var/lock/subsys/httpd
        rm -f /var/run/httpd.pid
        ;;
  status)
        status httpd
        ;;
  restart)
        $0 stop
        $0 start
        ;;
  reload)
        echo -n "Reloading httpd: "
        [ -f /var/run/httpd.pid ] && {
            kill -HUP `cat /var/run/httpd.pid`
            echo -n httpd
        }
        echo
        ;;
  *)
        echo "Usage: $0 {start¦stop¦restart¦reload¦status}"
        exit 1
esac

exit 0
```

Speedups with Squid

Some people have dubbed the World Wide Web the World Wide Wait because it can take so long to download Web pages across the Internet. One way to increase the download speed is to store a copy of a requested page on the local server and then have a browser check the local server first. This procedure is called caching, and under Linux, you can use a program called Squid to perform this caching.

> **NOTE**
>
> *Macmillan's New World Dictionary of Computer Terms* defines a cache as a memory area in which parts of information are copied. Information that is likely to require reading goes to the cache, where the system can access it more quickly.

Squid caches Web data, FTP data, and some DNS information, thus speeding up access to this data. Squid accepts requests for this data rather than sends the request on to the specified server (a process called proxying). The program then checks its internal cache, and if the data is there, it streams the data to the requesting client. If the data is not there, Squid contacts the sever that does have the data and downloads the data to the cache. After downloading the data, the program then streams the data to the client.

The Squid system consists of the following components:

`squid` The main cache/proxy server.

`dnsserver` Squid spawns a number of `dnsserver` processes, each of which can perform a single, blocking Domain Name System (DNS) lookup. This reduces the amount of time the cache waits for DNS lookups.

`ftpget` This process retrieves FTP data.

Squid is based on the Harvest Project funded by ARPA and is available for non-commercial use under the GNU General Public License. For more information on Squid, check out `http://squid.nlanr.net/Squid`.

Installing Squid

You can find the Squid RPM either on the Red Hat Linux installation media, on the Red Hat FTP server, or at `http://squid.nlanr.net/Squid/`. You can install it like any other RPM with the command-line `rpm` tool or with `glint`, the X Window package management utility. To install the package using `rpm`, execute

```
rpm -i latest_squid.rpm
```

where *latest_squid.rpm* is the name of the latest Apache RPM (currently squid-1.1.21-5.i386.rpm.)

NOTE

The Apache server installed by default is not SSL compliant, so it does not provide any security for the Web site. This is mostly due to the export restrictions of the U.S. Government and patents held by RSA. However, Apache SSL is available outside the U.S. Commercial Apache-based SSL servers are available from both Red Hat and StrongHold.

Configuring Squid

To run a cache, you basically need to customize the `squid.conf` configuration file, located at `/usr/local/squid/etc/squid.conf`, and then start the cache by running

```
/usr/local/squid/bin/squid
```

There is a WWW interface to the Cache Manager. To use this interface, you must copy the `cachemgr.cgi` program into your `httpd` server's `cgi-bin` directory. Listing 9.2 provides a simple configuration file from `http://cache.is.co.za/squid/initial/basic.conf.txt`, a useful Web site for admins running Squid.

LISTING 9.2 `squid.conf`

```
#squid.conf -  a very basic config file for squid

#Turn logging to its lowest level
debug_options ALL,1

#defines a group (or Access Control List) that includes all IP
#addresses
acl all src 0.0.0.0/0.0.0.0

#allow all sites to connect to us via HTTP
http_access allow  all

#allow all sites to use us as a sibling
icp_access  allow  all
```

continues

LISTING 9.2 CONTINUED

```
#test the following sites to check that we are connected
dns_testnames internic.net usc.edu cs.colorado.edu mit.edu yale.edu

#run as the squid user
cache_effective_user squid squid
#otherwise, you can uncomment the line below and comment out the one
➥above.
#       this will run as use "nobody" with the group "nogrtoup"
cache_effective_user nobody nogroup
```

This is enough information to get Squid up and running on your system, but for more complete information, check out the FAQ at

`http://squid.nlanr.net/Squid/FAQ/FAQ.html`

Hosting Virtual Hosts

One of the more popular services to provide with a Web server is to host a virtual domain, also known as a virtual host. A virtual domain is a complete Web site with its own domain name, as if it's a standalone machine, but it's hosted on the same machine as other Web sites. Apache implements this ability in a simple way with directives in the `http.conf` configuration file. Before configuring the Web server, you must configure your Red Hat system to handle multiple hosts.

Adding Virtual Hosts

Currently, a big portion of browsers surfing the Internet only understand `http` version 1.0. Why is this important? These browsers cannot distinguish virtual hosts served by a server running on a machine assigned only one IP address. For most of the world to see your virtual domain, each domain must have a unique IP number, and this IP number must be bound to the machine hosting the domain. For example, your Red Hat box can have the IP numbers 10.1.1.5, 10.1.1.6, 10.1.1.8, and 10.1.1.134 pointing to it. These IPs can be bound to `www.virthost1.com` (10.1.1.5), `www.virthost2.com` (10.1.1.6), and so on.

The first step in binding these IPs is to have a DNS entry on your name server pointing to them. A name record might have the following form:

```
virtdomain1.org. IN  SOA ns.netwharf.com. root.netwharf.com. (
                                1998020702
                                10800
                                3600
                                604800
```

```
                                        86400 )

;; Name Servers
virtdomain1.org.    IN      NS      ns.netwharf.com.
virtdomain1.org.    IN      NS      rtp2.intrex.net.

localhost             IN  A     127.0.0.1
www                   IN  A     10.1.1.5
www                   IN  MX    10 ns.netwharf.com.
www                   IN  MX    20 www.netwharf.com.
www                   IN  MX    30 rtp2.intrex.net.
virtdomain1.org.        IN  MX    10 ns.netwharf.com.
virtdomain1.org.        IN  MX    20 www.netwharf.com
virtdomain1.org.        IN  MX    30 rtp2.intrex.net.
```

This DNS record maps the IP 10.1.1.5 to the site `www.virtdomain1.org`, so if you ping `www.virtdomain1.org`, you see the IP 10.1.1.5.

The next step is to use the `ifconfig` command to bind the IP to the host onto a network device on your Web server box. You use the following syntax to bind the IP:

```
/sbin/ifconfig eth0:count virtdomain
```

`eth0` is the network device, and *`count`* is just a numeric value used to identify the host to the network system. *`virtdomain`* is the IP of virtual domain you want to host on this computer. To bind an IP to your current Web server box for the `www.tacket.org` site, you use the following command as the superuser:

```
/sbin/ifconfig eth0:1 10.1.1.5
```

After binding the IP to the your system, you then need to add a route to your network so that others can find you. You use the `route` command to update the system's routing tables:

```
/sbin/route add -host 10.1.1.5 dev eth0:1
```

`add` instructs the system to add the following route to the table for the host indicated by the IP address 10.1.1.5. The parameter `dev eth0:1` indicates which device to use for this route.

Configuring Virtual Hosts

Once you've set up the physical computer to handle the virtual hosts, getting Apache to serve up that site's Web pages is simpler. Virtual hosts are configured using the `VirtualHost` directive in `httpd.conf`. They have the following format:

```
<VirtualHost www.virthost1.com>
DocumentRoot /home/virthost1/public_html
```

```
TransferLog /home/virthost1/logs/access.virthost1
ErrorLog /home/virthost1/logs/error.virthost1
</VirtualHost>
```

The value in the `VirtualHost` tag, `www.virthost1.com`, is the hostname, which Apache looks up to get an IP address. Any directives placed within this directive apply only to requests made to this hostname. The `DocumentRoot` indicates the directory where the owner of `www.virthost1.com` places the Web content for the site.

CAUTION

If you plan to run a large number of virtual hosts on your system, you should consider sending all logged information to the standard Apache log files instead of to individual files. The reason is that you may reach your system's file descriptor limit (typically 64 per process) because you would be consuming one file descriptor per log file. Symptoms of this problem include error messages such as "unable to fork()," no information being written to the log files, or poor response to `http` requests.

Configuration File Listings

For your convenience, I provide listings of the various configuration files I discuss in this chapter. You might notice some differences between the files listed here and configuration files of source you download from the Internet. These differences are normal because newer versions of the server might have been released since this printing.

Listing 9.3 shows the server configuration file.

LISTING 9.3 `conf/httpd.conf`

```
# This is the main server configuration file. See URL
➥http://www.apache.org/
# for instructions.

# Do NOT simply read the instructions in here without understanding
# what they do, if you are unsure consult the online docs. You have been
# warned.

# Originally by Rob McCool

# ServerType is either inetd, or standalone.

ServerType standalone
```

```
# If you are running from inetd, go to "ServerAdmin".

# Port: The port the standalone listens to. For ports < 1023, you will
# need httpd to be run as root initially.

Port 80

# HostnameLookups: Log the names of clients or just their IP numbers
#   e.g.   www.apache.org (on) or 204.62.129.132 (off)
HostnameLookups on

# If you wish httpd to run as a different user or group, you must run
# httpd as root initially and it will switch.

# User/Group: The name (or #number) of the user/group to run httpd as.
#  On SCO (ODT 3) use User nouser and Group nogroup
User nobody
Group #-1

# ServerAdmin: Your address, where problems with the server should be
# e-mailed.

ServerAdmin you@your.address

# ServerRoot: The directory the server's config, error, and log files
# are kept in

ServerRoot /etc/httpd

# BindAddress: You can support virtual hosts with this option. This option
# is used to tell the server which IP address to listen to. It can either
# contain "*", an IP address, or a fully qualified Internet domain name.
# See also the VirtualHost directive.

#BindAddress *

# ErrorLog: The location of the error log file. If this does not start
# with /, ServerRoot is prepended to it.

ErrorLog logs/error_log

# TransferLog: The location of the transfer log file. If this does not
# start with /, ServerRoot is prepended to it.

TransferLog logs/access_log

# PidFile: The file the server should log its pid to
PidFile logs/httpd.pid
```

continues

LISTING 9.3 CONTINUED

```
# ScoreBoardFile: File used to store internal server process information
ScoreBoardFile logs/apache_status

# ServerName allows you to set a host name which is sent back to clients
➥for
# your server if it's different than the one the program would get (i.e.
➥use
# "www" instead of the host's real name).
#
# Note: You cannot just invent host names and hope they work. The name you
# define here must be a valid DNS name for your host. If you don't
➥understand
# this, ask your network administrator.

#ServerName new.host.name

# CacheNegotiatedDocs: By default, Apache sends Pragma: no-cache with each
# document that was negotiated on the basis of content. This asks proxy
# servers not to cache the document. Uncommenting the following line
➥disables
# this behavior, and proxies will be allowed to cache the documents.

#CacheNegotiatedDocs

# Timeout: The number of seconds before receives and sends time out
#  n.b. the compiled default is 1200 (20 minutes !)

Timeout 400

# KeepAlive: The number of Keep-Alive persistent requests to accept
# per connection. Set to 0 to deactivate Keep-Alive support

KeepAlive 5

# KeepAliveTimeout: Number of seconds to wait for the next request

KeepAliveTimeout 15

# Server-pool size regulation.  Rather than making you guess how many
# server processes you need, Apache dynamically adapts to the load it
# sees --- that is, it tries to maintain enough server processes to
# handle the current load, plus a few spare servers to handle transient
# load spikes (e.g., multiple simultaneous requests from a single
# Netscape browser).

# It does this by periodically checking how many servers are waiting
# for a request.  If there are fewer than MinSpareServers, it creates
# a new spare.  If there are more than MaxSpareServers, some of the
# spares die off.  These values are probably OK for most sites --
```

```
MinSpareServers 5
MaxSpareServers 10

# Number of servers to start --- should be a reasonable ballpark figure.

StartServers 5

# Limit on total number of servers running, i.e., limit on the number
# of clients who can simultaneously connect --- if this limit is ever
# reached, clients will be LOCKED OUT, so it should NOT BE SET TOO LOW.
# It is intended mainly as a brake to keep a runaway server from taking
# Unix with it as it spirals down...

MaxClients 150

# MaxRequestsPerChild: the number of requests each child process is
#  allowed to process before the child dies.
#  The child will exit so as to avoid problems after prolonged use when
#  Apache (and maybe the libraries it uses) leak.  On most systems, this
#  isn't really needed, but a few (such as Solaris) do have notable leaks
#  in the libraries.

MaxRequestsPerChild 30

# Proxy Server directives. Uncomment the following line to
# enable the proxy server:

#ProxyRequests On

# To enable the cache as well, edit and uncomment the following lines:

#CacheRoot /usr/local/etc/httpd/proxy
#CacheSize 5
#CacheGcInterval 4
#CacheMaxExpire 24
#CacheLastModifiedFactor 0.1
#CacheDefaultExpire 1
#NoCache adomain.com anotherdomain.edu joes.garage.com

# Listen: Allows you to bind Apache to specific IP addresses and/or
# ports, in addition to the default. See also the VirtualHost command

#Listen 3000
#Listen 12.34.56.78:80

# VirtualHost: Allows the daemon to respond to requests for more than one
# server address, if your server machine is configured to accept IP
➥packets
# for multiple addresses. This can be accomplished with the ifconfig
# alias flag, or through kernel patches like VIF.
```

continues

LISTING 9.3 CONTINUED

```
# Any httpd.conf or srm.conf directive may go into a VirtualHost command.
# See also the BindAddress entry.

#<VirtualHost host.foo.com>
#ServerAdmin webmaster@host.foo.com
#DocumentRoot /www/docs/host.foo.com
#ServerName host.foo.com
#ErrorLog logs/host.foo.com-error_log
#TransferLog logs/host.foo.com-access_log
#</VirtualHost>
```

Listing 9.4 shows the resource configuration file.

LISTING 9.4 conf/srm.conf

```
# With this document, you define the name space that users see for your
➥http
# server.  This file also defines server settings which affect how
➥requests are
# serviced, and how results should be formatted.

# See the tutorials at http://www.apache.org/ for
# more information.

# Originally by Rob McCool; Adapted for Apache

# DocumentRoot: The directory out of which you will serve your
# documents. By default, all requests are taken from this directory, but
# symbolic links and aliases may be used to point to other locations.

DocumentRoot /home/httpd/html

# UserDir: The name of the directory which is appended onto a user's home
# directory if a ~user request is received.

UserDir public_html

# DirectoryIndex: Name of the file or files to use as a pre-written HTML
# directory index.  Separate multiple entries with spaces.

DirectoryIndex index.html

# FancyIndexing is whether you want fancy directory indexing or standard

FancyIndexing on

# AddIcon tells the server which icon to show for different files or
➥filename
# extensions
```

```
AddIconByEncoding (CMP,/icons/compressed.gif) x-compress x-gzip

AddIconByType (TXT,/icons/text.gif) text/*
AddIconByType (IMG,/icons/image2.gif) image/*
AddIconByType (SND,/icons/sound2.gif) audio/*
AddIconByType (VID,/icons/movie.gif) video/*

AddIcon /icons/binary.gif .bin .exe
AddIcon /icons/binhex.gif .hqx
AddIcon /icons/tar.gif .tar
AddIcon /icons/world2.gif .wrl .wrl.gz .vrml .vrm .iv
AddIcon /icons/compressed.gif .Z .z .tgz .gz .zip
AddIcon /icons/a.gif .ps .ai .eps
AddIcon /icons/layout.gif .html .shtml .htm .pdf
AddIcon /icons/text.gif .txt
AddIcon /icons/c.gif .c
AddIcon /icons/p.gif .pl .py
AddIcon /icons/f.gif .for
AddIcon /icons/dvi.gif .dvi
AddIcon /icons/uuencoded.gif .uu
AddIcon /icons/script.gif .conf .sh .shar .csh .ksh .tcl
AddIcon /icons/tex.gif .tex
AddIcon /icons/bomb.gif core

AddIcon /icons/back.gif ..
AddIcon /icons/hand.right.gif README
AddIcon /icons/folder.gif ^^DIRECTORY^^
AddIcon /icons/blank.gif ^^BLANKICON^^

# DefaultIcon is which icon to show for files which do not have an icon
# explicitly set.

DefaultIcon /icons/unknown.gif

# AddDescription allows you to place a short description after a file in
# server-generated indexes.
# Format: AddDescription "description" filename

# ReadmeName is the name of the README file the server will look for by
# default. Format: ReadmeName name
#
# The server will first look for name.html, include it if found, and it
➥will
# then look for name and include it as plaintext if found.
#
# HeaderName is the name of a file which should be prepended to
# directory indexes.

ReadmeName README
```

continues

LISTING 9.4 CONTINUED

```
HeaderName HEADER

# IndexIgnore is a set of filenames which directory indexing should ignore
# Format: IndexIgnore name1 name2...

IndexIgnore */.??* *~ *# */HEADER* */README* */RCS

# AccessFileName: The name of the file to look for in each directory
# for access control information.

AccessFileName .htaccess

# DefaultType is the default MIME type for documents which the server
# cannot find the type of from filename extensions.

DefaultType text/plain

# AddEncoding allows you to have certain browsers (Mosaic/X 2.1+)
➥uncompress
# information on the fly. Note: Not all browsers support this.

AddEncoding x-compress Z
AddEncoding x-gzip gz

# AddLanguage allows you to specify the language of a document. You can
# then use content negotiation to give a browser a file in a language
# it can understand.  Note that the suffix does not have to be the same
# as the language keyword --- those with documents in Polish (whose
# net-standard language code is pl) may wish to use "AddLanguage pl .po"
# to avoid the ambiguity with the common suffix for perl scripts.

AddLanguage en .en
AddLanguage fr .fr
AddLanguage de .de
AddLanguage da .da
AddLanguage el .el
AddLanguage it .it

# LanguagePriority allows you to give precedence to some languages
# in case of a tie during content negotiation.
# Just list the languages in decreasing order of preference.

LanguagePriority en fr de

# Redirect allows you to tell clients about documents which used to exist
➥in
# your server's namespace, but do not anymore. This allows you to tell the
# clients where to look for the relocated document.
# Format: Redirect fakename url
```

```
# Aliases: Add here as many aliases as you need (with no limit). The
➥format is
# Alias fakename realname

#Alias /icons/ /usr/local/etc/httpd/icons/

# ScriptAlias: This controls which directories contain server scripts.
# Format: ScriptAlias fakename realname

#ScriptAlias /cgi-bin/ /usr/local/etc/httpd/cgi-bin/

# If you want to use server side includes, or CGI outside
# ScriptAliased directories, uncomment the following lines.

# AddType allows you to tweak mime.types without actually editing it, or
➥to
# make certain files to be certain types.
# Format: AddType type/subtype ext1

# AddHandler allows you to map certain file extensions to "handlers",
# actions unrelated to filetype. These can be either built into the server
# or added with the Action command (see below)
# Format: AddHandler action-name ext1

# To use CGI scripts:
#AddHandler cgi-script .cgi

# To use server-parsed HTML files
#AddType text/html .shtml
#AddHandler server-parsed .shtml

# Uncomment the following line to enable Apache's send-asis HTTP file
# feature
#AddHandler send-as-is asis

# If you wish to use server-parsed imagemap files, use
#AddHandler imap-file map

# To enable type maps, you might want to use
#AddHandler type-map var

# Action lets you define media types that will execute a script whenever
# a matching file is called. This eliminates the need for repeated URL
# pathnames for oft-used CGI file processors.
# Format: Action media/type /cgi-script/location
# Format: Action handler-name /cgi-script/location

# For example to add a footer (footer.html in your document root) to
# files with extension .foot (e.g. foo.html.foot), you could use:
```

continues

LISTING 9.4 CONTINUED

```
#AddHandler foot-action foot
#Action foot-action /cgi-bin/footer

# Or to do this for all HTML files, for example, use:
#Action text/html /cgi-bin/footer

# MetaDir: specifies the name of the directory in which Apache can find
# meta information files. These files contain additional HTTP headers
# to include when sending the document

#MetaDir .web

# MetaSuffix: specifies the file name suffix for the file containing the
# meta information.

#MetaSuffix .meta

# Customizable error response (Apache style)
#  these come in three flavors
#
#    1) plain text
#ErrorDocument 500 "The server made a boo boo.
#  n.b.  the (") marks it as text, it does not get output
#
#    2) local redirects
#ErrorDocument 404 /missing.html
#  to redirect to local url /missing.html
#ErrorDocument 404 /cgi-bin/missing_handler.pl
#  n.b. can redirect to a script or a document using server-side-includes.
#
#    3) external redirects
#ErrorDocument 402 http://other.server.com/subscription_info.html
#
```

Listing 9.5 shows the global access configuration file.

LISTING 9.5 conf/access.conf

```
# access.conf: Global access configuration
# Online docs at http://www.apache.org/

# This file defines server settings which affect which types of services
# are allowed, and in what circumstances.

# Each directory to which Apache has access can be configured with respect
# to which services and features are allowed and/or disabled in that
# directory (and its subdirectories).
```

```
# Originally by Rob McCool

# This should be changed to whatever you set DocumentRoot to.

<Directory /home/httpd/html>

# This may also be "None", "All", or any combination of "Indexes",
# "Includes", "FollowSymLinks", "ExecCGI", or "MultiViews".

# Note that "MultiViews" must be named *explicitly* --- "Options All"
# doesn't give it to you (or at least, not yet).

Options Indexes FollowSymLinks

# This controls which options the .htaccess files in directories can
# override. Can also be "All", or any combination of "Options",
➥"FileInfo",
# "AuthConfig", and "Limit"

AllowOverride None

# Controls who can get stuff from this server.

order allow,deny
allow from all

</Directory>

# /usr/local/etc/httpd/cgi-bin should be changed to wherever your
➥ScriptAliased
# CGI directory exists, if you have that configured.

<Directory /home/httpd/cgi-bin>
AllowOverride None
Options None
</Directory>

# Allow server status reports, with the URL of http://servername/status
# Change the ".nowhere.com" to match your domain to enable.

#<Location /status>
#SetHandler server-status

#order deny,allow
#deny from all
#allow from .nowhere.com
#</Location>

# You may place any other directories or locations you wish to have
# access information for after this one.
```

Summary

At this point, you should have a properly configured Apache server running. Several advanced options are available for Web sites running Apache, so you should check out the online documentation available at `http://www.apache.org/docs/`. Reading about the Apache project itself, at `http://www.apache.org/ABOUT_APACHE.html`, is also particularly interesting. If you are interested in Perl and CGI programming, you might want to take a look at the Apache/Perl integration project at `http://perl.apache.org/`. For more information on hosting virtual domains, see the Virtual-Services-HOWTO and the mini HOWTO IP-Alias. For more information on Squid, check out all the information available at the official Squid Web site at `http://squid.nlanr.net/Squid/FAQ/FAQ.html`. Finally, if you have other operating systems on other machines, remember that Apache is available for a variety of other platforms, including OS/2 and, on an experimental basis, 32-bit versions of Windows such as 98 and NT. Of course, real Web sites run on Red Hat!

CHAPTER

Internet News System

by Tim Parker

IN THIS CHAPTER

Usenet newsgroups are a fascinating and informative source of information, entertainment, news, and general chat. Usenet is one of the oldest components of the Internet and was popular long before the World Wide Web came on the scene. Usenet is still the most popular aspect of the Internet in terms of user interaction, offering a dynamic and often controversial forum for discussion on any subject.

Usenet newsgroups now number well over 100,000 groups dedicated to many different subjects. A full download of an average day's newsgroup postings takes several hundred megabytes of disk space and associated transfer time. Obviously, if you are going to access Usenet over anything slower than a T1 (1.544Mbps) line, you have to be selective in what you download. An analog modem simply can't download the entire Usenet feeds in a reasonable time. Selective access to newsgroups suits most users, however, because few (if any) users actually read all the postings on Usenet every day!

Providing access to the Usenet newsgroups is a natural purpose for Linux because newsgroups evolved under UNIX. To provide Usenet newsgroup access for yourself and anyone else accessing your machine, you need to set up newsgroup software on your system and get access to a source for downloading newsgroups. Any connection to the Internet gives you access to newsgroups, whether directly through your own gateway, through a news forwarding service, or through a third-party access service. Most Internet service providers (ISPs) can offer newsgroup downloads to you as part of their basic service. Typically, you choose which newsgroups you might be interested in from the complete list of all newsgroups, and those groups are transferred to your machine for reading. If you want to access a newsgroup you didn't download, a quick connection to your ISP lets you sample the postings.

In this chapter, you'll learn how to configure your Linux machine to download newsgroups from your Internet connection. You will also see how to install and configure common newsreaders, which users need to read postings in a newsgroup. There are several alternatives available for Linux access to newsgroups, so I chose the most common to show you how to configure on your Red Hat system.

Linux and Newsgroups

There are three ways to download newsgroups onto your Linux system: NNTP, C News, and INN. NNTP is the Network News Transfer Protocol, which is widely used over TCP/IP connections to ISPs or the Internet. C News was designed for downloading news through UUCP (UNIX to UNIX Copy) connections. INN (Internet News) is the most flexible and configurable method of downloading newsgroups and works especially well on larger systems or those where a lot of news is transferred. Unfortunately, INN is a little more complicated to configure than NNTP, but the added flexibility makes it a better choice for most system administrators. Because INN is included with most Linux systems, that's the choice I discuss.

Rich Saltz developed INN as an alternative to NNTP. One of the attractions of INN is that it doesn't care whether you are using TCP/IP or UUCP to transfer your newsgroups. INN handles both methods equally well.

Usenet newsgroup postings are sent from machine to machine across the Internet all the time. To send mail from one system to another, Usenet uses a technique called *flooding*. Flooding happens when one machine connects to another and essentially transfers all the postings in the newsgroups as one big block of data. The receiving machine then connects to another machine and repeats the process. In this way, all the postings in the newsgroups are transferred across the entire Internet. This is much better than maintaining a single source of newsgroup information on a server isolated somewhere on the Internet. Each machine that participates in the flooding has a list of all other machines that can send or receive newsgroup postings. Each connection is called a newsfeed. When you connect to an ISP and download newsgroup postings, you are creating a newsfeed between your machine and the ISP's, which in turn has a newsfeed to another machine somewhere on the Internet.

Every time a new posting is added to a newsgroup, the newsfeeds are used to transfer that posting. Each article has a list of all the machines that have received the posting, so it is easy to avoid transferring the same new posting to every machine on the Internet many times. The list of machines that have received the posting is called the path. Each posting also has a unique message ID, which prevents duplicate postings.

When you connect to your ISP and request newsgroup updates, one of two methods is usually used to ensure you don't get duplicate postings when you use your newsreader. The most common technique is called *ihave/sendme*, which uses a protocol to inform the machine at the other end of your newsfeed (such as your ISP's server) which message IDs you already have and which ones are lacking. Then, only the missing postings are transferred to your Linux machine.

The ihave/sendme protocol is excellent for updating a few newsgroups but starts to bog down dramatically when handling very large volumes of newsgroups. For this reason, a method called *batching* is used to transfer large newsgroup feeds. With batching, everything on one end of the newsfeed is transferred as a block. Your machine then sorts through the download, discarding any duplicates. Batching adds more overhead to your local Linux machine than ihave/sendme but involves a lot less messaging between the two ends of the newsfeeds.

Two other terms are used to describe the transfer of newsgroup postings from one machine to another, and these terms apply especially to smaller systems that don't download the entire newsfeed every day. Your system can download articles from the newsfeed using the ihave/sendme protocol, a technique called *pushing* the news. Alternatively, your machine can request specific postings or entire newsgroups from the newsfeed based on the date of arrival of the posting, a technique called *pulling* the news.

Before looking at how to download Usenet newsgroups to your machine, there is one alternative you might want to consider if you don't use Usenet a lot or you have limited connection time to the newsfeed. That approach is interacting with a news server on a remote network, reading the postings on that server instead of downloading them to your machine. Many ISPs allow you to choose whether to download newsgroups to your machine or to read them on the server. Obviously, if you are reading on the server, you must be connected all the time, but this might be a better choice if you do not do a lot of Usenet surfing or you have limited disk space on your machine.

INN Hardware and Software Requirements

INN doesn't impose too many hardware requirements; most Linux-capable hardware is sufficient to run INN. If you do download a lot of newsgroup postings, however, slow processors will be affected. Because INN often works in background, your foreground tasks get slower while INN crunches away in background. This is usually not a problem with 80486 or better CPUs running Red Hat Linux.

There are no extra RAM requirements for INN, although the more RAM, the better, to avoid swapping. If you download only a dozen newsgroups a day, then Linux needs no extra RAM. You should have swap space allocated on your system as a RAM overflow, but there is no need to expand swap space just for INN unless the existing swap space is very small (less than half your physical RAM, for example).

Disk space can be a problem if you don't have a lot to spare. Downloading newsgroups can eat up disk space at an alarming rate, even if you download only a few groups a day. Because newsgroup postings are not automatically deleted after you read them, the effect is cumulative. This is especially a problem with newsgroups that contain binary information such as compiled programs or pictures. A typical newsgroup download can range from a few kilobytes to several megabytes. Some of the binary newsgroups get many megs daily, all of which accumulate over a week or so to huge amounts of disk space. It is not unusual for a week's complete download of all the newsgroups to use more than a gigabyte of disk space, so you must be careful about which newsgroups you select to download.

Modems are another issue, and the speed of your modem directly impacts how many newsgroups you can download in a reasonable amount of time. Obviously, the faster your modem, the better. A 56Kbps modem will download much more data in a minute than a 9,600bps modem. That doesn't mean you need to junk your existing slower modems and replace them. The determining factor for your connection is the amount of data you will be transferring. If you download less than a dozen non-binary newsgroups a day, a 9,600bps modem is just fine. When you start downloading megabytes of data a day, as often happens with binary-laden newsgroups, you need a much faster connection to keep the download time to a minimum. Any of today's 56Kbps modems will suit your purposes for typical Usenet downloads of a few dozen non-binary newsgroups. When you start downloading large amounts of news, you should look at faster connections such as ISDN (128Kbps), T1 (1.544Mbps), or T3 (4Mbps). Fractional use of ISDN and T1 lines are available for a reasonable cost these days, but the overall expenses of the line and routers are usually more than the newsgroup reading is worth to end users.

Software requirements for INN are simple: You need INN and a configured connection to a newsfeed source (such as UUCP or TCP/IP to an ISP). INN is supplied with Red Hat Linux, and you can also obtain it from most Linux FTP and Web sites.

INN

INN was originally designed for handling news on very large systems with complex connections and configuration problems. INN contains an NNTP component but is noticeably faster when downloading and handling newsgroups than NNTP alone. Luckily, INN can be quickly configured for most basic Linux setups. I look at setting up INN on a typical Red Hat Linux system using a dial-up connection to an ISP using TCP/IP because this is the most common configuration. One problem with INN is a lack of good documentation. To date, no one has spent the time to produce a good public-domain how-to file about configuring and maintaining INN on Linux systems, although the Red Hat INN package contains nine helpful files named `INN-faq_part1` through `INN-faq_part9`, which are installed in the `/usr/doc` directory.

INN uses a daemon called `innd` to control its behavior. Another daemon, `nnrpd`, is used to provide newsreader services. When you boot your machine, `innd` usually starts up right away. Every time a user launches a newsreader, a copy of `nnrpd` is started.

Installing INN

To install INN, you can start with either the source code (usually obtained from a Web or FTP site) or a precompiled binary included in the Red Hat INN package. Precompiled binaries are much easier because they save the hassle of running a C compiler to produce the binary from source code.

NOTE

If you are working with INN source code instead of a precompiled binary, you should carefully read any `readme` files included in the source distribution. They will describe the steps involved in compiling the INN software for your system. A `makefile` will accompany the source code and may need modification to suit your system. The version of INN shipping with Red Hat Linux when this chapter was written was 1.7.2.

To install your precompiled INN binaries on the system and properly configure it for secure operation, follow these steps:

1. Check your `/etc/passwd` file for a user called `news`. If one does not exist, create the `news` user. The user `news` should belong to a group called `news`. The home directory and startup command can be anything because they are not used by the system. The `news` user is created to allow INN to run as a non-user and non-root login for better system security. This account should exist by default on Red Hat systems.
2. Check the `/etc/group` file for a group called `news`. If one does not exist, create it. The `news` login should be the only user in the `news` group. Providing a dedicated group for INN access enhances system security. This group should exist by default on Red Hat systems.
3. INN often sends mail to the news logins, so you might want to create an alias for the usernames `news` and `usenet` to root, postmaster, or whatever other login you want these messages to be sent to. The alias file is kept in `/etc/aliases`. When you add aliases, make sure to run the `/usr/bin/newaliases` command afterward so that the added aliases will take effect.
4. Check to see if INN is already installed on your system by typing

   ```
   rpm -q inn
   ```

   If no installed package is found, install the INN package from the directory containing RPM files by issuing the following command:

   ```
   rpm -i inn-1.7.2-7.i386.rpm
   ```

   Installing the package will cause the creation of two files called `/etc/rc.d/init.d/innd` and `/etc/rc.d/rc.news`. These files will be used by `init` to start news services each time you boot, and once installed, they are executed automatically during the boot process unless explicitly disabled or removed.

5. The INN RPM file will install INN and newsgroup support into the `/usr/lib/news` directory. Most newsreaders expect news to dwell in `/usr/lib/news` by default, but if you need to use a newsreader that doesn't follow this convention, you might want to use symbolic links to duplicate `/usr/lib/news` elsewhere.
6. The INN RPM will install the INN configuration files into the `/etc/news` directory and will add several files to the `/etc/cron.*` directories to be run by `cron`. The `/etc/cron.daily/inn-cron-expire` file will call the `news.daily` program once per day to expire (remove) old articles and to clean and maintain the INN logs. The `/etc/cron.daily/inn-cron-rnews` file will download new articles to your system once per day. The `/etc/cron.hourly/inn-cron-nntpsend` file will send articles created on your system to your outgoing news server once every hour.

   Once the INN package has successfully been installed, you can start news services by typing

   ```
   /etc/rc.d/init.d/innd start
   ```
7. If you are uncomfortable starting INN on a running system, you can reboot your machine now, and INN should start automatically as a part of the boot process.

Once the INN package is installed and ready to go, you still need to check the configuration information to make sure everything will run smoothly when `innd` or `nntpd` (the NNTP daemon) connects to the newsfeed.

NOTE

INN is very particular about its user and group setup and file permissions in general. As a general rule, don't modify any INN file permissions at all, or you might find the package ceases to work properly.

Configuring INN

Configuring INN can take hours because it is a complex package allowing many newsfeeds at once. Worried? Don't be, because for a simple connection to an ISP through TCP/IP or UUCP, you can configure INN in a few minutes. Most of the work was already done when you installed the package.

Follow these steps to check and configure your INN setup, being careful not to corrupt any files or change permissions as you go:

1. Edit the `/etc/news/hosts.nntp` file. This file lists all the newsfeeds that your system connects to and is read by the INN daemon. Enter the names of IP addresses (preferable) of the newsfeed machines, one newsfeed on a line. Because most systems will have only a single newsfeed, add the name or IP address of the newsfeed followed by the colon. If a password is required by the machine to which you connect for your newsfeed, enter the password after the colon:

   ```
   news_server1: goodnews
   ```

2. If you allow other machines on your local area network, or machines connecting through a remote access server on your machine, to read news collected by your system, you need to add their names to your `/etc/news/nnrp.access` file. This file is read when the `nnrpd` daemon starts for each person invoking a newsreader. The `nnrp.access` file contains a list of all the machines that are allowed to read news from your server and follows this syntax:

   ```
   name:perms:user:password:newsgroup
   ```

   name is the address of the machine that you are allowing to read news. (You can use wildcards to allow entire subnets.) *perms* is the permissions and has one of the following values: `Read` (for read-only access), `Post` (to allow posting of messages), or `Read Post` (for both `Read` and `Post`). The *user* field is used to authenticate a username before it is allowed to post, and the *password* accomplishes the same task. To prevent a user from posting messages through your server, leave *user* and *password* as spaces so they can't be matched.

   The *newsgroup* field is a pattern of newsgroup names that can be either read or not read, depending on how you set up the contents. Access to newsgroups uses wildcards, so `comp*` allows access to all newsgroups starting with comp, whereas `!sex` disables access to any newsgroups starting with the word sex. The default setting in the `nnrp.access` file is to prevent all access. To allow all users in the domain `tpci.com` to read and post news with no authentication required, you add this line to `nnrp.access`:

   ```
   *.tpci.com:Read Post:::*
   ```

   To open the news system to everyone on your system regardless of domain name, use an asterisk instead of a domain name.

After setting the `hosts.nntp` and `nnrp.access` files, you should be able to use INN to download news and access it with a newsreader (assuming you've granted yourself permission in the `nnrp.access` file). A lot of complexity can be introduced into INN's configuration file, but keeping it simple tends to be the best method. As your experience grows, you can modify the behavior of the newsfeeds, but start with as simple an access approach as possible to allow testing of the news system first. After you set up INN, the next step is to provide users with a newsreader.

Configuring trn

Many newsreaders are available for Linux systems, but the perennial favorite remains trn. This is an old package but is simple to use, fast, and efficient. You might not need a newsreader at all if you have Web services on your system. Many Web browsers allow access to newsgroups either in your own news directory or through a connection to an ISP's newsfeed.

The primary advantage of trn over the earlier rn (read news) package is that trn lets you follow threads. A *thread* in a newsgroup is a continuing discussion with one primary subject. Before trn came along, you had to read news in consecutive order from first to last, trying to assemble several different conversations into logical groups as you went. When trn became available, you could start with one thread or subject and read all the postings about that subject and then move on to another subject, regardless of the chronological order in which the postings were made.

Threads are usually handled automatically without requiring any special user interaction, although there is some work performed behind the scenes on your newsfeed. Some newsgroups do not support threading, but most do. If threads are available, you can follow the thread from start to finish, or jump out and change threads at any time.

The trn newsreader is easy to install as a binary package; an RPM is included with Red Hat Linux. To see if trn is already installed on your system, type

```
rpm -q trn
```

If no package by that name is found, you can install the trn package from the directory containing RPM files by issuing the following command:

```
rpm -i trn-3.6-12.i386.rpm
```

There really is no special configuration required for trn to run. When the binary is available on your system, it will check for the newsgroup information in /usr/lib/news and present it to you. In the past, trn wasn't capable of forming threads on its own. Because of this, external threading utilities such as mthreads or overview were once popular. As of version 3.0, however, trn supports direct threading without the need for external thread utilities, so most users now use trn as a standalone program.

Summary

In this chapter, you've seen how to install and configure the Internet News service, INN. The steps involved may seem a little overwhelming, but if you take them slowly and check everything carefully, you'll be surprised how little time it takes to have a functional newsfeed on your Linux machine. Remember that you do need a connection available to a newsfeed before you complete and test the INN configuration. Setting up TCP/IP and UUCP connections are explained elsewhere in this book.

The Domain Name Service

By Sriranga Veeraraghavan

In This Chapter

Referring to hosts by their IP addresses is convenient for computers, but humans have an easier time working with names. Obviously, we need some sort of translation table to convert IP addresses to hostnames. With millions of machines on the Internet and new ones popping up every day, it would be impossible for everyone to keep this sort of table up-to-date. This is where DNS comes in.

The Domain Name Service (DNS) is the system by which each site maintains only its own mapping of IP addresses to machine names. Each site puts this mapping into a publicly accessible database so that anyone can find the IP address corresponding to a hostname in the site by simply querying the site's database.

To access this database, you need to run a DNS server for your site. A DNS server is also known as a nameserver (NS). These servers come in three varieties:

- Primary
- Secondary
- Caching

If you are connecting to an existing network (through your school or company network, for example), you only need to run a caching server. If, on the other hand, you are setting up a new site to be accessed through the Internet, you need to set up a primary server. Secondary servers become important as your site grows to the point that the primary server can no longer handle the load from queries.

This chapter shows how to configure each of these nameservers and gives you an overview of the tasks involved in maintaining a DNS database.

A Brief History of the Internet

To understand the Domain Name System, it is important to know a little about the history of the Internet and its precursor, ARPAnet.

The Internet began in the late 1960s as an experimental wide-area computer network funded by the Department of Defense's Advanced Research Projects Agency (ARPA). This network, called ARPAnet, was intended to enalbe government scientists and engineers to share expensive computing resources. During this period only government users and a handful of computers were ever connected to ARPAnet. It remained that way until the early 1980s.

In the early 1980s, two main developments led to the popularization of ARPAnet. The first was the development of the Transmission Control Protocol and the Internet Protocol (TCP/IP). TCP/IP standardized connectivity to the ARPAnet for all computers. The second was U.C. Berkeley's version of UNIX, known as BSD. BSD was the first UNIX distribution to include TCP/IP as a networking layer. Because BSD was available to other universities at minimal cost, the number of computers connecting to ARPAnet soared.

All of a sudden, thousands of computers were connected to a network that had been designed to handle a few computers. In many cases, these new computers were simultaneously connected to a university network and to ARPAnet. At this point, it was decided that the original ARPAnet would become the backbone of the entire network, which was being called the Internet.

In 1988, the Defense Department decided the ARPAnet project had continued long enough and stopped funding it. The National Science Foundation (NSF) then supported the Internet until 1995, when private companies such as BBNPlanet, MCI, and Sprint took over the backbone.

Now millions of computers and millions of users are on the Internet, and the numbers keep rising.

The hosts.txt File

In the early days, when there were only a few hundred computers connected to the ARPAnet, every computer had a file called hosts.txt. UNIX modified the name to /etc/hosts. This file contained all the information about every host on the network, including the name-to-address mapping. With so few computers, the file was small and could be maintained easily.

The maintenance of the hosts.txt file was the responsibility of SRI-NIC, located at the Stanford Research Institute in Menlo Park, California.

When administrators wanted a change to the hosts.txt file, they emailed the request to SRI-NIC, which incorporated the request once or twice a week. This meant the administrators also had to periodically compare their hosts.txt file against the SRI-NIC hosts.txt file, and if the files were different, the administrators had to FTP a new copy of the file.

As the Internet started to grow, the idea of centrally administering hostnames and deploying the hosts.txt file became a major issue. Every time a new host was added, a change had to be made to the central version, and every other host on ARPAnet had to get the new version of the file.

In the early 1980s, SRI-NIC called for the design of a distributed database to replace the hosts.txt file. The new system was known as the Domain Name System (DNS). ARPAnet switched to DNS in September 1984, and it has been the standard method for publishing and retrieving hostname information on the Internet ever since.

DNS is a distributed database built on a hierarchical domain structure that solves the inefficiencies inherent in a large monolithic file such as hosts.txt. Under DNS, every computer that connects to the Internet connects from an Internet domain. Each Internet domain has a nameserver that maintains a database of the hosts in its domain and handles requests for hostnames. When a domain becomes too large for a single point of management, subdomains can be delegated to reduce the administrative burden.

The /etc/hosts File

Although DNS is the primary means of name resolution, the /etc/host file is still found on most machines. It can help to speed up the IP address lookup of frequently requested addresses such as the IP address of the local machine or of the nameserver. Also, during boot time, machines need to know the mapping of some hostnames to IP addresses (for example, your NIS servers) before DNS can be referenced. The IP address-to-hostname mapping for these hosts is kept in the /etc/hosts file.

Following is a sample /etc/hosts file:

```
# IP Address    Hostname    Alias
127.0.0.1       localhost
192.168.42.7    vestax      www
192.168.42.8    mailhub     mailhub.domain.com
192.168.42.6    technics
```

The leftmost column is the IP address to be resolved. The next column is the hostname corresponding to that IP address. Any subsequent columns are aliases for that host. In the second line, for example, the address `192.168.42.7` is for the host `vestax`. Another name for `vestax` is `www`. The domain name is automatically appended to the hostname by the system; however, many people append it themselves for clarity (for example, `www.domain.com`).

At the very least, you need to have the entries for

- Localhost
- Your NIS server (if you use NIS or NIS+)
- Any systems from which you mount disks
- The host itself

In this example, `localhost` is the first line, followed by `vestax`, which is a WWW server. The machine `mailhub` is used by `sendmail` for mail transfers. Finally, there is `technics`, the name of the machine from which the /etc/hosts file came.

Getting Started with DNS

This section shows you how to configure DNS clients. Then we look at some of the tools used to test and configure DNS.

Configuring the DNS Client: /etc/resolv.conf

Every machine in your network is a DNS client. To know which DNS server to use, you need to configure the file /etc/resolv.conf. This file should look something like this:

```
search domain.com
nameserver 192.168.42.1
```

Here `domain.com` is the domain name of the site, and the IP address listed after `nameserver` is the address of the DNS server that should be contacted. You can have up to three `nameserver` entries, each of which will be tried sequentially until one of them returns an answer.

> **NOTE**
>
> You must supply the nameserver's IP address, not its hostname. After all, how is the resolver going to know what the nameserver's IP address is until it finds the nameserver?

The Software of DNS

To configure a DNS for your site, you need to be familiar with the following tools:

- `named`
- The resolver library
- `nslookup`
- `traceroute`

named

The `named` daemon needs to run on DNS servers to handle queries. If `named` cannot answer a query, it forwards the request to a server that can. Along with queries, `named` is responsible for performing zone transfers. Zone transferring is the method by which changed DNS information is propagated across the Internet. You need to install the `named` daemon from the `BIND` distribution, available from `http://www.redhat.com`. It is also on the CD-ROM that comes with this book. The filename is

```
bind-4.9.5p1-2.i386.rpm
```

The Resolver Library

The resolver library enables client programs to perform DNS queries. This library is built in to the standard library under Linux.

nslookup

The `nslookup` command is a utility invoked from the command line to ensure that both the resolver and the DNS server being queried are configured correctly. It does this by resolving either a hostname into an IP address or an IP address into a domain name. To use `nslookup`, simply provide the address you want to resolve as a command line argument. For example:

```
nslookup rane.domain.com
```

The result should look something like this:

```
[root@vestax /root]# nslookup rane.domain.com
Server: numark.domain.com
Address: 192.168.42.1

Non-authoritative answer:
Name: rane.domain.com
Address: 192.168.42.8
```

traceroute

The `traceroute` utility enables you to determine the path a packet is taking across your network and into other networks. This is very useful for debugging network connection problems, especially when you suspect the trouble is located in someone else's network.

Using the ICMP protocol (same as `ping`), `traceroute` looks up each machine along the path to a destination host and displays the corresponding name and IP address for that site. With each name is the number of milliseconds each of the three tiers took to get to the destination.

Preceding each name is a number that indicates the distance to that host in terms of *hops*. The number of hops to a host indicates the number of intermediate machines that had to process the packet. As you can guess, a machine that is 1 or 2 hops away is usually much closer than a machine that is 30 hops away.

To use `traceroute`, give the destination hostname or IP address as a command-line argument. For example:

```
traceroute www.hyperreal.org
```

should return something similar to the following:

```
traceroute to hyperreal.org (204.62.130.147), 30 hops max, 40 byte packets
 1  fe0-0.cr1.NUQ.globalcenter.net (205.216.146.77)  0.829 ms  0.764 ms
➥0.519 ms
 2  pos6-0.cr2.SNV.globalcenter.net (206.251.0.30)  1.930 ms  1.839 ms
➥1.887 ms
 3  fe1-0.br2.SNV.globalcenter.net (206.251.5.2)  2.760 ms  2.779 ms
➥2.517 ms
 4  sl-stk-17-H10/0-T3.sprintlink.net (144.228.147.9)  5.117 ms  6.160 ms
➥6.109 ms
 5  sl-stk-14-F0/0.sprintlink.net (144.228.40.14)  5.453 ms  5.985 ms
➥6.157 ms
 6  sl-wired-2-S0-T1.sprintlink.net (144.228.144.138)  10.987 ms  25.130
➥ms  11.831 ms
 7  sf2-s0.wired.net (205.227.206.22)  30.453 ms  15.800 ms  21.220 ms
 8  taz.hyperreal.org (204.62.130.147)  16.745 ms  14.914 ms  13.018 ms
```

If you see any start characters (such as *) instead of a hostname, that machine is likely unavailable for a variety of reasons, with network failure and firewall protection being the most common. Also be sure to note the time it takes to get from one site to another. If you feel your connection is excessively slow, it might be just one connection in the middle that is slowing you down and not the site itself.

By using `traceroute`, you can also get a good measure of the connectivity of a site. If you are in the process of evaluating an ISP, try doing a `traceroute` from its site to a number of other sites, especially to large communications companies such as Sprint and MCI. Count how many hops and how much time per hop it takes to reach its network.

Configuring DNS Servers

As mentioned earlier, DNS comes in three flavors:

- Primary
- Secondary
- Caching

Primary DNS servers are the most authoritative of the three. When a DNS server is primary for a domain, it is considered to have the most up-to-date records for all the hosts in that site.

Secondary DNS servers are not quite as authoritative as primary. Typically, backup or offsite DNS servers for a domain are configured as secondary; hence, they don't receive the updates as quickly as the primary servers do. For all practical purposes, though, they are considered authoritative.

Caching DNS servers are not authoritative at all. When a query is made to a caching server for the first time, the query is forwarded to an authoritative server. If that server is not authoritative over the domain being queried, the request is forwarded until the authoritative server answers the query and returns it to the caching server. The caching server keeps the entry in its local cache and continues to return that answer until the entry expires.

All DNS servers should be configured to perform caching functions.

Depending on your site's configuration, you might not need your own nameserver. For instance, if you are connecting to an already existing network, there might already be a nameserver for you to use. On the other hand, if you are setting up a new department, you might want to set up a caching server for your local machines to reduce the load on your site's primary server.

CACHING NAMESERVERS AND PPP

If you plan to set up and use a PPP connection, you should definitely set up your own caching DNS server. This will reduce the load on your PPP connection.

Another way to reduce the load on your PPP connection is to have your ISP handle primary DNS resolution for your. This way, your local machine does not have to spend time answering DNS queries, and your PPP link is not slowed with these requests.

In such a setup, your machine would be `myhost.isp.com` instead of `myhost.mydomain.com`.

The /etc/named.boot File

The /etc/named.boot file is read in when `named` is started. Each line in this file begins with a keyword or a semicolon indicating the line is a comment. The format of the file is

```
; Comments begin with the semicolon
directory   directory_name
cache     .           filename
primary     domain    filename
secondary   domain    ip_addr filename
forwarders  ip_addr   [...]
```

The `directory` keyword tells `named` where any filenames mentioned in the configuration are located in the system.

The `cache` keyword makes `named` perform caching functions. The file listed at the end of the cache line contains a list of all the root DNS servers on the Internet. These root servers are needed to prime `named`'s cache. You can get the latest list of root servers from the InterNIC at

```
ftp://rs.internic.net/domain/named.cache
```

Lines beginning with `primary` indicate that the server is a primary DNS server for the listed `domain`. The entries for that server are listed in the file noted at the end of the line.

As you can predict, lines beginning with `secondary` make `named` behave as a secondary DNS server for the specified `domain`. This entry requires two parameters for a given domain:

- The IP address of the primary nameserver
- The file into which this nameserver should cache the entries pulled from the primary server

Depending on how the primary server is configured, the cached data is updated periodically via a zone transfer.

The `forwarders` line tells `named` where DNS queries should be forwarded if it cannot resolve queries on its own. If you are running a caching-only server, this should be the secondary or primary server for your site. If you are primary for your site, this should forward to your ISP's DNS server.

Primary Nameserver Configuration Files

The primary line in the /etc/named.boot file points to a file that contains the information needed for `named` to be primary for the specified domain. The file format for these configuration files is unfortunately a bit tricky and requires care when you're setting it up. Be especially careful with periods—a misplaced period can quickly become difficult to track down.

The format of each line in the configuration file is as follows:

```
name    IN    record_type    data
```

Here *`name`* is the hostname you are dealing with. Any hostnames that do not end in a period automatically get the domain name appended to them.

The second column, `IN`, is actually a parameter telling `named` to use the Internet class of records. Two other classes exist:

- `CH` for ChaosNet
- `HS` for Hesiod

ChaosNet has long been obsolete, and HS was meant to be a replacement for NIS but has been overshadowed by NIS+.

The third and fourth columns, *record_type* and *data*, respectively, indicate what kind of record you are dealing with and the parameters associated with it. There are eight possible records:

SOA	Start of authority
NS	Nameserver
A	Address record
PTR	Pointer record
MX	Mail exchanger
CNAME	Canonical name
RP and TXT	The documentation entries

SOA: Start of Authority

The SOA record starts the description of a site's DNS entries. The format of this entry is as follows:

```
domain.com. IN ns1.domain.com. hostmaster.domain.com. (
    1997082401          ; serial number
    10800               ; refresh rate in seconds (3 hours)
    1800                ; retry in seconds (30 minutes)
    1209600             ; expire in seconds (2 weeks)
    604800 )            ; minimum in seconds (1 week)
```

The first line begins with the domain for which this SOA record is authoritative. This entry is followed by IN to indicate that the Internet standard is being used. The column after the IN is the primary nameserver for this domain. Finally, the last column specifies the email address for the person in charge. Note that the email address is not in the standard *user@domain.com* form, but instead the @ symbol is replaced by a period. A good practice is to create the mail alias hostmaster at your site and have all mail sent to it and forwarded to the appropriate people.

At the end of the first line is an open parenthesis. This tells named that the line continues on to the next line, thereby making the file easier to read.

The five values presented in subsequent lines detail the characteristics of this record. The first line is the record's serial number. Whenever you make a change to any entry in this file, you need to increment this value so that secondary servers know to perform zone transfers. Typically, the current date in the form YYYYMMDDxx is used, where YYYY is the year, MM is the month, DD is the day, and xx is the revision done that day. This allows for multiple revisions in one day.

The second value is the refresh rate in seconds. This value tells the secondary DNS servers how often they should query the primary server to see if the records have been updated.

The third value is the retry rate in seconds. If the secondary server tries to contact the primary DNS server to check for updates but cannot contact it, the secondary server tries again after *retry* seconds.

When secondary servers have cached the entry, the fourth value indicates to them that if they cannot contact the primary server for an update, they should discard the value after the specified number of seconds. One to two weeks is a good value for this.

The final value, the `minimum` entry, tells caching servers how long they should wait before expiring the entry if they cannot contact the primary DNS server. Five to seven days is a good guideline for this entry.

Don't forget to place a closing parenthesis after the fifth value.

NS: Nameserver

The `NS` record specifies the authoritative nameservers for a given domain. For example:

```
IN NS    ns1.domain.com.
IN NS    ns2.domain.com.
```

Note that if the domain name for the nameserver applies to the current `SOA` record, you do not need to specify the `name` field in the DNS record.

In this example, the domain, `domain.com`, has two nameservers, `ns1.domain.com` and `ns2.domain.com`. These are fully qualified hostnames, so they need the period to suffix them. Without the period, `named` evaluates their value to be `ns1.domain.com.domain.com`, which is *not* what you're looking for.

A: Address Record

The address record is used for providing translations from hostnames to IP addresses. There should be an `A` record for each machine that needs a publicly resolvable hostname. A sample entry using the `A` record is

```
toybox    IN A        192.168.42.59
```

In this example, the address is specified for the host `toybox`. Because this hostname is not suffixed by a period, `named` assumes it is in the same domain as the current SOA record. Thus, the hostname is `toybox.domain.com`.

PTR: Pointer Record

The pointer record, also known as the reverse resolution record, tells named how to turn an IP address into a hostname. PTR records are a little odd in that they should not be in the same SOA as your A records. You will see why when you configure a small primary DNS server later in this section.

A PTR record looks like this:

```
59.42.168.192.  IN PTR  toybox.domain.com.
```

Notice that the IP address to be reverse-resolved is in reverse order and is suffixed with a period.

MX: Mail Exchanger

The mail exchanger record enables you to specify which host in your network is in charge of receiving mail from the outside. sendmail uses this record to determine the correct machine to which mail needs to be sent. The format of an MX record looks like this:

```
domain.com.     IN MX 10    mailhub
                IN MX 50    mailhub2
```

The first column indicates the hostname for which mail is received. In this case, it is for domain.com. Based on the previous examples, you might have noticed that you have yet to specify a machine that answers to domain.com., yet the sample MX record shows you can accept mail for it. This is an important feature of DNS; you can specify a hostname for which you accept mail without that hostname's having an A record.

As expected, the IN class is the second column. The third column specifies that this line is an MX record. The number after the MX indicates a priority level for that entry. Lower numbers mean higher priority. In this example, sendmail will try to communicate with mailhub first. If it cannot successfully communicate with mailhub, it will try mailhub2.

CNAME: Canonical Name

The CNAME record makes it possible to alias hostnames via DNS. This is useful for giving common names to servers. For example, we are used to Web servers having the hostname www, as in www.domain.com. However, you might not want to name the Web server this at all. On many sites, the machines have a theme to the naming of hosts, and placing www in the middle of that might appear awkward.

To use a CNAME, you must have another record for that host—such as an A or MX record—that specifies its real name. For example:

```
toybox     IN A        192.168.42.59
www        IN CNAME    toybox
```

In this example, toybox is the real name of the server and www is its alias.

RP and TXT: The Documentation Entries

Providing contact information as part of your database is often useful—not just as comments, but as actual records that can be queried by others. You can accomplish this by using the RP and TXT records.

TXT records are free-form text entries in which you can place whatever information you deem fit. Most often, you will only want to give contact information. Each TXT record must be tied to a particular hostname. For example:

```
domain.com.     IN TXT "Contact: Heidi S."
                IN TXT "Systems Administrator/Ring Master"
                IN TXT "Voice: (800) 555-1212"
```

Because TXT records are free-form, you are not forced to place contact information there. As a result, the RP record was created, which explicitly states who is the responsible person for the specified host. For example:

```
domain.com.         IN RP heidis.domain.com. domain.com.
```

The first column states for which host the responsible party is set. The second column, IN, defines this record to use the Internet class. RP designates this to be a responsible party record. The fourth column specifies the email address of the person who is actually responsible. Notice that the @ symbol has been replaced by a period in this address, much as in the SOA record. The last column specifies a TXT record that gives additional information. In this example, it points back to the TXT record for domain.com.

Configuring a Caching DNS Server

To get a caching nameserver running, you need two files in place. The first is the /etc/named.boot file, which should look like this:

```
directory /etc/dns
cache     .     root-servers
```

This configuration communicates that the data files are kept in the /etc/dns directory and that the root-servers file in that directory contains the IP addresses of the root DNS servers for priming the cache. You can obtain the most recent list of root servers from

```
ftp://rs.internic.net/domain/named.cache
```

Note that this configuration does not forward any queries it cannot answer to another server. If you have a primary server at your site, you might want to add a forwarders line to your /etc/named.boot file.

When you have the necessary files in place, all you need to do is restart the nameserver with the following command:

```
/usr/sbin/named.restart
```

Configuring a Primary and a Secondary DNS Server

In this example, you configure a primary DNS server for domain.com. Your sample domain has a handful of hosts in it and does secondary DNS for another company, `ally.com`. For this configuration, four files are needed in addition to the /etc/named.boot file.

The /etc/named.boot file for this server is

```
directory /etc/dns
cache     .                                        root-servers
primary     domain.com                             domain.hosts
primary     42.168.192.IN-ADDR.ARPA                domain.reverse
primary     0.0.127.IN-ADDR.ARPA                   local.reverse
secondary   ally.com                172.16.1.1     ally.hosts.cache
secondary   16.172.IN-ADDR.ARPA 172.16.1.1         ally.reverse.cache
```

The first two lines are straight from your caching server. This was done so that it would perform the caching functions necessary for better performance. The third line specifies the domain for which you are primary and the file containing the corresponding DNS records.

The fourth line is related to the `PTR` record mentioned earlier. So far, your /etc/named.boot file has specified only the DNS records that enable the translation of names into IP addresses. However, a good practice is to allow for the reverse translation to take place. In fact, some sites on the Internet will not allow you to connect with them unless they can make that reverse resolution.

The second column in the fourth line specifies the network for which you are providing reverse resolution. All reverse mappings exist in the `IN-ADDR.ARPA` domain, thereby eliminating any possible confusion regarding the number's purpose. The network and subnetwork parts of the IP address are placed in reverse order to follow the standard way domain names are written. Domain names describe the hostname, then the subnetwork, and then the network, whereas IP addresses describe the network, subnetwork, and finally hostname. Placing the IP address in reverse follows the convention established by the actual host and network names.

The last column in the fourth line simply tells you which file contains the reverse-mapping information. Because reverse mappings require their own `SOA` records, they need to be kept in a separate file from the forward mappings.

The fifth line of the /etc/named.boot file is the reverse-mapping information for the localhost.

The sixth and seventh lines specify that your server does secondary DNS for `ally.com`. The third column makes these entries a little different because they specify the primary DNS server for `ally.com`. It is this specified server from which your secondary server will fill its cache. The last column specifies where the cache files for `ally.com` will stay on the system.

TIP

It is common for sites to pick a naming scheme for all their hosts. This tends to make remembering names easier, especially as the site grows in size. For example, the east wing of the office might use names of famous music bands to name their machines, and the west wing might use names of Star Trek characters. This also makes locating a machine by its name easier.

Listing 13.1 contains the `domain.hosts` file.

LISTING 13.1 THE `domain.hosts` FILE

```
; forward mappings for the domain.com. hosts file
; update history:
;    August 6, 1997 - sshah@domain.com
;                     Setup primary DNS for domain.com.

@             IN SOA      domain.com. hostmaster.domain.com. (
                          1997080600    ; serial number
                          10800        ; refresh rate (3 hours)
                          1800            ; retry (30 minutes)
                          1209600        ; expire (2 weeks)
                          604800 )        ; minimum (1 week)
              IN NS       ns1.domain.com
              IN NS       ns2.domain.com
              IN MX 10    mailhub.domain.com
numark        IN A        192.168.42.1
ns1           IN CNAME    numark
domain.com.   IN CNAME    numark
```

continues

LISTING 13.1 CONTINUED

```
mtx             IN A        192.168.42.2
ns2             IN CNAME    mtx
pioneer         IN A        192.168.42.3
denon           IN A        192.168.42.4
atus            IN A        192.168.42.5
technics        IN A        192.168.42.6
vestax          IN A        192.168.42.7
www             IN CNAME    vestax
rane            IN A        192.168.42.8
mailhub         IN CNAME    rane
```

Did you notice the use of the @ symbol instead of the domain name? You can use this shortcut because the domain name is specified in the /etc/named.boot file.

An additional note regarding names: As mentioned in the preceding tip, using themes in naming machines is helpful from a management perspective. Listing 13.1 uses the names of companies that make professional audio gear. In keeping with this sort of theme, however, you might run into an instance in which outsiders expect certain names for systems such as your Web server. By default, most people expect Web servers to begin with www, as in www.domain.com. Although you can name the machine www, two issues arise:

- This breaks the naming theme. If your site is large enough, this can become a problem.
- This can get cumbersome. If you want to start using a new Web server, you have to change all the machine's configurations accordingly. Changing the CNAME entry in your DNS to point to a new Web server is much easier.

Listing 13.2 contains the domain.reverse file.

LISTING 13.2 THE domain.reverse FILE

```
; reverse mappings for domain.com
; revision history: sshah@domain.com, Aug. 6, 1997
@               IN SOA    domain.com. hostmaster.domain.com. (
                          1997080600    ; serial number
                          10800        ; refresh rate (3 hours)
                          1800            ; retry (30 minutes)
                          1209600        ; expire (2 weeks)
                          604800 )        ; minimum (1 week)
                IN NS     ns1.domain.com
                IN NS     ns2.domain.com
192.168.42.1    IN PTR    numark
192.168.42.2    IN PTR    mtx
```

```
192.168.42.3      IN PTR      pioneer
192.168.42.4      IN PTR      denon
192.168.42.5      IN PTR      atus
192.168.42.6      IN PTR      technics
192.168.42.7      IN PTR      vestax
192.168.42.8      IN PTR      rane
```


Finally, Listing 13.3 contains the `local.reverse` file.

LISTING 13.3 THE `local.reverse` FILE

```
; local.reverse
@           IN SOA    domain.com. hostmaster.domain.com. (
                      1997080600    ; serial number
                      10800        ; refresh rate (3 hours)
                      1800            ; retry (30 minutes)
                      1209600        ; expire (2 weeks)
                      604800 )        ; minimum (1 week)
            IN NS     ns1.domain.com
            IN NS     ns2.domain.com
1           IN PTR    localhost.domain.com.
```

Troubleshooting and Debugging DNS

One of the main debugging tools you have with `in.named` is having the daemon dump its cached database to a text file. To have `in.named` dump its cache, you must send the daemon an `INT` signal. The file /etc/named.pid contains the process ID of `in.named`. The following command sends the INT signal to `in.named`:

```
kill -INT  `cat /etc/named.pid`
```

The file /var/tmp/named_dump.db will contain the cache information that was dumped. The cache file will look identical to a zone database file.

The `in.named` daemon also supports debug logging. To start the daemon logging, send the daemon a `USR1` signal like this:

```
kill -USR1  `cat /etc/named.pid`
```

The logging information is logged in the /var/tmp/named.run file. If the `USR1` signal is sent to the daemon, the verbosity of the logging information increases. To reset the debug level to `0`, send the daemon a `USR2` signal.

The HUP signal can be sent to the named daemon each time a zone database is changed. The HUP signal re-reads the databases without having to kill and restart the `in.named` daemon. The following example sends the HUP signal to `in.named`:

```
kill -HUP  `cat /etc/named.pid`
```

RESTARTING BIND AFTER MAKING CHANGES

If alterations are made to the /etc/named.boot file, the `in.named` daemon must be stopped and restarted to see the changes.

Summary

This chapter covered the historical motivations for the creation of DNS, as well as different types of nameservers and demonstrated a sample DNS query. We have examined the creation and maintenance of the DNS database files. We have also examined the configuration and troubleshooting of DNS. With the material covered in this chapter, you should have a good idea of how name resolution works on the Internet.

CHAPTER

The Network Information Service

by Steve Shah

In This Chapter

The Network Information Service (NIS) is a simple, generic client/server database system. Under Linux, however, the most common use for it is sharing password and group files across a network. This chapter covers the setup of both master and slave NIS servers as well as the configuration needed for clients to use them.

NIS, developed by Sun Microsystems as part of its SunOS operating system, was originally known as "The Yellow Pages," or YP for short. Unfortunately, the name Yellow Pages had already been trademarked, and the resulting lawsüit forced the name change to NIS. You will soon discover that all the NIS commands are still prefixed with `yp`.

The NIS protocol was made public, and implementations of it quickly spread to other variations of UNIX. Linux has supported NIS from its onset. Because Linux follows the NIS standard, it can work with other flavors of UNIX as either the NIS server or client.

Recently, NIS has been updated to NIS+. NIS+ addresses many of the concerns with NIS, most notably in the areas of security. As of this writing, Linux support for NIS+ through the NYS libraries has been weak. Server support is not ready, and the client software isn't complete. Because it is still developmental, I do not cover NIS+ here.

Understanding NIS

As you configure your network, you will find that some of your configuration files are not host specific, but they require frequent updating. `/etc/passwd` and `/etc/group` are two that come to mind. NIS enables you to set up a master server where these files are stored and then configure each machine on your network as clients to this server. Whenever a client needs to fetch an entry from the `/etc/passwd` file, it consults the NIS server instead.

For a file to be sharable via NIS, two prerequisites must be met. First, the file must be tabular with at least one entry that is unique across the entire file. In the `/etc/passwd` file, this entry is either the login or UID. Second, the file in its raw form must be a straight text file.

With the criteria met, the files are converted into DBM files, a simple database format allowing for quick searches. You must create a separate DBM for each key to be searched. In the `/etc/passwd` file, for instance, you need the database to be searchable by login and by UID. The result is two DBM files, `passwd.byname` and `passwd.byuid`.

The original text file, along with the DBM files created from it, is maintained at the NIS master server. Clients that connect to the server to obtain information do not cache any returned results.

NIS Domains

NIS servers and clients must be in the same NIS domain to communicate with one another. Note that the NIS domain is not the same as a DNS domain, although it is valid for them share the same name.

TIP

You should maintain separate names for your NIS and DNS domains for two reasons. First, it is easier for you to differentiate what you're talking about when discussing problems with anyone else. Second, having separate names makes it more difficult for potential intruders to understand the internal workings of your machines from the outside.

Both the clients and servers bind themselves to a domain; hence, a client can belong to only one NIS domain at a given time. Once bound, clients send a broadcast to find the NIS server for the given domain.

The Different Servers

So far, you might have noticed that I've referenced the NIS server explicitly as the "master" server. The two kinds of NIS servers are master servers and slave servers.

Master NIS servers are the actual truth holders. They contain the text files used to generate the DBM files, and any changes to the database must be made to these files.

Slave NIS servers are designed to supplement master NIS servers by taking some of the load off. When a file is updated on the server, a server push is initiated, and the slave NIS server gets an updated copy of the DBM files.

CAUTION

Like any network service, NIS might have bugs that can allow unauthorized access to your system. It is prudent to keep track of security reports and obtain patches when they become available. The two best places to start are the Computer Emergency Response Team Web site at `www.cert.org` and the `comp.os.linux.announce` newsgroup. Both provide a moderated source of information that you can use to maintain your system.

Installing the Software

If you didn't install the NIS software during the initial setup process, you need to install it now. Start by mounting the Red Hat CD-ROM. I assume that the CD-ROM is in the `/mnt/cdrom` directory.

Access the `/mnt/cdrom/RedHat/RPMS` directory:

```
[root@server /root]# cd /mnt/cdrom/RedHat/RPMS
```

Install the RPMS `yp-tools-1.4.1-2.i386.rpm`, `ypbind-3.3-7.i386.rpm`, and `ypserv-1.3.1-2.i386` with the following commands:

```
[root@server RPMS]# rpm -i yp-tools-1.4.1-2.i386.rpm
[root@server RPMS]# rpm -i ypbind-3.3-7.i386.rpm
[root@server RPMS]# rpm -i ypserv-1.3.1-2.i386.rpm
```

Configuring a Master NIS Server

Before you configure the server software, you need to decide whether you are going to set up any slave servers. If you are, you need to know their hostnames before continuing. Along with the names of your NIS servers, you need to decide on a domain name at this point. Remember that this domain name is not the same as your DNS domain name and for clarity purposes should be set differently.

With this information, you are ready to begin. First, you need to set the domain name with the `domainname` command:

```
[root@vestax /etc]# domainname audionet.domain.com
```

Although this will work for the moment, you do need to change a startup configuration file so that this happens every time your system reboots. The `/etc/rc.d/init.d/ypserv` script that was installed as part of the RPM looks for the domain name to be set in the `/etc/sysconfig/network` file. Simply add the following line:

```
NIS_DOMAIN=audionet.domain.com
```

With the domain name set, you can decide what files you want to share via NIS, as well as their filenames. You do this by editing `/var/yp/Makefile`. As the name implies, NIS maintains its maps by using the `make` utility. Although familiarity with how this tool works is useful, it isn't mandatory to configure NIS.

Begin by loading `/var/yp/Makefile` into your favorite editor. Scroll past the lines that read

```
# These are files from which the NIS databases are built. You may edit
# these to taste in the event that you wish to keep your NIS source files
# separate from your NIS server's actual configuration files.
```

Below this segment of text, you will see lines that resemble the following:

```
GROUP        = $(YPPWDDIR)/group
PASSWD       = $(YPPWDDIR)/passwd
etc...
```

NOTE

As you scroll down the file, you will notice several parameters you can set to alter the behavior of the NIS server. For the time being, you probably shouldn't alter anything except for those items I discuss in this section. If you are feeling adventurous, read the comments associated with each line and have fun with it.

This section tells NIS where your database files are located. The `$(YPPWDDIR)` string is a variable that was set to `/etc` at the top of the `Makefile`. Although it is possible to change this to another directory, you should probably keep it there for consistency. The string that comes after `$(YPPWDDIR)` is the name of the file in `/etc` that will become shared through NIS. Most of these entries can remain the same. The few that you want to change are `GROUP`, `PASSWD`, `SHADOW`, `ALIASES`, and possibly `HOSTS`.

The `GROUP` line shows that the file for controlling group information is at `/etc/group`. You might want to keep your local group file on the server separate from your NIS group file because your local group file could contain server-specific groups that you don't want to share across NIS, such as the `www` group for your Web server.

The same holds true for the other lines as well, especially the `PASSWD` line. A simple convention you can use to indicate that the file is being shared across NIS is to suffix it with a `.yp`. The resulting line looks something like the following:

```
PASSWD          = $(YPPWDDIR)/passwd.yp
```

NOTE

By default, the NIS server will not distribute any password entries with a UID or GID below 500. To change this, look for the line reading `MINUID=500` in the makefile. Right below it is `MINGID=500`. Changing their values will change the minimum UIDs and GIDs. Unless you already have a UID/GID numbering system that includes values below 500, you will probably want to keep this setting as is.

With the filenames you want set, you can now determine which files to distribute. Scroll down the makefile past the following block:

```
# If you don't want some of these maps built, feel free to comment
# them out of this list.
```

Your cursor should be at the following line:

```
all:  ypservers passwd group hosts rpc services netid protocols mail \
        # shadow publickey # netgrp networks ethers bootparams \
        # amd.home auto.master auto.home
```

This line specifies which maps will be made available via NIS. The # symbol after shadow is the comment symbol. The second and third lines are commented out.

Before making any changes to this line, you should make a copy of it and comment the copy out. The result looks something like the following:

```
#all:  ypservers passwd group hosts rpc services netid protocols mail \
#        # shadow publickey # netgrp networks ethers bootparams \
#        # amd.home auto.master auto.home

all:  ypservers passwd group hosts rpc services netid protocols mail \
        # shadow publickey # netgrp networks ethers bootparams \
        # amd.home auto.master auto.home
```

By commenting out the line, you can retain a copy of it just in case something goes wrong. You can always refer to the copy and see how the line looked before things were changed. With the copy in place, go ahead and begin your changes.

The only files you need to distribute for your network are `ypservers`, `passwd`, `group`, `hosts`, `rpc`, `services`, `netid`, `protocols`, and `mail`. This distribution is already set so you don't need to change anything.

NOTE

What are those other lines for? Good question! They are other databases that some sites distribute as well. As you need specific entries in that list, you can simply uncomment them and include them for distribution to your clients. At some sites, NIS is used to distribute other kinds of information, so you can create custom entries. You can even use NIS to make a company-wide telephone directory.

Unless you are comfortable with makefiles, you should leave the remainder of the file alone. Save the makefile and quit the editor.

You are ready to initialize your NIS database with the `/usr/lib/yp/ypinit` command. When invoked, this command prompts for the name of any NIS slave servers you want to set up. For this example, select `denon` to be the slave NIS server.

Remember that you do not have to set up a slave NIS server. Setting up a slave server is only useful if you have a large number of NIS clients and you need to distribute the load they generate.

To initialize the master server, use the following:

```
 [root@vestax /root]# /usr/lib/yp/ypinit -m
At this point, we have to construct a list of the hosts which will run NIS
servers. vestax is in the list of NIS server hosts. Please continue to add
the names for the other hosts, one per line. When you are done with the
list, type a <control D>.
    next host to add:  vestax
    next host to add:  denon
    next host to add: <CTRL-D>
The current list of NIS servers looks like this:

vestax
denon

Is this correct?  [y/n: y]  y
We need some minutes to build the databases...
Building /var/yp/audionet.domain.com/ypservers...
Running /var/yp/Makefile...
NIS Map update started on Mon May  5 22:16:53 PDT 1997
make[1]: Entering directory '/var/yp/audionet.domain.com'
Updating passwd.byname...
Updating passwd.byuid...
Updating hosts.byname...
Updating hosts.byaddy...
Updating group.byname...
Updating group.bygid...
Updating netid.byname...
Updating protocols.bynumber...
Updating protocols.byname...
Updating rpc.byname...
Updating rpc.bynumber...
Updating services.byname...
Updating mail.aliases...
make[1]: Leaving directory '/var/yp/audionet.domain.com'
NIS Map update completed
```

If anywhere in the middle of the output you received a message like the following instead,

```
make[1]:***No rule to make target '/etc/shadow', needed by 'shadow.byname'.
Stop.
make[1]: Leaving directory '/var/yp/audionet.domain.com'
```

it means that you are missing one of the files you listed in the makefile. Check that you edited the makefile as you intended, and then make sure that the files you selected to be shared via NIS actually do exist. After you've made sure of these, you do not need to rerun `ypinit` but instead can simply rerun `cd /var/yp;make`.

Starting the Daemons on Boot

To start the NIS server automatically at boot time, you need to create a symbolic link from the runlevel 3 startup directory. To do this, type the following:

```
[root@client /root]# cd /etc/rc.d/rc3.d
[root@client rc3.d]# ln -s ../init.d/ypserv S60ypserv
```

The `yppasswdd` daemon allows users from NIS clients to change their passwords on the NIS server. To start this program automatically at boot time, you need to type the following:

```
[root@client /root]# cd /etc/rc.d/rc3.d
[root@client rc3.d]# ln -s ../init.d/yppasswdd S61yppasswdd
```

If you want to start the daemons by hand so you don't need to reboot, simply run

```
[root@client /root]# /etc/rc.d/init.d/ypserv
start;/etc/rc.d/init.d/yppasswdd
```

```
➥start
```

You now have a NIS master server. Time to test the work with an NIS client.

Configuring an NIS Client

Compared to configuring an NIS server, NIS clients are trivial. You must deal with only four files, one of which is only one line long.

Begin by creating the `/etc/yp.conf` file. This file needs only two lines, one to specify the NIS domain name and the other to specify the NIS server hostname. The format of this file is

```
domain domainname server nis_server
```

`domainname` is the name of your NIS domain, and *`nis_server`* is the server's hostname. For this example, this file should look like the following:

```
domain audionet.domain.com server vestax.domain.com
```

The next step is to edit the `/etc/sysconfig/network` file to set the NIS domainname for boot time. To do this, simply add the line

```
NISDOMAIN=domainname
```

domainname is the same as specified in the /etc/yp.conf file (in this case, audionet.domain.com).

The last file that needs to be changed is the /etc/nsswitch.conf file. This is slightly more involved than the previous files; however, a default file comes with the Red Hat installation. This file is used to configure which services are used to determine information such as hostnames, password files, and group files.

Begin by opening /etc/nsswitch.conf with your favorite editor. Scroll past the comments (those lines beginning with the # symbol). You should see something like this:

```
passwd:    files nis
shadow:    files nis
group:    files nis

hosts:    files nis dns

services:     files [NOTFOUND=return] nis
etc...
```

The first column indicates the file in question. In the first line, this is passwd. The next column indicates the source for the file. This can be one of six options:

Option	*Description*
nis	Uses NIS to determine this information.
yp	Uses NIS to determine this information (alias for nis).
dns	Uses DNS to determine this information (only applicable to hosts).
files	Uses the file on the local machine to determine this information (for example, /etc/passwd).
[NOTFOUND=return]	Stops searching if the information has not been found yet.
nis+	Uses NIS+. (You won't use this because of the incomplete support for NIS+ under Linux.)

The order these are placed in the /etc/nsswitch.conf file determines the search order used by the system. For example, in the hosts line, the order of the entries are files nis dns, indicating that hostnames are first searched for in the /etc/hosts file, then via NIS in the map hosts.byname, and finally by DNS via the DNS server specified in /etc/resolv.conf.

In almost all instances, you want to search the local file before searching through NIS or DNS. This allows a machine to have local characteristics (such as a special user listed in

/etc/passwd) while still using the network services being offered. The notable exception to this is the netgroup file that by its very nature should come from NIS.

Modify the order of your searches to suit your site's needs and save the configuration file.

Now that all the files are in place, set up the client daemon to automatically start at boot time. You do this by creating a symbolic link from /etc/rc.d/rc.3/S60ypbind to /etc/rc.d/init.d/ypbind. The exact commands are

```
[root@client /root]# cd /etc/rc.d/rc3.d
[root@client rc3.d]# ln -s ../init.d/ypbind S60ypbind
```

Testing the Client

Because of the way NIS works under Red Hat, you do not need to reboot to start NIS client functions. To see if you can communicate with the NIS server, start by setting the domainname by hand. You can do this with the command

```
[root@client /root]# domainname nis_domain
```

nis_domain is the NIS domain name. In the test case, it is audionet.domain.com. Now, start the NIS client daemon, ypbind, with the command

```
[root@client /root]# /etc/rc.d/init.d/ypbind start
```

With the NIS client and server configured, you are ready to test your work:

```
ypcat passwd
```

If your configuration is working, you should see the contents of your NIS server's /etc/passwd.yp file displayed on your screen (assuming, of course, that you chose that file to be shared via NIS for your passwd file). If you received a message such as

```
No such map passwd.byname. Reason: can't bind to a server which serves
domain
```

you need to double-check that your files have been properly configured.

TIP

As a precautionary measure, you should schedule a reboot while you are with the machine to ensure that it does start and configure the NIS information correctly. After all, your users will not be happy if after a power failure, your machine does not come back up correctly without assistance.

Configuring an NIS Secondary Server

After you've decided to configure a machine as an NIS secondary server, you start by configuring it as an NIS client machine. Verify that you can access the server maps via the `ypcat` command.

Now you are ready to tell the master server that a slave server exists. To do this, edit the `/var/yp/ypservers` file so that the slave server you are setting up is included in the list. If you configured your master server with the name of the slave server during the `ypinit -m` phase, you do not need to do this.

You can now initialize the slave server by running the command

```
/usr/lib/yp/ypinit -s master
```

where *`master`* is the hostname for the NIS master server. In this example, it's `vestax`. The output should look something like the following:

```
We will need some minutes to copy the databases from vestax.
Transferring mail.aliases...
Trying ypxfrd ... not running
Transferring services.byname...
Trying ypxfrd ... not running
Transferring rpc.bynumber...
Trying ypxfrd ... not running
[etc...]

denon.domain.com's NIS database has been set up.
If there were warnings, please figure out what went wrong, and fix it.

At this point, make sure that /etc/passwd and /etc/group have
been edited so that when the NIS is activated, the databases you
have just created will be used, instead of the /etc ASCII files.
```

Don't worry about the `Trying ypxfrd...not running` message. This happens because you haven't set the NIS master server to run the YP map transfer daemon `rpc.ypxfrd`. In fact, you never set it up to do so; instead, use a server push method where the NIS master server pushes the maps to all the NIS slaves whenever there is an update.

To set the NIS master to do the actual push, you need to change its makefile a little. On the master server, edit the makefile so that the line `NOPUSH="True"` is changed to read `#NOPUSH="True"` and the line that reads `DOMAIN = 'basename \'pwd\''` is changed to `DOMAIN='/bin/domainname'`.

Now for the big test: On the NIS master server, run `cd /var/yp;make all` to force all the maps to be rebuilt and pushed. The output should look something like the following:

```
Updating passwd.byname....
Pushed passwd.byname map.
Updating passwd.byuid...
Pushed passwd.byuid map.
Updating hosts.byname...
Pushed hosts.byname.
Updating hosts.byaddr...
Pushed hosts.byaddr.
[etc...]
```

On the NIS slave server, change the `/etc/yp.conf` file so that the `ypserver` is set to point to the slave server. Run the command `ypcat passwd`, and see whether your NIS password file is displayed. If so, you're set. The NIS slave server is configured.

If you're having problems, trace through your steps. Also, be sure to reboot the machine and see if your NIS slave server still works correctly. If it doesn't come back up, be sure that the changes you made to the boot sequence when installing `ypserv` were correct.

TIP

If your NIS client or slave server seems to have a hard time finding other hosts on the network, be sure that the `/etc/nsswitch.conf` file is set to resolve hosts by file before NIS. Then, be sure that all the important hosts needed for the NIS servers to set themselves up are in their own local `/etc/hosts` file.

Using NIS-isms in Your `/etc/passwd` File

The most popular use of NIS is to keep a global user database so that it is possible to grant access to any machine at your site to any user. Under Red Hat Linux, this behavior is implicit for all NIS clients.

Sometimes, however, you do not want everyone accessing certain systems, such as those used by personnel. You can fix this access by using the special token + in your `/etc/passwd` file. By default, NIS clients have the line `+::::::` at the end of their `/etc/passwd` file, thereby allowing everyone in NIS to log in to the system. To arrange that the host remains an NIS client but does not grant everyone permission, change the line to read `+::::::/bin/false`. This will allow only people with actual entries in the `/etc/passwd` file for that host (for example, `root`) to log in.

To allow a specific person to log in to a host, you can add a line to the /etc/passwd file granting this access. The format of the line is *+username*:::::: where *username* is the login of the user you want to grant access to. NIS will automatically grab the user's passwd entry from the NIS server and use the correct information for determining the user information (for example, UID, GID, GECOS, and so on). You can override particular fields by inserting the new value in the *+username*:::::: entry. For example, if the user sshah uses /usr/local/bin/tcsh as his shell, but the host he needs to log in to keeps it in /bin/tcsh, you can set his /etc/passwd entry to +sshah::::::/bin/tcsh.

Using Netgroups

Netgroups are a great way to group people and machines into nice neat names for access control. A good example of using this feature is for a site where users are not allowed to log in to server machines. You can create a netgroup for the system administrators and let in members of the group through a special entry in the /etc/passwd file.

Netgroup information is kept in the /etc/netgroup file and shared via NIS.

The format of a netgroups file is

```
groupname member-list
```

groupname is the name of the group being defined, and the *member-list* consists of other group names or tuples of specific data. Each entry in the *member-list* is separated by a whitespace.

A tuple containing specific data comes in the form

```
(hostname, username, domain name)
```

hostname is the name of the machine for which that entry is valid, *username* is the login of the person being referenced, and *domain name* is the NIS domain name. Any entry left blank is considered a wildcard; for example, (technics,,,) implies everybody on the host technics. An entry with a dash in it (-) means that there are no valid values for that entry. For example, (-,sshah,) implies the user sshah and nothing else. This is useful for generating a list of users or machine names for use in other netgroups.

In files where netgroups are supported (such as /etc/passwd), you reference them by placing an @ sign in front of them. If you want to give the netgroup sysadmins consisting of (-,sshah,) (-,heidis,) permission to log in to a server, you add the line

```
+@sysadmins
```

to your /etc/passwd file.

An example of a full netgroups file follows:

```
sysadmins    (-,sshah,) (-,heidis,) (-,jnguyen,) (-,mpham,)
servers      (numark,-,) (vestax,-,)
clients      (denon,-,) (technics,-,) (mtx,-,)
research-1   (-,boson,) (-,jyom,) (-,weals,) (-,jaffe,)
research-2   (-,sangeet,) (-,mona,) (-,paresh,) (-,manjari,) (-,jagdish,)
consultants  (-,arturo,)
allusers       sysadmins research-1 research-2 consultants
allhosts       servers clients
```

Some Troubleshooting Tips

If the NIS software isn't behaving as you think it should, you can check a few some things:

- Make sure the processes are running. Use `ps auxw` to list all the running processes. Make sure you see the appropriate processes running, regardless of whether the machine is a client, a server, or both.
- Check system logs (in `/var/log`) to see if there are any messages indicating peripheral problems that could be affecting your configuration.
- If the processes appear to be running but are not responsive, kill them and restart them. In some rare circumstances, the daemon may be misbehaving and need to be restarted.
- Make sure `/etc/nsswitch.conf` is configured properly. This is a common problem.
- If you are trying to start the daemons by hand, make sure you are logged in as `root`.

When encountering problems, slow down, take a short break, and then retrace your steps. It's amazing how often simply slowing down helps you find problems.

Summary

In this chapter, I covered the installation and configuration of NIS master servers, secondary servers, and clients. In addition to the setup of NIS itself, I discussed common "NIS-isms" and netgroups. The lessons learned from these sections puts a powerful tool in your hands.

Some key points to remember are

- Use `ypinit` to set up NIS master servers and secondary servers.
- The `/var/yp` directory contains the makefile necessary to update NIS information.

- Consider separating NIS files from your regular system files for clarity.
- NIS servers need the `ypserv` daemon.
- NIS clients need the `ypbind` daemon.
- `yppasswdd` allows users on NIS clients to change their passwords.
- Schedule a reboot to test all your changes.

Although it isn't the most exciting feature to come along in recent history, NIS is one of the most useful of the core network services. In conjunction with other services, NIS gives you the ability to create a seamless system for all of your users.

CHAPTER

The Network File System

by Steve Shah

In This Chapter

The Network File System, or NFS, is the means by which UNIX systems share their disk resources. What makes NFS really useful is its ability to function in a heterogeneous environment. Most if not all UNIX variants have support for NFS, and for not too much money, you can find NFS support for Microsoft Windows, making it a good choice for sharing disks.

NFS was originally developed by Sun Microsystems during the 1980s. It shared its design and made the protocol a standard, which eliminated any interoperability conflicts with other operating systems. Linux supported NFS before version 1.0 was released.

A key feature of NFS is its robust nature. It is a *stateless protocol*, meaning that each request made between the client and server is complete in itself and does not require knowledge of prior transactions. Because of this, NFS cannot tell the difference between a very slow host and a host that has failed altogether. This allows for servers to go down and come back up without having to reboot the clients. If this doesn't make much sense, don't worry about it. Understanding the underlying protocol isn't necessary to set up and successfully run an NFS server.

NOTE

In Chapter 14, "Samba," you'll read about how Linux can share its disks with Windows machines. NFS and Samba are *not* the same. They are two different protocols with two fundamentally different views on how disks should be shared. One of the many things that makes Linux great is its ability to support both means of sharing disks at the same time. In fact, it is a common situation for Linux servers to share disks with each other through NFS and then with Windows-based clients with Samba at the same time.

CAUTION

NFS's design by nature is, unfortunately, insecure. Although taking some steps provides a moderate level of security to protect you from the common user pretending to be an evil hacker, there is not much more you can do. Any time you share a disk via NFS with another machine, you need to give the users of that machine (especially the root user) a certain amount of trust. If you believe that the person you are sharing the disk with is untrustworthy, you need to explore alternatives to NFS for sharing data and disk space.

Keep up with security bulletins from both Red Hat and the Computer Emergency Response Team (CERT). You can find these bulletins on Red Hat's site at www.redhat.com, CERT's site at www.cert.org, or the moderated newsgroup comp.security.announce.

Installing NFS

Although the NFS software comes preinstalled with Red Hat Linux, you need to be aware of what the software is and what each specific program does. This is important when troubleshooting problems and configuring NFS-related tools such as the automounter.

Three programs provide NFS server services:

`rpc.portmapper` This program does not directly provide NFS services itself; however, it maps calls made from other machines to the correct NFS daemons.

`rpc.nfsd` This daemon is what translates the NFS requests into actual requests on the local filesystem.

`rpc.mountd` This daemon's services request to mount and unmount filesystems.

NOTE

The `rpc.nfsd` and `rpc.mountd` programs need only run on your NFS servers. In fact, you might find it prudent to not run them at all on your client machines for security concerns and to free resources that might otherwise be consumed by them. NFS clients do not need any special NFS software to run. They should, however, run the `rpc.portmapper` program because it provides RPC functionality to programs other than NFS.

By default, these programs are installed and loaded at boot time. To check for this, use the `rpcinfo` command as follows:

```
rpcinfo -p
```

This will display all the registered RPC programs running on your system. To check which RPC programs are registered on a remote host, use `rpcinfo` such as

```
rpcinfo -p hostname
```

where *hostname* is the name of the remote host you want to check. The output for a Linux host running NFS appears something like the following:

```
[root@vestax /root]# rpcinfo -p
  program   vers   proto   port
   100000      2     tcp    111    portmapper
   100000      2     udp    111    portmapper
   100005      1     udp    821    mountd
   100005      1     tcp    823    mountd
   100003      2     udp   2049    nfs
   100003      2     tcp   2049    nfs
```

Starting and Stopping the NFS Daemons

You might run across instances when you need to stop NFS and restart it later. You can do this using the startup scripts that are executed at boot time and shutdown. NFS's scripts are in `/etc/rc.d/init.d/nfs`.

To start the NFS services, run the following as root:

```
[root@vestax /root]# /etc/rc.d/init.d/nfs start
```

To stop NFS services, run the following as root:

```
[root@vestax /root]# /etc/rc.d/init.d/nfs stop
```

Configuring NFS Servers and Clients

The two key files to NFS are `/etc/exports` and `/etc/fstab`. The `exports` file is configured on the server side. This file specifies which directories are to be shared with which clients and each client's access rights. The `fstab` file is configured on the client side and specifies which servers to contact for certain directories as well as where to place them in the directory tree.

Setting Up the `/etc/exports` File

The `/etc/exports` file specifies which directories to share with which hosts on the network. You only need to set up this file on your NFS servers.

The `/etc/exports` file follows this format:

```
/directory/to/export     host1(permissions) host2(permissions)
            ➥host3(permissions) host4(permissions)
```

```
#
# Comments begin with the pound sign and must be at the start of
# the line
#
/another/dir/to/export    host2(permissions) host5(permissions)
```

In this example, */directory/to/export* is the directory you want to make available to other machines on the network. You must supply the absolute pathname for this entry. On the same line, you list the hosts and what permissions they have to access. If the list is longer than the line size permits, you can use the standard continuation character (the backslash, \) to continue onto the next line.

You specify the names of the hosts in four ways:

- Their direct hostname.
- Using `@`*group* where *group* is the specific netgroup. Wildcard hosts in the group are ignored.
- Wildcards in the hostname. The asterisk (`*`) can match an entire network. For example, `*.engr.widgets.com` matches all hosts that end in `.engr.widgets.com`.
- IP subnets can be matched with address/netmask combinations. For example, to match everything in the 192.168.42.0 network where the netmask is 255.255.255.0, you use `192.168.42.0/24`.

Each host is given a set of access permissions. They are as follows:

`rw`	Read and write access.
`ro`	Read-only access.
`noaccess`	Denies access to all subdirectories below the listed directory. This is useful when you want to export most of a directory tree. You can export high in the tree and set a few exceptions rather than export a large number of small subdirectories.
`no_root_squash`	Acknowledge and trust the client's root account.

If you are familiar with the export file configurations of other flavors of UNIX, you know that this process is not similar. Whether one is better than the other is a holy war discussion best left to Usenet newsgroups.

After you set up your `/etc/exports` file, run the `exportfs` command with the `-a` option:

```
exportfs -a
```

This sends the appropriate signals to the `rpc.nfsd` and `rpc.mountd` daemons to reread the `/etc/exports` file and update their internal tables.

TIP

It is considered a good convention to place all the directories you want to export in the `/export` hierarchy. This makes the intent clear and self-documenting. If you need the directory to also exist elsewhere in the directory tree, use symbolic links. For example, if your server is exporting its `/usr/local` hierarchy, you should place the directory in `/export`, thereby creating `/export/usr/local`. Because the server itself will need access to the `/export/usr/local` directory, you should create a symbolic link from `/usr/local` pointing to the real location, `/export/usr/local`.

TIP

If you have an error in your `/etc/exports` file, it is reported when NFS starts up in `syslog`. Read the section on `syslog` in this book to find out more about this wonderful debugging tool.

Using `mount` to Mount an Exported Filesystem

To mount a filesystem, use the `mount` command:

```
mount servername:/exported/dir /dir/to/mount
```

`servername` is the name of the server from which you want to mount a filesystem, *`/exported/dir`* is the directory listed in its `/etc/exports` file, and *`/dir/to/mount`* is the location on your local machine where you want to mount the filesystem. For example, to mount `/export/home` from the NFS server `denon` to the directory `/home`, you use

```
mount denon:/export/home /home
```

Remember that the directory must exist in your local filesystem before anything can be mounted there.

You can pass options to the `mount` command. The most important characteristics are specified in the `-o` options. These characteristics follow:

`rw`	Read/write.
`ro`	Read-only.
`bg`	Background mount. Should the mount initially fail (the server is down, for instance), the mount process will place itself in the background and continue trying until it is successful. This is useful for filesystems

	mounted at boot time because it keeps the system from hanging at that mount if the server is down.
`intr`	Interruptible mount. If a process is pending I/O on a mounted partition, it will allow the process to be interrupted and the I/O call to be dropped.
`soft`	By default, NFS operations are "hard," meaning that they require the server to acknowledge completion before returning to the calling process. The soft option allows the NFS client to return a failure to the calling process after `retrans` number of retries.
`retrans`	Specifies the maximum number of retried transmissions to a soft-mounted filesystem.
`wsize`	Specifies the number of bytes to be written across the network at once. The default is `8192` (for example, `wsize=2048`). You shouldn't change this value unless you are sure of what you are doing. Setting this value too low or too high can have a negative impact on your system's performance.
`rsize`	Specify the number of bytes read across the network at once. Like `wsize`, the default is 8192 bytes. The same warning applies as well: Changing the value without understanding the effect can have a negative impact on your system's performance.

Here's an example of these parameters in use:

```
mount -o rw,bg,intr,soft,retrans=6 denon:/export/home /home
```


NOTE

There are many more options to the `mount` command; however, you will rarely ever see them. See the man page for `mount` for additional details.

CAUTION

Solaris NFS clients talking to Linux NFS servers seem to bring out a bug in the Linux NFS implementation. If you suddenly notice normal files being treated as directories or other such unusual behavior, change the `wsize` and `rsize` to 2048 when mounting the directory. This appears to fix the problem without hurting performance too drastically.

Unmounting a Filesystem

To unmount the filesystem, use the `umount` command:

```
umount /home
```

This will unmount the `/home` filesystem.

There is, of course, a caveat. If users are using files on a mounted filesystem, you cannot unmount it. All files must be closed before the unmount can happen, which on a large system can be tricky, to say the least. There are three ways to handle this:

- Use the `lsof` program (available at `ftp://vic.cc.purdue.edu/pub/tools/unix/lsof`) to list the users and their open files on a given filesystem. Then, either wait until they are done, beg and plead for them to leave, or kill their processes. Then, you can unmount the filesystem. This isn't the most desirable way to achieve an unmount, but you'll find that this is often the path you need to take.
- Use `umount` with the `-f` option to force the filesystem to unmount. This is often a bad idea because it confuses the programs (and users) who are accessing the filesystem. Files in memory that have not been committed to disk might be lost.
- Bring the system to single-user mode and then unmount the filesystem. Although this is the largest inconvenience, it is the safest way because no one loses any work. Unfortunately, on a large server, you'll have some angry users to contend with. (Welcome to system administration!)

Configuring the `/etc/fstab` File to Mount Filesystems Automatically

At boot time, the system will automatically mount the root filesystem with read-only privileges. This allows it to load the kernel and read critical startup files. However, after the system has bootstrapped itself, it will need guidance. Although it is possible for you to jump in and mount all the filesystems, it isn't realistic because you then have to finish bootstrapping the machine yourself, and even worse, the system might not come back online by itself. (Of course, if you enjoy coming into work at 2 a.m. to bring a system back up….)

To get around this, Linux uses a special file called `/etc/fstab`. This file lists all the partitions that need to be mounted at boot time and the directory where they need to be mounted. Along with that information, you can pass parameters to the `mount` command.

NOTE

NFS servers can also be NFS clients. For example, a Web server that exports part of its archive to, say, an FTP server can NFS mount from the server containing home directories at the same time.

Each filesystem to be mounted is listed in the `fstab` file in the following format:

```
/dev/device        /dir/to/mount        ftype parameters fs_freq fs_passno
```

The following items make up this line:

- *`/dev/device`* — The device to be mounted. In the case of mounting NFS filesystems, this comes in the form of *`servername:/dir/exported`*, where *`servername`* is the name of the NFS server, and *`/dir/exported`* is the directory that is exported from the NFS server—for example, `denon:/export/home`, where `denon` is the hostname of your NFS server and `/export/home` is the directory that is specified in the `/etc/exports` directory as being shared.
- *`/dir/to/mount`* — The location at which the filesystem should be mounted on your directory tree.
- *`ftype`* — The filesystem type. Usually, this is `ext2` for your local filesystems; however, NFS mounts should use the `nfs` filesystem type.
- *`parameters`* — These are the parameters you passed to `mount` using the `-o` option. They follow the same comma-delimited format. A sample entry looks like `rw,intr,bg`.
- *`fs_freq`* — This is used by `dump` to determine whether a filesystem needs to be dumped.
- *`fs_passno`* — This is used by the `fsck` program to determine the order to check disks at boot time.

Any lines in the `fstab` file that start with the pound symbol (#) are considered comments.

If you need to mount a new filesystem while the machine is live, you must perform the mount by hand. If you want this mount automatically active the next time the system is rebooted, you should add it to the `fstab` file.

There are two notable partitions that don't follow same set of rules as normal partitions. They are the swap partition and `/proc`, which use filesystem types `swap` and `proc`, respectively.

You do not mount the swap partition using the `mount` command. It is instead managed by the `swapon` command. For a swap partition to be mounted, you must list it in the `fstab` file. Once there, use `swapon` with the `-a` parameter, followed by the partition on which you've allocated swap space.

The `/proc` filesystem is even stranger because it really isn't a filesystem. It is an interface to the kernel abstracted into a filesystem format. Take a peek into it for a large amount of useful information regarding the inner workings of the kernel.

TIP

If you need to remount a filesystem that already has an entry in the `fstab` file, you don't need to type the `mount` command with all the parameters. Instead, simply pass the directory to `mount` as the parameter, as in

```
mount /dir/to/mount
```

where */dir/to/mount* is the directory that needs to be mounted. `mount` will automatically look to the `fstab` file for all the details, such as which partition to mount and which options to use.

If you need to remount a large number of filesystems that are already listed in the `fstab` file, you can use the `-a` option in `mount` to remount all the entries in `fstab`:

```
mount -a
```

If it finds that a filesystem is already mounted, no action on that filesystem is performed. If, on the other hand, it finds that an entry is not mounted, it will automatically mount it with the appropriate parameters.

CAUTION

When setting up servers that mount filesystems from other servers, be wary of *cross mounting*. Cross mounting happens when two servers mount each other's filesystems. This can be dangerous if you do not configure the `/etc/fstab` file to mount these systems in the background (via the `bg` option) because it is possible for these two machines to deadlock during their boot sequence as each host waits for the other to respond.

For example, let's say you want `host1` to mount `/export/usr/local` from `host2` and `host2` to mount `/export/home/admin` from `host1`. If both machines are restarted after a power outage, `host1` will try to mount the directory from `host2` before turning on its own NFS services. `host2` is, at the same time, trying to mount the directory from host1 before it turns on its NFS services. The result is that both machines wait forever for the other machine to start.

If you use the bg option in the /etc/fstab entry for both hosts, they would fail on the initial mount, place the mount in the background, and continue booting. Eventually, both machines would start their NFS daemons and allow each other to mount their respective directories.

Complete Sample Configuration Files

Listing 13.1 contains a complete /etc/exports file for a server.

LISTING 13.1 A COMPLETE /etc/exports FILE

```
#
# /etc/exports for denon
#
# Share the home dirs:
/export/home          technics(rw) pioneer(rw) vestax(rw)
           ➥atus(rw) rane(rw)

#
# Share local software
#
/export/usr/local     technics(rw,no_root_squash)
            ➥vestax(rw,no_root_squash)
            ➥pioneer(rw,no_root_squash)
            ➥atus(rw,no_root_squash)
            ➥rane(rw,no_root_squash)
```

Listing 13.2 contains a complete /etc/fstab file for a client.

LISTING 13.2 A COMPLETE /etc/fstab FILE

```
#
# /etc/fstab for technics
#

/dev/hda1                /                  ext2 rw            0
0
/dev/hda2                swap               swap
/dev/hda3                /usr               ext2 rw            0
0
```

continues

THE NETWORK FILE SYSTEM

LISTING 13.2 CONTINUED

```
/dev/hda4                    /var                 ext2 rw                 0
0
denon:/export/home           /home                nfs  rw,bg,intr,soft 0
0
denon:/export/usr/local      /usr/local           nfs  rw,bg,intr,soft 0
0
rane:/export/mail            /var/spool/mail      nfs  rw,bg,intr,soft 0
0
```

Summary

In this chapter, you learned how to

- Start and stop NFS servers
- Mount and unmount directories
- Create and maintain the configuration files for clients and servers

A rather straightforward tool, NFS is one of the power features that lets you work not only with other Linux systems, but with other variants of UNIX as well. From a user's standpoint, it provides a seamless bridge between clients and servers so that they can keep to their tasks instead of trying to remember the drive letter for their home directory.

CHAPTER 1

Samba

by Jack Tackett, Jr.

IN THIS CHAPTER

This chapter gives you the information you need to install, configure, and use the Session Message Block (SMB or Samba) protocol services under Linux. With Samba, you can share a Linux filesystem with Windows 95, 98, or NT. You can share a Windows 95, 98, or NT FAT filesystem with Linux. You can also share printers connected to either Linux or a system with Windows 95, 98, or NT.

Samba is the protocol used by Microsoft's operating systems to share files and printer services. Microsoft and Intel developed the SMB protocol system in 1987, and later, Andrew Tridgell ported the system to various UNIX systems and Linux.

NOTE

Microsoft is currently proposing another file sharing standard, Common Internet File System (CIFS). The standard has been submitted to the Internet Engineering Task Force, but CIFS has yet to be widely adopted and does not currently exist for Linux.

The Samba suite consists of several components. The `smbd` daemon provides the file and print services to SMB clients, such as Windows for Workgroups, Windows NT, or LAN Manager. The configuration file for this daemon is described in `smb.conf`. The `nmbd` daemon provides NetBIOS nameserving and browsing support. You can also run `nmbd` interactively to query other name service daemons.

The SMB client program implements a simple FTP-like client. This is useful for accessing SMB shares on other compatible servers such as Windows machines and can also be used to allow a UNIX box to print to a printer attached to any SMB server, such as a PC running Windows 98.

The `testparm` utility allows you to test your `smb.conf` configuration file. The `smbstatus` utility allows you to tell who is currently using the `smbd` server.

Installing Samba

You can install Samba during the Red Hat installation from CD-ROM or later using RPM. If you need to install the package, first download the current version from Red Hat's Web site (`http://www.redhat.com`) or locate the package on your CD-ROM. You can then install the package (the current version is `samba-1.9.18p10-2.i386.rpm`) with the following command:

```
rpm -ivh samba-1.9.18p5-1.i386.rpm
```

The package should contain all the files needed, including the two primary programs smbd and nmbd, to run samba.

Configuring Samba

The main configuration file, smb.conf, is located in /etc. Listing 14.1 provides the default listing shipped with Red Hat 5.2.

NOTE

The ; character at the beginning of a line indicates the line is a comment that is to be ignored when processed by the Samba server.

LISTING 14.1 THE SAMPLE smb.conf SAMBA CONFIGURATION FILE

```
; The global setting for a Red Hat default install
; smbd re-reads this file regularly, but if in doubt stop and restart it:
; /etc/rc.d/init.d/smb stop
; /etc/rc.d/init.d/smb start
;====================== Global Settings
=====================================
[global]

; workgroup = NT-Domain-Name or Workgroup-Name, eg: REDHAT4
   workgroup = WORKGROUP

; comment is the equivalent of the NT Description field
   comment = Red Hat Samba Server

; volume = used to emulate a CDRom label (can be set on a per share basis)
   volume = RedHat4

; printing = BSD or SYSV or AIX, etc.
   printing = bsd
   printcap name = /etc/printcap
   load printers = yes

; Uncomment this if you want a guest account
;  guest account = pcguest
   log file = /var/log/samba-log.%m
; Put a capping on the size of the log files (in Kb)
   max log size = 50

; Options for handling file name case sensitivity and / or preservation
```

continues

LISTING 14.1 CONTINUED

```
; Case Sensitivity breaks many WfW and Win95 apps
;   case sensitive = yes
    short preserve case = yes
    preserve case = yes

; Security and file integrity related options
   lock directory = /var/lock/samba
   locking = yes
   strict locking = yes
;   fake oplocks = yes
   share modes = yes
; Security modes: USER uses Unix username/passwd, SHARE uses WfW type
passwords
;        SERVER uses a Windows NT Server to provide authentication
services
   security = user
; Use password server option only with security = server
;   password server = <NT-Server-Name>

; Configuration Options ***** Watch location in smb.conf for side-effects
*****
; Where %m is any SMBName (machine name, or computer name) for which a
custom
; configuration is desired
;   include = /etc/smb.conf.%m

; Performance Related Options
; Before setting socket options read the smb.conf man page!!
   socket options = TCP_NODELAY
; Socket Address is used to specify which socket Samba
; will listen on (good for aliased systems)
;   socket address = aaa.bbb.ccc.ddd
; Use keep alive only if really needed!!!!
;   keep alive = 60

; Domain Control Options
; OS Level gives Samba the power to rule the roost. Windows NT = 32
;       Any value < 32 means NT wins as Master Browser, > 32 Samba gets it
;   os level = 33
; specifies Samba to be the Domain Master Browser
;   domain master = yes
; Use with care only if you have an NT server on your network that has
been
; configured at install time to be a primary domain controller.
;   domain controller = <NT-Domain-Controller-SMBName>
; Domain logon control can be a good thing! See [netlogon] share section
below!
;   domain logons = yes
; run a specific logon batch file per workstation (machine)
```

```
;   logon script = %m.bat
; run a specific logon batch file per username
;   logon script = %u.bat
; Windows Internet Name Serving Support Section
; WINS Support - Tells the NMBD component of Samba to enable its WINS
Server
;       the default is NO.
;   wins support = yes
; WINS Server - Tells the NMBD components of Samba to be a WINS Client
;       Note: Samba can be either a WINS Server, or a WINS Client, but NOT
both
;   wins server = w.x.y.z
; WINS Proxy - Tells Samba to answer name resolution queries on behalf of
a non
;       WINS Client capable client, for this to work there must be at
least one
;       WINS Server on the network. The default is NO.
;   wins proxy = yes

;============================ Share Declarations
==============================
[homes]
   comment = Home Directories
   browseable = no
   read only = no
   preserve case = yes
   short preserve case = yes
   create mode = 0750

; Un-comment the following and create the netlogon directory for Domain
Logons
; [netlogon]
;   comment = Samba Network Logon Service
;   path = /home/netlogon
; Case sensitivity breaks logon script processing!!!
;   case sensitive = no
;   guest ok = yes
;   locking = no
;   read only = yes
;   browseable = yes  ; say NO if you want to hide the NETLOGON share
;   admin users = @wheel

; NOTE: There is NO need to specifically define each individual printer
[printers]
   comment = All Printers
   path = /var/spool/samba
   browseable = no
   printable = yes
; Set public = yes to allow user 'guest account' to print
```

continues

LISTING 14.1 CONTINUED

```
   public = no
   writable = no
   create mode = 0700

;[tmp]
;   comment = Temporary file space
;   path = /tmp
;   read only = no
;   public = yes

; A publicly accessible directory, but read only, except for people in
; the staff group
;[public]
;   comment = Public Stuff
;   path = /home/samba
;   public = yes
;   writable = yes
;   printable = no
;   write list = @users

; Other examples.
;
; A private printer, usable only by fred. Spool data will be placed in
fred's
; home directory. Note that fred must have write access to the spool
directory,
; wherever it is.
;[fredsprn]
;   comment = Fred's Printer
;   valid users = fred
;   path = /homes/fred
;   printer = freds_printer
;   public = no
;   writable = no
;   printable = yes
;
; A private directory, usable only by fred. Note that fred requires write
; access to the directory.
;[fredsdir]
;   comment = Fred's Service
;   path = /usr/somewhere/private
;   valid users = fred
;   public = no
;   writable = yes
;   printable = no
;
; a service which has a different directory for each machine that connects
; this allows you to tailor configurations to incoming machines. You could
; also use the %u option to tailor it by user name.
```

```
; The %m gets replaced with the machine name that is connecting.
;[pchome]
;  comment = PC Directories
;  path = /usr/pc/%m
;  public = no
;  writeable = yes
;
;
; A publicly accessible directory, read/write to all users. Note that all
files
; created in the directory by users will be owned by the default user, so
; any user with access can delete any other user's files. Obviously this
; directory must be writable by the default user. Another user could of
course
; be specified, in which case all files would be owned by that user
instead.
;[public]
;   path = /usr/somewhere/else/public
;   public = yes
;   only guest = yes
;   writable = yes
;   printable = no
;
;
; The following two entries demonstrate how to share a directory so that
two
; users can place files there that will be owned by the specific users. In
this
; setup, the directory should be writable by both users and should have
the
; sticky bit set on it to prevent abuse. Obviously this could be extended
to
; as many users as required.
;[myshare]
;   comment = Mary's and Fred's stuff
;   path = /usr/somewhere/shared
;   valid users = mary fred
;   public = no
;   writable = yes
;   printable = no
;   create mask = 0765
```


The `smb.conf` file layout consists of a series of named sections. Each section starts with its name in brackets, such as `[global]`. Within each section, the parameters are specified by key/value pairs, such as `comment = Red Hat Samba Server`.

`smb.conf` consists of three special sections and one or more custom sections. The special sections are `[global]`, `[homes]`, and `[printers]`.

The [global] section

The global section controls parameters for the entire SMB server. This section also provides default values for the other sections:

```
[global]

; workgroup = NT-Domain-Name or Workgroup-Name, eg: REDHAT4
   workgroup = WORKGROUP

; comment is the equivalent of the NT Description field
   comment = Red Hat Samba Server

; volume = used to emulate a CDRom label (can be set on a per share basis)
   volume = RedHat4
```

The first line from the global section in Listing 14.1 defines the workgroup that this machine will belong to on your network. Next, the file specifies a comment for the system and identifies a volume label:

```
; printing = BSD or SYSV or AIX, etc.
   printing = bsd
   printcap name = /etc/printcap
   load printers = yes
```

The next entry tells the Samba server what type of printing system is available on your server. The next line indicates where the printer configuration file is located.

The next line instructs Samba to make available on the network all the printers defined in the printcap file:

```
; Uncomment this if you want a guest account
;  guest account = pcguest
   log file = /var/log/samba-log.%m
; Put a capping on the size of the log files (in Kb)
   max log size = 50
```

The next entry indicates a username for a guest account on your server. This account is used to authenticate users for Samba services available to guest connections.

The logfile entry specifies the location of the logfile for each client who accesses Samba services. The `%m` parameter tells the Samba server to create a separate logfile for each client. The `max log size` entry sets a maximum file size for the logs created.

The [homes] section

The `[homes]` section allows network clients to connect to a user's home directory on your server without having an explicit entry in the `smb.conf` file. When a service request is made, the Samba server searches the `smb.conf` file for the specific section corresponding to the service request. If the service is not found, then Samba checks whether there is a [homes] section. If the [homes] section exists, the password file is searched to find the home directory for the user making the request. Once this directory is found, the system shares it with the network:

```
[homes]
   comment = Home Directories
   browseable = no
   read only = no
   preserve case = yes
   short preserve case = yes
   create mode = 0750
```

The comment entry is displayed to the clients to let them know what shares are available. The browseable entry instructs Samba how to display this share in a network browse list. The read only parameter controls whether a user can create and change files in his home directory when shared across the network. The preserve case and short preserve case parameters instruct the server to preserve the case of any information written to the server. This is important because Windows filename are not typically case sensitive, but Linux filenames are case sensitive. The final entry sets the file permissions for any files created on the shared directory.

The [printers] section

The printers section defines how printing services are controlled if no specific entries are found in the smb.conf file. As with the [homes] section, if no specific entry is found for a printing service, Samba uses the printers section (if it's present) to allow a user to connect to any printer defined in /etc/printcap:

```
[printers]
   comment = All Printers
   path = /var/spool/samba
   browseable = no
   printable = yes
; Set public = yes to allow user 'guest account' to print
   public = no
   writable = no
   create mode = 0700
```

The comment, browseable, and create mode entries mean the same as those discussed earlier in the [homes] section. The path entry indicates the location of the spool file to be used when servicing a print request via SMB.

The printable value, if yes, indicates this printer resource can be used to print. The public entry controls whether the guest account can print.

Sharing Files and Print Services

After configuring your defaults for the Samba server, you can create specific shared directories limited to just certain groups of people or available to everyone. For example, let's say you want to make a directory available to only one user. To do so, you would create a new section and fill in the needed information. Typically, you'll need to specify the user, the directory path, and configuration information to the SMB server as shown here:

```
[jacksdir]
comment = Jack's remote source code directory
path = /usr/local/src
valid users = tackett
browseable = yes
public = no
writable = yes
create mode = 0700
```

This sample section creates a shared directory called `jacksdir`. The path to the directory on the local server is `/usr/local/src`. Because the `browseable` entry is set to `yes`, `jacksdir` will show up in the network browse list. However, because the `public` entry is set to `no`, only the user `tackett` can access this directory using Samba. You can grant access to more users by specifying them in the `valid users` entry.

Testing Your Configuration

After creating the configuration file, you should test it for correctness with the `testparm` program. `testparm` is a simple test program to check the `/etc/smb.conf` configuration file for internal correctness. If this program reports no problems, you can use the configuration file with confidence that `smbd` will successfully load the configuration file.

CAUTION

Using `testparm` is not a guarantee that the services specified in the configuration file will be available or will operate as expected. This kind of testing guarantees only that Samba is able to read and understand the configuration file.

`testparm` has the following command line:

```
testparm [configfile [hostname hostip]]
```

configfile indicates the location of the smb.conf file if it is not in the default location (/etc/smb.conf). The *hostname hostIP* optional parameter instructs testparm to see whether the host has access to the services provided in the smb.conf file. If you specify *hostname*, then you must specify the IP number of that host as well, or the results will be unpredictable.

The following illustrates sample output from running testparm. If there are any errors, the program will report them along with a specific error message:

```
[root@ns /etc]# testparm smb.conf ntackett 209.42.203.236
Load smb config files from smb.conf
Processing section "[homes]"
Processing section "[printers]"
Loaded services file OK.
Allow connection from ntackett (209.42.203.236) to homes
Allow connection from ntackett (209.42.203.236) to printers
Allow connection from ntackett (209.42.203.236) to lp
Allow connection from ntackett (209.42.203.236) to IPC$
```

Testing Your Printers with testprns

If you have configured your server to print to a printer on a Samba mount, you can test this configuration using the testprns command. testprns has the following command line:

```
testprns printername [printcapname]
```

printername is the name of the printer, and *printcapname* is the name specified in the /etc/printcap file. Because the testprns command is simple, it is recommended that you specify the *printcapname*. The following is sample output:

```
[root@ns /etc]# testprns lp
Looking for printer lp in printcap file /etc/printcap
Printer name lp is valid.
```

Testing with smbstatus

The smbstatus program reports on current Samba connections. smbstatus has the following command line:

```
smbstatus [-d] [-p] [-s configfile]
```

configfile is by default /etc/smb.conf. -d provides verbose output, and -p provides a list of current SMB processes. The -p option is useful if you are writing shell scripts using smbstatus. Following is sample output:

```
[root@ns /etc]# smbstatus
Samba version 1.9.18p5
```

```
Service      uid      gid      pid     machine
----------------------------------------------
No locked files
Share mode memory usage (bytes):
   102232(99%) free + 112(0%) used + 56(0%) overhead = 102400(100%) total
```

Running the Samba Server

The Samba server consists of two daemons, `smbd` and `nmbd`. The `smbd` daemon provides the file and print sharing services. The `nmbd` daemon provides NetBIOS name server support.

You can run the Samba server either from the `init` scripts or from `inetd` as a system service. Because Red Hat by default starts SMB services from the `init` scripts each time you boot, rather than as a service from `inetd`, you can use the command

```
/etc/rc.d/init.d/smb start¦stop
```

to start or stop the SMB server. Using the `init` scripts provides better response to SMB requests rather than continuously spawning the programs from `inetd`.

Accessing Shares with `smbclient`

The `smbclient` program allows Linux users to access SMB shares on other, typically Windows, machines. If you want to access files on other Linux boxes, you can use a variety of methods including FTP, NFS, and the r-commands such as `rcp`.

`smbclient` provides an FTP-like interface that allows you to transfer files with a network share on another computer running an SMB server. Unfortunately, unlike NFS, `smbclient` does not allow you to mount another share as a local directory.

`smbclient` provides command-line options to query a server for the shared directories available or to exchange files. For more information on all the command-line options, consult the man page for `smbclient`. Use the following command:

```
smbclient -L -I win.netwharf.com
```

to list all available shares on the machine `win.netwharf.com`. The `-L` parameter requests the list. The `-I` parameter instructs `smbclient` to treat the following machine name as a DNS specified entry, rather than as a NetBIOS entry.

To transfer a file, you must first connect to the Samba server using the following command:

```
smbclient '\\WORKGROUP\PUBLIC' -I win.netwharf.com -U tackett
```

The parameter `'\\WORKGROUP\PUBLIC'` specifies the remote service on the other machine. This is typically either a filesystem directory or a printer. The `-U` option allows you to specify the username you want to connect with. Samba prompts you for a password if this account requires one and then places you at the prompt:

```
smb: \
```

where \ indicates the current working directory.

From this command line, you can issue the commands shown in Table 14.1 to transfer and work with files.

TABLE 14.1 SMBCLIENT COMMANDS

Command	*Parameters*	*Description*
`?` or `help`	[command]	Provides a help message on command or in general if no command is specified.
`!`	[shell command]	Executes the specified shell command or drops the user to a shell prompt.
`cd`	[directory]	Changes to the specified directory on the server machine (not the local machine). If no directory is specified, `smbclient` will report the current working directory.
`lcd`	[directory]	Changes to the specified directory on the local machine. If no directory is specified, `smbclient` will report the current working directory on the local machine.
`del`	[files]	The specified files on the server are deleted if the user has permission to do so. Files can include wildcard characters.
`dir` or `ls`	[files]	Lists the indicated files. You can also use the command `ls` to get a list of files.
`exit` or `quit`	none	Exits from the `smbclient` program.
`get`	[remotefile] [local name]	Retrieves the specified *`remotefile`* and saves the file on the local server. If *`local name`* is specified, the copied file will be saved with this filename rather than the filename on the remote server.
`mget`	[files]	Copy all the indicated files, including those matching any wildcards, to the local machine.
`md` or `mkdir`	[directory]	Creates the specified directory on the remote machine.

TABLE 14.1 CONTINUED

Command	*Parameters*	*Description*
`rd` or `rmdir`	[directory]	Removes the specified directory on the remote machine.
`put`	[file]	Copies the specified file from the local machine to the server.
`mput`	[files]	Copies all the specified files from the local machine to the server.
`print`	[file]	Prints the specified file on the remote machine.
`queue`	none	Displays all the print jobs queued on the remote server.

Summary

At this point, you should have a properly configured Samba server up and running. Several advanced options are available for Samba and the various programs that make up the Samba suite. For more information about Samba, read the Samba how-to on your distribution CD-ROM at `/doc/HOWTO/SMB-HOWTO`. Finally, you can find a large amount of information on Samba at
http://samba.anu.edu.au/samba/docs/smb_serv/html/smb_se.html.

System Administration and Management

IN THIS PART

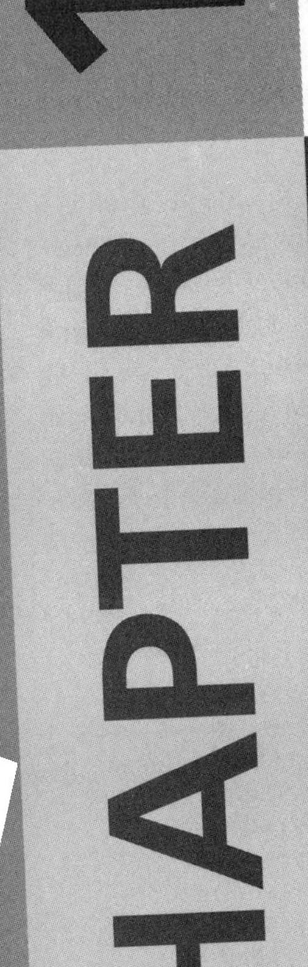

Filesystems, Disks, and Other Devices

by David Pitts

In This Chapter

One of the simplest and most elegant aspects of Linux design is the way that everything is represented as a file. Even the devices on which files are stored are represented as files.

Hardware devices are associated with drivers that provide a file interface; the special files representing hardware devices (or just *devices*) are kept in the directory `/dev`. Devices are either block devices or character devices.

A *character device* is one from which you can read a sequence of characters—for example, the sequence of keys typed at a keyboard or the sequence of bytes sent over a serial line. A *block device* is one that stores data and offers access to all parts of it equally; floppy and hard disks are block devices. Block devices are sometimes called *random access devices,* just as character devices are sometimes called *sequentially accessed devices*. With the latter, you can get data from any random part of a hard disk, but you have to retrieve the data from a serial line in the order it was sent.

When you perform some operation on a file, the kernel can tell that the file involved is a device by looking at its file mode (not its location). The device nodes are distinguished by different major and minor device numbers. The *major device number* indicates to the kernel which of its drivers the device node represents. (For example, a block device with major number 3 is an IDE disk drive, and one with the major device number 8 is a SCSI disk.) Each driver is responsible for several instances of the hardware it drives, and these are indicated by the value of the minor device number. For example, the SCSI disk with the minor number 0 represents the whole "first" SCSI disk, and the minor numbers 1 to 15 represent 15 possible partitions on it. The `ls` command prints the major and minor device numbers for you:

```
$ ls -l --sort=none /dev/sda{,?,??} /dev/sdb
brw-rw----   1 root     disk       8,   0 Sep 12  1994 /dev/sda
brw-rw----   1 root     disk       8,   1 Sep 12  1994 /dev/sda1
brw-rw----   1 root     disk       8,   2 Sep 12  1994 /dev/sda2
brw-rw----   1 root     disk       8,   3 Sep 12  1994 /dev/sda3
brw-rw----   1 root     disk       8,   4 Sep 12  1994 /dev/sda4
brw-rw----   1 root     disk       8,   5 Sep 12  1994 /dev/sda5
brw-rw----   1 root     disk       8,   6 Sep 12  1994 /dev/sda6
brw-rw----   1 root     disk       8,   7 Sep 12  1994 /dev/sda7
brw-rw----   1 root     disk       8,   8 Sep 12  1994 /dev/sda8
brw-rw----   1 root     disk       8,   9 Sep 12  1994 /dev/sda9
brw-rw----   1 root     disk       8,  10 Sep 12  1994 /dev/sda10
brw-rw----   1 root     disk       8,  11 Sep 12  1994 /dev/sda11
brw-rw----   1 root     disk       8,  12 Sep 12  1994 /dev/sda12
brw-rw----   1 root     disk       8,  13 Sep 12  1994 /dev/sda13
brw-rw----   1 root     disk       8,  14 Sep 12  1994 /dev/sda14
brw-rw----   1 root     disk       8,  15 Sep 12  1994 /dev/sda15
brw-rw----   1 root     disk       8,  16 Sep 12  1994 /dev/sdb
```

The obscure option (--sort=none) with this `ls -l` command ensures that the devices are presented in correct order. If you use only `ls -l`, the entries are sorted alphabetically, and `/dev/sda10` comes before `/dev/sda2`.

The `b` at the far left of the output of this command indicates that each of these entries is block devices. (Character devices are indicated by a `c`.) The major and minor device numbers appear just before the time field, separated by commas. (This is the position normally occupied in `ls -l` output by the file's size.)

Block Devices

If you had just one file of data to store, you could put it directly on a block device and read it back. Block devices have some fixed capacity, however, and you would need some method of marking the end of your data. Block devices behave in most respects just like ordinary files, except that although an ordinary file has a length determined by how much data is in it, the "length" of a block device is its total capacity. If you write a megabyte to a 100MB block device and read back its contents, you get the 1MB of data followed by 99MB of its previous contents. Bearing in mind this restriction, several UNIX utilities encode the amount of data available in the file's data rather than the file's total length and hence are suitable for storing data directly on block devices—for example, `tar` and `cpio`, which are suitable for everybody, and `dump`, which is suitable only for the system administrator (because it requires read access to the block device underlying the data to be backed up). To back up the entire contents of your home directory to floppy disk, type the following:

```
$ tar cf /dev/fd0 $HOME
```

or

```
$ find $HOME -print0 | cpio --create -0 --format=crc >/dev/fd0
```

The `-print0` and `-0` options for `find` and `cpio` ensure that the names of the files to be backed up that `find` sends to `cpio` are separated by ASCII NULs, rather than newlines. This ensures that any filenames containing a newline are correctly backed up.

NOTE

The only characters that are illegal in UNIX filenames are the slash and the ASCII NUL.

These backup utilities are written specifically to write their backups to any kind of file; in fact, they were designed for sequentially accessed character devices, such as tape drives.

Filesystems

When you have more than one item of data, it is necessary to have some method of organizing files on the device. These methods are called *filesystems*. Linux enables you to choose any organizational method to marshal your files on its storage device. For example, you can use the MS-DOS filesystem on a floppy or the faster `ext2` filesystem on your hard disk.

Many different filesystems are supported by Linux; the `ext2` filesystem is used most because it is designed for Linux and is very efficient. Other filesystems are used for compatibility with other systems; for example, it's common to use the `msdos` and `vfat` filesystems on floppies (these are the native filesystems of MS-DOS and Windows 95). Under Red Hat Linux 5.2, some filesystems are built into the kernel:

```
$ cat /proc/filesystems
        ext2
        msdos
nodev   proc
nodev    autofs
```

Some filesystems are available as loadable modules:

```
$ ls /lib/modules/'uname -r'/fs
ext.o     isofs.o  ncpfs.o  smbfs.o  ufs.o     vfat.o
hpfs.o    minix.o  nfs.o    sysv.o   umsdos.o  xiafs.o
```

Some of these (`nfs`, `ncpfs`, and `smbfs`) are network filesystems that don't depend on block devices. Network filesystems are covered in Chapter 17, "TCP/IP Network Management." Other filesystems are supported by Linux but are not provided by the standard kernel .

The `mount` Command

To mount a block device onto the filesystem, use the `mount` command. You need to specify what device contains the filesystem, what type it is, and where in the directory hierarchy to mount it.

A `mount` command looks like this:

```
mount [-t type] [-o options] device mount-point
```

device must be a block device, or, if it contains a colon, it can be the name of another machine from which to mount a filesystem (see Chapter 17). *mount-point* should be an existing directory; the filesystem will appear at this position. (Anything previously in that directory will be hidden.) The filesystem type and options are optional, and the variety and meaning of options depend on the type of filesystem being mounted. If the filesystem you want to mount is specified in the /etc/fstab file, you need to specify only the mount point or the device name; the other details are read from /etc/fstab by mount. Here is an example of the mount command being used:

```
# mount /dev/fd1 -t vfat /mnt/floppy
mount: block device /dev/fd1 is write-protected, mounting read-only
# ls /mnt/floppy
grub-0.4.tar.gz
# umount /mnt/floppy
# ls /mnt/floppy
filesystem not mounted
```

In this example, I mounted a floppy containing a vfat filesystem at the mount point /mnt/floppy (and got an informational message). The directory /mnt/floppy already existed. I used ls to see what was on the disk and unmounted it again. I then ran ls again, and the response I got was simply the name of a file that I leave in the directory /mnt/floppy on my hard disk to remind me that there currently is nothing mounted there. This hint enables me to distinguish a written floppy from an empty floppy that is mounted. I can also use the df command to see what filesystems are mounted.

Mounting a vfat floppy like this causes the Linux kernel to automatically load the vfat driver into the kernel while it was needed. These drivers are loaded by the kernel module handler, and when they become unused after the filesystem is unmounted, they are unloaded to recover the memory that they occupied. See Chapter 28, "Configuring and Building Kernels," for more information about kernel modules.

Potential Problems with mount

Any one of several things can cause the mount command to fail:

- Incorrect device name—It is possible to specify an incorrect device name (that is, a device file that does not exist or one for which a driver is not available in the kernel or for which the hardware is not present).
- Unreadable devices—Devices can be unreadable either because the devices themselves are bad (for example, empty floppy drives or bad media) or because you have insufficient permissions to mount them. Filesystems, other than those sanctioned by the administrator by listing them with the option user in /etc/fstab, are forbidden to ordinary users and require root privilege to mount them.

- Bad mount point—Trying to mount a device at a mount point that does not already exist will not work.
- Other errors—Still more error conditions are possible but unlikely (for example, exceeding the compiled-in limit to the number of mounted filesystems) or self-explanatory (for example, most usage errors for the `mount` command itself). There are some more unlikely error messages that chiefly relate to the loopback devices.

When you mount a filesystem, the point at which it is to be mounted (that is, the mount point) must be a directory. This directory doesn't have to be empty, but after the filesystem is mounted, anything "underneath" it is inaccessible. Linux provides a *singly rooted* filesystem, in contrast to those operating systems that give each filesystem a separate drive letter. Although this might seem less flexible, it is *more* flexible because the size of each block device (that is, hard disk or whatever) is hidden from programs, and things can be moved around. For example, if you have some software that expects to be installed in `/opt/umsp`, you can install it in `/big-disk/stuff/umsp` and make `/opt/umsp` a symbolic link. There is also no need to edit a myriad of configuration files that are using the wrong drive letter after you install a new disk drive, for example.

Many options govern how a mounted filesystem behaves; for example, it can be mounted read-only. There are options for filesystems such as `msdos` that don't have any concept of users. The filesystems enable you to give each file a particular file mode (for security or to allow access by everyone). When you mount an `nfs` filesystem, there is so much flexibility available that the options have a separate manual page (`man nfs`), although the defaults are perfectly reasonable. The `nfs` filesystem is explained in more detail in Chapter 17.

Table 15.1 contains options useful for `mount` in alphabetical order. Unless otherwise indicated, these options are valid for all filesystem types, although asking for asynchronous writes to a CD-ROM is no use. Options applicable only to NFS filesystems are not listed here; refer to the `nfs` manual page for those.

TABLE 15.1 `mount` OPTIONS

`async`	Write requests for the filesystem normally should wait until the data has reached the hardware; with this option, the program continues immediately instead. This does mean that the system is slightly more prone to data loss in the event of a system crash, but, on the other hand, crashes are rare with Linux. This option speeds up NFS filesystems to a startling extent. The opposite of this option is `sync`.

`auto`	Indicates to `mount` that it should mount the device when given the `-a` flag. This flag is used by the startup scripts to make sure that all the required filesystems are mounted at boot time. The opposite of this option is `noauto`.
`defaults`	Turns on the options `rw`, `suid`, `dev`, `exec`, `auto`, `nouser`, and `async`.
`dev`	Allows device nodes on the system to be used. Access to devices is completely determined by access rights to the on-disk device node. Hence, if you mount an `ext2` filesystem on a floppy and you have previously placed a writable `/dev/kmem` device file on the disk, then you've just gained read/write access to kernel memory. System administrators generally prevent this from happening by mounting removable filesystems with the `nodev` `mount` option.
`exec`	Indicates to the kernel that it should allow the execution of programs on the filesystem. This option is more frequently seen as `noexec`, which indicates to the kernel that execution of programs on this filesystem shouldn't be allowed. This is generally used as a security precaution or for NFS filesystems mounted from another machine that contain executable files of a format unsuitable for this machine (for example, intended for a different CPU).
`noauto`	Opposite of `auto`.
`nodev`	Opposite of `dev`.
`noexec`	Opposite of `exec`.
`nosuid`	Opposite of `suid`.
`nouser`	Opposite of `user`.
`remount`	Allows the `mount` command to change the flags for an already-mounted filesystem without interrupting its use. You can't unmount a filesystem that is currently in use, and this option is basically a workaround. The system startup scripts, for example, use the command `mount -n -o remount,ro /` to change the root filesystem from read-only (it starts off this way) to read/write (its normal state). The `-n` option indicates to `mount` that it shouldn't update `/etc/fstab` because it can't do this while the root filesystem is still read-only.
`ro`	Mounts the filesystem read-only. This is the opposite of the option `rw`.
`rw`	Mounts the filesystem read/write. This is the opposite of the option `ro`.
`suid`	Allows the set user ID and set group ID file mode bits to take effect. The opposite of this option is `nosuid`. The `nosuid` option is more usual; it is used for the same sorts of reasons that `nodev` is used.

continues

TABLE 15.1 mount OPTIONS

`sync`	All write operations cause the calling program to wait until the data has been committed to the hardware. This mode of operation is slower but a little more reliable than its opposite, asynchronous I/O, which is indicated by the option `async`.
`user`	Allows ordinary users to mount the filesystem. When there is a `user` option in `/etc/fstab`, ordinary users indicate which filesystem they want to mount or unmount by giving the device name or mount point; all the other relevant information is taken from the `/etc/fstab` file. For security reasons, `user` implies the `noexec`, `nosuid`, and `nodev` options.

NOTE

One of the defaults for filesystems is that they are mounted `async`. This matters in that the operating system will return control before it actually reads or writes a file. Many people have erred by pulling a disk out of the drive too soon, causing a read or write not to occur and errors to occur.

Options are processed by the `mount` command in the order they appear on the command line (or in `/etc/fstab`). Thus, it is possible to allow users to mount a filesystem and then run set user ID executables by using the options `user, suid` in that order. Using them in reverse order (`suid, user`) wouldn't work because the `user` option would turn off the `suid` option again.

Many other options available are all specific to particular filesystems. All the valid options for `mount` are detailed in its manual page. An example is the `umask` flag for the `vfat` and `fat` filesystems, which allows you to make all the files on your MS-DOS or Windows partitions readable (or even writable if you prefer) for all the users on your Linux system.

Setting Up Filesystems

When the kernel boots, it attempts to mount a `root` filesystem from the device specified by the kernel loader, LILO. The `root` filesystem is initially mounted read-only, and the boot process proceeds as described in Chapter 6, "System Startup and Shutdown." During the boot process, the filesystems listed in the filesystem table `/etc/fstab` are mounted. This file specifies which devices are to be mounted, what kinds of filesystems they contain, at what point in the filesystem the mount takes place, and any options governing how they are to be mounted. The format of this file is described in `fstab`.

The Red Hat File System Manager

An easy way of setting up filesystem entries in `/etc/fstab` is to use the configuration tool File System Manager in the Red Hat Control Panel (although you can invoke it separately as `fstool`). The File System Manager is shown in Figure 15.1.

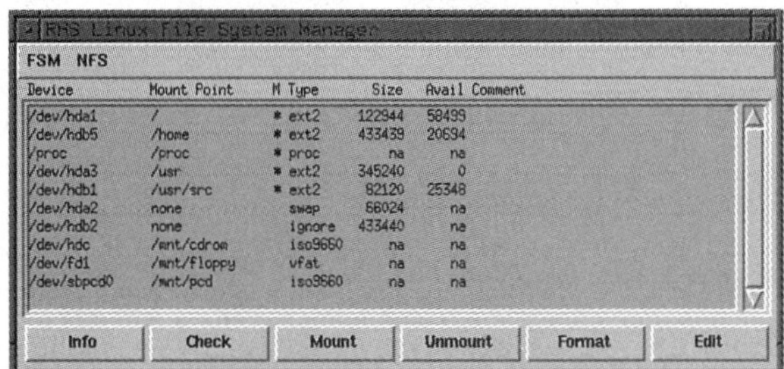

FIGURE 15.1
The File System Manager.

When you start `fstool`, it produces a window that contains all the entries in `/etc/fstab`. Each entry shows the device name, mount point, filesystem type, size, space used, and space available. Additionally, each mounted filesystem is marked with an asterisk. The Info button displays extra information about the highlighted filesystem (the same information that is indicated in `/etc/fstab` and in the output of the `df` command).

Filesystems can be mounted or unmounted with the two buttons Mount and Unmount. Any errors that occur are shown in a dialog box; this can happen if, for example, you try to mount a CD-ROM when there is no disk in the drive. (Go ahead and try it.) The Format button works only for hard disk partitions, for which it runs `mkfs`. (See the section "Creating New Filesystems" later in this chapter.) Other media (for example, floppy disks) are formatted differently (See the section "Floppy Disks" later in this chapter.)

The Check button works only for unmounted `ext2` and `minix` filesystems. If you get the error `fsck: command not found`, this just means that the directory `/sbin` is not on your path, and you should be able to fix this by running `su - root`. (You might also need to do `export DISPLAY=:0.0` if that is necessary.) Checking a filesystem can take a while, and the result is shown in a dialog box afterward. It is unusual for errors to be shown for hard disk filesystems here because these are checked at boot time and don't get corrupted during the normal operation of Linux.

The NFS menu is used to add and remove NFS network mounts, which are explained in Chapter 17. You can exit the File System Manager by selecting the Quit option from the FSM menu.

Editing /etc/fstab Manually

The filesystem table /etc/fstab is just a text file; it is designed to have a specific format that is readable by humans and not just computers. It is separated into columns by tabs or spaces. (It doesn't matter which you use.) You can edit it with your favorite text editor; it doesn't matter which. You must take care, however, if you modify it by hand because removing or corrupting an entry will make the system unable to mount that filesystem the next time it boots. For this reason, I make a point of saving previous versions of this file using the Revision Control System (a very useful program; see the manual page for rcs).

My /etc/fstab looks like this:

```
#
# /etc/fstab
#
# You should be using fstool (control-panel) to edit this!
#
#<device> <mountpoint> <filesystemtype> <options>    <dump> <fsckorder>

/dev/hda1     /             ext2      defaults          1      1
/dev/hdb5     /home         ext2      defaults,rw       1      2
/dev/hda3     /usr          ext2      defaults          1      2
/dev/hdb1     /usr/src      ext2      defaults          1      3

/dev/hdc      /mnt/cdrom    iso9660   user,noauto,ro    0      0
/dev/sbpcd0   /mnt/pcd      iso9660   user,noauto,ro    0      0
/dev/fd1      /mnt/floppy   vfat      user,noauto       0      0

/proc         /proc         proc      defaults
/dev/hda2     none          swap      sw
```

The first four entries are the ext2 filesystems composing my Linux system. When Linux is booted, the root filesystem is mounted first; all the other local (that is, non-network) filesystems are mounted next. Filesystems appear in /etc/fstab in the order they are mounted; /usr must appear before /usr/src, for example, because the mount point for one filesystem exists on the other. The following three filesystems are all removable filesystems (two CD-ROMs and a floppy drive). These have the noauto option set so that they are not automatically mounted at boot time. The removable devices have the user option set so that I can mount and unmount them without having to use su all the time. The CD-ROMs have the filesystem type iso9660, which is the standard filesystem for CD-ROMs, and the floppy drive has the filesystem type vfat because I often use it for interchanging data with MS-DOS and Windows systems.

The last two filesystems are special; the first (/proc) is a special filesystem provided by the kernel as a way of providing information about the system to user programs. The information in the /proc filesystem is used to make utilities such as ps, top, xload, free, netstat, and so on work. Some of the "files" in /proc are really enormous (for example, /proc/kcore), but don't worry; no disk space is wasted. All the information in the /proc filesystem is generated on-the-fly by the Linux kernel as you read it. You can tell that they are not real files because, for example, root can't give them away with chown.

The final "filesystem" isn't, in fact, a filesystem at all; it is an entry that indicates a disk partition used as swap space. Swap partitions are used to implement virtual memory. Files can also be used for swap space. The names of the swap files go in the first column where the device name usually goes.

The two numeric columns on the right relate to the operation of the dump and fsck commands. The dump command compares the number in column 5 (the *dump interval*) with the number of days since that filesystem was last backed up so that it can inform the system administrator that the filesystem needs to be backed up. Other backup software—for example, Amanda—can also use this field for the same purpose. (You can find Amanda at the URL http://www.amanda.org.) Filesystems without a dump interval field are assumed to have a dump interval of zero, denoting "never dump." For more information, see the manual page for dump.

The sixth column is the fsck pass and indicates which filesystems can be checked in parallel at boot time. The root filesystem is always checked first, but after that, separate drives can be checked simultaneously because Linux is a multitasking operating system. There is no point, however, in checking two filesystems on the same hard drive at the same time because this results in a lot of extra disk head movement and wasted time. All the filesystems that have the same pass number are checked in parallel from 1 upward. Filesystems with a 0 or missing pass number (such as the floppy and CD-ROM drives) are not checked at all.

Creating New Filesystems

When you install Red Hat Linux, the installation process makes some new filesystems and sets up the system to use them.

Many operating systems don't distinguish between the preparation of the device's surface to receive data (formatting) and the building of new filesystems. Linux does distinguish between the two, principally because only floppy disks need formatting in any case and also because Linux offers as many as half a dozen different filesystems that can be created (on any block device). Separately providing the facility of formatting floppy disks in each of these programs is poor design and requires you to learn a different way of doing it for each kind of new filesystem. The process of formatting floppy disks is dealt with separately. (See the section "Floppy Disks" later in this chapter.)

Filesystems are initially built by a program that opens the block device and writes some structural data to it so that when the kernel tries to mount the filesystem, the device contains the image of a pristine filesystem. This means that both the kernel and the program used to make the filesystem must agree on the correct filesystem structure.

Linux provides a generic command, `mkfs`, that enables you to make a filesystem on a block device. In fact, because UNIX manages almost all resources with the same set of operations, `mkfs` can be used to generate a filesystem inside an ordinary file! Because this is unusual, `mkfs` asks for confirmation before proceeding. When this is done, you can even mount the resulting filesystem using the loop device. (See the section "Mounting Filesystems on Files" later in this chapter.)

Because of the tremendous variety of filesystems available, almost all the work of building the new filesystem is delegated to a separate program for each; however, the generic `mkfs` program provides a single interface for invoking them all. It's not uncommon to pass options to the top-level `mkfs` (for example, `-V` to make it show what commands it executes or `-c` to make it check the device for bad blocks). The generic `mkfs` program also enables you to pass options to the filesystem-specific `mkfs`. Most of these filesystem-dependent options have sensible defaults, and you normally do not want to change them. The only options you might want to pass to `mke2fs`, which builds `ext2` filesystems, are `-m` and `-i`. The `-m` option specifies how much of the filesystem is reserved for root's use (for example, for working space when the system disk would otherwise have filled completely). The `-i` option is more rarely exercised and is used for setting the balance between inodes and disk blocks; it is related to the expected average file size. As stated previously, the defaults are reasonable for most purposes, so these options are used only in special circumstances:

```
# mkfs -t ext2 /dev/fd1
mke2fs 1.10, 24-Apr-97 for EXT2 FS 0.5b, 95/08/09
Linux ext2 filesystem format
Filesystem label=
360 inodes, 1440 blocks
72 blocks (5.00) reserved for the super user
First data block=1
Block size=1024 (log=0)
Fragment size=1024 (log=0)
1 block group
8192 blocks per group, 8192 fragments per group
360 inodes per group

Writing inode tables: done
Writing superblocks and filesystem accounting information: done
```

```
# mount -t ext2 /dev/fd1 /mnt/floppy
# ls -la /mnt/floppy
total 14
drwxr-xr-x   3 root     root          1024 Aug  1 19:49 .
drwxr-xr-x   7 root     root          1024 Jul  3 21:47 ..
drwxr-xr-x   2 root     root         12288 Aug  1 19:49 lost+found
# umount /mnt/floppy
```

Here, you see the creating and mounting of an `ext2` filesystem on a floppy. The structure of the filesystem as specified by the program's defaults are shown. There is no volume label, and there are 4096 bytes (4KB) per inode ($360 \times 4 = 1440$). The block size is 1KB, and 5 percent of the disk is reserved for root. These are the defaults (which are explained in the `mke2fs` manual page). After you have created a filesystem, you can use `dumpe2fs` to display information about an `ext2` filesystem, but remember to pipe the result through a pager such as `less` because this output can be very long.

After creating the filesystem on this floppy, you can include it in the filesystem table by changing the existing line referring to a `vfat` filesystem on `/dev/fd1` to the following:

```
/dev/fd1       /mnt/floppy    ext2   user,sync,errors=continue 0 0
```

The first three columns are the device, mount point, and filesystem type, as shown previously. The options column is more complex than previous ones. The `user` option indicates that users are allowed to mount this filesystem. The `sync` option indicates that programs writing to this filesystem wait while each write finishes and only then continue. This might seem obvious, but it is not the normal state of affairs. The kernel normally manages filesystem writes in such a way as to provide high performance. (Data still gets written to the device of course, but it doesn't necessarily happen immediately.) This is perfect for fixed devices such as hard disks, but for low-capacity removable devices such as floppy disks, it's less beneficial. Normally, you write a few files to a floppy and then unmount it and take it away. The unmount operation must wait until all data has been written to the device before it can finish (and the disk can then be removed). Having to wait like this is off-putting, and there is always the risk that someone might copy a file to the floppy, wait for the disk light to go out, and remove it. With asynchronous writes, some buffered data might not have yet been written to disk. Hence, synchronous writes are safer for removable media.

The `ext2` filesystem has a configurable strategy for errors. If an `ext2` filesystem encounters an error (for example, a bad disk block) there are three possible responses to the error:

Remount the device read-only. For filesystems that contain mostly nonessential data (for example, `/tmp`, `/var/tmp`, or news spools), remounting the filesystem read-only so that it can be fixed with `fsck` is often the best choice.

Panic. Continuing regardless in the face of potentially corrupted system configuration files is unwise, so a kernel panic (that is, a controlled crash—or emergency landing, if you prefer) can sometimes be appropriate.

Ignore it. Causing a system shutdown if a floppy disk has a bad sector is a little excessive, so the `continue` option tells the kernel to "carry on regardless" in this situation. If this actually does happen, the best thing to do is to use the `-c` option of `e2fsck`, for example, with `fsck -t ext2 -c /dev/fd1`. This runs `e2fsck`, giving it the `-c` option, which invokes the command `badblocks` to test the device for bad disk blocks. After this is done, `e2fsck` does its best to recover from the situation.

Repairing Filesystems

Some disk data is kept in memory temporarily before being written to disk for performance reasons. (See the previous discussion of the `sync` mount option.) If the kernel does not have an opportunity to actually write this data, the filesystem can become corrupted. This can happen in several ways:

- The storage device (for example, a floppy disk) can be manually removed before the kernel has finished with it.
- The system might suffer a power loss.
- The user might mistakenly turn off the power or accidentally press the reset button.

As part of the boot process, Linux runs the `fsck` program, whose job it is to check and repair filesystems. Most of the time, the boot follows a controlled shutdown (see the manual page for `shutdown`), and in this case, the filesystems will have been unmounted before the reboot. In this case, `fsck` says that they are "clean." It knows this because before unmounting them, the kernel writes a special signature on the filesystem to indicate that the data is intact. When the filesystem is mounted again for writing, this signature is removed.

If, on the other hand, one of the disasters listed takes place, the filesystems will not be marked "clean," and when `fsck` is invoked, as usual, it will notice this and begin a full check of the filesystem. This also occurs if you specify the `-f` flag to `fsck`. To prevent errors creeping up on it, `fsck` also enforces a periodic check; a full check is done at an interval specified on the filesystem itself (usually every 20 boots or 6 months, whichever comes sooner), even if it was unmounted cleanly.

The boot process (see Chapter 6) checks the root filesystem and then mounts it read/write. (It's mounted read-only by the kernel; `fsck` asks for confirmation before operating on a read/write filesystem, and this is not desirable for an unattended reboot.) First, the root filesystem is checked with the following command:

```
fsck -V -a /
```

Then, all the other filesystems are checked by executing this command:

```
fsck -R -A -V -a
```

These options specify that all the filesystems should be checked (`-A`) except the root filesystem, which doesn't need checking a second time (`-R`), and that operations produce informational messages about what it is doing as it goes (`-V`), but that the process should not be interactive (`-a`). The latter is specified because, for example, there might not be anyone present to answer any questions from `fsck`.

In the case of serious filesystem corruption, the approach breaks down because there are some things that `fsck` will not do to a filesystem without your say-so. In this case, it returns an error value to its caller (the startup script), and the startup script spawns a shell to allow the administrator to run `fsck` interactively. When this happens, this message appears:

```
***An error occurred during the file system check.
***Dropping you to a shell; the system will reboot
***when you leave the shell.
Give root password for maintenance
(or type Control-D for normal startup):
```

This is a troubling event, particularly because it might well appear if you have other problems with the system—for example, a lockup (leading you to press the reset button) or a spontaneous reboot. None of the online manuals are guaranteed to be available at this stage because they might be stored on the filesystem whose check failed. This prompt is issued if the root filesystem check failed or the filesystem check failed for any of the other disk filesystems.

When the automatic `fsck` fails, you need to log in by specifying the root password and run the `fsck` program manually. When you have typed in the root password, you are presented with the following prompt:

```
(Repair filesystem) #
```

You might worry about what command to enter here or indeed what to do at all. At least one of the filesystems needs to be checked, but which one? The preceding messages from `fsck` should indicate which, but it isn't necessary to go hunting for them. You can give `fsck` a set of options that tells it to check *everything* manually, and this is a good fallback:

```
fsck -A -V ; echo == $? ==
```

This is the same command as the previous one, but the `-R` option is missing, in case the root filesystem needs to be checked, and the `-a` option is missing, so `fsck` is in its "interactive" mode. This might enable a check to succeed just because it can now ask you questions. The purpose of the `echo == $? ==` command is to unambiguously interpret the outcome of the `fsck` operation. If the value printed between the equals signs is less than 4, all is well. If this value is `4` or more, more recovery measures are needed. The meanings of the various values follow:

`0`	No errors.
`1`	Filesystem errors corrected.
`2`	System should be rebooted.
`4`	Filesystem errors left uncorrected.
`8`	Operational error.
`16`	Usage or syntax error.
`128`	Shared library error.

If this does not work, it might be because of a *corrupted superblock*; `fsck` starts its disk check and if this is corrupted, it can't start. By good design, the `ext2` filesystem has many backup superblocks scattered regularly throughout the filesystem. Suppose the command announces that it has failed to clean some particular filesystem—for example, `/dev/fubar`. You can start `fsck` again using a backup superblock by using the following command:

```
fsck -t ext2 -b 8193 /dev/fubar
```

`8193` is the block number for the first backup superblock. This backup superblock is at the start of block group 1. (The first is numbered 0.) There are more backup superblocks at the start of block group 2 (16385) and block group 3 (24577); they are spaced at intervals of 8,192 blocks. If you made a filesystem with settings other than the defaults, these might change. `mke2fs` lists the superblocks that it creates as it goes, so that is a good time to pay attention if you're not using the default settings. There are further things you can attempt if `fsck` is still not succeeding, but these situations are rare and usually indicate hardware problems so severe that they prevent the proper operation of `fsck`. Examples include broken wires in the IDE connector cable and similar nasty problems. If this command still fails, you might seek expert help or fix the disk in a different machine.

These extreme measures are unlikely; a manual `fsck`, in the unusual circumstance where it is actually required, almost always fixes things. After the manual `fsck` has worked, the root shell that the startup scripts provide has done its purpose. Type `exit` to exit it. At this point, to make sure that everything goes according to plan, the boot process is started again from the beginning. This second time around, the filesystems should all be error-free and the system should boot normally.

Hardware

There are block devices under Linux for representing all sorts of random access devices: floppy disks, hard disks (XT, EIDE, and SCSI), Zip drives, CD-ROM drives, ramdisks, and loopback devices.

Hard Disks

Hard disks are large enough to make it useful to keep different filesystems on different parts of the hard disk. The scheme for dividing these disks is called *partitioning*. Although it is common for computers running MS-DOS to have only one partition, it is possible to have several different partitions on each disk. The summary of how the disk is partitioned is kept in its *partition table*.

The Partition Table

A hard disk might be divided like this:

Device Name	*Disk*	*Partition*	*Filesystem*	*Mounted At*
`/dev/hda1`	1	1	`ext2`	`/`
`/dev/hda3`	1	3	`ext2`	`/usr`
`/dev/hdb1`	2	1	`ext2`	`/usr/src`
`/dev/hdb5`	2	5	`ext2`	`/home`

Note that the partitions on the first disk have names starting with `/dev/hda` and those on the second have names starting with `/dev/hdb`. These prefixes are followed by the number of the partition.

> **NOTE**
>
> All is not quite as simple as it could be in the partition table, however. Early hard disk drives on PCs were quite small (about 10MB), so you were limited to only a small number of partitions, and the format of the partition table originally allowed for only four partitions. Later on, this was too great a restriction, and the *extended partition* was introduced as a workaround.
>
> Inside each extended partition is another partition table. This enables the extended partition to be divided, in the same way, into four *logical partitions*. Partitions that aren't inside an extended partition are sometimes referred to as *primary partitions*.

Running `fdisk -l` shows that my first hard disk is divided like this:

Device	*Begin*	*Start*	*End*	*Blocks*	*ID*	*System*
/dev/hda1	1	1	244	122944	83	Linux native
/dev/hda2	245	245	375	66024	82	Linux swap
/dev/hda3	376	376	1060	345240	83	Linux native

In this case, there are three primary partitions, of which one is a swap partition.

Disk Geometry

The units of the table in the last section are *cylinders*. The partition table allocates a consecutive block of cylinders to each partition. The term *cylinder* itself dates from the days when it was possible to remove a disk pack from a UNIX machine and point to the various parts. That can't be done here, so here's another way of looking at it.

Imagine that a hard disk is in fact a stack of pizzas. Each of the pizzas is a *platter*, a disk-shaped surface with a magnetic coating designed to hold magnetic encodings. Both sides of these platters are used. These platters rotate around the spindle, like the spindle in a record player. (Don't put pizzas on a record player!) The hard disk has a movable arm containing several *disk heads*. Each side of each platter has a separate disk head. If you were to put your fingers between the pizzas while keeping them straight, your fingers are the same as the arrangement of the heads on the arm. All the parts of the platters that the heads pass over in one rotation of the disk is called a *cylinder*. The parts of a single platter that one head passes over in one rotation is called a *track*. Each track is divided into *sectors*, as if the pizzas had been already sliced for you. The layout of a disk, its *geometry*, is described by the number of cylinders, heads, and sectors comprising the disk. Another important feature is the rotational speed of the disk; generally, the faster it is, the faster the hard disk can read or write data.

You can discover the geometry of one of your hard disks by using the `hdparm` command, and typical output might look like this:

```
# /sbin/hdparm -g /dev/hdc

/dev/hdc:
 geometry     = 6232/16/63, sectors = 6281856, start = 0
```

As you can see from the geometry specified in this example, this is the drive discussed previously.

> **NOTE**
>
> IBM PCs with older BIOSs can have difficulty with large disks; see the Linux Large-Disk mini how-to.

Floppy Disks

Floppy disks are removable low-capacity storage media. As storage devices, they are far slower than hard disks, but they have the advantage of being removable, which makes them good media for transporting modest amounts of data.

The block devices corresponding to the floppy disks begin with the letters `fd`; `/dev/fd0` is the first, and any additional ones have increasing numbers. There are many possible formats for a floppy disk, and the kernel needs to know the format (geometry) of a disk to read it properly. Linux can usually work out the correct format, so the automatic devices `/dev/fd0` (plus `/dev/fd1` and so on for extra floppy drives) are usually sufficient, but if for some reason it is necessary to specify the exact format, further device names are provided. The device `/dev/fd0H1440`, for example, denotes a 1.44MB high-density floppy. There are many more devices indicating obscure formats, both older lower-capacity formats and other nonstandard extra–high-capacity formats. You can even create your own floppy disk formats using the `serfdprm` program.

The most common reason to use the specific-format device names is that you are formatting a floppy for the first time. In this situation, the disk is not yet readable, so the kernel will not be able to autoprobe an existing format. You need to use the name `/dev/fd0H1440`, for example, to denote a high-density 3.5-inch disk in the first floppy drive. For device names representing other formats, refer to the `fd` manual page. Section 4 of the manual is devoted to devices.

The process of formatting a floppy is completely destructive to the data on it, and because it requires writing to the actual device itself, it requires root privileges. It is done like this:

```
# fdformat /dev/fd0H1440
Double-sided, 80 tracks, 18 sec/track. Total capacity 1440 kB.
Formatting ... done
Verifying ... done
```

After you have formatted a floppy, don't forget to use `mkfs` to build a filesystem on it. (See the section "Creating New Filesystems" earlier in this chapter.)

Another popular way of accessing floppy disks is to use the `mtools` package, which is a suite of programs designed to enable the user to manipulate DOS-format disks without needing to mount them. The commands are designed specifically to be similar to MS-DOS commands. Windows 95 filesystems are also supported. You will find an introduction to the use of `mtools` in the `mtools` manual page. You can also use `mtools` to access hard disks and disk image files, and it supports many nonstandard disk formats.

CD-ROM Drives

The CD-ROM drive is fundamentally another kind of read-only block device. They are mounted in just the same way as other block devices. CD-ROMs almost always contain standard ISO 9660 filesystems, often with some optional extensions. There is no reason, however, why you should not use any other filesystem. Once you have mounted your CD-ROM, it behaves like any other read-only filesystem.

You can set up and mount your CD-ROM drive using the Red Hat File System Manager, as explained previously, or by using the `mount` command:

```
# mount /dev/cdrom -t iso9660 /mnt/cdrom
```

The directory `/mnt/cdrom` is a common place to mount one's CD-ROM drive under Red Hat Linux because it is where the graphical package manager Glint expects to find the contents of the Red Hat installation CD-ROM, for example.

The device name `/dev/cdrom` is commonly used as a symbolic link to the actual device name corresponding to the CD-ROM because at the time the CD-ROM drive became available for the PC, there was no cheap standard interface for these devices. Each manufacturer chose or invented an interfacing scheme that was incompatible with everyone else's. For this reason, there are about a dozen different drivers for CD-ROM drives available in the Linux kernel. SCSI would have been a sensible standard to use, but although SCSI CD-ROM drives are available, they're not particularly popular.

The ATAPI standard arrived in time to ensure that all non-SCSI CD-ROM drives at quad speed or faster use a standard interface, so the situation is far simpler for new CD-ROM drives. Support for ATAPI CD-ROMs is handled by one driver for all drives. The ATAPI standard also provides for very large hard disk drives and tape drives. ATAPI CD-ROM drives are attached to IDE interfaces, just like hard disks, and they have the same set of device names as hard disk devices.

Because CD-ROMs come already written, there is no need to partition them. They are accessed using the device names for whole-disk devices: `/dev/hda`, `/dev/hdb`, and so on.

The ISO 9660 standard specifies a standard format for the layout of data on CD-ROMs. It restricts filenames to no more than 32 characters, for example. Most CD-ROMs are written with very short filenames for compatibility with MS-DOS. To support certain UNIX features such as symbolic links and long filenames, developers created a set of extensions called *Rock Ridge*, and the Linux kernel will automatically detect and use the Rock Ridge extensions.

CD-ROM drives also usually support the playing of audio CDs, and there are many Linux programs for controlling the CD-ROM drive in the same way as you might control a CD player. The multimedia package on the Red Hat 5.2 CD-ROM contains the `xplay-cd` program for playing CDs. To make it work, you need to set the `/dev/cdrom` symbolic link to point to your real CD-ROM device.

Loopback Devices

Loopback devices enable you to store new filesystems inside regular files. You might want to do this to prepare an emulated hard disk image for DOSEMU, an install disk, or just to try a filesystem of a new type or an ISO9660 CD-ROM image before writing it to the CD writer.

Mounting Filesystems on Files

Under UNIX, you need root permissions to change the system's filesystem structure; even if you own a file and the mount point on which you want to mount it, only root can do this, unless the `user` option has been specified in `/etc/fstab` for this filesystem.

When a filesystem is mounted using the loopback driver, the file containing the filesystem plays the role of the block device in the `mount` command and `/etc/fstab`. The kernel talks to the block device interface provided by the loopback device driver, and the driver forwards operations to the file:

```
# mount $(pwd)/rtems.iso -t iso9660 -o ro,loop /mnt/test
# ls -F /mnt/test
INSTALL    LICENSE    README    SUPPORT    c/    doc/    rr_moved/
# mount ¦ grep loop ¦ fold -s
/home/james/documents/books/Sams/Linux-Unleashed-2/ch9/tmp/rtems.iso on
/mnt/test type iso9660 (ro,loop=/dev/loop0)
# umount /mnt/test
```

Once the loopback filesystem is mounted, it's a normal filesystem.

Using Encrypted Filesystems

Loopback filesystems offer even more features—encryption, for example. A loopback filesystem can be configured to decrypt data from the block device on-the-fly so that the data on the device is useless to people even if they can read it—unless they have the password. The `mount` command prompts for the password at the appropriate time. To make this work, first you have to use `mkfs` to generate a filesystem on the encrypted block device; `losetup` is used to associate a loop device and encryption method with the block device you want to use (in the following case, a floppy drive):

```
# /sbin/losetup -e DES /dev/loop0 /dev/fd1
Password:
Init (up to 16 hex digits):
# /sbin/mkfs -t ext2 -m0 /dev/loop0
mke2fs 1.10, 24-Apr-97 for EXT2 FS 0.5b, 95/08/09
Linux ext2 filesystem format
Filesystem label=
360 inodes, 1440 blocks
0 blocks (0.00) reserved for the super user
First data block=1
Block size=1024 (log=0)
Fragment size=1024 (log=0)
1 block group
8192 blocks per group, 8192 fragments per group
360 inodes per group

Writing inode tables: done
Writing superblocks and filesystem accounting information: done
# losetup -d /dev/loop0
```

As shown previously, `losetup`'s `-e` option associates an encryption method and block device with a loopback device. The `-d` option deletes this association and erases the stored encryption key.

When the filesystem has been created on the encrypted device, it can be mounted in a manner similar to the normal case:

```
# /sbin/losetup -d /dev/loop0
# mount /dev/fd1 -t ext2 -o loop=/dev/loop0,encryption=DES /mnt/test
Password:
Init (up to 16 hex digits):
# ls /mnt/test
lost+found
```

Usually, the whole process of using an encrypted filesystem can be set up for ordinary users by adding the appropriate line to `/etc/fstab`:

```
$ mount /mnt/test
Password:
Init (up to 16 hex digits):
$ ls -ld /mnt/test
drwxrwxrwx  3 james  root    1024 Sep 14 22:04 /mnt/test
```

In this example, root has enabled users to mount encrypted filesystems by including

```
/dev/fd1    /mnt/test    ext2    user,loop,encryption=DES
```

in `/etc/fstab`. Additionally, ownership of the top-level directory on the floppy disk has been given to the user `james` because, presumably, it is his floppy disk. If root had not done this, `james` would have been able to mount his filesystem but not read it. It was an essential step, but it turns out that in this example, root has made a fatal mistake. As well as changing the ownership of the filesystem's root directory, root has changed the directory's mode as well. This means that once the unsuspecting `james` has supplied his secret password, any user on the system can read and write the files on the floppy. This underlines the fact that encryption alone is not sufficient for safety. Careful thought is also essential.

In the previous case, the file ownerships and permissions have turned out to be more of a hindrance than a help. It is probably better to use an MS-DOS filesystem on the encrypted device because ownership is automatically given away to the user mounting the disk and the file modes are set correctly:

```
$ ls -ld  /mnt/floppy/
drwxr-xr-x 2 james  users   7168 Jan  1  1970 /mnt/floppy/
```

However, there are still two problems with this strategy. First, it is not possible to make an encrypted filesystem easily on a floppy because the `mkfs.msdos` program needs to know the geometry for the device on which it is creating the filesystem and the loopback device drivers don't really have geometries. Second, once your encrypted `ext2` filesystem is mounted, the superuser can still read your data.

The encryption methods outlined previously are not available in standard kernels because most useful forms of encryption technology are not legally exportable from the United States. However, they are already available outside the United States at the URL
`ftp://ftp.replay.com/crypto/linux/all/linux-crypt-kernelpatches.tar.gz`.

This site is in Holland. You need to apply these patches to your kernel and recompile it in order to use the DES and IDEA encryption methods with loopback devices. The patches were made against version 2.0.11 of the Linux kernel, but they work perfectly well with the kernel supplied with Red Hat Linux 5.2.

To summarize, encrypted filesystems can be useful for some kinds of data (for example, for storing digital signatures for important system binaries in such a way that they can't be tampered with), but their usefulness to users other than root is limited. Of course, all the ordinary file encryption mechanisms are still available to and useful for ordinary users.

Other Block Devices

Although hard disks, floppy disks, and CD-ROM drives are probably the most heavily used block devices, there are other kinds of block devices, including ramdisks and Zip drives.

Ramdisks

Ramdisks are block devices that store their data in RAM rather than on a disk. This means they are very fast; nevertheless, ramdisks are rarely used with Linux because Linux has a very good disk caching scheme, which provides most of the speed benefit of a ramdisk but not the fixed cost in memory.

The most common use for ramdisks, then, is to serve as a root filesystem while Linux is being installed. A compressed filesystem image is loaded into a ramdisk, and the installation process is run from this disk. The ramdisk's filesystem can be larger than a single floppy because the image is compressed on the floppy.

Although ramdisks are useful with operating systems lacking effective disk buffering, they offer little performance advantage under Linux. If you want to try a ramdisk, they work just like any other block device. For example, to mount a ramdisk as `/tmp`, you add

```
/dev/ram     /tmp        ext2    defaults    0 0
```

to `/etc/fstab` and then create and mount an `ext` filesystem with the following:

```
/sbin/mkfs -t ext2 /dev/ram
mount /tmp
```

Any performance benefits from doing this are hard to find, but you might find that this helps in unusual circumstances.

The principal advantage of ramdisks is that they provide great flexibility in the boot process. Although it is possible to recompile a kernel including support for your hardware, it makes the initial installation process difficult. Historically, programmers worked around this problem by providing dozens of different installation boot disks, each with support for one or two items of boot hardware (SCSI cards and CD-ROM drives, for example).

A simpler solution is to exploit loadable kernel modules. Instead of having separate boot disks for each type of hardware, all containing different kernels, it is simple to provide just one boot disk containing a modular kernel and the module utilities themselves.

A compressed filesystem is loaded from the floppy disk into a ramdisk by the kernel loader, LILO, at the same time the kernel is loaded. The kernel mounts this filesystem and runs a program (`/linuxrc`) from it. This program then mounts the "real" root filesystem and exits, enabling the kernel to remount the real root filesystem on `/`. This system is convenient to set up, and the process of creating initial ramdisks had been automated by Red Hat Software. (See the manual page for `mkinitrd`.) Red Hat Linux systems whose root filesystem is on a SCSI device have a modular kernel and boot by this method.

Zip Drives

Zip drives are drives providing removable 100MB cartridges. They come in three varieties: parallel port (PPA), IDE, and SCSI. All are supported, but the parallel port version is slowest; it is also a SCSI drive but with a proprietary parallel port interface, for which the Linux kernel provides a driver. Hence, both kinds of drive appear as SCSI disks.

Because they're just standard (but removable) SCSI or IDE disks, most aspects of their use are similar to those for other block devices. Red Hat Linux 5.2 comes with support for both the SCSI and PPA varieties. You can find further information in the Zip-Drive mini how-to (which explains how to install your Zip drive), and the Zip-Install mini how-to, which explains how to install Red Hat Linux onto a Zip drive.

Character Devices

Character devices offer a flow of data that must be read in order. Whereas block devices enable a seek to select the next block of data transferred, for example, from one edge or the other of a floppy disk, character devices represent hardware that doesn't have this capability. An example is a terminal, for which the next character to be read is whatever key you type at the keyboard.

In fact, because there are only two basic types of devices, block and character, all hardware is represented as one or the other, rather like the animal and vegetable kingdoms of biological classification. Inevitably, this means that a few devices don't quite fit into this classification scheme. Examples include tape drives, generic SCSI devices, and the special memory devices such as `/dev/port` and `/dev/kmem`.

> **NOTE**
>
> Network interfaces are represented differently; see Chapter 17.

Parallel Ports

Parallel ports are usually used for communicating with printers, although they are versatile enough to support other things too—for example, Zip drives, CD-ROM drives, and even networking.

The hardware itself offers character-at-a-time communication. The parallel port can provide an interrupt to notify the kernel that it is now ready to output a new character, but because printers are usually not performance-critical on most PCs, this interrupt is often borrowed for use by some other hardware, often sound hardware. This has an unfortunate consequence: The kernel often needs to poll the parallel hardware, so driving a parallel printer often requires more CPU work than it should.

The good news is that if your parallel printer interrupt is not in use by some other hardware, it can be enabled with the printer driver configuration program `tunelp`. The `-i` option for `tunelp` sets the IRQ for use with each printer device. You might set the IRQ for the printer port to 7 like this:

```
# /usr/sbin/tunelp /dev/lp1 -i 7
/dev/lp1 using IRQ 7
```

If this results in the printer ceasing to work, going back to the polling method is easy:

```
# /usr/sbin/tunelp /dev/lp1 -i 0
/dev/lp1 using polling
```

The best way to test a printer port under Red Hat Linux is from the Control Panel's Printer Configuration tool (`/usr/bin/printtool`). The Tests menu offers the option of printing a test page directly to the device rather than via the normal printing system. This is a good starting point. You can find more information on setting up printers in Chapter 16, "Printing with Linux."

Tape Drives

Tape drives provide I/O of a stream of bytes to or from the tape. Although most tape drives can be repositioned (that is, rewound and wound forward like audio or video tapes), this operation is very slow by disk standards. Although access to a random part of the tape is at least feasible, it is very slow, so the character device interface is workable for using tape drives.

For most UNIX workstations, the interface of choice for tape drives is SCSI because this fits in well with the SCSI disks and so on. SCSI provides the ability to plug in a new device and start using it. (Of course, you can't do this with the power on.) SCSI has traditionally been more expensive than most other PC technologies, so it wasn't used for many tape drives developed for use with PCs. Several interfaces have been used for tape drives for IBM PCs:

Type	*Device Names*	*Major Number*
SCSI	`/dev/st*`	9
Floppy	`/dev/rft*`	27
QIC-02	`/dev/rmt`	12
IDE	`/dev/ht*`	37
Parallel Port	(Currently unsupported)	

All these tape drives have the feature that when the device is closed, the tape is rewound. All these drives except the QIC-02 drive have a second device interface with a name prefixed with `n`—for example `/dev/nst0`, `/dev/nst3`, or `/dev/nht0`. All these devices support the magnetic tape control program, `mt`, which is used for winding tapes past files, rewinding them, and so on. Many commands, particularly the more advanced `mt` commands, are only available for SCSI tape drives.

Apart from the `mt` command for the basic control of a tape drive, there are many commands that you can use for storing and retrieving data on tape. Because the character devices are "just files," you could use `cat` to store data on the tape, but this is not very flexible. A great many programs are particularly or partly designed with tape drives in mind:

`tar` — This is widely used for creating archives in regular files but was originally created for making tape backups. In fact, `tar` stands for *tape archiver*. Archives made by `tar` can be read on a wide variety of systems.

`cpio` — Another program principally intended for backups and so on, `cpio` stands for copy in–out. The GNU version of `cpio`, which is used by Linux distributions, supports eight different data formats—some of which are varieties of its "native" format, two are varieties of `tar` archives, and some are obsolete. If you want to unpack an unknown archive, `cpio`, along with `file` and `dd`, is very useful.

`dump` — The `dump` utility is of use only to system administrators because it backs up an `ext2` filesystem by raw access to the block device on which the filesystem exists. (For this reason, it is better to do this when the filesystem is either not mounted or is mounted read-only.) This has the advantage, among other things, that the access times of the backed-up directories are left unmodified. (GNU `tar` will also do this.) Although tapes written with `dump` are not always readable on other versions of UNIX, unlike those written by `tar` and `cpio`, `dump` is a popular choice.

`dd` — Designed for blockwise I/O, `dd` is a general-purpose tool for doing file manipulations and can often be useful.

`afio` — A variant of `cpio`, `afio` compresses individual files into the backup. For backups, this is preferable to `tar`'s compression of the whole archive because a small tape error can make a compressed `tar` archive useless, although a `tar` archive that isn't compressed doesn't have this vulnerability. `afio` isn't widely used outside the Linux world.

Amanda	Amanda is a powerful backup system that schedules, organizes, and executes backups for you. It uses either `tar` or `dump` to do the actual work and will effortlessly allow you to automate all the backups for one machine or a multitude. One of its most useful features is its ability to perform fast backups across the network from several client machines to a single server machine containing a tape drive. More information about Amanda is available at the URL `http://www.cs.umd.edu/projects/amanda/`; RPMs of Amanda are available on the Red Hat FTP site.
BRU	BRU (Backup and Restore Utility) is a commercial product for making backups.

Terminals

The *terminal* is the principal mode of communication between the kernel and the user. When you type keystrokes, the terminal driver turns them into input readable by the shell or whatever program you are running.

For many years, UNIX ran only on serial terminals. Although most computers now also have video hardware, the terminal is still a useful concept. Each window in which you can run a shell provides a separate *pseudo-terminal*, each one rather like a traditional serial terminal. Terminals are often called `ttys` because the device nodes for many of them have names like `/dev/tty*`.

The terminal interface is used to represent serial lines to "real" terminals, to other computers (via modems), mice, printers, and so on. The large variety of hardware addressed by the terminal interface has led to a wide range of capabilities offered by the terminal device driver, and explaining all the facilities offered could easily occupy an entire chapter. This section just offers an overview of the facilities.

For more complete information on terminals and serial I/O, refer to the Linux Documentation Project's excellent how-to documents. These are provided on the Red Hat Linux 5.2 CD-ROM and are also available on the Web at `http://sunsite.unc.edu/LDP/`. Specific how-tos dealing with this are the Serial how-to, Section 9 of the Hardware how-to, and the Serial Port Programming mini how-to. Many documents deal with using modems for networking. They are mentioned later in the chapter in the section "Using Modems."

The Terminal Device Driver

The terminal device driver gathers the characters you type at the keyboard and sends them to the program you're working with, after some processing. This processing can involve gathering the characters into batches a line at a time and taking into account the special meanings of some keys you might type.

Some special keys of this sort are used for editing the text that is sent to the program you're interacting with. Much of the time, the terminal driver is building a line of input that it hasn't yet sent to the program receiving your input. Keys that the driver will process specially include the following:

Return (CR) or Line Feed (LF)

CR is usually translated into LF by the terminal driver. (See the `icrnl` option in the manual page for `stty`.) This ends the current line, which is then sent to the application. (It is waiting for terminal input, so it wakes up.)

Backspace/Delete

Only one of these two keys can be selected as the erase key, which erases the previous character typed. For more information, read the Linux Keyboard Setup mini how-to.

End-of-File, Usually Ctrl+D

When a program is reading its standard input from the keyboard, and you want to let it know that you've typed everything, you press Ctrl+D. ("Usually" indicates that this option is shell dependent and may differ depending upon which shell you are using.)

Word-Erase, Usually Ctrl+W

This combination deletes the last word you typed.

Kill-Line, Usually Ctrl+U

This kills the entire line of input so that you can start again.

Interrupt, Usually Ctrl+C

This kills the current program. Some programs block this at times when the program might leave the terminal in a strange state if it were unexpectedly killed.

Suspend, Usually Ctrl+Z

This key sends a suspend signal to the program you're using. The result is that the program is stopped temporarily, and you get the shell prompt again. You can then put that program (job) in the background and do something else. See Chapter 25, "Shell Programming," for more information.

Quit, Usually Ctrl+\ (Ctrl+Backslash)

Sends a Quit signal to the current program; programs that ignore Ctrl+C can often be stopped with Ctrl+\, but programs ignoring Ctrl+C are often doing so for a reason.

Stop, Usually Ctrl+S, and Start, Usually Ctrl+Q

These keys stop and restart terminal output temporarily, which can be useful if a command produces a lot of output, although it can often be more useful to repeat the command and pipe it through `less`.

You can examine many other terminal modes and settings with the `stty` command. This command has a built-in set of sensible settings for terminals, and typing `stty` to find the current settings usually shows you only the differences from its "sane" settings:

```
$ stty
speed 9600 baud; line = 0;
```

TIP

If you ever find that your terminal state is messed up, you can usually fix it with the command `$ stty sane` and Ctrl+J. Note that you finish the command Ctrl+J, rather than Enter (which is the same as Ctrl+M). The `icrnl` option might have been turned off. This is fixed again with `stty sane`. GNU `bash` will always cope with CRs that have not been converted to LF anyway, but some other programs won't.

If this still doesn't work, and the screen font appears to have been changed, type `$ echo`, press Ctrl+V and Esc, type `c`, and press Ctrl+J. You press Ctrl+V to make the terminal driver pass the next key without processing. You can get a similar effect by typing `$ reset` and pressing Ctrl+J, but the program `reset` is only available if the `ncurses` package is installed.

Programs can turn off the processing that the line driver does by default; the resulting behavior (raw mode) allows programs to read unprocessed input from the terminal driver (for example, CR is not mapped to LF), and control characters don't produce the signals described in the table earlier in this section. The `stty sane` command will return things to normal.

Serial Communications

Although the terminal interfaces used most commonly under Linux are the console driver and the pseudo-terminals driven by programs such as `xterm`, `script`, and `expect`, the original terminal interface involved serial communications. In fact, this still lingers; a pseudo-`tty` associated with an `xterm` window still has an associated baud rate as shown in the example in the section "The Terminal Device Driver." Changing this baud rate has no actual effect. For real serial ports, however, the baud rate and many other parameters have a direct relevance. The device nodes relating to the serial ports are composed of two "teams," with the names /dev/cua* and /dev/ttyS*. Starting with version 2.2 of the kernel (which includes the one with this book), /dev/ttyS* is the "correct" name to use. /dev/cua* will, most likely, disappear from the next version or two. The device nodes allow you to use the same serial hardware for both incoming and outgoing serial connections, as explained later in the section "Using Modems."

Configuring the Serial Ports

Serial port configuration is mostly done either with the stty command or directly by programs using the interface outlined in the termios manual page. The stty command offers almost all the configuration possibilities provided by termios; however, there are configuration issues for serial hardware that are not addressed by stty. The setserial command allows the configuration of the correct IRQ settings for each serial port and of extra-fast baud rates that the standard termios specification doesn't provide. For more detailed information, refer to the Linux Serial how-to and the manual page for setserial.

Using Modems

Modems (other than "WinModems") are very flexible devices. They allow dial-up terminal access and wide area networking, and they also often allow you to send and receive faxes or voice mail. The two "teams" of serial device nodes mentioned earlier are intended specifically for good modem support, and they look like this:

```
$ ls -l /dev/ttyS* /dev/cua* /dev/mo*
crw-rw----    1 root     uucp       5,  64 Jan  1  1980 /dev/cua0
crw-rw----    1 root     uucp       5,  65 Jan  1  1980 /dev/cua1
crw-rw----    1 root     uucp       5,  66 Jan  1  1980 /dev/cua2
crw-rw----    1 root     uucp       5,  67 Jan  1  1980 /dev/cua3
lrwxrwxrwx    1 root     uucp            4 Jun  7 14:16 /dev/modem -> cua2
lrwxrwxrwx    1 root     root           10 Sep  6  1996 /dev/mouse ->
➥/dev/ttyS0
crw-r--r--    1 root     root       4,  64 Nov  1 08:56 /dev/ttyS0
crw-r--r--    1 root     root       4,  65 May 29  1995 /dev/ttyS1
crw-r--r--    1 root     root       4,  66 Jan  1  1980 /dev/ttyS2
crw-r--r--    1 root     root       4,  67 Jan  1  1980 /dev/ttyS3
```

The /dev/cua* devices are intended for use for dialing out, and the /dev/ttyS* devices are intended for dialing in. A process such as getty can be waiting for an open system call to complete (that is, waiting for the modem to signal that there is an incoming call) on the /dev/ttyS0 device while you are opening the corresponding device /dev/cua0, which refers to the same hardware. Because there can't be an incoming call on that line while you're using the modem, getty continues to wait. Lock files keep everyone from trying to use the same device at the same time.

These days, internetworking is the most common use for modems. Many resources will help you set up your machine for Internet access via a modem. See the section "Connecting to the Net with PPP" in Chapter 17. Other resources include the Red Hat PPP Tips document, which can be found in the support section of Red Hat's Web site, the EzPPP package, and the ISP-Hookup and PPP how-tos. A large number of useful mini how-tos each help with more specific things; these include the Diald, Dip+SLiRP+CSLIP, Dynamic-IP-Hacks, IP-Masquerade, PPP-over-ISDN, PPP-over-minicom, SLIP+proxyARP, and Tiny-News Linux mini how-tos. If, on the other hand, you send and receive email by UUCP rather than Internet protocols, you should read the Linux UUCP how-to and the Linux Sendmail+UUCP mini how-to.

Generic SCSI Devices

Not all SCSI devices are hard disks, CD-ROM drives, or tape drives. Some are optical scanners, CD-ROM recorders, or even electron microscopes. The kernel can't possibly abstract the interfaces for all possible SCSI devices, so it gives user programs direct access to SCSI hardware via the generic SCSI devices. These enable programs to send arbitrary SCSI commands to hardware. Although this arrangement offers the opportunity of wreaking havoc by mistake, it also offers the capability of driving all sorts of interesting hardware, of which the principal examples are CD-ROM recorders. The SCSI device nodes all have names starting with `/dev/sg`. SCSI commands are sent to the devices by writing data to the device, and the results are read back by reading from the device.

CD-ROM Recorders

CD-ROM recorders are devices for recording data on special media that can be read in ordinary CD-ROM drives. There are two stages in the writing of a CD: generating the CD image and writing that image to the media.

The surface of a CD-R (recordable CD) is only writable once, so if `mkisofs` worked like the other `mkfs` tools, it would always generate image files representing empty CDs. For this reason, `mkisofs` populates the filesystem with files as it generates the image file.

The CD image file is produced by the `mkisofs` program, which generates the structures for an ISO 9660 filesystem and populates it with the files from a directory tree. CDs are not writable in the same sense as block devices; this is why they are not actually block devices. The image file must be written to the CD-R with a specialized program, `cdwrite`, which understands all the various proprietary schemes used for driving CD writers. All the CD writers supported by Linux (as of version 2.0.30 of the kernel) are SCSI devices, so the kernel accommodates this by providing access to the generic SCSI device interface that enables a program to send SCSI commands to these devices.

While *burning* (writing) a CD, it is usually important that the flow of data to the writer keeps up with the speed at which the writer is going; otherwise, if the writer runs out of data to write, the CD-R is ruined. For this reason, it is usual to use `mkisofs` to generate an image file and then separately use `cdwrite` to write this image file to the CD writer.

It is possible to use a pipe to send the data from `mkisofs` directly to `cdwrite`. This often works either because a fast machine can ensure that `mkisofs` supplies the data fast enough to keep the CD writer busy or because the CD writer is not sensitive to data underruns. (Some of the more expensive ones have internal hard disks to which the data is written during an intermediate stage.) This technique is not recommended, however, because the generation of the intermediate image file has other benefits; it enables you to test your CD image before the final writing of the data takes place.

Testing CD Images

Just as you can use `mkfs` to create a filesystem inside an ordinary file, you can mount filesystems contained in ordinary files by using the loopback device driver described previously. The first example of mounting a loopback filesystem is a demonstration of how you can test a CD image.

Other Character Devices

Several other varieties of character devices, such as `/dev/null`, are used frequently.

The Controlling Terminal Device—/dev/tty

Most processes have a controlling terminal, particularly if they were started interactively by a user. The *controlling terminal*, which I refer to as simply `/dev/tty`, is used for initiating a conversation directly with the user (for example, to ask him something). An example is the `crypt` command:

```
$ fmt diary.txt ¦ crypt ¦ mail -s Diary confidant@linux.org
Enter key:
$
```

Here, the `crypt` command has opened `/dev/tty` to obtain a password. It was not able to use its own standard output to issue the prompt and its standard input to read the password because they are being used for the data to be encrypted.

NOTE

Of course, it's unusual to send email encrypted with `crypt`. A better choice is probably PGP. PGP is available in RPM format from `ftp://ftp.replay.com//pub/linux/redhat`.

More useful examples are commands that need to ask the operator something even if the input and output are redirected. A case in point is the `cpio` command, which prompts the operator for the name of a new tape device when it runs out of space. See the section "`/dev/null` and Friends" later in this chapter for another example.

Nonserial Mice

Many computers have bus or PS/2 mice instead of serial mice. This arrangement has the advantage of keeping both of the two standard serial ports free, but the disadvantage of using up another IRQ. These devices are used by `gpm` and the X Window system, but most other programs don't interact with them directly. Setting up your system with these mice is easy; the Red Hat Linux installation process pretty much takes care of it for you. If you have problems with your mouse, however, you should read the manual page for `gpm` and the Linux BusMouse how-to.

Audio Devices

There are several audio-related device nodes on Linux systems, and they include the following:

`/dev/sndstat`	Indicates the status of the sound driver
`/dev/audio*`	Sun-compatible audio output device
`/dev/dsp*`	Sound sampling device
`/dev/mixer`	For control of the mixer hardware on the sound card
`/dev/music`	A high-level sequencer interface
`/dev/sequencer*`	A low-level sequencer interface
`/dev/midi*`	Direct MIDI port access

Setting up the sound driver under Linux can sometimes be difficult, but the Linux Sound how-to provides useful advice.

Random Number Devices

Many program features require the generation of apparently random sequences. Examples include games, numerical computations, and various computer-security–related applications. Numerical computing with random numbers requires that the sequence of random numbers be repeatable but also that the sequence "look" random. Games require apparently random numbers, but the quality of the random numbers is not quite as critical as for numerical computation programs. The system libraries produce repeatable sequences of "pseudo-random" numbers that satisfy these requirements well.

On the other hand, in many aspects of computer security, it is advantageous to generate numbers that really are random. Because you can assume that an attacker has access to the same sorts of random number generators that you do, using them is not very safe; an attacker can use these generators to figure out what random number you'll use next. Sequences that are genuinely random must in the end be produced from the real world and not from the internals of some computer program. For this reason, the Linux kernel keeps a supply of random numbers internally. These numbers are derived from very precise timings of the intervals between "random" external events—for example, the user's key presses on the keyboard, mouse events, and even some interrupts (such as from the floppy disk drive and some network cards). These "real" random numbers are used in security-critical contexts—for example, the choosing of TCP sequence numbers.

NOTE

The Linux kernel uses these methods to produce TCP sequence numbers that are more difficult to guess than those of any other implementation at the time of writing. This improves the security of TCP connections against "hijacking."

The two random number devices differ in what happens when the rate of reading exceeds the rate at which random data is collected inside the kernel. The `/dev/random` device makes the calling program wait until some more randomness arrives, and the `/dev/urandom` device falls back on the difficult-to-guess MD5 hash to produce a stream of random data. When more random information arrives later, it is added to the randomness of `/dev/urandom`. To summarize, `/dev/random` doesn't sacrifice quality in favor of speed, but `/dev/urandom` does.

`/dev/null` and Friends

In the following segment, the special devices `/dev/full` and `/dev/null` first simulate a tape-full condition and then discard the output:

```
$ echo diary.txt | cpio -o >/dev/full
Found end of tape.  To continue, type device/file name when ready.
/dev/null
52 blocks
```

In the real world, when the tape on `/dev/st0` becomes full, you probably just change the tape in the drive and type `/dev/st0` a second time. However, `/dev/full` is occasionally useful for testing purposes, and `/dev/null` is used all the time for discarding unwanted output. The device `/dev/full` produces a stream of zero bytes when read. (`/dev/null`, on the other hand, produces no output at all.)

Memory Devices

The memory devices have the same major device number as /dev/null and /dev/full but are used differently. They are as follows:

/dev/mem	Provides access to physical memory
/dev/kmem	Provides access to the kernel's virtual memory
/dev/port	Provides access to I/O ports

These devices are not frequently used in many programs; the X Window system's X server uses memory mapping on /dev/mem to access the video memory, and many programs use /dev/port to access I/O ports on those architectures that have a separate I/O space. (Many modern processors do not.)

Virtual Console Screen Devices

The virtual console screen devices exist to provide screen capture capabilities for virtual consoles (VCs). They are not readable by ordinary users; hence, other users cannot eavesdrop on your session.

There are two sets of device nodes for this purpose:

```
$ ls -l /dev/vcs[012] /dev/vcsa[012]
crw--w----   1 root     tty        7,   0 Sep 27  1995 /dev/vcs0
crw--w----   1 root     tty        7,   1 Sep 27  1995 /dev/vcs1
crw--w----   1 root     tty        7,   2 Sep 27  1995 /dev/vcs2
crw--w----   1 root     tty        7, 128 Sep 27  1995 /dev/vcsa0
crw--w----   1 root     tty        7, 129 Sep 27  1995 /dev/vcsa1
crw--w----   1 root     tty        7, 130 Sep 27  1995 /dev/vcsa2
```

Each set is numbered from 0 to 63, corresponding to the numbering system for the /dev/tty* console devices. The device /dev/vcs0, like the device dev/tty0, always refers to the currently selected VC.

The /dev/vcs* files provide a snapshot of what is in view on the corresponding VC. This snapshot contains no newlines because there are none actually on the screen; after all, a newline character just moves the cursor. To make the captured data into the kind of thing you usually see in text files or send to printers, you need to add newlines in the appropriate places. This can be done with dd:

```
$ dd cbs=80 conv=unblock </dev/vcs1 | lpr
```

This command works only if the screen is 80 columns wide. This is not always true; the kernel can set up a different video mode at boot time, and you can use the SVGATextMode command to change it at any time.

You can overcome this problem by using the other set of devices, `/dev/vcsa*`. Reading from these devices gives a header, followed by the screen data with attribute bytes. The header consists of two bytes indicating the screen size (height first), followed by two bytes indicating the cursor position. The screen data is provided at a rate of two bytes per character cell, the first containing the attribute byte and the second containing the character data (as with `/dev/vcs*`). You can use this data to provide full-color screen dumps and so on. The following script uses `/dev/vcsa1` to determine the width of the VC and to get the conversion of `/dev/vcs1` right:

```
#! /bin/sh

# Insist on exactly one argument (the VC number to dump)
[ $# -eq 1 ] || { echo "usage: $0 [vc-number]" >&2; exit 1 }

vc=$1 # Which VC to dump.

# Extract the VC's width from the second byte of the vcsa device.
# Th "unpack" expression extracts the value of the second
# character of the input (the vcsa device).
width='perl -e 'print unpack("x%C",<>);' < /dev/vcsa${vc}'

# Use dd(1) to convert the output now that we know the width.
dd cbs=${width} conv=unblock </dev/vcs${vc}
```

Summary

This chapter introduces the topics of character and block devices and filesystem administration and gives an overview of the hardware accessed via the special files in the directory `/dev`. You can find further information from the Linux Documentation Project material at `http://sunsite.unc.edu/LDP`. Much of the LDP material is also provided on the CD-ROM accompanying this book.

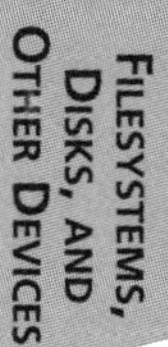

CHAPTER

Printing with Linux

by Bill Ball

In This Chapter

This chapter shows you how to use your printer with Linux. A number of programs, files, and directories are integral to supporting printing under Linux, but you'll find that with little effort, you'll be able to get to work and print nicely formatted documents or graphics.

If you can print to your printer from DOS, Windows 98, or Windows NT, don't worry! Chances are you'll be able to print under Linux, and you'll probably be pleasantly surprised by the additional printing capabilities you won't find in the commercial operating system installed on your PC.

As a Red Hat Linux user, you'll be especially pleased because the kind folks in North Carolina have hidden the ugly and gory details of installing and using a printer and have made the process a snap!

Printer Devices

Under Linux, each piece of your computer's hardware is abstracted to a device file (hopefully with an accompanying device driver in the kernel; see Chapter 15, "Filesystems, Disks, and Other Devices," for more details). Printer devices, traditionally named after line printers, are character mode devices and will be found in the /dev directory. Some of these are shown in Table 16.1.

Table 16.1 PARALLEL PRINTER DEVICES

Device Name	*Printer*	*Address*
`/dev/lp0`	First parallel printer	`0x3bc`
`/dev/lp1`	Second parallel printer	`0x378`
`/dev/lp2`	Third parallel printer	`0x278`

Serial printers are assigned to serial devices such as `/dev/ttySX`, where X is a number from 0 to 3. Quite a few `tty` devices are listed in /dev. Generally, if you're going to use a serial printer, you'll have to use the `setserial` command to make sure the printer's serial port is set to the fastest baud rate your printer supports.

In some special cases, such as using an old Apple LaserWriter as a serial printer (it has a Diablo print-wheel emulation mode using the Courier font), you must define your own printer or edit an entry in the /etc/printcap database. Sometimes you can manipulate the printer to get a higher speed. For example, here's a 10-year-old trick, posted to the `comp.laser-printers` newsgroup by Dale Carstensen, for increasing the serial port speed of the Apple LaserWriter Plus to 19200:

```
%!
0000 % Server Password
statusdict begin 25 sccbatch 0 ne exch 19200 ne or
{ serverdict begin exitserver} {pop end stop} ifelse
statusdict begin
25 19200 0 setsccbatch
end % note—next line has an actual CTRL-D
```

See Appendix D in the *RedBook*, Adobe's PostScript language reference manual, for more information about LaserWriters, or peruse `comp.laser-printers` for hints on setting up your laser printer. Also check the /usr/lib/ghostscript/doc directory for information about 25 PostScript printer utilities included in the Ghostscript distribution.

Most users, however, have a printer attached to the parallel printer port, so I'll concentrate on /dev/lp.

What Printer Should I Use with Linux?

Nearly any printer that uses your computer's serial or parallel port should work; however, printers using Printing Performance Architecture (PPA), such as the HP 720, 820, or 1000-series printers, should be avoided. These printers require a special software driver (available only for Win95 at the time of this writing).

A PostScript printer is the best printer to use with Linux because many programs and text utilities used with Linux and ported from other Unix systems output graphics and text as PostScript. However, another great reason to use Linux, and Red Hat's distribution of Linux, is that through the magic of software, your $129 inkjet printer can also print PostScript documents—even in color. That's a bargain!

You'll find excellent support for many different printers. Red Hat Linux comes with a special configuration tool, called `printtool`, that directly supports more than 30 printers (see "The RHS Linux Print System Manager" later in this chapter). The Ghostscript interpreter, included with Red Hat Linux, is an integral part of Linux printing for many users and supports nearly 100 different printers. Table 16.2 lists Ghostscript drivers and supported printers. For the latest list of supported printers and other information, see Ghostscript's home page at `http://www.cs.wisc.edu/~ghost/printer.html`.

Table 16.2 GHOSTSCRIPT DRIVERS AND SUPPORTED PRINTERS

Driver	*Printer(s)*
bj10e	Canon BJ10e
bj200	Canon BJC-210, 240, 250, 70, 200
bjc600	Canon BJC-600, 610, 4000, 4100, 4200,4300, 4550, 210, C2500240, 70
bjc800	BJC-800, 7000
cdeskjet	HP DeskJet 500C
cdj500	HP DeskJet 400, 500C, 540C, 690C, 693C
cdj550	HP DeskJet 550C, 560C, 600, 660C, 682C, 683C, 693C, 694C, 850, 870C
cdj850	HP DeskJet 850, 855, 870Cse, 870Cxi, 890C, 672C, 680
cdjcolor	(24-bit color for cdj500 supported printers)
cdjmono	HP DeskJet 500C, 510, 520, 540C, 693C
deskjet	HP DeskJet, Plus
djet500	HP DeskJet 500, Portable
lj4dith	HP DeskJet 600
ljet4	HP DeskJet 600, 870Cse; LaserJet 5, 5L, 6L, Oki OL410ex
ljetplus	NEC SuperScript 860
pjxl300	HP PaintJet XL300, HP DeskJet 600, 1200C, 1600C
r4081	Ricoh 4081, 6000 laser printers
stcolor	Epson Stylus Color, Color II, 500, 600, 800
uniprint	Canon BJC 610, HP DeskJet 550C, NEC P2X, Epson Stylus Color, II, 500, 600, 800, 1520

In general, if you have a printer that supports some form of printer control language (PCL), you shouldn't have problems.

How Do I Print?

First, check to see that your printer is plugged in, turned on, and attached to your computer's parallel port. Pass-through parallel port cables shouldn't pose a problem, but don't expect to be able to use your printer while you're using your CD-ROM, QuickCam, SCSI adapter, or tape, ZIP, or SyQuest drive if attached to a pass-through cable.

For starters, try a simple

```
# ls >/dev/lp1
```

Chances are your printer will activate and its print head will move, but when you look at the printout, you might see a staircase effect, with each word on a separate line, moving across the page. Don't worry—this is normal and tells you that you can at least access your printer. Later in this chapter, you'll find out how to fine-tune your printing.

If you're unable to print, try using

```
# cat /proc/devices
```

to see if the `lp` device driver loaded or compiled into your kernel. You should see something like the following:

```
Character devices:
 1 mem
 2 pty
 3 ttyp
 4 ttyp
 5 cua
 6 lp
 7 vcs
10 misc
14 sound
63 pcmcia
Block devices:
 1 ramdisk
 2 fd
 3 ide0
 9 md
22 ide1
```

You can also try the `tunelp` command, which sets various parameters to "tune" your printer port or lets you know if your printer device is using interrupts or polling for printing. Try using

```
# tunelp /dev/lp1
```

and you might see something like the following:

```
/dev/lp1 using polling
```

Or you can try

```
# tunelp /dev/lp1 -s
```

and you might see

```
/dev/lp1 status is 223, on-line
```

If `tunelp` reports "No such device or address," or if you do not find an `lp` character device, see Chapter 28, "Configuring and Building Kernels."

The RHS Linux Print System Manager

If you want to install, modify, or delete a local, remote, or LAN printer, you're going to love the `printtool` program. Found in /usr/bin, `printtool` is a graphical interface printer setup program you can call up from the command line or through the Red Hat `control-panel` program.

The `control-panel` and `printtool` programs run under X, so you'll have to first fire up X and then type

```
# printtool
```

from a terminal window. The main `printtool` dialog then comes up. Click the Add button and you'll be asked to select a local, remote, or LAN manager printer (see Figure 16.1).

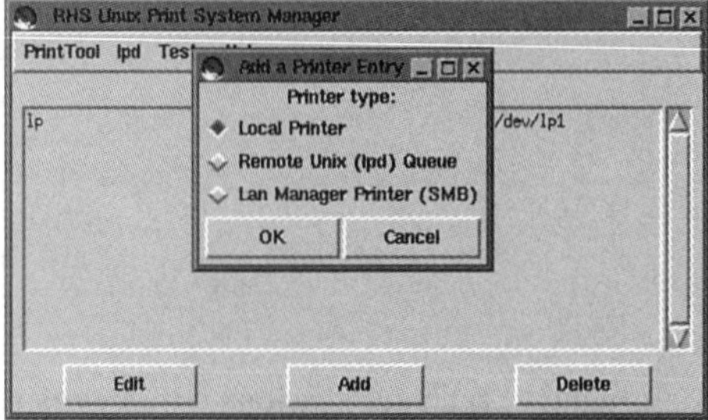

FIGURE 16.1
The `printtool` *Add a Printer Entry dialog.*

Remote and LAN Printers

To set up a remote printer, you'll need the following, according to the `printtool` program's help information:

- The hostname of the remote machine hosting the printer
- The printer queue name of the printer on the remote machine

This means you can send documents to other printers anywhere. Using Red Hat's `printtool` command to set up remote printing creates a remote printer entry in /etc/printcap. For details about a remote printer entry, see the `printcap` man page and look for the `rm` and `rp` capabilities. But you should also know there are other, possibly easier ways to print to remote printers, such as using the `rlpr` command. For more information, read Grant Taylor's *Linux Printing HOWTO* under /usr/doc/HOWTO.

Before you can print to a LAN printer, you *must* have Server Message Block services enabled (through the smbd daemon, part of the SAMBA software package) and have the `smbprint`/`smbclient` command installed under the /usr/bin directory. You must also be connected to a Windows network and have printer sharing enabled under Windows.

For example, under Windows 95, navigate to the Network device in the Control Panel (available through the Settings menu item in the Start menu). Press the File and Print Sharing button, select "I want to be able to allow others to print to my printers," and press the OK button. Then press the Identification tab at the top of the Network window, note the name of your computer, and close the window.

Next, open the Printers folder, right-click on the printer you would like to share, and select the Sharing menu item. Select Shared As, enter a Shared Name and a password, and press the OK button. You'll need the name and password information when you run `printtool`. To set up a LAN printer, you'll need the following (according to `printtool`):

- Printer server name
- Printer server IP number
- Printer name
- Printer user
- Printer password

This information is entered in a dialog that pops up after you select the type of printer you want to set up. You can also select the type of printer through the Select button at the Input Filter field (similar to that shown in Figure 16.3).

NOTE

Check Chapter 17, "TCP/IP Network Management," for tips on printing through Apple LocalTalk networks and Chapter 14, "Samba," for information on setting up other services through Server Message Block (SMB) Windows-based networks. Need more detailed instructions on how to print from Red Hat Linux to a printer on a Windows 95/98/NT system or to print on a Linux printer from Windows 95? Browse to http://www.redhat.com/support/docs/rhl/Samba-Tips. You'll also find the latest information about Samba at `http://samba.anu.edu.au/samba`.

After you fill out your LAN printer's information and press the OK button, `printtool` creates a printer entry in your system's printer-capabilities database, /etc/printcap (see Linux printing commands later in this chapter). The printer entry might look something like this:

```
##PRINTTOOL3## SMB cdj500 300x300 letter {} DeskJet500 1 1
lp0:\
        :sd=/var/spool/lpd/lp0:\
        :mx#0:\
        :sh:\
        :if=/var/spool/lpd/lp0/filter:\
        :af=/var/spool/lpd/lp0/acct:\
        :lp=/dev/null:
```

NOTE

You'll receive a warning before you create a LAN printer for Red Hat Linux with `printtool`. You should know that when you use `printtool` to create a LAN printer entry, a file named `.config`, containing the Share (server) name, the printer user name, and the password, is created under the `/var/spool/lpd` directory, or spool directory. This file is not encrypted, and anyone on your system can read it!

Before you can print to your LAN printer, you should have an active network connection. You can then use the –P option of the `lpr` command, followed by your new LAN printer's name and the name of the file you'd like to print. Using the `/etc/printcap` entry given earlier for lp0, to print a file called myfile.txt, use `lpr` like this:

```
# lpr -Plp0 myfile.txt
```

You can also use the `smbprint` command, part of Andrew Tridgell's collection of programs in the Samba software package, to print to a LAN printer. The `smbprint` command is a shell script, found under the /usr/bin directory, that uses the `smbclient` command to send files to a shared printer. In fact, a modified version of `smbprint` is used as Red Hat's printer filter when you create a LAN printer entry with `printtool`. For details about `smbclient`, see its man page.

Local Printers

For now, I'll assume you're going to set up a parallel port printer attached directly to your computer. To do so, run `printtool` and then click the Add button, select Local, and click the OK button.

Linux then tries to load the parallel printing module, lp.o, if you haven't compiled parallel printing support into your kernel. An Info dialog appears, telling you what parallel printer devices have been detected (see Figure 16.2). If `printtool` reports that no device was found, check to make sure your printer cable is correctly attached and your printer is turned on.

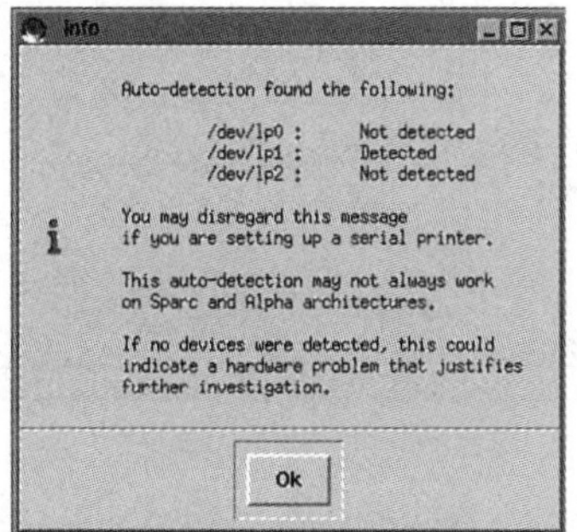

FIGURE 16.2
The printtool printer device auto-detection dialog informs you if Linux found an attached local printer.

Click OK. If you'd like to give your printer a name, type a name in the Names field. If you want to limit the size of any spooled printer files (because you don't have enough space on your hard drive), enter a number (such as 1024 for one megabyte). After you have finished, click the Select button in the Edit Local Printer Entry dialog (see Figure 16.3).

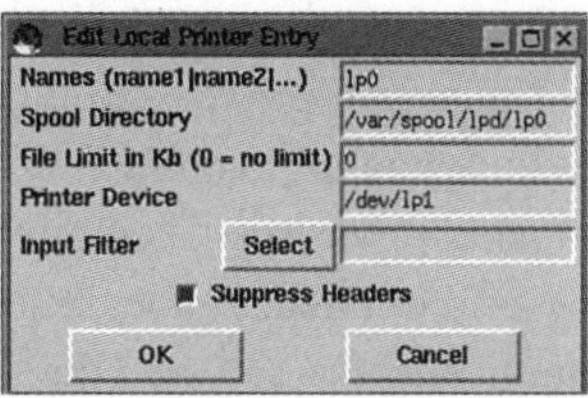

FIGURE 16.3
The printtool printer device main configuration dialog allows you to name printers and limit the size of spooled printer files.

A large dialog appears, called Configure Filter, with a list of more than 30 popular printers to choose from (see Figure 16.4). Pick your printer or a printer close to yours, and then click the OK button.

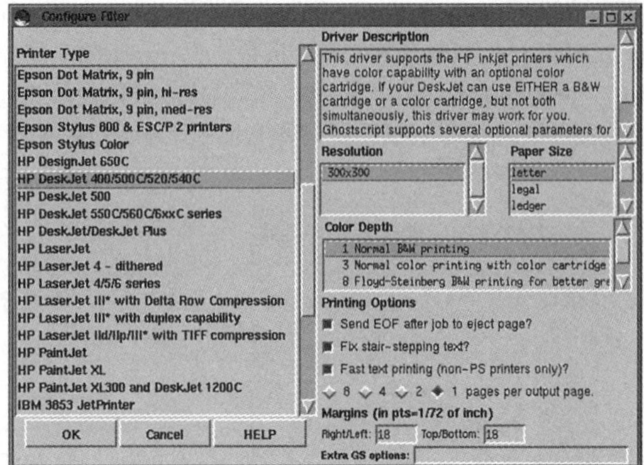

FIGURE 16.4
The printtool printer Configure Filter dialog provides for custom settings of your printer.

The dialog disappears and you can click OK on the Edit Local Printer Entry dialog. The printer you defined should now appear under the list of Printer Queues in the main `printtool` dialog. Select it and then select an ASCII or PostScript test from the Tests menu.

The ASCII test page prints two lines of text, followed by a centered paragraph of text. The PostScript test page prints a half-inch and one-inch border, a logo, and a color scale (grayscale on a black-and-white printer).

The `printtool` program (written in the Python language—see Chapter 34, "Programming in Python") works by first defining your printer and then inserting the definition into an /etc/printcap entry, along with a pointer to a filter script (written in bash—see Chapter 25, "Shell Programming") in the /var/spool/lpd directory. The filter and associated scripts reside in a directory, or printer queue, under /var/spool/lpd, with either a name you choose or an assigned default, such as `lp0`. See the sample /etc/printcap database file later in this chapter.

You can use `printtool` to add, edit, or delete printers. Another nice feature is the ability to assign a size limit to spooled files, which can be helpful if you have limited disk space or don't want users to fill up your filesystem. If you have a printer that requires you to change the print cartridge so you can print black-and-white or color pages, you'll find `printtool` indispensable. Try it!

By the way, although the current version of `printtool`, 3.27, creates a backup of your /etc/printcap database each time you make a change, it does not delete the associated printer queue, or spool directory, when you delete a printer. One disconcerting `printtool` bug is that while you're printing, at least with a kernel using polling, your printer's parallel port will not be detected if you run `printtool` to install a printer. Perhaps this will be fixed in a newer version.

Linux Printing Commands

Of course, you don't have to use the `printtool` command to set up your printer. You can edit /etc/printcap directly, but you should know what you're doing and understand `printcap`'s format. This file, an ASCII database of your system's local and networked printers, describes the capabilities of each printer in detail. For full details, see the `printcap` man page for commands and the `termcap` man page for the file's layout.

In fact, you can have multiple entries for each printer, which is helpful if you want to print on different size papers, print color or black-and-white documents, or change printer trays.

Linux uses the 4.3BSD line printer spooling system. This system has a number of features and associated programs to support background printing, multiple local and networked printers, and control of the printers and queued documents.

The main files used in the Linux printer spooling system are as follows:

```
/etc/printcap
/usr/sbin/lpd
/usr/sbin/lpc
/usr/bin/lpr
/usr/bin/lprm
/usr/bin/lpq
/dev/printer
```

When you first boot Linux, the shell script `lpd.init`, under /etc/rc.d/init.d/, starts `lpd`, the printer daemon. This program, a printer server, runs in the background, waiting for print requests. When a request is detected (on `/dev/printer`), a copy of `lpd` is created, while the original daemon continues to wait for more requests.

Print requests are started with the `lpr` command. For example, the command line

```
# lpr myfile.txt
```

will print your document to a file in the /var/spool/ directory. Other print-spooling commands can help you track your request. If you're printing a large document or a number of smaller files, you can see a list of print jobs running by using the `lpq` command. For example, to print a number of files at once, use

```
# lpr .x*
```

followed by

```
# lpq
```

This outputs the following:

```
Rank   Owner      Job  Files                                   Total Size
active root       301  .xboing-scores, .xinitrc                1366 bytes
```

If you want to stop the preceding print job, use the `lprm` command, followed by the job number, as in the following:

```
# lprm 301
dfA071Aa01088 dequeued
dfB071Aa01088 dequeued
cfA071Aa01088 dequeued
```

This shows that `lprm` has removed the spool files from the printer's spool directory under /var/spool/lpd.

If you want to disable or enable a printer and its spooling queue, rearrange the order of any print jobs, or find out the status of printers, you can use `lpc` from the command line or interactively, but you must be logged in as root or as a superuser (through the `su` command). See the `lpc` man page for details.

Simple Formatting

Of course, printing directory listings or short text files is fine, but default printouts of longer files require formatting with borders, headers, and footers. To get a nicer document with text files, use the `pr` command.

The `pr` command has 19 command-line options to help you format documents for printing. For example,

```
# pr +9 -h CONFIDENTIAL DOCUMENT -o 5 < myfile.txt ¦ lpr
```

will print your document, starting at page 9, with a header containing the date, time, words "CONFIDENTIAL DOCUMENT," and page number, with a left margin of 5 spaces.

Want to save paper? Try using the `mpage` command. This program, run from the command line of your console or a terminal window, can print multiple pages of text on a single sheet of paper. The command

```
# mpage -2 myfile.txt ¦ lpr
```

will print two consecutive pages of your document on each sheet of paper, putting a nice hairline border around the paper's margins. See the `mpage` manual page for details and other options.

Another text formatter you might want to try is the `fmt` command; see its man page for details.

Other Helpful Printer Programs and Filters

Printer filters work by defining and inserting printer definitions into your /etc/printcap file. Embedded in each printer description is a pointer (pathname) to a script or program containing the filter to be run before output to the printer. See the `printcap` man page and the sample /etc/printcap listing later in this chapter.

APSfilter

Even if, as a Red Hat user, you're spoiled by the `printtool` program, you will at times need to use other programs or scripts to help set up or manage printing. If you can't or don't want to run X, but want to easily install printing services for HP or PostScript printers, one great solution is the printing filter package called APSfilter, by Andreas Klemm and Thomas Bueschgens. Installing APSfilter is a snap, and it's even easier to use.

APSfilter works well with all Linux printing applications. Two added benefits are that it prints two formatted pages in Landscape mode on a single page when you print text documents, saving you paper, and "automagically" recognizes the following documents and graphic formats: `xfig`, `pbm`, `pnm`, `tiff`, `jpeg`, `gif`, Sun rasterfile, PostScript, `dvi`, raw ASCII, `gzip`, and compressed.

One downside is that APSfilter's printing of grayscale is not as good as the grayscale printing offered by the `printtool` program's setup (at least on HP DeskJets). Hopefully, this will be fixed in the next version.

BubbleTools

If you have a Canon Bubble Jet, IBM Proprinter X24E, Epson LQ1550, or Epson Stylus, Olav Wolfelschneider's BubbleTools printer drivers can help you. This filter program converts a number of graphics formats, including Group 3 Fax, for this series of 360-dpi printers.

magicfilter

Another printer filter similar to APSfilter is H. Peter Anvin's magicfilter, which detects and converts documents for printing through a combination of a compiled C filter and a printer configuration file.

HPTools

Have a Hewlett-Packard printer? If so, you might want to try Michael Janson's HPTools to manage your printer's settings. The main tool is the `hpset` command, which sports more than 13 command-line options you can use to control your printer. For example, to save money on print cartridges by using less ink, you can use `hpset` to tell your printer to print in the economy mode with

```
# hpset -c econ ¦ lpr
```

The hpset command also has an interactive mode, so you can test your printer, set different default fonts, or perform other software control of your printer, such as bi- or unidirectional printing.

You can find APSfilter, BubbleTools, HPTools, and magicfilter, along with nearly 50 different Linux printing utilities, at `http://sunsite.unc.edu/pub/Linux/system/Printing`.

PostScript Printers

If you want a print spooler specifically designed for PostScript printers, give Dave Chappell's PPR a try. PPR works with printers attached to parallel, serial, and AppleTalk (LocalTalk) ports, along with other network interfaces. PPR also works much like other non-PostScript printer filters and converts a number of graphics file formats for printing.

You can find PPR at `ftp://ppr-dist.trincoll.edu/pub/ppr/`.

Enhanced Printer Spooler

The future of Linux printing has arrived, and its name is `LPRng`. This print spooler software, descended from the 4.3BSD release but rewritten from the ground up, offers a host of benefits and features in the areas of distribution, setup, use, and security. Some of these are as follows:

- GNU GPL (General Public License) distribution for freedom from restrictive copyrights
- Backward printer filter compatibility
- Enhanced security with a permissions database
- Improved diagnostics
- Multiple printers on a single queue
- Simplified client and server printer configuration files
- Simplified printer database

You will find the latest copy of LPRng at the site ftp://dickory.sdsu.edu/pub/LPRng (along with other neat printing utilities) or at http://www.astary.com/lprng/LPRng.html.

System Accounting

Want to know how much printing you or your users have been doing and at what cost? Should your printer's name be "TreeEater"? See the man pages for the pac command, which you can use to track usage and costs. You'll also need to read the man pages for the printcap database to see how to enable printer use accounting.

Infrared Printer Support

For those users fortunate enough to have a printer with infrared support (such as the HP 340Cbi or Canon BJC80) and a Linux system with an infrared port (such as a laptop), here is good news: You can print without a printer cable! Recent efforts in Linux device driver development have yielded infrared printing (and networking) support.

You'll need to download the latest Linux/IR snapshot (such as linux-irda-1998-07-21.tar.gz) from http://www.cs.uit.no/~dagb/irda/irda.html. To use infrared printing with Linux you must have module support enabled for your kernel (see Chapter 28, "Configuring and Building Kernels"). Here are the basic steps to enable infrared printing:

- Download the Linux/IR distribution.
- Build the modules.
- Install the modules.
- Load the needed module(s).
- Create your system's infrared printer device.

After you have installed the software, the easiest way to print is to create a printer entry in your /etc/printcap printer database or to use a filter program, such as APSfilter (mentioned earlier).

For a detailed HOWTO, see Werner Heuser's Linux IR-mini-HOWTO, available at http://www.userpage.fu-berlin.de/~r2d2c3po/ir_howoto.cgi or through the Linux-IR project home page listed earlier.

Some Program Tips

The following are some helpful tips to help you print documents or set up applications for easier printing.

emacs

Want to print directly from `emacs`? To print the entire buffer, unformatted or formatted, press Esc+X, type **`lpr-buffer`**, and press Enter, or press Esc+X, type **`print-buffer`**, and press Enter. Just make sure you set the `lpr-switches` variable in your `.emacs` file to point to the correct printer in your /etc/printcap file.

You'll find `emacs`, along with its Help files and documentation, on your Red Hat Linux CD-ROM.

Applixware for Linux

Applixware, a fully integrated suite of office tools and development environment, is a newcomer to the Linux scene but a veteran UNIX application. If you want to create, import, edit, and print documents with ease, this product is a good bet.

Here's a tip on how to set up your printer for Applixware you won't find in the program's manuals. Go to Applixware Preferences and select Printing. In the Printing Preferences dialog that comes up, set Default Printer Type to PostScript, as shown in Figure 16.5. Then scroll down the list of preferences at the bottom of the dialog to Pathname of Your Printer Aliases File. Click in the Value text area and enter the path of the file (/etc/printers). Then create a simple ASCII file containing a list of printers defined in your /etc/printcap file. (You are using X with virtual desktops so you can do a lot of different things at once, aren't you? If not, see Chapter 4, "X Window.")

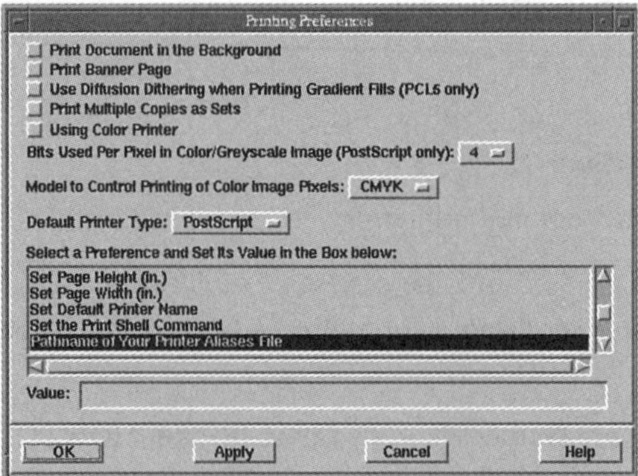

FIGURE 16.5
The Applixware Printer Preferences dialog.

For example, here's a sample /etc/printcap for an HP DeskJet 500, created following installation and setup using `printtool`. Note that `printtool` offered four different modes for the printer (normal black-and-white printing, normal color printing with color cartridge, Floyd-Steinberg black-and-white printing for better grayscale, and Floyd-Steinberg color printing for best, but slow):

```
### /etc/printcap
###
### Please don't edit this file directly unless you know what you are
doing!
### Be warned that the control-panel printtool requires a very strict
format!
### Look at the printcap(5) man page for more info.
###
### This file can be edited with the printtool in the control-panel.
##
##PRINTTOOL3## LOCAL cdj500 300x300 letter {} DeskJet500 8 1
DJ500greyscale:\
    :sd=/var/spool/lpd/lp0:\
    :mx#0:\
    :sh:\
    :lp=/dev/lp1:\
    :if=/var/spool/lpd/lp0/filter:
##PRINTTOOL3## LOCAL cdj500 300x300 letter {} DeskJet500 24 {}
DJ500colorbest:\
    :sd=/var/spool/lpd/lp0:\
    :mx#0:\
    :sh:\
    :lp=/dev/lp1:\
    :if=/var/spool/lpd/lp0/filter:
##PRINTTOOL3## LOCAL cdj500 300x300 letter {} DeskJet500 3 {}
DJ500colornormal:\
    :sd=/var/spool/lpd/lp0:\
    :mx#0:\
    :sh:\
    :lp=/dev/lp1:\
    :if=/var/spool/lpd/lp0/filter:
##PRINTTOOL3## LOCAL cdj500 300x300 letter {} DeskJet500 1 1
DJ500mononormal:\
    :sd=/var/spool/lpd/lp0:\
    :mx#0:\
    :sh:\
    :lp=/dev/lp1:\
    :if=/var/spool/lpd/lp0/filter:
```

From this listing, create and save the file `/etc/printers` with the following four lines:

```
DJ500greyscale
DJ500colorbest
DJ500colornormal
DJ500mononormal
```

Then, under Applixware, save the preferences by clicking the OK button and then the Dismiss button.

Now, when you start to print from, say, Applix Words, you'll see these four printers listed in your Print dialog. Select an appropriate printer, make sure PostScript is selected in the Class pop-up menu, and uncheck the Print to File box. When you click OK, your file will immediately print, using the fonts and formatting of your Applix Words document.

Other Helpful Programs

The following are short descriptions of just a few of the programs offering handy printing services available either in your Red Hat distribution or for Linux. You'll find some of these indispensable.

xv

One great tool that does a lot more than just print graphics is John Bradley's program, `xv`, which runs under X. It can read and export nearly 18 graphics file formats, and even comes in a scanner-driver version so you can scan and immediately print. You can print a quick copy of a graphic with the click of a button.

`pbm` Utilities

To translate or manipulate your graphics files into a multitude of different formats or effects for printing, try one of Jef Poskanzer's numerous `pbm` utilities. At last count there were nearly 40 programs. See the `pbm` and `pnm` man pages for pointers.

gv

Most of the convenience of having PostScript documents print automatically on cheap inkjet printers under Linux derives from Aladdin Enterprises' interpreter, `gs`, or Ghostscript. However, Johannes Plass's X client, gv, based on Tim Theisen's much-beloved Ghostview, is another one of those "insanely great" programs that come with nearly every Linux distribution.

You can use gv, like the older Ghostview, to preview or print `.ps` files. This program features multiple levels of magnification and landscape and portrait modes, and prints PostScript files too.

Troubleshooting and More Information

I'll offer some general tips on troubleshooting printing, and then give some pointers to more information. You should not have trouble with printing under Linux, but if you can't seem to get started, try some of these hints:

- Make sure your printer cable is properly connected to your computer and printer.
- Make sure your printer is on.
- Verify that you initially wanted printer support when you installed Linux or if you've rebuilt your Linux kernel.
- Make sure the kernel daemon is active (this loads the printer driver module when needed).
- Ensure you have the `lp.o` module available and installed on your system (usually under the /lib/modules/2.0.XX directory, where XX is the kernel version installed on your system).
- Avoid PPA or Windows-only printers until hardware manufacturers offer better support.
- Make sure you select the correct printer filter for your printer with the `printtool` command.
- If you're using a Zip drive, you might have to first unmount any mounted Zip disks and then unload the ppa.o kernel module first.

Still having problems? See the man pages for `tunelp`, `printcap`, `lpd`, `lpr`, `lpq`, `lprm`, and `lpc`. Curiously, there is no man page for the `printtool` program, but its Help menu shows some general information and troubleshooting tips.

Information on how to use APSfilter is under the aps/doc source directory in a number of files.

For information about the BSD printing system, read Ralph Campbell's abstract, "4.3BSD Line Printer Spooler Manual," which is part of the 4.4BSD *System Manager's Manual*, tabbed section 7.

For an excellent introduction to `LPRng`, see Patrick Powell's abstract "LPRng—An Enhanced Printer Spooler." This 13-page document, in PostScript or text format, includes the history, architecture, configuration, operation, and algorithm of the spooler software. You can find it or the LPRng FAQ at `http://www.astart.com/lprng/LPRng.html` or look at the files Intro.txt or Intro.ps in the DOC directory of the `LPRng` sources.

To join the LPRng mailing list, send a subscribe message to plp-request@iona.ie.

For detailed information about printing under Linux, you'll need to read *The Linux Printing HOWTO* by Grant Taylor. *The Linux Printing HOWTO* contains a host of great tips, tricks, traps, and hacks concerning printing under Linux, including setups for serial printers and network printing.

Also read *The Linux Printing Usage HOWTO* by Mark Komarinski, under /usr/doc/HOWTO/mini.

And don't forget to peruse the following newsgroups for information about printers, PostScript, or Linux printing:

```
comp.lang.postscript
comp.laser-printers
comp.os.linux.hardware
comp.os.linux.setup
comp.periphs.printers
comp.sources.postscript
comp.sys.hp.hardware
```

Summary

In this chapter, you've learned about Linux printer devices, how to print simple files, and even a little about the latest Linux development, infrared printing. I've also shown you the RHS Linux Print System Manager and some Linux printing commands for simple formatting of text files. Hopefully, you'll also try some of the other printer programs and filters. Use this chapter's information as a starting point to explore the printing features of Red Hat Linux, and push your printer to the max!

CHAPTER

TCP/IP Network Management

by David Pitts

IN THIS CHAPTER

Although a standalone system can be quite interesting and very useful, you cannot harness the true power of a UNIX system until you attach it to a network. This chapter covers the various means and tools you will need to get your system on a network.

An Introduction to Networking

TCP/IP (Transmission Control Protocol/Internet Protocol) was the first widely used networking protocol under UNIX and has been an integral part of Linux since its creation. The success of TCP/IP was the result of many things, but three in particular: the United States Department of Defense's involvement in creating the protocol and establishing a wide area network with it (the predecessor to what has become the Internet), the availability of the protocol specifications to anyone in the world, and finally, the nature of TCP/IP itself: robust and untied to any particular physical medium.

What Is an IP Number?

An IP number is what uniquely identifies a network interface. If your network is private, you only need to worry about address uniqueness within your own network. If, however, your network is attached to the Internet, you do need to worry about having a unique address across the entire Internet.

An IP address consists of four numbers, ranging from 0 to 255 and separated by dots. A valid address looks something like `192.168.3.12`. This is sometimes called the *dotted address*; however, it is more frequently referred to as the *IP address*. Although coming up with an address might appear simple, you need to be aware of some restrictions.

TIP

You might have noticed I've specified that IP addresses need to be unique to a network interface, not a host, because it is possible for a single host to have multiple network interfaces. Although you should keep this distinction in mind, *network interface* and *host* mean the same thing in most cases and are used interchangeably. In the examples in this chapter, each host has only one network interface; hence, I use the term *host* more often.

A TCP/IP Primer

The range of addresses available has been broken up into three segments: classes A, B, and C. Each class is determined by the first number in the IP address. (More accurately, it is determined by the first few bits of the address, but as you can see, picking out the ranges in decimal is much easier for us humans.) The classes and ranges are shown in Table 17.1.

TABLE 17.1 IP CLASSES AND RANGES

Class	*Range*	*Comment*
A	1 to 126	Each class A network is capable of holding 16 million addresses.
B	128 to 191	Each class B network is capable of holding 65 thousand addresses.
C	192 to 223	Each class C network is capable of holding 254 addresses.
Reserved	224 to 255	

Within these class ranges are several special addresses. The one you will see most frequently is `127.0.0.1`, the *loopback address*. The loopback address, also known as *localhost*, is a network address that points back to the machine from which it originated. This is useful for establishing and testing network services on a machine without having to connect to a network.

Depending on the class, a network can hold a varying number of hosts within it. For class A networks, the first number in dotted notation shows which network. The subsequent three numbers identify the hosts. In class B networks, the first two dotted numbers identify the network, leaving the last two numbers to identify the hosts. Finally, class C networks use the first three numbers to identify the network and the last number to identify the hosts.

If the host part of the network address is all zeros, that address refers to the entire network, not just one host. Hence, a host's IP address should not have a zero in it.

Within each address class, special addresses are designated for internal networks, networks not directly connected to the Internet. Machines that are behind firewalls, for example, can use these addresses for communicating with one another. The ranges for these addresses are

Class A	`10.0.0.0`
Class B	`172.16.0.0` to `172.31.0.0`
Class C	`192.168.0.0` to `192.168.255.0`

For all the examples in this chapter, I use the class C network `192.168.42.0`.

Determining which IP address to use is highly site dependent. If you are attaching your machine to an established network, you need to contact your network administrator to establish which IP address you should use. This includes connecting to an Internet service provider (ISP) that will be assigning you an address.

If, on the other hand, you are establishing a local area network at home or behind a firewall, you should use one of the established private ranges. These are chunks of IP addresses that have been put aside by the InterNIC so that no publicly accessible network can use them.

NOTE

So far, I've only used IP addresses to identify machines on a network. How is it, then, that you can use names to find machines across the Internet? Simple. Most sites set up a special mapping between hostnames and their IP numbers. Many programs are designed to automatically use names instead of IP addresses, because they are much easier for humans to digest. Imagine trying to remember `192.168.42.7` instead of `www.domain.com`!

TIP

Details of the TCP/IP theory are beyond the scope of this chapter. For additional information regarding TCP/IP theory, check out the Sams book *TCP/IP Blueprints* (ISBN: 0-672-31055-4) by Robin Burk, Martin Bligh, Thomas Lee, et al.

Subnetworking

Imagine trying to network a site with hundreds, if not thousands, of machines. Now try to imagine the resulting mess of network addresses, cables, and traffic. Attempting to manage such a beast would only leave you with a migraine and a fistful of hair.

Realizing this would eventually happen, the creators of TCP/IP included the capability to break a network down into subnetworks for easier management. Each subnetwork, or *subnet* for short, has its own *broadcast address* and *network mask*. The broadcast address is used to send messages to all the machines within a particular subnet. The network mask, or *netmask* for short, tells how many machines are in a subnet and their corresponding network addresses.

If you are joining an existing network, you should be given this information. If, on the other hand, you are setting up your own network, you need to determine these numbers on your own.

Computing Netmasks

An IP address is composed of a total of 32 bits. Every 8 bits makes up one number in the dotted address. Although many sites set up their netmasks across an 8-bit boundary, smaller sites are finding it necessary to allocate fewer than 254 addresses to a site. This means less intuitive netmasks.

As I mentioned earlier, IP addresses are divided into two parts, the network address and the host address. Depending on the class of the address, a particular network can include anywhere from 254 to 16 million addresses. To subnet these address ranges, a certain part of the host address must be allocated to the subnetwork address. By counting the number of bits it takes to compose the network and subnet address, you can figure out how many bits are in the netmask.

For example, if you are in the network `192.168.42.0` (equal to `11000000.10101000.00101010.00000000`) and you don't need to subnet at all, you would see that 24 bits are needed to make the netmask. Hence, the netmask for this network is `255.255.255.0` (equal to `11111111.11111111.11111111.00000000` in binary).

Suppose you do wish to subnet the network, and you want to break it down into eight subnets, each with 32 addresses. Remember that for each subnet, you need one network address and one broadcast address; hence, each subnet can only contain 30 addresses. Table 13.2 shows how to determine the netmask based on how many subnets you have.

TABLE 13.2 *SUBNET* NETMASKS

Subnets	*Hosts on the Subnet*	*Netmask*
2	126	`255.255.255.128` (`11111111.11111111.11111111.10000000`)
4	62	`255.255.255.192` (`11111111.11111111.11111111.11000000`)
8	30	`255.255.255.224` (`11111111.11111111.11111111.11100000`)
16	14	`255.255.255.240` (`11111111.11111111.11111111.11110000`)
32	6	`255.255.255.248` (`11111111.11111111.11111111.11111000`)
64	2	`255.255.255.252` (`11111111.11111111.11111111.11111100`)

Although you can encode your netmask such that the subnet part of the address does not consume the bits in the suggested order, figuring out each host's address becomes very tricky and cumbersome. This is not a recommended practice.

Determining the Broadcast Address

After you have the network mask determined, you can easily determine the broadcast address.

Begin by taking the network address along with the subnetwork component. In your sample network, this would be `192.168.42.0`. Because you need 24 bits (the first three dotted numbers) to identify the network, hold those bits constant and make the remainder bits all 1. This turns the sample address into `192.168.42.255`.

The Next Generation of IP, IPv6

If you're quick with figures, you might have realized that IP numbers have 32 bits, thereby providing us with 4+ billion possible IP addresses. Quite a few addresses, isn't it? Seems we should be set for a long time.

Not quite. Because of the way addresses are segmented between classes A, B, C, and reserved, and because of the problem with liberal policies on IP address assignment early in the Internet's life, we're quickly running out of available IP addresses. With every new movie having a new IP address for its domain name and network connectivity becoming cheap enough for small businesses, predictions are that we will run out of IP addresses not too long after the year 2000.

Luckily, a solution has been developed to cope with this. IPv6 is the successor to the current IPv4 standard. (IPv5 was an experimental real-time stream protocol.) IPv6 tackles many of IPv4's problems, such as inadequate address space, no security, an overly complex structure, no support for a large number of options, and no special tags indicating the type of service in use.

IPv6 solves the address space problem by expanding the address field to 128 bits. The idea behind this was that the address space should allow for an inefficient scheme of address assignment (similar to the idea behind class A, B, and C addresses in IPv4) but still provide for billions of possible hosts on each subnetwork.

A resolution for the security issue was also designed into IPv6. With commerce on the Internet growing at phenomenal rates, security mechanisms needed to be integrated into the network protocol itself instead of letting them remain above the protocol. Authentication and privacy were serious considerations in IPv6's design.

Multimedia has also been taking the Internet by storm. Entertainment services want to broadcast their services in real-time audio and video. By tagging the packets of data with a datatype field, routers across the Internet know to give priority to those packets needing real-time transmission. (If this subject interests you, look into the RSVP protocol at `http://www.ietf.org`.)

The last major revision of IPv6 was to simply include the information needed in each packet of data. This allows routers to process more packets per second without a demand for faster (and more costly) hardware.

As of this writing, Red Hat Linux doesn't support IPv6 because most people are sticking with IPv4 for their connectivity needs. An IPv6 package is available for Linux if you are interested in experimenting with it or possibly joining the 6Bone, a small network of IPv6 systems on the Internet. (Check out their site at `http://www-6bone.lbl.gov/6bone`.)

Getting a New IP Address

If you're planning to join the Internet with your new Linux box for the first time, you need two things:

- An Internet service provider (ISP) who is providing a connection to the Internet
- An unused IP range and domain name

Often, your ISP will assist you with all the steps involved in getting your machine connected, but it's always a good idea for you to know the steps involved.

The easiest way to join the Internet is to have an existing account on someone else's network. A good start would be the ISP you're planning to join. This will give you an opportunity to evaluate the ISP's services and determine if its connection to the Internet is fast enough for your needs.

When you've decided to go with a particular ISP, the ISP needs to set up its machines to respond to connection requests for your desired domain name. (Note that your ISP doesn't need to provide content, just the name service.) With your ISP ready to handle the domain, you begin your registration with the InterNIC.

The InterNIC is an organization that keeps track of all allocated domain names and their corresponding IP address ranges. Whenever a new site wants to have its own domain name, it must be allocated from the InterNIC. If the new site also needs an IP range allocated to it, the InterNIC takes care of that as well. (Typically, the InterNIC allocates IP ranges to ISPs, and the ISPs pass them on to you.)

Not too long ago, you could simply ask the InterNIC to allocate a domain name, and it would do it. However, with the recent boom of commercialization, the rules have changed so you must have an ISP responding to your desired domain name before InterNIC will allocate the domain. (In other words, you cannot request `my-new-domain.com` without having a server ready to respond to requests made on that domain.) Along with each new domain is an annual fee of $100.

To request a new domain name, visit the InterNIC's Web site at `http://www.internic.net`. You have to work with your ISP when doing this. The InterNIC can take up to one week to process your request and allocate the domain name.

When your new domain name is allocated and the InterNIC has announced it to all of the nameservers across the Internet, your site is ready to accept connections.

The Network Card Solution

If you are using a network card to join a network, configuring it is a straightforward task. This section shows how to use the `netcfg`, `ifconfig`, and `route` commands to do this.

NOTE

You must be the root user to run all the commands used in this section, because they change kernel parameters. You can run some of these programs as a normal user for gaining status information; I point out these programs.

Stock Network Configuration

Red Hat Linux comes with networking enabled. The easiest way to get started with networking is to configure it as part of your installation. If you are not familiar with the information requested, you can skip it and reconfigure it later with the `netcfg` program.

Begin by starting up the X Window environment and running `netcfg` from an `xterm` window. The opening window should look something like Figure 17.1.

If your Hostname and Domain entries already have entries in them, don't worry. That just means you've already set these values during the installation. If not, enter the appropriate information for your hostname and domain name. If you are unsure of these, contact your local network administrator to find out.

The Search for Hostnames in Additional Domains box should be left blank unless you want to be able to specify hostnames from multiple domains without having to use their fully qualified domain names. This is usually a bad idea.

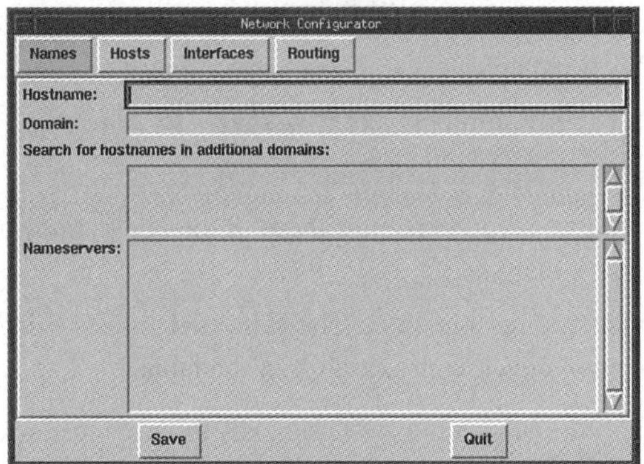

FIGURE 17.1
The Network Configurator Names menu.

The Nameservers box is important. This will tell your network where to resolve hostnames that are not local to your network. Each line should contain the IP address of every DNS server you want to query (with a maximum of three). Again, if you do not know this information, contact your network administrator and ask. If you are the network administrator, read Chapter 11.

When you finish entering this information, click the Hosts button at the top of the window. The window changes to look like Figure 17.2.

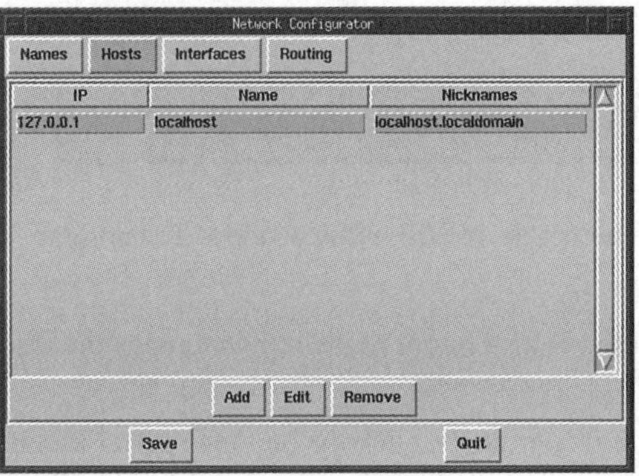

FIGURE 17.2
The Network Configurator Hosts menu.

This is what will become the /etc/hosts file (see Chapter 11, "The Domain Name Service," for detailed information.) This file essentially provides a mapping from hostnames to IP numbers. At the very least, you should provide mappings for any machines on your network necessary as part of your startup procedure (such as servers). For example, if you want to add an entry for the host `vestax`, whose IP address is `192.168.42.7`, you do the following:

1. Click the Add button (toward the bottom of the window) to open the Edit /etc/hosts window, which has three entries.
2. In the first box (for the IP number), enter `vestax`'s IP address.
3. In the Name box, enter the name `vestax`.
4. If `vestax` has any aliases, you can enter them in the Nicknames box. If there are no aliases, leave that box blank.
5. Click Done to finish adding this entry. The Edit `/etc/hosts` window closes, and the main window now shows your addition in the table.

After you have entered all the hosts your system needs to know at startup time, click the button labeled Interfaces at the top of the window. The window changes to look like Figure 17.3.

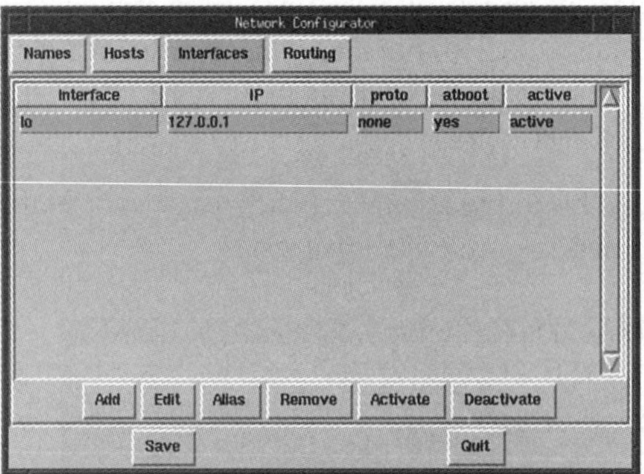

FIGURE 17.3
The Network Configurator Interface menu.

You can configure an ethernet device from this window. To configure your ethernet card, do the following:

1. Click the Add button at the bottom of the screen to open the Choose Interface window.
2. In the Choose Interface window, click the button to select Ethernet and then click OK. The Choose Interface window disappears and the Edit Ethernet/Bus Interface window appears.
3. In the Edit Ethernet/Bus Interface window, click the IP box and enter the IP address of your machine. The Netmask box automatically fills, based on the address you provide in the IP box. If this is not correct, click the Netmask box and make the necessary corrections.

4. If you want this interface to automatically start at startup time, click the Activate Interface at Boot Time button and leave the Allow Any User To (De)activate Interface box unselected. Allowing non-root users to configure network settings is a very bad practice.
5. The Interface Configuration Protocol enables you to select alternative methods (`bootp` or DHCP) to configure your network interface. Unless you have been instructed by a network manager to use these protocols, leave this box blank.
6. Click Done to bring up a new window asking whether you wish to save the current configuration. Click Save to keep your addition. Both windows close, leaving you at the original Network Configurator window, this time showing your new network interface.

With your interface defined, you can now set routes and gateways for your machine. Click the Routing button at the top of the window. This changes the Network Configurator window to look like Figure 17.4.

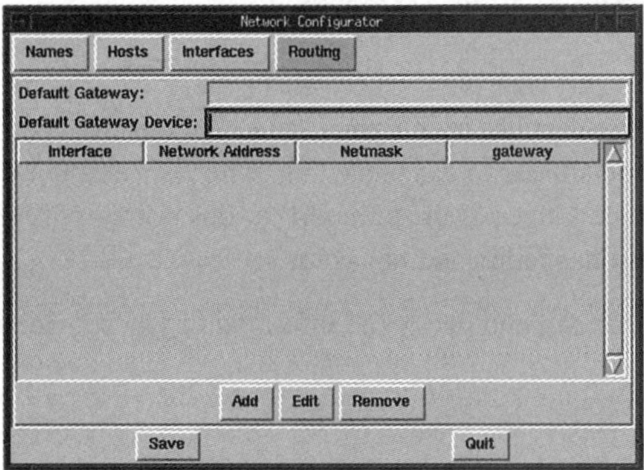

FIGURE 17.4
The Network Configurator Routing menu.

To set up your routing information, follow these steps:

1. Click in the Routing box and enter the IP address of your gateway to the rest of the network. If you do not have a gateway machine (for example, if you're configuring a local area network without an Internet connection), you can leave this blank.
2. If you do have a gateway, enter the device name from which the gateway will be accessed. Most likely, this will be the device name you configured in the Interface part of the Network Configurator window. If you are using an ethernet card, this will most likely be `eth0`.
3. Click Save and then click Quit to exit the `netcfg` program.

Your system now has the necessary scripts configured to establish your network connection. Before you can claim victory, you need to test the connection. Enter the following command to start the network connection:

```
/etc/rc.d/init.d/network stop;/etc/rc.d/init.d/network start
```

This restarts your network connection. Try pinging a machine in your immediate network by using the `ping` command, like this:

```
ping IP_Address
```

IP_Address is the IP address of the machine you are trying to ping. If you placed the IP address to hostname mapping in the Hosts section in `netcfg`, you can use the hostname instead. This should return output similar to the following:

```
PING 192.168.42.1 (192.168.42.1): 56 data bytes
64 bytes from 192.168.42.1: icmp_seq=0 ttl=255 time=1.0 ms
64 bytes from 192.168.42.1: icmp_seq=1 ttl=255 time=3.5 ms
-- 192.168.42.1 ping statistics --
2 packets transmitted, 2 packets received, 0% packet loss
round-trip min/avg/max = 1.0/24.4/47.8 ms
```

Note that in order to get `ping` to stop, you need to press Ctrl+C.

If you have an Internet connection, try pinging a machine outside your network. The resulting output should be similar to the preceding, with the notable exception that the time measurements will be longer. If the ping fails at this point, try another host; it could be the other machine that has failed and not yours.

If the pings fail, restart `netcfg` and verify the information you provided it.

Using `ifconfig`

`ifconfig` is the tool used to set up and configure your network card. If you used the Red Hat installation package, this might already be configured for you. You should, however, understand this command in the event you need to configure the network by hand after a system crash.

The purpose of `ifconfig` is to set up and configure the network interfaces. Typically, this is done early in the startup sequence so that any other network services that need to be started know how to communicate with the rest of the world.

The format of the `ifconfig` command is

```
ifconfig interface IP_address options
```

NOTE

The `ifconfig` command takes parameters in a slightly different way than most commands. Each parameter should not be prefixed by a minus sign (-) unless you are turning that function off. If you are setting a parameter, such as the netmask, simply use `netmask` followed by the netmask you want to set—for example, `netmask 255.255.255.0`.

`interface` is the network device you want to set up. If you are using ethernet, this will be `eth`, followed by a number designating which ethernet card you are using. The numbering starts from zero (the first ethernet card in your system will be `eth0`). *`IP_address`* is the address you want to assign to your machine. Use the dotted notation and remember not to assign it the network address or broadcast address.

These are the only required options for configuring a network device. `ifconfig` uses the default netmask and broadcast address based on the class of your *`IP_address`* setting. The default netmask and broadcast addresses, however, will only be correct if you are subnetting along an 8-bit boundary.

To set the netmask and broadcast address, use the parameters `netmask` and `broadcast`, respectively, followed by the address you want to set for them.

Here is a sample `ifconfig`:

```
ifconfig eth0 192.168.42.2 netmask 255.255.255.0 broadcast 192.168.42.255
```

As with most other UNIX commands, there is no output if it is successful. To see what the currently configured cards are, simply run `ifconfig` without any parameters:

```
[root@vestax /root]# ifconfig

lo        Link encap:Local Loopback
          inet addr:127.0.0.1  Bcast:127.255.255.255  Mask:255.0.0.0
          UP BROADCAST LOOPBACK RUNNING  MTU:3584  Metric:1
          RX packets:10984 errors:0 dropped:0 overruns:0
          TX packets:10984 errors:0 dropped:0 overruns:0

eth0      Link encap:10Mbps Ethernet  HWaddr 00:60:97:C3:D0:C9
          inet addr:192.168.42.2 Bcast:192.168.42.255 Mask:255.255.255.0
          UP BROADCAST RUNNING MULTICAST  MTU:1500  Metric:1
          RX packets:1995581 errors:1 dropped:1 overruns:0
          TX packets:1361726 errors:0 dropped:0 overruns:0
          Interrupt:11 Base address:0x6100
```

The first network card listed here is the `lo` device, which is the loopback device. I'm not terribly interested in that entry, although it should be there. The second entry shows how the `eth0` network card is currently configured. `Link encap` tells you it is configured as a 10Mbps ethernet card. The `HWaddr` tells you the hardware address of that particular ethernet card (also known as the MAC address). On the second line of the output is the `inet addr`, the address you have configured the card to answer to. On the same line are the respective broadcast and netmask addresses. The third line of the output shows which options have been enabled on the card from the `ifconfig` command. You should recognize the `BROADCAST` option because you explicitly set it. The others are default options I'll cover shortly. The fourth line contains information regarding the number of packets that have been received. In this example, about 1.9 million packets have been received, 1 packet had an error, 1 packet was dropped, and no packets were overruns. (Overruns are packets that are too long.) In the line below is the same information for packets transmitted. The last line provides the configuration information for the hardware.

Optional Parameters to `ifconfig`

The following parameters are optional on the `ifconfig` command line:

- `up` This tells `ifconfig` to activate the network interface and begin sending and receiving packets.
- `down` This option enables you to shut the interface down after it has been activated, useful for shutting down an active card when you're troubleshooting network-related problems.
- `arp` ARP (Address Resolution Protocol) enables you to map a network card's hardware address to its IP address. Protocols such as DHCP use this to find machines on a subnet without having to know an IP address first. Note that the ARP will only work within your immediate subnet and will not transfer through routers. By default, this option is turned on. To turn it off, place a minus sign in front of it (`-arp`).
- `mtu N` The MTU (Maximum Transfer Unit) sets the size of each ethernet packet to *N*, where *N* is the number of bytes in each packet. For ethernet, this defaults to 1500, and you shouldn't change it unless you are sure of what you are doing.

Using `route`

To communicate with machines outside your local area network, you need to use a router. This device is the link between your network and the rest of the world. When you need to communicate to a machine outside of your LAN, your host sends the message to the router, which forwards it on through the outside network. The same is true for packets coming in from the outside network. The router receives the packet and forwards it to your host.

If you used the Red Hat installation procedure for configuring your network, this has already been configured for you. For a host connected to the Internet, you should have—at the very least—three possible routes: a loopback, a route to your LAN, and a default route to your router. By running `route` without any parameters, you can see your current routing table. The format of the `route` command is

```
route cmd type target_ip netmask gateway options
```

where *`cmd`* is either `add` or `del`, depending on whether you want to add or delete a route. If you use `del`, you then only need the *`target_ip`* parameter, which specifies the IP address for which you are routing.

If, on the other hand, you used the `add` command, you need to specify *`type`* to be either `-net` or `-host`, where `-net` is a network to which you are routing and `-host` is a specific host to which you are routing.

The *`target_ip`* address specifies either the network or host IP address for which you are routing. The special keyword for this option is `default`. If you specify `default` instead of an actual IP address, all packets that do not have a specific route listed in the route table will be sent to this route.

`netmask` enables you to specify the netmask to the network to which you are routing. Note that this only applies when you're using the `-net` option. The `netmask` option is used like this: `netmask` *`mask_number`*, where *`mask_number`* is the actual netmask in dotted notation.

`gateway` specifies which gateway to use for sending packets to *`target_ip`*. For example, if your default route points to the Internet (a likely situation), your gateway setting should point to your router connecting to the Internet. For example, if the router is `192.168.42.1`, you would specify this option as `gw 192.168.42.1`. You can use hostnames if you want to, so long as they appear in the /etc/hosts file (see Chapter 11 for details.)

The options available in addition to the ones already stated are as follows:

- `-n` Uses numerical addresses instead of trying to resolve IP addresses to hostnames. This is used when invoking `route` without either the `add` or `del` parameter so that you can see which routes are currently set.
- `dev ethn` Specifies the device onto which a routed packet should go. This is only useful if you have a *multihomed* system (a machine with multiple network cards).

The ethn parameter specifies the interface's name. This option should always be at the end of the command line.

Examples of Using route

In this example, the default route is set up to go to 192.168.42.1, your router:

```
route add -net default gw 192.168.42.1
```

(You'll find that many routers are set up such that their IP addresses end in .1. This isn't a rule, but a common practice.) Because this is a -net, the netmask is computed automatically.

Assuming your machine is set up as 192.168.42.12 with a netmask of 255.255.255.0, this route points to your own local area network:

```
route add -net 192.168.42.0 dev eth0
```

This keeps the router from having to send packets back to your network after they've sent to it as the default route. The last parameter, dev eth0, specifies that the 192.168.42.0 network is connected to the first ethernet device in the system.

Understanding the route Table

When route is invoked without a parameter, it displays your current routing table. The output should look something like this:

```
[root@denon /root]# route
Kernel IP routing table
Destination      Gateway        Genmask        Flags   Metric   Ref   Use
➥Iface
192.168.42.0     *              255.255.255.0  U       0        0     2
➥eth0
loopback         *              255.0.0.0      U       0        0     3
➥lo
default          192.168.42.1   0.0.0.0        UG      0        0     0
➥eth0
```

Destination is the destination network or host address for packets, and Gateway is the gateway host (typically a router) used to get to the destination. An * character is displayed if no gateway is set. Flags describe the characteristic of the route. It is possible to have more than one characteristic, as in the default route. The possible flags are

U	The route is up.
H	The route is a host.
G	The route is through a gateway.

`Metric` gives the route a weight, a lower weight being a faster route. This is only useful for dynamic routing, so you will usually see this as `0`. The `Ref` column states the number of references to the route. Because this information is not used in the Linux kernel, it is always `0`. `Use` tells you how many times this route has been looked up by your system. `Iface` is the network interface the route uses.

Adding a PLIP Interface with the `netcfg` Tool

To connect a system to a network, you must use some type of interface. For temporary connections, most people use a modem and must configure either a PPP connection or a SLIP connection (see Chapter 18, "Connecting to the Internet," for more on these). For a more permanent connection, you need to use either a parallel connection or an ethernet connection.

What Is PLIP?

The Parallel Line Internet Protocol (PLIP) provides a point-to-point connection (like SLIP), but it uses the faster parallel ports to provide higher speeds.

Adding the Interface

Adding the PLIP interface by using the `netcfg` tool is a simple process. Here are the steps for configuring a PLIP connection:

1. First, you must have X Window up so that you can use `netcfg`. If you do not have X Window configured, refer to Chapter 4, "The X Window System."
2. Launch `netcfg`.
3. Click the INTERFACES button in the Network Configuration main window.
4. Click the ADD button in the Interfaces screen to open the Choose Interface dialog.
5. Select PLIP and click OK to open the Edit PLIP Interface dialog.
6. In the IP field, type the local machine's IP address.
7. In the Remote IP field, type the remote machine's IP address.
8. In the Netmask field, enter the network mask for the local machine's IP address.
9. If you want the PLIP interface to be active when your machine starts up, select Activate Interface At Boot Time.

10. Click DONE. In the window that asks whether you want to save the current configuration, click YES.
11. The new PLIP entry (probably `plip0`) should now appear in the Interface screen. To activate it, click the Activate button.

Adding an Ethernet Interface with the `netcfg` Tool

Ethernet is the other way of connecting a system to a network for long periods of time. Ethernet is, in fact, the most common way of connecting machines to a network. Using an ethernet connection is also fairly cheap (a two-system ethernet network can be put together for less than $100 for the two cards, the hub, and the cables).

Unlike PLIP, which uses the parallel port already available on all systems, ethernet requires its own special port. On most systems, this means you have to purchase an ethernet card to go into your system. My original intention at this point was to list many of the supported cards usable by Red Hat Linux. Unfortunately—or fortunately, depending on your point of view—this list is changing so rapidly that by the time this book comes out, the list would be out of date. Suffice it to say that most, if not all, major brands of ethernet cards are supported. When in doubt, check Red Hat's Web site at `http://www.redhat.com` for a list of supported cards and hardware.

Adding the Interface

Adding an ethernet interface is almost identical to adding a PLIP interface. The difference is that instead of having only two machines on the network, your machine becomes one of potentially endless numbers of machines on the network.

1. First, you must have X Window up to use `netcfg`. If you do not have X Window configured, refer to Chapter 4.
2. Launch `netcfg`.
3. Click the INTERFACES button in the Network Configuration main window (see Figure 17.1).
4. Click the ADD button to open the Choose Interface dialog (see Figure 17.2).
5. In the Choose Interface window, click ethernet to open the Edit Ethernet dialog.
6. In the IP field, type the IP address of the interface. If the ethernet interface is the primary network interface, enter the machine's IP address.
7. In the Netmask field, type the network mask for the IP address you entered in step 6.

8. If you want the ethernet interface to be active when your machine starts, select Activate Interface At Boot Time.
9. Unless you need the capability of starting remote machines by using this interface as the address of the boot server, leave Configure Interface with BOOTP unselected.

Setting Up a Router

The steps given in the previous section for configuring your ethernet interface do not finish making your system "network-aware." If you want your computer to actually talk to other computers, you must also set up the routing. In any network, there must be one machine that knows how to route packets to the other machines on the network.

Setting up a router is discussed earlier in this chapter, but the basic steps are:

1. Add a route to yourself.
2. Add a route to all hosts in your subnet.
3. Configure a route to hosts outside your subnet.

Dynamic Host Configuration Protocol (DHCP)

DHCP is a way of automatically getting networking information from a DHCP server. Version 5 of Red Hat Linux comes with a `dhcpcd` (DHCP client daemon) that is compliant with RFC2131—the current latest RFC concerning DHCP. It gets an IP address and other network information (netmask, nameserver, and so on) and tries to configure the network interface automatically. It also tries to renew the lease time (again, following RFC2131's specifications).

The current version of DHCP for Red Hat is RFC1541-compliant when the `-r` option is specified. The `dhcpcd` that comes with Red Hat Linux runs with many DHCP servers. Although a complete list can be obtained from the Web site, here are five DHCP server daemons I know are compatible with Red Hat's DHCP client daemons:

- ISC's dhcpd-BETA-5.15
- DHCP server on Windows NT server 3.51
- DHCP server version 1.3b by WIDE project
- DHCP server in the SolarNet PC-Admin 1.5 package
- DHCP server used in Time Warner Cable's Internet Access Service

Installing DHCP

Steps 1 and 2 assume you want the latest version of DHCP.

1. Get the latest version. Try MIT's FTP site:

```
ftp://tsx-11.mit.edu/pub/linux/distributions/redhat/redhat-5.1/
➥updates/i386/
```

> **NOTE**
>
> This version has probably changed. Make sure you get the latest version for your level of Red Hat Linux.

2. From the file list displayed, download the file dhcpcd-0.65-3.i386.rpm. (If the file has been updated after this was written, the filename might have changed slightly.)
3. If you need network connectivity only occasionally, you can start `dhcpcd` from the command line (you need to be root to execute it) by typing **`/usr/sbin/dhcpcd`**. To "turn off" `dhcp`, type the following line (again, as root):

   ```
   /usr/sbin/dhcpcd -k
   ```

   If you want to be connected to the network at all times, and would like `dhcp` to start at startup time, follow the rest of the these directions. If you're only going to use the network on occasion, you just need to create the resolv.conf file below.
4. After your network interface is configured, type

   `ifconfig`

   You should get something like this:

   ```
   lo   Link encap:Local Loopback
        inet addr:127.0.0.1  Bcast:127.255.255.255  Mask:255.0.0.0
        UP BROADCAST LOOPBACK RUNNING  MTU:3584  Metric:1
        RX packets:302 errors:0 dropped:0 overruns:0 frame:0
        TX packets:302 errors:0 dropped:0 overruns:0 carrier:0 coll:0

   eth0 Link encap:Ethernet  HWaddr 00:20:AF:EE:05:45
         inet addr:24.128.53.102  Bcast:24.128.53.255
         Mask:255.255.254.0
         ^^^^^^^^^^^^^^^^^^^^^^
         UP BROADCAST NOTRAILERS RUNNING MULTICAST  MTU:1500  Metric:1
         RX packets:24783 errors:1 dropped:1 overruns:0 frame:1
         TX packets:11598 errors:0 dropped:0 overruns:0 carrier:0 coll:96
         Interrupt:10 Base address:0x300
   ```

If you have some normal number under `inet addr`, you are set. `dhcpcd` is a daemon and will stay running as long as you have your machine on. Every three hours, it will contact the DHCP server and try to renew the IP address lease. It will log all the messages to the syslog (/var/adm/syslog) in case you need to check up on it.

5. One final thing. You need to specify your nameservers in one of two ways. Either you can put them in the /etc/resolv.conf, or `dhcpcd` will obtain the list from the DHCP server and build a resolv.conf in /etc/dhcpc. I decided to use `dhcpcd`'s resolv.conf by doing the following:

   a. Back up your old /etc/resolv.conf:

   ```
   mv /etc/resolv.conf /etc/resolv.conf.OLD
   ```

   b. If directory /etc/dhcpc doesn't exist, create it:

   ```
   mkdir /etc/dhcpc
   ```

   c. Make a link from /etc/dhcpc/resolv.conf to /etc/resolv.conf:

   ```
   ln -s /etc/dhcpc/resolv.conf /etc/resolv.conf
   ```


NetaTalk

With the NetaTalk program, your UNIX box looks like an AppleTalk fileserver on a LAN. NetaTalk exports a piece of the UNIX filesystem via the AppleTalk protocol. Using NetaTalk, Macintosh computers can mount UNIX volumes as if they were standard AppleTalk network drives.

NetaTalk comes with Red Hat Linux, but it is not compiled as part of the kernel. The following steps show you how to compile a kernel with NetaTalk services.

NOTE

Red Hat already contains a precompiled AppleTalk support. Confirm this by checking your configuration with a `make menuconfig` from the /usr/src/linux/ directory.

NOTE

You also need to have TCP/IP up and running on the network card you plan to use for AppleTalk. Kernel AppleTalk support doesn't contain all the framing code necessary to run AppleTalk alone.

You should have experience compiling a kernel. If you don't, look through your Kernel-HOWTO docs (/usr/doc/faq/howto/Kernel-HOWTO.gz in Red Hat Linux) with the command `zless /usr/doc/faq/howto/Kernel-HOWTO.gz` or see Chapter 28, "Configuring and Building Kernels."

Configuring the Kernel for AppleTalk

To configure the kernel for AppleTalk, perform the following steps.

1. Go to your Linux source root directory (/usr/src/linux).
2. Type **`make config`** (or **`make menuconfig`**).
3. Answer the questions corresponding to your setup.
4. Be sure to answer yes when asked if you want to configure AppleTalk DDP support.
5. Do a make dep; make clean to set up your source code for compile. Make a new kernel.

   If you haven't done this before, consult your Kernel-HOWTO docs. Kernels are made with different commands, depending on the results you want. (When I compile, I use the command make `zImage`.)

NOTE

You can build AppleTalk support as a module if you like.

6. Copy your old kernel somewhere in case the new kernel you just compiled decides to hate you and grind to a screeching halt.
7. Install your new kernel and restart your system on it.

CAUTION

If you mess something up, your system will not come up! Consult your HOWTO docs for kernel installation.

Configure the Options

This configuration is for the AppleTalk file services. It does not go into the various print options.

1. Make yourself an atalkd.conf file. In the NetaTalk source directory under etc/atalkd, find a file called etc.atalkd.conf. Usually this file is edited and copied to your NetaTalk DESTDIR/etc (/usr/local/atalk/etc) directory and renamed atalkd.conf.
2. Make yourself an AppleVolumes.default and an AppleVolumes.system file. These files tell the system which directories to offer as AppleShare volumes. In the NetaTalk source directory under etc/afpd, find two files called etc.AppleVolumes.default and etc.AppleVolumes.system. Usually these files are edited and copied to your NetaTalk DESTDIR/etc (/usr/local/atalk/etc) directory and renamed AppleVolumes.default and AppleVolumes.system, respectively.
3. Edit your /etc/services file to include the following AppleTalk services:
   - rtmp 1/ddp # Routing Table Maintenance Protocol
   - nbp 2/ddp # Name Binding Protocol
   - echo 4/ddp # AppleTalk Echo Protocol
   - zip 6/ddp # Zone Information Protocol

   The /etc/services file tells your computer what service to use when network requests go in or out. If you are using NIS (Network Information System, formerly known as Yellow Pages or YP), don't add these lines to the services file. Add them to your NIS master machine's maps and push them.
4. In your source distribution, edit your `rc.atalk` script to launch your AppleTalk services. Here's what I use:

```
ATALKDIR="/usr/local/atalk"
echo 'Starting AppleTalk fileserver...'
${ATALKDIR}/etc/atalkd
echo -n 'atalkd'
${ATALKDIR}/bin/nbprgstr -p 4 `hostname¦sed 's/\..*$//'`:Workstation
${ATALKDIR}/bin/nbprgstr -p 4 `hostname¦sed 's/\..*$//'`:NetaTalk
echo -n ' nbprgstr'
${ATALKDIR}/etc/afpd
echo ' afpd.'
```

NOTE

It is important not to launch any of these services in the background; their network data structures need time to stabilize.

5. Set AppleTalk services to automatically start when the system restarts. In the source distribution directory, move the rc.atalk file to your /etc/rc.d directory and make it executable:

   ```
   chmod 755 /etc/rc.d/rc.atalk
   ```

6. In your /etc/rc.d directory, edit the file rc.local to launch the `rc.atalk` script. Add the following line to your rc.local:

   ```
   /etc/rc.d/rc.atalk
   ```

7. For users to mount the volumes you have created on your Linux box, they need to have a valid shell account on the Linux system. AppleShare limits passwords to 8 characters, so you want to add users to your Linux system with passwords of 8 characters or less. A valid shell account means that something such as /bin/sh or /bin/tcsh is at the end of that user's entry in the /etc/passwd file. If you just pipe to /dev/null, the user will not be able to log in. Root logins are prohibited by NetaTalk, and for good reason. Just don't!

Start the Server

Assuming everything has been installed and configured correctly, you should have no problem turning on AppleTalk services.

Fire up AppleTalk server. In your /etc/rc.d directory, run the script `rc.atalk`. Now sit back and wait a minute or so as the system checks out the network and sets itself up. The `rc.atalk` script is usually run at system startup time.

Summary

As you've seen in this chapter, adding network access and networking tools to your system is a fantastic asset. And with Red Hat Linux, sharing data through these networking tools is relatively straightforward, which is impressive, considering the power they add to your system.

Here's a summary of this chapter's main points:

- An IP address is the number that uniquely identifies a machine across a network.
- The `netcfg` tool is used to configure basic network services, such as setting up the network card or PPP connection, establishing routes, setting the hostname and DNS information, and setting up the /etc/hosts file.
- If you need to hand-configure your network interface, use the `ifconfig` command to set up the IP number, netmask, and broadcast address.
- When configuring a network by hand, don't forget to set the routing table with the `route` command. Without it, your machine will not know where to send packets.
- PLIP and ethernet enable your machine to connect to other machines on the network. Red Hat Linux has all the support necessary for doing this and for easily configuring these connections with the `netcfg` program.
- DHCP enables your machine to configure itself for the network. When you enable DHCP, the system itself will check out IPs, configure netmasks, and even define nameservers for the system.
- NetaTalk is the UNIX implementation of AppleTalk. NetaTalk makes your UNIX box look like an AppleTalk fileserver on a LAN by exporting a piece of the UNIX filesystem via the AppleTalk protocol.

After you have configured your machine and you're accessing the network, have fun with it! You will quickly find uses for the network access you could never even dream about on a standalone system. A word of warning, though—after you put your machine on a network, you will never want to take it offline.

Connecting to the Internet

by Tim Parker

IN THIS CHAPTER

Connections from a Linux system to an ISP (Internet service provider) are usually made through a modem using either PPP (Point to Point Protocol) or SLIP (Serial Line Interface Protocol). Both PPP and SLIP allow you to transfer mail, surf the World Wide Web, use FTP, and access all the other features of the Internet. Both PPP and SLIP use the TCP/IP network protocol, and because TCP/IP and UNIX evolved together, Linux is particularly adept at handling PPP and SLIP.

In this chapter, you will learn how to easily set up your Linux system to use PPP and SLIP. You probably will not want to set up both PPP and SLIP because most ISPs use PPP only. PPP is the faster of the two protocols, but sometimes you will need to use SLIP. Before setting up either PPP or SLIP, you need to create a *dummy interface* so that your machine knows about itself in a networking sense and because most protocols require this dummy interface to work properly.

Setting Up the Dummy Interface

A dummy interface is used by TCP/IP to assign an IP address to your machine, which is required for both SLIP and PPP. The reason for a dummy interface is simple: When you connect to an ISP, your IP address is often assigned dynamically, and you never know what the IP address will be in advance. This can cause problems for TCP/IP routines in your kernel that need to know an IP address to function properly. When you assign an IP address—the dummy interface IP address—to your machine, TCP/IP is happy. The need for an IP address internally is most important when you are not connected to your ISP because many applications that are network-aware (such as email, newsreaders, and so on) need to have some IP address to connect to, even if it doesn't lead anywhere. This dummy interface IP address does not conflict with the one assigned by your ISP.

Fortunately, setting up a dummy interface is simple. All that is required is a couple of commands to create the interface and a couple more commands to test that the interface is working, and you're done. The file that Linux uses to store all network IP address information is called /etc/hosts, and every system should have one (even if it is empty).

The `/etc/hosts` file is an ASCII file that provides two pieces of information to the TCP/IP drivers and applications: an IP address and the names associated with that IP address. Usually, you will find the `/etc/hosts` file has a single line in it when you install Linux without network support:

```
127.0.0.1 localhost
```

This line essentially tells TCP/IP that a special interface called `localhost` is assigned the IP address `127.0.0.1`. The `localhost` interface is called the dummy interface because it is not a real address. This interface is also called the loopback interface because it leads back to the same machine.

NOTE

The terms *localhost*, *loopback*, and *dummy interface* all refer to the use of the IP address `127.0.0.1` to refer to the local machine. The term *loopback interface* indicates that to the networking drivers, it looks as though the machine is talking to a network that consists of only one machine. In internal terms, the kernel sends network traffic out one port and back in to another on the same machine. Dummy interface indicates that the interface doesn't really exist to the outside world, only to the local machine.

`127.0.0.1` is a special IP address reserved for the local machines on all networks. Every networked Linux machine has this IP address for its localhost. If you display the contents of your `/etc/hosts` file and this line already exists, then the dummy interface is already set up for you and you can skip this section. If the `/etc/hosts` file doesn't exist or this line is not in the file, you have to set up the interface yourself. If your machine has an IP address other than `127.0.0.1` in your `/etc/hosts` file, and the interface `127.0.0.1` is not there, then you do not have the localhost interface set up.

NOTE

When you installed Linux, you may have chosen a networking boot image. If you did, the dummy interface was probably set up automatically. If you chose a nonnetworking boot image, you will have to manually add the dummy interface.

To create the dummy interface, your Linux system needs the networking software installed. The installation happens automatically with most root and boot images, even if the network interfaces are not configured.

Begin the dummy interface setup by editing (or creating, if it doesn't exist) the `/etc/hosts` file, and add the following line:

```
127.0.0.1 localhost
```

The number of spaces between the IP address and the name localhost does not matter, as long as there is at least one. Make sure you enter the IP address exactly as shown, with no spaces between the parts of the dotted-quad notation. If you already had an IP address in the `/etc/hosts` file for your local machine but no localhost entry with this IP address, you still need to add this line. The localhost line is usually the very first line in the `/etc/hosts` file.

After updating the `/etc/hosts` file, you need to tell TCP/IP about the new interface. To set up the dummy interface, issue the following commands when you are logged in as `root`:

```
ifconfig lo 127.0.0.1
route add 127.0.0.1
```

The first command tells the system to add an interface called the `localhost` (`lo` is the short form for localhost) with an IP address of `127.0.0.1`. The second command adds the IP address `127.0.0.1` to an internal table that keeps track of routes to different addresses.

After you have issued these two commands, the dummy interface should be created and ready to use. A machine reboot is usually helpful to ensure the proper configurations are read. To test the dummy interface, use the `ifconfig` command again with the name of the interface (`lo` for localhost) to tell you statistics about the interface. The command and a sample output look like this:

```
$ ifconfig lo
lo        Link encap:Local Loopback
          inet addr:127.0.0.1  Bcast:127.255.255.255  Mask:255.0.0.0
          UP BROADCAST LOOPBACK RUNNING  MTU:2000  Metric:1
          RX packets:0 errors:0 dropped:0 overruns:0
          TX packets:12 errors:0 dropped:0 overruns:0
```

This output shows that the loopback interface is active and running, that it has been assigned the IP address `127.0.0.1`, that the broadcast mask of `255.0.0.0` is used, and that the interface hasn't had much traffic. Don't worry about the errors in the last couple of lines: You haven't used the interface yet, so no meaningful statistics are available.

As a check that your kernel knows about the interface and that your machine responds to the IP address `127.0.0.1` and the name `localhost`, you can use the `ping` command to check that the interface is responding properly:

```
$ ping localhost
PING localhost (127.0.0.1): 56 data bytes
64 bytes from 127.0.0.1: icmp_seq=0 ttl=255 time=0.8 ms
64 bytes from 127.0.0.1: icmp_seq=1 ttl=255 time=0.7 ms
```

```
64 bytes from 127.0.0.1: icmp_seq=2 ttl=255 time=0.7 ms
64 bytes from 127.0.0.1: icmp_seq=3 ttl=255 time=0.7 ms
64 bytes from 127.0.0.1: icmp_seq=4 ttl=255 time=0.7 ms

--- localhost ping statistics ---
5 packets transmitted, 5 packets received, 0% packet loss
round-trip min/avg/max = 0.7/0.7/0.8 ms
```

To stop the output from the `ping` command, you press Ctrl+C. You should get similar results using either the name `localhost` or the IP address `127.0.0.1` (because they both refer to exactly the same interface, according to the `/etc/hosts` file).

If you get the message

```
$ ping localhost
unknown host
```

then the interface is not set up properly and you should check the `/etc/hosts` file and the `ifconfig` command to make sure you installed the interface properly. Repeating the installation steps should correct the problem. After you complete those simple steps and tests, the dummy interface is ready to be used by your system, its applications, and both PPP and SLIP.

Setting Up PPP

Most ISPs allow the use of PPP instead of SLIP. This is good for you because PPP is a faster and more efficient protocol. PPP and SLIP are both designed for two-way networking. In other words, your machine talking to one other machine—usually your ISP—and no other machines at the time. PPP is not a replacement for a local area network protocol such as TCP/IP, but PPP can coexist with TCP/IP. Setting up PPP on your system is not as scary as you might suspect. You can do it through a configuration utility or manually from the command line. Both approaches produce the same results, and using the command line offers the advantage that you get to understand what is going on.

PPP uses two components on your system. The first is a daemon called `pppd`, which controls the use of PPP. The second is a driver called the high-level data link control (HDLC), which controls the flow of information between two machines. A third component of PPP is a routine called `chat` that dials the other end of the connection for you when you want it to.

> **NOTE**
>
> PPP is a complex protocol with many tunable parameters. Fortunately, most of these parameters concern things you will never care about, so you can ignore all those underlying details in the vast majority of installations. Unless you plan to use PPP to connect to the Internet all day (and there are better choices for that), you will do fine using the default settings PPP employs.

Installing PPP

PPP was most likely installed for you when you installed Linux. If it wasn't, you need to load the package before you can continue to configure the system for PPP use. The PPP library and files are included with practically every CD-ROM distribution of Linux, and you can obtain the most recent versions from the usual Linux Web and FTP sites.

You can use Red Hat's RPM to load the PPP package quickly with the following command line:

```
rpm -ivh /cdrom/Redhat/Rpms/ppp-2_3_.rpm
```

where the path to the PPP ROM file is fully specified in the command line. The full path depends on where you have mounted your CD-ROM. This example is for a Red Hat 5.2 CD-ROM mounted on the directory /cdrom. You should check the CD-ROM directory first to find out which version of PPP is included with your system. The most recent version is shown in the sample command line as 2.3.

Alternatively, you can use the RPM package to list all available packages and select the PPP package from the list. Red Hat will then install the package, relink the kernel, and tell you to reboot the system.

Setting Up a PPP User Account

To help protect your system from hackers and break-in attempts from your ISP (remember that if your machine can communicate to the Internet, users on the Internet can communicate with your machine), it is advisable to set up a special user login for PPP. This step is optional but highly recommended.

You can add the new user account for PPP (usually just called `ppp` for convenience) using any of the user administration scripts you want, or you can simply edit the /etc/passwd file and add the user yourself. Because the PPP login does not have a home directory per se, you don't need to create mail boxes and other paraphernalia normally created by a user administration script. The line you want to add to the /etc/passwd file looks like this:

```
ppp:*:301:51:PPP account:/tmp:/etc/ppp/pppscript
```

This creates a user called ppp with no password (the asterisk in the second field can't be matched). The user ID is 301 in this example, but you can substitute any unused user ID. The group ID is best set to a new group called ppp, although this is not necessary. The fourth field is a comment that describes the account's purpose. The home directory is set to /tmp in this case because you don't want to keep files in the ppp account home directory. The last field in the /etc/passwd entry is used for a startup script. In this case, I've created a new script called /etc/ppp/pppscript, which takes care of starting PPP properly. You will have to create this script yourself. The contents of pppscript should look like this:

```
#!/bin/sh
mesg n
stty -echo
exec pppd -detach silent modem crtscts
```

The first line invokes the Bourne shell to run the script. The second line suppresses messages for this login. The third line stops the remote from echoing everything back. The fourth line invokes the pppd daemon with some options that control its behavior. (You'll look at the pppd daemon in more detail in a few moments). Make sure the file pppscript is executable.

Setting Up chat

Because you are going to use a modem to connect to your ISP, you need to tell PPP about the modem and how to use it. PPP uses a program called chat to handle all these details. (You can use utilities other than chat, but experience has shown that chat is the most foolproof of the options, as well as one of the easiest to set up quickly.) The chat utility takes a lot of its features from the UUCP program, which makes it familiar for many veteran system administrators.

The chat utility requires a command line that tells it what number to call to connect to your ISP and what types of login responses are required. All of this information is placed on a single-line chat script. These lines are often stored in files to prevent you from having to type the commands every time you want to access the Internet.

Here's a typical chat script for a connection to an ISP:

```
"" ATZ OK ATDT2370400 CONNECT "" ogin: ppp word: guessme
```

chat scripts are always set up as a conversation between the chat utility and the modem. The script parts are separated by spaces, with the chat instruction and the expected reply one after another. This chat script tells chat the following: Expect nothing from the modem to start (the two quotation marks), then send the string ATZ, and wait for the reply OK. After OK is received, chat sends the string ATDT2370400 to dial out to the ISP's number. When a CONNECT string is received back from the modem, send nothing and wait for the string ogin: from the ISP. (This covers all the case types such as login and Login). After getting ogin:, send the login ppp and wait for word (the end of password) and send the password guessme. After that, chat terminates and hands control over to PPP.

You can see in the script how the conversation goes through with each end (the modem and chat) taking turns communicating. You will need to set up a chat script like this in a file with your ISP's number and the proper login and password. Place it in an ASCII file. To call the file, use the chat command:

```
chat -f filename
```

where *filename* is the name of the chat script file. The chat command has a lot of options for handling error conditions from your modem and the ISP, but these all complicate the script quite a bit. The easiest modifications are to build in handling for both a busy signal from the modem (the ISP's line was busy) or a no-carrier message from the modem (when it couldn't connect properly). To handle both these error conditions in the script and have chat terminate when these conditions occur, modify the script to look like this:

```
ABORT BUSY 'NO CARRIER' "" ATZ OK ATDT2370400 CONNECT "" ogin: ppp word:
guessme
```

The two ABORT sequences in front of the older script tell chat to terminate if either the BUSY or NO CARRIER messages are sent by the modem. Make sure you use quotation marks around the two words in NO CARRIER; otherwise, chat thinks these are two different parts of the script.

Configuring pppd

As mentioned earlier, most of the functions of PPP are controlled by a daemon called pppd. When chat has connected to a remote system and chat terminates cleanly, it hands control of the connection over to pppd. It is the pppd daemon that handles all the communications from this point forward.

The pppd daemon is usually started with arguments for the modem device and the speed of the connection. If you want to start pppd manually from the command line, your command looks like this:

```
pppd /dev/cua0 38400 crtscts defaultroute
```

This line tells pppd to use the serial port /dev/cua0 (COM1) to connect at 38,400bps. The crtscts option tells pppd to use hardware handshaking on the connection, and defaultroute tells pppd to use the local IP address for the connection.

Because most ISPs assign you a dynamic IP address when you connect, you can't hard-code the address into the pppd command line. The pppd daemon can accept any IP address the remote connection wants if you modify the command line like this:

```
pppd /dev/cua0 38400 crtscts IP_address:
```

where you substitute whatever IP address your machine has (even 127.0.0.1) before the colon. The colon with nothing after it tells pppd to accept whatever IP address the remote sends as the other end of the connection.

The pppd daemon accepts options from configuration files if they exist. The most common configuration file for PPP is stored as /etc/ppp/options, although you may use any path and filename you want. The default settings in the /etc/ppp/options file look like this:

```
# /etc/ppp/options: global definitions
domain merlin.com
auth                    # force authentication
usehostname             # use local hostname for authentication
lock                    # use file locking UUCP-style
```

The first line gives the local domain name, and you should edit it to suit your domain (if you have one). The second and third lines force authentication to prevent misuse. The fourth line tells pppd to use UUCP-like file locking, which works well to prevent device problems. You can add any other valid pppd options to this file, but these suffice for most setups.

Combining chat and pppd

The way I've described setting up chat and pppd, you have to take two steps to connect to an ISP: Use chat to establish the connection and then launch pppd to use PPP over the connection. There is a way to take both steps with one command line, which can be added to the pppscript I talked about earlier in this section. By calling chat from the pppd command line, you can simplify the entire process. Here's a modification of the pppd command line that accomplishes this:

```
pppd connect "chat -f chatfile" /dev/cua0 38400 -detach crtscts modem
defaultroute
```

With this command, pppd will call chat with the filename chatfile (or whatever you called your chat script file), create the link, and then finish establishing pppd. You must have the path to your `chat` file easily found by `chat` or specify the full pathname in the command line. As mentioned, you can substitute this line for the `pppd` line in the `pppscript` file, and then the connection will be established in one step.

After these few steps, your system is ready to use PPP to dial out to your ISP. As long as the `chat` script has all the instructions for connecting to the ISP's modem bank, PPP will start properly once a connection is established.

Setting Up SLIP

SLIP is used by some ISPs that don't support PPP. You may also find SLIP supported by some online services that don't use the Internet, such as bank access programs and stock trading. SLIP is usually installed automatically as part of the Linux kernel, as is a modification of SLIP called CSLIP (Compressed SLIP).

To use SLIP, you need to dedicate a port to it. This means that the port cannot be used by other applications. This is necessary because of the way SLIP handles ports, which causes conflicts if shared with other programs.

NOTE

Most Linux versions, including Red Hat, install SLIP by default when the kernel is installed. However, if you do not have SLIP installed, you need to rebuild the kernel. As part of the configuration routine for the kernel, you will be asked if you want to include SLIP or CLSIP as part of the kernel. Answer yes, let the kernel relink, reboot the machine, and SLIP is now part of your kernel. A quick way to check whether SLIP is installed is to examine the /proc/net/dev file for a line starting with `sl0`. If the line exists, SLIP is installed.

Configuring SLIP

The fastest way to configure SLIP is to use the `slattach` program. This requires the name of the port that SLIP will use (which has a modem attached for the connection, usually). The command to set up `slattach` is

```
slattach /dev/cua0 &
```

In this case, I've configured the /dev/cua0 port (COM1) as the SLIP port. You can use any other port attached to your system. The ampersand at the end of the line puts the `slattach` program in background so that you can get your shell prompt back.

When you run slattach, the port is renamed to /dev/sl0 to show it is the first SLIP device. It doesn't matter what device name you used for the serial port; the first SLIP device is always called /dev/sl0. This can lead to some confusion if you are using /dev/cua2, for example, which becomes /dev/sl0. If more than one SLIP port is created, they are numbered increasingly as /dev/sl1, /dev/sl2, and so on. Linux usually supports up to eight SLIP lines, but it is unlikely you will need this many.

Linux uses CSLIP by default for most SLIP lines because it packs more information in the same space as SLIP. If your ISP or whomever you are connecting to does not support CSLIP, you need to force Linux to use only SLIP. You can do this on the `slattach` line like this:

```
slattach -p slip /dev/cua0 &
```

This tells `slattach` to use only the SLIP protocol. Other valid arguments after the `ñp` option are `cslip` (for CSLIP), `adaptive` (which adjusts to whatever is at the other end of the connection), and `slip6` (an older 6-bit version of SLIP).

Now that the SLIP device has been created, you need to tell the Linux kernel about it, using the `ifconfig` program for setting up the dummy interface. The `ifconfig` line to establish the interface requires the name of the remote system:

```
ifconfig sl0 mymachine-slip pointopoint remotemachine
```

`sl0` is the name of the interface (`/dev/sl0` in this case), *`mymachine`*`-slip` is the local name of the SLIP interface (you should substitute your machine's name, such as `merlin-slip` or `darkstar-slip`), `pointopoint` tells `ifconfig` the interface is a point-to-point connection (not to be confused with PPP), and *`remotemachine`* is the name of the machine at the other end of the connection. For example, if the remote machine's name is `darkstar` and your machine's name is `dogbert`, the `ifconfig` command looks like this:

```
ifconfig sl0 dogbert-slip pointopoint darkstar
```

The next step is to issue the `route` command to add the route to the remote machine to the system databases. The syntax is the same as when you set up the dummy interface:

```
route add darkstar
```

in this case, adding a route to the remote machine called `darkstar`. You should substitute whatever the remote machine is called.

> **NOTE**
>
> Many ISPs don't tell you their remote machine's names. That's fine because these machine names are only placeholders. You can substitute any name you want that identifies the other end of the connection.

Summary

In this chapter, you've seen how to set up PPP and SLIP for use with your Internet connections. You can also use PPP and SLIP for any machine-to-machine connection, so you can create a small network with a friend if you want. PPP and SLIP are mostly transparent to you once the interfaces are properly set up.

CHAPTER

Getting Started with Red Hat Linux

by Bill Ball

In This Chapter

This chapter covers the basics of getting started on a Red Hat Linux installation and takes a look at the organization of the files on a system along with the installation of packaged software using Red Hat Package Manager.

Organization

A Red Hat Linux installation is usually very nicely organized and fully featured in comparison with other UNIX and Linux distributions. This is because Red Hat complies with the Linux filesystem standard (FSSTND). A complete description of the standard is available at `http://www.pathname.com/fhs/`.

A feature of FSSTND is that the root directory, `/`, is very clean and only holds the most essential files. My `/` looks something like the following:

```
bin/          etc/          lost+found/  sbin/         var/
boot/         home/         mnt/         tmp/
dev/          lib/          proc/        usr/
```

The following sections cover the types of files contained in most of these directories. The /dev, /proc, and /boot directories and their contents are covered in Chapter 15, "Filesystems, Disks, and Other Devices."

/bin and /sbin

Most of the essential programs for using and maintaining a UNIX or Linux system are stored in the /bin and /sbin directories. The *bin* in the names of these directories comes from the fact that executable programs are binary files.

The /bin directory is usually used to hold the most commonly used essential user programs, such as

- `login`
- Shells (`bash`, `ksh`, `csh`)
- File manipulation utilities (`cp`, `mv`, `rm`, `ln`, `tar`)
- Editors (`ed`, `vi`)
- Filesystem utilities (`dd`, `df`, `mount`, `umount`, `sync`)
- System utilities (`uname`, `hostname`, `arch`)

In addition to these types of programs, the /bin directory might also contain GNU utilities such as `gzip` and `gunzip`.

The /sbin directory is used to hold essential maintenance or system programs, such as the following:

- fsck
- fdisk
- mkfs
- shutdown
- lilo
- init

The main difference between the programs stored in /bin and /sbin is that nearly all of the programs in /sbin are executable only by root (one exception is the `ifconfig` command).

/etc

The /etc directory is normally used to store the systemwide configuration files required by many programs. Some of the important files in /etc are as follows:

- passwd
- shadow
- fstab
- hosts
- inittab
- motd
- profile
- shells
- services
- lilo.conf

The first two files in this list, /etc/passwd and /etc/shadow, are files that define the authorized users for a system. The /etc/passwd file contains all of the information about a user except the encrypted password, which is contained in /etc/shadow for security reasons. Manually editing these files is not recommended. To add or change user information, follow the procedures covered in Chapter 20, "Administrative Essentials."

The next file on the list, /etc/fstab, contains a list of devices the system knows how to mount automatically. A line from this file looks something like the following:

```
/dev/hda1       /                   ext2     defaults 1 1
```

The first part, /dev/hda1, indicates the device to mount (in this case the first partition of the internal hard drive, hda). The second part, /, indicates where to mount the device. The entry ext2 indicates what type of filesystem the device contains, while the rest of the entries are mount options (the default options are specified for this device).

This file contains at least two other entries, one for `swap` and another for /proc. On many systems, /etc/fstab also contains entries for CD-ROMs, floppy disks, zip disks, and other mountable media.

To add, delete, or change mount information, use Red Hat's File System Manager, covered in Chapter 15.

The file /etc/hosts contains a list of IP addresses and the corresponding hostnames (and aliases). This list is used to resolve the IP address of a machine when its name is given. A sample entry might look like the following:

```
10.8.11.2       kanchi
```

NOTE

The /etc/inittab, or initialization table, is another important file under the /etc directory. This text file contains directions for how you normally start Linux and is discussed in Chapter 6, "System Startup and Shutdown."

/etc/motd is the file in which the system administrator puts the message of the day (hence the name motd). Usually it contains information related to the system, such as scheduled downtime or upgrades of software, but it can contain anything. The contents of this file are usually displayed at login.

/etc/profile is the default initialization file for users whose shell is either `sh`, `ksh`, or `bash` (the default shell for Red Hat Linux). Mostly it is used for settings variables such as `PATH` and `PS1`, along with such things as the default `umask`. The /etc/profile file is not meant to be used in place of personal initialization files and should be kept small because it is used by scripts as well as users.

The file /etc/shells also pertains to shells. It is a list of "approved" shells for users. One of its primary uses is to prevent people from accidentally changing their shells to something unusable.

In /etc/services is a list of the services that run on the various ports on the system. The entries will look something like the following:

```
telnet          23/tcp
http            80/tcp
```

The first entry is the name of the service, the second entry is the port on which the service runs, and the final entry is the type of service. From the preceding lines you can see that Telnet runs on port 23 and HTTP runs on port 80, which are the standard ports for those services.

The last file on the list is /etc/lilo.conf. This file contains a description of the behavior of the system at boot time, along with a list of all of the bootable images on the system (see Chapter 3, "LILO," for more information).

Two important subdirectories are also in /etc:

X11

rc.d

The X11 subdirectory of /etc contains the configuration files for the X server and the various window managers such as `fvwm`, `mwm`, and `twm`. Most window manager packages add their configuration files into a directory located under /etc/X11. An exception to this is a Red Hat Linux installation with the CDE (Common Desktop Environment) installed. The CDE is covered in Chapter 5, "Window Managers."

The rc.d subdirectory of /etc contains initialization scripts that run when Linux is loaded or shut down. Some of the scripts contain commands to load modules; others handle general boot behavior.

In addition to the files discussed, many other configuration files are found in the /etc directory. The process of modifying and maintaining configuration files is covered in Chapter 20, "Administrative Essentials," and Chapter 21, "Advanced System Administration."

/home

The /home directory is where all home directories for all users on a system are stored. This includes home directories for actual users (people) and for users such as HTTPD. An interesting feature of Linux is that the home directory for the user root is usually stored as /home/root. This is different from many UNIX systems, where / is the home directory for the user root.

/mnt

By convention, the /mnt directory is the directory under which removable media such as CD-ROMs, floppy disks, Zip disks, or Jaz disks are mounted. Usually the /mnt directory contains a number of subdirectories, each of which is a mount point for a particular device type. On my system, the /mnt directory looks like the following:

```
cdrom/      floppy/     zip/
```

By using subdirectories under /mnt to house all of your mounted removable media, you keep the / directory clean.

/tmp and /var

The /tmp and /var directories are used to hold temporary files or files with constantly varying content.

The /tmp directory is usually a dumping ground for files that only need to be used briefly and can afford to be deleted at any time. It usually is quite unstructured, but on a multiuser system, most users abide by the convention of creating a personal directory (named the same as their username) in /tmp for storing their temporary files. The most common use of /tmp (other than as a location for throwaway files) is as a starting point for building and installing programs.

The /var directory is a bit more structured than /tmp and usually looks something like the following:

```
catman/     local/      log/        nis/        run/        tmp/
lib/        lock/       named/      preserve/   spool/      yp/
```

Of these directories, the /var/log directory is one of the directories with which all users should be familiar because most of the messages generated by the system are stored in it. On my system, /var/log contains the following files:

```
./          dmesg       maillog     savacct     spooler     wtmp
../         httpd/      messages    secure      usracct
cron        lastlog     pacct       sendmail.st uucp/
```

Of these files, the following are very helpful when attempting to diagnose system problems:

- dmesg contains the messages displayed when the system was last booted.
- messages contains all messages displayed at boot time since the system was first booted.

For example, one helpful way to diagnose problems, such as establishing a Point-to-Point Protocol connection, is to use the `tail` command to pipe the last few lines of /var/log/messages through a pager (such as `less`) like this

```
# tail /var/log/messages | less
```

/usr

By convention, the /usr directory is where most programs and files directly relating to users of the system are stored. It is in some ways a miniversion of the / directory. On my system, the /usr directory looks like this:

```
X11/        etc/              libexec/    share/
X11R6/      games/            local/      src/
X386@       i486-linuxaout/   man/        tmp@
bin/        include/          openwin/
dict/       info/             opt/
doc/        lib/              sbin/
```

The contents of the various directories are briefly described in the following paragraphs.

The /usr/bin and /usr/sbin directories hold the vast majority of the executables available on a system. The function and type of the executables placed into these directories follow the same general convention as for /bin and /sbin. However, in many cases, unless you are logged in as the root operator, you won't be able to run commands from the /usr/sbin or /sbin directories because these programs might act on important system files.

The /usr/opt or /opt directories under Linux are equivalent to the /opt directory in Solaris. Optional software packages are usually installed in /opt; for example, the Applixware Office Suite, the K Desktop Environment (KDE), and the latest version of WordPerfect for Linux are stored under the /opt directory.

The /usr/X11 and /usr/X11R6 directories and subdirectories contain all of the X Window-related files, such as man pages, libraries, and executables. Red Hat Linux systems contain only /usr/X11R6, the 6th revision of the X Window version 11.

Although X is the primary windowing environment under Linux, other Linux installations might contain the /usr/openwin directory for storing files that use open windows. This includes programs such as `olwm`, `textedit`, and `workman`.

The /usr/local directory is the location where local programs, man pages, and libraries are installed. At many sites, most of the directories in /usr are kept the same on every computer, but anything that needs to be installed on a particular machine is placed in /usr/local, thus identifying these files as local files and making maintenance of large numbers of systems easier.

Finally, one of the most useful directories under /usr is /usr/dict, where the local dictionary for the system, called /usr/dict/words, is stored. Most versions of /usr/dict/words contain about 25,000 words, but some can be as large as a hundred thousand or more. In Red Hat Linux, the words file is a symbolic link to the file linux.words. The main dictionary for Red Hat's default spelling checker, ispell, resides under the /usr/lib/ispell directory, but you can force ispell to use /usr/dict/words with the `-l` command-line option.

The Red Hat Package Manager (RPM)

One of the most powerful and innovative utilities available in Red Hat Linux is RPM, the Red Hat Package Manager. It can be used to install, uninstall, upgrade, query, verify, and build software packages.

A software package built with RPM is an archive of files and some associated information, such as a name, a version, and a description. Following are a few of the advantages of RPM packages over the traditional `tar.gz` method of software distribution:

- Upgrading—A new version of the software can be installed without losing customization files.
- Uninstalling—A software package that installs files in several locations can be cleanly removed.
- Verification—After installation, a package can be verified to be in working order.
- Querying—Information about what package a file belongs to can be easily obtained.

In addition to these features, RPM is available for many flavors of Linux and UNIX, making it one of the emerging utilities for distributing software packages.

Major Modes and Common Options

The major modes in which RPM can be run are the following:

- Install (`rpm -i`)
- Uninstall (`rpm -e`)
- Query (`rpm -q`)
- Verify (`rpm -V`)

The options to invoke the major modes are given in parentheses. These major modes are covered in detail in subsequent sections.

All of these major modes understand the following options:

`-vv`	Prints out all debugging information; useful to see what exactly RPM is doing
`--quiet`	Prints out very little information, only error messages

In addition to these, a few other "minor" modes are useful. These are as follows:

Version (rpm ---version)

Help (rpm ---help)

Showrc (rpm ---showrc)

Rebuilddb (rpm --rebuilddb)

The version mode, invoked as

```
# rpm --version
```

prints out a line containing version information, similar to this:

```
RPM version 2.3.11
```

The help mode prints out an extensive help message and is invoked as follows:

```
# rpm --help
```

Because the message is long, it is handy to have a large `xterm` or to pipe the output to `more`. To get a shorter help message, just type

```
# rpm
```

This prints out a usage message. The showrc mode

```
# rpm --showrc
```

prints out a list of variables that can be set in the files /etc/rpmrc and $HOME/.rpmrc. The default values are adequate for most installations.

The `rebuilddb` option is used to rebuild the database RPM uses to keep track of which packages are installed on a system. It is invoked as follows:

```
# rpm --rebuilddb
```

The database files are usually stored in /var/lib/rpm/. In most cases, the database files do not need to be rebuilt very often.

Installing Packages

One of the major uses of RPM is to install software packages. The general syntax of an `rpm` install command is

```
rpm -i [options] [packages]
```

where *options* can be one of the common options given earlier or one of the install options covered in the following list, and *packages* is the name of one or more RPM package files. Some of the install options are as follows:

`-v`	Prints out what RPM is doing.
`-h` or `--hash`	Prints out 50 hash marks (`#`) as the package is installed.
`--percent`	Prints out percentages as files are extracted from the package.
`--test`	Goes through a package install, but does not install anything; mainly used to catch conflicts.
`--excludedocs`	Prevents the installation of files marked as documentation, such as man pages.
`--includedocs`	Forces files marked as documentation to be installed; this is the default.
`--nodeps`	No dependency checks are performed before installing a package.
`--replacefiles`	Allows for installed files to be replaced with files from the package being installed.
`--replacepkgs`	Allows for installed packages to be replaced with the packages being installed.
`--oldpackage`	Allows for a newer version of an installed package to be replaced with an older version.
`--force`	Forces a package to be installed.

When giving options to RPM, regardless of the mode, all of the single-letter options can be lumped together in one block. For example, the command

```
# rpm -i -v -h kernel-2.0.30-3.i386.rpm
```

is equivalent to

```
# rpm -ivh kernel-2.0.30-3.i386.rpm
```

All options starting with `--` must be given separately, however.

Now look at a couple of examples of installing RPM packages. The first example installs `vim` (the improved version of `vi`) from the package:

```
vim-4.5-2.i386.rpm
```

This package follows the standard naming convention for RPM packages, which is

name-version-release.arch.rpm

where *name* is the package's name, *version* is the package's version, *release* is the package's release level, *arch* is the hardware architecture the package is for, and rpm is the default extension. This naming scheme is quite handy because some of the essential information about a particular package can be determined from just looking at its name.

For the vim package, say you are installing vim version 4.5, release 2, for a computer with the i386 architecture. Go ahead now and install this package. With the Red Hat CD-ROM on /mnt/cdrom, the package you want is

```
/mnt/cdrom/RedHat/RPMS/vim-4.5-2.i386.rpm
```

First, cd into the appropriate directory. Then, to install it, type the following at the prompt (#):

```
# rpm -ivh vim-4.5-2.i386.rpm
```

As the package is installed, the output looks like the following:

```
vim                          #################
```

When the install is finished, 50 hash marks are displayed.

In this example I used the hash character (#) to indicate the root prompt because only root can properly install packages for an entire system. If you try to install this package as a user other than root, an error similar to the following will be generated:

```
failed to open //var/lib/rpm/packages.rpm
error: cannot open //var/lib/rpm/packages.rpm
```

Now, to install the X11 version of vim from the package, type:

```
/mnt/cdrom/RedHat/RPMS/vim-X11-4.2-8.i386.rpm
```

If you try using

```
# rpm -ivh vim-X11-4.2-8.i386.rpm
```

you will get the following error:

```
package vim-X11-4.2-8 is already installed
error: vim-X11-4.2-8.i386.rpm cannot be installed
```

To install this package, use the --replacepkgs option:

```
# rpm -ivh --replacepkgs vim-X11-4.5-2.i386.rpm
```

Occasionally, the files install by one package conflict with the files of a previously installed package. If you have vim version 4.2 installed, the following message will be generated:

```
/bin/vim conflicts with file from vim-4.2-8
/usr/share/vim/vim_tips.txt conflicts with file from vim-4.2-8
error: vim-4.5-2.i386.rpm cannot be installed
```

If you want to install these files anyway, the --replacefiles option can be added to the command.

Another type of conflict sometimes encountered is a dependency conflict when a package you are installing requires certain other packages to function correctly. For example, when I try to install the package

```
# rpm -ivh dosemu-0.66.2-1.i386.rpm
```

I get the following dependency errors:

```
failed dependencies:
kernel >= 2.0.28 is needed by dosemu-0.66.2-1
dosemu = 0.64.1 is needed by xdosemu-0.64.1-1
```

This indicates two things. I need to upgrade my kernel to 2.0.28, and if I install a newer version of `dosemu`, I also need to install a newer version of `xdosemu`. Although it is usually not a good idea to ignore dependency problems, using the `--nodeps` option causes RPM to ignore these errors and install the package.

Upgrading Packages

RPM's upgrade mode provides an easy way to upgrade existing software packages to newer versions. Upgrade mode is similar to install mode:

```
rpm -U [options] [packages]
```

`options` can be any of the install options or any of the general options.

Here is an example of how to upgrade packages. On my system I am currently running `emacs` version 19.31, but I want to upgrade to the newer `emacs` version 19.34. To upgrade, I use the following command:

```
# rpm -Uvh emacs-19.34-4.i386.rpm
```

The upgrade mode is a combination of two operations, `uninstall` and `install`. First, RPM uninstalls any older versions of the requested package, and then it installs the newer version. If an older version of the package does not exist, RPM simply installs the requested package.

An additional advantage of using `upgrade` over manually installing and uninstalling is that `upgrade` automatically saves configuration files. For these reasons, some people prefer to use `upgrade` rather than `install` for all package installations.

Uninstalling Packages

The `uninstall` mode of RPM provides for a clean method of removing files belonging to a software package from many locations.

Many packages install files in /etc, /usr, and /lib, so removing a package can be confusing, but with RPM an entire package can be removed as follows:

```
rpm -e [options] [package]
```

options is one of the options listed later in this section, and *package* is the name of the package to be removed. For example, if I want to remove the package for dosemu, the command is as follows:

```
# rpm -e dosemu
```

The name specified here for the package is just the name of the package, not the name of the file that was used to install the package. If I had asked for

```
# rpm -e dosemu-0.64.1-1.i386.rpm
```

the following error would have been generated:

```
package dosemu-0.64.1-1.i386.rpm is not installed
```

Another common error encountered while trying to uninstall packages is a dependency error when a package that is being uninstalled has files required by another package. For example, when I try to remove dosemu from my system, I get the following error:

```
removing these packages would break dependencies:
dosemu = 0.64.1 is needed by xdosemu-0.64.1-1
```

This means the package xdosemu will not function properly if the package dosemu is removed. If I still want to remove this package, I can give RPM the --nodeps option to make it ignore dependency errors.

The other useful option is the --test option, which causes RPM to go through the motions of removing a package without actually removing anything. Usually there is no output from an uninstall, so the -vv option is given along with the --test option to see what would happen during an uninstall. For example,

```
# rpm -e -vv --test xdosemu
```

produces the following output on my system:

```
D: counting packages to uninstall
D: opening database in //var/lib/rpm/
D: found 1 packages to uninstall
D: uninstalling record number 1650520
D: running preuninstall script (if any)
D: would remove files test = 1
D: /usr/man/man1/xtermdos.1 - would remove
D: /usr/man/man1/xdos.1 - would remove
D: /usr/bin/xtermdos - would remove
D: /usr/bin/xdos - would remove
D: /usr/X11R6/lib/X11/fonts/misc/vga.pcf - would remove
D: running postuninstall script (if any)
D: script found - running from file /tmp/02695aaa
```

```
+ PATH=/sbin:/bin:/usr/sbin:/usr/bin:/usr/X11R6/bin
+ export PATH
+ [ -x /usr/X11R6/bin/mkfontdir ]
+ cd /usr/X11R6/lib/X11/fonts/misc
+ /usr/X11R6/bin/mkfontdir
D: would remove database entry
```

As you can see, the files that would have been removed are clearly indicated in the output.

Querying Packages

The querying mode in RPM allows for determining the various attributes of packages. The basic syntax for querying packages is

```
rpm -q [options] [packages]
```

where *options* is one or more of the query options listed later in this section. The most basic query is one similar to

```
# rpm -q kernel
```

On my system, this prints out the following line for the kernel package:

```
kernel-2.0.27-5
```

In a manner similar to `uninstall`, RPM's `query` mode uses the name of the package, not the name of the file in which the package came.

Now for a few more sample queries. If you want to get a list of all files "owned" by the kernel package, you can use the `-l` option:

```
# rpm -ql kernel
```

This outputs the following list of files on my system:

```
/boot/System.map-2.0.27
/boot/module-info
/boot/vmlinuz-2.0.27
```

In addition to getting a list of the files, you can determine their state by using the `-s` option:

```
# rpm -qs kernel
```

This option gives the following information about the state of files in my kernel package:

```
normal        /boot/System.map-2.0.27
normal        /boot/module-info
normal        /boot/vmlinuz-2.0.27
```

If any of these files reported a state of missing, there would probably be problems with the package.

In addition to the state of the files in a package, the documentation files and the configuration files can be listed. To list the documentation that comes with the dosemu package, use the following:

```
# rpm -qd dosemu
```

This produces the following list:

```
/usr/man/man1/dos.1
```

To get the configuration files for the same package, you use the following query:

```
# rpm -qc dosemu
```

This results in the following list:

```
/etc/dosemu.conf
/var/lib/dosemu/hdimage
```

In addition to these queries, complete information about a package can be determined by using the info option. For example,

```
# rpm -qi kernel
```

gives the following information about the installed kernel package:

```
Name        : kernel              Distribution: Red Hat Linux Vanderbilt
Version     : 2.0.27              Vendor: Red Hat Software
Release     : 5                   Build Date: Sat Dec 21 21:06:28 1996
Install date: Thu Jul 17 14:10:52 1997    Build Host: porky.redhat.com
Group       : Base/Kernel         Source RPM: kernel-2.0.27-5.src.rpm
Size        : 565900
Summary     : Generic linux kernel
Description : This package contains the Linux kernel that is
➥used to boot and run your system. It contains few device
➥drivers for specific hardware. Most hardware is instead
➥supported by modules loaded after booting.
```

Here is a summary of the query options:

-l	Lists all files in a package
-s	Lists the state of files in a package
-d	Lists all files in a package that are marked as documentation
-c	Lists all files in a package that are marked as configuration
-i	Lists the complete information for a package

If any of these options (except `-i`) are given along with a `-v` option, the files are listed in `ls -l` format. For example,

```
# rpm -qlv kernel
```

outputs the following:

```
-rw-r--r---     root     root     104367 Dec 21 21:05 /boot/System.map-
2.0.27
-rw-r--r---     root     root      11773 Dec 21 21:05 /boot/module-info
-rw-r--r---     root     root     449760 Dec 21 21:05 /boot/vmlinuz-2.0.27
```

In addition to the preceding, RPM understands the following query options:

`-a`	Lists all installed packages
`-f` *file*	Lists the package that owns the specified file
`-p` *package*	Lists the package name of the specified package

Verifying Packages

Verifying packages is an easy way to determine any problems with an installation. In verification mode, RPM compares information about an installed package against information about the original package, which is stored in the package database at install time.

The basic syntax for verifying a package is as follows:

```
rpm -V [package]
```

If a package is verified correctly, RPM does not output anything. If RPM detects a difference between the installed package and the database record, it outputs an 8-character string, where tests that fail are represented by a single character and tests that pass are represented by a period (.). The characters for failed tests are as follows:

Character	*Failed Test*
`5`	MD5 Sum
`S`	File Size
`L`	Symlink
`T`	Mtime
`D`	Device
`U`	User
`G`	Group
`M`	Mode (permissions and file type)

For example, on my system, verifying the bash package by using

```
# rpm -V bash
```

fails as follows:

```
.M..L...   /bin/bash
....L...   /bin/sh
```

This indicates that the size of my bash is different from the information stored in the database. This is okay on my system because I have recompiled bash.

In addition, you can use the query option -f to verify a package containing a particular file, which is helpful when diagnosing problems with programs. For example, if ksh is behaving peculiarly,

```
# rpm -Vf /bin/ksh
```

will verify the package ksh came in. If any of the tests fail, you will be closer to understanding the source of the problems.

Introduction to glint

The most common way most users interact with RPM is via glint, the graphical Linux installation tool. glint is an X-based interface for RPM that allows for installing, uninstalling, querying, and verifying packages via a graphical "file manager" interface.

glint is accessible from the command line of an X11 terminal window or the Control Panel application that comes with Red Hat Linux. To launch glint, simply type

```
# glint
```

at the prompt. glint accepts no command-line options. While glint is loading, a message such as

```
Glint Graphical Package Manager -- version 2.1.5 Copyright (d) 1996
➥Red Hat Software
➥This may be freely redistributed under the terms of the GNU Public
License
```

appears in the terminal window. After glint has loaded, a window similar to Figure 19.1 appears.

From this window, packages can be selected and queried, verified, uninstalled, or installed. When you click the Available button, all packages available for installation from the default location (/mnt/cdrom/RedHat/RPMS) are listed in the Available Packages window, shown in Figure 19.2.

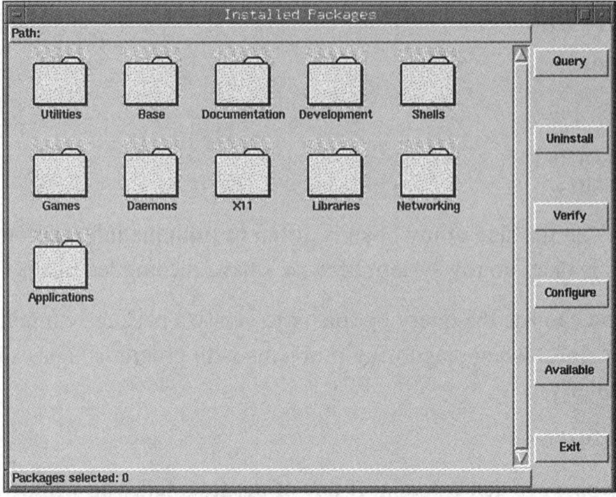

FIGURE 19.1
The primary `glint` *window.*

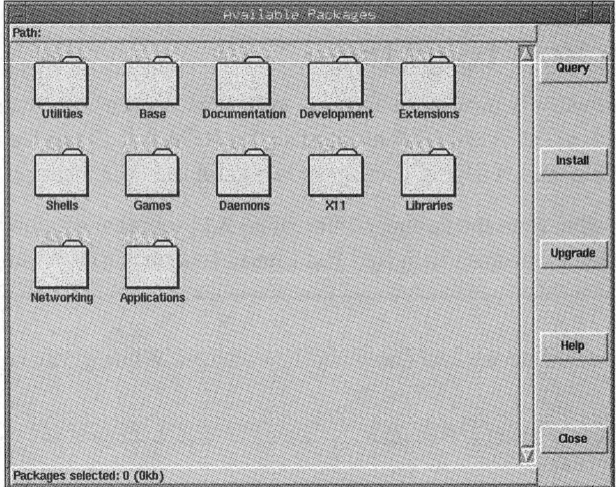

FIGURE 19.2
The Available Packages `glint` *window.*

By navigating through the folders, you can select and install different packages. As an example, take a look at installing the `vim` package.

To install the `vim` package, first launch `glint`. Then, in the Installed Packages window, click the Available button. When the Available Packages window appears, select the Applications folder and then the Editors folder, and click the package `vim-4.5-2`, which becomes highlighted (see Figure 19.3).

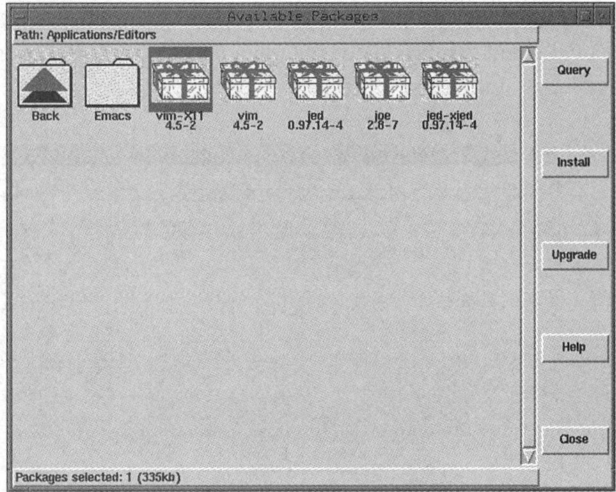

FIGURE 19.3 *Available Packages with* `vim` *selected.*

When a package is highlighted, it can be installed by clicking the Install button. You can install many packages at once by highlighting more than one package.

When you click the Install button, the Installing dialog box appears (see Figure 19.4). This dialog shows the progress of the installation.

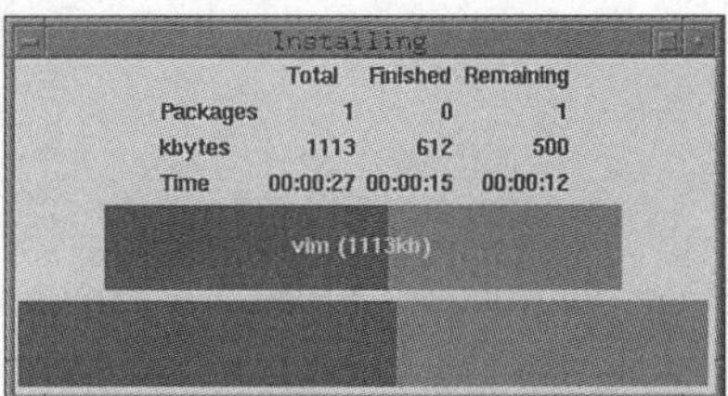

FIGURE 19.4 *The Installing dialog.*

When `vim` has been installed, it is removed from the Available Packages window.

In this example, I assumed that the available packages were stored in the default location mentioned earlier, but often that is not the case. You can change this location by first clicking the Configure button in the primary `glint` window (refer to Figure 19.1). Then, in the Configuration dialog, enter the different location where the package files are located (see Figure 19.5).

FIGURE 19.5 *Changing the package location.*

`glint` also provides a nice front end for querying packages. `glint` executes most of the queries automatically and displays the results in a tabular form. For example, a query of the `vim` package looks similar to Figure 19.6.

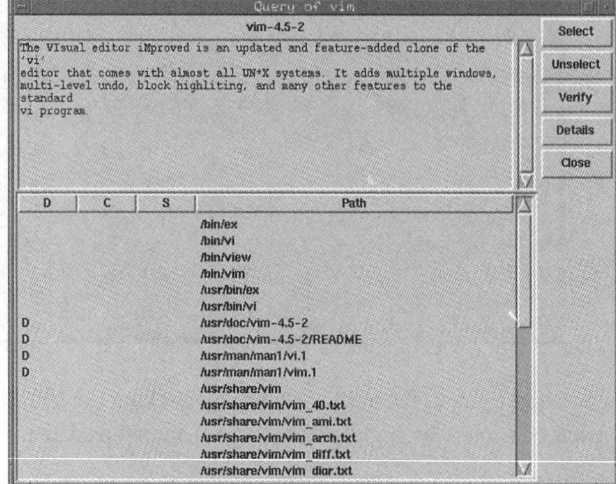

FIGURE 19.6
Query of the `vim` *package.*

In this format, descriptions of the package and all of its files, marked by type, are clearly visible. In some respects, it is easier to use than the command-line queries.

Red Hat Tools

Red Hat Linux is one of the best Linux distributions because of the wealth of specialized administrative tools included in each release. Table 19.1 lists a number of Red Hat tools. The table includes the name, if the tool requires X11 or is available in Red Hat's control-panel client, and a short description.

> **NOTE**
>
> Veteran Red Hat Linux users should note that the former Red Hat filesystem tool, `fstool`, and Red Hat Linux 5.0's `cabaret` filesystem tool are no longer supported or distributed. The newer Linux configuration tool, `linuxconf` (discussed later in "Using the `linuxconf` Command"), replaces these programs.

TABLE 19.1 RED HAT LINUX SOFTWARE TOOLS

Name	*Requires X11*	*Control-panel*	*Description*
Xconfigurator			Configure the X Window System
chkconfig(non-gui)			View status of services and runlevels
comanche	X	X	Configure Apache Web server
fetchmailconf	X	X	Configure email retrieval
glint	X	X	Graphical interface to rpm
helptool	X	X	Search manual pages
kbdconfig			Configure your keyboard
kernelcfg	X	X	Load, unload kernel modules
linuxconf		X	Total configuration tool for Red Hat Linux
modemtool	X	X	Create /dev/modem symbolic link
mouseconfig			Configure your mouse
netcfg	X	X	Install, configure, administer network interfaces
ntsysv			Configure system services
printtool	X	X	Install, configure printers
setup			Dialog for ntsysv, X, kbd, mouse, snd, and time config tools
sndconfig			Configure your sound card
timeconfig			Set your timezone
timetool	X	X	Set system date, time
tksysv	X	X	Configure system services

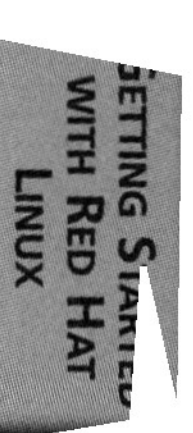

These tools represent the future of Linux system administration—point-and-click convenience. Many of these programs feature built-in help, and all aim to make the care and feeding of your Linux system easier.

NOTE

A number of Red Hat's system tools or their interfaces are written in the Python programming language. For example, one of the most powerful, `glint`, is a graphical interface to the rpm software package management tool. For more information about Python, see Chapter 34, "Programming in Python."

Using the `control-panel` Client

The `control-panel` tool is a graphical interface that hosts a number of Red Hat tools (see Figure 19.7 and Table 19.1). You must be the root operator to use all except one of the `control-panel` programs (`helptool`), and the control panel can only be used during X11 sessions. The `control-panel` client can be started from the command line of an X11 terminal window like this

```
# control-panel &
```

FIGURE 19.7
The X11 `control-panel` client is a graphical interface to Red Hat Linux tools.

You can use the `control-panel` client as a vertical or horizontal toolbar by selecting File, Change Orientation. Although the client initially sports a line of square buttons, you can find out what they do by moving your X11 pointer over each button to see a pop-up text string. The next sections briefly describe each control-panel tool.

Configuring Apache with the Comanche Tool

The Comanche tool, also available from the command line of an X terminal window as the `comanche` command, is a graphical interface to configuring the Apache Web server. If you click on the Comanche tool button in the control panel or type the command **`comanche`** on the command line, its main dialog appears, as shown in Figure 19.8.

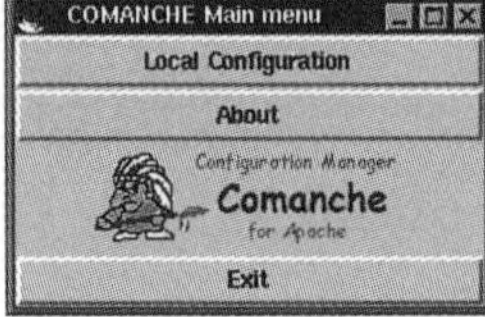

FIGURE 19.8
The comanche tool is a graphical interface to configuring the Apache Web server for Linux.

Configuring Fetchmail with the fetchmailconf Tool

The fetchmailconf tool, also available from the command line of an X terminal window as the `fetchmailconf` command, is a graphical interface to configuring electronic mail retrieval for users on your system. If you click on the Fetchmailconf tool button in the control panel or type the command **`fetchmailconf`** on the command line, its main dialog appears, as shown in Figure 19.9.

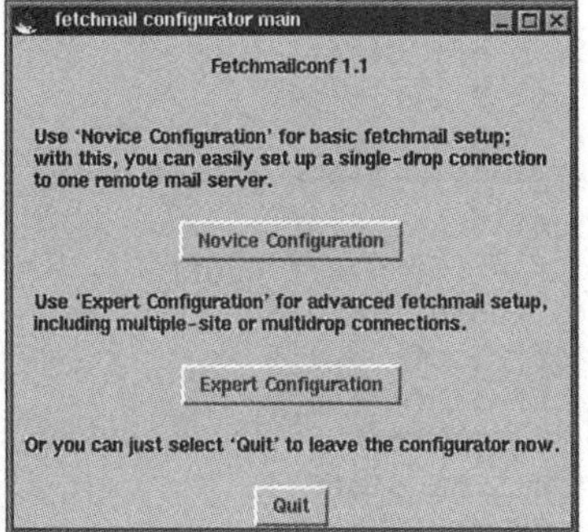

FIGURE 19.9
The `fetchmail-conf` tool is a graphical interface to setting up email services on your system.

Configuring Linux Runlevels with the tksysv Tool

The tksysv tool, also available from the command line of an X terminal window as the `tksysv` command, is a graphical interface to configuring what services you'd like to start or stop during each Linux runlevel (see Chapter 6 for more information about how Red Hat Linux uses runlevels). Click on the Tksysv tool button in the control panel or type the command **`tksysv`** on the command line, and its main dialog appears, as shown in Figure 19.10.

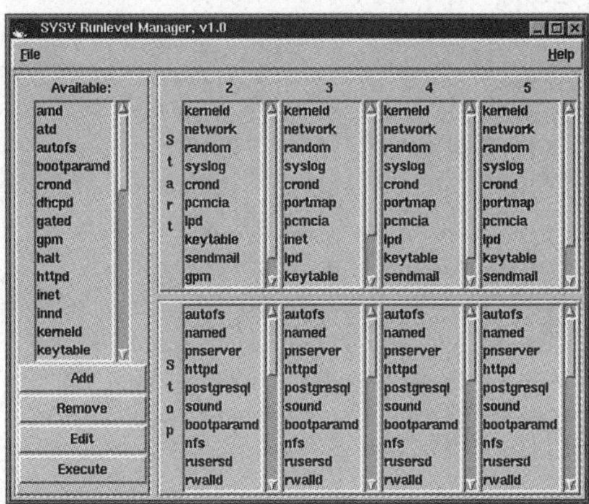

FIGURE 19.10
The `tksysv` tool is a handy interface to customizing system services for Linux.

Checking Runlevels with the `chkconfig` Command

Another handy Red Hat tool you can use in conjunction with `tksysv` is the `chkconfig` command. This command, which does not require X, can be used from the command line of your console and reports on the status of the services as shown by `tksysv`. The `chkconfig` command can also, like `tksysv`, add or remove new services, list each service for each runlevel, configure runlevels, or check system services. For example, to see the current state of your system and which services are started or stopped for each runlevel, use the `chkconfig --list` option like this

```
# chkconfig --list
amd 0:off 1:off 2:off 3:off 4:off 5:off 6:off
httpd 0:off 1:off 2:off 3:off 4:off 5:off 6:off
atd 0:off 1:off 2:off 3:off 4:off 5:off 6:off
autofs 0:off 1:off 2:off 3:off 4:off 5:off 6:off
named 0:off 1:off 2:off 3:off 4:off 5:off 6:off
bootparamd 0:off 1:off 2:off 3:off 4:off 5:off 6:off
snmpd 0:off 1:off 2:off 3:off 4:off 5:off 6:off
dhcpd 0:off 1:off 2:off 3:off 4:off 5:off 6:off
gated 0:off 1:off 2:off 3:off 4:off 5:off 6:off
gpm 0:off 1:off 2:on 3:on 4:on 5:on 6:off
network 0:off 1:off 2:on 3:on 4:on 5:on 6:off
nfsfs 0:off 1:off 2:off 3:off 4:off 5:off 6:off
random 0:off 1:on 2:on 3:on 4:on 5:on 6:off
innd 0:off 1:off 2:off 3:off 4:off 5:off 6:off
keytable 0:off 1:off 2:on 3:on 4:on 5:on 6:off
lpd 0:off 1:off 2:on 3:on 4:on 5:on 6:off
mars-nwe 0:off 1:off 2:off 3:off 4:off 5:off 6:off
mcserv 0:off 1:off 2:off 3:off 4:off 5:off 6:off
kerneld 0:off 1:on 2:on 3:on 4:on 5:on 6:off
inet 0:off 1:off 2:off 3:on 4:off 5:off 6:off
nfs 0:off 1:off 2:off 3:off 4:off 5:off 6:off
pcmcia 0:off 1:off 2:on 3:on 4:on 5:on 6:off
pnserver 0:off 1:off 2:off 3:off 4:off 5:off 6:off
portmap 0:off 1:off 2:off 3:on 4:on 5:on 6:off
postgresql 0:off 1:off 2:off 3:off 4:off 5:off 6:off
sound 0:off 1:off 2:off 3:off 4:off 5:off 6:off
routed 0:off 1:off 2:off 3:off 4:off 5:off 6:off
rusersd 0:off 1:off 2:off 3:off 4:off 5:off 6:off
rwalld 0:off 1:off 2:off 3:off 4:off 5:off 6:off
rwhod 0:off 1:off 2:off 3:off 4:off 5:off 6:off
smb 0:off 1:off 2:off 3:off 4:off 5:off 6:off
sendmail 0:off 1:off 2:on 3:on 4:on 5:on 6:off
syslog 0:off 1:off 2:on 3:on 4:on 5:on 6:off
crond 0:off 1:off 2:on 3:on 4:on 5:on 6:off
ypbind 0:off 1:off 2:off 3:off 4:off 5:off 6:off
ypserv 0:off 1:off 2:off 3:off 4:off 5:off 6:off
yppasswdd 0:off 1:off 2:off 3:off 4:off 5:off 6:off
```

As you can see, chkconfig reports on nearly 40 different system services. You can use chkconfig to start, stop, or reassign services for each runlevel.

CAUTION

Don't reconfigure your system's services indiscriminately! Make sure you know what you're doing before using the chkconfig, tksysv, or ntsysv (discussed later) commands! Stopping your services or reconfiguring them to incorrect runlevels might render your system unusable. Definitely read Chapter 6 before using these commands. Also make sure to read the documentation or man pages for each service before configuring your runlevels.

Setting the Time and Date with the Timetool Command

The Timetool command, also available from the command line of an X terminal window as timetool, is a graphical interface to setting your system's date and time. If you click on the Timetool button in the control panel or type the command **timetool** on the command line, its main dialog appears, as shown in Figure 19.11.

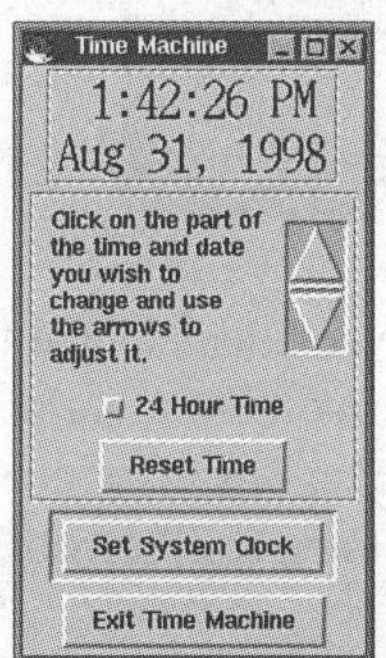

FIGURE 19.11
The timetool client is a graphical interface to setting your system's date and time.

Note that this command is different from the timeconfig command (discussed later), which can be used to set your system's timezone.

Configuring Your Printers with the Printtool Client

The Printtool client, also available from the command line of an X terminal window as the printtool command, is a graphical interface to installing or configuring printers for Linux. Click on the Printtool button in the control panel or type the command **printtool** on the command line, and its main dialog appears, as shown in Chapter 16, "Printing with Linux." Be sure to read Chapter 16 for more complete information on using this client.

Configuring Network Devices with the `netcfg` Tool

The `netcfg` tool, also available from the command line of an X terminal window as the `netcfg` command, is a graphical interface to managing critical network information for your system. If you click on the `netcfg` tool button in the control panel or type the command **`netcfg`** on the command line, its main dialog appears, as shown in Figure 19.12.

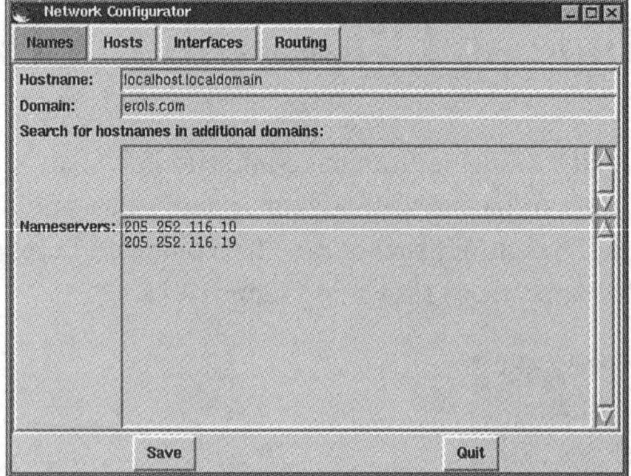

FIGURE 19.12
The `netcfg` tool is a graphical interface to configuring and managing your system's network information and services.

You can use `netcfg` to assign your system's hostname and domain and to specify the addresses of your system's Domain Name servers (for more information about DNS, see Chapter 11, "The Domain Name Service"). This tool also sets up or configures network interfaces such as Point-to-Point Protocol, Serial-line Interface Protocol, Parallel-line Interface Protocol, ethernet, or others.

NOTE

Want to know more about using `netcfg`? See Chapter 17, "TCP/IP Network Management," for more details about setting up interfaces for PLIP or ethernet networks. To learn more about using `netcfg` for setting up PPP or SLIP, see Chapter 18, "Connecting to the Internet."

Getting Help with the `helptool` Client

The `helptool` client, also available from the command line of an X terminal window as `helptool`, can be used by all users (not just the root operator) to search the Linux file system for documentation, manual pages, or GNU info files related to entered queries. If you click on the `helptool` button in the control panel or type the command **`helptool`** on the command line, its main dialog appears, as shown in Figure 19.13 (which shows the results for a search on the phrase "gcc").

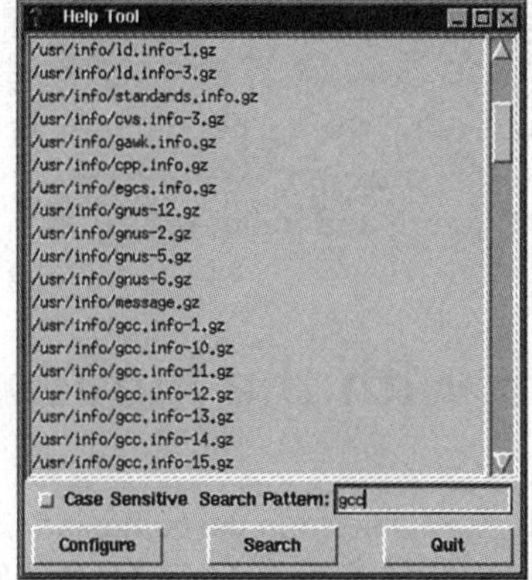

FIGURE 19.13
`helptool` *is a graphical query interface to searching your system for information documents.*

You can also configure the `helptool` client to search for random documents, GNU info files, or system manual pages. Click the helptool's Configure button, and you can tell `helptool` where to search for documents on your system (or other mounted filesystems). To use `helptool`, enter a command name or phrase into the search field and click the Search button. If related documents are found, you can double-click on a listed document to display the document in a new window. If you double-click on a man page, the new window uses the `man` command to show the document. If you double-click on a GNU info file, the new window uses the `info` command.

Configuring Your Linux Kernel with the `kernelcfg` Tool

The `kernelcfg` tool, also available from the command line of an X terminal window as the `kernelcfg` command, is a graphical interface to the kerneld daemon and several Linux kernel module commands, such as `init`, `lsmod`, `insmod`, or `rmmod`. If you click on the kernelcfg tool button in the control panel or type the command **`kernelcfg`** on the command line, its main dialog appears, as shown in Figure 19.14.

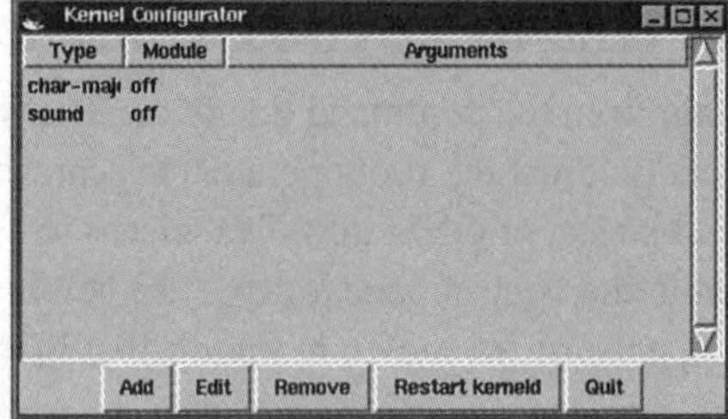

FIGURE 19.14
The `kernelcfg` *client is a graphical interface to loading or unloading modules from your Linux kernel.*

> **NOTE**
>
> For more detailed information about using the `kernelcfg` tool, or for instructions on how to build and install kernel code modules or even compile a new Linux kernel, see Chapter 28, "Configuring and Building Kernels."

Creating /dev/modem with the modemtool Client

The modemtool client, a simple tool also available from the command line of an X terminal window as the `modemtool` command, creates a symbolic link called /dev/modem that points to your modem's serial port. If you click on the modemtool button in the control panel or type the command **`modemtool`** on the command line, its main dialog appears, as shown in Figure 19.15.

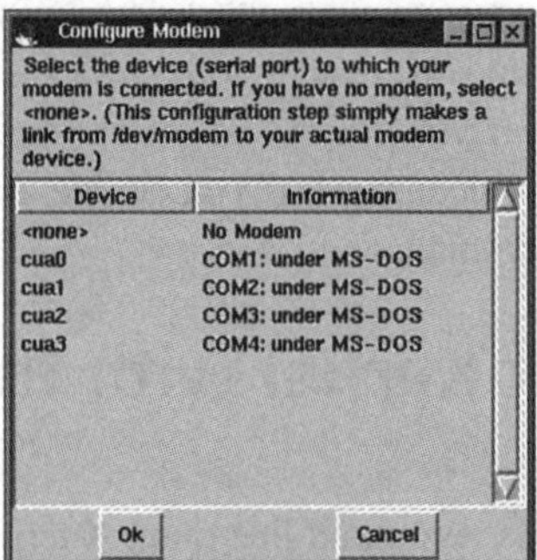

FIGURE 19.15
The `modemtool` *client is a graphical tool used to create a symbolic link for your system's modem.*

Using Red Hat's setup Command

The `setup` command, found under the /usr/sbin directory, is an earlier Red Hat tool the root operator can use to configure a variety of hardware and software services for Linux.

Unlike a number of other Red Hat tools, `setup` and the programs that run under its graphical interface—such as `Xconfigurator`, `mouseconfig`, `ntsysv`, `sndconfig`, and `timeconfig`—do not require X11. Start the program from the command line of your console (or an X11 terminal window) like this

```
# setup
```

A main dialog appears, as shown in the Figure 19.16. Navigate through the dialog by using the up- or down-arrow keys or the Tab key. After you've highlighted a desired program, navigate to the Run button (or press the F1 key). To quit setup, navigate to the Quit button (or press the F12 key).

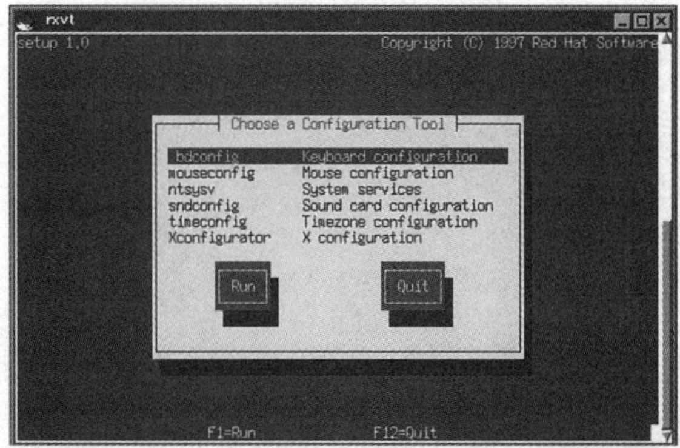

FIGURE 19.16
The `setup` *command is a graphical shell for several Red Hat tools.*

The following sections discuss the various setup commands, except the `Xconfigurator` command, which is used to configure the X Window System for Linux. For details about `Xconfigurator`, see Chapter 4, "X Window."

Configuring Your Keyboard with the `kbdconfig` Command

The `kbdconfig` command is a graphical interface you can use to choose the type of keyboard used with your computer. If you select kbdconfig from setup's window or type **`kbdconfig`** on the command line, its main dialog appears, as shown in Figure 19.17.

Configuring Your Mouse with the `mouseconfig` Command

The `mouseconfig` command is a graphical interface you can use to choose the type of pointing device used with your computer. If you select mouseconfig from setup's window, or type **`mouseconfig`** on the command line, its main dialog appears, as shown in Figure 19.18.

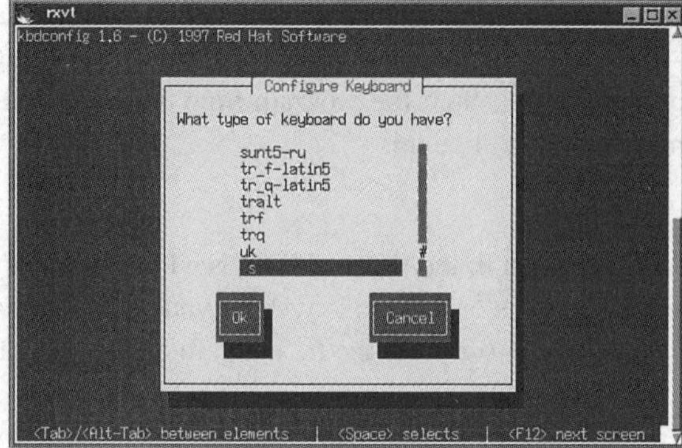

FIGURE 19.17
The `kbdconfig` *command selects the type of keyboard used by your system.*

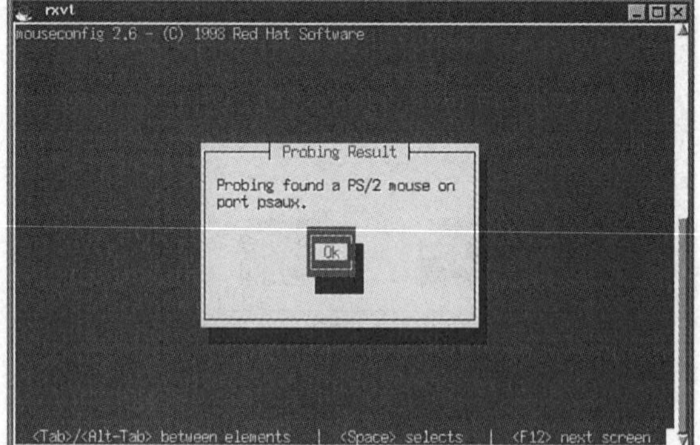

FIGURE 19.18
The `mouseconfig` *command is used to select or configure your Linux system's mouse.*

`mouseconfig` automatically probes your system for the type of pointing device attached unless you use its `--noprobe` command-line option. If you use this option, a dialog appears, as shown in Figure 19.19, listing 11 choices from which you can pick your device.

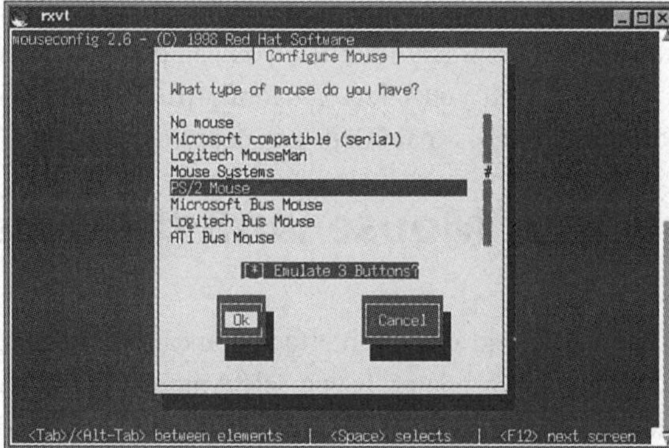

FIGURE 19.19
The `mouseconfig` *command offers a choice of 11 mouse devices.*

NOTE

`mouseconfig`'s option to emulate three buttons is especially handy if you use the X Window System and want to copy and paste text. See Chapter 4 to see how to configure X11 to use your mouse, or read the `gpm` man page to learn about using a mouse server for the console window.

Configuring Your Sound Card with the `sndconfig` Command

The `sndconfig` command is a graphical interface to selecting and configuring your system's sound card. Select sndconfig from setup's main window or type **`sndconfig`** from the command line to displays its main dialog, as shown in Figure 19.20.

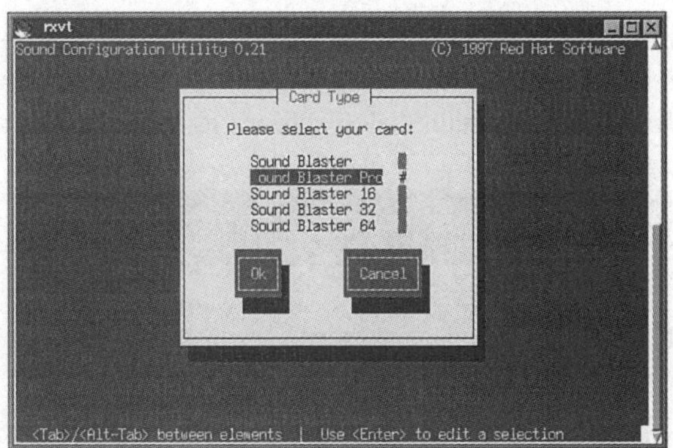

FIGURE 19.20
The `sndconfig` command can be used to select or configure your system's sound card.

If you have a sound card similar to one listed in `sndconfig`'s dialog, select the card and then click the OK button. A dialog appears, asking for your card's settings. After you fill out this information and click the OK button, `sndconfig` tries to play a sample sound (actually Linus Torvald pronouncing "Linux") called sample.au in the /usr/share/ sndconfig. directory.

NOTE

Make sure you have your soundcard's technical information on hand before using the `sndconfig` command, but if your soundcard is not supported, or if `sndconfig` fails to properly configure Linux to use your card, you do have other

continues

options. First, read the Sound-HOWTO document under the /usr/doc/HOWTO directory. If you have a Soundblaster AWE card, read the mini-HOWTO document Soundblaster-AWE under the /usr/doc/HOWTO/mini directory. You can then try to either rebuild the sound support modules or rebuild your Linux kernel to support your card (see Chapter 28). Don't feel like using this approach? Then use the Open Sound System from 4Front Technologies. OSS is a relatively inexpensive commercial software package that automatically detects and configures loadable code modules for your soundcard. You can also download a 30-day trial version to try before you buy. Navigate to `http://www.4front.tech.com` for more information.

Configuring System Services with the `ntsysv` Command

The `ntsysv` command is a graphical interface to configuring which system services to start or stop. If you select ntsysv from the setup command's dialog, or type the command **`ntsysv`** on the command line, its main dialog appears, as shown in Figure 19.21.

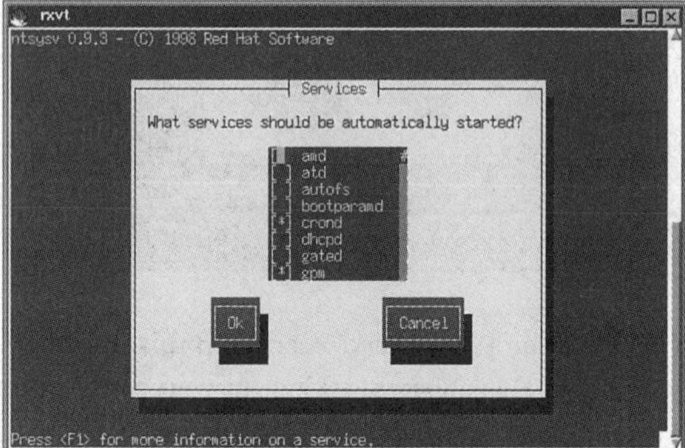

FIGURE 19.21
With the `ntsysv` command, you can start or stop 38 different system services.

Setting the System Timezone with the `timeconfig` Command

The `timeconfig` command is a graphical interface to configuring the system timezone. If you select timeconfig from the setup command's dialog, or type the command **`timeconfig`** on the command line, its main dialog appears, as shown in Figure 19.22.

FIGURE 19.22
The `timeconfig` *command enables you to set the timezone for your Linux system.*

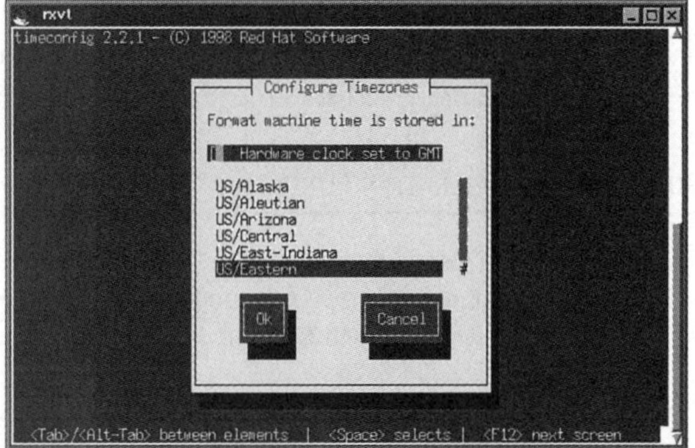

Using the `linuxconf` Command

You were first introduced to the `linuxconf` tool in Chapter 6. You should know, however, that the screenshots, such as Figure 6.3, show how `linuxconf` looks when run from the command line of your console or without installation of the GNOME graphic libraries. If you install GNOME (see Chapter 5 for more information) and then use `linuxconf` during an X session, the linuxconf dialogs will look radically different.

Start an X session, install the GNOME libraries by using the `glint` command, and then type the command **`linuxconf`** on the command line to see its main dialog appear, as shown in Figure 19.23.

FIGURE 19.23
You can use the `linuxconf` *command with or without X11 for nearly complete administration of your Linux system.*

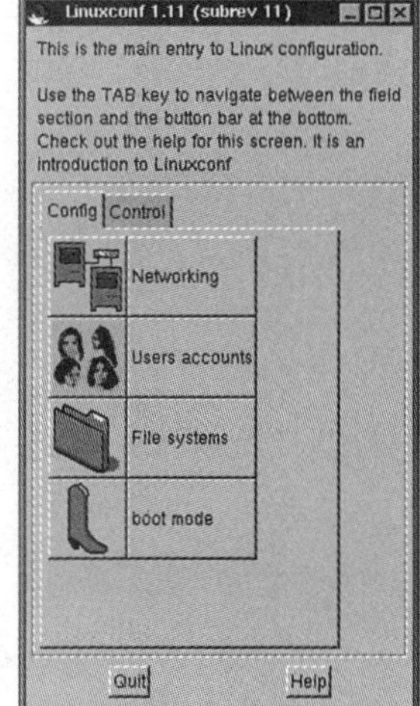

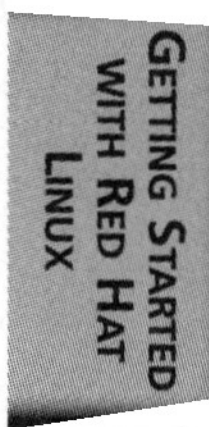

The `linuxconf` command enables you to configure and control many different aspects and services. As shown in Figure 19.23, its functions are grouped on the Config and Control tabs in the main dialog. Table 19.2 lists `linuxconf`'s configuration functions.

TABLE 19.2 LINUXCONF'S CONFIGURATION FUNCTIONS

Category	*Functions*
Networking	Basic host info, name server specs, routing, gateways, NIS configuration, IPX interface setup, PPP, SLIP, PLIP, NFS, uucp, IP aliasing, network host definitions, linuxconf's net access
Users accounts	User accounts, group definitions, root password, special network accounts (such as email only), passwords, user shells, PPP or SLIP shells
File systems	Access of local and NFS volumes, swap file, quota configuration, file permissions checks
Boot mode	Configuration or changes to LILO, default kernel

However, only half of linuxconf's usability is in its system configuration options. If you select the Control tab, you find access to five groups of control options. These options and functions are listed in Table 19.3, and the Control menu is shown in Figure 19.24.

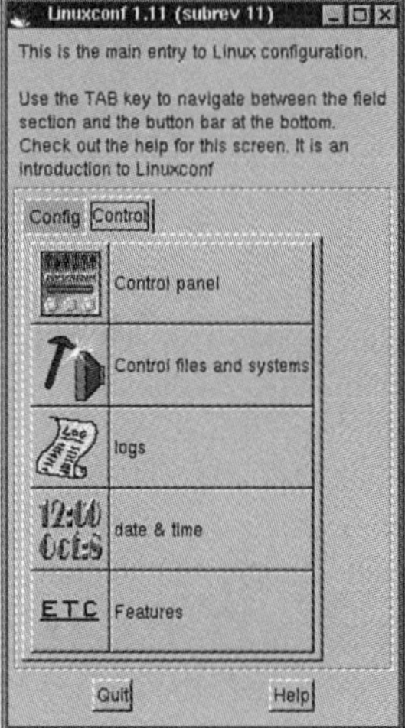

FIGURE 19.24
The linuxconf Control menu enables activation of custom configurations of your Linux system.

TABLE 19.3 LINUXCONF'S CONTROL FUNCTIONS

Category	*Function*
Control Panel	Activate current system configuration, reboot Linux, activate system services, configure root crontab, save configuration, change current configuration, control PPP/SLIP/PLIP links
Control files and system	Control linuxconf's behavior, load or specify add-ons, specify different configurations (such as home or office system setups)
logs	Control boot messages, linuxconf logs
date & time	Set system timezone, date, time
Features	Set linuxconf's keyboard, layout, interface mode

As you can see from Tables 19.2 and 19.3, `linuxconf` has many features and uses. For example, you can define different system configurations and then shift your Linux system into a different mode, depending on your needs. If you're a laptop Linux user, you can have several configurations—one for home, in which you have your own Internet Service Provider (and related phone, DNS and other entries); one for the office, in which you might use an ethernet connection, with different network addresses; and one for the road, in which you might use an entirely different networking dial-up scheme.

The ability to use `linuxconf` to create custom system configurations is an exciting approach to using Linux. With a couple of mouse clicks and keyboard presses, you can turn your system into a desktop machine or an Internet email or Web server. Of course, setting up these configurations takes time and effort, but you'll only have to come up with a working system once, because you can save each configuration for later use. Value-added resellers or Linux consultants develop their own `linuxconf` configuration files, with custom menus and added features, which are stored in named directories under the /etc/linuxconf/archive directory.

For example, the default `linuxconf` installed with Red Hat Linux comes with two configurations, Office and Home-Office, both found under the /etc/linuxconf/archive directory. Under the Home-Office directory, a directory called etc contains six more directories and 43 configuration files. By using the tree command, you can see linuxconf's directory structure:

```
# tree
.
`-- etc
    |-- X11
    |   |-- XF86Config,v
    |   `-- XMetroconfig,v
    |-- XF86Config,v
```

```
|-- Xaccel.ini,v
|-- amd.conf,v
|-- auto.master,v
|-- bootparams,v
|-- conf.linuxconf-amd,v
|-- conf.linuxconf-autofs,v
|-- conf.linuxconf-base,v
|-- conf.linuxconf-bootparamd,v
|-- conf.linuxconf-crond,v
|-- conf.linuxconf-dialout,v
|-- conf.linuxconf-gated,v
|-- conf.linuxconf-gpm,v
|-- conf.linuxconf-hardware,v
|-- conf.linuxconf-httpd,v
|-- conf.linuxconf-inet,v
|-- conf.linuxconf-keytable,v
|-- conf.linuxconf-mars-nwe,v
|-- conf.linuxconf-netaccess,v
|-- conf.modules,v
|-- crontab,v
|-- fstab-local,v
|-- gated.conf,v
|-- httpd
|   `-- conf
|       |-- access.conf,v
|       |-- httpd.conf,v
|       `-- srm.conf,v
|-- inetd.conf,v
|-- lilo.conf,v
|-- networks,v
|-- nwserv.conf,v
|-- nwserv.stations,v
|-- passwd.htmlintro,v
|-- ppp
|   `-- pap-secrets,v
|-- quota.conf,v
|-- services,v
|-- shells,v
|-- sysconfig
|   |-- clock,v
|   |-- keyboard,v
|   |-- mouse,v
|   `-- ptpdev.list,v
`-- syslog.conf,v

6 directories, 43 files
```

These files were generated by `linuxconf` through menu definitions and dialog entries, although they're nothing more than regular text files. You can define your own configurations through the `linuxconf` Control menus. For more information about this program, you can look in the /usr/doc/linuxconf directory. However, `linuxconf` has extensive built-in help, and nearly all dialogs have a Help button (the main help information can be found in the /usr/lib/linuxconf/help.eng directories for English readers).

Summary

This chapter has covered the basic structure of a Red Hat Linux installation, along with the use of RPM, the Red Hat Package Manager, and many of Red Hat's graphical-interface administration tools. From this starting point, the rest of the Red Hat Linux world waits to be explored and enjoyed.

Administrative Essentials

by David Pitts

In This Chapter

Today, system administrators are at a premium. They are demanding, and receiving, high salaries. It does not matter whether the systems are Windows NT, Novell NetWare, or UNIX. Part of the reason is simply supply and demand. The number of knowledgeable system administrators is low, and the demand for them is high. The other reason concerns whether the system administrators are indeed *knowledgeable*. The market is flooded with system administrators with few skills or training. People are entering the field because of the high pay. Many of them come with a willingness to learn, but unfortunately, training them is a long-term, multi-thousand dollar investment that corporations are incurring with no guarantee of a return on their investment. This scenario is particularly accurate when it comes to UNIX systems.

UNIX is a large and complicated operating system. It is also very powerful. Every aspect of the system is under the direct control of the system administrator. What is it a system administrator does? Here is a breakdown of some of the tasks a system administrator must handle on a day-to-day basis:

- Account management
- Assisting programmers
- Assisting users with problems
- Data backup and restoration
- Meetings, both formal and informal
- Performance monitoring and tuning
- Problem determination
- Software installation and configuration
- System automation
- System configuration and management
- System integrity and other security issues
- System startup and shutdown
- User education

Handling the All-Powerful Root Account

Although system administrators do all the things in the preceding list, they don't do them as system administrators, per se; they do them as a special user called root, also known as the superuser (`su`). Root is a special user account that is on every UNIX system. This special user has full access to the system. The system ignores all permissions when dealing with root, providing read, write, and execute permissions to every file and device known to the system.

What does this mean in practical terms? The command `rm -r /` run as root will delete the entire system. It also means that root has access to all data. This is important when it comes to backing up and restoring data, performing system maintenance, and even performing security tasks. Many commands, with certain parameters, are ideal to hand off to the users; bringing up print queues is a good example. Unfortunately, the same commands, with different parameters, could take down the print queues or delete other users' printouts. The root account is all-powerful. It can be used to keep the system up and running as a stable environment; it can also destroy the system and all data contained therein.

It is because of this ability to manipulate the system that, as system administrator, you should take great care when you are using the root account—not only when you are dealing with the system, but also when you are dealing with passwords. A password is the only identification that the computer has to determine whether people attempting to log on with certain user IDs are who they say they are. Anyone who gets root's password can control the system. This also means that a Red Hat Linux system left unsecured can be booted from disk and have its root password changed.

That is correct; you can change the root password this easily:

1. Boot the system with the boot disk.
2. Mount the root partition.
3. Edit the `/etc/passwd` file to remove any password for root.
4. Reboot from the hard disk.
5. Set a new password for root.

This process is nice and convenient if the Red Hat system happens to be a system in someone's home with no other purpose than teaching the user how to use UNIX. But this process is a problem for a Red Hat system used as an ISP in an unsecured location in a public building.

Because of the power of the root account, no user on the system who has access to the root password should log in as root. To perform a task that requires root authority, the user should `su` to root (this is explained in greater detail in Chapter 19, "Getting Started with Red Hat Linux"), perform the task, and then return to his normal account. This procedure helps to ensure two things. First, it keeps users from accidentally performing actions that they did not intend but that are allowed by root. Second, it provides logging. The `/etc/login.defs` is the file that defines, among other things, the `su` log, the failed login log, and the list of who logged in last. Although logging does not stop an action, it will at least help to determine who performed the action.

Maintaining the System—Implementing Changes

The overall function of any system administrator is to keep the system up and running. Not only does this mean applying the latest updates of software, adding and replacing hardware, and adding new software, but it also means being part soothsayer, part instructor, and part detective. The system administrator must

- Understand how things work
- Know where to find things
- Plan processes
- Have a back-out plan and know when to use it
- Make changes in small increments
- Test all changes
- Communicate effectively and in a timely fashion

Each of these seven tasks can be daunting. For example, it takes years of training and practice to understand how everything works, and just about the time you figure out everything, it changes. The learning curve is steep and the changes are inevitable, but does this mean that you ignore this area? Of course it doesn't. Without an understanding of how things work, you cannot accomplish the other items effectively. As a system administrator, you must be careful not to spend too little or too much time in any one of these areas.

Fortunately, you can tackle the first two tasks at a later time. As two of the primary reasons for this book, they are covered throughout. The other five items are examined in more detail in the following sections.

Planning Processes

Red Hat is a complicated operating system. Many files and processes are dependent on other files and processes. Therefore, when you are preparing to make a change to the system, it only makes sense to define a process for the task. The amount of planning and documenting required for the task should obviously depend on the complexity of the task, but it should at least touch on the following items.

First, you should list some kind of description of the task. Second, provide documentation of how this task is going to affect the system, including, but not limited to, the files and processes affected. The third item should be a test plan. Finally, plan some way to back out of the change—to restore the system to its previous configuration.

Creating a Back-Out Plan

Creating the back-out plan is the most important part of making a change to a system. In determining the back-out plan, consider how long the task will take, how long testing will take, and how long it will take to back out of the current process and return to the former process. An important part of the back-out plan is a decision point—a predetermined point when you decide to continue with the current process or to implement the back-out plan. This could be a decision based on a time limit, a lack of system resources, malfunctioning equipment, poorly written software, or any other problem that requires returning to the old process.

Making Changes in Small Increments

It is easier to back out of small changes than it is to back out of big and multiple changes. It is also easier to plan a series of smaller changes than it is to plan one large change. Diagnosing problems is considerably easier when fewer things are changed than when a large number of things are changed. If you can break a task down into several small tasks, each with individual test plans and back-out plans, then the job becomes much simpler.

Developing a Test Plan

You must test each change to a system. Even a small change, such as moving a file from one location to another, should have a test plan. The test plan should be appropriate to the task. In the example of moving a file, the test plan could be as simple as the following:

1. Are there users or processes dependent upon the file?
2. If yes, can the users or processes still access the file?
3. If no, make it available (change permissions, add directory to path, create link, and so on).
4. Does it do what it is supposed to do?
5. If yes, okay; if no, fix it.

A task as simple as moving a file requires five steps to properly test. Imagine the difficulty of testing a large change.

Communicating Effectively and in a Timely Manner

Communicating the result of changes to the system is the final element of a successful system change. Success does not necessarily mean that the task was completed without errors. In fact, it could mean that the task could not be completed and the back-out plan was successfully implemented. Communication also means letting the users know in advance about a change that affects them.

Communication, on a larger level, is any information passed between one user and another, whether it's one-way communication or a dialog back and forth. Although it is imperative to have this communication before, during, and after a system change, communication does not have to stop nor should it stop there. Some system administrators communicate birthdays, local news, jokes, and just about anything else to users on a regular basis.

You can use many different tools to communicate with users. To decide which tool to use, you need to determine the purpose of the communication. For example, if you are about to shut down a system, you need to communicate that information only to the users currently logged on to the system. If on the other hand, you want to announce a birthday, you need to be announce that information either to all users or to all users who log on to the system that day. Perhaps a user is remotely logged on to a system and is having problems. A user with only one phone line cannot call in the problem without disconnecting. This situation requires an entirely different form of communication. The following sections discuss several different tools for communication; some are commands, and others are concepts. In addition, I give examples to illustrate which tool is best for the particular need. I discuss the following communication tools in the upcoming sections:

- `write`: One-way communication with another user currently logged on the system.
- Echo to the device: One-way communication with another user currently logged on the system.
- `wall`: One-way communication with all other users currently logged on the system.
- `talk`: Interactive two-way communication with another user currently logged on the system.
- `mesg`: Message reception (`talk` and `write`) from other nonroot users currently logged on the system.
- `motd`: Message of the day received by users when they log on to the system.
- Electronic mail: Sending messages to and receiving messages from users whether or not they are currently logged on to the system.

- Pre-login message `/etc/issue`: Displaying the message on a terminal at time of login. Users do not have to log on to see this message.

write

The `write` command enables a user to write a message to a terminal. The syntax is the command followed by the user ID of the person to whom you want to write. This places you in a write shell. Anything you type, until you hit Ctrl+C, is echoed to that user's display. For example, I tried to write a message to my friend Rich, who was logged on to `mk.net`:

```
shell:/home/dpitts$ write rbowen
Hello Rich.  How are you today?
shell:/home/dpitts$
```

I didn't receive a reply.

I wasn't sure that I was doing it right, so I tried to send a message to myself. Before I did, I turned off my `mesg` (`mesg n`). Here's what happened:

```
shell:/home/dpitts$ write dpitts
write: you have write permission turned off.
```

As a further test, I turned my `mesg` on (`mesg y`) and tried again:

```
shell:/home/dpitts$ mesg y
shell:/home/dpitts$ write dpitts

Message from dpitts@shell on ttyp0 at 20:10 ...
hello
hello
It enters what I type, and then echoes it back to me.
It enters what I type, and then echoes it back to me.
type <ctrl>c
type <ctrl>c
EOF
shell:/home/dpitts$
```

It displayed everything that I typed and then echoed it back to me with `write`. That is why there are two identical lines. Had this gone to another terminal, I would have seen what I typed, and when I hit Enter, the message would have been sent to the user I had indicated.

You will notice that when I received the message, I got an initial line that told me who the message was from, the `tty` (terminal type) I was on, and the time (local to the server):

```
Message from dpitts@shell on ttyp0 at 20:10 ...
```

Holding down the Control key and pressing the C key disconnected me from the `write` program, indicated by the last line showing the end of the file (`EOF`).

NOTE

The `write` command writes to a terminal. The operating system doesn't think that it is input. Therefore, even in an editing session when text gets overwritten by the `write` command, the text does not really exist. (On most editors, Ctrl+L will restore the original screen.) This also means that a person cannot send commands to your terminal and have the computer execute them. It is strictly an output operation on the receiver's end.

Echo to the Device

Echoing to a device is similar to using the `write` command. It has a similar result in that it writes output to a device (such as a terminal), but it uses a different mechanism, and thus, potentially, has different results. Let me see if I can send some output to someone's terminal as I log on to `mk.net`.

First, I look to see who is logged on:

```
shell:/home/dpitts$ who -u
root      ttyp1    Aug 13 10:01 00:05 (laptop.mk.net)
rbowen    ttyp2    Aug 13 17:29 00:44 (rbowen.is.lex.da)
dpitts    ttyp3    Aug 13 18:13   .   (d13.dialup.seane)
```

I am logged on (`dpitts`), the system administrator is logged on (`root`) and my good friend Rich Bowen is logged on (`rbowen`).

Next, I try to echo a comment and send it to my terminal type:

```
shell:/home/dpitts$ echo hello >/dev/tty/p3
bash: /dev/tty/p3: Not a directory
```

Oops, I did it wrong. I should have sent it to `/dev/ttyp3`, like this:

```
shell:/home/dpitts$ echo hello /dev/ttyp3
hello /dev/ttyp3
```

Nope, that was wrong again; although it did go to my terminal (because of the `echo` command), what I needed to do was to take the output and send it to the device `/dev/ttyp3`, not have it echo `/dev/ttyp3` back to me. Therefore, I should have done it like this:

```
shell:/home/dpitts$ echo hello> /dev/ttyp3
hello
```

Well, I finally got it right. Now to send it to Rich:

```
shell:/home/dpitts$ echo hello rich > /dev/ttyp2
bash: /dev/ttyp2: Permission denied
```

Permission denied! I wonder why that happened? Let me look at the permissions on his device:

```
shell:/home/dpitts$ ls -la /dev/ttyp2
crw--w----    1 rbowen   tty        3,   2 Aug 13 18:14 /dev/ttyp2
```

Well, I am not the owner of the device, and I am not in the group `tty`. The permissions for the rest of the world indicates no read, write, or execute. That is why I did not have permission to write to his terminal type.

Even though I could `write` to `rbowen`, I did not have the permission to send something directly to his terminal.

wall

Sometimes, administrators need to send a message to all the users currently logged on to the system. This type of communication is typically used when the administrator needs to inform everyone about something that affects them. One time the `wall` command is typically used is when a system is about to shut down. The system administrator, instead of just blowing everyone off the system, might want to give them time to close their applications and save their data. The `wall` command stands for *write all*. Just like the `write` command, it only sends the text to the terminal, and the computer does not treat the text as input from that user. The standard for `wall` is that it gets its information to display from a file. You can either use this method or use a less-than sign to send it information from the command line. In the following example, I have a small file that says "system shutting down!" The system was not really shutting down, so I made sure no one was logged on first. (I didn't want to upset anyone.) When a `wall` command is issued, the output goes to everyone currently logged on, including the person issuing the command.

Here's how I checked to see who was logged on:

```
shell:/home/dpitts$ who
dpitts   ttyp1    Aug 24 00:10 (d4.dialup.seanet)
```

Good, I was the only one logged on. Therefore, I issued the following command:

```
shell:/home/dpitts$ wall test
Broadcast Message from dpitts@shell
(/dev/ttyp1) at 0:11 ...
system shutting down!
```

Note that the output indicates that it is a broadcast message from `dpitts@shell`. It also mentions the terminal I am on and the current time. It then gives the message. This information is important if something unfortunate were about to happen and you wanted to respond. If the output were anonymous (as it is when writing to a device), then the people receiving the information would not know to whom to respond.

talk

Writing to a device, either with `write`, `wall`, or literally to the device, is strictly one-way communication. One-way communication has its benefits but also has its drawbacks. For example, what if the person receiving the data wants to respond to the message? She could use a series of `write` commands or the `talk` command. The `talk` command notifies the second person that you want to talk. The command tells the other person what to type to finish initializing a `talk` session.

When the session is established, each person receives a split window. When the first person types information on the top window, it is echoed in the bottom window of the second person's display and vice versa. Also, displaying in both windows happens as each letter is typed. As one person types, the other person sees the information.

mesg

The `mesg` command was briefly mentioned in the discussion on `write`. The `mesg` command is used to allow or disallow others from writing or walling messages to you. Of course, root overrides this authority. The syntax for that command is `mesg y` or `mesg n`. The `y` parameter allows the communication, and the `n` parameter disallows the communication with normal users.

motd

The `motd` (*message of the day*) command is a good way to pass information on to whomever happens to log in that particular day. Typically, it is a reminder or an announcement of some type. Many companies use it to announce birthdays and other days of significance or to remind users of an event or telephone number to call. The `motd` command is a good way to communicate if the information is either not that important or only important to a person if he or she logs in.

The `motd` is actually a file that has its contents displayed upon login. The file is kept in the `/etc` directory and is called `motd` (`/etc/motd`). For example, when I log in to `mk.net`, I get the following message:

```
Welcome to shell.mk.net!
```

Electronic Mail

Electronic mail is quickly becoming the medium by which most communication occurs between people these days. Many companies now consider email to be a necessary element and spend great amounts of money making sure that people receive their electronic mail.

Electronic mail is a great way of communicating with others when time is not a critical factor. It can be sent to individuals or to entire lists of people. One of the benefits of electronic mail is that information can be passed to one or more individuals whenever they happen to log in and check their mail. Another benefit of electronic mail is that it can be sent to other people on other servers. If you are connected to the Internet, you can send email practically anywhere.

Pre-Login Message

The `/etc/issue` file contains the message that is displayed when a Telnet session is initiated. Following the issue statement, the session prompts for the login and password. This pre-login message is a good place to put something that you want everyone to see before they log in to the system. This could include a notice that printers are not working or an explanation of the purpose of the workstation where they are trying to log on. The following example is the pre-login message I get when I log on to `mk.net`:

```
/etc/issue pre-login message
**  MK Computer Associates  **
**    UNIX shell server     **
**      (shell.mk.net)      **
** Login on this machine is **
**  restricted to web site  **
**  development activities  **
**     ONLY, thank you.     **

shell login:
```

As you can see from the pre-login message, this particular server is restricted to Web site development activities (`ONLY`). I know, in this case, that I should not use this server to perform engineering computations, for example.

Although the `/etc/issue` file can be as long as you want it to be, it is best to keep it short. If it is too long, people won't read it and it will scroll off their screens; those who might have read it will probably not take the time to scroll back to see what, if anything, they missed.

Getting Help

One of the things that all system administrators realize at some point is that they cannot possibly know everything about the operating system; it is too complex and it changes on a regular basis. A good system administrator, however, knows where to turn to get help. Because you are reading this book, you have at least started on your way to being a good system administrator. This book unleashes many of the tools and "secrets" of the Red Hat Linux operating system. With a book of this type, the index is very important. A book like this is not bought to be read from cover to cover, like a good C.S. Lewis novel, but is intended to be a resource guide—a place to go to find specific answers to specific questions. The following sections discuss the places you can turn to get help.

Man Pages

The man pages are like the Marines: They are your first lines of defense. Man pages contain the online version of the Red Hat UNIX reference manuals. They provide definitions and explanations of commands. In addition, they provide optional parameters for commands to perform specific functions. After all of the explanations are examples, and finally, other commands that are similar or relate to the command you looked up.

The format of the man pages is as follows:

Name
Synopsis
Description
Command-Line Options
See Also
Bugs

Over time, especially in Linux, people have customized the man pages to include other optional fields. Some of these fields are Author, Sort Keys, Updating, and Notes. The additions have been made to enhance the pages. For example, the Author section many times includes the email address of the author, which is handy if the command is not working as you expected it to. (Remember, none of Linux was taken from AT&T's UNIX, so small differences do exist, even in the "standard" commands.)

Probably the one thing to point out to new man page users is the syntax used for showing the Synopsis of the command. There are several standards that are followed in writing commands that are used in the man pages. Here's the Synopsis for the `ps` command:

```
SYNOPSIS
ps  [-]  [lujsvmaxScewhrnu]  [txx]  [O[+¦-]k1[[+¦-]k2...]] [pids]
```

Anything in square brackets ([ ]) is optional. Note that the only thing not optional in this command is the command itself. Therefore, you can issue the `ps` command without any options and you will receive a snapshot of the current processes.

The `[…]` means that the `[…]` is an optional argument. Many commercial versions of UNIX require a dash to indicate that what follows are arguments. This is not true for the Red Hat Linux version of the `ps` command. The next set of characters (between the next set of square brackets) indicates that any of these parameters can be added to the `ps` command. For example, a common set of parameters to add to the `ps` command is `-la`, which displays a long list of all (including hidden) files.

The man pages are not a singular file or directory of Linux manuals. Instead, the man pages are a set of directories, each containing a section of the man pages. These directories contain the raw data for the man pages. Red Hat Linux has eight sections of man pages. In addition, each section has corresponding `catn` subdirectories that store processed versions of the man pages. When a man page is accessed, the program that formats the man pages saves a copy of the formatted man page in the `catn` (`/etc/catn`) directories. This saves time in the future because the next time a user requests a man page for a specific subject that has been accessed before, the formatting does not have to be repeated but can be displayed from the previously formatted page. The following shows what information appears within each section:

Section	*Content*
1	User commands
2	System calls
3	Functions and library routines
4	Special files, device drivers, and hardware
5	Configuration files and file formats
6	Games and demos
7	Miscellaneous: character sets, filesystem types, datatype definitions, and so on
8	System administration commands and maintenance commands

The `man` command searches the sections in a predefined order: 1, 6, 8, 2, 3, 4, 5, and 7. It checks for commands first, followed by system calls and library functions, and then the other sections.

There is a special way of accessing the man pages so that all pages listing a certain piece of data are displayed: using the keyword search for man pages (`man -k`). To use this searching capability, you must first issue the command `catman -w`. This command (which takes a little while to process) indexes the man pages so that the keyword search will work.

One of the benefits of man pages is that you can add your own local man pages. A friend of mine did not know how to do this, so he wrote a Perl program called `man.pl` that performed a similar function. It was a shame that he didn't have this book to tell him it could be done! Adding man pages is a wonderful way of documenting tools that you write for use at your site. Two directories are left blank for that purpose. They are the `mann` directory and the `cat` directory (`/usr/man/mann` and `/usr/man/cat`).

The simplest way of making a man page is to place some text in a file describing the command or topic. However, it is fairly easy to make a more elaborate page that looks like a normal man page. Man pages are designed for the `nroff` text formatter and have text and `nroff` directives intermingled.

The best way to figure out what the different directives do is to look at a man page and see how it is laid out. To do this with Linux, you must first gunzip the file. Once gunzipped, the file can be looked at with a text editor. All the different directives begin with a period (or dot). Table 20.1 lists many of the `nroff` directives and explanations about what they do.

TABLE 20.1 `nroff` DIRECTIVES

Directive	*Explanation*
`.B`	Uses bold type for the text (entire line is bolded).
`.fi`	Starts autofilling the text (adjusting the text on the lines).
`.I`	Uses italicized type for the text (entire line is italicized).
`.IP`	Starts a new indented paragraph.
`.nf`	Stops autofilling the text (adjusting the text on the lines).
`.PP`	Starts a new paragraph.
`.R`	Uses Roman type for text given as its arguments.
`.SH`	Section heading (names are uppercase by convention).
`.TH`	Title heading (arguments are command name and section).
`.TP` *n*	Tagged paragraph (uses a hanging indent). The *n* specifies the amount to indent.

When testing the man page, you can simulate an actual man page call to the file with the following command:

```
$ nroff -man <file> ¦ more
```

The man pages are not the only place that a resourceful system administrator can turn for answers. You also have the Internet. On the Internet, you can find email services, Web pages describing how to do things, and newsgroups.

Email

With email, you can send questions to people you know who are doing similar work. For example, when I get stuck writing Perl scripts, I send a note to Rich. He drops everything and responds immediately to my questions. (Yeah, right!) The point is, some people you associate with can assist with your problems or point you on your way to success. If you don't know anyone who is working with Red Hat Linux, you can do two things. First, find new friends—obviously the ones you have are holding you back—and secondly, you can email newsgroups.

Red Hat Mailing Lists and Newsgroups

Many mailing lists and newsgroups are available to assist you with your problems. After you have been using Linux for awhile, you might even be able to answer some questions. Newsgroups are a great source of information. Before I list newsgroups that are available to you, I want to first mention the Red Hat mailing lists (`http://www.redhat.com/support/mailing-lists`).

> **NOTE**
>
> A *newsgroup* is a place where you can download and read postings. When you are on a *mailing list*, you are sent postings either in bulk or as they come in.

These lists are maintained and monitored by Red Hat. Currently, there are 13 different lists. Direct from Red Hat's Web page, here they are:

- `redhat-list`

  For the general discussion of topics related to Red Hat Linux.
- `redhat-digest`

  The digest version of the `redhat-list`. Instead of getting mail that goes to the `redhat-list` as individual messages, subscribers to this list receive periodic volumes that include several posts at once.
- `redhat-announce-list`

  The most important list; all Red Hat users should make it a point to subscribe. Here, security updates and new RPMs are announced. It is very low traffic and moderated for your convenience.

- `redhat-install-list`

  For the general discussion of installation-related topics only. This can include appropriate hardware, problems with hardware, package selection, and so on.

- `redhat-ppp-list`

  For the general discussion of PPP under Red Hat. This includes configuration, installation, changes, and so on.

- `redhat-devel-list`

  General discussion of software development under Red Hat Linux. This is where we announce the availability of alpha- and beta-quality software that is available for testing purposes (with the exception of RPM, which has its own list).

- `sparc-list`

  SPARC-specific issues only. This can be kernel development, SILO, and so on.

- `axp-list`

  Alpha-specific issues only. This can be kernel development, MILO, and so on.

- `rpm-list`

  Discussion of RPM-related issues. This can be RPM usage in general, RPM development using `rpmlib`, RPM development using shell scripts, porting RPM to non-Linux architectures, and so on.

- `applixware-list`

  Applixware discussion only. Mostly related to installation, usage, macro writing, and so on.

- `cde-list`

  CDE discussion only. Mostly related to installation and usage.

- `forsale-list`

  Posting for-sale and wanted items of a computer nature. This includes software and hardware and should be limited to items that work with Linux.

- `post-only`

  This "list" is a fake list. It has no posting address, only a request address (`post-only-request@redhat.com`). You can subscribe to this list to be allowed to post to any of the Red Hat mailing lists without receiving any mail from them. We do not allow posts from folks who aren't subscribed to the list, but frequently, people want to read the list via local gateways and don't need to subscribe themselves. This way, you just subscribe to `post-only` to be allowed to post to any list.

Each of these lists has a subscription address, the list address with `-request` on the end of it. For example, for the `redhat-list`, you send your subscription or unsubscription request to `redhat-list-request@redhat.com`. For the RPM list, you use `rpm-list-request@redhat.com`. All you need to send is the word `subscribe` in the subject line of your message to subscribe and `unsubscribe` in the subject line to unsubscribe. You can leave the body of the message empty.

NOTE

To unsubscribe from the `redhat-digest`, send your request to `redhat-digest-request@redhat.com`, not `redhat-list-request`.

Other Newsgroups

Other newsgroups require a newsreader. Most of the current browsers supply some kind of newsreader. There are somewhere around 15,000 to 20,000 newsgroups. Following is a list of some of interest to Linux users:

```
alt.os.linux.caldera                alt.os.linux
alt.fido.linux                      alt.uu.comp.os.linux.questions
comp.os.linux.announce              comp.os.linux.advocacy
comp.os.linux.development.apps      comp.os.linux.answers
comp.os.linux.hardware              comp.os.linux.development.systems
comp.os.linux.misc                  comp.os.linux.m68k
comp.os.linux.setup                 comp.os.linux.networking
linux.act.680x0                     comp.os.linux.x
linux.act.apps                      linux.act.admin
linux.act.chaos_digest              linux.act.bbsdev
linux.act.configs                   linux.act.compression
linux.act.debian                    linux.act.c-programming
linux.act.doc                       linux.act.dec_alpha
linux.act.fsf                       linux.act.findo
linux.act.fsstnd                    linux.act.gcc
linux.act.ibcs2                     linux.act.interviews
linux.act.kernel                    linux.act.linux-bbs
linux.act.linuxnews                 linux.act.localbus
linux.act.mca                       linux.act.mips
linux.act.mumail                    linux.act.newbie
```

```
linux.act.normal                linux.act.ftp
linux.act.hams                  linux.act.ibsc2
linux.act.japanese              linux.act.laptops
linux.act.linuxbsd              linux.act.linuxss
linux.act.lugnuts               linux.act.mgr
linux.act.msdos                 linus.act.net
linux.act.new-channels          linux.act.nys
linux.act.oasg-trust            linux.act.oi
linux.act.pkg                   linux.act.postgres
linux.act.ppp                   linux.act.promotion
linux.act.qag                   linux.act.scsi
linux.act.serial
linux.act.sound                 linux.act.seyon
linux.act.sysvpkg-project       linux.act.svgalib
linus.act.term                  linux.act.tape
linux.act.userfs                linux.act.tktools
linux.act.wabi                  linux.act.uucp
linux.act.x11                   linux.act.word
linux.admin.isp
```

The preceding list consists of maybe a third of the actual newsgroups that specifically deal with Linux. Most of the others are similar to those listed. It is probably best to scan the newsgroups that you have access to for `Linux`.

In addition to newsgroups, myriad Web pages are devoted to Linux, and specifically, Red Hat. When I performed a search on WebCrawler (`www.webcrawler.com`) for `Linux`, I saw 9,107 documents; searching on `Linux AND Redhat`, I saw 294 documents. Considering so many choices and the volatility of the Web, it might be helpful if I point out and briefly describe a few Web resources I believe will be around awhile.

The first one, which should be obvious, is Red Hat's home page at `http://www.redhat.com`. It is, of course, the first place to look for any information concerning Red Hat Linux.

Another great source for information about Linux (as well as every other type of UNIX) is `http://www.ugu.com`, the UNIX Guru Universe page. According to the site's front page, it is "the largest single point UNIX resource on the Net!" This Web site is highly configurable and provides a great deal of information on everything of value to the UNIX community.

The Linux Documentation Project (`http://sunsite.unc.edu/LDP/linux.html`) has a tremendous number of links, providing everything from general Linux information, to Linux user groups, to Linux development projects. Although I do not think there is much, if anything, unique about this site, it is complete. It has information on just about everything associated with Linux.

Knowing how much the Web changes on a day-to-day basis, I am reluctant to share any more Web sites. If you visit the three sites I mention, I think at least one of the three will have a current link to the location that can answer your question.

Problem Solving—Logs

Many times, when trying to diagnose a problem, it is helpful to look at log files of various activities. As an example, consider the following scenario.

You are the administrator of a server connected to the Internet. When you try to log in with your user ID (after all, you don't log in as root but `su` to root), you find that you cannot log in.

Perhaps the problem is as simple as mistyping your password. In this case, a simple second attempt at logging in will fix the problem. Of course, if that were the problem, you wouldn't be reading this book.

Perhaps you forgot your password. This is a common error, especially when a password has just been changed.

NOTE

Writing down new passwords is not a good idea because it gives other people access to your account.

For a forgotten password, you could simply log in as root (or get the system administrator) and change the password.

Perhaps someone logged on to your system as you and changed your password. How would you know this? This is one of the places where logs come in handy. You can examine certain logs, depending on the information needed. Probably the first file to check is the `login.access` file.

login.access

The login.access file is used to control login access. The file is nothing more than a table that is checked each time a person attempts to log in. The table is scanned for the first entry that matches the user/host or user/tty combination. The table is a colon-delimited list of permissions, users, and origins (host or tty).

The permission is either a plus sign (+) or a minus sign (-). A plus sign indicates that the user has permission to access, and a minus sign indicates that the user does not have permission to access.

The user is the user ID of the person either being restricted or allowed access to the machine from that location. The option ALL indicates all users. You can use the ALL option in conjunction with the EXCEPT option. The EXCEPT option allows for certain users to be excluded from the ALL option. You can also include groups as valid users. This is a way to restrict or allow access to the system for users who have similar job functions. The group file is searched only when the name does not match the user logged in. An interesting twist is that it does not check primary groups but instead checks secondary groups in the /etc/groups file.

The origin is where the user is logging in from. The option ALL indicates all locations. You can use the ALL option in conjunction with the EXCEPT option to allow exceptions to the ALL option.

The login.access file is used many times to restrict access to the console. Following are some examples of allowing access and denying access to various groups. The first example is used to restrict access to the console to all but a few accounts:

```
-:ALL EXCEPT admin shutdown sync:console
```

The next example disallows nonlocal logins to the privileged accounts in the group wheel:

```
-:wheel:ALL EXCEPT LOCAL
```

The following is an example of disallowing certain accounts to log in from anywhere:

```
-:bertw timp wess lorenl billh richb chrisb chrisn:ALL
```

This last example allows all other accounts to log in from anywhere.

Other Files That Deny or Allow Users or Hosts

Another file that will deny hosts from accessing the computer is the /etc/hosts.deny file. The hosts.deny file describes the names of the hosts that are not allowed to use the local INET services. These INET services are defined by the /usr/sbin/tcpd server.

The /etc/hosts.lpd file describes the names of the hosts that are considered "equivalent" to the current host. This equivalence means that the hosts listed are trusted enough to allow rsh commands. Typically, a system that is directly connected to the Internet only has an entry of localhost.

syslog.conf

The file /etc/syslog.conf is used to define where messages and logs go. The default syslog.conf file that comes with RedHat follows. The file is a standard text file with comments beginning with a pound sign (#):

```
$ cat /etc/syslog.conf
# Log all kernel messages to the console.
# Logging much else clutters up the screen.
#kern.*                                  /dev/console

# Log anything (except mail) of level info or higher.
# Don't log private authentication messages!
*.info;mail.none;news.none;authpriv.none                  /var/log/messages

# The authpriv file has restricted access.
authpriv.*                               /var/log/secure

# Log all the mail messages in one place.
mail.*                                   /var/log/maillog

# Everybody gets emergency messages, plus log them on another
# machine.
*.emerg                                   *

# Save mail and news errors of level err and higher in a
# special file.
uucp,news.crit                               /var/log/spooler

#
# INN
#
news.=crit                                            /var/log/news/news.crit
news.=err                                             /var/log/news/news.err
news.notice
/var/log/news/news.notice

$
```

From the sample segment, you will notice that the use of wildcards is acceptable. For instance, anything that is mail.* is logged to /var/log/maillog. For system administration, the most important files are the ones found in /var/log/messages. This file is a combination of su log, syslog, and other logs found on other UNIX type systems. An example of part of that log follows:

```
$ cat /var/log/messages
Aug 15 11:15:33 localhost kernel: scsi : 1 host.
Aug 15 11:15:33 localhost kernel: (scsi0:0:-1:-1) Scanning channel for
➥devices.
Aug 15 11:15:33 localhost kernel: (scsi0:0:6:0) Synchronous at
➥5.0MHz,offset 15.
Aug 15 11:15:33 localhost kernel: Vendor: MATSHITA Model: CD-R CW-7501
➥Rev: 1.4D
Aug 15 11:15:33 localhost kernel: Type:   CD-ROM       ANSI SCSI revision:
➥02
Aug 15 11:15:33 localhost kernel: Detected scsi CD-ROM sr0 at scsi0,
➥channel 0,
id 6, lun 0
Aug 15 11:15:33 localhost kernel: VFS: Mounted root (ext2 filesystem)
➥readonly.
Aug 15 11:15:33 localhost kernel: Trying to unmount old root ... okay
Aug 15 11:15:33 localhost kernel: Adding Swap: 120956k swap-space
➥(priority -1)
Aug 15 11:15:33 localhost kernel: Soundblaster audio driver Copyright (c)
➥by Hannu Savolainen 1993-1996
Aug 15 11:15:38 localhost PAM_pwdb[347]: (su) session opened for user
➥postgres
by (uid=100)
Aug 15 11:15:39 localhost PAM_pwdb[347]: (su) session closed for user
➥postgres
Aug 15 11:16:48 localhost PAM_pwdb[420]: (login) session opened for
➥user root by (uid=0)
Aug 15 11:16:48 localhost login[420]: ROOT LOGIN ON tty1
Aug 15 11:17:05 localhost PAM_pwdb[420]: (login) session closed for user
➥root
```

This file is logging startup information—such as mounting filesystems, loading audio drivers, and so on—as well as access information—root login on tty1, session closed for user root, and so on.

Adding Users

There are two ways to add users to a system. The first is to manually edit the appropriate files, including the /etc/passwd file and the /etc/group file. The second method is to use Red Hat's user configuration tools. The use of a configuration tool is the preferred method because it limits the mistakes (always a good idea!), and you don't have to understand the process or be familiar with the editor. Because you are reading this book, the second reason—understanding the process and familiarizing yourself with the editor—becomes moot because we tell you how.

Manually adding a user is a simple process, involving the following six steps:

1. Edit `/etc/passwd`.
2. Edit `/etc/group`.
3. Create a home directory.
4. Copy files from `/etc/skel` to the new home.
5. Change ownerships and permissions.
6. Set the password.

Editing etc/passwd

The first task is to edit the `/etc/passwd` file, adding the new user to the list. Technically, it is the second thing you should do. The real first thing you should do is copy the `/etc/passwd` file to a backup file in case you make a mistake. The `/etc/passwd` file should be owned by root and the group ID should be set to zero (root or system). The permissions for the file should be set so that root has read and write permissions, and everyone else (including group) should only have read access (`644` in hex).

Each user must have a distinct username and password from a security perspective. Each should also have a unique user ID number. The rest of the information associated with a user doesn't have to be unique, and in some cases, is exactly the same as that of other users. The format of the `/etc/passwd` file is a series of seven segments delimited by colons:

```
username : password : user ID : group ID : comment : home directory :
➥login command
```

The default `/etc/passwd` file looks like this when Red Hat Linux is first installed:

```
root::0:0:root:/root:/bin/bash
bin:*:1:1:bin:/bin:
daemon:*:2:2:daemon:/sbin:
adm:*:3:4:adm:/var/adm:
lp:*:4:7:lp:/var/spool/lpd:
sync:*:5:0:sync:/sbin:/bin/sync
shutdown:*:6:0:shutdown:/sbin:/sbin/shutdown
halt:*:7:0:halt:/sbin:/sbin/halt
mail:*:8:12:mail:/var/spool/mail:
news:*:9:13:news:/usr/lib/news:
uucp:*:10:14:uucp:/var/spool/uucppublic:
operator:*:11:0:operator:/root:/bin/bash
games:*:12:100:games:/usr/games:
man:*:13:15:man:/usr/man:
postmaster:*:14:12:postmaster:/var/spool/mail:/bin/bash
nobody:*:-1:100:nobody:/dev/null:
ftp:*:14:50::/home/ftp:/bin/bash
```

If there is nothing to be entered into a field, that field is left blank (see the `ftp` entry). There will still be a colon delimiting the field from the other fields. Following is a short description of each of the fields:

username	A unique identifier for the user
password	The user's encrypted password
user ID (UID)	The unique number that identifies a user to the operating system
group ID (GID)	The unique number that identifies the user's group
comment	The information displayed when a person is fingered, usually the user's name
home directory	The directory in which the user is placed upon login
login command	The command executed when the user logs in, usually a shell

The following sections give more detailed descriptions of the contents of these fields.

The Username

The username is a single string. Usually, it is eight characters or fewer. This username uniquely identifies the user, and it should be easy for the user to identify and remember. The system identifies the user by this name. Typically, a combination of the letters of the first and last name composes the username. (Mine is `dpitts` on many systems.)

Although there are traditions (corporate folklore) about how the username is designated, the computer does not care what the username is, as long as it is unique. In fact, you can use underscores, periods, numbers, and some special characters in the username. Also, case makes a difference; `dpitts` is different from `dpittS` or `DPitts`.

Passwords

The system stores the user's encrypted password in the `passwords` field. If the system is using a shadow password system, the value placed in this field is an `x`. A value of `*` blocks login access to the account because `*` is not a valid character for an encrypted field. This field should never be edited (after it is set up) by hand; you should use a program such as `passwd` so that proper encryption takes place. If this field is changed by hand, the old password is no longer valid and, more than likely, will have to be changed by root.

If the system is using a shadow password system, a separate file called `/etc/shadow` contains passwords (encrypted, of course).

The User ID

Every username has a number associated with it. This number, also called the UID, is used by the system to identify everything owned by the user. All processes, files, and so on associated with the user are identified in this manner. The valid range for the user ID is zero and up. Therefore, the account `nobody` from the `/etc/passwd` file listing earlier in this chapter has an invalid UID because it is `-1`.

Comments

The `comment` field is used by other programs to identify the user. Typically, the user's real name is placed in this field. Many times, the user's telephone number is also placed here. One thing to keep in mind concerning this field is that anyone can read it. You should not put anything in this field that you do not want everyone who has access to your system to see. This field is sometimes called the GECOS field after the operating system that first used it.

In addition to users having access to this field, certain utilities use this field as an identifier as well. `sendmail`, for example, can access this field to show who is sending the mail. `finger` displays this information upon request.

The Home Directory

The home directory field tells the system where to dump the user, if the login is successful. Typically, this directory is the home directory of the user, but it does not have to be. The system does not care where the directory points, as long as that user can enter it.

Typically, the home directories are grouped together for convenience. The standard directory, under which all users are placed, is `/home`. My directory might be `/home/dpitts` and `rbowen`'s directory would be `/home/rbowen`. Some systems, and some companies, use a different location for grouping home directories. Some alternative locations I have seen are `/u`, `/user`, `/s`, and `/usr`.

The Login Command

The login command is the command that is executed when the user first logs in. In most cases, it is a shell command. In other cases, it might be a front-end interface or a single application. If this field is left blank, the system will default to `/bin/bash` shell.

Red Hat allows two different ways for the users to change the login command: the `chps` command and the `passwd -s` command. Both of these commands look exactly alike in their implementation. Both ask for a password and then ask what to change the login command to. Before your security hairs on the back of your neck start to stand straight up, a file called `/etc/shells` has the same ownership and permissions as the

/etc/passwd file. In this file, the system administrator defines which login commands are acceptable. Because of the permissions, every user has access to read the file, but not to change it. The following is an example of an /etc/shells file:

```
shell:/home/dpitts$ cat /etc/shells
/bin/sh
/bin/bash
/bin/tcsh
/bin/csh
/bin/ash
/bin/zsh
```

As you can see, the only login command the user can change to are shells. Following is an example of both the chsh command and the passwd -s command. As always, the password is not displayed.

```
shell:/home/dpitts$ chsh
Password:
Changing the login shell for dpitts
Enter the new value, or press return for the default
Login Shell [/bin/bash]:
shell:/home/dpitts$ passwd -s
Password:
Changing the login shell for dpitts
Enter the new value, or press return for the default
Login Shell [/bin/bash]: /bin/bash
shell:/home/dpitts$
```

Editing /etc/group

After the /etc/passwd file has been set up, the next step is to define the groups that that user is associated with. Every user is associated with at least one group. A group is a collection of users thrown together for a particular purpose. This purpose could be job function—programmer, system administrator, accountant, or engineer—or the users could all have access to a special device—scanner, color printer, or modem.

There is no limit to the number of groups on a system. In fact, the default /etc/group file contains 18 groups:

```
root::0:root
bin::1:root, bin, daemon
daemon::2:root,bin,daemon
sys::3:root,bin,adm
tty::5:
disk::6:root,adm
lp::7:lp
mem::8:
kmem::9:
wheel::10:root
```

```
floppy::11:root
mail::12:mail
news::13:news
uucp::14:uucp
man::15:man
users::100:games
nogroup::-1:
```

Each line contains four segments and, like the `passwd` file, is delimited by colons:

`group name : password : group ID : users`

If there is nothing to be entered into a field, that field is left blank (notice the *`password`* field). There will still be a colon delimiting the field from the other fields. Following is a short description of each of the fields:

group name	A unique identifier for the group
password	Usually left blank or an `*`, but a password can be assigned
group ID	The unique number that identifies a group to the operating system
users	A list of all user IDs that belong to that group

As with the `/etc/passwd` file, there are two ways of editing this file. The first way is with a script, such as `addgroup` or `groupadd`; the second way is to manually edit the file with a text editor. (By the way, always make sure you make a backup copy of the file before you edit it.) When adding groups to this file, just follow the format of the other files. Add a unique group, assign it a password if necessary, give it a unique group ID, and then list the users associated with that group. The users, by the way, are separated with commas. If the line is not in the correct format or is incorrect in some other way, the users might not be able to use that group ID.

If the system were using a shadow password system, the password field would be moved to `/etc/shadow.group`, and an `x` would be assigned to the field.

When finished editing the `/etc/group` file, double-check its permissions. It should be owned by root, and its group should be `root` or `sys` (a group ID of `0`). The permissions should be read and write for owner and read for everyone else (`644` in hex).

The list of groups does not need to be in any particular order. The list of users in each group is also irrelevant. Red Hat Linux will search the entire file until it comes to the line it is looking for.

Although users can be in several groups, Linux only allows them to be active in a single group at any given time. The starting group, commonly called the primary group, is the group identified in the `/etc/passwd` file. If a user wants to switch to another group (and he or she is in the group according to `/etc/group`), the user must issue the `newgrp` command to switch.

Removing a group or a user from a group is as simple as editing the `/etc/group` file and removing either the entire line or the particular user you want removed. You should also check the `/etc/passwd` file to make sure that there are no users defined to the group you just deleted.

Creating a Home Directory and Copying Files to the New Home

After a new user has been added to the `/etc/passwd` file and the `/etc/group` file, the next step is to create the user's new home directory. For the rest of this chapter, assume that the home directory is `/home/username`.

To create the directory, go to the `/home` directory (`cd /home`), and issue the `mkdir` command. The parameter passed to the `mkdir` command is the directory you want to correct. In the following example, I am creating a user directory for `tpowell`:

```
shell:/home/dpitts$ cd /home
shell:/home/dpitts$ mkdir tpowell
```

I now have a directory for my friend Tim. Now that I have the directory, I need to copy the files from `/etc/skel` to the new home. This is accomplished with the `cp` command, as shown in the following example:

```
shell:/home/dpitts$ cp /etc/skel/*  /home/tpowell
```

Changing Ownerships and Permissions

Now that the basic files are placed in the new user's account, it is time to give the files and the new home directory to the new user and give the files the correct file permissions. Of course, an individual site might differ in the security placed on the files and directories. The following is a general guideline of the commands that need to be executed:

1. `cd /home/new_users_name ex. cd /home/tpowell`
2. `chown -R username.group ex. chown -R tpowell.user`
3. `chmod -R go=u, go-w`
4. `chmod go= .`

Setting the Password

Issue the `passwd` command as root, and set the password of the new user. After you have set this password, the account will work. If you are creating dummy accounts, you might not want to set the password.

Changing User Properties

There are a few commands for changing various properties of an account. The `chsh` command, used to change the login command, is mentioned earlier in this chapter. In addition to it (and the `passwd -s`), you can use two other commands:

`chfn`	Changes the full name field (the comment field)
`passwd`	Changes the password

The superuser (root) can use these commands to change the properties of any account. Normal users (those whose UIDs do not correspond to 0) can only change the properties of their own account.

Temporarily Disabling a User

Sometimes, it is necessary to temporarily disable a user's account. Many times, you do not want to remove it, just make it inaccessible instead. One of the ways I have seen people do this is to change the user's password. Although this works, it also causes confusion for the user, who doesn't know what is going on.

A better way of disabling the account is to change the login command set in the `/etc/passwd` file. Make a special program called a `tail` script:

```
#!/usr/bin/tail +2
This account has been temporarily closed due to <whatever reason>.
Please call the system administrator at 555-1212 to discuss this
➥situation.
```

The first two characters of the first line (`#!`) tell the kernel that the rest of the line is a command that needs to be run to interpret this file. (If you are accustomed to shell programming or Perl programming, this ought to look familiar.) The `tail` command outputs the last two lines of the file (which happens to be everything except the first line that executed the program).

If our friend `tpowell` has not logged in to his account for 90 days, the system administrator would write something like this:

```
# chsh -s /usr/local/lib/no-login/old tpowell
# su - tpowell
This account has been closed due to inactivity.
Please call the system administrator at 555-1212 to discuss this
➥situation.
#
```

By using the `su` command to switch to `tpowell`, I was able to test and make sure that I had issued the command correctly and that it said what I wanted it to say. It worked.

Red Hat's User Configuration Tools

If you are using the X Window system, Red Hat has provided you (as root) with a tool for adding users to the system. From the control panel, you can click the tool (see Figure 20.1).

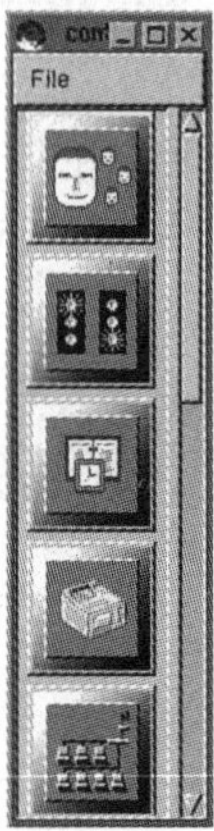

FIGURE 20.1
User and Group Configuration icon.

By clicking the User and Group Configuration Tool icon, you have the option of configuring users or groups. The default is users.

Users

Once you have clicked the User and Group Configuration Tool icon, the interface shown in Figure 20.2 will appear.

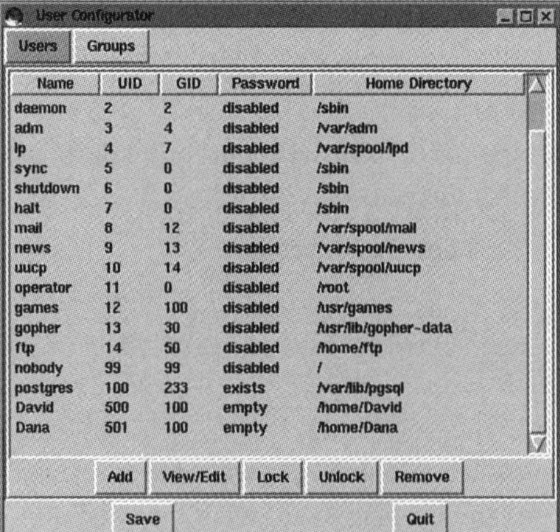

User Configurator
Users
Groups
Name UID GID Password Home Directory
daemon 2 2 disabled /sbin
adm 3 4 disabled /var/adm
lp 4 7 disabled /var/spool/lpd
sync 5 0 disabled /sbin
shutdown 6 0 disabled /sbin
halt 7 0 disabled /sbin
mail 8 12 disabled /var/spool/mail
news 9 13 disabled /var/spool/news
uucp 10 14 disabled /var/spool/uucp
operator 11 0 disabled /root
games 12 100 disabled /usr/games
gopher 13 30 disabled /usr/lib/gopher-data
ftp 14 50 disabled /home/ftp
nobody 99 99 disabled /
postgres 100 233 exists /var/lib/pgsql
David 500 100 empty /home/David
Dana 501 100 empty /home/Dana
Add
View/Edit
Lock
Unlock
Remove
Save
Quit

FIGURE 20.2
User and Group configuration.

The default screen shows the current users. You will notice that the Users tab at the top is darker than the Groups tab. An explanation of the password entries is given in Table 20.2.

TABLE 20.2 PASSWORD ENTRIES

Password Status	*Description*
`disabled`	This means that the account is locked. Users cannot log in to this account.
`empty`	This means that the account is active but that there is no password required to log in as this user. (This can be a dangerous situation, especially on a network.) This is the default password entry.
`exists`	This means that the account is active and that there is an existing password for this user. Unless security is not an issue, there should always be a password associated with each user.

Across the bottom of the screen are five tabs. These tabs are the actions that can be performed to a user. The first option, add, will bring up another window for adding a user (see Figure 20.3).

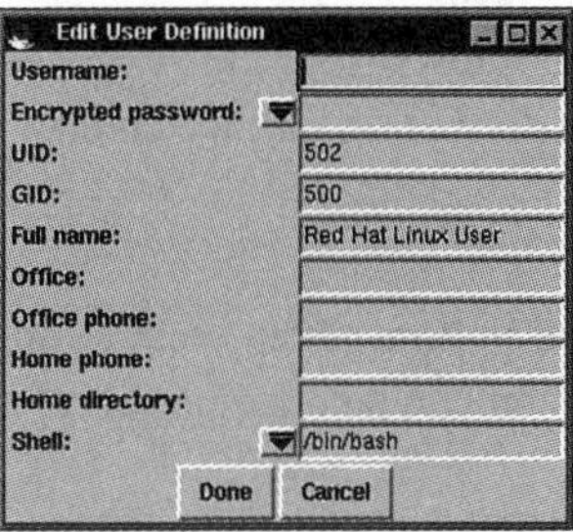

FIGURE 20.3
Edit User Definition.

The only field that must be filled in is the username. Each user should have a unique username. Although there are no standards for usernames, you should have a standard for your system. Some examples I have used are dpitts, dspitts, davidp, davidpitts, or even a completely random name such as xx6855 or a combination such as dsp6855. On my system at home, I simply use David and my wife uses Dana. Of course, on our home system, we are not connected to a network, so there is little concern of security issues. (In actuality, if it were not that several games use the username to record high scores, we would have only one user ID for the two of us to share.)

Add User

When you add a user, the system automatically grabs a few pieces of information. First of all, it calculates the next available UID for the new user. (The first user added to a system will get 500 by default.) Then, it assigns the default group ID (GID), which is `500-users`. The default home location will be `/home/<username>`.

View/Edit User

When you view/edit a user, the screen shown in Figure 20.4 comes up.

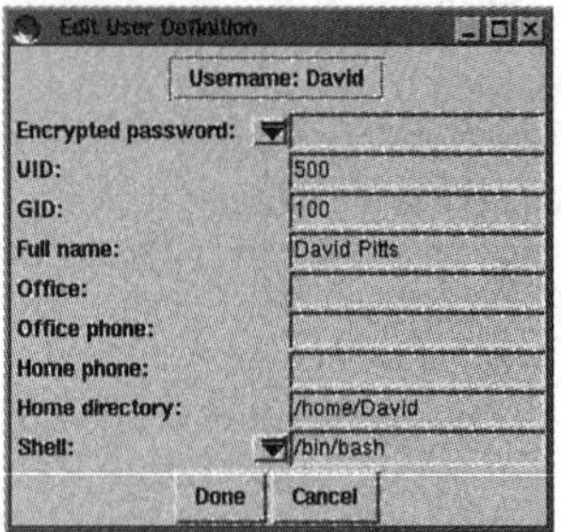

FIGURE 20.4
Edit User Definition, Screen 2.

The system fills in all the information that it knows from the `/etc/passwd` file. You, as root, have the option of editing any of the information on the screen.

Lock

When you lock an account, you have several options about what to do with that user's account. As you can tell from Figure 20.5, you can take care of all of the data pertaining to that particular user.

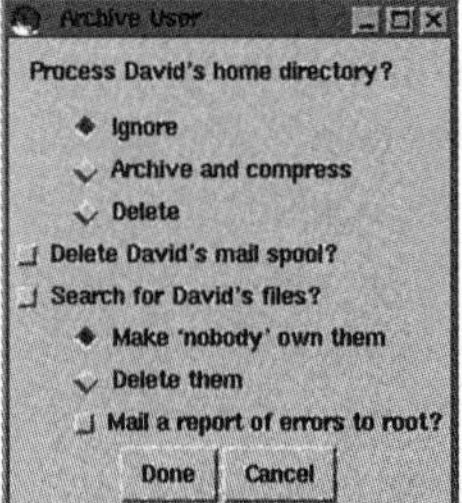

FIGURE 20.5
Lock (Archive) User.

The first section asks what to do with the home directory. The options are to ignore it, which leaves it just the way it is; archive and compress it, in case the data is needed later; or delete the data. You can choose only one option.

Next, what should you do with the user's mail? Your choices are to leave it alone (the default value) or to delete it.

The third section is what to do with other files on the system owned by that user. Your options are to search the system and change the ownership so that "nobody" owns them or to delete them.

Finally, the last option is whether to send mail to root with any errors received. By default, no errors are sent to the system administrator.

Unlock

The unlock option is used for an account that you have previously locked. Figure 20.6 shows what is involved with this option.

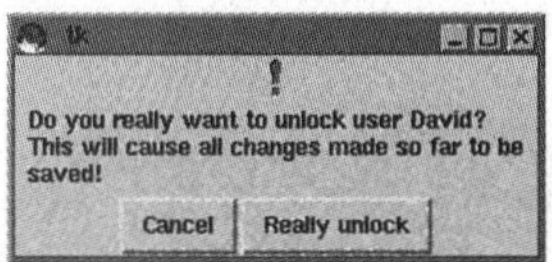

FIGURE 20.6
Unlock user.

Basically, the only options you have here are to unlock it or not. Basically, it is just a double-check to make sure that this is really what you want to do.

Remove

You can remove accounts by either clicking the remove tab or clicking the lock tab. In either case, the same window pops up except that the name of the screen changes to Delete User instead of Archive User (see Figure 20.7).

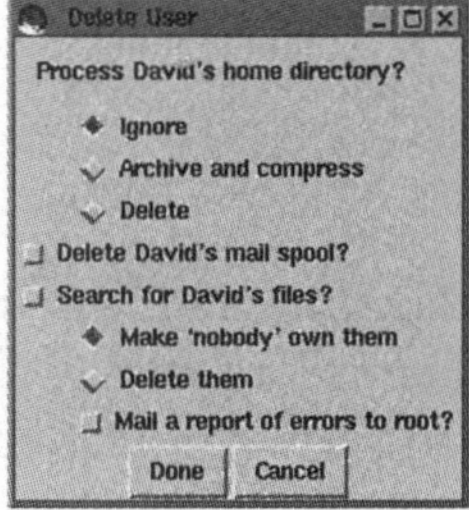

FIGURE 20.7
Delete user.

As you can tell, Red Hat's tool for dealing with users is very good and complete. The tools for dealing with groups are just as good.

Groups

When you click the Groups tab along the top of the User Configurator screen, you see the screen shown in Figure 20.8.

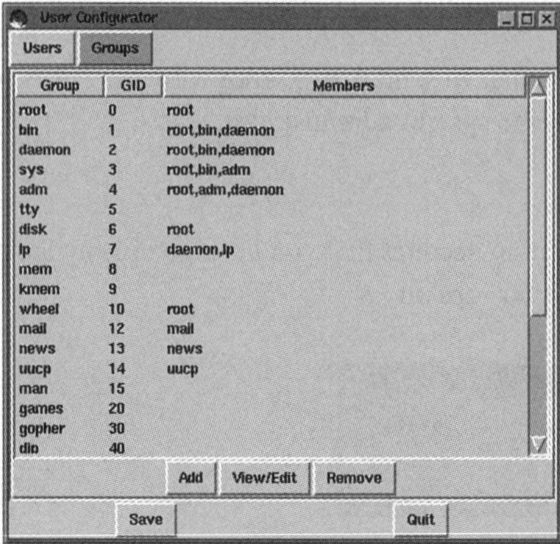

FIGURE 20.8
Group configuration.

There are three options for dealing with groups. You can add, edit/view, and remove them. There are fewer additional windows as well.

Add Groups

When you click the Add Groups tab, the window shown in Figure 20.9 pops up.

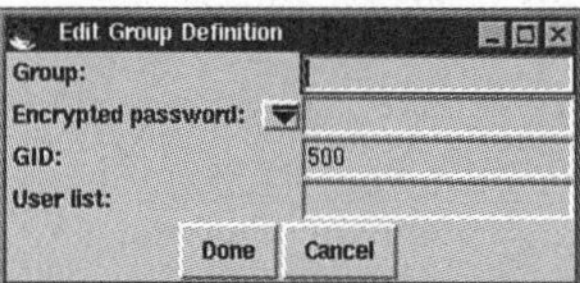

FIGURE 20.9
Edit Group Definition.

Like adding users, the only field that needs to be filled in is the name of the group. The system grabs the next available group ID (GID), beginning with 500. At the time that you add a group, you can also add users to that group by placing their usernames in the "user list" field. When you are finished, you click the Done tab.

Edit/View Groups

The screen for editing groups is similar to the one for adding users (see Figure 20.10).

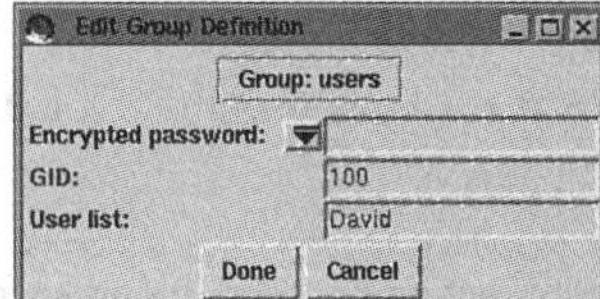

FIGURE 20.10
Edit Group Definition, Screen 2.

Because you must highlight a group to edit it, the group name is not editable and is just listed at the top for reference's sake. Everything else about this screen is the same as the Add Group window, including the title.

Remove

There is no screen associated with removing groups. Because groups do not "own" files, the only options are to remove it or not. Personally, I think it is strange that they make you confirm when you want to unlock a user, but there is no similar confirmation screen when you remove a group. When you highlight a group and click the Remove tab, it simply goes away.

The Login and How to Become a Specific User

When logging in via a terminal, `init` makes sure there is a `getty` program for the terminal connection. `getty` listens at the terminal and waits for the user to notify that he or she is ready to log in. When it notices a user, `getty` outputs a welcome message (`/etc/issue`), prompts for a username, and runs the `login` program. The `login` program checks for the existence of the `/etc/nologin` file. If it exists, logins are disabled. If it does not exist, the `login` program gets the username as a parameter and prompts the user for the password. The password is compared to the password on file for the user. If all of this matches up, `login` starts the login command identified in the `/etc/passwd` file. If it does not match up, either the program will give the user another chance to enter the user ID and password, or the program will terminate the process. When `init` notices that the process terminated, it starts a new `getty` for the terminal.

After the login command is run, and assuming there is a place to send standard output, the `login` program outputs the contents of `/etc/motd` and checks for electronic mail. You can turn off these two steps by placing an empty file in your home directory called `.hushlogin`. Use the following command:

```
shell:/home/dpitts$touch .hushlogin
shell:/home/dpitts$
```

The touch command says to update the file passed as a parameter with the current date and time. If that file does not exist, it creates it with nothing in it. It is this second part that has the desired effect.

NOTE

If the file /etc/nologin exists, logins are disabled. This file is usually created by shutdown. All failed login attempts are logged in the system log file (syslog). It also logs all logins by root. Current logins are listed in the /var/run/utmp file and logged in the /var/log/wtmp file.

The su Command

The su command (su stands for switch user) is used to switch from one user to another. If no user is given as a parameter, the su command assumes a switch to the root user account. If the - parameter is used, all environment variables for the user switched to are read. If not, the environment variables of the real user are kept. The su command switches the effective username. It does not change the actual username.

If a normal user switches to another user, the system will ask for the password of the user being switched to. If root attempts to switch to another user, the system switches to that user without the necessary password.

Searching

Sometimes when you are on a system, it is nice to know who else is on the system. Other times, it is nice to know other information about a user, such as whether the user is currently logged on to the system. The next sections discuss the who command and the finger command, list possible reasons they are used, and explain where the information comes from.

who

The who command checks the /var/run/utmp file to create its information. The /var/run/utmp command keeps track of who is currently logged on. Other than mere curiosity's sake, there are other reasons why you might care who is logged on. One possible reason is system performance. If you are getting really bad system performance, you will probably want to see who is logged on and what the logged-on user is doing. The who command tells who, and the ps command tells what. Of course, to communicate with users with write or talk, you need to know whether that user is logged on.

The -u parameter for who adds the column for how long it has been since that login has been active. In the following example, there are two users. The first has not done anything for 15 minutes. The second (me) is currently running a command (gee, I bet it is the who -u command):

```
shell:/home/dpitts$ who -u
wsheldah  ttyp0    Sep  1 12:55 00:15 (d3.dialup.lexne)
dpitts   ttyp1    Sep  1 17:06   .   (a20.dialup.seane)
```

The output is a space-delimited line with the following elements (who -u):

```
user id <space> terminal logged in <space> Date logged in (month/day)
➥<space>
time logged in <space> inactive time <space> where logged in from
```

finger

The finger command checks some system and user-defined files and reports the information it finds. The output is explained after this example of a finger command:

```
shell:/home/dpitts$ finger dpitts
Login: dpitts                              Name: MCA Financial Systems
Directory: /home2/dpitts                   Shell: /bin/bash
On since Mon Sep  1 17:06 (EDT) on ttyp1 from a20.dialup.seane
Mail forwarded to dpitts@seanet.com
No mail.
Plan:
David Pitts
Systems Administrator, Consultant, Author
shell:/home/dpitts$
```

First, the finger command reads and interprets the /etc/passwd file. From that file, it gives the login ID, the comment field, the home location, and the login command issued. In addition, it checks /var/run/utmp, and if the person is logged in, it displays how long, on which terminal, and from where. After it gives this information, it then checks for the existence of a .forward file. If one exists, it displays its information. Next, it checks to see whether the user has any mail waiting to be read. It then checks for a .plan file in the user's home directory. The .plan file contains information that the user wants to have displayed when another user looks him up. This can be any ASCII information.

As you can tell, the finger command gives quite a bit of publicly available information. The files that are accessed (passwd, .plan, and .forward) need information in them that is appropriate for any user who can access the system to see.

Summary

This chapter gives you a glimpse of the importance of planning an activity and providing all the necessary steps involved in changing a system. These steps are even more vital in a production system. As a reminder, a system administrator should

- Understand how things work
- Know where to find things
- Plan processes
- Have a back-out plan and know when to use it
- Make changes in small increments
- Test all changes
- Communicate efficiently and effectively

Communication is the key to success in system administration, as it is with life. You have many tools to enable you to communicate with other users on the system.

Advanced System Administration

by David Pitts

In This Chapter

A large portion of this book is devoted to advanced system administration, including script and automation development, configuring and building kernels, network management, security, and many other tasks. One task not addressed thus far is performance analysis. This chapter looks at the initial steps of performance analysis, showing how to determine CPU, memory, and paging space usage. I examine two tools for acquiring snapshots of the system—`vmstat` and `top`—and two tools for watching resources graphically—`Xosview` and `Xload`.

Basic Performance Analysis

Basic performance analysis is the process of identifying performance bottlenecks and involves a number of steps. The first step is to look at the big picture: Is the problem CPU- or I/O-related? If it is a CPU problem, what is the load average? You should probably check what processes are running and who is causing the problem. If it is an I/O problem, is it paging or normal disk I/O? If it is paging, then increasing memory might help. You can also try to isolate the program or the user causing the problem. If it is a disk problem, is the disk activity balanced? If you have only one disk, you might want to install a second.

The next section looks at several tools that you can use to determine the answers to the preceding questions.

Determining CPU Usage with `vmstat`

CPU usage is the first test on the list. There are many different ways to obtain a snapshot of the current CPU usage. The one I focus on here is `vmstat`. The `vmstat` command gives you several pieces of data, including the CPU usage. The following is the syntax for the command:

```
$ vmstat interval [count]
```

`interval` is the number of seconds between reports, and *`count`* is the total number of reports to give. If the count is not included, `vmstat` will run continuously until you stop it with Ctrl+C or kill the process.

Here is an example of the output from `vmstat`:

```
shell:/home/dpitts$ vmstat 5 5
 procs                  memory    swap        io    system         cpu
 r b w   swpd  free  buff cache  si  so   bi   bo   in   cs  us  sy  id
 0 0 0   1104  1412 10032 36228   0   0   10    8   31   15   7   4  24
 0 0 0   1104  1736 10032 36228   0   0    0    3  111   18   1   1  99
 0 0 0   1104  1816 10032 36228   0   0    0    1  115   23   2   2  96
 0 1 0   1104  1148 10096 36268   8   0    7    4  191  141   4   6  91
 0 0 0   1104  1868  9812 35676   6   0    2   10  148   39  25   4  70
```

The first line of the report displays the average values for each statistic since boot time. It should be ignored. For determining CPU used, you are interested in the last three columns, as indicated by the cpu heading. They are us, sy, and id:

CPU	*Description*
us	Percentage of CPU cycles spent on performing user tasks.
sy	Percentage of CPU cycles spent as system tasks. These tasks include waiting on I/O, performing general operating system functions, and so on.
id	Percentage of CPU cycles not used. This is the amount of time the system was idle.

A high CPU time (or low idle time) is not necessarily indicative of an overall CPU problem. It could be that a number of batch jobs running just need rearranged. To determine that there is actually a CPU problem, it is important to monitor the CPU percentages for a significant period of time. If the percentages are high during this time, then there is definitely a problem.

Next, look at a different section of the vmstat output. If the problem is not CPU related, check whether it is a problem with paging or normal disk I/O. To determine whether it is a memory problem, look at the headings memory and swap:

```
shell:/home/dpitts$ vmstat 5 5
 procs                      memory    swap          io     system         cpu
 r b w   swpd   free   buff cache  si  so    bi    bo   in    cs  us  sy  id
 1 0 0   1096   1848   4580 37524   0   0     9     8    8    17   7   3  29
 1 0 0   1096   1424   4580 37980   0   0    92    10  125    24  94   4   3
 2 0 0   1096    864   4536 38408   0   0   112    31  146    42  93   2   5
 2 0 0   1096    732   4360 38480  10   0    98     7  146    48  97   3   1
```

Memory	*Description*
swpd	The amount of virtual memory used (KB)
free	The amount of idle memory (KB)
buff	The amount of memory used as buffers (KB)
cache	The amount of memory left in the cache (KB)

Swap	*Description*
si	The amount of memory swapped in from disk (KB/s)
so	The amount of memory swapped to disk (KB/s)

The most important of these fields is the swap in column. This column shows paging that has previously been swapped out, even if it was done before the vmstat command was issued.

The `io` section is used to determine whether the problem is with blocks sent in or out of the device:

```
shell:/home/dpitts$ vmstat 5 5
 procs                      memory    swap          io     system         cpu
 r b w   swpd   free   buff  cache  si  so    bi    bo   in    cs  us  sy  id
 1 0 0   1096   1848   4580 37524   0   0     9     8    8    17   7   3  29
 1 0 0   1096   1424   4580 37980   0   0    92    10  125    24  94   4   3
 2 0 0   1096    864   4536 38408   0   0   112    31  146    42  93   2   5
 2 0 0   1096    732   4360 38480  10   0    98     7  146    48  97   3   1
```

The `io` section is described in the following table:

IO	*Description*
`bi`	The blocks sent to a block device (blocks/s)
`bo`	The blocks received from a block device (blocks/s)
`cs`	The number of context switches per second

These fields run from several to several hundred (maybe even several thousand). If you are having a lot of in and out block transfers, the problem is probably here. Keep in mind, however, that a single reading is not indicative of the system as a whole; it's just a snapshot of the system at that time. There are three states in which the processes can exist. They are runtime, uninterrupted sleep, and swapped out:

Procs	*Description*
`r`	The number of processes waiting for runtime
`b`	The number of processes in uninterrupted sleep
`w`	The number of processes swapped out but otherwise able to run

The number of processes waiting for runtime is a good indication that there is a problem. The more processes waiting, the slower the system. More than likely, you won't look at `vmstat` unless you already know there is a bottleneck somewhere, so the `r` field doesn't give you much vital information.

top

The `top` command provides another tool for identifying problems with a Linux system. The `top` command displays the `top` CPU processes. More specifically, `top` provides an ongoing look at processor activity in real time. It displays a listing of the most CPU-intensive tasks on the system and can provide an interactive interface for manipulating processes. The default is to update every five seconds. The following is an example of the output from `top`:

```
  1:36am  up 16 days,  7:50,  3 users,  load average: 1.41, 1.44, 1.21
60 processes: 58 sleeping, 2 running, 0 zombie, 0 stopped
CPU states: 89.0% user,  8.5% system, 92.4% nice,  3.9% idle
Mem:  63420K av, 62892K used,   528K free, 32756K shrd,  6828K buff
Swap: 33228K av,  1096K used, 32132K free                38052K cached
PID USER     PRI  NI  SIZE  RSS SHARE STATE  LIB %CPU %MEM   TIME COMMAND
```

The following table explains each field:

Field	*Description*
`up`	The time the system has been up and the three load averages for the system. The load averages are the average number of processes ready to run during the last 1, 5, and 15 minutes. This line is just like the output of `uptime`.
`processes`	The total number of processes running at the time of the last update. This is also broken down into the number of tasks that are running, sleeping, stopped, and zombied.
`CPU states`	The percentage of CPU time in user mode, system mode, niced tasks, and idle. (*Niced* tasks are only those whose `nice` value is negative.) Time spent in niced tasks is also counted in system and user time, so the total is more than 100 percent.
`Mem`	Statistics on memory usage, including total available memory, free memory, used memory, shared memory, and memory used for buffers.
`Swap`	Statistics on swap space, including total swap space, available swap space, and used swap space. This and `Mem` are just like the output of `free`.
`PID`	The process ID of each task.
`USER`	The username of the task's owner.
`PRI`	The priority of the task.
`NI`	The `nice` value of the task. Negative `nice` values are lower priority.
`SIZE`	The size of the task's code plus data plus stack space, in kilobytes.
`RSS`	The total amount of physical memory used by the task, in kilobytes.
`SHARE`	The amount of shared memory used by the task.
`STATE`	The state of the task, either `S` for sleeping, `D` for uninterrupted sleep, `R` for running, `Z` for zombies, or `T` for stopped or traced.

continues

Field	Description
TIME	Total CPU time the task has used since it started. If cumulative mode is on, this also includes the CPU time used by the process's children that have died. You can set cumulative mode with the S command-line option or toggle it with the interactive command S.
%CPU	The task's share of the CPU time since the last screen update, expressed as a percentage of total CPU time.
%MEM	The task's share of the physical memory.
COMMAND	The task's command name, which is truncated if tasks have only the name of the program in parentheses (for example, (getty)).

As you can probably tell from the server used to obtain the data, there are no current bottlenecks in the system.

free is another good command for showing the amount of memory that is used and memory that is free:

```
shell:/home/dpitts$ free
             total       used       free     shared    buffers     cached
Mem:         63420      61668       1752      23676      13360      32084
-/+ buffers:            16224      47196
Swap:        33228       1096      32132
```

The first line of output (Mem:) shows the physical memory. The total column does not show the physical memory used by the kernel, which is usually about a megabyte. The used column shows the amount of memory used. The free column shows the amount of free memory. The shared column shows the amount of memory shared by several processes. The buffers column shows the current size of the disk buffer cache. The cached column shows how much memory has been cached off to disk.

The last line (Swap:) shows similar information for the swapped spaces. If this line is all zeroes, your swap space is not activated.

To activate a swap space, use the swapon command. The swapon command tells the kernel that the swap space can be used. The location of the swap space is given as the argument passed to the command. The following example shows starting a temporary swap file:

```
$ swapon /temporary_swap
```

To automatically use swap spaces, list them in the /etc/fstab file. The following example lists two swap files for the /etc/fstab:

```
/dev/hda8 none swap sw 0 0
/swapfile none swap sw 0 0
```

To remove a swap space, use the `swapoff` command. Usually, this is necessary only when using a temporary swap space.

CAUTION

If swap space is removed, the system will attempt to move any swapped pages into other swap space or to physical memory. If there isn't enough space, the system will freak out but will eventually come back. During the time that it is trying to figure out what to do with these extra pages, the system will be unavailable.

Graphical Tools

`Xosview` and `Xload` are two tools with graphical interfaces that monitor the conditions of the system.

Xosview

`Xosview` is a tool that you can run at all times, and it makes only a small performance hit on the system. `Xosview` looks like Figure 21.1.

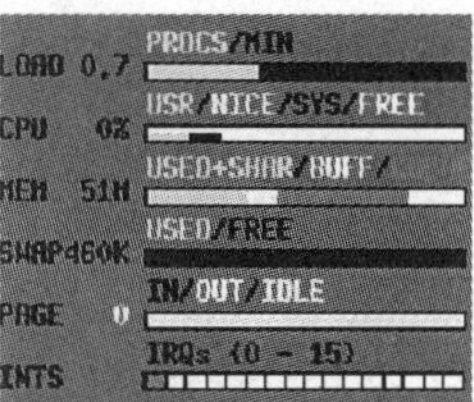

FIGURE 21.1
`Xosview`

There are six fields associated with this graphical tool:

Load—The load is shown as a two-color graph. The first part is the load average of the processes, and the second is the background. If the load average is above 1.0, the color will change. On my system, the color below the 1.0 average is an aquamarine color; if it goes above the 1.0 average, it changes to gray.

CPU—The CPU meter shows four different fields: usr, nice, sys, and free. In the figure, you can see that the user is using some of the system, and the system is using some of the system, but overall, the system is not being used even 1 percent.

Mem—The mem section shows the total amount of real memory being used. The used+shar section shows how much is used by the user. The next color is the amount in the buffer, the next color is the cache, and what is left is white. This entire bar represents 100 percent of your memory.

Swap—This meter shows how much data is being swapped out to the hard disk. The used will be in one color; the free in another. If you have a lot of real memory, you should not have much in swap. Having memory in swap is perfectly fine; it should not worry you. If, however, you run out of swap space, your system will start to thrash. (See "How Much Swap Is Enough?" later in this chapter for more information.)

Page—This bar shows how much paging is going on between memory and swap. There are three colors here. Typically, the darkest color is paging in (putting pages into swap), the middle color is paging out (taking pages out of swap and back to real memory), and the lightest color is idle. As with the swap meter, paging in and out is not a bad thing but needs to be watched just the same.

Ints (interrupts)—This bar shows interrupts as they are being used. If the IRQ is busy, the "light" turns red. For example, when I move my mouse, the 13th light lights up, indicating that the 12th interrupt is being used. (Computers start numbering at 0, not 1). The graph shows 16 interrupts.

Xload

The `Xload` program is a graphical representation of the system load average, shown as a histogram. With many versions of the X Window programs, a similar histogram is displayed along with the virtual windows you have available. Figure 21.2 shows the `Xload` program.

FIGURE 21.2
`Xload`

As with all histograms, the top limit is 100 percent and the bottom is 0 percent. As you can tell, the system load average goes up and down as users ask the system to perform tasks.

How Much Swap Is Enough?

A common question asked by people who are designing a system for the first time is, "How much swap space is enough?" Some people estimate that you should have twice as much swap space as you have physical memory. Following this method, if you have a system with 16MB of memory, you will set up 32MB of swap space. Depending on how much physical memory you have, this number can be way out of line. For example, my system has 64MB of physical memory, so I should configure 124MB of paging space. I say that this is unnecessary. I prefer to use a slightly more complex strategy for determining the amount of swap space needed.

Determining the amount of swap space you need is a simple four-step program. First, admit that you have a memory problem. No, sorry; that is a different program. The four steps are as follows:

1. Estimate your total memory needs. Consider the largest amount of space you will need at any given time. Consider what programs you will be running simultaneously. A common way of determining this is to set up a bogus swap space (quite large) and load as many programs as you estimate will run at the same time. Then, check how much memory you have used. A few things typically don't show up when a memory check is performed. The kernel, for example, will use about a megabyte of space.
2. Add a couple megabytes as a buffer for those programs that you did not think you would use but found out later that in fact you will.
3. Subtract the amount of physical memory you have from this total. The amount left is the amount of swap space needed to run your system with all the memory in use.
4. If the total from Step 3 is more than approximately three times the amount of physical memory you have, you will probably have problems. Given the relatively inexpensive cost of physical memory, it is worthwhile to add more physical memory.

Sometimes these calculations show that you don't need any swap space; my system with 64MB of RAM, for example. I followed the steps and came up with about 40MB of memory need. It is a good policy to create some space anyway. Linux uses the swap space so that as much physical memory as possible is kept free. It swaps out memory pages that have not been used for a while so that when the memory is needed, it is available. The system will not have to wait for the memory to be swapped out.

Momma Always Said to Be Nice!

I grew up with two older brothers and one younger one. Many times, Momma asked one or more of us to be nice! Sometimes, the same is true for our processes. The `renice` command is used to alter the priority of running processes.

By default in Red Hat Linux, the `nice` value is `0`. The range of this is `-20` to `20`. The lower the value, the faster the process runs. The following example shows how you display the `nice` value by using the `nice` command. My shell is running at the default value of `0`. To check this another way, I issue the `ps -l` command. The `NI` column shows the `nice` value:

```
shell:/home/dpitts$ nice
0
shell:/home/dpitts$ ps -l
```

```
 FLAGS    UID    PID   PPID PRI   NI    SIZE    RSS WCHAN          STA TTY TIME
➥COMMAND
    100    759  3138  3137    0    0    1172    636 force_sig      S   p0  0:00 -
➥bash
 100000    759  3307  3138   12    0     956    336                R   p0  0:00 ps
➥-l
```

I change the nice value by using the renice command. The syntax of the command follows:

```
renice priority [[-p] pid ...] [[-g] pgrp ...] [[-u] user ...]
```

In the following example, the shell's nice value is changed to a value of 5. This means that any process with a lower value will have priority on the system:

```
shell:/home/dpitts$ renice 5 3138
3138: old priority 0, new priority 5
shell:/home/dpitts$ nice
5
shell:/home/dpitts$ ps -l
 FLAGS    UID    PID   PPID PRI   NI    SIZE    RSS WCHAN          STA TTY TIME
➥COMMAND
    100    759  3138  3137    5    5    1172    636 force_sig      S N p0  0:00 -
➥bash
 100000    759  3319  3138   14    5     968    368                R N p0  0:00 ps
➥-l
```

The owner of the process (and root) has the ability to change the nice value to a higher value. Unfortunately, the reverse is not also true:

```
shell:/home/dpitts$ renice -5 3138
renice: 3138: setpriority: Permission denied
```

Only root has the capability to lower a nice value. This means that even though I set my shell to a nice value of 5, I cannot lower it even to the default value.

The renice command is a wonderful way of increasing the apparent speed of the system for certain processes. This is a trade-off, however, because the processes that are raised will now run slower.

Summary

Computers slow down significantly when they run out of memory. If they try to do too much at one time, they seem slow. As a system administrator, your job is to determine whether the system is actually slow or just seems slow. The difference is significant. If the system seems slow, the problem is usually a matter of adjusting the times that certain processes run. Using cron and at helps you schedule certain activities when the system is otherwise idle.

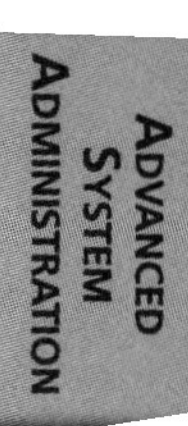

If the system is actually slow—that is, waiting on processes all the time, with consistent IO waits—then it is time to invest in more equipment. The other option is to just live with it. (Get your users to buy off on that one!) As system administrator, your job is to keep performance at an acceptable level. With tools such as `vmstat` and `top`, this task is much simpler. Graphical tools such `Xosview` and `Xload` are also good tools that take up few resources and give you a picture of what is going on.

Sacrificing speed in certain processes is another way of increasing the apparent speed of other processes. The basic concept is that each process gets a certain piece of the processing pie. Certain processes can have a smaller, or larger, piece of the processing pie. The amount of processing that can be completed never changes. The change is how much processing time each process gets. Mainframes call this *cycling*. The lower the `nice` value, the more cycles the process gets each time the processor comes to do its work.

GNU Project Utilities

by Bill Ball

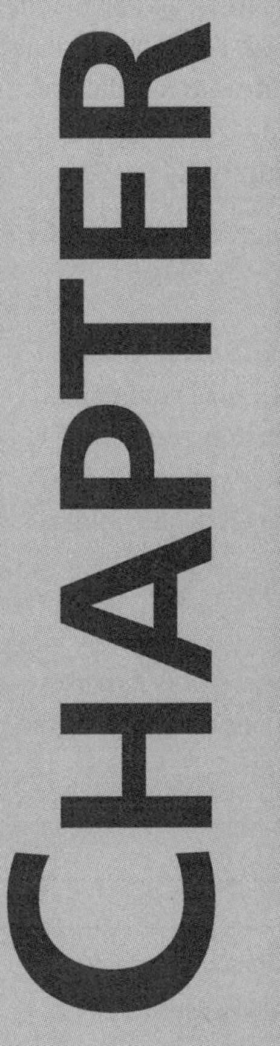

In This Chapter

GNU (stands for "GNU's not UNIX") is a UNIX-compatible software system distributed by the Free Software Foundation, founded by Richard Stallman. The GNU Project utilities are the GNU implementation of familiar UNIX programs such as `mv`, `cp`, and `ls`. The GNU Project includes hundreds of commands, utilities, and collections of commands and documentation in its distributions. Indeed, without the efforts of the hundreds of programmers who have contributed their time and expertise in developing these programs, the Red Hat Linux experience would be a lot less enriching and productive.

The GNU versions of these programs generally run faster, provide more options, have fewer arbitrary limits, and are POSIX.2-compliant.

The GNU project utilities are distributed in several parts. The `bin` utilities, `diff` utilities, and `shar` (shell archive) utilities are primarily used in development work. The most frequently used utilities—the file utilities, find utilities, shell utilities, and text utilities—are covered in this chapter.

The true power of the GNU Project utilities is that they enable users to break down complex tasks and solve them piece by piece, quickly and easily. Table 22.1 lists the various GNU Project Software Distributions. You'll find nearly all of this software installed on your Red Hat Linux system, either automatically when you installed Linux or through updates using the `rpm` command or Glint software maintenance client for X11.

Most, but not all of these programs have a corresponding manual page, usually read by a command like this one, which displays the manual page for the `cat` command:

```
# man cat
```

If you do not find a manual page for a command, try using the GNU `info` command, which searches for corresponding information about a program from compressed GNU info-format compressed files (found under the /usr/info directory after you install Red Hat Linux). For example, if you don't find information about `as`, the GNU assembler, you can try using the info command like this:

```
# info as
```

If the information is found, the `info` command displays information in info's hypertext-like format. For the latest news and update information about GNU utilities, such as the file, text, or shell collections, look under the /usr/doc directory.

TABLE 22.1 VARIOUS GNU PROJECT SOFTWARE DISTRIBUTIONS

Distribution	*Description*
am-utils	Various network and filesystem utilities (such as hostname or mount)
as	An essential program development utility—the GNU assembler

Distribution	Description
autoconf	A programming utility to create configuration scripts for source code
automake	Programming utilities for creating Makefiles
bash	The Bourne Again shell
bfd	The GNU Binary File Descriptor library
binutils	Binary utilties, many used for programming (for example, `ar`, `ranlib`, `strip`)
bison	The GNU bison command (a parser generator like `yacc`)
ccmode	Emacs support for source-code editing
cl	Common Lisp support for GNU Emacs Lisp
cpp	The essential C preprocessor
cvs	Part of the Concurrent Versions System, a front-end to the Revision Control System
cvsclient	Description of the cvs protocol
dc	A reverse-polish command-line calculator
diff	A collection of programs to report on differences between files
dired-x	Support for directory-editing for GNU emacs
dvips	A DVI-to-PostScript translator
ed	A line editor
ediff	Mutiple-file comparision and merging
egcs	The experimental GNU C compiler system
emacs	The Edit Macros editor from GNU
find	Filesystem search and operation utilities
fontname	TeX font names
forms	Database forms entry support for GNU emacs
gasp	A programming utility—the GNU assembler preprocessor
gcc	The essential programming utility—the GNU C compiler
gdb	A programming utility—the GNU debugger
gdbint	Internals to GNU debugger
gdbm	A library of database routines for programmers
gdk	A library of graphics routines for programmers
gettext	Utilities for the GNU gettext programming routines
git	Interactive tools

continues

TABLE 22.1 CONTINUED

Distribution	Description
gmp.info	A multiple-precision arithmetic library of software routines
gnus	Usenet newsreading in emacs
gpm	A library of routines for mouse support in text-mode consoles (including the gpm daemon)
gprof	Program-profiling support routines
gtk	A library of graphics routines for the GNU Image Processor (GIMP)
gzip	A collection of file-compression programs
indent	A programming utility to format source code
info	Utilities to prepare and read GNU info-format text files
kpathsea	A library of program utilities for directory searches
ld	An essential programming command—the GNU linker
libc	A collection of library routines needed by nearly all commands
libtool	Script and information to support shared software libraries
linux-faq	The Linux FAQ with Answers (/usr/doc/FAQ)
m4	The GNU macro processor
make	A programming utility used to build programs from scripts
message	Support for electronic mail and newsreading for GNU emacs
mgetty	Login monitoring programs (supporting voice mail, faxing, and so on)
mh-e	GNU emacs support routines for MH electronic mail
mtools	A collection of programs to access and manipulate DOS disks
pdb	Support for the GNU Image Processor (GIMP)
psacct	A suite of process-accounting utilities
readline	A collection of software input routines
sc	Electronic mail message reply support routines for emacs and gnus
screen	The GNU screen multiplexer
sh-utils	Shell utilities (such as date, printenv, tee, and who)
sharutils	A series of shell-archive tools (includes uuencode and uudecode)
stabs	Information about debugging tools and formats
standards	Programming standards for GNU programs
tar	The tape archive command
texinfo	Texinfo documentation translation, preparation, and printing utilities
textutils	Text utilities (such as `cat`, `head`, `sort`, `tail`, and so on)

Distribution	Description
time	The GNU time utility (for timing command execution)
umb-scheme	The UMB Scheme interpreter
vip	Vi-emulation support for GNU emacs
viper	Vi-emulation support for GNU emacs (19.29)
zsh	The Z shell, compatible with the Bourne shell (sh)

File Utilities

This section covers the major GNU file-management utilities. Table 22.2 lists the programs included in the GNU file utilities distribution, along with a short description of each.

TABLE 22.2 GNU FILE UTILITIES

Command	Description
chgrp	Change a user's group membership
chmod	Change file permissions
chown	Change file or directory ownerships
cp	Copy file(s) or directories
dd	Convert files during copy operations
df	Show free space on filesystems
dir	List the contents of a directory
du	Show disk usage
install	Install programs
ln	Create hard or symbolic links
ls	List the contents of a directory
mkdir	Create a directory
mkfifo	Create named pipes
mknod	Create special files, such as devices
mv	Rename (move) file(s) or directories
mvdir	(Not included with Red Hat Linux)
rm	Delete (remove) file(s)
rmdir	Delete (remove) a directory

continues

TABLE 22.2 CONTINUED

Distribution	*Description*
sync	Flush filesystem cache buffers to disk
touch	Create or update files
vdir	List the contents of a directory

Listing Directory Contents

The GNU file utilities include three programs for listing directory contents and information about files: `ls`, `dir`, and `vdir`. The biggest difference among these three programs is in their default behavior: `dir` is equivalent to `ls -C`, and `vdir` is equivalent to `ls -l`.

The default behavior of `ls` (invoked with no arguments) is to list the contents of the current directory. If a directory is given as an argument, its contents are listed nonrecursively (files starting with a period [`.`] are omitted). For filename arguments, just the name of the file is printed. By default, the output is listed alphabetically.

The GNU version of `ls` supports all of the standard options and also introduces the major feature of color-coding files.

The variable `$LS_COLOR` (or `$LS_COLOUR`) is used to determine the color scheme. If `$LS_COLOR` is not set, the color scheme is determined from the system default stored in the file `/etc/DIR_COLORS`. This variable can be set by hand, but it is much easier to have the program `dircolors` set it by issuing the following command:

```
# eval `dircolors`
```

To aid in customizing the color scheme, `dircolors` supports a `-p` option that prints out the default configuration. Redirecting the output to a file creates a valid dircolors init file. The command

```
# dircolors -p > .dircolorsrc
```

creates a file .dircolorsrc, which can be customized. After the file .dircolorsrc is customized, `$LS_COLORS` can be set by issuing this command:

```
# eval `dircolors .dircolorsrc`
```

Putting this line in an init file (.profile or .cshrc) and then having the alias

```
alias ls="ls --colors" (sh,bash,ksh)
alias ls "ls --colors" (csh,tcsh)
```

ensures that the custom color scheme is used for `ls`.

Listing 22.1 is an excerpt from a .dircolorsrc file that implements bold text for directories and normal text for all other types of files. If any of these file types are left out, default values are substituted for them. The comments describe the color values that can be used.

LISTING 22.1 EXCERPT FROM A .DIRCOLORSRC FILE

```
# Below are the color init strings for the basic file types. A color init
# string consists of one or more of the following numeric codes:
# Attribute codes:
# 00=none 01=bold 04=underscore 05=blink 07=reverse 08=concealed
# Text color codes:
# 30=black 31=red 32=green 33=yellow 34=blue 35=magenta 36=cyan 37=white
# Background color codes:
# 40=black 41=red 42=green 43=yellow 44=blue 45=magenta 46=cyan 47=white
NORMAL 00      # global default
FILE   00      # normal file
DIR    01      # directory
LINK   00      # symbolic link
FIFO   00      # pipe
SOCK   00      # socket
BLK    00      # block device driver
CHR    00      # character device driver
ORPHAN 00      # symlink to nonexistent file
EXEC   00      # executables
```

To implement colors, simply specify the scheme as

```
FILE_TYPE attribute codes;text codes;background codes
```

This line indicates all links are red with a white background:

```
LINK 00;31;47
```

Another feature of the `--color` option is that files with extensions can also be colorized. For example, to make all `JPG` files underlined, put the following line into the `.dircolors` file:

```
.jpg 04
```

Any file extension can be used. Some people like to have archive files (.uu, .tar, .tar.gz, .gz, .Z, .z, .tgz) in one color and picture files (.jpg, .jpeg, .gif) in another.

File Operations

The next set of commands in the file utilities are the utilities used for basic file operations, such as copying and moving files.

File operations commands such as `cp`, `mv`, `rm`, and `ln` are familiar to all UNIX users. The GNU versions of these commands support all the standard options along with a few additional options for safety and convenience. These options are as follows:

`-b` or `--backup`	Makes backups of files that are about to be overwritten or removed. Without this option, the original versions are destroyed. (Not available in `rm`.)
`-s suffix` or `--suffix=suffix`	Appends suffix to each backup file made if a backup option is specified. (Not available in `rm`.)
`-v` or `--verbose`	Prints out the filename before acting on it.

In terms of safety, the backup options are like the `-i` option (interactive mode)—they frequently prevent mishaps, and you definitely want to avoid mishaps. What's the most dangerous command and command-line options to use with Red Hat Linux? What command has caused more untold misery than nearly any other program? What command, if allowed to run unchecked, will destroy not only your Linux installation, but possibly all other mounted filesystems? The `rm` command, of course! This command is especially dangerous with the `-fr` option, followed by the root directory, like this:

```
# rm -fr /*
```

By default, the suffix for the backups is the tilde (~), but this can easily be changed by setting the variable `$SIMPLE_BACKUP_SUFFIX`. Setting this variable also avoids having to give the `-s` option each time.

Another useful command for copying files is the `install` command. It is frequently used to install compiled programs and is familiar to programmers who use `make`; however, `install` also can be useful for the casual user because it can be used to make copies of files and set attributes for those files.

Changing File Attributes

In addition to having a name, contents, and file type, every file in UNIX has several other pieces of information associated with it. The most commonly encountered of these are the file's owner, group, permissions, and timestamps. All of the pieces of information stored about a file make up its attributes.

The four commands `chown`, `chgrp`, `chmod`, and `touch` enable users to change file attributes.

The `chown` command is used to change the owner or group of a file, depending on how it is invoked. The basic syntax is

```
chown [options] [owner] [ [:.] [group] ] [files]
```

where either *owner* or *group* is optional and the separator can be either a . or a :. Thus, a command of the form

```
# chown ranga:users *
```

or

```
# chown ranga.users *
```

changes the owner of all files in the current directory to `ranga` and the group of all the files in the current directory to `users`, provided that `ranga` was a valid username and `users` was a valid group name. To find out which usernames and group names are valid, check in the files /etc/passwd and /etc/group.

In addition to giving usernames and group names, `uid` (user IDs) and `gid` (group IDs) can be given to `chown`. The command

```
# chown 500:100 foo.pl
```

changes the owner of foo.pl to the user with `uid 500` and the group of foo.pl to the group with `gid 100`. When using numeric IDs, make sure the IDs are valid, as `chown` only works for valid names.

If only the owner of a file (or files) needs to be changed, the group name or group ID can be omitted. For example,

```
# chown larry: camel.txt llama.txt
```

changes the owner of the files camel.txt and llama.txt to `larry`.

Similarly, if only the group of a file (or files) needs to be changed, the username or `uid` can be omitted. Thus,

```
# chown :100 bar.sh
```

changes only the group of bar.sh to `100`. If only a group change is required, the `chgrp` command can be used. Its basic syntax is

```
chgrp [options] [group] [files]
```

where *group* can be either the `gid` or a group name. To change the group of bar.sh to `100` with the `chgrp` command, the command would be

```
# chgrp 100 bar.sh
```

In addition to changing the owner and group of a file, it is often necessary to change the permissions of the owner, the group, and the "world" in respect to files. This is done via the `chmod` command. The basic syntax is

```
chmod [options][[g][u][o][a]][-/+/=][[r][w][x]][files]
```

where the letters g, u, o, and a (called the user part) specify whose access to the file is modified; the -, +, and = operators (called the operator part) specify how the access is changed; and the letters r, w, and x (called the permissions part) specify the permissions.

The letters in the user part have the following meanings:

u	The user who owns the file
g	Other users who are in the file's group
o	All other users
a	All users; the same as ugo

The functions of the operators are as follows:

+	Adds the specified permissions to the file
-	Removes the specified permissions from the file
=	Sets the permissions on the file to the specified permissions

The letters in the permissions part have the following meanings:

r	Permission to read the file
w	Permission to write to the file
x	Permission to execute the file

Here are a few examples to illustrate the use of chmod. To give the world read access to all files in a directory, use this command:

```
# chmod a+r *
```

Instead of a, you could also use guo. To stop anyone except the owner of .profile from writing to it, use this:

```
# chmod go-w .profile
```

To be a file miser, use this:

```
# chmod go-rwx ~/*
```

When specifying the user part or the permissions part, the order in which the letters are given is irrelevant. Thus the commands

```
# chmod guo+rx *
```

and

```
# chmod uog+xr *
```

are equivalent.

If more than one set of permission changes need to be applied to a file or files, you can use a comma-separated list; for example,

```
# chmod go-w,a+x a.out
```

removes the group and world write permissions on `a.out` and adds the execute permission for everyone.

The commands `chown`, `chgrp`, and `chmod` accept the following options:

`-c` or `--changes`	Describes files to which a change was made
`-f`, `--silent`, or `--quiet`	Prints no output or errors
`-v` or `--verbose`	Describes the actions done to each file
`-R` or `--recursive`	Recursively applies changes to a directory and its contents

The final file attribute that often needs to be changed is the timestamp. This can be changed via the `touch` command. The `touch` command is normally used to change the access or modification times of a file, but can also be used to create empty files. The basic syntax is

```
touch [options] [files]
```

By default, `touch` changes the access and modification times of a file to the current time and creates files that do not exist. For example,

```
# touch foo bar blatz
```

results in the files `foo`, `bar`, and `blatz` having their access and modification times changed to the current time. If either `foo`, `bar`, or `blatz` does not exist, `touch` tries to create the file. The only limitation is that `touch` cannot change files the current user does not own or for which the user does not have write permissions.

Some of the options `touch` understands are as follows:

`-a`, `--time=atime`, or `--time=access`	Changes access time only
`-c`	Doesn't create files that don't exist
`-m`, `--time=mtime`, or `--time=modify`	Changes modification time only
`--date=time`	Uses `time` instead of current time
`-r file` or `--reference=file`	Uses the times from `file` instead of the current time

One of the common uses of `touch` is to create a large number of files quickly for testing scripts that read and process filenames.

Disk Usage

The GNU disk usage utilities, `df` and `du`, are quite similar to their UNIX counterparts but implement a few nice options that make their output much easier to read and understand.

By default, both programs produce output in terms of blocks, which vary depending on the local machine (strict POSIX machines use 512 bytes per block, while others use 1024 bytes per block), but their output can be changed to be in kilobytes, megabytes, or gigabytes. The output options are as follows:

`-k` or `--kilobytes`	Prints in 1KB (1024-byte) blocks
`-m` or `--megabytes`	Prints in 1MB (1,048,576 bytes) blocks
`-h` or `--human-readable`	Appends a letter to indicate size (*K* for kilobytes, *M* for megabytes, *G* for gigabytes)

Find Utilities

The find utilities enable users to find files that meet given criteria and perform actions on those files. The three main utilities are `locate`, `find`, and `xargs`. The `locate` and `find` commands are used to locate files, and `xargs` is used to act on those files.

`locate`

The `locate` command is the simplest and fastest command available for finding files. It does not actually search the filesystem; instead, it searches through filename databases that contain a list of files that were in particular directory trees when the databases were last updated. Typically, the databases are updated nightly and thus are reasonably up-to-date for executables and libraries.

The basic syntax for `locate` is

```
locate [string1 ... stringN]
```

Any number of files can be specified, and `locate` runs through the database files and prints a list of matches. For example,

```
# locate bash emacs
```

prints a list of files that contain either of the strings `bash` or `emacs`. Some matches on my system include

```
/usr/bin/bashbug
/usr/local/bin/bash
/usr/local/man/man1/bash.1
```

```
/usr/lib/zoneinfo/Africa/Lumumbashi
/usr/doc/minicom-1.75-2/doc/Todo.emacskey.dif
/usr/local/bin/emacs
/usr/share/emacs/19.34/etc/emacs.1
```

In addition, `locate` also properly handles shell wildcards. Thus,

`# locate *[mM]akefile`

prints a list of `makefiles` on the system.

NOTE

Although not part of a GNU distribution, you'll find at least two other utilities installed on your Red Hat Linux system that also help locate, find, or point to commands and files. See the man pages for the `whereis` and `whatis` commands. The `whereis` command returns the location of binary, source, or man pages for programs. The `whatis` command returns a short description of a command derived from its man page.

If the filename databases are not being updated regularly on a system, the system administrator can update the databases by running the `updatedb` command manually. Usually, simply running `updatedb` without any options and waiting for it to finish is adequate, but sometimes it is necessary to specify the directories that should and should not be included. To facilitate this, `updatedb` understands the following options:

`--localpaths=path`	A list of non-network directories to put in the database; the default is `/`.
`--netpaths=path`	A list of network directories to put in the database; the default is `none`.
`--prunepaths=path`	A list of directories not to put in the database; the default is `'/tmp /usr/tmp /var/tmp /afs'`

find

The `find` command is much more powerful than `locate` and can be given extensive options to modify the search criteria. Unlike `locate`, `find` actually searches the disk (local or remote); thus, it is much slower but provides the most up-to-date information. The basic syntax of `find` is

`find` ***`directory`*** **`[`*`options`*`]`**

The most basic usage of `find` is to print the files in a directory and its subdirectories:

```
find directory -print
```

After learning about the `find` command, many new users quickly implement an alias or function as a replacement for `locate`:

```
find / -print | grep $1
```

Generally, this is a bad idea because most systems have network drives mounted, and `find` tries to access them, causing not only the local machine to slow down, but also remote machines. To exclude other filesystems during a find run, try using the –xdev option, like this:

```
# find / -name Makefile -print -xdev
```

This searches for any file named Makefile, starting at the root directory, but won't search other mounted or network-mounted filesystems, such as NFS (possibly mounted under the /mnt directory). Here's the correct way to get output such as `locate` from `find`:

```
find directories -name name -print
```

For example, use this line to find all `makefiles` in /usr/src/:

```
# find /usr/src -name "[mM]akefile" -print
```

The `-name` option accepts all shell metacharacters. An alternative to the preceding method for finding all files named `Makefile` or `makefile` is to use the non–case-sensitive `-iname` option instead of `-name`. You must use quotation marks to prevent your shell from misinterpreting wildcard characters (such as ? or *). For the truly adventurous, `find` also supports a `-regex` option.

In addition to specifying which filenames to find, `find` can be told to look at files of a specific size, type, owner, or permissions.

To find a file by size, use the following option:

```
-size n[bckw]
```

where *n* is the size and the letters stand for

b	512-byte blocks (default)
c	Bytes
k	Kilobytes (1024 bytes)
w	2-byte words

For example, to find all files in /usr larger than 100KB, use

```
# find /usr -size 100k
```

To find files by type, use the following option:

```
-type x
```

where *x* is one of the following letters:

b	Block (buffered) special
c	Character (unbuffered) special
d	Directory
p	Named pipe (FIFO)
f	Regular file
l	Symbolic link
s	Socket

Therefore, to find all symbolic links in /tmp, use the following:

```
# find /tmp -type l
```

In addition to simply printing out the filename, `find` can be told to print file information by specifying the `-ls` option. For example,

```
# find /var -name "log" -ls
```

produces the following output:

```
42842 1 drwxr-xr-x 2 root root 1024 Jul 17 14:29 /var/log/httpd
157168 1 -rw-r--r-- 1 root nobody 4 Aug 14 17:44 /var/run/httpd.pid
```

The output is similar in form to the output from `ls -il`.

The last option of interest for `find` is the `-exec` option, which allows for the execution of a command on each filename that matches the previous criteria. The basic syntax of the `-exec` option is

```
-exec [command [options]] '{}' ';'
```

The `-exec` option uses the string `'{}'` and replaces it with the name of the current file that was matched. The `';'` string is used to tell `find` where the end of the executed command is. For example, the following makes a list of all files that contain the word `foo` in the Linux source files:

```
# find /usr/src/linux -name "*.c" -exec grep -l foo '{}' ';'
```

(Note that the preceding command should appear all on one line.)

xargs

One of the biggest limitations of the -exec command is that it can only run the specified command on one file at a time. The xargs command solves this problem by enabling users to run a single command on many files at one time. In general, it is much faster to run one command on many files, because this cuts down on the number of commands that need to be started. Here's how to modify the preceding example to count the number of files with foo in them:

```
# find /usr/src/linux -name "*.c" -exec grep -l foo '{}' ';' ¦ wc -l
```

(Note that this command should appear all on one line.)

My version of the sources (780 files) included 27 files with the word foo in them, and it took about 44 seconds to find that out.

Now let's modify the command to run with xargs. First, you need to replace the -exec grep foo '{}' ';' part with an xargs to avoid having to start new greps for each file. The basic syntax for xargs is

```
xargs [options] [command [options]]
```

You don't need to specify filenames to xargs because it reads these from the standard input, so the xargs command is

```
xargs grep -l foo
```

To get a list of files for xargs to give to grep, use find to list the files in /usr/src/linux that end in .c:

```
# find /usr/src/linux -name "*.c"
```

Then attach the standard output of find to the standard input of xargs with a pipe:

```
# find /usr/src/linux -name "*.c" ¦ xargs grep -l foo
```

Finally, tack on a wc -l to get a count, and you have

```
# find /usr/src/linux -name "*.c" ¦ xargs grep -l foo ¦ wc -l
```

On my system, this took about 29 seconds, so xargs works considerably faster. The difference becomes even greater when more complex commands are run and the list of files is longer.

You need to be careful about filenames that contain spaces in them. Many people believe spaces are not valid characters in UNIX filenames, but they are, and handling them correctly is becoming an issue of greater importance because today many machines are able to mount and read disks from systems that frequently use spaces in filenames.

I routinely mount Macintosh HFS disks (Zip, floppy, hard disk), and many files on these disks have spaces in their filenames. The spaces confuse `xargs`, because it uses the newline (`\n`) and space characters as filename delimiters. The GNU version of `xargs` provides a pretty good workaround for this problem with the `--null` and `-0` options, which tell `xargs` to use the `null` character (`\0` or `\000`) as the delimiter. To generate filenames that end in `null`, `find` can be given the `-print0` option instead of `-print`.

As an illustration, here is an `ls` of my Macintosh's Zip Tools disk:

```
./              .resource/      Desktop DB*     System Folder/ ../
.rootinfo       Desktop DF*     Utilities/ .finderinfo/    Applications/
Icon:0d*
```

Notice that the Desktop DB and Desktop DF files have spaces in them, as does the System Folder directory. If I wanted to run through this Zip disk and remove all files that end in `prefs copy`, I would normally try

```
# find /mnt/zip -name "*prefs copy" -print ¦ xargs rm
```

This won't work, because I have a filename with spaces, but if I add `-print0`, I can do it with no problems:

```
# find /mnt/zip -name "*prefs copy" -print0 ¦ xargs rm
```

Two other useful options for `xargs` are the `-p` option, which makes `xargs` interactive, and the `-n args` option, which makes `xargs` run the specified command with only `args` number of arguments.

Some people wonder why there is a `-p` option. The reason is that `xargs` runs the specified command on the filenames from its standard input, so interactive commands such as `cp -i`, `mv -i`, and `rm -i` don't work right. The `-p` option solves that problem. In the preceding example, the `-p` option would have made the command safe because I could answer yes or no to each file. Thus, the command I typed was the following:

```
# find /mnt/zip -name "*prefs copy" -print0 ¦ xargs -p rm
```

Many users frequently ask why `xargs` should be used when shell command substitution archives the same results. The drawback with commands such as

```
# grep -l foo `find /usr/src/linux -name "*.c"`
```

is that if the set of files returned by `find` is longer than the system's command-line length limit, the command will fail. The `xargs` approach gets around this problem because `xargs` runs the command as many times as is required, instead of just once.

Shell Utilities

The GNU shell utilities are a package of small shell programming utilities. Table 22.3 lists the programs included in the package, along with a short description.

TABLE 22.3 GNU SHELL UTILITIES

Command	*Description*
basename	Strip filenames of directory info and suffixes
chroot	Root directory interactive shell or command execution
date	Show or change current date and time
dirname	Strip filenames of non-directory suffixes
echo	Print message, string of characters
env	Print or show current environment variables
expr	Expression evaluator
factor	Prime number generator
false	Shell scripting utility
groups	Show a user's groups
hostname	Show name of system
id	Display user and group IDs
logname	Show a user's login name
nice	Assign program execution priority
nohup	Run commands after logoff
pathchk	File and directory permission check utility
printenv	Print or show current environment variables
printf	Format and print data
pwd	Print current working directory
seq	Output sequences of numbers
sleep	Timed-delay program
stty	Terminal line settings utility
su	Become root, other user; run commands as another user
tee	Save portion of pipelined command
test	Shell script utility
true	Shell script utility
tty	Show terminal file name

Command	*Description*
uname	Show some of or all system information
users	Show currently logged-in users
who	Show currently logged-in users
whoami	Print current user name
yes	Repeatedly echo a string of characters

Who's Who in GNU

One of the first things many people do when they log on to a new machine is to see who else is logged on. The GNU shell utilities provide the commands `who` and `users` to give information about which users are currently logged on and what they are doing. The `users` command just prints out a list of names of people who are logged on. The `who` command is much more sophisticated.

NOTE

Want to save a few letters of typing if you need to use the `who` command? If you don't need all features of who, try `w`, which also shows who is logged on to your system.

In addition to giving information about who is logged on, `who` makes it possible to find out how long people have been idle, when they logged on, and if they are allowing other people to talk. Some of the options `who` recognizes are as follows:

`-H` or `--heading`	Prints a heading
`-T`, `-w`, or `--mesg`	Adds user message status as `+`, `-`, or `?`
`-i`, `-u`, or `--idle`	Adds user idle time as *`HOURS:MINUTES`*, `.`, (less than a minute), or `old` (greater than a day)

One of the useful features of `who` over `users` is that because `who` outputs one user entry per line, it can be used with such commands as `grep` or `sed` to process and format its output with ease (although you can use `gawk`, `perl`, or `tr` to format the user command's output).

The `id` Commands

The next set of frequently used commands are the `id` commands.

Knowing your own uid and gid and having the ability to determine other users' uids and gids are very handy skills.

Almost all users know about the commands whoami and groups, but many have never heard of id, which encompasses the functionality of the other two and adds the capability to determine user information about other people on the system.

By default, the id command prints out all identification information about the current user. When I run id on my system, I get (as myself)

```
uid=500(ranga) gid=100(users) groups=100(users)
```

But I can also run id on my brother's login name:

```
# id vathsa
```

and I get

```
uid=501(vathsa) gid=100(users) groups=500(vathsa)
```

I could have determined all of the preceding information by looking in /etc/passwd, but id is a much easier way of accomplishing the task.

In addition, the output of id can be tailored by using the following options:

-g or --group	Prints only the group ID
-G or --groups	Prints only the supplementary groups
-n or --name	Prints a name instead of a number
-r or --real	Prints the real ID instead of the effective ID
-u or --user	Prints only the user ID

Thus, the groups command is really just id -Gn and the whoami program is just id -un.

A related command is logname, used to determine the username that was used to log in. The logname command becomes useful if a user (usually the sysadmin) logs in to the system as different people and uses su extensively.

Checking What System You're Running

Everyone should know how to check for what system they are running. The command to use is uname, and it comes with a whole host of options. Usually, the most useful option is -a, which prints all of the information uname knows about. On my computer, uname -a prints

```
Linux kanchi 2.0.29 #4 Sat Jul 19 10:36:15 PDT 1997 i586
```

This is a complete summary of my system and even includes the version of the kernel I am running and when I last compiled it, along with my current architecture. Some of the other options for uname are

-m or --machine	Prints the machine (hardware) type
-n or --nodename	Prints the machine's network node hostname (usually the same as hostname)
-r or --release	Prints the operating system release
-s or --sysname	Prints the operating system name
-v	Prints the operating system version

Environment Variables and Shell Functions

The *environment* is a list of variables and shell functions the shell passes to every process that is started. Knowing about the environment and managing it properly are important because it affects the execution of many programs.

The two main commands for getting information and controlling the environment are printenv and env. If invoked without arguments, both commands will print a list of all of the current environment variables and shell functions.

The difference between the two is that env is used to manipulate the environment given to a process, and printenv is used to simply list information about the environment.

The primary use of env is to start a subshell or process in a clean environment when the current environment needs to be preserved. For example,

```
# env -i $0
```

starts another shell in a clean environment. The env command can also be used to set the environment:

```
# env DISPLAY=kanchi:0.1 netscape &
```

The preceding line starts up Netscape on my second display without affecting my environment. The options env understands are as follows:

-u or --unset=NAME	Removes named variable from the environment
-i or --ignore-environment	Starts with an empty environment

Text Utilities

The GNU text utilities contain programs that enable easy manipulation of large amounts of text. The programs in this distribution are listed in Table 22.4.

TABLE 22.4 GNU TEXT UTILITIES

Command	*Description*
cat	Display, copy, append input to designated file
cksum	Generate checksum of input file
comm	Compare two sorted input streams of text
csplit	Split input text according to designated patterns
cut	Remove designated fields of input text stream
expand	Convert tabs in input text to designated number of spaces
fmt	Simple text formatter
fold	Line-wrap utility for input text
head	Display designated number of lines from head of file
join	Merge lines of two files
md5sum	Checksum generator for message digests
nl	Number lines of input text
od	Octal, decimal, hexadecimal dump utility
paste	Merge lines in varying order from file(s)
pr	Format text file for viewing or printing
sort	Arrange input in alphabetical, dictionary, or reverse order
split	Break input text into pieces
sum	Generate checksum of a file
tac	Print appended files in reverse order
tail	Print designated number of lines from end of input
tr	Character, string transliteration utility
unexpand	Convert input's spaces to tabs
uniq	Remove adjacent, duplicate strings from input
wc	Count input's characters, words and lines

The `head` and `tail` Commands

What's a cat without a head and a tail? A very bad deal. Every `cat` should come with a `head` and a `tail`. Every GNU `cat` comes with them, so if you have one of those old system V cats, upgrade (it's easier than bathing your cat).

Seriously, at certain times it is nice to be able to output entire files at once or to squeeze multiple blank lines in a file into one line, but most often more control over which lines are displayed is required. The `head` and `tail` commands provide this control.

The head command shows the first ten (or n if -n is given) lines of its standard input. This is useful for viewing the tops of large README files, but its real power is in daily applications.

Take the following problem. Every day a list of the five largest mail spool files needs to be generated. The easiest solution is easier to see if the problem is broken down. First, to generate a list of the mail spool files and their sizes, use

```
# ls -1 /var/spool/mail
```

Next, to sort the list by size, give ls the -S (sort by size) option:

```
# ls -1S /var/spool/mail
```

To get a list of the five largest mail spool files, pipe the output of ls into head -5:

```
# ls -1S ¦ head -5
```

On my system, I get this list:

```
root
ranga
vathsa
amma
anna
```

Say you also want the five *oldest* mail spool files. Start with ls -1 again, but this time give the -t (sort by last accessed time) option instead of the -S option:

```
# ls -1t /var/spool/mail
```

To get the bottom five, use tail instead of head:

```
# ls -1t /var/spool/mail ¦ tail -5
```

On my system, I get (there are only five users on my system) this list:

```
anna
root
amma
vathsa
ranga
```

As a quick check with ls -l reveals, in this list the files are listed newest to oldest; to reverse the order, use tac (the reverse of cat):

```
# ls -1t /var/spool/mail ¦ tail -5 ¦ tac
```

On my system, I get this list:

```
ranga
vathsa
amma
```

```
root
anna
```

One other handy feature of `tail` is the `-f` option, which allows for examining files while they are growing. Often I have to look at the log files generated by programs I am debugging, but I don't want to wait for the program to finish, so I start the program and then `tail -f` the log file. Another common use for `tail -f` is

```
# tail -f /var/log/httpd/access_log
```

which can be used to watch the HTTP requests made for their system.

The `split` Command

The `split` command is probably one of the handiest commands for transporting large files. One of its most common uses is to split up compressed source files (to upload in pieces or fit on a floppy disk). The basic syntax is

```
split [options] filename [output prefix]
```

where the options and output prefix are optional. If no output prefix is given, `split` uses the prefix `x` and labels output files as `xaa`, `xab`, `xac`, and so on. By default, `split` puts 1000 lines in each of the output files (the last file can be fewer than 1000 lines), but because 1000 lines can mean variable file sizes, the `-b` or `--bytes` option is used. The basic syntax is

```
-b bytes[bkm]
```

or

```
--bytes=bytes[bkm]
```

where *`bytes`* is the number of bytes of size:

`b`	512 bytes
`k`	1KB (1024 bytes)
`m`	1MB (1,048,576 bytes)

Thus,

```
# split -b1000k JDK.tar.gz
```

splits the file JDK.tar.gz into 1000KB pieces. To get the output files to be labeled `JDK.tar.gz.`, you would use the following:

```
# split -b1000k JDK.tar.gz JDK.tar.gz.
```

This creates 1000KB files that could be copied to a floppy disk or uploaded one at a time over a slow modem link.

When the files reach their destination, you can join them by using `cat`:

```
# cat JDK.tar.gz.* > JDK.tar.gz
```

A useful command for confirming whether a split file has been joined correctly is `cksum`. Historically, it has been used to confirm if files have been transferred properly over noisy phone lines.

`cksum` computes a cyclic redundancy check (CRC) for each filename argument and prints out the CRC along with the filename and number of bytes in the file. The easiest way to compare the CRC for the two files is to get the CRC for the original file

```
# cksum JDK.tar.gz > JDK.crc
```

and then compare it to the output `cksum` for the joined file.

Counting Words

Counting words is a handy thing to be able to do, and there are many ways to do it. Probably the easiest is the `wc` command, which stands for "word count," but `wc` only prints the number of characters, words, or lines. What if you need a breakdown by word? It's a good problem, and one that serves to introduce the next set of GNU text utilities.

Here are the commands you need:

`tr`	Transliterate; changes the first set of characters it is given into the second set of characters it is given; also deletes characters
`sort`	Sorts the file (or its standard input)
`uniq`	Prints out all of the unique lines in a file (collapses duplicates into one line and optionally gives a count)

I used this chapter as the text for this example. First, this line gets rid of all the punctuation, braces, and so on, in the input file:

```
# tr '!?":;[]{}(),.' ' ' < ~/docs/ch16.doc
```

This demonstrates the basic use of `tr`:

```
# tr 'set1' 'set2'
```

It takes all of the characters in `set1` and transliterates them to the characters in `set2`. Usually, the characters themselves are used, but the standard C escape sequences work also (as you will see).

I specified `set2` as ' ' (the space character) because words separated by these characters need to remain separate. The next step is to transliterate all capitalized versions of words together because the words *To* and *to, The* and *the*, and *Files* and *files* are really the same word. To do the transliteration, tell tr to change all capital characters "A–Z" into lower-case characters "a–z":

```
# tr '!?":;[]{}(),.' ' ' < ~/docs/ch16.doc ¦
tr 'A-Z' 'a-z'
```

I broke the command into two lines, with the pipe character as the last character in the first line so the shell (sh, bash, ksh) will do the right thing and pipe to the next line. Reading and cutting and pasting from an xterm is easier this way, also, but it won't work under csh or tcsh unless you start one of the preceding shells.

Multiple spaces in the output can be squeezed into single spaces with

```
# tr '!?":;[]{}(),.' ' ' < ~/docs/ch16.doc ¦
tr 'A-Z' 'a-z' ¦  tr -s ' '
```

To get a count of how many times each word is used, you need to sort the file. In the simplest form, the sort command sorts each line, so you need to have one word per line to get a good sort. This code deletes all of the tabs (\t) and newlines (\n) and then changes all of the spaces into newlines:

```
# tr '!?":;[]{}(),.' ' ' < ~/docs/ch16.doc ¦
tr 'A-Z' 'a-z' ¦ tr -s ' ' ¦ tr -d '\t\n' ¦ tr ' ' '\n'
```

Now you can sort the output, so simply tack on the sort command:

```
# tr '!?":;[]{}(),.' ' ' < ~/docs/ch16.doc ¦
tr 'A-Z' 'a-z' ¦ tr -s ' ' ¦ tr -d '\t\n' ¦ tr ' ' '\n' ¦ sort
```

You could eliminate all repeats at this point by giving sort the -u (unique) option, but you need a count of the repeats, so use the uniq command. By default, the uniq command prints out "the unique lines in a sorted file, discarding all but one of a run of matching lines" [man page uniq(1)]. uniq requires sorted files because it only compares consecutive lines. To get uniq to print out how many times a word occurs, give it the -c (count) option:

```
# tr '!?":;[]{}(),.' ' ' < ~/docs/ch16.doc ¦
tr 'A-Z' 'a-z' ¦ tr -s ' ' ¦ tr -d '\t\n' ¦
tr ' ' '\n' ¦ sort ¦ uniq -c
```

Next you need to sort the output again, because the order in which the output is printed is not sorted by number. This time, to get sort to sort by numeric value instead of string comparison and have the largest number printed first, give sort the -n (numeric) and -r (reverse) options:

```
# tr '!?":;[]{}(),.' ' ' < ~/docs/ch16.doc ¦
tr 'A-Z' 'a-z' ¦ tr -s ' ' ¦ tr -d '\t\n' ¦
tr ' ' '\n' ¦ sort ¦ uniq -c ¦ sort -rn
```

The first few lines (ten actually—I piped the output to head) look like this:

```
389 the
164 to
127 of
115 is
115 and
111 a
 80 files
 70 file
 69 in
 65 '
```

Note that the tenth most common word is the single quotation character, but I said we took care of the punctuation with the very first tr. Well, I lied (sort of); we took care of all of the characters that would fit between quotation marks, and a single quotation mark won't fit. So why not just backslash escape that sucker? Well, not all shells can handle that properly.

What's the solution?

The solution is to use the predefined character sets in tr. The tr command knows several character classes, and the punctuation class is one of them. Here is a complete list (names and definitions) of class names, from the man page for uniq(1):

alnum	Letters and digits
alpha	Letters
blank	Horizontal whitespace
cntrl	Control characters
digit	Digits
graph	Printable characters, not including space
lower	Lowercase letters
print	Printable characters, including space
punct	Punctuation characters
space	Horizontal or vertical whitespace
upper	Uppercase letters
xdigit	Hexadecimal digits

The way to invoke tr with one of these character classes is '[:classname:]'. To get rid of punctuation, use the punct class:

```
# tr '[:punct:]' ' ' < ~/docs/ch16.doc ¦
tr 'A-Z' 'a-z' ¦ tr -s ' ' ¦ tr -d '\t\n' ¦
tr ' ' '\n' ¦ sort ¦ uniq -c ¦ sort -rn
```

Here's some of the new output:

```
405 the
170 to
136 a
134 of
122 and
119 is
 80 files
 74 file
 72 in
 67 or
```

The numbers are different for some of the words because I have been running the commands and writing the chapter at the same time.

I could also have replaced `'A-Z'` and `'a-z'` with the `upper` and `lower` classes, also, but there is really no advantage to using the classes, and the ranges are much more illustrative of the process.

Summary

This chapter covered the four major GNU utilities packages and the major commands in each of these packages. As you have seen in the various examples, the real power of these packages lies in their capability to help users break complex tasks down and solve them quickly.

Backup and Restore

by Bill Ball

In This Chapter

CHAPTER

Data is important, made valuable by both the time it took to create it and the uniqueness of the data. Therefore, you should take care not to lose that data.

Data can be lost in several different ways. The first is through carelessness. I do not know how many times I have restored data for people who have been in the wrong directory when they issued an `rm -r` command. The second way data can be lost is through hardware failure. Although newer hard drives are more reliable than the older ones, they still fail, and data is lost. A third way data is lost is faulty software. Too many times I have programmed a tool to perform a task, only to have the tool destroy my data instead of manipulating it. These days, programs are often released before they are ready. If there is a bug, the people who developed the software put out a patch; still, the data—and the time it took—are both gone. Finally, the earth can just swallow up entire buildings, or there can be earthquakes, or tornadoes, or volcanoes, or hurricanes, or aliens from outer space.

Backups can protect your investment in time and in data, but only if you are actually successful in backing up and keeping the information; therefore, part of a successful backup procedure is a test strategy to spot-check backups. The easiest way to spot-check your backups is to perform a restore with them, which you should attempt *before* it is actually needed.

Backups can take many forms. At one time, I worked for a company that had six servers. Their backup method was to `tar` servers and store a copy of that `tar` on another server. In addition, they did tape backups of the servers, which included the online version of the backups. These tape backups were used for disaster recovery purposes and kept off-site. This example shows a couple of different ways to perform backups—storing tarred copies on other machines and storing copies on tape backup (and keeping the copies off-site). The combination of these two methods provides a fairly reliable way of doing backups, covering everything from the simple "Oops, I accidentally deleted your database" to "Godzilla just stepped on our building, and we need the data back in less than two days!"

You need to understand the difference between a backup and an archive. A good backup strategy involves both forms of data protection. *Backups* are file operations to save your data at regular intervals, either in whole or incrementally (see "Backup Strategy," later in this chapter). *Archives* are file operations to save your data for long periods of time. For example, the CD-ROM included with this book is an archive of the free portions of Red Hat Linux.

This chapter covers what the qualities of a good backup are and the process of selecting a good backup medium and a backup tool. Finally, backup strategies are considered, including incremental and full backups and when to perform each.

Qualities of a Good Backup

Obviously, in the best of all possible worlds, backups would be perfectly reliable, always available, easy to use, and really fast. In the real world, trade-offs must be made. For example, backups stored offsite are good for disaster recovery, but are not always available.

Above all, backups need to be reliable. A reliable backup medium will last for several years. Of course, if the backups are never successfully written to the backup medium, it does not matter how good the medium is.

Speed is more or less important, depending on the system. If a time window is available when the system is not being used and the backup can be automated, speed is not an issue. On the other hand, restoration might be an issue. The time it takes to restore the data is important as the need to have the data available.

Availability is a necessary quality. Performing regular backups does no good if, when they are needed, they are unavailable. Backups for disaster recovery would not be available to restore a single file accidentally deleted by a user. A good backup and recovery scheme includes both a local set of backups for day-to-day restores and an offsite set of backups for disaster recovery purposes.

Fast, available, reliable backups are no good if they are not usable. The tools used for backup and restoration need to be easy to use. This is especially important for restoration. In an emergency, the person who normally performs the backup and restores might be unavailable, and a nontechnical user might have to perform the restoration. Obviously, documentation is a part of usability.

Selecting a Backup Medium

Today, many choices of backup media exist, although the three most common types for a long time were floppy disks, tapes, and hard drives. Table 23.1 rates these media—and newer ones such as CD-ROM read-only and CD-ROM read-write—in terms of reliability, speed, availability, and usability.

Table 23.1 BACKUP MEDIUM COMPARISON

Media	*Reliability*	*Speed*	*Availability*	*Usability*
Floppy disks	Good	Slow	High	Good with small data; bad with large data
CD-ROM RO	Good	Slow	High	Read-only media; OK for archives
CD-ROM RW	Good	Slow	Medium	Read-write media; economical for medium-sized systems
Iomega Zip	Good	Slow	High	100MB storage; OK for small systems
Flash ROM	Excellent	Fast	Low	Very expensive; currently limited to less than 200MB
Tapes	Good	Medium to fast	High	Depending on the size of the tape, can be highly usable; tapes cannot be formatted under Linux
Removable HD	Excellent	Fast	High	Relatively expensive, but available in sizes up to 2GB
Hard drives	Excellent	Fast	High	Highly usable

Writable CDs are good for archival purposes, and some formats can be overwritten; however, the expense tends to be high if a large number of regular archives or backups must be made. Flopticals, with attributes of both floppy and optical disks, tend to have the good qualities of floppy disks and tapes and are good for single file restoration. Flopticals can hold a lot of data, but have not captured the consumer market; they are popular in high-end, large-scale computing operations. More popular removable media are Iomega Zip and Jaz drives, which come in 100MB Zip and 1–2GB Jaz form factors.

Selecting a Backup Tool

Many tools are available for making backups. In addition to numerous third-party applications, Red Hat Linux comes with some standard tools for performing this task. This section examines two of them, `tar` and `cpio`.

NOTE

If you're looking for more sophisticated backup software, you can also try AMANDA, the Advanced Maryland Automatic Network Disk Archiver. This free software from the University of Maryland at College Park can be used over a network to back up multiple computer filesystems to a single, large-capacity tape drive. Some features include graceful error recovery, compression, scheduling, encryption, and high-speed backup operation. For more information, see `http://www.amanda.org`.

`tar` and `cpio` are very similar. Both are capable of storing and retrieving data from almost any medium. In addition, both `tar` and `cpio` are ideal for small systems, which Red Hat Linux systems often are. For example, the following `tar` command saves all files under /home to the default tape drive:

```
$ tar -c /home
```

The `-c` option tells `tar` which directory it is gathering files from—/home in the preceding example.

`cpio`, although similar to the `tar` command, has several advantages. First, it packs data more efficiently. Second, it is designed to back up arbitrary sets of files (`tar` is designed to back up subdirectories). Third, `cpio` is designed to handle backups that span over several tapes. Finally, `cpio` skips over bad sections on a tape and continues, but `tar` crashes and burns.

NOTE

The GNU version of `tar` included with Red Hat Linux has several options useful for file compression and multivolume backup operations. If you use the `z` option in the `tar` command line, `tar` uses gzip compression or decompression. To perform a multivolume backup or restore, use `tar`'s `M` option on the command line. For example, to create a compressed backup of the /home directory using multiple floppy disks, use **`tar -cvzMf /dev/fd0 /home`**.

Backup Strategy

The simplest backup strategy is to copy every file from the system to a tape. This is called a full backup. Full backups by themselves are good for small systems, such as those typically used by Red Hat Linux users.

The downside of a full backup is that it can be time-consuming. Restoring a single file from a large backup such as a tape archive can be almost too cumbersome to be of value. Sometimes a full backup is the way to go, and sometimes it is not. A good backup and recovery scheme identifies when a full backup is necessary and when incremental backups are preferred.

NOTE

If you use your Red Hat Linux system for business, you should definitely have a backup strategy. Creating a formal plan to regularly save critical information, such as customer accounts or work projects, is essential to avoid financial disaster. Even more important: After you devise your backup plan, stick to it!

Incremental backups tend to be done more frequently. With an incremental backup, only those files that have changed since the last backup are backed up. Therefore, each incremental builds upon previous incremental backups.

UNIX uses the concept of a backup level to distinguish different kinds of backups. A full backup is designated as a level 0 backup. The other levels indicate the files that have changed since the preceding level. For example, on Sunday evening you might perform a level 0 backup (full backup). Then on Monday night you would perform a level 1 backup, which backs up all files changed since the level 0 backup. Tuesday night would be a level 2 backup, which backs up all files changed since the level 1 backup, and so on. This gives way to two basic backup and recovery strategies. Here is the first:

Sunday	Level 0 backup
Monday	Level 1 backup
Tuesday	Level 1 backup
Wednesday	Level 1 backup
Thursday	Level 1 backup
Friday	Level 1 backup
Saturday	Level 1 backup

The advantage of this backup scheme is that it requires only two sets of backup media. Restoring the full system from the level 0 backup and the previous evening's incremental can perform a complete restore. The negative side is that the amount backed up grows throughout the week, and additional media might be needed to perform the backup. Here is the second strategy:

Sunday	Level 0 backup
Monday	Level 1 backup

Tuesday	Level 2 backup
Wednesday	Level 3 backup
Thursday	Level 4 backup
Friday	Level 5 backup
Saturday	Level 6 backup

The advantage of this backup scheme is that each backup is relatively quick. Also, the backups stay relatively small and easy to manage. The disadvantage is that it requires seven sets of media. Also, to do a complete restore, you must use all seven sets.

When deciding which type of backup scheme to use, you need to know how the system is used. Files that change often should be backed up more often than files that rarely change. Some directories, such as /tmp, never need to be backed up.

Performing Backups with tar and cpio

A full backup with `tar` is as easy as

```
$ tar -c /
```

An incremental backup takes a bit more work. Fortunately, the `find` command is a wonderful tool to use with backups to find all files that have changed since a certain date. It can also find files that are newer than a specified file. With this information, it is easy to perform an incremental backup. The following command finds all files that have been modified *today* and backs up those files with the `tar` command to an archive on /dev/rmt1:

```
$ tar c1 `find / -mtime -1 ! -type d -print`
```

The `! -type d` says that if the object found is a directory, don't give it to the `tar` command for archiving. This is done because `tar` follows the directories, and you don't want to back up an entire directory unless everything in it has changed. Of course, the `find` command can also be used for the `cpio` command. The following command performs the same task as the preceding `tar` command:

```
$ find / -mtime -1 ¦ cpio -o >/dev/rmt1
```

As mentioned, the `find` command can find files that are newer than a specified file. The `touch` command updates the time of a file; therefore, it is easy to touch a file after a backup has completed. Then, at the next backup, you simply search for files that are newer than the file you touched. The following example searches for files that are newer than the file /tmp/last_backup and performs a `cpio` to archive the data:

```
$ find / -newer /tmp/last_backup -print ¦ cpio -o > /dev/rmt0
```

With `tar`, the same action is completed this way:

```
$ tar c1 `find / -newer /tmp/last_backup -print`
```

NOTE

You will want to touch the file before you start the backup. This means you have to use different files for each level of backup, but it ensures that the next backup gets any files modified during the current backup.

Performing Backups with Red Hat's rhbackup Command

The `rhbackup` command, by Donnie Barnes of Red Hat Software, Inc., is found under the /usr/bin directory. This small shell script uses a number of Linux commands, such as `mt`, `mail`, `rsh`, and `tar`, and can be used to perform backups of your system, or other systems across a network, from the command line of a console terminal window. The main configuration file for `rhbackup` is /etc/sysconfig/tape. This file contains default settings for such things as:

- Name of the tape device to use (default is /dev/nst0)
- Who to email error messages to (default is root)
- The name, location and format of log files (/var/log/backup)
- The name of the backup table file (/etc/backuptab)

The `rhbackup` script's default backup table file, /etc/backuptab, contains directions about the different network computers and what files to either include or exclude from your backup. Before you use `rhbackup`, edit its default settings to suit your specific hardware and backup strategy. If you don't have a tape drive, you'll definitely need to change the default device setting in `rhbackup's` tape file. You should also edit `rhbackup's` backuptab file to include those directories or files you'd like excluded from your backups. Entries in backuptab look like this:

```
<your hostname> <directory to backup> <exclusion pattern>
```

Use the `rhbackup` command with one of its three command-line options:

- `–full`—To perform a full backup of the specified directories
- `–test`—To test the connectivity of network backup operations
- `–incremental`—To back up only newer files from the specified directories

Details about the `rhbackup` program can be found in its man page.

Performing Backups with the taper Script

The `taper` script, included with Red Hat Linux, is a backup and restore program with a graphical interface you can use to maintain compressed or uncompressed archives on tapes or removable media. Using `taper` is easy; the format of a `taper` command line looks like this:

```
# taper <-T device> <type> <option>
```

You first need to decide what type of device (or medium) you'd like to use with `taper`. This program supports a number of devices, which are listed in Table 23.2 along with the command lines to use.

Table 23.2 DEVICE SUPPORT BY TAPER

Device	*Type*	*Command Line*
/dev/zftape	Floppy tape driver	**# taper –T z**
/dev/ftape	Floppy tape driver	**# taper –T f**
/dev/fd0	Removable floppy drive	**# taper –T r**
/dev/sda4	Removable Zip drive	**# taper –T r –b /dev/sda4**
/dev/sda	SCSI tape drive	**# taper –T s**

After you start `taper` from the command line of your console or an X11 terminal window (you must be the root operator), you'll see a main menu of options to back up, restore, re-create, verify, set preferences, or exit, as shown in Figure 23.1.

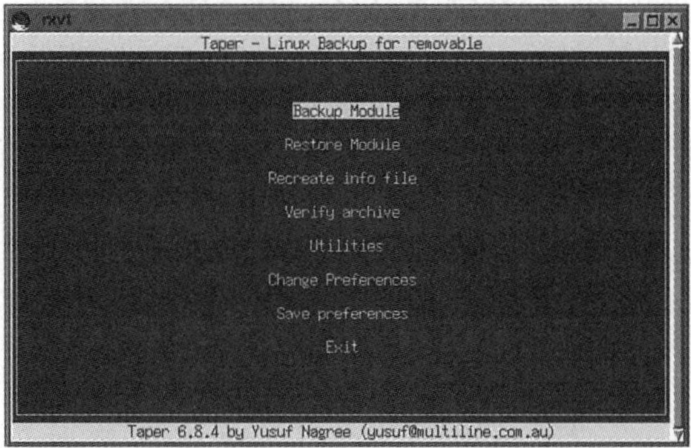

FIGURE 23.1.
The `taper` script offers a graphical interface to back up and restore operations for Linux.

Navigate through `taper`'s menus with your up or down arrow keys, and press the Enter key to make a selection. If you're not sure what keys to use, press the question mark (?) to have `taper` show a concise Help screen.

Start the backup process by selecting files or directories for your backup. First, highlight the Backup Module menu item and then press the Enter key. The `taper` script checks the status of the device you've specified on the command line and then looks for an existing tape archive on the device. If none is found, `taper` asks you to name the volume and then give a name for the new archive. You'll then see a directory listing similar to that in Figure 23.2.

FIGURE 23.2.
The `taper` script offers selective backup and restoration of your directories or files.

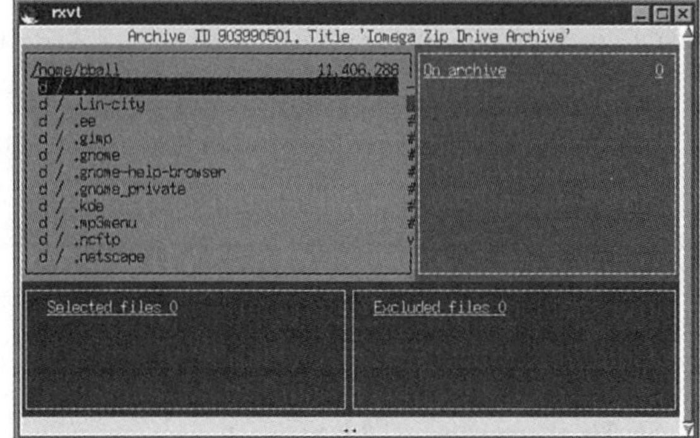

Next, navigate through the listings or directories, using the i or I key to select files or directories to back up. When you finish, press the f or F key to start backing up your files. The `taper` script has many features and can be customized through preference settings in its main menu. For detailed information, see its documentation under the /usr/doc/taper directory.

Performing Backups with BRU-2000

Red Hat Linux users who purchase the commercial distribution of Red Hat Linux will find a copy of Enhanced Software Technologies' BRU-2000-PE on the CD-ROM. BRU-2000-PE is a "personal edition" of a more complete, commercial network backup and restore program that features

- Command-line or graphical interface for X11
- Error detection during backup
- Data integrity verification following backup operations
- Backup and restore operations of live filesystems
- Built-in help
- Automatic recognition of compressed files (so archives don't become larger by trying to compress already compressed files or directories)
- Background mode, so backups can be scheduled

This software includes two commands: `bru` for backing up from the console and `xbru` for a graphical interface during X11 sessions. BRU-2000 uses several files and directories on your Linux file system. Much of the graphical interface support is found under the /usr/lib/bru directory, and the support file /etc/brutab is used to specify different backup devices.

The BRU-2000-PE software is installed by using the `rpm` or `glint` command (or during an initial installation of the commercial version of Red Hat Linux).

To do a full or incremental backup of your system, you must run BRU-2000 as the root operator. To use the graphical interface version, start the program by typing **`xbru`** at the command line of an X11 terminal window to see the main dialog as shown in Figure 23.3.

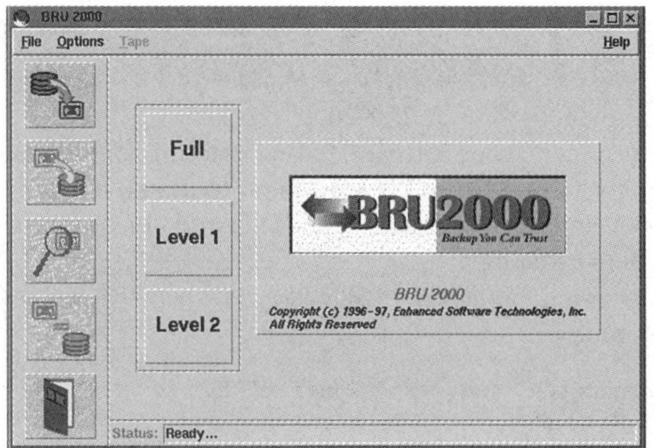

FIGURE 23.3
The BRU-2000 program is a commercial backup and restore program for nearly 20 operating systems, including Linux.

The program first checks the status of the default backup device, but you can configure the program to use one of more than 37 different devices for backup. You can also define new devices, such as Iomega Zip drives, to use for storing tape archives. To configure BRU-2000 to use a Zip disk as a backup device, select the Configure BRU menu item from the File menu. A new dialog appears, as shown in Figure 23.4.

FIGURE 23.4
To configure a new backup device for BRU-2000, select the Devices tab in its Configuration dialog.

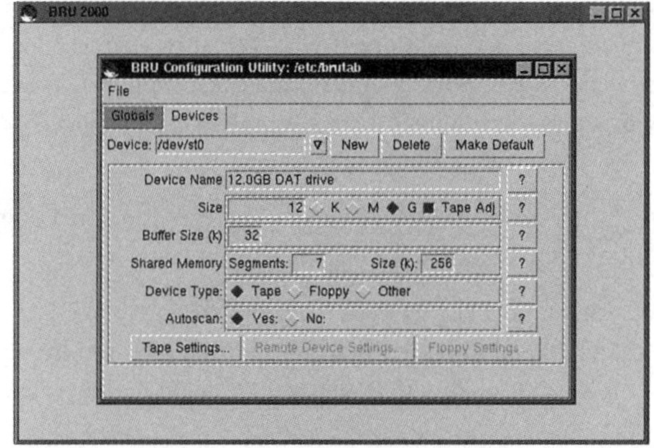

NOTE

If you have an older version of BRU-2000, check http://www.estinc.com/`brutabs.html` for important updated device table files such as jazzip.fix and zip.bt. You'll need them to use an Iomega Zip or Jaz disk with BRU-2000. First, you should add the following lines to the file /usr/lib/bru/unmounttape.tcl:

```
if [string match "/dev/hd*" $device] {
     exit 0
 }
 if [string match "/dev/sd*" $device] {
     exit 0
 }
```

Select the Devices tab and then select the New button. A New Device window appears, as shown in Figure 23.5. Type in the name of your Zip disk's device (for example, **`/dev/sda4`**), select the Device type as OTHER, and press the Create button. You can then type in a description of your Zip drive in the Device name field and set the size of the device as 95MB. Press the Save button, followed by the Exit button.

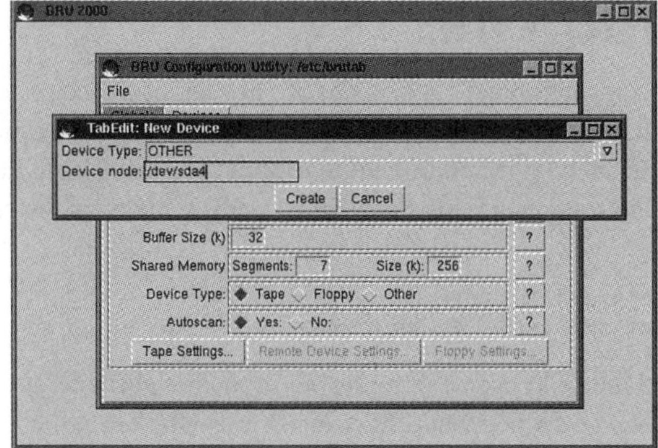

FIGURE 23.5
The New Device dialog is used to select a new backup device or create a new one for BRU-2000.

To select which files or directories to back up, either select Backup from the File menu or press the top button in BRU-2000's main dialog (as shown in Figure 23.3). A directory and file selection dialog appears, as shown in Figure 23.6. You can then choose the files or directories by highlighting the name and then pressing the Add button. When finished, press the Start Backup button to begin operation. If you want to use file compression or set other options, use the Options button before backing up.

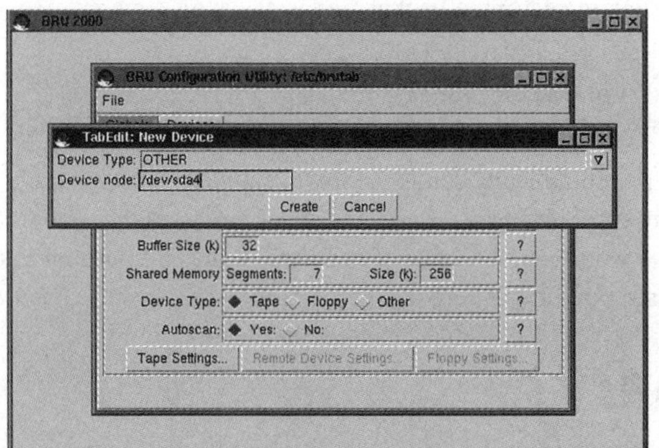

FIGURE 23.6
BRU-2000 offers numerous backup options and a selective file and directory backup dialog.

BRU-2000 has many options and features. After you finish your backup, you can restore your archive, test its integrity, and even view the contents of your archives. For more details, read BRU-2000's bru man page, check the /bru directory after installation, or browse to `http://www.estinc.com`.

Restoring Files

Backing up files is a good thing, but backups are like an insurance policy. When it is time for them to pay up, you want it all, and you want it now! To get the files, you must restore them. Fortunately, it is not difficult to restore files with either `tar` or `cpio`. The following command restores the file /home/alana/bethany.txt from the current tape in the drive:

```
$ tar -xp /home/alana/bethany.txt
$ cpio -im `*bethany.txt$` < /dev/rmt0
```

The `-p` in `tar` and the `-m` in `cpio` ensure that all of the file attributes are restored along with the file. By the way, when you restore directories with `cpio`, the `-d` option creates subdirectories. The `tar` command creates subdirectories automatically.

What Is on the Tape?

When you have a tape, you might not know what is on it. Perhaps you are using a multiple-level backup scheme and you don't know which day the file was backed up. Both `tar` and `cpio` offer a way of creating a table of contents for the tape. The most convenient time to create this TOC file, of course, is during the actual backup. The following two lines show how to perform a backup and at the same time create a table of contents file for that tape:

```
$ tar -cv / > /tmp/backup.Monday.TOC
$ find / -print ¦ cpio -ov > /dev/rmt0 2> /tmp/backup.Monday.TOC
```

The `cpio` backup automatically sends the list to standard error; therefore, this line just captures standard error and saves it as a file. By the way, if the > in the `tar` command is replaced with the word `tee`, the table of contents is not only written to the file; it is also printed to standard output (the screen).

Summary

Backups are important, but being able to restore the files is more important. Nothing will cause a lump to appear in the throat faster than trying to restore a system, only to find that the backups failed. As with any administrative task performed on a system, backups require a good plan, proper implementation, good documentation, and lots of testing. An occasional spot-check of a backup could save hours, if not days, of time.

CHAPTER

System Security

by David Pitts

In This Chapter

Security is one of the hottest topics in any system debate. How do you make your site more secure? How do you keep the hackers out of your system? How do you make sure your data is safe from intruders? How do you keep your company's secrets secret?

Your system is as secure as its weakest point. This is an old saying, and one that is still true. I am reminded of an Andy Griffith TV show in which the town drunk is sleeping off another episode in the jail. After he is sober, he looks around at the bars on the windows, the barred walls, and the gate. "A pretty secure jail," I thought, until the town drunk pushed open the door, said good-bye to Barney, and left. So much for the security!

Many times, systems are as secure as that jail. All the bars and locks are in place, but the door is left open. This chapter takes a look at some of the bars and locks and explains how to lock the door. More important, though, it explains how to conduct a security audit and where to go to get more information.

Security comes in many forms. Passwords and file permissions are your first two lines of defense. After that, things get difficult. Security breaches take many forms. To understand your particular system and the security issues relevant to your system, you should first develop a security audit.

Thinking About Security—An Audit

A security audit has three basic parts, each with many things to think about. First, you need to develop a plan, a set of security aspects to be evaluated. Second, you need to consider the tools available for evaluating the security aspects and choose ones that are suitable to your system. The third part of a security audit is knowledge-gathering—not only how to use the system, but what the users are doing with the system, break-in methods for your system, physical security issues, and much more. The following sections look at each of these three pieces of the audit and offer some direction about where to go for more information.

A Plan

The plan can be as complex as a formal document or as simple as a few notes scribbled on the back of a java receipt. Regardless of the complexity, the plan should at least list what aspects of the system you are going to evaluate, and how. This means asking two questions:

- What types of security problems could we have?
- Which ones can we (or should we) attempt to detect or fix?

To answer these questions, a few more questions might be necessary concerning the following areas:

- Accountability
- Change control and tracking
- Data integrity, including backups
- Physical security
- Privacy of data
- System access
- System availability

Based on discussion of these topics, a more detailed plan can be developed. As always, there will trade-offs; for example, privacy of data could mean that only certain people can log on to the system, which affects system access for the users. System availability is always in conflict with change control. For example, when do you change that failing hard drive on a 7×24 system? The bottom line is that your detailed plan should include a set of goals, a way of tracking the progression of the goals (including changes to the system), and a knowledge base of what types of tools are needed to do the job.

Tools

Having the right tools always makes the job easier—especially true when you are dealing with security issues. A number of tools are available on the Internet, including tools to check passwords, check system security, and protect your system. Some major UNIX-oriented security organizations assist the UNIX/Red Hat Linux user groups in discussing, testing, and describing tools available for use. CERT, CIAC, and the Linux Emergency Response Team are excellent sources of information for both the beginner and advanced system administrator.

The following list introduces many of the available tools. This should be a good excuse, however, to surf the Net and see what else is available.

`cops` — A set of programs: each checks a different aspect of security on a UNIX system. If any potential security holes do exist, the results are either mailed or saved to a report file.

`crack` — A program designed to find standard UNIX 8-character DES-encrypted passwords by standard guessing techniques.

`deslogin` — A remote login program that can be used safely across insecure networks.

`findsuid.tar.Z` — Finds changes in `setuid` (set user ID) and `setgid` (set group ID) files.

`freestone`	A portable, fully functional firewall implementation.
`gabriel`	A `satan` detector. `gabriel` gives the system administrator an early warning of possible network intrusions by detecting and identifying `satan`'s network probing.
`ipfilter`	A free packet filter that can be incorporated into any of the supported operating systems, providing IP packet-level filtering per interface.
`ipfirewall`	An IP packet-filtering tool, similar to the packet-filtering facilities provided by most commercial routers.
`kerberos`	A network authentication system for use on physically insecure networks. It allows entities communicating over networks to prove their identities to each other while preventing eavesdropping or replay attacks.
`merlin`	Takes a popular security tool (such as `tiger`, `tripwire`, `cops`, `crack`, or `spi`) and provides it with an easy-to-use, consistent graphical interface, simplifying and enhancing its capabilities.
`npasswd`	`passwd` replacement with password sanity check.
`obvious-pw.tar.Z`	An obvious password detector.
`opie`	Provides a one-time password system for POSIX-compliant, UNIX-like operating systems.
`pcheck.tar.Z`	Checks format of /etc/passwd; verifies root default `shell` and `passwd` fields.
Plugslot Ltd.	PCP/PSP UNIX network security and configuration monitor.
`rsaeuro`	A cryptographic toolkit providing various functions for the use of digital signatures, data encryption, and supporting areas (PEM encoding, random number generation, and so on).
`rscan`	Allows system administrators to execute complex (or simple) scanner scripts on one (or many) machines and create clean, formatted reports in either ASCII or HTML.
`satan`	The security analysis tool for auditing networks. In its simplest (and default) mode, `satan` gathers as much information about remote hosts and networks as possible by examining such network services as `finger`, NFS, NIS, `ftp` and `tftp`, and `rexd`.
`ssh`	Secure shell—a remote login program.
`tcp` wrappers	Can monitor and control remote access to your local `tftp`, `exec`, `ftp`, `rsh`, `telnet`, `rlogin`, `finger`, and `systat` daemons.

`tiger`	Scans a system for potential security problems.
`tis` firewall toolkit	Includes enhancements and bug fixes from version 1.2 and new proxies for HTTP/Gopher and X11.
`tripwire`	Monitors system for security break-in attempts.
`xp-beta`	An application gateway of X11 protocol. It is designed to be used at a site that has a firewall and uses SOCKS and/or CERN WWW Proxy.
`xroute`	Routes X packets from one machine to another.

As you can see, a few tools exist for your use. If you want a second reason for looking at these tools, keep in mind that people trying to break into your system know how to—and do—use these tools. This is where the knowledge comes in.

Knowledge Gathering

Someone once said a little knowledge goes a long way. As stated in the chapter opening, all the bells and whistles can be there, but if they are not active, they do no good. It is, therefore, important that the system staff, the users, and the keepers of the sacred root password all follow the security procedures put in place—that they gather all the knowledge necessary to adhere to those procedures.

I was at the bank the other day, filling out an application for a car loan. The person assisting me at the bank was at a copy machine in another room (I could see her through the window). Another banking person, obviously new, could be heard from his office, where he was having problems logging in to the bank's computer. He came out and looked around for the bank employee helping me. When he did not see her, I got his attention and pointed him toward the copy area. He thanked me and went to her and asked for the system's password because he could not remember it. She could not remember the password. He went back to his desk, checked a list of telephone numbers hanging on the wall by his phone, entered something into the computer, and was in. About that time, my bank person came out of the copy area, stuck her head in his office, and said that she recalled the password. He said he had it. She asked if he had done with the password what they normally do. He looked at his phone list and said yes. She left and returned to me at her desk.

This scenario is true. The unfortunate thing about it, besides the fact that at least two customers—the person with the employee trying to log in to the system and I—saw the whole thing, is that they didn't know, nor did they care, that others might be listening. To them it was business as usual. What can be learned from this? *Don't write down passwords!*

Not only should passwords not be written down, they should not be easily associated with the user. I'll give you two examples that illustrate this point. The first involves a wonderful man from the Middle East with whom I worked on a client site. He has three boys. As a proud father, he talks about them often. When referring to them individually, he uses their first names. When referring to them cumulatively, he calls them "three boys." His password (actually, he uses the same password for all his accounts) is `threeboys`.

The second example comes from one of the sweetest people I have met in the industry. She is an unmarried person with no children. On her desk is a little stuffed cow named Chelsea. I do not remember the significance of the name, but I remember that she really likes dairy cows. Her password is—you guessed it—`chelsea`. These peoples' passwords are probably still `threeboys` and `chelsea`.

File security is another big issue. The use of `umask` (file creation masks) should be mandated. It should also be set to the maximum amount possible. Changing a particular file to give someone else access to it is easy. Knowing who is looking at your files is difficult, if not impossible. The sensitivity of the data, of course, would certainly determine the exact level of security placed on the file. In extremely sensitive cases, such as employees' personnel records, encryption of the files might also be necessary.

After an audit has been done, you should have an excellent idea of what security issues you need to be aware of and which issues you need to track. The next section shows you how to track intruders.

Danger, Will Robinson, Danger!

I used to love watching *Lost in Space*. On that show was a life-sized robot that would declare, "Danger, Will Robinson, danger!" when there was some danger. Unfortunately, no such robot warns of danger on our systems. (Although some tools exist, they are nowhere near as consistent as that robot was!)

If you have a lot of extra disk space, you can turn on auditing, which records all user connects and disconnects from your system. If you don't rely on auditing, you should scan the logs often. A worthwhile alternative might be to write a quick summary script that gives an account of the amount of time each user is on the system.

Unfortunately, there are too many holes to block them all. Measures can be placed to plug the biggest of them, but the only way to keep a system secure is locking a computer in a vault, allowing no one access to it and no connectivity outside of the vault. The bottom line is, if users want into your system, and they are good enough, they can get in. What you have to do is prepare for the worst.

Preparing for the Worst

The three things that can be done to a system, short of physically removing it, are stealing data, destroying data, and providing easier access for next time. Physically, an intruder can destroy or remove equipment or, if very creative, even add hardware. Short of chaining the system to the desk, there is not much you can do to prevent theft. Physical security is beyond the scope of this book, anyway. What is within the scope of this book is dealing with the data and dealing with additional access measures.

Data should be backed up on a regular basis. The backed-up information, depending on how secure it needs to be, can be kept on a shelf next to the system or in a locked vault at an alternative location. A backup is the best way of getting back data that has been destroyed.

Most of the time, though, data is not just destroyed. A more common problem is that the data is captured. This could be actual company secrets or system configuration files. Keeping an eye on the system files is very important. Another good idea is to occasionally search for programs that have `suid` or `sgid` capability. It might be wise to search for `suid` and `sgid` files when the system is first installed, so later searches can be compared to this initial list.

`suid` and `sgid`

Many people talk about `suid` (set user ID) and `sgid` (set group ID) without clearly understanding them. The concept behind these powerful, yet dangerous, tools is that a program (not a script) is set to run as the owner or group set for the program, not as the person running the program. For example, say you have a program with `suid` set, and its owner is root. Users running the program run that program with the permissions of the owner instead of their own permissions. The `passwd` command is a good example of this. The file /etc/passwd is writable by root and readable by everyone. The `passwd` program has `suid` turned on; therefore, anyone can run the `passwd` program and change her password. Because the program is running as the user root, not the actual user, the /etc/passwd file can be written to.

The same concept holds true for `sgid`. Instead of the program running with the permissions and authority of the group associated with the person calling the program, the program is run with the permissions and authority of the group associated with the program.

How to Find `suid` and `sgid` Files

The `find` command once again comes in handy. With the following command, you can search the entire system, looking for programs with their `suid` or `sgid` turned on:

```
find / -perm -200 -o -perm -400 -print
```

SYSTEM SECURITY

Running the preceding `find` command when you first load a system is probably best, saving its output to a file readable only by root. Future searches can be performed and compared to this "clean" list of `suid` and `sgid` files to ensure that only the files that are supposed to have these permissions really do.

Setting `suid` and `sgid`

The set user ID and set group ID can be powerful tools for giving users the ability to perform tasks without the other problems that could arise if a user has the actual permissions of that group or user. However, these can be dangerous tools as well. When considering changing the permissions on a file to be either `suid` or `sgid`, keep in mind these two things:

- Use the lowest permissions needed to accomplish the task.
- Watch for back doors.

Using the lowest permissions means not giving a file an `suid` of root if at all possible. Often, a less privileged person's access can be configured to do the task. The same goes for `sgid`. Many times, setting the group to the appropriate non-sys group accomplishes the same task while limiting other potential problems.

Back doors come in many forms. A program that allows a shell is a back door. Multiple entrances and exits to a program are back doors. Keep in mind that if a user can run an `suid` program set to root and the program contains a back door (users can get out of the program to a prompt without actually exiting the program), the system keeps the effective user ID as what the program is set to (root), and the user now has root permissions.

With that said, how do you set a file to have the effective user be the owner of the file, or the effective group be the group of the file, instead of running as the user ID or the user's group ID of the person invoking the file? The permissions are added with the `chmod` command, as follows:

```
chmod u+s file(s)
chmod g+s file(s)
```

The first example sets `suid` for the file(s) listed. The second example sets `sgid` to the file(s) listed. Remember, `suid` sets the effective ID of the process to the owner associated with the file, and `sgid` sets the effective group's ID of the process to the group associated with the file. These cannot be set on nonexecutables.

File and Directory Permissions

As I stated in the introduction to this chapter, file and directory permissions are the basics for providing security on a system. These, along with the authentication system, provide the basis for all security. Unfortunately, many people do not know what permissions on directories mean, or they assume they mean the same thing they do on files. The following section describes the permissions on files; after that, the permissions on directories are described.

Files

The permissions for files are split into three sections: the owner of the file, the group associated with the file, and everyone else (the world). Each section has its own set of file permissions, which provide the ability to read, write, and execute (or, of course, to deny the same). These permissions are called a file's *filemode*. Filemodes are set with the `chmod` command.

The permissions of the object can be specified in two ways—the numeric coding system or the letter coding system. Using the letter coding system, the three sections are referred to as `u` for user, `g` for group, and `o` for other or `a` for all three. The three basic types of permissions are `r` for read, `w` for write, and `x` for execute. Combinations of `r`, `w`, and `x` with the three groups provide the permissions for files. In the following example, the owner of the file has read, write, and execute permissions, and everyone else has read access only:

```
shell:/home/dpitts$ ls -l test
-rwxr--r--    1 dpitts   users          22 Sep 15 00:49 test
```

The command `ls -l` tells the computer to give you a long (`-l`) listing (`ls`) of the file (`test`). The resulting line is shown in the second code line and tells you a number of things about the file. First, it tells you the permissions. Next, it tells you how many links the file has. It then tells you who owns the file (`dpitts`) and what group is associated with the file (`users`). Following the ownership section, the date and timestamp for the last time the file was modified is given. Finally, the name of the file is listed (`test`). The permissions are actually made up of four sections. The first section is a single character that identifies the type of object listed. Check Table 24.1 to determine the options for this field.

TABLE 24.1 OBJECT TYPE IDENTIFIER

Character	*Description*
-	Plain file
b	Block special file
c	Character special file
d	Directory

continues

TABLE 24.1 CONTINUED

Character	*Description*
`l`	Symbolic link
`p`	Named pipe
`s`	Socket

Following the file type identifier are the three sets of permissions: `rwx` (owner), `r--` (group), and `r--` (other).

NOTE

A small explanation needs to be made as to what read, write, and execute actually mean. For files, a user who has read capability can see the contents of the file, a user who has write capability can write to it, and a user who has execute permission can execute the file. If the file to be executed is a script, the user must have read and execute permissions to execute the file. If the file is a binary, just the execute permission is required to execute the file.

Directories

The permissions on a directory are the same as those used by files: read, write, and execute. The actual permissions, however, mean different things. For a directory, read access provides the capability to list the names of the files in the directory but does not allow the other attributes to be seen (owner, group, size, and so on.). Write access provides the capability to alter the directory contents. This means the user could create and delete files in the directory. Finally, execute access enables the user to make the directory the current directory.

Table 24.2 summarizes the differences between the permissions for a file and those for a directory.

TABLE 24.2 FILE PERMISSIONS VERSUS DIRECTORY PERMISSIONS

Permission	*File*	*Directory*
`r`	View the contents	Search the contents
`w`	Alter file contents	Alter directory contents
`x`	Run executable file	Make it the current directory

Combinations of these permissions also allow certain tasks. For example, I already mentioned that it takes both read and execute permission to execute a script. This is because the shell must first read the file to see what to do with it. (Remember the `#! /local/bin/perl` tells the shell to execute the `/local/bin/perl` executable, passing the rest of the file to the executable.) Other combinations allow certain functionality. Table 24.3 describes the combinations of permissions and what they mean, both for a file and for a directory.

TABLE 24.3 COMPARISON OF FILE AND DIRECTORY PERMISSION COMBINATIONS

Permission	*File*	*Directory*
`---`	Cannot do anything with it.	Cannot access it or any of its subdirectories.
`r--`	Can see the contents.	Can see the contents.
`rw-`	Can see and alter the contents.	Can see and alter the contents.
`rwx`	Can see and change the contents, as well as execute the file.	Can list the contents, add or remove files, and make the directory the current directory (`cd` to it).
`r-x`	If a script, can execute it. Otherwise, provides read and execute permission.	Provides capability to change to directory and list contents, but not to delete or add files to directory.
`--x`	Can execute if a binary.	Users can execute a binary they already know about.

As stated, the permissions can also be manipulated with a numeric coding system. The basic concept is the same as the letter coding system. As a matter of fact, the permissions look exactly alike—the difference is the way the permissions are identified. The numeric system uses binary counting to determine a value for each permission and sets them. Also, the `find` command can accept the permissions as an argument, using the `-perm` option. In that case, the permissions must be given in their numeric form.

With binary, you count from the right to the left. Therefore, if you look at a file, you can easily come up with its numeric coding system value. The following file has full permissions for the owner and read permissions for the group and the world:

```
shell:/home/dpitts$ ls -la test
-rwxr--r--   1 dpitts   users         22 Sep 15 00:49 test
```

This would be coded as `744`. Table 24.4 explains why.

TABLE 24.4 NUMERIC PERMISSIONS

Permission	*Value*
Read	4
Write	2
Execute	1

Permissions use an additive process; therefore, a person with read, write, and execute permissions to a file would have a `7` (4+2+1). Read and execute would have a value of `5`. Remember, there are three sets of values, so each section would have its own value.

Table 24.5 shows both the numeric system and the character system for the permissions.

TABLE 24.5 COMPARISON OF NUMERIC AND CHARACTER PERMISSIONS

Permission	*Numeric*	*Character*
Read-only	4	`r--`
Write-only	2	`-w-`
Execute-only	1	`--x`
Read and write	6	`rw-`
Read and execute	5	`r-x`
Read, write, and execute	7	`rwx`

Permissions can be changed by using the `chmod` command. With the numeric system, the `chmod` command must be given the value for all three fields. Therefore, to change a file to read, write, and execute for everyone, you would issue the following command:

```
$ chmod 777 <filename>
```

To perform the same task with the character system, you would issue the following command:

```
$ chmod a+rwx <filename>
```

Of course, more than one type of permission can be specified at one time. The following command adds write access for the owner of the file and adds read and execute access to the group and everyone else:

```
$ chmod u+w,og+rx <filename>
```

The advantage the character system provides is that you do not have to know the previous permissions. You can selectively add or remove permissions without worrying about the rest. With the numeric system, each section of users must always be specified. The downside of the character system is apparent when complex changes are being made. Looking at the preceding example (`chmod u+w,og+rx <filename>`), an easier way might have been to use the numeric system and replace all those letters with three numbers: `755`.

How suid and sgid Fit into This Picture

The special-purpose access modes `suid` and `sgid` add an extra character to the picture. Before looking at what a file looks like with the special access modes, check Table 24.6 for the identifying characters for each of the modes and a reminder about what they mean.

TABLE 24.6 SPECIAL-PURPOSE ACCESS MODES

Code	*Name*	*Meaning*
s	suid	Sets process user ID on execution
s	sgid	Sets process group ID on execution

`suid` and `sgid` are used on executables; therefore, the code is placed where the code for the executable would normally go. The following file has `suid` set:

```
$ ls -la test
-rwsr--r--    1 dpitts   users          22 Sep 15 00:49 test
```

The difference between setting the `suid` and setting the `sgid` is the placement of the code. The same file with `sgid` active would look like this:

```
$ ls -la test
-rwxr-sr--    1 dpitts   users          22 Sep 15 00:49 test
```

To set the `suid` with the character system, you execute the following command:

```
$ chmod u+s <filename>
```

To set the `sgid` with the character system, you execute the following command:

```
$ chmod g+s <filename>
```

To set the `suid` and the `sgid` using the numeric system, use these two commands:

```
$ chmod 2### <filename>
$ chmod 4### <filename>
```

In both instances, you replace the `###` with the rest of the values for the permissions. The additive process is used to combine permissions; therefore, the following command adds `suid` and `sgid` to a file:

```
$ chmod 6### <filename>
```

NOTE

A sticky bit is set by using `chmod 1### <filename>`. If a sticky bit is set, the executable is kept in memory after it has finished executing. The display for a sticky bit is a `t`, placed in the last field of the permissions. Therefore, a file that has been set to `7777` would have the following permissions: `-rwsrwsrwt`.

The Default Mode for a File or Directory

The default mode for a file or directory is set with the `umask`, which uses the numeric system to define its value. To set the `umask`, you must first determine the value you want the files to have. For example, a common file permission set is `644`, with which the owner has read and write permission and the rest of the world has read permission. After the value is determined, you subtract it from `777`. Keeping the same example of `644`, the value would be `133`. This value is the `umask` value. Typically, this value is placed in a system file that is read when a user first logs on. After the value is set, all files created will set their permissions automatically, using this value.

Passwords—A Second Look

The system stores the user's encrypted password in the /etc/passwd file. If the system is using a shadow password system, the value placed in this field is `x`. A value of `*` blocks login access to the account, as `*` is not a valid character for an encrypted field. This field should never be edited by hand (after it is set up), but a program such as `passwd` should be used so proper encryption takes place. If this field is changed, the old password is no longer valid and more than likely will have to be changed by root.

NOTE

If the system is using a shadow password system, a separate file exists called /etc/shadow that contains passwords (encrypted, of course).

A password is a secret set of characters set up by the user and known only by the user. The system asks for the password, compares the input to the known password, and, if there is a match, confirms the user's identity and lets the user access the system. It cannot be said enough: Do not write down your password. A person who has a user's name and password is, from the system's perspective, that user, with all of that user's rights and privileges.

Related WWW Sites

Table 24.7 shows the more standard locations to find some of the tools discussed in this chapter. Other Web sites have these tools as well, but these were chosen because they will probably still be around when this book is published and you are looking for the information. As a matter of fact, I checked these sites a year after originally putting them here for the 2nd edition, and only two entries needed to be changed for the 3rd edition.

TABLE 24.7 WWW SITES FOR TOOLS

Tool	*Address*
cops	ftp://ftp.cert.org/pub/tools/cops
crack	ftp://ftp.cert.org/pub/tools/crack
deslogin	ftp://ftp.uu.net/pub/security/des
findsuid.tar.Z	ftp://isgate.is/pub/unix/sec8/findsuid.tar.Z
freestone	ftp.soscorp.com/pub/sos/freestone
gabriel	ftp://ftp.best.com/pub/lat
ipfilter	http://cheops.anu.edu.au/~avalon/ip-filter.html
ipfirewall	ftp://ftp.nebulus.net/pub/bsdi/security
kerberos	http://www.contrib.andrew.cmu.edu/usr/db74/kerberos.html
merlin	http://ciac.llnl.gov/
obvious-pw.tar.Z	ftp://isgate.is/pub/unix/sec7/obvious-pw.tar.Z
pcheck.tar.Z	ftp://isgate.is/pub/unix/sec8/pcheck.tar.Z
Plugslot Ltd.	http://www.var.org/~greg/PCPPSP.html
rsaeuro	ftp://ftp.ox.ac.uk/pub/crypto/misc/
rscan	http://www.umbc.edu/rscan/
satan	http://www.fish.com/satan
Secure Telnet	ftp://idea.sec.dsi.unimi.it/cert-it/stel.tar.gz
ssh	http://www.cs.hut.fi/ssh/
tcp wrappers	ftp://ftp.win.tue.nl/pub/security/
telnet (encrypted)	ftp.tu-chemnitz.de/pub/Local/informatik/sec_tel_ftp/
tiger	ftp://wuarchive.wustl.edu/packages/security/TAMU/
tis firewall	ftp://ftp.tis.com/pub/firewalls/toolkit/toolkit
tripwire	ftp://wuarchive.wustl.edu/packages/security/tripwire/

continues

TABLE 24.7 CONTINUED

Tool	*Address*
`xp-beta`	`ftp://ftp.mri.co.jp/pub/Xp-BETA/`
`xroute`	`ftp://ftp.x.org/contrib/utilities/`

Summary

Security is only as good as the users' willingness to follow the policies. This is, on many systems and in many companies, where the contention comes in. The users just want to get their jobs done. The administrators want to keep undesirables out of the system. The corporate management wants to keep the corporate secrets secret. Security is, in many ways, the hardest area in which to get users to cooperate, but is, in fact, the most important. Users who write down or share passwords, poorly written software, and maliciousness are the biggest security problems.

For the administrator in charge of the system, I can only offer this advice: The best user will only follow the policies you follow. If you have poor security habits, they will be passed along. On the other hand, people generally rise to the minimum level they see exhibited or expected. The job of the administrator is to go beyond the call of duty and gently point out improvements, while at the same time fighting the dragons at the back gate trying to get into the system.

Automation, Programming, and System Modification

PART IV

IN THIS PART

Shell Programming

by Bill Ball

In This Chapter

When you enter commands from the command line, you are entering commands one at a time and getting a response from the system. From time to time you will need to execute more than one command, one after the other, and get the final result—you can do so with a *shell program* or *shell script*. A shell program is a series of Linux commands and utilities that have been put into a file by using a text editor. When you execute a shell program, the commands are interpreted and executed by Linux one after the other.

You can write shell programs and execute them like any other command under Linux. You can also execute other shell programs from within a shell program if they are in the search path. A shell program is like any other programming language and has its own syntax. You can define variables and assign various values and so on. These are discussed in this chapter.

Your Red Hat Linux CD-ROM that accompanies this book comes with a rich assortment of capable, flexible, and powerful shells. These shells have numerous built-in commands, configurable command-line prompts, and features such as command-line history and editing. Table 25.1 lists each shell, along with its description and location in your Red Hat Linux file system.

Table 25.1 SHELLS WITH RED HAT LINUX

Name	*Description*	*Location*
`ash`	A small shell	/bin/ash
`ash.static`	A version of ash not dependent on software libraries	/bin/ash.static
`bash`	The Bourne Again SHell	/bin/bash
`bsh`	A symbolic link to ash	/bin/bsh
`csh`	The C shell, a symbolic link to tcsh	/bin/csh
`ksh`	The public-domain Korn shell	/bin/ksh, /usr/bin/ksh
`pdksh`	A symbolic link to ksh	/usr/bin/pdksh
`rsh`	The restricted shell(for network operation)	/usr/bin/rsh
`sh`	A symbolic link to bash	/bin/sh
`tcsh`	A csh-compatible shell	/bin/tcsh
`zsh`	A compatible csh, ksh, and sh shell	/bin/zsh

Creating and Executing a Shell Program

Say you want to set up a number of aliases whenever you log on. Instead of typing all of the aliases every time you log on, you can put them in a file by using a text editor such as `vi`, and then execute the file.

Here is a list of what is contained in a sample file created for this purpose, `myenv`:

```
alias ll 'ls -l'
alias dir 'ls'
alias copy 'cp'
```

`myenv` can be executed in a variety of ways under Linux.

You can make `myenv` executable by using the `chmod` command as follows, and then execute it as you would any other native Linux command:

```
# chmod +x myenv
```

This turns on the executable permission of `myenv`. You need to ensure one more thing before you can execute `myenv`—the file `myenv` must be in the search path. You can get the search path by executing

```
# echo $PATH
```

If the directory where the file `myenv` is located is not in the current search path, you must add the directory name in the search path.

Now you can execute the file `myenv` from the command line as if it were a Linux command:

```
# myenv
```

NOTE

The first line in your shell program should start with a pound sign (#). The pound sign tells the shell that the line is a comment. Following the pound sign, you must have an exclamation point (!), which tells the shell to run the command following the exclamation point and to use the rest of the file as input for that command. This is common practice for all shell scripting. For example, if you write a shell script for `bash`, the first line of your script would contain `#!/bin/bash`.

A second way to execute myenv under a particular shell, such as pdksh, is as follows:

```
# pdksh myenv
```

This invokes a new pdksh shell and passes the filename myenv as a parameter to execute the file.

> **NOTE**
>
> The pdksh shell, originally by Eric Gisin, is a public-domain version of the ksh shell, and is found under the /usr/bin directory as a symbolic link. In Red Hat Linux, pdksh is named ksh. Two symbolic links, /usr/bin/pdksh and /usr/bin/ksh, point to the pdksh shell. For more information about pdksh, see the /usr/doc/pdksh directory or the ksh man page.

You can also execute myenv from the command line as follows:

Command Line	*Environment*
# . myenv	pdksh and bash
# source myenv	tcsh

The dot (.) is a way of telling the shell to execute the file myenv. In this case, you do not have to ensure that execute permission of the file has been set. Under tcsh, you have to use the source command instead of the dot (.) command.

After executing the command myenv, you should be able to use dir from the command line to get a list of files under the current directory, and ll to get a list of files with various attributes displayed. However, the best way to use the new commands in myenv is to put them into your shell's login or profile file. For Red Hat Linux users, the default shell is bash, so make these commands available for everyone on your system by putting them in the file profile under the /etc directory.

> **NOTE**
>
> If you find you'd prefer to use a shell other than bash after logging into Red Hat Linux, use the chsh command. You'll be asked for your password and the location and name of the new shell (from Table 25.1). The new shell will become your default shell (but only if its name is in the list of acceptable system shells in /etc/shells).

Variables

Linux shell programming is a full-fledged programming language and as such supports various types of variables. Variables have three major types: environment, built-in, and user.

Environment variables are part of the system environment, and you do not have to define them. You can use them in your shell program; some of them, such as PATH, can also be modified within a shell program.

Built-in variables are provided by the system; unlike environment variables, you cannot modify them.

User variables are defined by you when you write a shell script. You can use and modify them at will within the shell program.

A major difference between shell programming and other programming languages is that in shell programming, variables are not typecast; that is, you do not have to specify whether a variable is a number or a string and so on.

Assigning a Value to a Variable

Say you want to use a variable called `lcount` to count the number of iterations in a loop within a shell program. You can declare and initialize this variable as follows:

Command	*Environment*
`lcount=0`	`pdksh` and `bash`
`set lcount = 0`	`tcsh`

NOTE

Under `pdksh` and `bash`, you must ensure that the equals sign (=) does not have space before and after it.

As shell programming languages do not use typed variables, the same variable can be used to store an integer value one time and a string another time. This is not recommended, however, and you should be careful not to do this.

To store a string in a variable, you can use the following:

Command	*Environment*
`myname=Sanjiv`	pdksh and bash
`set myname = Sanjiv`	tcsh

The preceding can be used if the string does not have embedded spaces. If a string has embedded spaces, you can do the assignment as follows:

Command	*Environment*
`myname='Sanjiv Guha'`	pdksh and bash
`set myname = 'Sanjiv Guha'`	tcsh

Accessing Variable Values

You can access the value of a variable by prefixing the variable name with a `$` (dollar sign). That is, if the variable name is `var`, you can access the variable by using `$var`.

If you want to assign the value of `var` to the variable `lcount`, you can do that as follows:

Command	*Environment*
`lcount=$var`	pdksh and bash
`set lcount = $var`	tcsh

Positional Parameters

It is possible to write a shell script that takes a number of parameters at the time you invoke it from the command line or from another shell script. These options are supplied to the shell program by Linux as *positional parameters*, which have special names provided by the system. The first parameter is stored in a variable called `1` (number 1) and can be accessed by using `$1` within the program. The second parameter is stored in a variable called `2` and can be accessed by using `$2` within the program, and so on. One or more of the higher numbered positional parameters can be omitted while you're invoking a shell program.

For example, if a shell program `mypgm` expects two parameters—such as a first name and a last name—you can invoke the shell program with only one parameter, the first name. However, you cannot invoke it with only the second parameter, the last name.

Here's a shell program called `mypgm1`, which takes only one parameter (a name) and displays it on the screen:

```
#Name display program
```

```
if [ $# == 0]
then
   echo "Name not provided"
else
   echo "Your name is "$1
```

If you execute `mypgm1` as follows in `pdksh` and `bash`:

```
# . mypgm1
```

you get the following output:

```
Name not provided
```

However, if you execute `mypgm1` as follows:

```
# . mypgm1 Sanjiv
```

you will get the following output:

```
Your name is Sanjiv
```

The shell program `mypgm1` also illustrates another aspect of shell programming, the built-in variables. In `mypgm1`, the variable `$#` is a built-in variable and provides the number of positional parameters passed to the shell program.

Built-in Variables

Built-in variables are special variables Linux provides to you, which can be used to make decisions within a program. You cannot modify the values of these variables within the shell program.

Some of these variables are

`$#`	Number of positional parameters passed to the shell program
`$?`	Code of the last command or shell program executed within the shell program
`$0`	The name of the shell program
`$*`	A single string of all arguments passed at the time of invocation of the shell program

To show these built-in variables in use, here is a sample program called `mypgm2`:

```
#my test program
echo "Number of parameters is "$#
echo "Program name is "$0
echo "Parameters as a single string is "$*
```

If you execute mypgm2 from the command line in pdksh and bash as follows:

```
# . mypgm2 Sanjiv Guha
```

you get the following result:

```
Number of parameters is 2
Program name is mypgm2
Parameters as a single string is Sanjiv Guha
```

Special Characters

Some characters have special meaning to Linux shells, so using them as part of variable names or strings causes your program to behave incorrectly. If a string contains such special characters, you also have to use escape characters (backslashes, discussed below) to indicate that the special characters should not be treated as special characters.

Some of these special characters are shown in Table 25.2.

Table 25.2 SPECIAL SHELL CHARACTERS

Character	*Explanation*
$	Indicates the beginning of a shell variable name
|	Pipes standard output to next command
#	Starts a comment
&	Executes a process in the background
?	Matches one character
*	Matches one or more characters
>	Output redirection operator
<	Input redirection operator
`	Command substitution (the backquote or backtick—the key above the Tab key on most keyboards)
>>	Output redirection operator (to append to a file)
[ ]	Lists a range of characters
[a-z]	Means all characters a through z
[a,z]	Means characters a or z
. *filename*	Executes the file *filename*
Space	Delimiter between two words

A few characters deserve special note. They are the double quotes ("), the single quotes ('), the back slash (\), and the backtick (`), all discussed in the following sections. Also note you can use input and output redirection from inside your shell scripts. Be sure to use output redirection with care when testing your shell programs, as you can easily overwrite files!

Double Quotes

If a string contains embedded spaces, you can enclose the string in double quotes (") so the shell interprets the whole string as one entity instead of more than one. For example, if you assigned the value of `abc def` (`abc` followed by one space followed by `def`) to a variable called `x` in a shell program as follows, you would get an error because the shell would try to execute `def` as a separate command.

Command	*Environment*
`x=abc def`	`pdksh` and `bash`
`set x = abc def`	`tcsh`

What you need to do is surround the string in double quotes:

Command	*Environment*
`x="abc def"`	`pdksh` and `bash`
`set x  = "abc def"`	`tcsh`

The double quotes resolve all variables within the string. Here is an example for `pdksh` and `bash`:

```
var ="test string"
newvar="Value of var is $var"
echo $newvar
```

Here is the same example for `tcsh`:

```
set var = "test string"
set newvar = "Value of var is $var"
echo $newvar
```

If you execute a shell program containing these three lines, you get the following result:

```
Value of var is test string
```

Single Quotes

You can surround a string with single quotes (') to stop the shell from resolving a variable. In the following example, the double quotes in the preceding example have been changed to single quotes.

pdksh and bash:

```
var ='test string'
newvar='Value of var is $var'
echo $newvar
```

tcsh:

```
set var = 'test string'
set newvar = 'Value of var is $var'
echo $newvar
```

If you execute a shell program containing these three lines, you get the following result:

```
Value of var is $var
```

As you can see, the variable var did not get resolved.

Backslash

You can use a backslash (\) before a character to stop the shell from interpreting the succeeding character as a special character. Say you want to assign a value of $test to a variable called var. If you use the following command, a null value is stored in var.

Command	*Environment*
var=$test	pdksh and bash
set var = $test	tcsh

This happens because the shell interprets $test as the value of the variable test. No value has been assigned to test, so var contains null. You should use the following command to correctly store $test in var:

Command	*Environment*
var=\$test	pdksh and bash
set var = \$test	tcsh

The backslash (\) before the dollar sign ($) signals to the shell to interpret the $ as any other ordinary character and not to associate any special meaning to it.

Backtick

You can use the backtick (`) character to signal the shell to execute the string delimited by the backtick. This can be used in shell programs when you want the result of execution of a command to be stored in a variable. For example, if you want to count the number of lines in a file called test.txt in the current directory and store the result in a variable called var, you can use the following command:

Command	*Environment*
`var=`wc -l test.txt``	`pdksh` and `bash`
`set var = `wc -l test.txt``	`tcsh`

Comparison of Expressions

The way the logical comparison of two operators (numeric or string) is done varies slightly in different shells. In `pdksh` and `bash`, a command called `test` can be used to achieve comparisons of expressions. In `tcsh`, you can write an expression to accomplish the same thing.

pdksh and bash

This section covers comparisons using the `pdksh` or `bash` shells. Later in the chapter, the section "`tcsh`" contains a similar discussion for the `tcsh` shell.

The syntax of the `test` command is as follows:

```
test expression
```

or

```
[ expression ]
```

Both forms of `test` commands are processed the same way by `pdksh` and `bash`. The `test` commands support the following types of comparisons:

- String comparison
- Numeric comparison
- File operators
- Logical operators

String Comparison

The following operators can be used to compare two string expressions:

`=`	To compare if two strings are equal
`!=`	To compare if two strings are not equal
`-n`	To evaluate if the string length is greater than zero
`-z`	To evaluate if the string length is equal to zero

Next are some examples comparing two strings, `string1` and `string2`, in a shell program called `compare1`.

```
string1="abc"
string2="abd"
if [ string1 = string2 ] then
   echo "string1 equal to string2"
else
   echo "string1 not equal to string2"
fi

if [ string2 != string1 ] then
   echo "string2 not equal to string1"
else
   echo "string2 equal to string1"
fi

if [ string1 ] then
   echo "string1 is not empty"
else
   echo "string1 is empty"
fi

if [ -n string2 ] then
   echo "string2 has a length greater than zero"
else
   echo "string2 has length equal to zero"
fi

if [ -z string1 ]
   echo "string1 has a length equal to zero"
else
  echo "string1 has a length greater than zero"
fi
```

If you execute `compare1`, you get the following result:

```
string1 not equal to string2
string2 not equal to string1
string1 is not empty
string2 has a length greater than zero
string1 has a length greater than zero
```

If two strings are not equal in size, the system pads the shorter string with trailing spaces for comparison. That is, if the value of `string1` is `abc` and that of `string2` is `ab`, `string2` will be padded with trailing spaces for comparison purposes—that is, it will have a value of `ab `.

Number Comparison

The following operators can be used to compare two numbers:

`-eq`	To compare if two numbers are equal
`-ge`	To compare if one number is greater than or equal to the other number
`-le`	To compare if one number is less than or equal to the other number
`-ne`	To compare if two numbers are not equal
`-gt`	To compare if one number is greater than the other number
`-lt`	To compare if one number is less than the other number

The following examples compare two numbers, `number1` and `number2`, in a shell program called `compare2`.

```
number1=5
number2=10
number3=5

if [ number1 -eq number3 ] then
   echo "number1 is equal to number3"
else
   echo "number1 is not equal to number3"
fi

if [ number1 -ne number2 ] then
   echo "number1 is not equal to number2"
else
   echo "number1 is equal to number2"
fi

if [ number1 -gt number2 ] then
   echo "number1 is greater than number2"
else
   echo "number1 is not greater than number2"
fi

if [ number1 -ge number3 ] then
   echo "number1 is greater than or equal to number3"
else
   echo "number1 is not greater than or equal to number3"
fi

if [ number1 -lt number2 ] then
   echo "number1 is less than number2"
else
   echo "number1 is not less than number2"
```

```
fi

if [ number1 -le number3 ] then
   echo "number1 is less than or equal to number3"
else
   echo "number1 is not less than or equal to number3"
fi
```

When you execute the shell program compare2, you get the following results:

```
number1 is equal to number3
number1 is not equal to number2
number1 is not greater than number2
number1 is greater than or equal to number3
number1 is less than number2
number1 is less than or equal to number3
```

File Operators

The following operators can be used as file comparison operators:

-d	To ascertain if a file is a directory
-f	To ascertain if a file is a regular file
-r	To ascertain if read permission is set for a file
-s	To ascertain if the name of a file has a length greater than zero
-w	To ascertain if write permission is set for a file
-x	To ascertain if execute permission is set for a file

Assume that a shell program called compare3 contains a file called file1 and a subdirectory dir1 under the current directory. Assume file1 has a permission of r-x (read and execute permission) and dir1 has a permission of rwx (read, write, and execute permission).

The code for compare3 would look like this:

```
if [ -d dir1 ] then
   echo "dir1 is a directory"
else
   echo "dir1 is not a directory"
fi

if [ -f dir1 ] then
   echo "file1 is a regular file"
else
   echo "file1 is not a regular file"
fi

if [ -r file1 ] then
   echo "file1 has read permission"
else
```

```
   echo "file1 does not have read permission"
fi

if [ -w file1 ] then
   echo "file1 has write permission"
else
   echo "file1 does not have write permission"
fi

if [ -x dir1 ] then
   echo "dir1 has execute permission"
else
   echo "dir1 does not have execute permission"
fi
```

If you execute the file `compare3`, you get the following results:

```
dir1 is a directory
file1 is a regular file
file1 has read permission
file1 does not have write permission
dir1 has execute permission
```

Logical Operators

Logical operators are used to compare expressions using the rules of logic; the characters represent `NOT`, `AND`, and `OR`.

`!`	To negate a logical expression
`-a`	To logically `AND` two logical expressions
`-o`	To logically `OR` two logical expressions

tcsh

As stated earlier, the comparisons are different under `tcsh` than they are under `pdksh` and `bash`. This section explains the same concepts as the section "`pdksh` and `bash`" but uses the syntax necessary for the `tcsh` shell environment.

String Comparison

The following operators can be used to compare two string expressions:

`==`	To compare if two strings are equal
`!=`	To compare if two strings are not equal

The following examples compare two strings, `string1` and `string2`, in the shell program `compare1`:

```
set string1 = "abc"
set string2 = "abd"

if  (string1 == string2)  then
   echo "string1 equal to string2"
else
   echo "string1 not equal to string2"
endif

if  (string2 != string1)  then
   echo "string2 not equal to string1"
else
   echo "string2 equal to string1"
endif
```

If you execute `compare1`, you get the following results:

```
string1 not equal to string2
string2 not equal to string1
```

Number Comparison

These operators can be used to compare two numbers:

>=	To compare if one number is greater than or equal to the other number
<=	To compare if one number is less than or equal to the other number
>	To compare if one number is greater than the other number
<	To compare if one number is less than the other number

The next examples compare three numbers, `number1`, `number2`, and `number3`, in a shell program called `compare2`:

```
set number1 = 5
set number2 = 10
set number3 = 5

if  (number1 > number2)  then
   echo "number1 is greater than number2"
else
   echo "number1 is not greater than number2"
endif

if  (number1 >= number3) then
   echo "number1 is greater than or equal to number3"
else
   echo "number1 is not greater than or equal to number3"
```

```
endif

if  (number1 < number2)  then
   echo "number1 is less than number2"
else
   echo "number1 is not less than number2"
endif

if  (number1 <= number3) then
   echo "number1 is less than or equal to number3"
else
   echo "number1 is not less than or equal to number3"
endif
```

Executing the shell program `compare2`, you get the following results:

```
number1 is not greater than number2
number1 is greater than or equal to number3
number1 is less than number2
number1 is less than or equal to number3
```

File Operators

These operators can be used as file comparison operators:

`-d`	To ascertain if a file is a directory
`-e`	To ascertain if a file exists
`-f`	To ascertain if a file is a regular file
`-o`	To ascertain if a user is owner of a file
`-r`	To ascertain if read permission is set for a file
`-w`	To ascertain if write permission is set for a file
`-x`	To ascertain if execute permission is set for a file
`-z`	To ascertain if file size is zero

The following examples are based on a shell program called `compare3` that contains a file called file1 and a subdirectory dir1 under the current directory. Assume that file1 has a permission of `r-x` (read and execute permission) and dir1 has a permission of `rwx` (read, write, and execute permission).

The following is the code for the `compare3` shell program:

```
if  (-d dir1) then
   echo "dir1 is a directory"
else
   echo "dir1 is not a directory"
endif

if (-f dir1)  then
   echo "file1 is a regular file"
```

```
else
   echo "file1 is not a regular file"
endif

if (-r file1) then
   echo "file1 has read permission"
else
   echo "file1 does not have read permission"
endif

if (-w file1) then
   echo "file1 has write permission"
else
   echo "file1 does not have write permission"
endif

if (-x dir1) then
   echo "dir1 has execute permission"
else
   echo "dir1 does not have execute permission"
endif

if (-z file1) then
   echo "file1 has zero length"
else
   echo "file1 has greater than zero length"
endif
```

If you execute the file `compare3`, you get the following results:

```
dir1 is a directory
file1 is a regular file
file1 has read permission
file1 does not have write permission
dir1 has execute permission
file1 has greater than zero length
```

Logical Operators

Logical operators are used with conditional statements. These operators are used to negate a logical expression or to perform logical `AND`s and `OR`s.

`!`	To negate a logical expression
`&&`	To logically `AND` two logical expressions
`||`	To logically `OR` two logical expressions

Iteration Statements

Iteration statements are used to repeat a series of commands contained within the iteration statement.

The for Statement

The `for` statement has a number of formats. The first format is as follows:

```
for curvar in list
do
    statements
done
```

This form should be used if you want to execute *`statements`* once for each value in *`list`*; for each iteration, the current value of the list is assigned to `vcurvar`. *`list`* can be a variable containing a number of items or a list of values separated by spaces. This format of the `for` statement is used by `pdksh` and `bash`.

The second format is as follows:

```
for curvar
do
    statements
done
```

In this form, the *`statements`* are executed once for each of the positional parameters passed to the shell program. For each iteration, the current value of the positional parameter is assigned to the variable `curvar`.

This form can also be written as follows:

```
for curvar in "$@"
do
    statements
done
```

Remember that `$@` provides you a list of positional parameters passed to the shell program, all strung together.

Under `tcsh`, the `for` statement is called `foreach`. The format is as follows:

```
foreach curvar (list)
    statements
end
```

In this form, *`statements`* are executed once for each value in *`list`* and, for each iteration, the current value of *`list`* is assigned to `curvar`.

Suppose you want to create a backup version of each file in a directory to a subdirectory called backup. You can do the following in pdksh and bash:

```
for filename in `ls`
do
   cp $filename backup/$filename
   if [ $? -ne 0 ] then
      echo "copy for $filename failed"
   fi
done
```

In the preceding example, a backup copy of each file is created; if the copy fails, a message is generated.

The same example in tcsh is as follows:

```
foreach filename (`ls`)
   cp $filename backup/$filename
   if $? -ne 0 then
      echo "copy for $filename failed"
   fi
end
```

The while Statement

The while statement can be used to execute a series of commands while a specified condition is true. The loop terminates as soon as the specified condition evaluates to false. It is possible that the loop will not execute at all if the specified condition evaluates to false right at the beginning. You should be careful with the while command, as the loop will never terminate if the specified condition never evaluates to false.

In pdksh and bash, the following format is used:

```
while expression
do
    statements
done
```

In tcsh, the following format is used:

```
while (expression)
    Statements
end
```

If you want to add the first five even numbers, you can use the following shell program in pdksh and bash:

```
loopcount=0
result=0
while [ $loopcount -lt 5 ]
do
   loopcount = `expr $loopcount + 1`
   result = `$result + ($loopcount * 2)`
done

echo "result is $result"
```

In tcsh, this program can be written as follows:

```
set loopcount = 0
set result = 0
while ( $loopcount < 5 )
   set loopcount  =  `expr $loopcount + 1`
   set result  =  `$result + ($loopcount * 2)`
end

echo "result is $result"
```

The until Statement

The until statement can be used to execute a series of commands until a specified condition is true. The loop terminates as soon as the specified condition evaluates to true.

In pdksh and bash, the following format is used:

```
until expression
do
    statements
done
```

As you can see, the format is similar to the while statement.

If you want to add the first five even numbers, you can use the following shell program in pdksh and bash:

```
loopcount=0
result=0
until [ $loopcount -ge 5 ]
do
   loopcount = `expr $loopcount + 1`
   result = `$result + ($loopcount * 2)`
done

echo "result is $result"
```

The example here is identical to the example for the while statement, except the condition being tested is just the opposite of the condition specified in the while statement.

The tcsh command does not support the until statement.

The repeat Statement (tcsh)

The `repeat` statement is used to execute only one command a fixed number of times.

If you want to print a hyphen (-) 80 times on the screen, you can use the following command:

```
repeat  80 echo '-'
```

The select Statement (pdksh)

The `select` statement is used to generate a menu list if you are writing a shell program that expects input from the user online. The format of the `select` statement is as follows:

```
select  item in itemlist
do
    Statements
done
```

`itemlist` is optional. If not provided, the system iterates through the entries in `item` one at a time. If, however, `itemlist` is provided, the system iterates for each entry in `itemlist`, and the current value of `itemlist` is assigned to `item` for each iteration, which then can be used as part of the statements being executed.

If you want to write a menu that gives the user a choice of picking a `Continue` or a `Finish`, you can write the following shell program:

```
select  item in Continue Finish
do
   if [ $item = "Finish" ] then
      break
   fi
done
```

When the `select` command is executed, the system displays a menu with numeric choices to the user—in this case, `1` for `Continue`, and `2` for `Finish`. If the user chooses `1`, the variable `item` contains a value of `Continue`; if the user chooses `2`, the variable `item` contains a value of `Finish`. When the user chooses `2`, the `if` statement is executed and the loop terminates.

The shift Statement

The `shift` statement is used to process the positional parameters, one at a time, from left to right. As you remember, the positional parameters are identified as `$1`, `$2`, `$3`, and so on. The effect of the `shift` command is that each positional parameter is moved one position to the left and the current `$1` parameter is lost.

The format of the `shift` command is as follows:

```
shift  number
```

The parameter *number* is the number of places to be shifted and is optional. If not specified, the default is `1`; that is, the parameters are shifted one position to the left. If specified, the parameters are shifted *number* positions to the left.

The `shift` command is useful when you are writing shell programs in which a user can pass various options. Depending on the specified option, the parameters that follow can mean different things or might not be there at all.

Conditional Statements

Conditional statements are used in shell programs to decide which part of the program to execute depending on specified conditions.

The `if` Statement

The `if` statement evaluates a logical expression to make a decision. An `if` condition has the following format in `pdksh` and `bash`:

```
if [ expression ] then
    Statements
elif [expression ] then
    Statements
else
    Statements
fi
```

The `if` conditions can be nested. That is, an `if` condition can contain another `if` condition within it. It is not necessary for an `if` condition to have an `elif` or `else` part. The `else` part is executed if none of the expressions specified in the `if` statement and optional in subsequent `elif` statements are true. The word `fi` is used to indicate the end of the `if` statements, which is very useful if you have nested `if` conditions. In such a case you should be able to match `fi` to `if` to ensure that all `if` statements are properly coded.

In the following example, a variable `var` can have either of two values: `Yes` or `No`. Any other value is an invalid value. This can be coded as follows:

```
if [ $var = "Yes" ] then
   echo "Value is Yes"
elif [ $var = "No" ] then
   echo "Value is No"
else
   echo "Invalid value"
```

```
fi
```

In tcsh, the if statement has two forms. The first form, similar to the one for pdksh and bash, is as follows:

```
if (expression) then
    Statements
else if (expression) then
    Statements
else
    Statements
endif
```

The if conditions can be nested—that is, an if condition can contain another if condition within it. It is not necessary for an if condition to have an else part. The else part is executed if none of the expressions specified in any of the if statements are true. The optional if (else if (*expression*) then) part of the statement is executed if the condition following it is true and the previous if statement is not true. The word endif is used to indicate the end of the if statements, which is very useful if you have nested if conditions. In such a case you should be able to match endif to if to ensure that all if statements are properly coded.

Remember the example of the variable var having only two values, Yes and No, for pdksh and bash? Here is how it would be coded with tcsh:

```
if ($var == "Yes") then
   echo "Value is Yes"
else if ($var == "No" ) then
   echo "Value is No"
else
   echo "Invalid value"
endif
```

The second form of if condition for tcsh is as follows:

```
if (expression) command
```

In this format, only a single command can be executed if the expression evaluates to true.

The case Statement

The case statement is used to execute statements depending on a discrete value or a range of values matching the specified variable. In most cases, you can use a case statement instead of an if statement if you have a large number of conditions.

The format of a case statement for pdksh and bash is as follows:

```
case str in
   str1 | str2)
```

```
      Statements;;
   str3¦str4)
      Statements;;
   *)
      Statements;;
esac
```

You can specify a number of discrete values—such as `str1`, `str2`, and so on—for each condition, or you can specify a value with a wildcard. The last condition should be `*` (asterisk) and is executed if none of the other conditions are met. For each of the specified conditions, all of the associated statements until the double semicolon (`;;`) are executed.

You can write a script that will echo the name of the month if you provide the month number as a parameter. If you provide a number other than one between 1 and 12, you will get an error message. The script is as follows:

```
case $1 in
   01 ¦ 1) echo "Month is January";;
   02 ¦ 2) echo "Month is February";;
   03 ¦ 3) echo "Month is March";;
   04 ¦ 4) echo "Month is April";;
   05 ¦ 5) echo "Month is May";;
   06 ¦ 6) echo "Month is June";;
   07 ¦ 7) echo "Month is July";;
   08 ¦ 8) echo "Month is August";;
   09 ¦ 9) echo "Month is September";;
   10) echo "Month is October";;
   11) echo "Month is November";;
   12) echo "Month is December";;
   *) echo "Invalid parameter";;
esac
```

You need to end the statements under each condition with a double semicolon(`;;`). If you do not, the statements under the next condition will also be executed.

The format for a `case` statement for `tcsh` is as follows:

```
switch (str)
   case str1¦str2:
      Statements
      breaksw
   case str3¦str4:
      Statements
      breaksw
   default:
      Statements
      breaksw
endsw
```

You can specify a number of discrete values—such as `str1`, `str2`, and so on—for each condition, or you can specify a value with a wildcard. The last condition should be `default` and is executed if none of the other conditions are met. For each of the specified conditions, all of the associated statements until `breaksw` are executed.

The example that echoes the month when a number is given, shown earlier for `pdksh` and `bash`, can be written in `tcsh` as follows:

```
switch  ( $1 )
   case 01 | 1:
      echo "Month is January"
      breaksw
   case 02 | 2:
      echo "Month is February"
      breaksw
   case 03 | 3:
      echo "Month is March"
      breaksw
   case 04 | 4:
      echo "Month is April"
      breaksw
   case 05 | 5:
      echo "Month is May"
      breaksw
   case 06 | 6:
      echo "Month is June"
      breaksw
   case 07 | 7:
      echo "Month is July";;
      breaksw
   case 08 | 8:
      echo "Month is August";;
      breaksw
   case 09 | 9:
      echo "Month is September"
      breaksw
   case 10:
      echo "Month is October"
      breaksw
   case 11:
      echo "Month is November"
      breaksw
   case 12:
      echo "Month is December"
      breaksw
   default:
      echo "Invalid parameter"
      breaksw
endsw
```

You need to end the statements under each condition with `breaksw`. If you do not, the statements under the next condition will also be executed.

Miscellaneous Statements

You should be aware of two other statements: the `break` statement and the `exit` statement.

The `break` Statement

The `break` statement can be used to terminate an iteration loop, such as a `for`, `until`, or `repeat` command.

The `exit` Statement

`exit` statements can be used to exit a shell program. You can optionally use a number after `exit`. If the current shell program has been called by another shell program, the calling program can check for the code and make a decision accordingly.

Functions

As with other programming languages, shell programs also support *functions*. A function is a piece of shell program that performs a particular process that can be used more than once in the shell program. Writing a function helps you write shell programs without duplication of code.

Following is the format of a function in `pdksh` and `bash` for function definition:

```
func(){
   Statements
}
```

You can call a function as follows:

```
func param1 param2 param3
```

The parameters *`param1`*, *`param2`*, and so on are optional. You can also pass the parameters as a single string—for example, `$@`. A function can parse the parameters as if they were positional parameters passed to a shell program.

An example is a function that displays the name of the month or an error message if you pass a month number. Here is the example, in `pdksh` and `bash`:

```
Displaymonth() {
   case $1 in
      01 | 1) echo "Month is January";;
      02 | 2) echo "Month is February";;
      03 | 3) echo "Month is March";;
      04 | 4) echo "Month is April";;
      05 | 5) echo "Month is May";;
      06 | 6) echo "Month is June";;
      07 | 7) echo "Month is July";;
      08 | 8) echo "Month is August";;
      09 | 9) echo "Month is September";;
      10) echo "Month is October";;
      11) echo "Month is November";;
      12) echo "Month is December";;
      *) echo "Invalid parameter";;
   esac
}

displaymonth 8
```

The preceding program displays the following:

```
Month is August
```

Summary

In this chapter, you have been introduced to the syntax of shell programming, and you have learned how to write a shell program. Shell programs can be used to write programs that do simple things, such as setting a number of aliases when you log on, or complicated things, such as customizing your shell environment.

CHAPTER 26

gawk Programming

by Bill Ball

IN THIS CHAPTER

gawk, or GNU awk, is one of the newer versions of the awk programming language created for UNIX by Alfred V. Aho, Peter J. Weinberger, and Brian W. Kernighan in 1977. The name awk comes from the initials of the creators' last names. Kernighan was also involved with the creation of the C programming language and UNIX; Aho and Weinberger were involved with the development of UNIX. Because of their backgrounds, you will see many similarities between awk and C.

Several versions of awk exist: the original awk, nawk, POSIX awk, and—of course—gawk. nawk was created in 1985 and is the version described in *The awk Programming Language*. POSIX awk is defined in the *IEEE Standard for Information Technology, Portable Operating System Interface, Part 2: Shell and Utilities Volume 2*, ANSI-approved, April 5, 1993. (IEEE is the Institute of Electrical and Electronics Engineers, Inc.) GNU awk is based on POSIX awk.

Red Hat Linux users will find that the awk command, under both the /bin and /usr/bin directories, is actually a symbolic link to the /bin/gawk program. In addition to a short manual page for (g)awk included under the /usr/man/man1 directory, a wealth of information about (g)awk programming can be found under the /usr/doc/gawk directory.

If you only need a short, quick-reference guide to gawk, thank Specialized Systems Consultants, Inc. (SSC, the publishers of *Linux Journal*) for their five-color awk guide, found in the file awkcard.ps. For a more thorough and scholarly dissertation about using gawk, see Arnold D. Robbins's 335-page *Gawk User Manual* in the file gawk.ps. Both documents (in PostScript format) can be read online or printed by using the gv X11 PostScript viewer from the command line of an X11 terminal window like this:

```
# gv /usr/doc/gawk*/*.ps
```

The awk language (in all of its versions) is a pattern-matching and processing language with a lot of power. It will search a file (or multiple files) for records that match a specified pattern. When a match is found, a specified action is performed. As a programmer, you do not have to worry about opening, looping through the file reading each record, handling end-of-file, or closing the file when done. These details are handled automatically for you.

Creating short awk programs is easy because of this functionality—many of the details are handled by the language automatically. Its many functions and built-in features handle many of the tasks of processing files.

Applications

You'll find many possible uses for awk, including extracting data from a file, counting occurrences within a file, and creating reports.

The basic syntax of the awk language matches the C programming language; if you already know C, you know most of awk. In many ways, awk is an easier version of C because of the way it handles strings and arrays (dynamically). If you do not know C yet, learning awk will make learning C a little easier.

awk is also very useful for rapid prototyping or trying out an idea that will be implemented in another language, such as C. Instead of having to worry about some of the minute details, you can let the built-in automation take care of them, and you can worry about the basic functionality.

TIP

awk works with text files, not binary. Because binary data can contain values that look like record terminators (newline characters)—or not have any values at all—awk gets confused. If you need to process binary files, look into Perl or use a traditional programming language such as C.

Features

Like the UNIX environment, awk is flexible, contains predefined variables, automates many of the programming tasks, provides the conventional variables, supports the C-formatted output, and is easy to use. awk lets you combine the best of shell scripts and C programming.

With usually many different ways to perform the same task within awk, programmers get to decide which method is best suited to their applications. Many of the common programming tasks are automatically performed with awk's built-in variables and functions. awk automatically reads each record, splits it up into fields, and performs type conversions whenever needed. The way a variable is used determines its type—you have no need (or method) to declare variables of any type.

Of course, the "normal" C programming constructs such as `if/else`, `do/while`, `for`, and `while` are supported. awk doesn't support the `switch/case` construct but does supports C's `printf()` for formatted output and also has a `print` command for simpler output.

awk Fundamentals

Unlike some of the other UNIX tools (shell, grep, and so on), awk requires a program (known as an awk script). This program can be as simple as one line or as complex as several thousand lines. (I developed an awk program that summarizes data at several levels with multiple control breaks; it is just short of 1000 lines.)

The awk program can be entered a number of ways—on the command line or in a program file. awk can accept input from a file, piped in from another program, or even directly from the keyboard. Output normally goes to the standard output device, but that can be redirected to a file or piped into another program. Output can also be sent directly to a file instead of standard output.

Using awk from the Command Line

The simplest way to use awk is to code the program on the command line, accept input from the standard input device, and send output to the standard output device (screen). Listing 26.1 shows this in its simplest form; it prints the number of fields, or words, in the input record or individual line, along with the record itself, for the text from file.txt.

LISTING 26.1 SIMPLEST USE OF awk

```
$ cat file.txt | gawk '{print NF ": " $0}'
6: Now is the time for all
7: Good Americans to come to the Aid
3: of Their Country.
16: Ask not what you can do for awk, but rather what awk can do for you.
$ _
```

> **NOTE**
>
> The entire awk script is contained within single quotes (') to prevent the shell from interpreting its contents. The single quotes are a requirement of the operating system or shell, not the awk language.

NF is a predefined variable set to the number of fields on each record. $0 is that record. The individual fields can be referenced as $1, $2, and so on.

You can also store your awk script in a file and specify that filename on the command line by using the -f flag. If you do that, you don't have to contain the program within single quotes.

NOTE

gawk and other versions of awk that meet the POSIX standard support the specification of multiple programs through the use of multiple -f options. This enables you to execute multiple awk programs on the same input. Personally, I tend to avoid this just because it gets a bit confusing.

You can also use the normal UNIX shell redirection or just specify the filename on the command line to accept the input from a file instead of the keyboard:

```
$ gawk '{print NF ": " $0}' < inputs
$ gawk '{print NF ": " $0}' inputs
```

Multiple files can be specified by just listing them on the command line, as shown in the second form above—they will be processed in the order specified. Output can be redirected through the normal UNIX shell facilities to send it to a file or pipe it into another program:

```
$ gawk '{print NF ": " $0}' > outputs
$ gawk '{print NF ": " $0}' | more
```

Of course, both input and output can be redirected at the same time.

One of the ways I use awk most commonly is to process the output of another command by piping its output into awk. For example, if I wanted to create a custom listing of files containing only the filenames and then the permissions, I would execute a command like:

```
$ ls -l | gawk '{print $NF, " ", $1}'
```

$NF is the last field (which is the filename—I am lazy and didn't want to count the fields to figure out its number). $1 is the first field. The output of ls -l is piped into awk, which processes it for me.

If I put the awk script into a file (named lser.awk) and redirected the output to the printer, I would have a command that looks like:

```
$ ls -l | gawk -f lser.awk | lp
```

I tend to save my awk scripts with the file type (suffix) of .awk just to make them obvious when I'm looking through a directory listing. If the program is longer than about 30 characters, I make a point of saving it, because there is no such thing as a "one time only" program, user request, or personal need.

CAUTION

If you forget the `-f` option before a program filename, your program will be treated as if it were data.

If you code your `awk` program on the command line but place it after the name of your data file, it will also be treated as if it were data.

What you will get is odd results.

See the section "Commands On-the-Fly" later in this chapter for more examples of using `awk` scripts to process piped data.

Patterns and Actions

Each `awk` statement consists of two parts: the pattern and the action. The pattern decides when the action is executed and, of course, the action is what the programmer wants to occur. Without a pattern, the action is always executed (the pattern can be said to "default to true").

Two special patterns (also known as blocks) are `BEGIN` and `END`. The `BEGIN` code is executed before the first record is read from the file and is used to initialize variables and set up such things as control breaks. The `END` code is executed after end-of-file is reached and is used for any cleanup required (for example, printing final totals on a report). The other patterns are tested for each record read from the file.

The general program format is to put the `BEGIN` block at the top, then any pattern/action pairs, and finally, the `END` block at the end. This is not a language requirement—it is just the way most people do it (mostly for readability reasons).

`BEGIN` and `END` blocks are optional; if you use them, you should have a maximum of one each. Don't code two `BEGIN` blocks, and don't code two `END` blocks.

The action is contained within braces (`{ }`) and can consist of one or many statements. If you omit the pattern portion, it defaults to true, which causes the action to be executed for every line in the file. If you omit the action, it defaults to `print $0` (print the entire record).

The pattern is specified before the action. It can be a regular expression (contained within a pair of slashes (`/ /`)) that matches part of the input record or an expression that contains comparison operators. It can also be compound or complex patterns that consist of expressions and regular expressions combined or of a range of patterns.

Regular Expression Patterns

The regular expressions used by awk are similar to those used by grep, egrep, sed, and the UNIX editors ed, ex, and vi. They are the notations used to specify and match strings. A regular expression consists of *characters* (such as the letters *A*, *B*, and *c* that match themselves in the input) and *metacharacters*. Metacharacters are characters that have special (meta) meaning; they do not match themselves but perform some special function.

Table 26.1 shows the metacharacters and their behavior.

TABLE 26.1 REGULAR EXPRESSION METACHARACTERS IN awk

Metacharacter	*Meaning*
\	Escape sequence (next character has special meaning, \n is the newline character and \t is the tab). Any escaped metacharacter will match to that character (as if it were not a metacharacter).
^	Starts match at beginning of string.
$	Matches at end of string.
/^$/	Matches a blank line.
.	Matches any single character.
[ABC]	Matches any one of A, B, or C.
[A-Ca-c]	Matches any one of A, B, C, a, b, or c (ranges).
[^ABC]	Matches any character other than A, B, and C.
Desk¦Chair	Matches any one of Desk or Chair.
[ABC][DEF]	Concatenation. Matches any one of A, B, or C that is followed by any one of D, E, or F.
*	[ABC]*—Matches zero or more occurrences of A, B, or C.
+	[ABC]+—Matches one or more occurrences of A, B, or C.
?	[ABC]?—Matches to an empty character or any one of A, B, or C.
()	Combines regular expressions. For example, (Blue¦Black)berry matches to Blueberry or Blackberry.

All of these can be combined to form complex search strings. Typical search strings can be used to search for specific strings (Report Date) or strings in different formats (may, MAY, May) or as groups of characters (any combination of upper- and lowercase characters that spell out the month of May). These look like the following:

```
/Report Date/  { print "do something" }
/(may)¦(MAY)¦(May)/ { print "do something else" }
/[Mm] [Yy]/ { print "do something completely different" }
```

Comparison Operators and Patterns

The comparison operators used by awk are similar to those used by C and the UNIX shells. They are the notation used to specify and compare values (including strings). A regular expression alone will match to any portion of the input record. By combining a comparison with a regular expression, you can test specific fields.

Table 26.2 shows the comparison operators and their behavior.

TABLE 26.2 COMPARISON OPERATORS IN awk

Operator	*Meaning*
==	Is equal to
<	Less than
>	Greater than
<=	Less than or equal to
>=	Greater than or equal to
!=	Not equal to
~	Matched by regular expression
!~	Not matched by regular expression

This enables you to perform specific comparisons on fields instead of the entire record. Remember that you can also perform comparisons on the entire record by using $0 instead of a specific field.

Typical search strings can be used to search for a name in the first field (Bob) and compare specific fields with regular expressions:

```
$1 == "Bob"    { print "Bob stuff" }
$2 ~ /(may)¦(MAY)¦(May)/ { print "May stuff" }
$3 !~ /[Mm] [Aa] [Yy]/ { print "other May stuff" }
```

Compound Pattern Operators

The compound pattern operators used by awk are similar to those used by C and the UNIX shells. They are the notations used to combine other patterns (expressions or regular expressions) into a complex form of logic.

Table 26.3 shows the compound pattern operators and their behavior.

TABLE 26.3 COMPOUND PATTERN OPERATORS IN awk

Operator	*Meaning*
&&	Logical AND
||	Logical OR
!	Logical NOT
( )	Parentheses—used to group compound statements

If I wanted to execute some action (print a special message, for instance) if the first field contained the value "Bob" and the fourth field contained the value "Street", I could use a compound pattern that looks like:

```
$1 == "Bob" && $4 == "Street" {print"some message"}
```

Range Pattern Operators

The range pattern is slightly more complex than the other types—it is set true when the first pattern is matched and remains true until the second pattern becomes true. The catch is that the file needs to be sorted on the fields that the range pattern matches; otherwise, it might be set true prematurely or end early.

The individual patterns in a range pattern are separated by a comma (,). If you have 26 files in your directory with the names A to Z, you can show a range of the files as shown in Listing 26.2.

LISTING 26.2 RANGE PATTERN EXAMPLE

```
$ ls | gawk '{$1 == "B", $1 == "D"}'
B
C
D
$ ls | gawk '{$1 == "B", $1 <= "D"}'
B
$ ls | gawk '{$1 == "B", $1 > "D"}'
```

continues

LISTING 26.2 CONTINUED

```
B
C
D
E
$ _
```

The first example is obvious—all of the records between B and D are shown. The other examples are less intuitive, but the key to remember is that the pattern is completed when the second condition is true. The second gawk command only shows the B, because C is less than or equal to D (making the second condition true). The third gawk shows B through E, because E is the first one that is greater than D (making the second condition true).

Handling Input

As awk reads each record, it breaks the record down into fields and then searches for matching patterns and the related actions to perform. It assumes that each record occupies a single line (the newline character, by definition, ends a record). Lines that are just blanks or are empty (just the newline) count as records, but with very few fields (usually zero).

You can force awk to read the next record in a file (cease searching for pattern matches) by using the next statement. next is similar to the C continue command—control returns to the outermost loop, which, in awk, is the automatic read of the file. If you decide you need to break out of your program completely, you can use the exit statement, which acts as though the end-of-file was reached and passes control to the END block (if one exists). If exit is in the END block, the program immediately exits.

By default, fields are separated by spaces. It doesn't matter to awk whether there is one or many spaces—the next field begins when the first nonspace character is found. You can change the field separator by setting the variable FS to that character. To set your field separator to the colon (:), which is the separator in /etc/passwd, code the following:

```
BEGIN { FS = ":" }
```

The general format of the file looks something like the following:

```
david:!:207:1017:David B Horvath,CCP:/u/david:/bin/ksh
```

If you want to list the names of everyone on the system, use the following:

```
$ gawk —field-separator=: '{ print $5 }' /etc/passwd
```

You will then see a list of everyone's name. In this example, I set the field separator variable (FS) from the command line, using the gawk format command-line options (--field-separator=:). I could also use -F :, which is supported by all versions of awk.

The first field is $1, the second is $2, and so on. The entire record is contained in $0. You can get the last field (if you are lazy like me and don't want to count) by referencing $NF. NF is the number of fields in a record.

Coding Your Program

The nice thing about awk is that, with a few exceptions, it is free format—like the C language. Blank lines are ignored. Statements can be placed on the same line or split up in any form you like. awk recognizes whitespace, much as C does. The following two lines are essentially the same:

```
$1=="Bob"{print"Bob stuff"}
$1      ==      "Bob"        {      print     "Bob stuff"      }
```

Spaces within quotes are significant because they appear in the output or are used in a comparison for matching. The other spaces are not. You can also split up the action (but you have to have the left brace on the same line as the pattern):

```
$1      ==      "Bob"        {
                                  print     "Bob stuff"
                             }
```

You can have multiple statements within an action. If you place them on the same line, you need to use semicolons (;) to separate them (so awk can tell when one ends and the next begins). Printing multiple lines looks like the following:

```
$1      ==      "Bob"        {
                                  print     "Bob stuff"; print     "more stuff";
                                  ➥print    "last stuff";
                             }
```

You can also put the statements on separate lines. When you do that, you don't need to code the semicolons, and the code looks like the following:

```
$1      ==      "Bob"        {
                                  print     "Bob stuff"
                                  print     "more stuff"
                                  print     "last stuff"
                             }
```

Personally, I am in the habit of coding the semicolon after each statement because that is the way I have to do it in C. To awk, the following example is just like the previous (but you can see the semicolons):

```
$1      ==      "Bob"           {
                                    print     "Bob stuff";
                                    print     "more stuff";
                                    print     "last stuff";
                                }
```

Another thing you should make use of is comments. Anything on a line after the pound sign or octothorpe (#) is ignored by awk. These are notes designed for the programmer to read and aid in the understanding of the program code. In general, the more comments you place in a program, the easier it is to maintain.

Actions

The actions of your program are the part that tells awk what to do when a pattern is matched. If there is no pattern, it defaults to true. A pattern without an action defaults to `{print $0}`.

All actions are enclosed within braces (`{ }`). The left brace should appear on the same line as the pattern; other than that, there are no restrictions. An action consists of one or many actions.

Variables

Except for simple find-and-print types of programs, you are going to need to save data, which is done through the use of variables. Within awk, the three types of variables are field, predefined, and user-defined. You have already seen examples of the first two—`$1` is the field variable that contains the first field in the input record, and `FS` is the predefined variable that contains the field separator.

User-defined variables are ones you create. Unlike many other languages, awk doesn't require you to define or declare your variables before using them. In C, you must declare the type of data contained in a variable (such as `int`—integer, `float`—floating-point number, `char`—character data, and so on). In awk, you just use the variable; awk attempts to determine the data in the variable by how it is used. If you put character data in the variable, it is treated as a string; if you put a number in, it is treated as numeric.

awk also performs conversions between the data types. If you put the string `"123"` in a variable and later perform a calculation on it, it will be treated as a number. The danger of this is, what happens when you perform a calculation on the string `"abc"`? awk attempts to convert the string to a number, gets a conversion error, and treats the value as

TIP

Initialize all variables in a BEGIN action like this:

```
BEGIN {total = 0.0; loop = 0; first_time = "yes"; }
```

a numeric zero! This type of logic error can be difficult to debug.

Like the C language, awk requires that variables begin with an alphabetic character or an underscore. The alphabetic character can be upper- or lowercase. The remainder of the variable name can consist of letters, numbers, or underscores. It would be nice (to yourself and anyone else who has to maintain your code after you are gone) to make the variable names meaningful. Make them descriptive.

Although you can make your variable names all uppercase letters, that is a bad practice because the predefined variables (such as NF or FS) are in uppercase. A common error is to type the predefined variables in lowercase (nf or fs)—you will not get any errors from awk, and this mistake can be difficult to debug. The variables won't behave like the proper, uppercase spelling, and you won't get the results you expect.

Predefined Variables

gawk provides you with a number of predefined (also known as built-in) variables. These are used to provide useful data to your program and can also be used to change the default behavior of gawk (by setting them to a specific value).

Table 26.4 summarizes the predefined variables in gawk. Earlier versions of awk don't support all of these variables.

TABLE 26.4 gawk PREDEFINED VARIABLES

Variable	*Meaning*	*Default Value (if any)*
ARGC	The number of command-line arguments	
ARGIND	The index within ARGV of the current file being processed	
ARGV	An array of command-line arguments	
CONVFMT	The conversion format for numbers	%.6g
ENVIRON	The UNIX environmental variables	
ERRNO	The UNIX system error message	

continues

TABLE 26.4 CONTINUED

Variable	*Meaning*	*Default Value (if any)*
`FIELDWIDTHS`	A whitespace-separated string of the width of input fields	
`FILENAME`	The name of the current input file	
`FNR`	The current record number	
`FS`	The input field separator	Space
`IGNORECASE`	Controls the case sensitivity	`0` (case-sensitive)
`NF`	The number of fields in the current record	
`NR`	The number of records already read	
`OFMT`	The output format for numbers	`%.6g`
`OFS`	The output field separator	Space
`ORS`	The output record separator	Newline
`RS`	The input record separator	Newline
`RSTART`	Start of string matched by match function	
`RLENGTH`	Length of string matched by match function	
`SUBSEP`	Subscript separator	`"\034"`

The `ARGC` variable contains the number of command-line arguments passed to your program. `ARGV` is an array of `ARGC` elements that contains the command-line arguments themselves. The first one is `ARGV[0]`, and the last one is `ARGV[ARGC-1]`. `ARGV[0]` contains the name of the command being executed (`gawk`). The `gawk` command-line options won't appear in `ARGV`—they are interpreted by `gawk` itself. `ARGIND` is the index within `ARGV` of the current file being processed.

The default conversion (input) format for numbers is stored in `CONVFMT` (conversion format) and defaults to the format string `"%.6g"`. See the section "`printf`" for more information on the meaning of the format string.

The `ENVIRON` variable is an array that contains the environmental variables defined to your UNIX session. The subscript is the name of the environmental variable for which you want to get the value.

If you want your program to perform specific code depending on the value in an environmental variable, you can use the following:

```
ENVIRON["TERM"] == "vt100"  {print "Working on a Video Tube!"}
```

If you are using a VT100 terminal, you will get the message `Working on a Video Tube!` Note that you only put quotes around the environmental variable if you are using a literal. If you have a variable (named `TERM`) that contains the string `"TERM"`, you leave the double quotes off.

The `ERRNO` variable contains the UNIX system error message if a system error occurs during redirection, read, or close.

The `FIELDWIDTHS` variable provides a facility for having fixed-length fields instead of using field separators. To specify the size of fields, you set `FIELDWIDTHS` to a string that contains the width of each field, separated by a space or tab character. After this variable is set, `gawk` splits up the input record based on the specified widths. To revert to using a field-separator character, you assign a new value to `FS`.

The variable `FILENAME` contains the name of the current input file. Because different (or even multiple files) can be specified on the command line, this provides you a means of determining which input file is being processed.

The `FNR` variable contains the number of the current record within the current input file. The variable is reset for each file that is specified on the command line and always contains a value that is less than or equal to the variable `NR`.

The character used to separate fields is stored in the variable `FS` with a default value of space or tab (although you can change this from the command line by using the -F option, followed by a different delimiter character, as in **-F","** to use a comma). You can change this variable with a command-line option or within your program. If you know your file will have some character other than a space as the field separator (for example, the /etc/passwd file in earlier examples, which uses the colon), you can specify it in your program with the `BEGIN` pattern.

You can control the case sensitivity of `gawk` regular expressions with the `IGNORECASE` variable. When set to the default (zero), pattern-matching checks the case in regular expressions. If you set it to a nonzero value, case is ignored (thus, the letter `A` matches to the letter `a`).

The variable `NF` is set after each record is read and contains the number of fields. The fields are determined by the `FS` or `FIELDWIDTHS` variables.

The variable `NR` contains the total number of records read. It is never less than `FNR`, which is reset to zero for each file.

The default output format for numbers is stored in `OFMT` and defaults to the format string

"%.6g". See the section "printf" for more information on the meaning of the format string.

The output field separator is contained in OFS with a default of space. This is the character or string that is output whenever you use a comma with the print statement, as in the following:

```
{print $1, $2, $3;}
```

This statement prints the first three fields of a file, separated by spaces. If you want to separate them by colons (like the /etc/passwd file), you simply set OFS to a new value: OFS=":".

You can change the output record separator by setting ORS to a new value. ORS defaults to the newline character (\n).

The length of any string matched by the match() function call is stored in RLENGTH. This is used in conjunction with the RSTART predefined variable to extract the matched string.

You can change the input record separator by setting RS to a new value. RS defaults to the newline character (\n).

The starting position of any string matched by the match() function call is stored in RSTART. This is used in conjunction with the RLENGTH predefined variable to extract the matched string.

NOTE

If you change a field ($1, $2, and so on) or the input record ($0), you will cause other predefined variables to change. If your original input record had two fields and you set $3="third one", NF will be changed from 2 to 3.

The SUBSEP variable contains the value used to separate subscripts for multidimension arrays. The default value is "\034", which is the double quote character (").

Strings

awk supports two general types of variables: *numeric* (which can consist of the characters 0 through 9, + or -, and the decimal [.]) and *character* (which can contain any character). Variables that contain characters are generally referred to as strings. A character string can contain a valid number, text such as words, or even a formatted phone number. If the string contains a valid number, awk automatically converts it and uses it as if it were a numeric variable; if you attempt to use a string that contains a formatted phone number as a numeric variable, awk attempts to convert and use it as a numeric variable—containing the value zero.

String Constants

A string constant is always enclosed within double quotes ("") and can be from zero (an *empty* string) to many characters long. The exact maximum varies by version of UNIX; personally, I have never hit the maximum. The double quotes aren't stored in memory. A typical string constant might look like the following:

```
"Red Hat Linux Unleashed, Third Edition"
```

You have already seen string constants used earlier in this chapter—with comparisons and the print statement.

String Operators

There is really only one string operator, and that is concatenation. You can combine multiple strings (constants or variables in any combination) by just putting them together. Listing 26.1 does this with the print statement, where the string ": " is prepended to the input record ($0).

Listing 26.3 shows a couple of ways to concatenate strings.

LISTING 26.3 CONCATENATING STRINGS EXAMPLE

```
$ gawk 'BEGIN{x="abc""def"; y="ghi"; z=x y; z2 = "A"x"B"y"C"; print x, y,
➥z, z2}'
abcdef ghi abcdefghi AabcdefBghiC
```

Variable x is set to two concatenated strings; it prints as abcdef. Variable y is set to one string for use with the variable z. Variable z is the concatenation of two string variables printing as abcdefghi. Finally, the variable z2 shows the concatenation of string constants and string variables printing as AabcdefBghiC.

If you leave the comma out of the print statement, all of the strings will be concatenated and will look like the following:

```
abcdefghiabcdefghiAabcdefBghiC
```

Built-in String Functions

In addition to the one string operation (concatenation), gawk provides a number of functions for processing strings.

Table 26.5 summarizes the built-in string functions in gawk. Earlier versions of awk don't support all of these functions.

TABLE 26.5 gawk BUILT-IN STRING FUNCTIONS

Function	*Purpose*
gsub(*reg*, *string*, *target*)	Substitutes *string* in *target* string every time the regular expression *reg* is matched.
index(*search*, *string*)	Returns the position of the *search* string in *string*.
length(*string*)	The number of characters in *string*.
match(*string*, *reg*)	Returns the position in *string* that matches the regular expression *reg*.
printf(*format*, *variables*)	Writes formatted data based on *format*; *variables* is the data you want printed.
split(*string*, *store*, *delim*)	Splits *string* into array elements of *store* based on the delimiter *delim*.
sprintf(*format*, *variables*)	Returns a string containing formatted data based on *format*; *variables* is the data you want placed in the string.
strftime(*format*, *timestamp*)	Returns a formatted date or time string based on *format*; *timestamp* is the time returned by the systime() function.
sub(*reg*, *string*, *target*)	Substitutes *string* in *target* string the first time the regular expression *reg* is matched.
substr(*string*, *position*, *len*)	Returns a substring beginning at *position* for *len* number of characters.
tolower(*string*)	Returns the characters in *string* as their lowercase equivalent.
toupper(*string*)	Returns the characters in *string* as their uppercase equivalent.

The gsub(*reg*, *string*, *target*) function enables you to globally substitute one set of characters for another (defined in the form of the regular expression *reg*) within *string*. The number of substitutions is returned by the function. If *target* is omitted, the input record, $0, is the target. This is patterned after the substitute command in the ed text editor.

The index(*search*, *string*) function returns the first position (counting from the left) of the *search* string within *string*. If *string* is omitted, 0 is returned.

The length(*string*) function returns a count of the number of characters in *string*. awk keeps track of the length of strings internally.

The match(*string*, *reg*) function determines whether *string* contains the set of characters defined by *reg*. If there is a match, the position is returned, and the variables RSTART and RLENGTH are set.

The printf(*format*, *variables*) function writes formatted data converting *variables* based on the *format* string. This function is very similar to the C printf() function. More information about this function and the formatting strings is provided in the section "printf" later in this chapter.

The split(*string*, *store*, *delim*) function splits *string* into elements of the array *store* based on the *delim* string. The number of elements in *store* is returned. If you omit the *delim* string, FS is used. To split a slash-delimited (/) date into its component parts, code the following:

```
split("08/12/1962", results, "/");
```

After the function call, results[1] contains 08, results[2] contains 12, and results[3] contains 1962. When used with the split function, the array begins with the element one. This also works with strings that contain text.

The sprintf(format, variables) function behaves like the printf function except it returns the result string instead of writing output. This function produces formatted data, converting variables based on the format string, and is very similar to the C sprintf() function. More information about this function and the formatting strings is provided in the "printf" section of this chapter.

The strftime(*format*, *timestamp*) function returns a formatted date or time based on the *format* string; *timestamp* is the number of seconds since midnight on January 1, 1970. The systime function returns a value in this form. The format is the same as the C strftime() function.

The sub(*reg*, *string*, *target*) function enables you to substitute one set of characters for the first occurrence of another (defined in the form of the regular expression *reg*) within *string*. The number of substitutions is returned by the function. If *target* is omitted, the input record, $0, is the target. This is patterned after the substitute command in the ed text editor.

The substr(*string*, *position*, *len*) function enables you to extract a substring based on a starting *position* and *length*. If you omit the *len* parameter, the remaining string is returned.

The tolower(*string*) function returns the uppercase alphabetic characters in *string*, converted to lowercase. Any other characters are returned without any conversion.

The `toupper(string)` function returns the lowercase alphabetic characters in *string*, converted to uppercase. Any other characters are returned without any conversion.

Special String Constants

awk supports special string constants that have special meaning or cannot be entered from the keyboard. If you want to have a double quote (") character as a string constant (`x = """`), how would you prevent awk from thinking the second one (the one you really want) is the end of the string? The answer is by escaping, or telling awk the next character has special meaning. This is done through the backslash (\) character, as in the rest of UNIX.

Table 26.6 shows most of the constants supported by gawk.

TABLE 26.6 gawk SPECIAL STRING CONSTANTS

Expression	*Meaning*
`\\`	The means of including a backslash
`\a`	The alert or bell character
`\b`	Backspace
`\f`	Formfeed
`\n`	Newline
`\r`	Carriage return
`\t`	Tab
`\v`	Vertical tab
`\"`	Double quote
`\xNN`	Indicates that *NN* is a hexadecimal number
`\0NNN`	Indicates that *NNN* is an octal (base 8) number

Arrays

When you have more than one related piece of data, you have two choices—you can create multiple variables, or you can use an array. An array enables you to keep a collection of related data together.

You access individual elements within an array by enclosing the subscript within brackets ([ ]). In general, you can use an array element anyplace you can use a regular variable.

Arrays in awk have special capabilities lacking in most other languages—they are dynamic, they are sparse, and the subscript is actually a string. You don't have to declare a variable to be an array, and you don't have to define the maximum number of elements—when you use an element for the first time, it is created dynamically. Because of this, a block of memory is not initially allocated. In normal programming practice, if you want to accumulate sales for each month in a year, 12 elements are allocated, even if you are only processing December at the moment. awk arrays are sparse; if you are working with December, only that element exists—not the other 11 (empty) months.

In my experience, the last capability is the most useful—that the subscript is a string. In most programming languages, if you want to accumulate data based on a string (for example, totaling sales by state or country), you need to have two arrays—the state or country name (a string) and the numeric sales array. You search the state or country name for a match and then use the same element of the sales array. awk performs this for you. You create an element in the sales array with the state or country name as the subscript and address it directly, as in the following:

```
total_sales["Pennsylvania"] = 10.15
```

This is much less programming and much easier to read (and maintain) than the "search one array and change another" method. The awk version is known as an associative array.

However, awk does not directly support multidimension arrays.

Array Functions

gawk provides a couple of functions specifically for use with arrays: in and delete. The in function tests for membership in an array. The delete function removes elements from an array.

If you have an array with a subscript of states and want to determine if a specific state is in the list, put the following within a conditional test (more about conditional tests in the "Conditional Flow" section):

```
"Delaware" in total_sales
```

You can also use the in function within a loop to step through the elements in an array (especially if the array is sparse or associative). This is a special case of the for loop and is described in the section "The for Statement," later in the chapter.

To delete an array element (the state of Delaware, for example), you code the following:

```
delete total_sales["Delaware"]
```

CAUTION

When an array element is deleted, it has been removed from memory. The data is no longer available.

Deleting elements in an array, or entire arrays, when you are finished with them is always good practice. Although memory is cheap and large quantities are available (especially with virtual memory), you will eventually run out if you don't clean up.

NOTE

You must loop through all loop elements and delete each one. You cannot delete an entire array directly; therefore, the following is not valid:

```
delete total_sales
```

Multidimension Arrays

Although awk doesn't directly support multidimension arrays, it does provide a facility to simulate them. The distinction is fairly trivial to you as a programmer. You can specify multiple dimensions in the subscript (within the brackets) in a form familiar to C programmers:

```
array[5, 3] = "Mary"
```

This is stored in a single-dimension array with the subscript actually stored in the form 5 SUBSEP 3. The predefined variable SUBSEP contains the value of the separator of the subscript components. The variable defaults to the double quote (" or \034) because the double quote is unlikely to appear in the subscript itself. Remember that the double quotes are used to contain a string; they are not stored as part of the string itself. You can always change SUBSEP if you need to have the double quote character in your multidimension array subscript.

If you want to calculate total sales by city and state (or country), you use a two-dimension array:

```
total_sales["Philadelphia", "Pennsylvania"] = 10.15
```

You can use the in function within a conditional:

```
("Wilmington", "Delaware") in total_sales
```

You can also use the `in` function within a loop to step through various cities.

Built-in Numeric Functions

gawk provides a number of numeric functions to calculate special values.

Table 26.7 summarizes the built-in numeric functions in gawk. Earlier versions of awk don't support all of these functions.

TABLE 26.7 gawk's BUILT-IN NUMERIC FUNCTIONS

Function	*Purpose*
`atan2(x, y)`	Returns the arctangent of y/x in radians
`cos(x)`	Returns the cosine of x in radians
`exp(x)`	Returns e raised to the x power
`int(x)`	Returns the value of x truncated to an integer
`log(x)`	Returns the natural log of x
`rand()`	Returns a random number between 0 and 1
`sin(x)`	Returns the sine of x in radians
`sqrt(x)`	Returns the square root of x
`srand(x)`	Initializes (seeds) the random number generator; `systime()` is used if x is omitted
`systime()`	Returns the current time in seconds since midnight, January 1, 1970

Arithmetic Operators

gawk supports a wide variety of math operations. Table 26.8 summarizes these operators.

TABLE 26.8 gawk ARITHMETIC OPERATORS

Operator	*Purpose*
`x^y`	Raises x to the y power
`x**y`	Raises x to the y power (same as x^y)
`x%y`	Calculates the remainder of x/y
`x+y`	Adds x to y
`x-y`	Subtracts y from x

continues

TABLE 26.8 CONTINUED

Operator	*Purpose*
`x*y`	Multiplies `x` times `y`
`x/y`	Divides `x` by `y`
`-y`	Negates `y` (switches the sign of `y`); also known as the unary minus
`++y`	Increments `y` by 1 and uses value (prefix increment)
`y++`	Uses value of `y` and then increments by 1 (postfix increment)
`--y`	Decrements `y` by 1 and uses value (prefix decrement)
`y--`	Uses value of `y` and then decrements by 1 (postfix decrement)
`x=y`	Assigns value of `y` to `x`. `gawk` also supports operator-assignment operators (`+=`, `-=`, `*=`, `/=`, `%=`, `^=`, and `**=`)

NOTE

All math in `gawk` uses floating point (even if you treat the number as an integer).

Conditional Flow

By its very nature, an action within a `gawk` program is conditional—executed if its pattern is true. You can also have conditional programs flow within the action through the use of an `if` statement.

The general flow of an `if` statement is as follows:

```
if (condition)
   statement to execute when true
else
   statement to execute when false
```

`condition` can be any valid combination of patterns shown in Tables 26.2 and 26.3. `else` is optional. If you have more than one statement to execute, you need to enclose the statements within braces (`{ }`), just as in the C syntax.

You can also stack `if` and `else` statements as necessary:

```
if ("Pennsylvania" in total_sales)
   print "We have Pennsylvania data"
```

```
else if ("Delaware" in total_sales)
   print "We have Delaware data"
else if (current_year < 2010)
   print "Uranus is still a planet"
else
   print "none of the conditions were met."
```

The Null Statement

By definition, `if` requires one (or more) statements to execute; in some cases, the logic might be straightforward when coded so the code you want executed occurs when the condition is false. I have used this when it would be difficult or ugly to reverse the logic to execute the code when the condition is true.

The solution to this problem is easy: Just use the null statement, the semicolon (`;`). The null statement satisfies the syntax requirement that `if` requires statements to execute; it just does nothing.

Your code will look something like the following:

```
if (($1 <= 5 && $2 > 3) || ($1 > 7 && $2 < 2))
   ;        # The Null Statement
else
   the code I really want to execute
```

The Conditional Operator

`gawk` has one operator that actually has three parameters: the conditional operator. This operator allows you to apply an if-test anywhere in your code.

The general format of the conditional statement is as follows:

```
condition ? true-result : false-result
```

Although this might seem like duplication of the `if` statement, it can make your code easier to read. If you have a data file that consists of an employee name and the number of sick days taken, for example, you can use the following:

```
{ print $1, "has taken", $2, "day" $2 != 1 ? "s" : "", "of sick time" }
```

This prints `day` if the employee only took one day of sick time and prints `days` if the employee took zero or more than one day of sick time. The resulting sentence is more readable. To code the same example using an `if` statement would be more complex and would look like the following:

```
if ($2 != 1)
   print $1, "has taken", $2, "days of sick time"
else
   print $1, "has taken", $2, "day of sick time"
```

Looping

By their very nature, awk programs are one big loop—reading each record in the input file and processing the appropriate patterns and actions. Within an action, the need for repetition often occurs. awk supports loops through the do, for, and while statements that are similar to those found in C.

As with the if statement, if you want to execute multiple statements within a loop, you must contain them in braces.

TIP

Forgetting the braces around multiple statements is a common programming error with conditional and looping statements.

The do Statement

The do statement (sometimes referred to as the do while statement) provides a looping construct that will be executed at least once. The condition or test occurs after the contents of the loop have been executed.

The do statement takes the following form:

```
do
   statement
while (condition)
```

statement can be one statement or multiple statements enclosed in braces. *condition* is any valid test like those used with the if statement or the pattern used to trigger actions.

In general, you must change the value of the variable in the condition within the loop. If you don't, you have a loop-forever condition because the test result (*condition*) never changes to become false.

Loop Control

You can exit a loop early if you need to (without assigning some bogus value to the variable in the condition). awk provides two facilities to do this: break and continue.

break causes the current (innermost) loop to be exited. It behaves as if the conditional test was performed immediately, with a false result. None of the remaining code in the loop (after the break statement) executes, and the loop ends. This is useful when you need to handle some error or early-end condition.

`continue` causes the current loop to return to the conditional test. None of the remaining code in the loop (after the `continue` statement) is executed, and the test is immediately executed. This is most useful when there is code you want to skip (within the loop) temporarily. The `continue` is different from the `break` because the loop is not forced to end.

The `for` Statement

The `for` statement provides a looping construct that modifies values within the loop. It is good for counting through a specific number of items.

The `for` statement has two general forms—the following:

```
for (loop = 0; loop < 10; loop++)
   statement
```

and:

```
for (subscript in array)
   statement
```

The first form initializes the variable (`loop = 0`), performs the test (`loop < 10`), and then performs the loop contents (*`statement`*). Then it modifies the variable (`loop++`) and tests again. As long as the test is true, *`statement`* will execute.

In the second form, *`statement`* is executed with `subscript` being set to each of the subscripts in *`array`*. This enables you to loop through an array even if you don't know the values of the subscripts. This works well for multidimension arrays.

`statement` can be one statement or multiple statements enclosed in braces. The condition (`loop < 10`) is any valid test like those used with the `if` statement or the pattern used to trigger actions.

In general, you don't want to change the loop control variable (`loop` or `subscript`) within the loop body. Let the `for` statement do that for you, or you might get behavior that is difficult to debug.

For the first form, the modification of the variable can be any valid operation (including calls to functions). In most cases, it is an increment or decrement.

> **TIP**
>
> This example shows the postfix increment. It doesn't matter whether you use the postfix (`loop++`) or prefix (`++loop`) increment—the results will be the same in our example. Do, however, understand that using postfix notation increments a variable before returning its value, while using prefix notation increments a variable after returning its value.

The for loop is a good method of looping through data of an unknown size:

```
for (i=1; i<=NF; i++)
    print $i
```

Each field on the current record will be printed on its own line. As a programmer, I don't know how many fields are in a particular record when I write the code. The variable NF lets me know as the program runs.

The while Statement

The final loop structure is the while loop. It is the most general, because it executes while the condition is true. The general form is as follows:

```
while(condition)
   statement
```

statement can be one statement or multiple statements enclosed in braces. *condition* is any valid test like those used with the if statement or the pattern used to trigger actions.

If the condition is false before the while is encountered, the contents of the loop are not executed. This is different from do, which always executes the loop contents at least once.

In general, you must change the value of the variable in the condition within the loop. If you don't, you have a loop-forever condition because the test result (*condition*) never changes to become false.

Advanced Input and Output

In addition to the simple input and output facilities provided by awk, you can take advantage of a number of advanced features for more complicated processing.

By default, awk automatically reads and loops through your program, but you can alter this behavior. You can force input to come from a different file or cause the loop to recycle early (read the next record without performing any more actions) or even just read the next record. You can even get data from the output of other commands.

On the output side, you can format the output and send it to a file (other than the standard output device) or as input to another command.

Input

You don't have to program the normal input loop process in awk. It reads a record and then searches for pattern matches and the corresponding actions to execute. If multiple files are specified on the command line, they are processed in order. It is only if you want to change this behavior that you have to do any special programming.

next and exit

The next command causes awk to read the next record and perform the pattern match and the corresponding action execution immediately. Normally, it executes all of your code in any actions with matching patterns. next causes any additional matching patterns to be ignored for this record.

The exit command in any action except END behaves as if the end of file was reached. Code execution in all pattern/actions is ceased, and the actions within the END pattern are executed. exit appearing in the END pattern is a special case—it causes the program to end.

getline

The getline statement is used to explicitly read a record. This is especially useful if you have a data record that looks like two physical records. It performs the normal field splitting (setting $0, the field variables, FNR, NF, and NR). It returns the value 1 if the read was successful and zero if it failed (end of file was reached). If you want to explicitly read through a file, you can code something like the following:

```
{ while (getline == 1)
  {
      # process the inputted fields
  }
}
```

You can also have getline store the input data in a field instead of taking advantage of the normal field processing by using the form getline *variable*. When used this way, NF is set to zero, and FNR and NR are incremented.

Input from a File

You can use getline to input data from a specific file instead of the ones listed on the command line. The general form is getline < "*filename*". When coded this way, getline performs the normal field splitting (setting $0, the field variables, and NF). If the file doesn't exist, getline returns -1; it returns 1 on success and 0 on failure.

You can read the data from the specified file into a variable. You can also replace *filename* with stdin or a variable that contains the filename.

NOTE

If you use getline < "filename" to read data into your program, neither FNR nor NR is changed.

Input from a Command

Another way of using the `getline` statement is to accept input from a UNIX command. If you want to perform some processing for each person signed on the system (send him or her a message, for instance), you can code something like the following:

```
{ while ("who -u" ¦ getline)
  {
      # process each line from the who command
   }
}
```

The `who` command is executed once, and each of its output lines is processed by `getline`. You could also use the form `"command" ¦ getline variable`.

Ending Input from a File or Command

Whenever you use `getline` to get input from a specified file or command, you should close it when you have finished processing the data. The maximum number of open files allowed to `awk` varies with the operating system version or individual account configuration (a command output pipe counts as a file). By closing files when you have finished with them, you reduce the chances of hitting the limit.

The syntax to close a file is simply

```
close ("filename")
```

where *`filename`* is the one specified on the `getline` (which could also be `stdin`, a variable that contains the filename, or the exact command used with `getline`).

Output

A few advanced features are available for output: pretty formatting, sending output to files, and piping output as input to other commands. The `printf` command is used for pretty formatting—instead of seeing the output in whatever default format `awk` decides to use (which is often ugly), you can specify how it looks.

printf

The `print` statement produces simple output for you. If you want to be able to format the data (producing fixed columns, for instance), you need to use `printf`. The nice thing about `awk printf` is that it uses syntax that is very similar to the `printf()` function in C.

The general format of the `awk printf` is as follows (the parentheses are only required if a relational expression is included):

```
printf format-specifier, variable1,variable2, variable3,..variablen
printf(format-specifier, variable1,variable2, variable3,..variablen)
```

Personally, I use the second form because I am so used to coding in C.

The variables are optional, but `format-specifier` is mandatory. Often you will have `printf` statements that only include `format-specifier` (to print messages that contain no variables):

```
printf ("Program Starting\n")
printf ("\f")          # new page in output
```

`format-specifier` can consist of text, escaped characters, or actual print specifiers. A print specifier begins with the percent sign (`%`), followed by an optional numeric value that specifies the size of the field and then by the format type (which describes the type of variable or output format). If you want to print a percent sign in your output, you use `%%`.

The field size can consist of two numbers separated by a decimal point (`.`). For floating-point numbers, the first number is the size of the entire field (including the decimal point) and the second number is the number of digits to the right of the decimal. For other types of fields, the first number is the minimum field size and the second number is the maximum field size (number of characters to actually print); if you omit the first number, it takes the value of the maximum field size.

The print specifiers determine how the variable is printed; there are also modifiers that change the behavior of the specifiers. Table 26.9 shows the print format specifiers.

TABLE 26.9 FORMAT SPECIFIERS FOR awk

Format	*Meaning*
`%c`	ASCII character
`%d`	An integer (decimal number)
`%i`	An integer, just like `%d`
`%e`	A floating-point number using scientific notation (1.00000E+01)
`%f`	A floating-point number (10.43)
`%g`	`awk` chooses between `%e` or `%f` display format (whichever is shorter), suppressing nonsignificant zeros
`%o`	An unsigned octal (base 8) number (integer)
`%s`	A string of characters
`%x`	An unsigned hexadecimal (base 16) number (integer)
`%X`	Same as `%x` but using ABCDEF instead of abcdef

NOTE

If you attempt to print a numeric value or variable using `%c`, it is printed as a character (the ASCII character for that value will print).

The format modifiers change the default behavior of the format specifiers. Listing 26.4 shows the use of various specifiers and modifiers.

LISTING 26.4 `printf` **FORMAT SPECIFIERS AND MODIFIERS**

```
printf("%d %3.3d %03.3d %.3d %-.3d %3d %-3d\n", 64, 64, 64, 64, 64, 64,
➥64)
printf("%c %c %2.2c %-2.2c %2c %-2c\n", 64, "abc", "abc", "abc", "abc",
➥"abc")
printf("%s %2s %-2s %2.2s %-2.2s %.2s %-.2s\n",
        "abc", "abc", "abc", "abc", "abc", "abc", "abc")
printf("%f %6.1f %06.1f %.1f %-.1f %6f\n",
        123.456, 123.456, 123.456, 123.456, 123.456, 123.456)

64 064 064 064 064  64 64
@ a  a a   a a
abc abc abc ab ab ab ab
123.456000  123.5 0123.5 123.5 123.5 123.456000
```

When using the integer or decimal (`%d`) specifier, the field size defaults to the size of the value being printed (two digits for the value 64). If you specify a field maximum size that is larger than that, you automatically get the field zero filled. All numeric fields are right-justified unless you use the minus sign (`-`) modifier, which causes them to be left-justified. If you specify only the field minimum size and want the rest of the field zero filled, you have to use the zero modifier (before the field minimum size).

When using the character (`%c`) specifier, only one character prints from the input, no matter what size you use for the field minimum or maximum sizes and no matter how many characters are in the value being printed. Note that the value `64` printed as a character shows up as `@`.

When using the string (`%s`) specifier, the entire string prints unless you specify the field maximum size. By default, strings are left-justified unless you use the minus sign (`-`) modifier, which causes them to be right-justified.

When using the floating (`%f`) specifier, the field size defaults to .6 (as many digits to the left of the decimal and 6 digits to the right). If you specify a number after the decimal in the format, that many digits print to the right of the decimal and `awk` rounds the number.

All numeric fields are right-justified unless you use the minus sign (-) modifier, which causes them to be left-justified. If you want the field zero filled, you have to use the zero modifier (before the field minimum size).

The best way to determine printing results is to work with them. Try the various modifiers and see what makes your output look best.

Output to a File

You can send your output (from `print` or `printf`) to a file. The following creates a new (or empties out an existing) file containing the printed message:

```
printf ("hello world\n") > "datafile"
```

If you execute this statement multiple times or other statements that redirect output to *datafile*, the output remains in the file. The file creation/emptying out only occurs the first time the file is used in the program.

To append data to an existing file, you use the following:

```
printf ("hello world\n") >> "datafile"
```

Output to a Command

In addition to redirecting your output to a file, you can send the output from your program to act as input for another command. You can code something like the following:

```
printf ("hello world\n") ¦ "sort -t , "
```

Any other output statements that pipe data into the same command will specify exactly the same command after the pipe character (¦), because that is how `awk` keeps track of which command is receiving which output from your program.

Closing an Output File or Pipe

Whenever you send output to a file or pipe, you should close it when you have finished processing the data. The maximum number of open files allowed to `awk` varies with the operating system version or individual account configuration (a pipe counts as a file). By closing files when you have finished with them, you reduce the chances of hitting the limit.

The syntax to close a file is simply

```
close ("filename")
```

where *`filename`* is the one specified on the output statement (which can also be `stdout`, a variable that contains the filename, or the exact command used with a pipe).

Functions

In addition to the built-in functions (for example, gsub or srand), gawk allows you to write your own. User-defined functions are a means of creating a block of code that is accessed in multiple places in your code. These functions can also be used to build a library of commonly used routines so you do not have to recode the same algorithms repeatedly.

User-defined functions are not a part of the original awk—they were added to nawk and are supported by gawk.

Using a function includes two parts: the definition and the call. The function definition contains the code to be executed (the function itself), and the call temporarily transfers from the main code to the function. The command execution is transferred back to the main code in two ways: implicit and explicit returns. When gawk reaches the end of a function (the right brace [}]), it automatically (implicitly) returns control to the calling routine. If you want to leave your function before the bottom, you can explicitly use the return statement to exit early.

Function Definition

The general form of a gawk function definition looks like the following:

```
function functionname(parameter list) {
     the function body
}
```

You code your function just as if it were any other set of action statements, and you can place it anywhere you would put a pattern/action set. If you think about it, the function *functionname(parameter list)* portion of the definition could be considered a pattern and *the function body* the action.

NOTE

gawk supports another form of function definition where the function keyword is abbreviated to func. The remaining syntax is the same:

```
func functionname(parameter list) {
     the function body
}
```

Listing 26.5 shows the defining and calling of a function.

LISTING 26.5 DEFINING AND CALLING FUNCTIONS

```
BEGIN { print_header() }

function print_header( ) {
   printf("This is the header\n");
   printf("this is a second line of the header\n");
}

This is the header
this is a second line of the header
```

The code inside the function is executed only once—when the function is called from within the `BEGIN` action. This function uses the implicit return method.

CAUTION

When working with user-defined functions, you must place the parentheses that contain the parameter list immediately after the function name when calling that function. When you use the built-in functions, this is not a requirement.

Function Parameters

Like C, `gawk` passes parameters to functions by value. In other words, a copy of the original value is made and that copy is passed to the called function. The original is untouched, even if the function changes the value.

Any parameters are listed in the function definition, separated by commas. If you have no parameters, you can leave the parameter list (contained in the parentheses) empty.

Listing 26.6 is an expanded version of Listing 26.5; it shows the pass-by-value nature of `gawk` function parameters.

LISTING 26.6 PASSING PARAMETERS

```
BEGIN { pageno = 0;
        print_header(pageno);
        printf("the page number is now %d\n", pageno);
}
```

continues

LISTING 26.6 CONTINUED

```
function print_header(page ) {
   page++;
   printf("This is the header for page %d\n", page);
   printf("this is a second line of the header\n");
}

This is the header for page 1
this is a second line of the header
the page number is now 0
```

The page number is initialized before the first call to the `print_header` function and incremented in the function. But when it is printed after the function call, it remains at the original value.

CAUTION

`gawk` does not perform parameter validation. When you call a function, you can list more or fewer parameters than the function expects. Any extra parameters are ignored, and any missing ones default to zero or empty strings (depending on how they are used).

TIP

You can take advantage of the lack of function parameter validation. It can be used to create local variables within the called function—just list more variables in the function definition than you use in the function call. I strongly suggest you comment the fact that the extra parameters are really being used as local variables.

A called function can change variables in the calling routines in several ways—through explicit return or by using the variables in the calling routine directly. (These variables are normally global, anyway.)

The `return` Statement (Explicit Return)

If you want to return a value or leave a function early, you need to code a `return` statement. If you don't code one, the function ends with the right brace (`}`). Personally, I prefer to code them at the bottom.

If the calling code expects a returned value from your function, you must code the `return` statement in the following form:

```
return variable
```

Expanding on Listing 26.6 to let the function change the page number, Listing 26.7 shows the use of the `return` statement.

LISTING 26.7 RETURNING VALUES

```
BEGIN { pageno = 0;
        pageno = print_header(pageno);
        printf("the page number is now %d\n", pageno);
}

function print_header(page ) {
   page++;
   printf("This is the header for page %d\n", page);
   printf("this is a second line of the header\n");
   return page;
}

This is the header for page 1
this is a second line of the header
the page number is now 1
```

The updated page number is returned to the code that called the function.

NOTE

The `return` statement allows you to return only one value back to the calling routine.

Writing Reports

Generating a report in awk entails a sequence of steps, with each step producing the input for the next step. Report-writing is usually a three-step process: Pick the data, sort the data, and make the output pretty.

Complex Reports

Using awk, you can quickly create complex reports. Performing string comparisons, building arrays on-the-fly, and taking advantage of associative arrays is much easier than coding in another language (such as C). Instead of having to search through an array for a match with a text key, that key can be used as the array subscript.

I have produced reports using awk with three levels of control breaks, multiple sections of reports in the same control break, and multiple totaling pages. The totaling pages were for each level of control break plus a final page; if the control break didn't have a particular type of data, the totaling page didn't have it either. If there was only one member of a control break, the totaling page for that level wasn't created. (This saved a lot of paper when there was really only one level of control break—the highest.)

This report ended up being more than 1,000 lines of awk code (nawk to be specific). It takes a little longer to run than the equivalent C program, but it took a lot less programmer time to create. Because it was easy to create and modify, it was developed by using prototypes. The users briefly described what they wanted, and I produced a report. They decided they needed more control breaks, and I added them; then they realized a lot of paper was wasted on totaling pages, so the report was modified as described.

Being easy to develop incrementally without knowing the final result made it easier and more fun for me. Because I could be responsive to user changes, the users were happy!

Extracting Data

As mentioned early in this chapter, many systems don't produce data in the desired format. When working with data stored in relational databases, two main ways are available for getting data out: Use a query tool with SQL or write a program to get the data from the database and output it in the desired form. SQL query tools have limited formatting ability but can provide quick and easy access to the data.

One technique I have found very useful is to extract the data from the database into a file that is then manipulated by an awk script to produce the exact format you need. When required, an awk script can even create the SQL statements used to query the database (specifying the key values for the rows to select).

The following example is used when the query tool places a space before a numeric field that must be removed for a program that will use the data in another system (mainframe COBOL):

```
{   printf("%s%s%-25.25s\n", $1, $2, $3);   }
```

awk automatically removes the field separator (the space character) when splitting the input record into individual fields, and the formatting %s string format specifiers in printf are contiguous (do not have any spaces between them).

Commands On-the-Fly

The capability to pipe the output of a command into another is very powerful because the output from the first becomes the input that the second can manipulate. A frequent use of one-line awk programs is the creation of commands based on a list.

The find command can be used to produce a list of files that match its conditions, or it can execute a single command that takes a single command-line argument. You can see files in a directory (and subdirectories) that match specific conditions with the following:

```
$ find . -name "*.prn" -print
```

This outputs

```
./exam2.prn
./exam1.prn
./exam3.prn
```

Or you can print the contents of those files with the following:

```
$ find . -name "*.prn" -exec lp {} \;
```

The find command inserts the individual filenames it locates in place of the {} and executes the lp command. But if you want to execute a command that requires two arguments (to copy files to a new name) or execute multiple commands at once, you can't do it with find alone. You can create a shell script that will accept the single argument and use it in multiple places, or you can create an awk single-line program:

```
$ find . -name "*.prn" -print | awk '{print "echo bak" $1;
➥print "cp " $1 " " $1".bak";}'
```

This outputs

```
echo bak./exam2.prn
cp ./exam2.prn ./exam2.prn.bak
echo bak./exam1.prn
cp ./exam1.prn ./exam1.prn.bak
echo bak./exam3.prn
cp ./exam3.prn ./exam3.prn.bak
```

To get the commands to actually execute, you need to pipe the commands into one of the shells. The following example uses the Korn shell; you can use the one you prefer:

```
$ find . -name "*.prn" -print ¦
     awk '{print "echo bak" $1; print "cp " $1 " " $1".bak";}' ¦
     ksh
```

This outputs

```
bak./exam2.prn
bak./exam1.prn
bak./exam3.prn
```

Before each copy takes place, the message is shown. This is also handy if you want to search for a string (using the `grep` command) in the files of multiple subdirectories. Many versions of the `grep` command don't show the name of the file searched unless you use wildcards (or specify multiple filenames on the command line). The following uses `find` to search for C source files, `awk` to create `grep` commands to look for an error message, and the shell `echo` command to show the file being searched:

```
$ find . -name "*.c" -print ¦
     awk '{print "echo " $1; print "grep error-message " $1;}' ¦
     ksh
```

The same technique can be used to perform `lint` checks on source code in a series of subdirectories. I execute the following in a shell script periodically to check all C code:

```
$ find . -name "*.c" -print ¦
     awk '{print "lint " $1 " > " $1".lint"}' ¦
     ksh
```

The `lint` version on one system prints the code error as a heading line and then the parts of code in question as a list below. `grep` shows the heading but not the detail lines. The `awk` script prints all lines from the heading until the first blank line (end of the `lint` section).

NOTE

Although you won't find the lint program included with your Red Hat Linux distribution, you can find a similar (and in many ways much more powerful) C syntax checker from the Massachusetts Institute of Technology (MIT) called `lclint`. Look at `http://sunsite.unc.edu/pub/Linux/devel/lang/c`. You'll find `lclint`, along with numerous other programming utilities you can install on your Red Hat Linux system.

When in doubt, pipe the output into more or less to view the created commands before you pipe them into a shell for execution.

One Last Built-in Function: system

One more built-in function, which doesn't fit in the character or numeric categories, is system. The system function executes the string passed to it as an argument, allowing you to execute commands or scripts on-the-fly when your awk code has the need.

You can code a report to automatically print to paper when it is complete. The code looks something like Listing 26.8.

LISTING 26.8 USING THE system FUNCTION

```
BEGIN { pageno = 0;
        pageno = print_header(pageno);
        printf("the page number is now %d\n", pageno);
}

# The production of the report would be coded here

END { close ("report.txt");
      system ("lpr -Pmyprinter report.txt");
}

function print_header(page ) {
   page++;
   printf("This is the header for page %d\n", page) > "report.txt";
   printf("this is a second line of the header\n")  > "report.txt";
}

This is the header for page 1
this is a second line of the header
the page number is now 0
```

The output is the same as that of Listing 26.6 except that the output shows up on the printer instead of the screen. Before printing the file, you have to close it.

> **NOTE**
>
> Be careful when using input or output redirection or requiring direct user input in your awk scripts. The code in Listing 26.8 is an example only. Ideally, the input would come from another awk-generated file.

Summary

This chapter has provided an introduction to the awk programming language and the GNU awk—gawk—a very powerful and useful language that enables you to search for data, extract data from files, create commands on-the-fly, or even create entire programs.

gawk is very useful as a prototyping language—you can create reports very quickly. After showing the reports to the user, you can make changes quickly, also. Although less efficient than a comparable program written in C, gawk is not so inefficient that you cannot create production programs. If efficiency is a concern with an awk program, it can be converted into C.

NOTE

If you'd like to try using an awk-to-C translator, try Eric S. Raymond's awk2c program. Although it doesn't support all of awk's features, you might find it useful and entertaining. Look for the file awk2c050.tgz at `http://sunsite.unc.edu/pub/Linux/utils/text`.

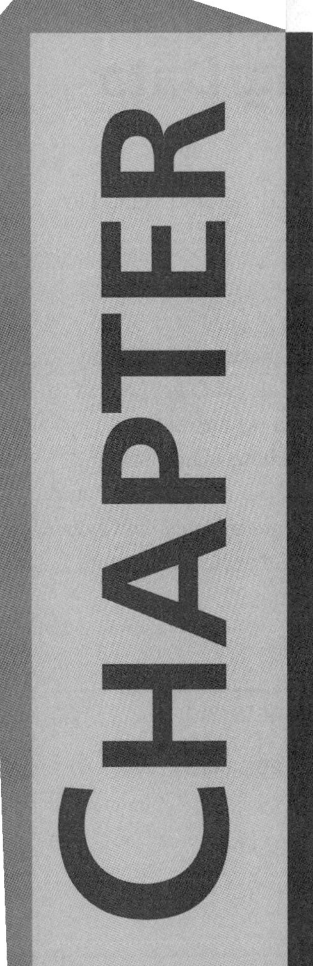

Automating Tasks

by Bill Ball

In This Chapter

"[T]he three great virtues of a programmer: *laziness*, *impatience*, and *hubris*."

—Wall and Schwartz, in *Programming Perl*

Automation enlists a machine—a Linux computer, in the present case—to perform jobs. What makes this definition live, however, and the true subject of this chapter, is *attitude*. The most important step you can take in understanding mechanisms of automation under Red Hat Linux is to adopt the attitude that the computer works for *you*. After you've done that, when you realize you're too lazy to type a telephone number that the machine should already know or too impatient to wait until midnight to start backups, and when you have enough confidence in your own creativity to teach the machine a better way, the technical details will work themselves out. This chapter offers more than a dozen examples of how small, understandable automation initiatives make an immediate difference. Let them lead you to your own successes.

First Example—Automating Data Entry

How can the details work out? Let's look at an example from the day before I started to write this chapter.

Problem and Solution

A client wanted to enhance an online catalog to include thumbnail pictures of the merchandise. After a bit of confusion about what this really meant, I realized that I needed to update a simple database table of products to include a new column (or attribute or value) that would specify the filenames of the thumbnails. The database management system has a couple of interactive front ends, and I'm a swift typist, so it probably would have been quickest to point and click my way through the 200 picture updates. Did I do that? Of course not—what happened later proved the wisdom of this decision. Instead, I wrote a shell script to automate the update, which is shown in Listing 27.1.

LISTING 27.1 A SHELL SCRIPT THAT UPDATES A DATABASE

```
# picture names seem to look like {$DIR/137-13p.jpg,$DIR/201-942f.jpg,...}
# The corresponding products appear to be {137-13P, 201-942F, ...}
DIR=/particular/directory/for/my/client

        # Will we use .gif-s, also, eventually?  I don't know.
for F in $DIR/*.jpg
do
```

```
        # BASE will have values {137-13p,201-942f, ...}
    BASE=`basename $F .jpg`
        # The only suffixes I've encountered are 'p' and 'f', so I'll
➥simply
        #     transform those two.
        # Example values for PRODUCT:  {137-13P, 201-942F, ...}
   PRODUCT=`echo $BASE ¦ tr pf PF`
        # one_command is a shell script that passes a line of SQL to the
➥DBMS.
   one_command update catalog set Picture = "'$DIR/$BASE.jpg'"
➥where Product = "'$PRODUCT'"
 done
```


As it turned out, the team decided within a couple days that the pictures needed to be in a different directory, so it was only a few seconds' work to update the penultimate line of the script and add a comment, such as

```
     ...
          # Do *not* include a directory specification in Picture; that
➥will be known
          #     only at the time the data are retrieved.
     one_command update catalog set Picture = "'$BASE.jpg'" where Product
➥= "'$PRODUCT'"
done
```

and rerun it. It's inevitable we'll someday have more pictures to add to the database or will want reports on orphaned pictures (those that haven't been connected yet to any product), and this same script, or a close derivative of it, will come into play again.

Analysis of the Implementation

Let's work through the example in Listing 27.1 in detail to practice the automation mentality.

Do you understand how the script in Listing 27.1 works? Chapter 25, "Shell Programming," explains shell processing, and Appendix B, "Important Linux Commands and Shell Operators," presents everything you're likely to need about the most commonly used UNIX utilities. You can always learn more about these by reading the corresponding man pages or any of the fine books available on shell programming. The most certain way to learn, of course, is to experiment on your own. For example, if you have any question about what `man tr` means by "…translation…," it's an easy matter to experiment, such as with

```
# tr pf PF <<HERE
abcopqOPQ
FfpPab
HERE
```

and conclude that you're on the right track when you see the following:

```
abcoPqOPQ
FFPPab
```

This is one of the charms of relying on shells for automation; it's easy to bounce between interaction and automation, which shapes a powerful didactic perspective and a check on understanding.

The sample product catalog script in Listing 27.1 is written for `sh` processing. I strongly recommend this be your target for scripts, rather than `ksh`, `csh`, or `bash`. I much prefer any of the latter for interactive, command-line use. In automating, however, when I'm often connecting to hosts that don't use Red Hat Linux, availability and esoteric security issues have convinced me to code using constructs that `sh` and therefore all the shells recognize. Default Red Hat Linux installations link `/bin/sh` and `/bin/bash`. All the work in this chapter is written so that it will function properly no matter what the details are of your host's configuration. Chapter 25 gives more details on the differences among shells.

Did I really include the inline comments, the lines that begin with `#`, when I first wrote the script in Listing 27.1? Yes. I've made this level of source-code documentation a habit, and it's one I recommend to you. If your life is at all like mine, telephones ring, coworkers chat, and power supplies fail; I find it easier to type this much detail as I'm thinking about it, rather than risk having to re-create my thoughts in case of an interruption. Also, it's *much* easier to pick up the work again days or weeks later. Writing for human readability also eases the transition when you pass your work on to others.

Listing 27.1 begins by assigning a shell variable `DIR` in Line 3. It's good practice to make such an assignment, even for a variable (apparently) used only once. It contributes to self-documentation and generally enhances maintainability; it's easy to look at the top of the script and see immediately what magic words or configuration in the outside environment (`/particular/directory/for/my/client`, in this case; see Line 3) the script depends on.

Many of the jobs you'll want to accomplish involve a quantifier: "change all…," "correct every…," and so on. The shell's looping constructs, `for` and `while`, are your friends. You'll make almost daily use of them.

`basename` and `tr` are universally available and widely used. `tr`, like many UNIX utilities, expects to read standard input. If you have information in shell variables, you can feed `tr` the information you want, either through a pipe from `echo`, as in

```
echo $VARIABLE | tr [a-z] [A-Z]
```

or an equivalent, or with a so-called `HERE` document, such as

```
tr [a-z] [A-Z] <<HERE
$VARIABLE
HERE
```

or perhaps by creating a temporary file:

```
echo $VARIABLE >$TMPFILE
tr [a-z] [A-Z] $TMPFILE
```

`one_command`, as invoked in Line 15 of Listing 27.1, is a two-line shell script I had written earlier in the day to process SQL commands. Why not inline the body of that script here? Although that's technically feasible, I have a strong preference for small, simple programs that are easy to understand and correspondingly easy to implement correctly. `one_command` already has been verified to do one small job reliably, so the script lets it do that job. This fits with the UNIX tradition that counsels combining robust toolkit pieces to construct grander works.

In fact, notice that the example in Listing 27.1 shows the shell's nature as a "glue" language. There's a small amount of processing within the shell in manipulating filenames, and then most of the work is handed off to other commands; the shell just "glues" together results. This is typical and is a correct style you should adopt for your own scripting.

Certainly, it was pleasant when the filenames changed and I realized I could rework one word of the script, rather than retype the 200 entries. As satisfying as this was, the total benefit of automation is still more profound. Even greater than saving my time are the improvements in quality, traceability, and reusability this affords. With the script, I control the data entering the database at a higher level and eliminate whole categories of error: mistyping, accidentally pushing a wrong button in a graphical user interface, and so on. Also, the script in Listing 27.1 records my procedure, in case it's later useful to audit the data. Suppose, for example, that next year it's decided I shouldn't have inserted any of these references to the database's `Picture` attribute. How many will have to be backed out? Useful answers—at most, the count of `$DIR/*.jpg`—can be read directly from the script; there's no need to rely on memory or speculate.

Tips for Improving Automation Technique

You're in charge of your career in automation. Along with everything else this chapter advises, you'll go farthest if you do the following:

- Improve your automation technique.
- Engineer well.

These tips have specific meaning in the rest of this chapter. Look for ways to apply them in all that follows.

Continuing Education

There are three important ways to improve your skill with automation techniques, which apply equally well whether you're using Perl, `cron`, Expect, or another mechanism:

- Scan the documentation.
- Read good scripts.
- Practice writing scripts.

Documentation has the reputation of being dry and even unreadable. It's important that you learn how to employ it. All the tools presented here have man pages, which you need to be comfortable using. Read these documents and reread them. Authors of the tools faced many of the challenges you do. Often, reading through the lists of options or keywords, you'll realize that particular capabilities apply exactly to your situation. Study the documentation with this in mind; look for the ideas that you can use. Give particular attention to commands you don't recognize. If some of them—`cu`, perhaps, or `od`—are largely superannuated, you'll realize in reading about others—such as `tput`, `ulimit`, `bc`, `nice`, or `wait`—that earlier users were confronted with just the situations that confound your own work. Stand on their shoulders and see farther.

NOTE

Want to know more about a command? There can be two other sources of information besides its man page. Red Hat Linux users should also check the `/usr/doc` directory, where there more than 230 programs have individual directories of additional information. You can also find more detailed information about a command if its man page indicates the program is part of the GNU software distribution. Use the info command in this way: `info` *<command>*.

It's important to read good programming. Aspiring literary authors find inspiration in Pushkin and Pynchon, not grammar primers; similarly, you'll go farthest when you read the best work of the best programmers. Look in the columns of computer magazines and, most importantly, the archives of software with freely available source. Good examples of coding occasionally turn up in Usenet discussions. Prize these; read them and learn from the masters.

All the examples in this chapter are written to be easy to use. They typically do one small task completely; this is one of the best ways to demonstrate a new concept. Although exception handling, and argument validation in particular, is important, it is beyond the scope of this chapter.

Crystallize your learning by writing your own scripts. All the documents you read will make more sense after you put the knowledge in place with your own experience.

Good Engineering

The other advice for those pursuing automation is to practice good engineering. This always starts with a clear, well-defined goal. Automation isn't an absolute good; it's only a method for achieving human goals. Part of what you'll learn in working through this chapter is how much, and how little, to automate.

When your goal is set, move as close to it as you can with components that are already written. "Glue" existing programs together with small, understandable scripting modules. Choose meaningful variable names. Define interfaces carefully. Write comments.

Shell Scripts

Although Chapter 25 covers the basic syntax and language of shell programming, let's look at a few additional examples of scripts that are often useful in day-to-day operation.

chstr

Users who maintain source code, client lists, and other records often want to launch a find-and-replace operation from the command line. It's useful to have a variant of `chstr` on UNIX hosts. Listing 27.2 gives one example.

LISTING 27.2 `chstr`—A SIMPLE FIND-AND-REPLACE OPERATION

```
########
#
# See usage() definition, below, for more details.
#
# This implementation doesn't do well with complicated escape
#     sequences. That has been no more than a minor problem in
#     the real world.
#
########
usage() {
     echo \
```

continues

LISTING 27.2 CONTINUED

```
"chstr BEFORE AFTER <filenames>
     changes the first instance of BEFORE to AFTER in each line of
➥<filenames>,
     and reports on the differences.
Examples:
     chstr TX Texas */addresses.*
     chstr ii counter2 *.c"
     exit 0
}

case $1 in
     -h¦-help)     usage;;
esac

if test $# -lt 3
then
     usage
fi

TMPDIR=/tmp
     # It's OK if more than one instance of chstr is run simultaneously.
     #     The TMPFILE names are specific to each invocation, so there's
     #     no conflict.
TMPFILE=$TMPDIR/chstr.$$

BEFORE=$1
AFTER=$2

     # Toss the BEFORE and AFTER arguments out of the argument list.
shift;shift

for FILE in $*
do
     sed -e "s/$BEFORE/$AFTER/" $FILE >$TMPFILE
     echo "$FILE:"
     diff $FILE $TMPFILE
     echo ""
     mv $TMPFILE $FILE
done
```

Most interactive editors permit a form of global search-and-replace, and some even make it easy to operate on more than one file. Perhaps that's a superior automation for your needs. If not, `chstr` is a minimal command-line alternative that is maximally simple to use.

WWW Retrieval

A question that arises frequently is how to automate retrieval of pages from the World Wide Web. This section shows the simplest of many techniques.

FTP Retrieval

Create a shell script, `retrieve_one`, with the contents of Listing 27.3 and with execution enabled (that is, command `chmod +x retrieve_one`).

LISTING 27.3 `retrieve_one`—AUTOMATING FTP RETRIEVAL

```
# Usage:  "retrieve_one HOST:FILE" uses anonymous FTP to connect
#     to HOST and retrieve FILE into the local directory.

MY_ACCOUNT=myaccount@myhost.com
HOST=`echo $1 ¦ sed -e "s/:.*//"`
FILE=`echo $1 ¦ sed -e "s/.*://"`
LOCAL_FILE=`basename $FILE`

     # -v:  report all statistics.
     # -n:  connect without interactive user authentication.
ftp -v -n $HOST << SCRIPT
     user anonymous $MY_ACCOUNT
     get $FILE $LOCAL_FILE
     quit
SCRIPT
```

`retrieve_one` is useful for such purposes as ordering a current copy of a FAQ into your local directory; start experimenting with it by making a request with the following:

```
# retrieve_one rtfm.mit.edu:/pub/usenet-by hierarchy/comp/os/linux/answers/
➥linux/faq/part1
```

HTTP Retrieval

For an HTTP interaction, let the Lynx browser do the bulk of the work. The Lynx browser that accompanies the Red Hat distribution is adequate for all but the most specialized purposes. In those cases, pick up a binary executable of the latest Lynx and simple installation directions at `http://www.crl.com/~subir/lynx/bin`. Although most Lynx users think of Lynx as an interactive browser, it's also handy for dropping a copy of the latest headlines, with live links, in a friend's mailbox with

```
# lynx -source http://www.cnn.com ¦ mail
someone@somewhere.com
```

To create a primitive news update service, script

```
NEW=/tmp/news.new
OLD=/tmp/news.old
URL=http://www.cnn.com
while true
do
     mv $NEW $OLD
     lynx -dump -nolist $URL >$NEW
     diff $NEW $OLD
          # Wait ten minutes before starting the next comparison.
     sleep 600
done
```

and launch it in the background (using the ampersand, `&`). Any changes in the appearance of CNN's home page will appear onscreen every 10 minutes. This simple approach is less practical than you might first expect because CNN periodically shuffles the content without changing the information. It's an instructive example, however, and a starting point from which you can elaborate your own scripts.

Conclusions on Shell Programming

Shells are glue; if there's a way to get an application to perform an action from the command line, there's almost certainly a way to wrap it in a shell script that gives you power over argument validation, iteration, and input-output redirection. These are powerful techniques and well worth the few minutes of study and practice it takes to begin learning them.

Even small automations pay off. My personal rule of thumb is to write tiny disposable one-line shell scripts when I expect to use a sequence even twice during a session. For example, although I have a sophisticated set of reporting commands for analyzing World Wide Web server logs, I also find myself going to the trouble of editing a disposable script such as `/tmp/r9`,

```
grep claird `ls -t /usr/cern/log/* | head -1` | grep -v $1 | wc -l
```

to do quick, ad hoc queries on recent hit patterns; this particular example reports on the number of requests for pages that include the string `claird` and exclude the first argument to `/tmp/r9`, in the most recent log.

cron and at Jobs

Red Hat Linux comes with several utilities that manage the rudiments of job scheduling. `at` schedules a process for later execution, and `cron` (or `crontab`—it has a couple of interfaces, and different engineers use both these names) periodically launches a process.

NOTE

The `crond` daemon is started when you boot Red Hat Linux and checks the `/etc/crontab` file and `/var/spool/cron` directory every minute, looking for assigned times at assigned times. The `/etc/cron.allow` and `/etc/cron.deny` files control who may use `crontab` on your system. For details, see the `crontab` man page. You can also control who can use the `at` command on your system with the `/etc/at.allow` and `/etc/at.deny` files, although by default, Red Hat Linux lets anyone use the `at` command. (No `/etc/at.deny` file initially exists.)

cron and find—Exploring Disk Usage

One eternal reality of system administration is that there's not enough disk space. The following sections offer a couple expedients recommended for keeping on top of what's happening with your system.

Cores

`cron` use always involves a bit of setup. Although Appendix B gives more details on `cron`'s features and options, I'll go carefully through an example here, one that helps track down core clutter.

You need at least one external file to start using the `cron` facility. Practice `cron` concepts by commanding first

```
# echo "0,5,10,15,20,25,30,35,40,45,50,55 * * * * date > `tty`"
➥>/tmp/experiment
```

then,

```
# crontab /tmp/experiment
```

and finally,

```
# crontab -l
```

The last of these gives you a result that looks something like the following:

```
0,5,10,15,20,25,30,35,40,45,50,55 * * * * date > /dev/ttyxx
```

Every five minutes, the current time will appear in the window from which you launched this experiment.

For a more useful example, create a `/tmp/entry` file with the single line

```
0 2 * * * find / -name "core*" -exec ls -l {} \;
```

Next, use the command

```
# crontab /tmp/entry
```

The result is that each morning, at 2:00, `cron` launches the core-searching job and emails you the results when finished. This is quite useful because Linux creates files `core*` under certain error conditions. These core images are often large and can easily fill up a distressing amount of space on your disk. With the preceding sequence, you'll have a report in your email inbox each morning, listing exactly the locations and sizes of a collection of files that are likely doing you no good.

User Space

Suppose you've experimented a bit and accumulated an inventory of `cron` jobs to monitor the health of your system. Now, along with your other jobs, you want your system to tell you every Monday morning at 2:10 which 10 users have the biggest home directory trees (`/home/*`). First, enter

```
# crontab -l >/tmp/entries
```

to capture all the jobs you've scheduled, and append the line

```
10 2 * * 1 du -s /home/* | sort -nr | head -10
```

to the bottom of `/tmp/entries`. Make the request

```
# crontab /tmp/entries
```

and `cron` will email the reports you seek.

at: Scheduling Future Events

Suppose you write a weekly column on cycles in the material world, which you deliver by email. To simplify legal ramifications involving financial markets, you make a point of delivering it at 5:00 Friday afternoon. It's Wednesday now, you've finished your analysis, and you're almost through packing for the vacation you're starting tonight. How do you do right by your subscribers? It only takes three lines of `at` scripting:

```
# at 17:00 Friday << COMMAND
   mail -s "This week's CYCLES report." mailing_list <
➥analysis.already_written
COMMAND
```

This schedules the `mail` command for later processing. You can log off from your session, and your Linux host will still send the mail at `17:00 Friday`, just as you instructed. In fact, you can even shut down your machine after commanding it `at ...`, and, as long as it's rebooted in time, your scheduled task will still be launched on the schedule you dictated.

Other Mechanisms: Expect, Perl, and More

Are you ready to move beyond the constraints of the UNIX shell? Several alternative technologies are free, easy to install, easy to learn, and more powerful—that is, with richer capabilities and more structured syntax—than the shell. A few examples will suggest what they have to offer.

Comparing Technologies

I'm often asked to compare different technologies for automation; as a service to readers, I've launched the page `http://starbase.neosoft.com/~claird/comp.lang.misc/portable_scripting.html`, which answers questions about choosing among different scripting languages. The most important principles are as follows:

- Choose a language that your friends (acquaintances, coworkers, correspondents, and so on) use.
- Choose a language that feels good to you.

With few exceptions, the capabilities of different languages are close enough that the social and psychological factors dominate.

Expect

Expect "is a must-know tool for system administrators and many others," according to a user testimonial that appears on the back cover of *Exploring Expect*, its standard reference. Why? Expect automates interactions, particularly those involving terminal control and time delays, that no other tool has attempted. Many command-line applications have the reputation for being unscriptable because they involve password entry and refuse to accept redirection of standard input for this purpose. That's no problem for Expect, however. After you install Expect (`http://starbase.neosoft.com/~claird/comp.lang.tcl/expect.html`), create a script `hold` with the contents of Listing 27.4.

LISTING 27.4 `hold`—A "KEEP-ALIVE" WRITTEN IN EXPECT

```
#!/usr /bin/expect

# Usage:  "hold HOST USER PASS".
# Action:  login to node HOST as USER.  Offer a shell prompt for
#     normal usage, and also print to the screen the word HELD
```

continues

LISTING 27.4 CONTINUED

```
#     every five seconds, to exercise the connection periodically.
#     This is useful for testing and using WANs with short time-outs.
#     You can walk away from the keyboard, and never lose your
#     connection through a time-out.
# WARNING:  the security hazard of passing a password through the
#     command line makes this example only illustrative.  Modify to
#     a particular security situation as appropriate.
set hostname [lindex $argv 0]
set username [lindex $argv 1]
set password [lindex $argv 2]

     # There's trouble if $username's prompt is not set to "...} ".
     #     A more sophisticated manager knows how to look for different
     #     prompts on different hosts.
set prompt_sequence "} "

spawn telnet $hostname

expect "login: "
send "$username\r"
expect "Password:"
send "$password\r"

     # Some hosts don't inquire about TERM.  That's another
     #     complexity to consider before widespread use
     #     of this application is practical.
     # Note use of global [gl] pattern matching to parse "*"
     #     as a wildcard.
expect -gl "TERM = (*)"
send "\r"

expect $prompt_sequence
send "sh -c 'while true; do; echo HELD; sleep 5; done'\r"
interact
```

I work with several telephone lines that are used with short timeouts, as a check on out-of-pocket expenses. I use a variant of the script in Listing 27.4 daily, for I often need that to hold one of the connections open.

Expect is an extension to `tcl`, so it is fully programmable with all the `tcl` capabilities that Chapter 33, "`tcl` and `tk` Programming," presents. For information about `tcl` and `tk` from its author, Dr. John Ousterhout, visit `http://www.sun.com/960710/cover/ousterhout.html`. For more information about Expect, visit `http://www.expect.org`. For a perspective on `tcl` that emphasizes the automation themes of this chapter, see the pages `http://starbase.neosoft.com/~claird/comp.lang.tcl/tcl.html` and `http://starbase.neosoft.com/~claird/comp.lang.tcl/expect.html`.

Perl

Chapter 31, "Perl Programming," presents Perl as the most popular scripting language for Red Hat Linux, apart from the shell. Its power and brevity take on particular value in automation contexts, as the page
`http://starbase.neosoft.com/~claird/comp.lang.perl.misc/perl.html`
emphasizes.

> **NOTE**
>
> For more information about Perl, or to get the latest release, browse `http://www.perl.com` or `http://www.perl.org`.

For example, if `/usr/local/bin/modified_directories.pl` contains

```
#!/usr/bin/perl

# Usage:  "modified_directories.pl DIR1 DIR2 ... DIRN"
# Output:  a list of all directories in the file systems under
#     DIR1 ... DIRN, collectively.  They appear, sorted by the
#     interval since their last activity, that is, since a file
#     within them was last created, deleted, or renamed.
# Randal Schwartz wrote a related program from which this is
#     descended.
use File::Find;
@directory_list = @ARGV;

     # "-M" abbreviates "time since last modification", while
     #      "-d" "... is a directory."
find (sub {$modification_lapse(File::Find::name} = -M if -d;},
➥directory_list);
foreach (sort{$modification_lapse{$a} <=> $modification_lapse{$b}} keys
➥%size) {
     # Tabulate the results in nice columns.
     printf "%5d:  %s\n", $modification_lapse{$_}, $_;
}
```

and you adjoin an entry such as

```
20 2 * * * /usr/local/bin/modified_directories.pl /
```

to your `crontab`, then each morning you'll receive an email report on the date each directory on your host was last modified. This can be useful both for spotting security issues when read-only directories have been changed (they'll appear unexpectedly at the top of the list) and for identifying dormant domains in the filesystem (at the bottom of the list) that might be liberated for better uses.

Other Tools

Many other general-purpose scripting languages effectively automate operations. Apart from Perl and `tcl`, Python deserves the most attention for several reasons, such as its portability and extensibility.

The next sections describe Python and several other special-purpose tools important in automation, such as Emacs, `procmail`, and `calendar`.

Python

Python can be of special interest to Red Hat Linux users. Python is object-oriented, modern, clean, portable, and particularly easy to maintain. If you are a full-time system administrator looking for a scripting language that will grow with you, consider Python. See Chapter 34, "Programming in Python," for more information. The official home page for Python is `http://www.python.org`.

Emacs

Emacs is one of the most polarizing lightning rods for religious controversy among computer users. Emacs has many intelligent and zealous users who believe it to be the ideal platform for all automation efforts. Its devotees have developed what was originally a screen editor into a tool with capabilities to manage newsgroup discussion, Web browsing, application development, general-purpose scripting, and much more. For the purposes of this chapter, what you need to know about Emacs follows:

- It's an editor that you ought to try at some point in your career.
- If you favor integrated development environments, Emacs can do almost anything you imagine. As an editor, it emulates any other editor, and its developers ensure that it always offers state-of-the-art capabilities in language-directed formatting, application integration, and development automation.

Even if the "weight" of Emacs (it's slow on startup and seems to require quite a bit of education and configuration) sways you against its daily use, keep it in mind as a paragon of how sophisticated programming makes common operations more efficient.

> **NOTE**
>
> The Emacs editor is included with Red Hat Linux. You can use Emacs with or without the X Window system. Type the word `emacs` on the command line of your console or an X11 terminal window, and press the Enter key. Then, run its built-in tutorial by pressing Ctrl+H and typing the `t` key.

procmail

Computer use has exploded in the Internet era. The most-indispensable, most-used Internet function is email. Can email be automated?

Yes, of course, and it's perhaps the single best return on your invested time to do so. Along with aliases, distribution lists, startup configurations, and the plethora of mail agents or clients with their feature sets, you'll want to learn about `procmail`. Suppose that you receive a hundred messages a day, that a fifth of them can be handled completely automatically, and that it takes at least three seconds of your time to process a single piece of email; those are conservative estimates, from the experience of the computer workers I know. A bit of `procmail` automation will save you at least a minute a day, or six hours a year. Even conservative estimates make it clear that an hour of setting up `procmail` pays for itself many times over.

Along with the man `procmail*` pages, serious study of `procmail` starts with the page `http://www.faqs.org/faqs/mail/filtering-faq`, Nancy McGough's "Filtering Mail FAQ." This gives detailed installation and debugging directions. To supplement it, I've launched the page `http://starbase.neosoft.com/~claird/comp.mail.misc/procmail.html` to keep you updated on the latest `procmail` news. Because your Red Hat Linux machine will almost certainly have a correctly configured `procmail`, you can immediately begin to program your personal use of it. As a first experiment, create exactly these files:

`~/.procmailrc`, with contents

```
VERBOSE=on
MAILDIR=$HOME/mail
PMDIR=$HOME/.procmail
LOGFILE=$PMDIR/log
INCLUDERC=$PMDIR/rc.testing
```

`~/.procmail/rc.testing`, holding

```
:0:
* ^Subject:.*HOT
SPAM.HOT
```

and ~/.forward, with

```
"¦IFS=' ' && exec /usr/local/bin/procmail -f ¦¦ exec 75 #YOUR_EMAIL_NAME"
```

After you create these three, set necessary permissions with the following:

```
# chmod 644 ~/.forward
# chmod a+x ~/.
```

Now, exercise your filter with the following:

```
# echo "This message 1." ¦ mail -s "Example of HOT SPAM." YOUR_EMAIL_NAME
# echo "This message 2." ¦ mail -s "Desired message." YOUR_EMAIL_NAME
```

What you now see in your mailbox is only one new item, the one with the subject `Desired message`. You also have a new file in your home directory, `SPAM.HOT`, holding the first message.

`procmail` is a robust, flexible utility that you can program to achieve even more useful automations than this. When you gain familiarity with it, it will become natural to construct rules that, for example, automatically discard obvious spam, sort incoming mailing-list traffic, and perhaps even implement pager forwarding, remote system monitoring, or FAQ responding. This can save you considerable time each day.

calendar

`calendar` is quite specialized, easy to use, and, because it matches a real-world need particularly well, very useful. `calendar` takes responsibility for sending messages to your screen to remind you of events or responsibilities. You can download `calendar` from `ftp://ftp.redhat.com/pub/contrib/i386`, file `calendar-8.4-3.i386.rpm`. Experiment with `calendar` by creating a local file called `calendar` (the command and the specification file have the same name, in general) with the following contents:

```
#include "/usr/lib/gcal-lib/calendar.holid"
Monday\tTake out trash.
Tuesday\tFeed dolphin.
Wednesday\tRe-synchronize orgone collector.
Thursday\tKaryotype produce from refrigerator.
Friday\tTake out trash.
Saturday\tPractice polo.
Sunday\tClimb Matterhorn.
```

Run `calendar`. You'll see a few historical events with current anniversaries and your own applicable daily chores. Three aspects of `calendar` give it dramatic power:

- You can run `calendar` automatically, using the techniques you've learned so far: For example, have `cron` put a reminder in your email every morning or invoke `calendar` from your shell's startup file so that it's run each time you log in.

- `calendar` has a sophisticated knowledge of calendars. It will, on request, remind you when it's the second Tuesday of the month, the day after Easter, or Mother's Day. See `man calendar` for details.
- The `#include` mechanism permits information-sharing. If your `calendar` begins

```
#include "/some/centrally/maintained/directory/calendar.bigboss"
#include "/some/centrally/maintained/directory/calendar.cafetaria"
/* My own stuff follows ... */
```

  the first reminders `calendar` gives you will be those for the company president and the lunch-time menu, with your personal events after.

Although `calendar` does a small job, it does it efficiently. Consider whether its capability to focus attention on the upcoming days' priorities matches your needs.

Internal Scripts

One more element of the automation attitude is to be on the lookout for opportunities within every application you use. Scripting has become a pervasive theme, and almost all common applications have at least a rudimentary macro or scripting capability. IRC users know about bots, Web browsers typically expose at least a couple of scripting interfaces, all modern PPP clients are scriptable, and even such venerable tools as `vi` and `ftp` have configuration, shortcut, and macro capabilities that enormously magnify productivity. If you use a tool regularly, take a few minutes to reread its presentation in this volume; chances are, you'll come up with a way to make your work easier and more effective.

Concluding Challenge for an Automater—Explaining Value

You've become knowledgeable and experienced in scripting your computer so that it best serves you. You know how to improve your skills in script writing. You've practiced different approaches enough to know how to solve problems efficiently. The final challenge in your automation career is this: How do you explain how good you have become?

This is a serious problem, and, as usual, the solution begins with attitude. You no longer pound at the keyboard to bludgeon technical tasks into submission; now, you operate in a more refined way and achieve correspondingly grander results. As an employee, you're much more valuable than the system administrators and programmers who reinvent wheels every day. In your recreational or personal use of Red Hat Linux, the computer is working for you, not the other way around, as it might have been when you started. Your attitude needs to adjust to the reality you've created by improving your productivity. Invest in yourself, whether by attending technical conferences where you can further promote your skills, negotiating a higher salary, or simply taking the time in your computer work to get things right. It's easy in organizations to give attention to crises and reward those visibly coping with emergencies. It takes true leadership to plan ahead, organize work so emergencies don't happen, and use techniques of automation to achieve predictable and manageable results on schedule.

One of the most effective tools you have in taking up this challenge is *quantification*. Keep simple records to demonstrate how much time you put into setting up backups before you learned about `cron`, or run a simple experiment to compare two ways of approaching an elementary database maintenance operation. Find out how much of your online time goes just to the login process and decide whether scripting that is justified. Chart a class of mistakes that you make and see whether your precision improves as you apply automation ideas.

In all cases, keep in mind you are efficient, perhaps extraordinarily efficient, because of the knowledge you apply. Automation feels good!

Summary

Automation offers enormous opportunities for using your Linux computer to achieve the goals you set. The examples in this chapter demonstrate that every Linux user can begin immediately to exploit the techniques and attitude of automation.

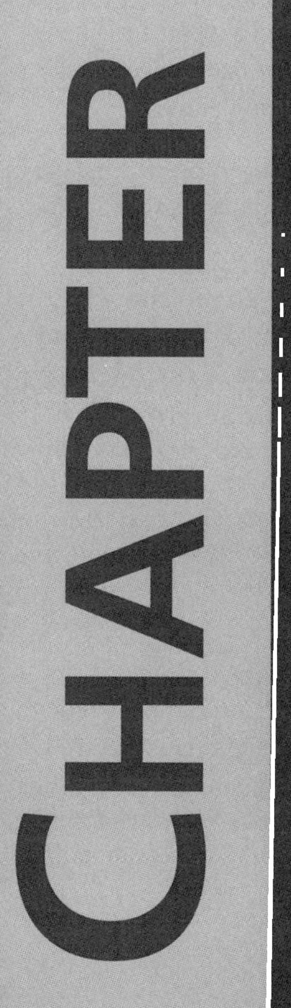

Configuring and Building Kernels

By Sriranga Veeraraghavan

In This Chapter

The kernel is the program that is loaded at startup time to provide an interface between the user-level programs and the hardware. It performs the actual task-switching that occurs in multitasking systems, handling requests to read and write to disks, dealing with the network interface, and managing memory. These functions give Linux the underlying behavior seen throughout the system.

Technically, Linux is only the kernel. The programs that surround it, such as the compilers, editors, windowing managers, and so on, make up the distribution. For example, Red Hat Linux is considered a *distribution* of Linux. Although several different distributions of Linux exist, the kernel is common to all of them.

The most recent version of Red Hat includes version 2.0.35 of the Linux kernel. This kernel is automatically installed and contains support for a large number of devices. Unless you have an unusual configuration, the standard-issue kernel from Red Hat should work on your machine without any changes.

Although the standard-issue kernel will work, you might need to add support for a new device or simply pare down the list of devices the kernel supports so that it takes less memory. Either way, you need to step through the kernel configuration process.

CAUTION

Recompiling a new kernel can be potentially dangerous. By doing so, you can easily deny yourself access to the system, so be sure to follow all the safety tips in this chapter. Being locked out of your own machine because of a silly mistake is extremely frustrating.

At the very least, you should have a startup disk ready. Test it and verify that it comes up just as you expect. Be familiar with the commands necessary to mount the root partition, make changes to key files, and rerun LILO.

An Introduction to the Linux Kernel

Now that you have an understanding of what the kernel does, you might find a need to reconfigure and build it. In this section, we discuss the kernel version numbers, acquiring the kernel source code, and installing it in the correct place.

Kernel Version Numbers

The version numbers of the kernel have more significance than might appear at first glance. The version number (for example, 2.0.35) is broken up into three parts:

- The major number
- The minor number
- The revision number

The major version number, 2 in this case, rarely changes. Every time the number increases, major improvements have been made in the kernel and upgrades are definitely warranted.

The minor number, 0 in this case, indicates the kernel's stability. Even-numbered kernels (0, 2, 4, and so on) are considered stable production-quality kernels, whereas odd-numbered kernels (1, 3, 5, and so on) are development kernels. When a kernel reaches a production version, no more features are added, and the only changes made to it are to fix any last-minute bugs. In contrast, odd-numbered kernels are actively being worked on. They contain experimental code and feature the latest developments. The side effect of these added features is the instability that might exist in them. Sometimes they are stable; at other times they have critical flaws. Odd-numbered kernels should be used only on systems on which users are comfortable trying out new features and can accept downtime incurred by frequent kernel upgrades.

The last number, which is the revision number, indicates the current patch level for this version of the release. During the development phase, new versions can be released as often as twice a week.

Acquiring the Source Tree

The CD-ROM that comes with this book contains an RPM for the kernel source tree. To use the source tree, simply install it, using the `rpm` package. You can find updated versions of the kernel source at `http://www.redhat.com` or from one of the following:

- `http://www.kernel.org`
- `ftp://ftp.cdrom.com/pub/linux/sunsite/kernel`
- `ftp://sunsite.unc.edu/pub/Linux/kernel`
- `ftp://tsx-11.mit.edu/pub/linux/sources/system`

The source tree comes in one large file named

`linux-X.X.XX.tar.gz`

Here *X.X.XX* is the version number of the kernel. In this chapter we will use version 2.0.35.

If you decide to download a more recent source tree instead of using the version on the CD-ROM, you need to decompress and untar it. You should do so in the /usr/src directory because symbolic links from /usr/include have already been set up. By manipulating the /usr/src directory so that /usr/src/linux always points to the most recent kernel, you don't have to fix the /usr/include directories every time you compile a new kernel.

To unpack the kernel, simply run

```
tar xzf linux-2.0.35.tar.gz
```

If you download a different version, substitute its filename for linux-2.0.35.tar.gz in the previous command. This command decompresses and untars the kernel into the directory:

```
/usr/src/linux
```

SYMBOLIC LINKS TO THE KERNEL SOURCES

If you have an older kernel in place, you might not want to remove the previous source tree. After all, if you need to revert to it, not having to download it again would be nice.

To avoid the need to download again, create a new directory titled linux-2.0.35, where 2.0.35 is the version number of the new kernel. Then create a symbolic link from /usr/src/linux to /usr/src/linux-2.0.35. By doing so, you can easily change the symbolic link to point to new kernels as they are released.

A pleasant side effect is that your /usr/include directories will always point to /usr/src/linux, which has the latest versions of the kernel header files.

If this is the first kernel you've compiled, be sure to take a few minutes to read the /usr/src/linux/README file. It contains up-to-the-minute details about the exact kernel you are working with, as well as problem-reporting information.

GETTING NEW DRIVERS

Because of the amount of concurrent development done in the Linux community, you might find that not all the drivers provided with the Linux kernel are the latest. If you have problems with a particular device, searching on the Internet for a more recent version of the driver is often worthwhile. A good place to start searching is

```
http://www.linuxhq.com
```

This site contains sources for the latest kernels and drivers, along with an extensive set of links to other Linux sites.

Patching the Source Tree

When a new version of the kernel source tree is released, a patch is released containing the differences between the latest version and its predecessor version. The patch is much smaller than the entire new source tree, making it a much quicker upgrade.

When you're patching the Linux kernel, keep in mind that patches apply to only one particular version of the Linux kernel. For example, if you have the 2.0.30 kernel, the only patch that should be applied to it is the patch for the version 2.0.31 kernel. If you want to bring your kernel up to version 2.0.35, you will need to apply four patches: 2.0.31, 2.0.32, 2.0.33, and 2.0.34. The patch files are available in the same directories as the kernel sources at the FTP and Web sites mentioned previously in this chapter.

After you download a patch, you need to use a combination of the `tar` and `patch` programs to make the changes. Begin by moving the patch into the /usr/src directory. After it is there, run these commands:

```
cd /usr/src
gzip -cd patch-XX.gz ¦ patch -p0
```

where *XX* is the version number of the patch you are applying. For example, to upgrade version 2.0.34 kernel sources, you would apply the following patch:

```
cd /usr/src
gzip -cd patch-2.0.35.gz ¦ patch -p0
```

After you apply the patch, check for any files ending in .rej in the /usr/src/linux directory. If any such files exist, verify that you applied the patch correctly. If you are sure you applied the patch correctly, watch for an update patch within a day or two. When an error occurs with the patch file, a new version of the patch appears quickly.

Modules

Modules are pieces of the kernel that are not loaded into memory at startup time. Instead, they are loaded on demand and removed from memory after a period of nonuse. Modules are commonly used for networking code on a machine that is not permanently connected, supporting devices not often used, and so on. Although you can make even commonly used kernel code a module, you might find that the overhead in reloading it often outweighs the benefits of its being removed from memory when not in use. Some common modules include AppleTalk, IPX, UFS, and HFS.

The Linux kernel as of version 2.0 has easy-to-use support for modules. Modules have, for all practical purposes, become transparent in their operation. If you are curious about the details of their operation, read the documentation that comes with the `insmod`, `rmmod`, `ksyms`, and `lsmod` programs.

Configuring the Linux Kernel

Now that you have the kernel source tree unpacked, you can begin the configuration.

CAUTION

Before making any key changes to a system, such as installing a new kernel, you should have a startup disk ready. In the unfortunate event that you configure something incorrectly (and everybody does eventually), you will need a way to get back into your system.

If you are only compiling a new kernel and not making any other key changes, you can simplify the emergency rescue process by making a backup of the kernel and modules on the root partition. Modify the /etc/lilo.conf file to allow you to restart to your currently working kernel as an option. This step is important because not all kernels work as advertised, especially if you are compiling a development kernel. It is much easier to revert to a working kernel stored on your root partition than it is to recover a system by restarting from a floppy disk.

You can configure the Linux kernel in one of three ways:

- `make config`
- `make menuconfig`
- `make xconfig`

The first (and original) method is to use the `make config` command. It provides you with a text-based interface for answering all the configuration options. You are prompted for all the options you need to set up your kernel. The text-based interface is a good backup for instances in which you don't have fancy screen control (for example, if your console is an old terminal for which you don't have a `termcap` setting); hence, you should be familiar with it.

More likely, however, you will have a standard PC console. If so, you can use the `make menuconfig` command, which provides all the kernel options in an easy-to-use menu.

For the sample configuration in this chapter, you will use the `make xconfig` command, which provides a full graphical interface to all the kernel options.

Starting the Configuration

For the sample configuration, assume that the system is a generic Pentium class PC with an EIDE hard drive, an IDE CD-ROM, an Adaptec 2940 SCSI card, and a 3Com 3C905 Ethernet card. The system will be used as a server, so we will compile version 2.0.35, which is a production kernel. We are not using a development kernel because this will be a production machine.

CAUTION

You should never use development kernels on production systems.

To start the configuration tool, change into the directory /usr/src/linux and invoke the following command:

```
make xconfig
```

This command generates some text in your terminal, and then a window similar to the one shown in Figure 28.1 appears.

The menu options, which are centered in the middle of the window, start with Code maturity level options and end with Kernel hacking. By using the four buttons below the menu, you can load or save configurations to disk for further work.

FIGURE 28.1
Kernel configuration main menu.

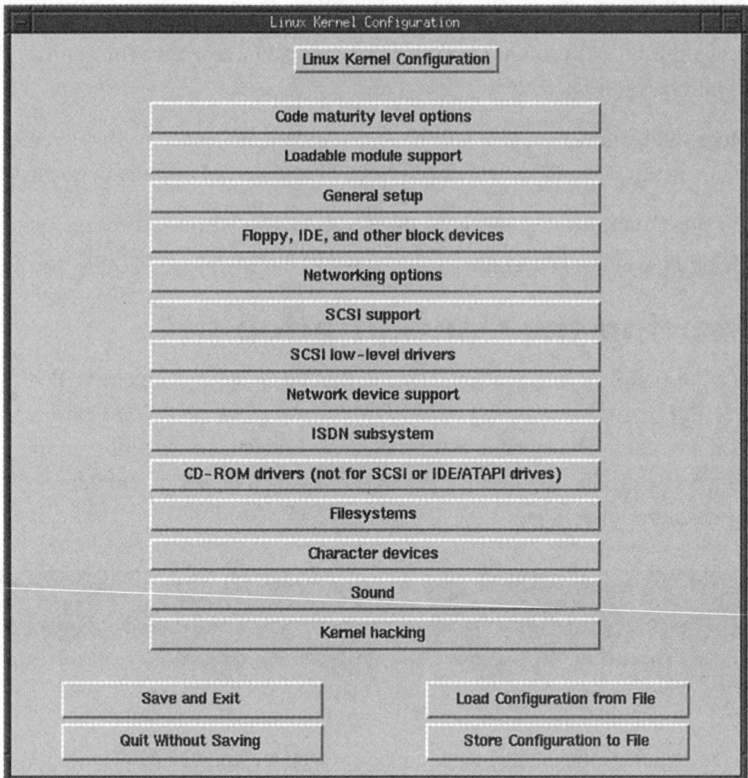

Stepping Through the Menus

Each top-level menu in the main window lets you access a list of options you can tag to compile into the kernel, compile as a module, or not include at all. Remember that each option you elect to compile into the kernel makes the kernel a little larger, thereby requiring more memory. In addition to adding support for key system functions into the kernel, such as network drivers and file system support for your startup drive, you should add only those features you will need on a constant basis. Features that are not often used, such as PPP support, are best compiled as modules.

Code Maturity Level

To start, take a close look at the menu under Code Maturity Level Options. Begin by clicking that menu. This action brings up the Code Maturity Level Options window, as shown in Figure 28.2.

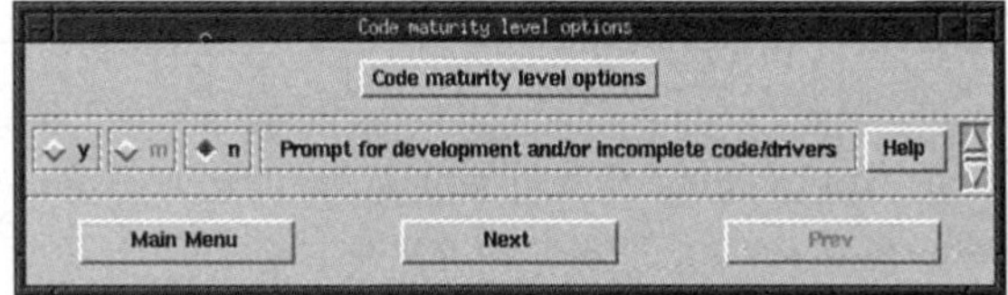

FIGURE 28.2
The Code Maturity Level Options menu.

At the top of the window is the title of the menu, and below the title is the list of options. This menu has only one option, Prompt for Development and/or Incomplete Code/Drivers.

To the left of this window are your choices for this particular option. The three choices for each option are:

- `y` for Yes. Selecting this option means that the corresponding code will be compiled into the kernel and always be loaded.
- `m` for Module. If this option is selected, the kernel will load the corresponding segment of code on demand. For example, if PPP support is compiled as a kernel module, when you initiate a PPP connection, the corresponding PPP code is loaded.
- `n` for No. Choosing the No option excludes this option from the kernel altogether.

As you can see in the current window, the Module option is faded out (grayed or dimmed). In this case, this particular option by itself doesn't add or remove anything from the kernel but instead serves as a guide to the rest of the configuration options. Because the kernel you are compiling is for use in a server, you should not try any experimental code, so be sure this option is set to `No`. Any experimental sections of the kernel will then be automatically grayed, thus making them not available for use.

As you go through the configuration, you'll likely come across options you don't know. As you upgrade kernels, you will find these are typically new options that someone has recently added but that are not well publicized. You can select a Help option that is located at the right of each option. Clicking the Help button opens a window describing the option. Simply click the OK button to close the Help window.

After you finish working with this menu, you can take one of three actions. You can click the Main Menu button to close the current window and return to the menu shown in Figure 5.1, you can click the Next button to go to the next configuration submenu, or you can click the Prev button to go to the previous configuration submenu.

Because this is the first configuration submenu, the Prev button is faded out in this window, leaving you access only to the Main Menu and Next buttons. Go ahead and click the Next button now.

Loadable Module Support

As discussed earlier, modules are chunks of the kernel that are loaded on demand. This feature gives you the benefit of being able to support features not often used, without taking up additional memory during periods of nonuse.

The Module Support submenu in this particular kernel version consists of three options, as you can see in Figure 28.3.

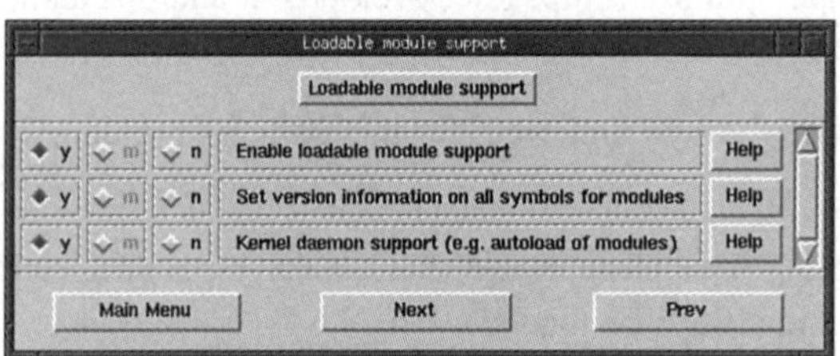

FIGURE 28.3
The Loadable Module Support menu.

You need to choose the first option, Enable Loadable Module Support, in order to enable support for loadable modules. Leave this option marked as `Yes` unless you have a specific reason not to have a moduleless kernel. Tagging it `No` dims the other two options.

The next option, Set Version Information on All Symbols for Modules, allows you to use modules originally compiled for a different version of the kernel in the current kernel if they are compatible. You should leave this option tagged `Yes`.

The last option, Kernel Daemon Support, you'll definitely want to leave tagged `Yes` if you are using modules. This way, the `kerneld` program can automatically load modules on demand instead of forcing you to explicitly load and unload modules by hand.

General Setup

On the General Setup submenu shown in Figure 28.4, you can configure several key elements of the kernel. Assume that these options should be tagged `Yes`, with the notable exception of Limit Memory to Low 16MB, which should be tagged `No`.

You should enable the first option, Kernel Math Emulation, only if you are compiling the kernel on a CPU that does not have a math coprocessor chip. This is applicable only to systems with i386dx, i386sx, or i486sx chips and no corresponding math coprocessors. All Pentium class machines have math coprocessor support built into them. Selecting `Yes` for this option increases the kernel size by 45 kilobytes. Kernel math support cannot be compiled as a module.

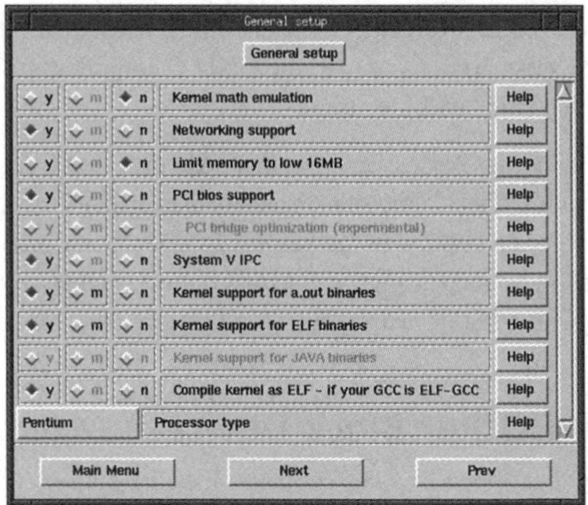

FIGURE 28.4
The General Setup menu.

If you plan to attach your machine to any kind of network, whether a LAN or via modem, you need to select `Yes` for Networking Support. Because Networking Support determines whether other options will be presented to you later and is not a feature in itself, you cannot select the Module option for it.

Some older motherboards had problems working with memory greater than 16MB. If your system exhibits this behavior, you should set Limit Memory to Low 16MB to `Yes`. Otherwise, leave it tagged `No`.

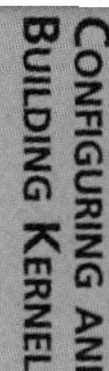

Unless you know for sure that all the programs you plan to run on the system do not require Inter-Process Communication (IPC, a method by which two programs running concurrently on one system can communicate with one another), you should set System V IPC to `Yes`. Many programs do not work unless this option is turned on. Because of the tight integration required between IPC and the kernel, this option cannot be compiled as a module.

When Linux was first created, programs it could run had to be in `a.out` format, which specifies how each program is structured internally and how the kernel needs to process the program while loading it into memory. For several reasons, the Linux development community decided to move to the ELF format. All recent development has been done using the ELF, with `a.out` quickly fading out of use. However, to ensure maximum compatibility with other programs, you should set both the Kernel Support for `a.out` Binaries and Kernel Support for ELF Binaries to `Yes`.

Because you opted not to use any experimental code in the Code Maturity Level Options submenu, the option for Kernel Support of Java Binaries is dimmed here.

The next-to-last option, Compile Kernel as ELF, should be tagged `Yes` if your version of `gcc` is ELF-compatible. Most versions of `gcc`, the GNU C compiler, are ELF-compatible (including the version that ships with this book).

The last option on this window, Processor Type, is a little different from the others. As you can imagine, this option doesn't require a Yes/No answer but instead a list of processors for which the compiler can optimize the kernel. To select your processor type, click the button to the left of the option (in Figure 5.4, this button is labeled Pentium) to generate a drop-down box with a list of processors. Click the processor type you have (or the closest one), and you're set.

Floppy, IDE, and Other Block Devices

The Floppy, IDE, and Other Block Devices submenu lists the options you have for basic device support for IDE and floppy drives as well as some older drive types (for example, MFM and RLL). As the kernel evolves, these options will change slightly.

You definitely should select `Yes` for Normal Floppy Disk Support, because you will have no way of accessing your floppy drives without it. Don't select No for this option because you're looking for a way to secure your floppy drives from nonroot users; instead change the permissions on /dev/fd0 to `0600`.

If you have an IDE hard drive like the sample system, you should select `Yes` for Enhanced IDE/MFM/RLL Disk/CDROM/Tape Support. Selecting No dims all the IDE options in the rest of the submenu. Because you're using this option, the next option—Old Harddisk (MFM/RLL/IDE) Driver—is dimmed.

The remainder of the IDE options are for support for specific chipsets. This information varies from machine to machine. When you're in doubt, selecting `Yes` for these options doesn't hurt, but it will result in a larger kernel. Each driver will automatically probe the system at startup time to determine whether it should or should not be activated.

You can select `Yes` for Loopback Device Support if you have a special need to mount a file as a file system. This is often used for testing an ISO9660 image before burning it to a CD. You should also select `Yes` for Loopback Device Support if you intend to use the Common Desktop Environment. For most people, however, this option should be tagged `No`.

The Multiple Devices Driver support option turns on a special driver that allows you to connect multiple partitions (even on different disks) together to work as one large partition. Unless you are a systems administrator configuring this item, you should set this option to `No`. If you plan to set up this feature, be sure to read the file:

```
/usr/src/linux/drivers/block/README.md
```

The options for using Linear (Append) Mode and RAID-0 (Striping) Mode are applicable only if you plan to use multiple device driver support.

RAM Disk Support is provided in the kernel to allow you to create virtual file systems in your system's memory. This feature is really useful only if you are creating a special kernel for use on startup disks. For most instances, select `No` for RAM Disk Support. Doing so automatically dims the Initial RAM Disk (initrd) Support option.

Unless you have a very old hard disk that you need to use with this machine, you should leave the XT Harddisk Support option tagged `No`. If you do need to support a very old hard disk, seriously consider making the investment in upgrading the device to something more current—if not for your performance, at least for the safety of the data.

Networking Options

Because of the rate at which network technology evolves, covering specifics is difficult because they become outdated too quickly. For this section on Networking options, we will cover the basics along with some security notes. For specific features, you should check the Help box attached to each option on the Networking Options submenu.

Before getting into details, you should have a clear idea of what sorts of networking features you expect your machine to offer. If your machine will spend a great deal of its time servicing requests or as a user's desktop machine, you should keep the network configuration simple and not provide any elaborate services. On the other hand, if the machine is destined to become a gateway/proxy service, you should pay attention to the details.

NOTE

Because of the rapid developments in the networking industry, many options are still experimental code. As a result, many of the Networking options will be dimmed if you opted not to use any experimental code in the kernel. Don't be alarmed.

Assuming that you do want to join the network, you must turn on two of the options. The first, of course, is TCP/IP Networking. Tagging this option `No` dims all the other options. The other option you must turn on is IP: Syn Cookies. Enabling this option is especially important if you are going to be attached to the Internet in one way or another, because it provides protection against SYN attacks. For additional details on SYN attacks and various other security-related issues, visit the CERT home page at `http://www.cert.org`.

The essence of many of the Networking options is the ability to configure Linux to act as either a router or a firewall. To access the firewall options, be sure to enable the Network Firewall, Network Aliasing, and IP: Forwarding/Gatewaying options. If you plan to use your Linux machine in this fashion, you will probably want to enable the IP: Accounting and IP: Optimize as Router Not Host options.

If you have trouble connecting to your Linux machine via Telnet from an older DOS system, you might want to select `Yes` for IP: PC/TCP Compatibility Mode. Turning on this option allows Linux to communicate with the older (and broken) software on the DOS side. The IP: Disable Path MTU Discovery option (normally enabled) can also be a cause of problems with older systems. Normally, Linux starts by sending larger packets of data across the network. If it finds a machine that cannot handle the larger size, it brings the size down until everyone is happy. Some older DOS machines with poorly written software don't handle this technique well and need to have this option disabled. If that is the case, check `Yes` for this option.

The IP: Reverse ARP option is useful if machines on the network use Address Resolution (ARP) to determine the network's IP address based on its Ethernet address. Typically, these types of clients are diskless. Enabling this option allows Linux to answer such queries. Look into running `rarp` for further information about this protocol.

Another security issue you will need to contend with, especially if you are attached to the Internet, is source-routed frames. IP allows for a machine originating a packet to specify the exact path of a packet from source to destination. This capability is rarely useful and is often used as a method of attacking machines across the Internet. Unless you are sure of what you're doing, you should select `Yes` for the IP: Drop Source Routed Frames option.

Along with these TCP/IP-centric options are a few other protocol options such as IPX and AppleTalk. If you work in a heterogeneous environment with Macintoshes and Windows/Novell-based PCs, you might want to enable these options, but doing so isn't required as long as the other machines can talk TCP/IP. The most common use of enabling AppleTalk, for example, is to be able to use AppleTalk printers.

SCSI Support

If you plan to use any SCSI devices on your system, you should select either `Yes` or `Module` for all the options on the SCSI Support submenu, as shown in Figure 28.5. If you're using SCSI disks, `Yes` is a better option than `Module`.

FIGURE 28.5
The SCSI support menu.

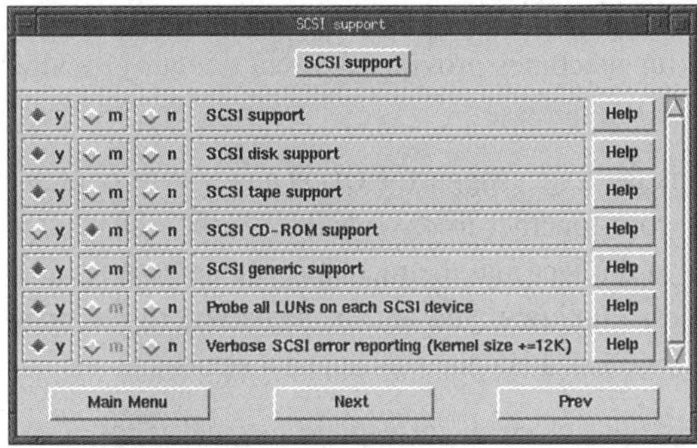

The only option worth explicitly mentioning on this submenu is Verbose SCSI Error Reporting (Kernel Size +=12K). When this option is enabled, detailed error messages are produced in the event of a failure. Although selecting this option costs some memory, it is often worthwhile when you need to debug an error condition quickly.

Because the sample system requires SCSI, select `Yes` for all options except SCSI CD-ROM Support, because you're using an IDE CD-ROM. If you are also using a SCSI CD-ROM, you might want to select the Module option, because most systems access the CD-ROM infrequently.

SCSI Low-Level Drivers

If you did not select `Yes` to SCSI in the SCSI Support submenu, you can skip the SCSI Low-Level Drivers submenu.

Like the submenu in Network support, the list of SCSI drivers supported by Linux increases regularly. For every SCSI card you have in your system, simply tag the option as either `Yes` if you intend to make heavy use of it or `Module` if it will have occasional use only.

After you select the driver you want, be sure to read the corresponding help. It might contain information about where to obtain current drivers and bug fixes.

Network Device Support

The Network Device Support submenu lists the drivers available for networking. This list includes the necessary drivers to control Ethernet cards, PPP connections, SLIP, and Token Ring.

To select any of the options in this screen, you must select `Yes` for the first option, Network Device Support. Checking `No` dims all the other options.

The next option, Dummy Net Driver Support, provides dummy network interfaces. This capability is often used for machines providing virtual domains in which each virtual interface receives its own IP address.

The last general option is for EQL Support. EQL is a means by which two modems using PPP or SLIP can work together to provide double the transfer speed. Your choice for this option is based on the fact that the machine you are connecting to can also support this capability. Unless you know you will be providing this support, be sure to check `No` for the EQL (Serial Line Load Balancing) Support option.

The rest of the options in this submenu correspond to specific types of network interfaces. Note that some of them are questions designed to make other options available to you. For example, if you select `Yes` for the 3Com Cards option, all of the supported 3Com cards become available for you to select.

ISDN Subsystem

The ISDN Subsystem submenu doesn't provide many options for ISDN users to configure. Most people should select `No` for the first option, ISDN Support. Doing so dims the other options in the submenu.

If you do need ISDN support, begin by selecting `Yes` for the first option so you can configure the other items on the submenu. Because of the nature of ISDN, be sure to find out whether your provider supports some of the options Linux supports.

CD-ROM Drivers

On the CD-ROM Drivers submenu, you can select the option to Support Non-SCSI/IDE/ATAPI CD-ROM Drives. As with the other lists of drivers, you need to select `Yes` for only the devices you have attached to your system.

Filesystems

Linux supports many filesystems, thereby allowing you to use disks from other operating systems without any conversion process. The most notable support is for the DOS-based file systems.

The filesystems available from the Filesystems submenu in version 2.0.35 of the kernel are given in Table 28.1.

TABLE 28.1 SUPPORTED FILE SYSTEMS

Filesystem	*Description*
Minix	This is the original Linux file system and is still used by startup disks and common floppy disks. This option should be tagged `Yes`.
Extended fs	This is the first successor to the Minix. It is no longer used. There is no good reason to enable support for this file system.
Second extended fs	This is the current default Linux file system. You should definitely select `Yes` for this option.
`xiafs` filesystem	This file system was introduced as a replacement for the Extended fs at the same time as the Second extended fs. It never really caught on and is rarely used today. Unless you have a specific need, you should select `No` for this option.
DOS FAT fs	This particular option isn't a file system but a foundation for other FAT-based file systems, such as MS-DOS FAT, VFAT (Windows 95), and `umsdos` support.
MS-DOS FAT fs	If you want to be able to access DOS-based systems from Linux, you need to set this option to `Yes`. This capability is especially useful for dual startup systems.
VFAT (Windows 95) fs	VFAT is an upgrade from the original MS-DOS FAT file system that includes support for long filenames. Again, if you are in a dual startup situation, having this capability is a good idea.
`umsdos`	This UNIX-like file system resides on top of the standard MS-DOS format. This capability is useful if you want to run Linux over your DOS partition occasionally. For a serious system, you should not need this support. For example, Red Hat Linux does not support running on a `umsdos` file system.
`/proc`	To simplify access to system information, the /proc file system was created to provide an intuitive interface. Although it appears to exist on your hard disk, it doesn't take up any actual space. Many programs rely on your having this capability in place, so be sure to include support for it.

continues

TABLE 28.1 CONTINUED

Filesystem	*Description*
NFS	The Network File System (NFS) support is needed if you intend to access remote file systems using this standard protocol. For a server, this capability is a must.
SMB	This network protocol was developed for Windows for Workgroups (also known as LanManager). This capability is useful only if you need to have direct access to Windows 95 or NT files as part of your file system. For most people, this option should be tagged `No`. For a server, you might want to select `Module` for this option because you never know where you're going to have to connect your machine.
NCP	NetWare support is done through the NCP protocol. Like SMB, this capability isn't terribly useful for most people; however, if you are in the process of transitioning away from Netware, selecting this option is a useful way to provide a seamless transition.
ISO9660	The ISO9660 file system is necessary if you intend to use CD-ROMs, because many CD-ROMs are encoded in this format. If you have a CD-ROM drive attached to your machine, be sure to select `Yes` for this option.
OS/2 HPFS	Support for the OS/2 file system, HPFS, is read-only under Linux. Most people should select `No` for this option.
System V and Coherent	These two file systems are from very old versions of UNIX and are useful only as a means of transitioning old data to new file systems. Most people should select `No` for this option.
Amiga FFS	The Amiga file system support is still considered experimental code and should be used with caution.
UFS	UFS is available on several other UNIX systems, most notably Solaris and SunOS. (Under SunOS, it was known as 4.2.) The support for this file system is read-only.

NOTE

If you plan to access a file system over the network, you do not need to support the remote file system directly. You do need to support NFS, however. For example, if you intend to mount a disk residing on a Solaris system, you do not need UFS support, only NFS.

In addition to the supported filesystems, several other file system modules are available for Linux. These modules must be compiled after you compile your kernel so that they contain the correct version information. Two of the most common are:

HFS: The Hierarchical File System used on the Apple Macintosh is available from:

`http://www-sccm.stanford.edu/Students/hargrove/HFS/`

NTFS: An alpha version with read-only support of the NT File System used by Microsoft Windows NT is available from:

`http://www.informatik.hu-berlin.de/~loewis/ntfs/index.html`

The Quota Support Option on this submenu is for people who need to limit the amount of disk space being used by each user. Currently, this capability is supported only with the second extended file system (ext2).

The last option in this submenu is for Mandatory Lock Support. Typically, file locking is done at the application level; however, there is an attempt to force locks on all files with this feature. The additional software to support this feature isn't available in the 2.0.x kernels, so do not enable this option unless you are certain of what you are doing.

Character Devices

Character devices work in a different manner than block devices. Block devices are typically devices such as disks and tape drives that transfer data in large chunks. In contrast, character devices transfer only one byte of data at a time. Typical character devices include keyboards, mice, and serial ports.

As its name implies, the Character Devices submenu is used to configure character devices in the kernel. This configuration is usually for your mouse, serial ports, and parallel ports, but a few unusual devices fall under this category as well.

To get basic support for your serial ports, you need to set the Standard/Generic Serial Support option to `Yes` or `Module`. Unless you have a specific serial card, such as an 8-port card, you do not need any additional serial support.

If you plan to use your printer or connect to a network via PLIP, be sure to set Parallel Printer Support to `Yes` also.

Mouse support comes in two flavors—you can use serial mice or bus mice. If you use a serial mouse, you do not need to explicitly turn on the Mouse Support option, because the Standard/Generic Serial Support covers this capability. If you use a bus mouse, you need to set Mouse Support (not serial mice) to `Yes` and indicate which particular mouse you have attached to the machine.

The remaining options in the Character Devices submenu are unusual and often unused features or hardware. Unless you explicitly know that your system uses them, select `No` for these options.

Sound

To enable sound card support in the kernel, begin by selecting `Yes` for the first option for Sound Card Support in the Sound submenu. By doing so, you can select which sound card you have in your system.

> **CAUTION**
>
> Before you attempt to configure kernel support for your sound card, make sure you have the correct IRQ and I/O Base Memory address.

After you select `Yes` for the appropriate sound card in your system, scroll down to the section for providing the appropriate IRQ, DMA, and Base I/O address information. Although the information required varies from card to card, you should be able to get this information from the manual or the on-card jumper settings.

To get a list of support hardware, including sound cards, consult the Red Hat support page located at

`http://www.redhat.com/support/docs/hardware.html`

Kernel Hacking

Because the Linux kernel is available in source code form, many people have taken an interest in its underlying functionality for one reason or another. To facilitate these people, additional debugging information can be compiled into the kernel by selecting `Yes` for the Kernel Profiling Support option.

As part of the profiling support, many functions are invoked with the intention of trying to force them to fail. This capability is useful during development to ensure that all possible paths of execution are exercised and tested. The result is a kernel that is less stable; hence, unless you truly understand the hows and whys of the kernel, you should leave the Kernel Profiling Support option tagged `No`.

Final Notes About Configuration

Configuring a kernel can be tricky. Be ready to spend some time learning the options and the effects each option has on others. You can easily misconfigure a kernel, so don't feel bad if integrating a new feature correctly takes a few tries. As with any learning endeav-

or, as you gain experience, you will be able to get the job done right more quickly and with less heartache.

After you set all your options, be sure to save the configuration and not just quit without saving. The options are then written to a file that is read as part of the compilation. Based on your selections, only the necessary components will be compiled.

Building and Installing the Kernel

Now that you have a configured kernel, you are ready to compile it. This process, known as "building the kernel," is much easier than the configuration process but takes much longer. Be prepared to wait.

Depending on system speed, available memory, and other processes, compiling the kernel can take from 10 minutes for a fast Pentium to 1.5 hours for a slow i386. The process will also slow down your system for other tasks. If you are sharing CPU time with other people, you might want to wait until the CPU is less busy before embarking on this task.

Building the Kernel

The magic command to start the build is as follows:

```
make dep;make clean;make zImage
```

This command actually contains three commands in one. The first command, `make dep`, takes your configuration and builds the corresponding dependency tree. This process determines what gets compiled and what doesn't. The next step, `make clean`, erases all previous traces of a compilation to avoid any mistakes in which the version of a feature gets tied into the kernel. Finally, `make zImage` does the full compilation. After the process is complete, the kernel is compressed and ready to be installed.

As the kernel compiles, all the commands necessary to do the actual compilation scroll down your screen. Although you don't need to understand the compilation process in detail, familiarity with C programming and Makefiles will be helpful in troubleshooting problems. If you do not have this sort of background, look out for messages such as:

```
make:***[directory/file.o] Error 1
```

where `[directory/file.o]` is the file at which the compilation failed. Take note of the first message starting with `gcc` after the preceding line. For example, if the output looks like:

```
gcc -D__KERNEL__ -I/usr/src/linux/include -Wall -Wstrict-prototypes -O2
➥-fomit-frame-pointer -fno-strength-reduce -pipe -m486 -malign-loops=2
➥-malign-jumps=2 -malign-functions=2 -DCPU=586  -c -o init/main.o
init/main.c
init/main.c:53: warning: function declaration isn't a prototype
init/main.c: In function `main':
init/main.c:53: storage class specified for parameter `_stext'
[...]
make:***[init/main.o] Error 1
```

you're interested in the line that says

```
init/main.c:53: warning function declaration isn't a prototype
```

Be sure to include this information when requesting help.

Before you can install the new kernel, you need to compile the corresponding modules. You do so by using the following command:

```
make modules
```

Again, watch for errors in the compilation.

Installing the Kernel

After the kernel and its corresponding modules are compiled, you're ready to start the installation.

Begin by checking the current /boot directory to see which kernels are presently installed. Most kernels' filenames begin with the `vmlinuz` string, but if you aren't sure, check the file

```
/etc/lilo.conf
```

to see which kernels are currently offered at startup time and their locations.

After you know what the current kernels are, copy the file

```
/usr/src/linux/arch/i386/boot/zImage
```

from the kernel source tree to /boot and give it an appropriate new name. For example, the sample kernel is the first kernel compiled with SCSI support in it, so you can use the following `copy` command:

```
cp /usr/src/linux/arch/i386/boot/zImage /boot/vmlinuz-2.0.35-scsi
```

The unique name enables you to see easily why that kernel is different from the others.

Installing the Modules

With the kernel in place, you're ready to start installing the appropriate kernel modules. As you do with the kernel, you should make a backup of the existing modules before installing the new ones.

To make a backup of the current modules, go into the /lib/modules directory and rename the current kernel version number to something else. For example, if the current version is 2.0.30, you can use the following:

```
cd /lib/modules
mv 2.0.30 2.0.30-working
```

This command renames the modules to 2.0.30-working so that, in the event the new modules don't work as advertised, you can erase the new ones and rename this directory to 2.0.30 to regain control of the system.

After you back up the modules, change back into the kernel source directory and type

```
make modules_install
```

to install the modules into the directory

`/lib/modules/`*`version_number`*

Here *`version_number`* is the version number of the kernel you just compiled.

Enabling the New Kernel

You need to edit the /etc/lilo.conf file to make your new kernel one of the startup time options. Do not remove the currently working kernel as an option—you will need it in case the new kernel doesn't work the way you expected. Remember to rerun `LILO` after making changes. Restart and then test your results.

Recovering from Faulty Kernels

While you're learning the nuances of the Linux kernel and its parameters, you might make some mistakes and need to recover the system in its prior state. If you backed up your kernels and modules, this process is relatively easy.

Begin by restarting the system into single user mode. At the `lilo:` prompt, select the previously working kernel to start with the kernel parameter `single`. As the system starts up, you will notice errors as part of the process. Don't worry; the errors are caused by the mismatched modules in the /lib/modules directory.

After you log in, go to the /lib/modules directory and erase the current module installation. For example, if you renamed your old modules 2.0.30-working and your new modules are 2.0.35, then use the following command:

```
rm -rf 2.0.35 ; mv 2.0.30-working 2.0.30
```

Using this command removes all the current modules for the broken kernel. With the broken programs gone, rename the stable kernel with its original name and restart. This procedure should give you full control of your system again.

Sometimes when loading your new kernel for the first time after a restart, an error message is produced, indicating that the kernel is too large. This happens because the kernel is compressed during the build procedure and then decompressed at startup time. Because of the nature of the Intel architecture, the kernel must be able to decompress within the first 1MB of memory. If the kernel cannot be decompressed, the system cannot start.

If you receive this message, restart and choose your old backup kernel to start from.

At this point you have two choices:

- You can reconfigure your kernel and trim down unnecessary items by either not including them or using them as modules.
- You can use `make bzImage` to build a kernel that can work around the kernel size limitation.

Summary

The kernel is the heart of Linux as well as one of its key features; other versions of UNIX have kernels three to four times the size without three to four times the functionality. Of course, this kernel provides the added benefit of the source code as well.

To keep up with the latest developments within the Linux community, you need to keep up with the latest kernel developments. The tools with which you configure and install the kernel have been refined a great deal, thereby making kernel upgrades and installation relatively straightforward tasks.

Like any other aspect of configuring Linux, understanding the details and nuances of the system are important to maintaining a healthy system. In particular, remember the following points:

- Be aware of which kernel version you install on systems. Critical systems should always get even version numbers.

- Make backups of both previous kernels and their corresponding modules. Locking yourself out of your system is a terrible way to waste an afternoon. In addition, keep a startup disk ready in case things go seriously wrong.
- Look for patches instead of downloading an entire new kernel. Using patches will save you a great deal of time.
- Read the /usr/src/linux/README file with each kernel distribution. This file will contain important information pertaining to the new release.
- Do not use any experimental code in a kernel destined for production use.
- Read the help information with each kernel option if you aren't sure about that option's functionality.
- Use `make dep;make clean;make zImage` to compile the kernel. Use `make modules;make modules_install` to compile and install modules.
- Compile infrequently used kernel features as modules to reduce kernel memory consumption. However, be sure to include key functions such as file system support for the root partition as part of the kernel—not a module.

Finally, don't be afraid of the kernel. Just be cautious, and you'll be fine.

CHAPTER

Network Programming

by Daniel Wilson

In This Chapter

"The computer industry has become firmly and irrevocably centered around the network during the past five years or so."

The preceding statement, and several thousand variations on it, has served as the opening for probably tens of thousands of magazine articles, editorials, and book chapters since 1995. The subject less frequently used as a topic is this: How are the applications that utilize these networks written? How do computers actually communicate over a network?

Networking and Linux are a natural combination. After all, Linux is a product of the Internet itself because most of the developers collaborated (and still do collaborate) across the world over email, the World Wide Web, and Usenet news. In addition, Linux is based on UNIX, one of the operating systems on which many common computer networking technologies were developed.

Linux's mature and fully functional networking features make it an excellent platform for networking programming. Because Linux provides full support for the sockets interface, most programs developed on other version of UNIX will build and run on Linux with little or no modification. Textbooks and documentation about UNIX networking are fully applicable to Linux, also.

This chapter uses Perl examples to introduce network programming concepts and shows how to create functioning network programs for Linux quickly and easily. Perl was selected because it enables you to focus on network programming concepts instead of application development issues and programming environments. The scripts referred to in the tutorials are also included on the CD-ROM that accompanies this book. Note that when these scripts were developed, the emphasis was on illustrating key network programming concepts, not programming style, robustness, or how to program in Perl. Only basic knowledge of Perl is required to understand the examples, and they are certainly clear enough for C or C++ programmers to follow. For detailed information on the Perl language and how to use it for a wide variety of tasks, see Chapter 31, "Perl Programming."

This chapter is by no means exhaustive, because the time and space allotted don't allow for coverage of concepts such as protocol layering and routing. This chapter is intended to serve as an introductory tutorial to network programming, with an emphasis on hands-on exercises.

Networking Concepts

This section covers the fundamentals of networking, including the necessary components of network communication. You will learn how these components are used to build a connection by following a simple program that retrieves networking information and uses it to connect to another program. By the end of this section, you should have a good understanding of network addresses, sockets, and the differences between TCP (Transmission Control Protocol) and its counterpart UDP (User Datagram Protocol).

Listing 29.1 contains a Perl function that creates a connection to a server by using TCP. You can find this function in network.pl on the CD-ROM.

LISTING 29.1 `makeconn()`—CREATING A TCP CONNECTION

```
sub makeconn

   my ($host, $portname, $server, $port, $proto, $servaddr);

   $host = $_[0];
   $portname = $_[1];

    #
    # Server hostname, port and protocol
    #
   $server = gethostbyname($host) or
       die "gethostbyname: cannot locate host: $!";
   $port = getservbyname($portname, 'tcp') or
       die "getservbyname: cannot get port : $!";
   $proto = getprotobyname('tcp') or
       die "getprotobyname: cannot get proto : $!";

    #
    # Build an inet address
    #
  $servaddr = sockaddr_in($port, $server);


    #
    # Create the socket and connect it
    #
  socket(CONNFD, PF_INET, SOCK_STREAM, $proto);
  connect(CONNFD, $servaddr) or die "connect : $!";

  return CONNFD;
}
```

I can summarize this procedure in three essential steps:

1. Build an address.
2. Create a socket.
3. Establish a connection.

The network address is built by retrieving address information in lines 11 and 13 and then assembling it in line 21. In line 27, you create the socket, using protocol information retrieved in line 15. (The protocol information, however, can actually be considered part of the address, as you'll see.) In line 28, you finally establish the connection.

Building Network Addresses

The steps involved in building a network address and connecting to it provide a framework for observing how network communication works. I'll spend some time covering each part of this process to better prepare for the hands-on tutorials. For a more in-depth look at TCP/IP and Networking, see Chapter 17, "TCP/IP Network Management."

If you've ever configured a PC or workstation for Internet connectivity, you have probably seen an *Internet address* (or *IP address*) similar to `192.9.200.10` or `10.7.8.14`. This is called *dotted-decimal format* and, like many things in computing, is a representation of network addresses that are intended to make things easier for humans to read. Computers, routers, and other internet devices actually use a 32-bit number, often called a *canonical address*, to communicate. When this number is evaluated, it is broken down into four smaller, 8-bit (one byte) values, much the way the dotted-decimal format consists of four numbers separated by decimals.

An *internetwork*, or *internet* for short, consists of two or more networks that are connected. In this case, the word *internet* refers to any two networks, not the *Internet*, which has become a proper name for the network that encompasses most of the world. The *Internet Protocol* (IP) was designed with this sort of topography in mind. For an internet address to be useful, it has to be capable of identifying not only a specific node (computer), but also the network on which the node resides. Both bits of information are provided in the 32-bit address. Which portion of the address is related to each component is decided by the *netmask* that is applied to the address. Depending on an organization's needs, a network architect can decide to have more networks or more addresses. For details on *subnetting* networks, see Chapter 17. For the sake of network programming, you only need to know what information is stored in an internet address and that individual workstation netmasks have to be correct for a message to be successfully delivered.

Dotted-decimal format is easier to read than 32-bit values (especially because many of the possible values can't be printed or would work out to some pretty ponderous numbers). Even so, most people would rather use names than numbers, finding `gandalf` or `www.yahoo.com` a lot easier to remember than `12.156.27.4` or `182.250.2.178`. For this reason, the notion of hostnames, domain names, and the domain name system was devised. You can get access to a database of name-to-number mappings through a set of *network library functions*, which provide host (node) information in response to names or numbers. For example, in line 11 of Listing 29.1, you retrieve the address associated with a name by using one of these functions, `gethostbyname()`.

Depending on the host configuration, `gethostbyname()` can retrieve the address associated with a name from a file (/etc/hosts), from the Domain Name System (DNS), or from the Network Information System (NIS or Yellow Pages). DNS and NIS (see Chapters 11, "The Domain Name Service," and 12, "The Network Information Service") are network-wide services administrators use to simplify network configuration. Adding and updating network address numbers from a central location (and maybe a backup location) is obviously a lot easier than updating files on every workstation in an organization. These systems are also useful for internetworks, because the address of a remote host can be determined by making a DNS request when it is needed, instead of exchanging configuration files in advance.

One other advantage of using names is that the address associated with a name can be changed without affecting applications. The application only needs to know the name; the address can be discovered at runtime.

To illustrate the use of the `gethostbyname()` function and the difference between dotted-decimal formatted addresses and canonical addresses, try the script in Listing 29.2, called `resolv` on the CD-ROM.

LISTING 29.2 `resolv`

```
1#!/bin/perl
2 use Socket;
3  $addr = gethostbyname($ARGV[0]);
4  $dotfmt = inet_ntoa($addr);
5  print "$ARGV[0]: numeric: $addr dotted: $dotfmt\n";
```

Line 2 uses the `Socket` module included with Perl 5 distributions. This module is required for all the sample code in this chapter, including Listing 29.1.

When you run this program, passing it a hostname for which you want information, you see something like the following:

```
$ ./resolv www.redhat.com
www.redhat.com: numeric:  symbol 199 \f "Courier" \s 8 Çsymbol 215 \f
"Symbol" \s 8 _w symbol 253 \f "Courier" \s 8 _ dotted: 199.183.24.253
```

Line 3 passes the name specified on the command line to `gethostbyname()`, which places the canonical address in `$addr`. This address is then passed to `inet_ntoa()`, which returns the same address in dotted-decimal format (`inet_ntoa` is an abbreviation for "internet number to ASCII"). You then print both values out in line 5. As you can see, the 32-bit address looks rather strange when printed.

NOTE

If your Linux workstation is not connected to the Internet, simply specify your own hostname to resolve or another hostname that is in your own /etc/hosts file or available to your workstation via DNS or NIS.

If your workstation is on the Internet and you see a different address for `http://www.redhat.com`, it just means the address has changed—after all, that is one of the reasons DNS was developed!

Network Services

Being able to locate a computer is a fundamental part of network communication, but it is not the only necessary component in an address. Why do you want to contact a specific host? Do you want to retrieve an HTML document from it? Do you want to log in and check mail? Most workstations, especially those running Linux or any other version of UNIX, provide more than one service to other nodes on a network.

Back in line 13 of Listing 29.1, you called the `getservbyname()` function, which provides the other value used to form the complete network address. This value, referred to as a *service port number*, is the portion of the address that specifies the service or program with which you want to communicate. The port number is a 16-bit integer that becomes part of the source and target (client or server) IP address your applications use to form a *connection endpoint*. If you execute a `netstat -a` you see multiple IP address pairs with their associated port numbers (the numbers might actually be replaced by the service port name from the /etc/services file). This combination of an IP address and a port number is called a *socket*.

Like host addresses, service ports can be referred to by name instead of number. `getservbyname()` retrieves the number associated with the specified name from the file /etc/services. (If NIS is available, the number can also be retrieved from a network database.) Port numbers listed in this database are called "well-known ports" (0 through 1023). In theory, any host can connect to one of these services on any machine, because the port numbers customarily remain consistent (for example, Telnet uses port 23 whether you use UNIX or Windows NT). Even though this is true 99% of the time, the /etc/services file can easily be altered, so watch out for corruption. Applications that don't rely on the well-known ports use what are called "ephemeral ports," considered available for any application to use. The port numbers used by applications don't have to be listed in or retrieved from this database; it's just considered a good idea to list them in /etc/services and share them in an effort to prevent conflicts.

After you have retrieved the two components necessary to build a fully qualified address, you provide them to the `sockaddr_in` function, which builds a `SOCKADDR_IN` structure for you. `SOCKADDR_IN` is the programmatic representation of a network address needed for most socket system calls.

Sockets

Before you can use your addressing information, you need a socket. The `socket()` function in line 27 of Listing 29.1 illustrates how to create one. Some explanation of what sockets are and the types first available to a program will help explain the function.

Sockets are an Application Programming Interface (API) used for network communication. This API was first available with BSD UNIX for the VAX architecture in the early 1980s, but has become prevalent in almost all UNIX versions and recently on Windows, along with a variety of other operating systems. System V Release 4 UNIX supports a different interface, called the Transport Layer Interface (TLI), and a TLI superset called X/Open Transport Interface (XTI), but even most system V Release 4 versions, such as Solaris 2.x and AT&T SVR4 UNIX, provide socket interfaces. Linux provides a full implementation of the socket interface.

Socket applications treat network connections (or to be more exact, connection endpoints) the same way most UNIX interfaces are handled—as file handles. The reason for the endpoint qualification is simple: not all network sessions are connected, and referring to all network streams as connections can be incorrect and misleading. As a matter of fact, after a network endpoint is created and bound or connected, it can be written to, read from, and destroyed by using the same functions as files. Because of this interface, socket programs tend to be portable between different versions of UNIX and frequently many other operating systems.

Protocols and Socket Types

The socket API is designed to support multiple protocols, called *domains* or *families*. Most UNIX versions support at least two domains: UNIX and Internet. (Two of the other domains are the Xerox Network system and the ISO protocol suite.) UNIX domain sockets use the local workstation file system to provide communication between programs running on the same workstation only. Internet domain sockets use the Internet Protocol (IP) suite to communicate over the network (as well as on the same machine). As you might guess, you will be concerned with Internet domain sockets.

In the following call to `socket()`, you specify the scalar variable in which you want to have the socket descriptor stored and three values that describe the type of socket you want to have created—the protocol family, the socket type, and the protocol. I've already covered which protocol family you will use, which is `PF_INET` for the Internet.

```
socket(CONNFD, PF_INET, SOCK_STREAM, $proto);
```

The possible socket types are `SOCK_STREAM`, `SOCK_DGRAM`, `SOCK_RAW`, `SOCK_RDM`, and `SOCK_SEQPACKET`. The last three are used for low-level, advanced operations and are beyond the scope of this chapter.

`SOCK_STREAM` sockets are connected at both ends, they are reliable, and the messages between them are sequenced. The terms "reliable" and "sequenced" have special meanings in networking. *Reliability* refers to the fact that the network guarantees delivery: an application can write a packet with the understanding that it will arrive at the other end unless the connection is suddenly broken by a catastrophic event, such as the unexpected shutting down of a host or a literal break in the network. *Sequencing* means that all messages are always delivered to the other application in the order in which they are sent (it does not mean they will *arrive* at the client or server machine in the order sent).

NOTE

A client application can mysteriously disappear(if a client machine is restarted or crashes) without performing an orderly shutdown of the connection. In this situation, your server could still be hanging around waiting for messages to be sent from the client. These are called *half-connections*, because your server believes the client is still there. If you think this could be a problem in your environment, try using the `keepalive` option, which periodically probes the client to see if it is still there. If the client is not found, the connection is shut down.

`SOCK_DGRAM` sockets support connectionless and unreliable datagrams. A *datagram* is typically a fixed-length, small message. Applications have no guarantees that datagrams will be delivered or, if they are, in what order. On the surface, it seems no application would ever want to use `SOCK_DGRAM`, but as you will see, many applications do, for good reasons.

The type of socket is very closely related to the protocol being used. In the case of the Internet suite, `SOCK_STREAM` sockets always implement TCP, and `SOCK_DGRAM` sockets implement UDP.

The characteristics of the TCP protocol match the characteristics of `SOCK_STREAM`. TCP packets are guaranteed to be delivered, barring a network disaster (the workstation on the other end of the connection drops out or the network itself suffers a serious, unrecoverable outage). Packets are always delivered to the application in the same order in which they were written by the sending application. Obviously, these properties make the job of a network developer easy because a message can be written and essentially forgotten, but there is a cost: TCP messages are much more expensive (demanding) than UDP messages in terms of both network and computing resources. The workstations at both ends of a session have to confirm that they have received the correct information, which results in more work for the operating system and more network traffic. Both systems also have to track the order in which messages were sent, and quite possibly have to store messages until others arrive, depending on the state of the network "terrain" between the two workstations. (New messages can arrive while others are being retransmitted because of an error.) In addition, the fact that TCP connections are just that—connections—has a price. Every conversation has an endpoint associated with it, so a server with more than one client has to arbitrate between multiple sockets, which can be very difficult. (See "I/O Multiplexing with TCP," later in this chapter, for details.)

UDP, like `SOCK_DGRAM`, is connectionless, which means the Transport Layer is not guaranteeing that every packet sent will make it to the destination machine. Try to envision UDP as a "Fire and Forget" protocol. In the past, it was considered unreliable, but with today's Local Area Networks (LANs), UDP is usually considered very reliable. Using UDP in a Wide Area Network (WAN) is usually more prone to error, because you have no idea of the reliability of the networks and machines your packets will pass through in a WAN.

With UDP, applications have to provide whatever reliability mechanisms are necessary for the job they are performing. For some applications, this is an advantage because all the mechanisms provided by TCP aren't always needed. For example, DNS, which uses UDP, simply sends a message and waits for a response for a predetermined interval; because DNS is a one-to-one message-to-response protocol, sequencing between client and server is not necessary. UDP is connectionless, so a server can use one socket to communicate with many clients. All clients write to the same address for the server, and the server responds individually by writing to specific client addresses.

UDP messages can also be broadcast to entire networks—a blessing to an application that needs to communicate one message to many users, but a curse for workstations that don't need the message but have to read it to figure out it isn't for them. Because UDP does not require a connection to be set up in advance, it is considered much quicker than TCP; however, vendors are getting better at speeding up TCP, so in the future this might not always be true.

Making a Connection

Logically, if you are creating a connection like that of the makeconn() function in Listing 29.1, you need to create a SOCK_STREAM socket with the TCP protocol information retrieved by getprotobyname() in line 15. Take a look at lines 27 and 28 from Listing 29.1, repeated here:

```
27:  socket(CONNFD, PF_INET, SOCK_STREAM, $proto);
28:  connect(CONNFD, $servaddr) or die "connect : $!";
```

After creating the socket in line 27, you then pass it to connect() with the address structure created by sockaddr_in(). The connect() function actually contacts the address specified in the structure and establishes the virtual circuit supported by TCP.

A TCP Client Example

Listing 29.3 puts makeconn() to work in a sample program. client1 can be found on the book's CD-ROM.

LISTING 29.3 client1

```
#!/usr/bin/perl
use Socket;
require "./network.pl";

$NETFD = makeconn($ARGV[0], $ARGV[1]);

#
# Get the message
#
sysread $NETFD, $message, 32768 or die "error getting message : $!";
print "$message \n";
close $NETFD;
```

Run this program with two command-line arguments, the name of a Linux host that is running sendmail and the mail port name, smtp:

```
$ ./client1 iest smtp
220 iest.home.mxn.com ESMTP Sendmail 8.8.5/8.8.5; Sat, 4 Oct 1997 18:25:08
-0400
```

This program uses makeconn() to connect to the sendmail program running on the named host and uses the sysread() function to read the greeting the host sends to a new client when it first connects.

sysread() is one of the functions used for extracting network messages from sockets. It is a wrapper for the UNIX read() system call. You cannot use the Perl read() function because it is designed for standard I/O, which uses buffering and other high-level features that interfere with network communications. In a real-world application, you would probably read messages with `sysread()` in and out of a buffer of your own, keeping careful track of what you had just read because you could be interrupted in a read call by a signal. (You would also install signal handlers.) As this example demonstrates, establishing a client connection and retrieving some data is pretty simple.

TIP

One of the benefits of using Perl for network programming is that it hides the issue of byte ordering between different architectures. Intel *x*86 chips and Sun SPARC chips, for example, represent values differently. The creators of the Internet introduced a concept of *network byte order*, in which programs are supposed to place values prior to transmission and then translate back to their network format when they read in messages. Perl does this for us.

A TCP Server Example

Now you'll write your own server to which `client1` can connect. First, you have to place a socket in the listen state by using `makelisten()`, another function defined in `network.pl`. `makelisten()` is shown in Listing 29.4.

LISTING 29.4 `makelisten()`

```
sub makelisten {

    my ($portname, $port, $proto, $servaddr);
    $portname = $_[0];

    #
    #  port and protocol
    #
    $port = getservbyname($portname, 'tcp') or
    die "getservbyname: cannot get port : $!";
    $proto = getprotobyname('tcp') or
    die "getprotobyname: cannot get proto : $!";

    #
    # Bind an inet address
    #
    socket(LISTFD, PF_INET, SOCK_STREAM, $proto);
```

continues

LISTING 29.4 CONTINUED

```
18:     bind (LISTFD, sockaddr_in($port, INADDR_ANY)) or die "bind: $!";
19:     listen (LISTFD, SOMAXCONN) or die "listen: $!";
20:     return LISTFD;
21: }
```

The `makelisten()` function creates a TCP socket, binds it to a local address, and then places the socket in the listen state.

Lines 9 and 11 retrieve the same information `makeconn()` retrieves to create a connection, with the exception of an internet address. `makelisten()` then creates an internet family `SOCK_STREAM` socket, which by definition is a TCP socket, but you specify this explicitly, as in `makeconn()`.

In line 18, the socket is bound to a local address. This tells the system that any messages sent to the specified service port and internet address should be relayed to the specified socket. You use `sockaddr_in()` to build an address from the service port retrieved with `getportbyname()` and with a special address that corresponds to all addresses on the workstation. In this way, connections can be made to all network interfaces and even over any dial-up interfaces on the workstation. This function shows a little laziness, in that it passes the `sockaddr_in()` function to `bind()` instead of calling it separately and saving the results.

There are some restrictions on what service ports can be bound. For historical reasons, only programs executing with superuser access can bind service ports numbered lower than 1024. Even if you find yourself on an operating system that bypasses this restriction, resist the temptation to use ports below 1024. You might find yourself needing to change your code when you either upgrade your OS level or port your application to an environment that enforces this restriction.

After the socket is bound, you can execute `listen()`, which notifies the system that you're ready to accept client connections.

`server1`, the program that uses `makelisten()`, is just as simple as the client and is shown in Listing 29.5. You can find it on the CD-ROM that accompanies this book.

LISTING 29.5 `server1`

```
#!/usr/bin/perl
  use Socket;
  require "./network.pl";

  $hello = "Hello world!";

  $LISTFD = makelisten("test");
```

```
  LOOP: while (1) {
    unless ($paddr = accept(NEWFD, $LISTFD)) {
    next LOOP;
    }
    syswrite(NEWFD, $hello, length($hello));
    close NEWFD;
}
```

In Listing 29.5, you simply place a socket in the listen state by using `makelisten()` and then enter a `while` loop that centers on the function `accept()`. The purpose of `accept()` is exactly as it sounds, to accept client connections. You pass two arguments to `accept()`: a new variable (`NEWFD`) that contains the socket identifier for the accepted connection and the socket (`$LISTFD`) that has been set up with `listen()`.

Whenever `accept()` returns a connection, you write a string to the new socket and immediately close it.

Before you can test your server, you need to add the entry for the test service it uses. Add the following three lines to the /etc/services file. You will have to be root to edit this file.

```
test            8000/tcp
test            8000/udp
test1           8001/udp
```

You have added three entries for your test programs, one for TCP and two others for UDP that you will use later.

Now, to test your server, you need to execute the following commands:

```
$ ./server1&
$./client1 iest test
Hello world!
```

iest is the hostname of your workstation. The server writes back your greeting and exits. Because the server is executing inside a `while` loop, you can run `./client1` repeatedly. When the test is finished, use `kill` to stop the server:

```
$ ps axl grep server1 l awk '{ print $1 }'
pid
$ kill pid
```

A UDP Example

To implement the same test in UDP, you have to set up a `SOCK_DGRAM` socket for both a client and a server. This function, `makeudpcli()`, can also be found in `network.pl` and is shown in Listing 29.6.

LISTING 29.6 `makeudpcli()`

```
sub makeudpcli {

    my ($proto, $servaddr);

    $proto = getprotobyname('udp') or
    die "getprotobyname: cannot get proto : $!";

    #
    # Bind a UDP port
    #
    socket(DGFD, PF_INET, SOCK_DGRAM, $proto);
    bind (DGFD,  sockaddr_in(0, INADDR_ANY)) or die "bind: $!";

    return DGFD;
}
```

In Listing 29.6, you retrieve the protocol information for UDP and then create a `SOCK_DGRAM` socket. You then bind it, but you tell the system to bind to any address and any service port; in other words, you want the socket named but don't care what that name is.

The reason for this extra `bind()` is quite straightforward. Because UDP is connectionless, special attention has to be made to addresses when you're sending and receiving datagrams. When datagram messages are read, the reader also receives the address of the originator so it knows where to send any replies. If you want to receive replies to your messages, you need to guarantee they come from a unique address. The call to `bind()` ensures that the system allocates a unique address for you.

Now that you have created a datagram socket, you can communicate with a server, using the program in Listing 29.7, `client2`, which can be found on the CD-ROM.

LISTING 29.7 `client2`

```
#!/usr/bin/perl

use Socket;
require "./network.pl";

$poke = "yo!";

 $NETFD = makeudpcli();

#
# Work out server address
#
```

```
13:  $addr = gethostbyname($ARGV[0]);
14:  $port = getservbyname($ARGV[1], 'udp');
15:
16:  $servaddr = sockaddr_in($port, $addr);
17:
18: #
19: # Poke the server
20: #
21:  send $NETFD, $poke, 0, $servaddr;
22:
23: #
24: # Recv the reply
25: #
26:  recv $NETFD, $message, 32768, 0 or die "error getting message : $!";
27:  print "$message \n";
28:  close $NETFD;
```

After you create the socket, you still have to resolve the server address, but instead of providing this address to the `connect()` function, you have to provide it to the `send()` function in line 21 so it knows where to, well, send the message. But why are you sending anything to the server at all? After all, in the TCP example in Listing 29.3, the communication is one way.

In the TCP example, the server sends a message as soon as you connect and then closes the session. The act of connecting is, in effect, a message from the client to the server. Because UDP lacks connections, you have to use a message from the client as a trigger for the conversation.

The server creates a UDP socket in a slightly different manner because it needs to bind a well-known port. It uses `getservbyname()` to retrieve a port number and specifies it as part of the call to `bind()`. Look at `makeudpserv()` in `network.pl` for details.

The server's main loop is actually pretty close to that of the TCP server and is shown in Listing 29.8.

LISTING 29.8 `server2`

```
#!/usr/bin/perl
#
#
use Socket;
require "./network.pl";

$hello = "Hello world!";

$LISTFD = makeudpserv("test");
```

continues

LISTING 29.8 CONTINUED

```
while (1) {
    $cliaddr = recv $LISTFD, $message, 32768, 0;
    print "Received $message from client\n";
    send $LISTFD, $hello, 0, $cliaddr;
}
```

Instead of waiting for a client by looping on the `accept()` function, the server loops on the `recv()` function. There is also no new socket to close after the reply is sent to the client.

When these programs are run, you see the following:

```
$ ./server2&
$./client2 iest test
Received yo! from client
Hello world!
```

So you see that from a programmer's standpoint, the differences between UDP and TCP affect not only the socket functions you use and how you use them, but also how you design your programs. Differences such as the lack of a connection and the lack of built-in reliability mechanisms must be seriously considered when you design an application. There is no guarantee, for example, that the server in this section ever receives your poke message. For that reason, a mechanism such as a timer would be employed in a real-world application.

Blocking Versus Nonblocking Descriptors

So far, all the examples in this chapter have relied on blocking I/O. Certain operations, such as reading, writing, and connecting or accepting connections, are set to block when they wait for completion, which brings a program (or thread) to a halt. After `server1` sets up a listen, for example, it enters the `while` loop and calls `accept()`. Until a client connects to the listening socket, the program is halted. It doesn't repeatedly call `accept()`; it calls it once and blocks. This condition is also true for `client2`, which blocks on the `recv()` call until the server replies. If the server is unavailable, the program will block forever. This is especially unwise for an application that uses UDP, but how can a timer be implemented if the call to `recv()` will never return?

Writing can also block on TCP connections when the receiver of the data hasn't read enough data to allow the current write to complete. To maintain reliability and proper flow control, the systems on both ends of a connection maintain buffers, usually about 8,192 bytes. TCP utilizes a "sliding window" mechanism to manage the transfer of data.

Look at it as a byte stream with a fixed size “window” sliding over the data stream. As packets are acknowledged from either the client or the server, the “window” moves forward until the data has been transmitted. If the buffers fill up from either connection (that is, window size equals 0), communications in that direction cease until data has passed from the buffer(s), up the protocol stack, and into the applications buffers. This is yet another concern for servers writing large messages to clients that aren’t running on very powerful systems or that are on remote networks with low bandwidth links. In these scenarios, one client can slow things down for everyone. Keep in mind, slow internet equipment can slow down your application as well. As a rule, the less data you must transfer via your application the better.

Blocking I/O is acceptable for programs that don’t have to maintain GUI interfaces and only have to maintain one communications channel. Needless to say, most programs cannot afford to use blocking communications.

I/O is said to be *nonblocking* when an operation returns an error or status code that cannot be completed. To demonstrate this, run `client2` without running the server. It will start and not return until you halt it by pressing Ctrl+C.

Now run `nonblock`:

```
$ ./nonblock
error getting message : Try again at ./nonblock line 30
```

You receive the `Try again` message from the `recv()` function.

`nonblock`, shown in Listing 29.9, is a modified version of `client2`, which is shown in Listing 29.7. Let’s see what changes were made to `client2` to remove blocking.

LISTING 29.9 `nonblock`

```
1: #!/usr/bin/perl
2: use Socket;
3: use Fcntl;
4: require "./network.pl";
5: $poke = "yo!";
6: $NETFD = makeudpcli();
7: fcntl $NETFD, &F_SETFL, O_NONBLOCK or die "Fcntl failed : $!\n";
8: (rest of file remains the same)
```

A new module, `Fcntl`, is added to the program in line 3, which provides an interface to the `fcntl(2)` system call. It is used to alter file descriptor properties, such as blocking and how certain signals are handled. In line 7, the last line of the modifications to `client2`, you set the `O_NONBLOCK` flag for the UDP socket. The rest of the program is unchanged.

When nonblocking I/O is used, the application designer has to be very careful when handling errors returned from `recv()`, `send()`, and other I/O-related functions. When no more data is available for reading or no more data can be written, these functions return error codes. As a result, the application has to be prepared to handle some errors as being routine conditions. This is also true of the C/C++ interfaces.

I/O Multiplexing with UDP

Frequently, applications need to maintain more than one socket or file descriptor. For example, many system services, such as Telnet, `rlogin`, and FTP, are managed by one process on Linux. To do this, the process `inetd` listens for requests for these services by opening a socket for each one. Other applications, such as Applix, Netscape, and Xemacs, monitor file descriptors for the keyboard, mouse, and perhaps the network.

Now set up an example that monitors the keyboard and a network connection. Listing 29.10 is contained in the file `udptalk`, which is included on the CD-ROM.

LISTING 29.10 `updtalk`

```
#!/usr/bin/perl

use Socket;
require "./network.pl";

 $NETFD = makeudpserv($ARGV[2]);

 $addr = gethostbyname($ARGV[0]);
 $port = getservbyname($ARGV[1], 'udp');

 $servaddr = sockaddr_in($port, $addr);

 $rin = "";
 vec($rin, fileno(STDIN), 1) = 1;
 vec($rin, fileno($NETFD), 1) = 1;

 while (1) {

    select $ready = $rin, undef, undef, undef;

    if (vec($ready, fileno(STDIN), 1) == 1) {
      sysread STDIN, $mesg, 256;
       send $NETFD, $mesg, 0, $servaddr;
    }
    if (vec($ready, fileno($NETFD), 1) == 1) {
        recv $NETFD, $netmsg, 256, 0;
       print "$netmsg";
       $netmsg = "";
```

```
29:       }
30: }
31:    close $NETFD;
```

To test this program, you must run it either in two windows on the same system or on two different systems. At one command-line session, execute the following command, where *iest* is the host on which the second command will be run:

```
$ ./udptalk iest test test1
```

On the second host, run the following command, where *iest* is the host where the first command was run:

```
$ ./udptalk iest test1 test
```

Each session waits for keyboard input. Each line typed at one program is printed by the other, after you press Enter.

To perform the two-way communication required for this exercise, both instances of `udptalk` have to bind a well-known port. To permit this on a single workstation, the program accepts two port names as the second and third command-line arguments. For obvious reasons, two programs cannot register interest in the same port.

In line 6 of Listing 29.10, `udptalk` uses `makeudpserv()` to create a UDP socket and bind it to a well-known port. For the examples here, I used 8000 for one copy and 8001 for the other.

In lines 8–11, you perform the usual procedure for building a network address. This will be the address to which the keyboard input is written.

Lines 13–15 build bit vectors in preparation for the `select()` function. In Perl, a *bit vector* is a scalar variable that is handled as an array of bits; in other words, instead of being evaluated as bytes that add up to characters or numbers, each individual bit is evaluated as a distinct value.

In line 13, you create a variable (`$rin`) and tell the Perl interpreter to clear it. You then use the `vec()` and `fileno()` functions to determine the file number for `STDIN` (the keyboard) and set that bit in `$rin`. Then you do the same for the socket created by `makeudpcli()`. Therefore, if `STDIN` uses file descriptor 1 (which is generally the case), the second bit in `$rin` is set to `1`. (Bit vectors, like other arrays, start numbering indexes at zero.) Fortunately, the `vec()` function can also be used to read bit vectors, so you can treat these data structures as opaque (and sleep a lot better at night for not knowing the details).

`select()` is a key function for systems programmers. Unfortunately, it suffers from an arcane interface that is intimidating in any language. System V UNIX has a replacement, `poll()`, that is a little easier to use, but it is not available on Linux or within Perl. The following is the function description for `select()`:

```
select readfds, writefds, exceptfds, timeout;
```

Like most of the UNIX system interface, this is virtually identical to `select()` in C/C++. `select()` is used for discovering which file descriptors are ready for reading, are ready for writing, or have an exceptional condition. An exceptional condition usually corresponds with the arrival of what is called *out-of-band* or urgent data. This sort of data is most frequently associated with TCP connections. When a message is sent out-of-band, it is tagged as being more important than any previously sent data and is placed at the top of the data queue. A client or server can use this to notify the process on the other end of a connection that it is exiting immediately.

The first three arguments are bit vectors that correspond to the file descriptors that you are interested in reading or writing to or that you are monitoring for exceptional conditions. If you aren't interested in a set of file descriptors, you can pass `undef` instead of a vector. In Listing 29.10, you aren't interested in writing or exceptions, so you pass `undef` for the second and third arguments.

When `select` returns, only the bits that correspond to files with activity are set; if any descriptors aren't ready when `select` returns, their settings are lost in the vector. For that reason, you have `select()` create a new vector and copy it into `$ready`. This is done by passing an assignment to `select()` as the first argument in line 19.

The last parameter is the time-out interval in seconds. `select()` waits for activity for this interval. If the interval expires with no activity occurring, `select()` returns with everything in the vector cleared. Because `undef` is supplied for *`timeout`* in line 19, `select()` blocks until a file is ready.

Inside the `while` loop entered in line 17, you call `select()`, passing it the bit vector built earlier and the new one to be created. When it returns, you check the vector by using `vec()` with pretty much the same syntax as you used to set the bits; however, because you are using `==` instead of `=`, `vec()` returns the value of the bit instead of setting it.

If the bit for `STDIN` is set, you read from the keyboard and send it to the other instance of `udptalk`. If the bit for the socket is set, you read from it and print it to the terminal. This sequence illustrates a very important advantage of the sockets interface—the program is extracting data to and from the network by using the same functions as the keyboard and screen.

This process is called *multiplexing* and is the loop at the core of many network-aware applications, although the actual mechanics can be concealed by sophisticated dispatchers or notifiers that trigger events based on which connection is ready to be read from or written to. Something else lacking in Listing 29.10 is the minimum amount of error checking and signal handling that cleans up connections when a quit signal is received.

I/O Multiplexing with TCP

To demonstrate TCP multiplexing, it is necessary to create different programs for the client and server. The server, `tcplisten`, is shown in Listing 29.11 and is the one that requires the most scrutiny. The client, `tcptalk`, is on the book's CD-ROM and won't be reprinted here because it resembles the server so closely. I'll explain how the client works as I cover the server.

LISTING 29.11 `tcplisten`

```
#!/usr/bin/perl

use Socket;
require "./network.pl";

 $NETFD = makelisten($ARGV[0]);

 while (1) {

    $paddr = accept(NEWFD, $NETFD);

    ($port, $iaddr) = sockaddr_in($paddr);

    print "Accepted connection from ", inet_ntoa($iaddr),
    " on port number ", $port, "\n";

    $rin = "";
    vec($rin, fileno(STDIN), 1) = 1;
    vec($rin, fileno(NEWFD), 1) = 1;

    while (1)

     select $ready = $rin, undef, undef, undef;

     if (vec($ready, fileno(STDIN), 1) == 1) {
        sysread STDIN, $mesg, 256;
        syswrite NEWFD, $mesg, length($mesg);
     }
     if (vec($ready, fileno(NEWFD), 1) == 1) {
```

continues

LISTING 29.11 CONTINUED

```
30:         $bytes = sysread NEWFD, $netmsg, 256;
31:         if ($bytes == 0) { goto EXIT; }
32:         print "$netmsg";
33:         $netmsg = "";
34:       }
35:     }
36:     EXIT: close NEWFD;
37:     print "Client closed connection\n";
38: }
39:
40: close $NETFD;
```

The server creates a listening socket in line 6 and then immediately enters a `while` loop. At the top of the loop is a call to `accept()`. Because you place this in a loop, the server can repeatedly accept client connections, like our other TCP server. The listen socket, `$NETFD`, can accept more than one connection, regardless of the state of any file descriptors cloned from it by using `accept()`.

`accept()` returns the address of the connecting client. You use this address in lines 12 and 14 to print out some information about the client. In line 12, you use `sockaddr_in()` to reverse-engineer the fully qualified address back into a network address and a service port. Then you use `print` to display it on the terminal. Note the call to `inet_ntoa()` embedded in the `print` command.

Next, you set up for a `select()` loop, using almost the same code as in Listing 29.10. There is, however, a key difference in the way the network connection is handled. You are reading with `sysread()` again, but you are saving the return value.

When a peer closes a TCP connection, the other program receives an end-of-file (EOF) indication. This is signified by marking the socket as ready for reading and returning zero bytes when it is read. By saving the number of bytes returned by `sysread()`, you are able to detect a closed connection and record it and then return to `accept()` at the top of the outer `while` loop.

The following is a server session, followed by the client session that is communicating with it. The client is `tcptalk`, which is included on the CD-ROM, as is a copy of `tcplisten`.

```
$ ./tcplisten test
Accepted connection from 10.8.100.20 on port number 29337
Hello, world.
Goodbye, cruel....
Client closed connection
```

```
$ ./tcptalk iest test
Hello, world.
Goodbye, cruel....
^C
```

Advanced Topics

Now we take some time to touch on a few more advanced topics.

One of the biggest issues for TCP applications is queuing messages. Depending on the nature of the data being transferred, the network bandwidth available, and the rate at which clients can keep pace with the data being delivered, data can queue up. Experienced application designers generally specify a queuing mechanism and the rules associated with it as part of the initial product description.

UDP applications have to wrestle with data reliability, and some schemes rely on message sequence numbers. All nodes involved in a transaction (or a series of transactions) keep track of a numbering scheme. When a node receives a message out of order, it sends a negative acknowledgment for the message it missed. This sort of scheme greatly reduces traffic when everything goes well but can become very expensive when things fall out of sequence.

Some applications can use asynchronous I/O to service network traffic and other tasks in a single application. This scheme registers interest in a signal that can be delivered whenever a file descriptor has data ready to be read. This method is not recommended, though, because only one signal can be delivered for all file descriptors (so `select()` would still be needed) and because signals are not reliable.

Security is always a big issue, regardless of the protocols being used. For that reason, applications that require a high level of security don't just rely on TCP to keep them secure. They tend to use encryption and authentication technologies as a means of securing data transmissions, including userids and passwords, over a LAN or WAN.

Summary

This chapter covered a lot of ground in a short time, introducing essential networking concepts such as the components of a network address and how an application can form an address from symbolic host and service names by looking them up with the resolver functions.

Sockets, the most commonly used network programming interface, are used throughout the chapter. This API enables you to treat network connections and data streams like files, which shortens the network programming learning curve and also makes applications easy to design and maintain.

The two most commonly used protocols on the Internet—TCP and UDP—were discussed here as well. TCP, a connection-oriented protocol, has very robust reliability mechanisms that allow an application to use the network without worrying too much about whether the messages it is sending are reaching the other end. This reliability does carry a price, however, because TCP comes with a certain degree of overhead in terms of speed and bandwidth. TCP also supports only two-way communication, so clients and servers that need to communicate with more than one node have to maintain multiple connections, which can be expensive.

UDP, on the other hand, is a connectionless, datagram-oriented protocol. By itself, UDP comes with virtually no overhead. A possible downside is that the applications themselves have to provide their own reliability mechanisms. UDP also supports broadcast, which can be convenient but also represents a potential problem for some networks.

This chapter introduced some of the fundamental concepts behind network applications. Using these concepts, you will be able to create some simple tools, or you can build on this information by utilizing some of the advanced information available on the Internet and in advanced texts.

The concepts and examples presented here can all be easily applied to C programming, because Perl essentially provides "wrappers" to the same system calls C uses for socket programming. All the functions used here have C equivalents and their own manual pages.

For more information on network programming, see the UNIX socket programming FAQs at `http://www.ibrado.com/sock-faq/`. This page includes a wealth of information, as well as pointers to other resources.

Helpful Programming Languages Overview

PART V

IN THIS PART

CHAPTER

C and C++ Programming

by Bill Ball

In This Chapter

UNIX shells support a wide range of commands that can be combined, in the form of scripts, into reusable programs. Command scripts for shell programs (and utilities such as `gawk` and Perl) are all the programming many UNIX users need to customize their computing environment.

Script languages have several shortcomings, however. To begin with, the commands a user types into a script are read and evaluated only when the script is being executed. Interpreted languages are flexible and easy to use, but they are inefficient because the commands must be reinterpreted each time the script is executed. Interpreted languages are also ill-suited to manipulate the computer's memory and I/O devices directly. Therefore, programs that process scripts (such as the various UNIX shells, the `awk` utility, and the Perl interpreter) are themselves written in the C and C++ languages, as is the UNIX kernel.

Many users find it fairly easy to learn a scripted, interpreted language because the commands can usually be tried out one at a time, with clearly visible results. Learning a language such as C or C++ is more complex and difficult because you must learn to think in terms of machine resources and the way actions are accomplished within the computer, rather than in terms of user-oriented commands.

This chapter introduces you to the basic concepts of C and C++ and demonstrates how to build some simple programs. Even if you don't go on to learn how to program extensively in either language, you will find that the information in this chapter will help you understand how kernels are built and why some of the other features of UNIX work the way they do. Additional resources are listed at the end of the chapter.

Introduction to C

C is the programming language most frequently associated with UNIX. Since the 1970s, the bulk of the operating system and its applications have been written in C. Because the C language doesn't directly rely on any specific hardware architecture, UNIX was one of the first portable operating systems. In other words, the majority of the code that makes up UNIX doesn't know and doesn't care about knowing what computer it is actually running on. Machine-specific features are isolated in a few modules within the UNIX kernel, which makes it easy for you to modify these when porting to a different hardware architecture.

C was first designed by Dennis Ritchie for use with UNIX on DEC PDP-11 computers. The language evolved from Martin Richard's BCPL, and one of its earlier forms was the B language, which was written by Ken Thompson for the DEC PDP-7. The first book on C was *The C Programming Language* by Brian Kernighan and Dennis Ritchie and was published in 1978.

In 1983, the American National Standards Institute (ANSI) established a committee to standardize the definition of C. The resulting standard is known as *ANSI C*, and it is the recognized standard for the language grammar and a core set of libraries. The syntax is slightly different from the original C language, which is frequently called K&R—for Kernighan and Ritchie. In this chapter, I will primarily address ANSI C.

Programming in C: Basic Concepts

C is a compiled, third-generation procedural language. *Compiled* means that C code is analyzed, interpreted, and translated into machine instructions at some time prior to the execution of the C program. These steps are carried out by the C compiler and, depending on the complexity of the C program, by the `make` utility. After the program is compiled, it can be executed over and over without recompilation.

The phrase *third-generation procedural* describes computer languages that clearly distinguish the data used in a program from the actions performed on that data. Programs written in third-generation languages take the form of a series of explicit processing steps, or procedures, that manipulate the contents of data structures by means of explicit references to their location in memory and manipulate the computer's hardware in response to hardware interrupts.

Functions in C Programs

In the C language, all procedures take the form of functions. Just as a mathematical function transforms one or more numbers into another number, a C function is typically a procedure that transforms some value or performs some other action and returns the results. The act of invoking the transformation is known as *calling* the function.

Mathematical function calls can be nested, as can function calls in C. When function calls are nested, the results of the innermost function are passed as input to the next function, and so on. Table 30.1 shows how nested calls to the square root function are evaluated arithmetically.

TABLE 30.1 NESTED OPERATIONS IN MATHEMATICS

Function	*Value*
`sqrt(256)`	16
`sqrt( sqrt(256) ) = sqrt(16)`	4
`sqrt( sqrt( sqrt(256) ) ) = sqrt(4)`	2

Figure 30.1 shows the way function calls are nested within C programs. In the figure, the `Main` function calls `Function 1`, which calls `Function 2`. `Function 2` is evaluated first, and its results are passed back to `Function 1`. When `Function 1` completes its operations, its results are passed back to the `Main` function.

FIGURE 30.1
Nesting function calls within C programs.

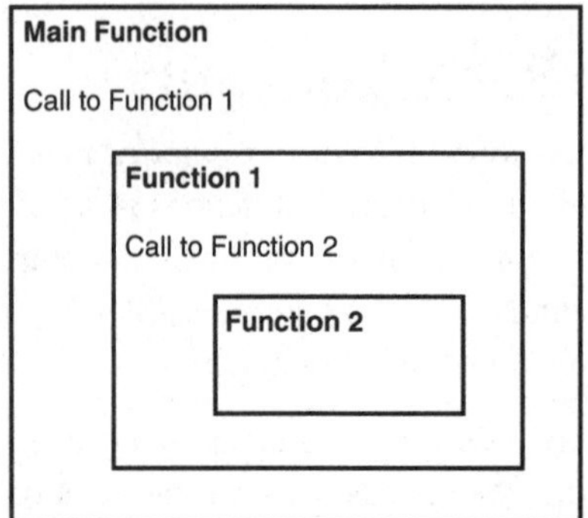

Nonfunctional procedures in other languages often operate on data variables that are shared with other code in the program. For instance, a nonfunctional procedure might update a program-wide `COUNT_OF_ERRORS` whenever a user makes a keyboard mistake. Such procedures must be carefully written, and they are usually specific to the program for which they were first created, because they reference particular shared data variables within the wider program.

A function, however, receives all the information it needs (including the location of data variables to use in each instance) when it is called. The function neither knows nor cares about the wider program context that calls it; it simply transforms the values found within the input variables (parameters), whatever they might be, and returns the result to whatever other function invokes it.

Because procedures written in C are implemented as functions, they don't need to know whether (or how deeply) they will be nested inside other function calls. This enables you to reuse C functions in many different programs without modifying them. For example, `Function 2` in Figure 30.1 might be called directly by the `Main` logic in a different C program.

An entire C program is itself a function that returns a result code, when executed, to the program that invokes it. This is usually a shell in the case of applications, but might also be any other part of the operating system or any other UNIX program. Because C programs are all structured as functions, they can be invoked by other programs or nested inside larger programs without needing to be rewritten in any way.

> **NOTE**
>
> C's feature of structuring programs as functions has heavily shaped the look and feel of UNIX. More than in most other operating environments, UNIX systems consist of many small C programs that call one another, are combined into larger programs, and are invoked by the user as needed. Instead of using monolithic, integrated applications, UNIX typically hosts many small, flexible programs. Users can customize their working environments by combining these tools to do new tasks.

Data in C Programs

The two kinds of data that are manipulated within C programs are *literal values* and *variables*. Literal values are specific, actual numbers or characters, such as `1`, `4.35`, or `a`. Variables are names associated with a place in memory that can hold data values. Each variable in C is typed; that is, each variable can hold only one kind of value. The basic datatypes include integers, floating-point (real) numbers, characters, and arrays. An *array* is a series of data elements of the same type; the elements are identified by the order in which they appear (by their place within the series).

You can define complex data structures as well. Complex data structures are used to gather a number of related data items together under one name. A terminal communications program, for example, might have a terminal control block (TCB) associated with each user who is logged on. The TCB typically contains data elements identifying the communications port, the active application process, and other information associated with that terminal session.

All the variables in a C program must be explicitly defined before they can be used.

Creating, Compiling, and Executing Your First Program

The development of a C program is an iterative procedure. Many UNIX tools familiar to software developers are involved in this four-step process:

1. Using an editor, write your code into a text file.
2. Compile the program.
3. Execute the program.
4. Debug the program.

Repeat the first two steps until the program compiles successfully. Then begin the execution and debugging. When I explain each of these steps in this chapter, you might find that some of the concepts seem strange, especially if you're a nonprogrammer. Remember that this chapter serves as only an introduction to C as a programming language. For more in-depth coverage of C, check out one of the resources listed at the end of this chapter in the section "Additional Resources."

The typical first C program is almost a cliché—the Hello, World program, which prints the simple line `Hello, World`. Listing 30.1 contains the source code of the program.

LISTING 30.1 SOURCE CODE OF THE HELLO, WORLD PROGRAM

```
main()
{
printf("Hello, World\n");
}
```

This program can be compiled and executed as follows:

```
$ gcc hello.c
$ ./a.out
Hello, World
$
```

NOTE

If the current directory is in your path, you could have executed `a.out` by typing

`a.out`

The Hello, World program is compiled with the `gcc` command, which creates a file `a.out` if the code is correct. Just typing **`a.out`** will run it. Notice that Listing 30.1 includes only one function, `main`. Every C program must have a `main` function; `main` is where the program's execution begins. The only statement in Listing 30.1 is a call to the `printf` library function, which passes the string `Hello, World\n`. (Functions are described in detail later in this chapter in the section "Functions.") The last two characters of the string, `\n`, represent the newline character.

NOTE

`a.out` is the default filename for executables (binaries) created by the C compiler under UNIX. This can be changed through the use of a command-line switch (see "GNU C/C++ Compiler Command-Line Switches" later in this chapter).

An Overview of the C Language

As with all programming languages, C programs must follow certain rules. These rules include how a program should appear and what the words and symbols mean; altogether, these are called the *syntax* of a programming language. Think of a program as a story. Within a story, each sentence must have a noun and a verb, put together with a particular syntax. Sentences form paragraphs, and the paragraphs tell the story. Similarly, C statements constructed with the correct syntax can form functions and programs.

Elementary C Syntax

Like all languages, C deals primarily with the manipulation and presentation of data. The language C evolved from, BCPL, dealt with data only as data. C, however, goes one step farther by using the concept of *datatypes*. The three basic datatypes are integers, floating-point numbers, and characters. Other datatypes are built from these.

Integers are the basic mathematical datatype. They can be classified as `long` and `short` integers, and their size is implementation dependent. With a few exceptions, integers are four bytes in length, and they can range from -2,147,483,648 to 2,147,483,647. In ANSI C, these values are defined in a header (`limit.h`) as `INT_MIN` and `INT_MAX`. The qualifier `unsigned` moves the range one bit higher to the equivalent of `INT_MAX` minus `INT_MIN`.

Floating-point numbers are used for more complicated mathematics, whereas integer mathematics is limited to integer results. For example, with integers, 3/2 equals 1. Floating-point numbers give a greater amount of precision to mathematical calculations than integers can; with floating-point numbers, 3/2 equals 1.5. Floating-point numbers can be represented by a decimal number, such as 687.534, or with scientific notation, such as 8.87534E+2. For larger numbers, scientific notation is preferred. For even greater precision, the type `double` provides a greater range. Again, specific ranges are implementation dependent.

Characters are usually implemented as single bytes, although some international character sets require two bytes. One common set of character representations is ASCII, which is found on most U.S. computers.

You use arrays for sequences of values that are often position dependent. An array is particularly useful when you need a range of values of a given type. Related to the array is the pointer. Variables are stored in memory, and a *pointer* is the physical address of that memory. In a sense, pointers and arrays are similar, except when a program is invoked. The space needed for an array's data is allocated when the routine that needs the space is invoked. For a pointer, the space must be allocated by the programmer, or the variable must be assigned by dereferencing a variable. The ampersand (`&`) is used to indicate dereferencing, and an asterisk (*) is used to indicate when the value pointed at is required. Here are some sample declarations:

`int i;`	Declares an integer
`char c;`	Declares a character
`char *ptr;`	Declares a pointer to a character
`double temp[16];`	Declares an array of double-precision floating-point numbers with 16 values

Listing 30.2 shows an example of a program with pointers.

LISTING 30.2 A PROGRAM WITH POINTERS

```
int i;
int *ptr;

i=5;
ptr = &i;
printf("%d %x %d\n", i,ptr,*ptr);
```

The output of this program is as follows:

```
5 f7fffa6c 5
```

NOTE

The middle value, `f7fffa6c`, is an address. This might be different on your system, because the pointer variable changes from version to version of the libraries.

A pointer is just a memory address and will tell you the address of any variable.

There is no specific type for a string. An array of characters is used to represent strings. They can be printed using an `%s` flag instead of `%c`.

Simple output is created by the `printf` function. `printf` takes a format string and the list of arguments to be printed. A complete set of format options is presented in Table 30.2. Format options can be modified with sizes. Check the `gcc` documentation (man page or info file) for the full specification.

TABLE 30.2 FORMAT CONVERSIONS FOR `printf`

Conversion	*Meaning*
`%%`	Percent sign
`%E`	Double (scientific notation)
`%G`	Double (format depends on value)
`%X`	Hexadecimal (letters are capitalized)
`%c`	Single character
`%d`	Integer
`%e`	Double (scientific notation)
`%f`	Double of the form `mmm.ddd`
`%g`	Double (format depends on value)
`%i`	Integer
`%ld`	Long integer
`%n`	Count of characters written in current `printf`
`%o`	Octal
`%p`	Print as a pointer
`%s`	Character pointer (string)
`%u`	Unsigned integer
`%x`	Hexadecimal

Some characters cannot be included easily in a program. Newlines, for example, require a special escape sequence because there cannot be an unescaped newline in a string. Table 30.3 contains a complete list of escape sequences.

TABLE 30.3 ESCAPE CHARACTERS FOR STRINGS

Escape Sequence	*Meaning*
`\"`	Double quote
`\'`	Single quote
`\?`	Question mark
`\\`	Backslash
`\a`	Audible bell
`\b`	Backspace

continues

TABLE 30.3 CONTINUED

Escape Sequence	*Meaning*
`\f`	Form feed (new page)
`\n`	Newline
`\ooo`	Octal number
`\r`	Carriage return
`\t`	Horizontal tab
`\v`	Vertical tab
`\xhh`	Hexadecimal number

A full program is a compilation of statements. Statements are separated by semicolons and can be grouped in blocks of statements surrounded by braces (curly brackets). The simplest statement is an assignment, in which a variable on the left side is assigned the value of an expression on the right.

Expressions

At the heart of the C programming language are *expressions*. These are techniques to combine simple values into new values. The three basic types of expressions are comparison, numerical, and bitwise.

Comparison Expressions

The simplest expression is a comparison. A comparison evaluates to a `true` or a `false` value. In C, `true` is a nonzero value and `false` is a zero value. Table 30.4 contains a list of comparison operators.

TABLE 30.4 COMPARISON OPERATORS

Operator	*Meaning*
`<`	Less than
`>`	Greater than
`==`	Equal to
`<=`	Less than or equal to
`>=`	Greater than or equal to
`||`	Logical OR
`&&`	Logical AND
`!`	Logical NOT

You can combine simple comparisons with ANDs and ORs to make complex expressions. For example, consider the definition of a leap year. In words, it is any year divisible by 4 except a year divisible by 100, unless that year is divisible by 400. Using `year` as the variable, you can define a leap year with the following expression:

```
((((year%4)==0)&&((year%100)!=0))||((year%400)==0))
```

On first inspection, this code might look complicated, but it isn't. The parentheses group the simple expressions with the ANDs and ORs to make a complex expression.

Mathematical Expressions

One convenient aspect of C is that expressions can be treated as mathematical values, and mathematical statements can be used in expressions. In fact, any statement—even a simple assignment—has values that can be used in other places as an expression.

The mathematics of C is straightforward. Barring parenthetical groupings, multiplication and division have higher precedence than addition and subtraction. The operators are standard and are listed in Table 30.5.

TABLE 30.5 MATHEMATICAL OPERATORS

Operator	*Meaning*
+	Addition
-	Subtraction
*	Multiplication
/	Division
%	Integer remainder

There are also *unary* operators, which affect a single variable. These are ++ (increment by one) and `--` (decrement by one) and are shorthand for `var = var + 1` and `var = var - 1`, respectively.

Shorthand can be used for situations in which you want to change the value of a variable. For example, if you want to add an expression to a variable called `a` and assign a new value to a, the shorthand `a += expr` is the same as `a=a+expr`. The expression can be as complex or as simple as required.

NOTE

Most UNIX functions take advantage of the truth values and return 0 for success. This enables a programmer to write code such as

```
if (function())
        {
        error condition
        }
```

The return value of a function determines whether the function worked.

Bitwise Operations

Because a variable is just a string of bits, many operations work on those bit patterns. Table 30.6 lists the bit operators.

TABLE 30.6 BIT OPERATORS

Operator	*Meaning*
&	Bitwise AND
|	Bitwise OR
~	Negation (one's complement)
<<	Bit shift left
>>	Bit shift right

A bitwise AND compares the individual bits in place. If both are 1, the value 1 is assigned to the expression. Otherwise, 0 is assigned. For a logical OR, 1 is assigned if either value is a 1. Bit shift operations move the bits a number of positions to the right or left. Mathematically, this is the same as multiplying or dividing by 2, but circumstances exist where the bit shift is preferred.

Bit operations are often used for masking values and for comparisons. A simple way to determine whether a value is odd or even is to perform a bitwise AND with the integer value 1. If it is `true`, the number is odd.

Statement Controls

With what you've seen so far, you can create a list of statements that are executed only once, after which the program terminates. To control the flow of commands, three types of loops exist in C. The simplest is the `while` loop. The syntax is

```
while (expression)
      statement
```

As long as the expression between the parentheses evaluates as nonzero—or `true` in C—the statement is executed. `statement` actually can be a list of statements blocked off with braces. If the expression evaluates to zero the first time it is reached, the statement is never executed. To force at least one execution of the statement, use a `do` loop. The syntax for a `do` loop is

```
do
        statement
        while (expression);
```

The third type of control flow is the `for` loop. This is more complicated. The syntax is

```
for(expr1;expr2;expr3) statement
```

When this expression is reached for the first time, `expr1` is evaluated, and then `expr2` is evaluated. If `expr2` is nonzero, `statement` is executed, followed by `expr3`. Then `expr2` is tested again, followed by the statement and `expr3`, until `expr2` evaluates to zero. Strictly speaking, this is a notational convenience, because a `while` loop can be structured to perform the same actions, as in the following:

```
expr1;
while (expr2) {
        statement;
        expr3
        }
```

Loops can be interrupted in three ways. A `break` statement terminates execution in a loop and exits it. `continue` terminates the current iteration and retests the loop before possibly reexecuting the statement. For an unconventional exit, you could use `goto`, which changes the program's execution to a labeled statement. According to many programmers, `goto` is poor programming practice, and you should avoid using it.

Statements can also be executed conditionally. Again, there are three different formats for statement execution. The simplest is an `if` statement. The syntax is

```
if (expr) statement
```

If the expression `expr` evaluates to nonzero, `statement` is executed. You can expand this with an `else`, the second type of conditional execution. The syntax for `else` is

```
if (expr) statement else statement
```

If the expression evaluates to zero, the second statement is executed.

NOTE

The second statement in an `else` condition can be another `if` statement. This situation might cause the grammar to be indeterminate if the structure

```
if (expr) if (expr) statement else statement
```

is not parsed cleanly.

As the code is written, the `else` is considered applicable to the second `if`. To make the `else` applicable to the first `if`, surround the second `if` statement with braces, as in the following:

```
if (expr) {if (expr) statement} else statement
```

The third type of conditional execution is more complicated. The `switch` statement first evaluates an expression. Then it looks down a series of `case` statements to find a label that matches the expression's value and executes the statements following the label. A special label `default` exists if no other conditions are met. If you want only a set of statements executed for each label, you must use the `break` statement to leave the `switch` statement.

This covers the simplest building blocks of a C program. You can add more power by using functions and by declaring complex datatypes.

If your program requires different pieces of data to be grouped on a consistent basis, you can group them into structures. Listing 30.3 shows a structure for a California driver's license. Note that it includes integer, character, and character array (string) types.

LISTING 30.3 AN EXAMPLE OF A STRUCTURE

```
struct license {
        char name[128];
        char address[3][128];
        int zipcode;
        int height, weight, month, day, year;
        char license_letter;
        int license_number;
        };

struct license newlicensee;
struct license *user;
```

Because California driver's license numbers consist of a single character followed by a seven-digit number, the license ID is broken into two components. Similarly, the new licensee's address is broken into three lines, represented by three arrays of 128 characters.

Accessing individual fields of a structure requires two different techniques. To read a member of a locally defined structure, you append a dot to the variable and then the field name, as in the following example:

```
newlicensee.zipcode=94404;
```

When using a pointer to a structure, you need `->` to point to the member (to reference the individual members):

```
user->zipcode=94404;
```

Interestingly, if the structure pointer is incremented, the address is increased not by `1`, but by the size of the structure.

Functions

Functions are an easy way to group statements and to give them a name. These are usually related statements that perform repetitive tasks such as I/O. `printf`, described above, is a function. It is provided with the standard C library. Listing 30.4 illustrates a function definition, a function call, and a function.

> **NOTE**
>
> The three-dot ellipsis simply means that some lines of sample code are not shown here to save space.

LISTING 30.4 AN EXAMPLE OF A FUNCTION

```
int swapandmin( int *, int *);          /* Function declaration */

...

int i,j,lower;

i=2; j=4;
lower=swapandmin(&i, &j);              /* Function call */

...
```

continues

LISTING 30.4 CONTINUED

```
int swapandmin(int *a,int *b)          /* Function definition */
{
int tmp;

tmp=(*a);
(*a)=(*b);
(*b)=tmp;
if ((*a)<(*b)) return(*a);
return(*b);
}
```

ANSI C and K&R differ most in function declarations and calls. ANSI C requires that function arguments be prototyped when the function is declared. K&R required only the name and the type of the returned value. The declaration in Listing 30.4 states that a function `swapandmin` will take two pointers to integers as arguments and that it will return an integer. The function call takes the addresses of two integers and sets the variable named `lower` to the return value of the function.

When a function is called from a C program, the values of the arguments are passed to the function. Therefore, if any of the arguments will be changed for the calling function, you can't pass only the variable—you must pass the address, too. Likewise, to change the value of the argument in the calling routine of the function, you must assign the new value to the address.

In the function in Listing 30.4, the value pointed to by `a` is assigned to the `tmp` variable. `b` is assigned to `a`, and `tmp` is assigned to `b`. `*a` is used instead of `a` to ensure that the change is reflected in the calling routine. Finally, the values of `*a` and `*b` are compared, and the lower of the two is returned.

If you include the line

```
printf("%d %d %d",lower,i,j);
```

after the function call, you will see `2 4 2` as output.

This sample function is quite simple, and it is ideal for a macro. A macro is a technique used to replace a token with different text. You can use macros to make code more readable. For example, you might use `EOF` instead of `(-1)` to indicate the end of a file. You can also use macros to replace code. Listing 30.5 is the same as Listing 30.4 except that it uses macros.

LISTING 30.5 AN EXAMPLE OF MACROS

```
#define SWAP(X,Y) {int tmp; tmp=X; X=Y; Y=tmp; }
#define MIN(X,Y) ((X<Y) ? X : Y )

...

int i,j,lower;

i=2; j=4;
SWAP(i,j);
lower=MIN(i,j);
```

When a C program is compiled, macro replacement is one of the first steps performed. Listing 30.6 illustrates the result of the replacement.

LISTING 30.6 AN EXAMPLE OF MACRO REPLACEMENT

```
int i,j,lower;

i=2; j=4;
{int tmp; tmp=i; i=j; j=tmp; };
lower= ((i<j) ? i : j );
```

The macros make the code easier to read and understand.

CAUTION

Macros can have side effects. Side effects occur because the programmer expects a variable to be evaluated once when it is actually evaluated more than once. Replacing the variable `i` with `i++` changes things dramatically:

```
lower=MIN(i++,j);
```

is converted to

```
lower= ((i++ < j) ? i++ : j );
```

As a result, the variable `i` can be incremented twice instead of once as the programmer expects.

Creating a Simple Program

For the next example, you write a program that prints a chart of the first 10 integers and their squares, cubes, and square roots.

Writing the Code

Using the text editor of your choice, enter all the code in Listing 30.7 and save it in a file called `sample.c`.

LISTING 30.7 SOURCE CODE FOR `sample.c`

```
#include <stdio.h>
#include <math.h>

main()
{
int i;
double a;

for(i=1;i<11;i++)
        {
        a=i*1.0;
        printf("%2d. %3d %4d %7.5f\n",i,i*i,i*i*i,sqrt(a));
        }
}
```

The first two lines are header files. The `stdio.h` file provides the function definitions and structures associated with the C input and output libraries. The `math.h` file includes the definitions of mathematical library functions. You need it for the square root function.

The `main` loop is the only function you need to write for this example. It takes no arguments. You define two variables: one is the integer `i`, and the other is a double-precision floating-point number called `a`. You don't have to use `a`, but you can for the sake of convenience.

The program is a simple `for` loop that starts at 1 and ends at 11. It increments `i` by 1 each time through. When `i` equals 11, the `for` loop stops executing. You also could have written `i<=10` because the expressions have the same meaning.

First, you multiply `i` by 1.0 and assign the product to `a`. A simple assignment would also work, but the multiplication reminds you that you are converting the value to a double-precision floating-point number.

Next, you call the `print` function. The format string includes three integers of widths `2`, `3`, and `4`. After the first integer is printed, you print a period. After the next integer is printed, you print a floating-point number that is seven characters wide with five digits following the decimal point. The arguments after the format string show that you print the integer, the square of the integer, the cube of the integer, and the square root of the integer.

Compiling the Program

To compile this program using the GNU C compiler, enter the following command:

```
$ gcc sample.c -lm
```

This command produces an output file called `a.out`. This is the simplest use of the C compiler. `gcc` is one of the most powerful and flexible commands of a UNIX system.

A number of different flags can change the compiler's output. These flags are often dependent on the system or compiler. Some flags common to all C compilers are described in the following paragraphs.

The `-o` flag tells the compiler to write the output to the file named after the flag. The `gcc -o sample sample.c` command puts the program in a file named `sample`.

> **NOTE**
>
> The output discussed here is the compiler's output, not the sample program. Compiler output is usually the program, and in every example here, it is an executable program.

The `-g` flag tells the compiler to save the symbol table (the data used by a program to associate variable names with memory locations) in the executable, which is necessary for debuggers. Its opposite is the `-O` flag, which tells the compiler to optimize the code—that is, to make it more efficient. You can change the search path for header files with the `-I` flag, and you can add libraries with the `-l` and `-L` flags.

The compilation process takes place in several steps:

1. First, the C preprocessor parses the file. To parse the file, it sequentially reads the lines, includes header files, and performs macro replacement.
2. The compiler parses the modified code for correct syntax. This builds a symbol table and creates an intermediate object format. Most symbols have specific memory addresses assigned, although symbols defined in other modules, such as external variables, do not.

3. The last compilation stage, linking, ties together different files and libraries and links the files by resolving the symbols that hadn't previously been resolved.

Executing the Program

The output from this program appears in Listing 30.8.

LISTING 30.8 OUTPUT FROM THE `sample.c` PROGRAM

```
$ sample
 1.   1    1 1.00000
 2.   4    8 1.41421
 3.   9   27 1.73205
 4.  16   64 2.00000
 5.  25  125 2.23607
 6.  36  216 2.44949
 7.  49  343 2.64575
 8.  64  512 2.82843
 9.  81  729 3.00000
10. 100 1000 3.16228
```

NOTE

To execute a program, just type its name at a shell prompt. The output will immediately follow.

Building Large Applications

C programs can be broken into any number of files, as long as no single function spans more than one file. To compile this program, you compile each source file into an intermediate object before you link all the objects into a single executable. The `-c` flag tells the compiler to stop at this stage. During the link stage, all the object files should be listed on the command line. Object files are identified by the `.o` suffix.

Making Libraries with `ar`

If several different programs use the same functions, they can be combined in a single library archive. The `ar` command is used to build a library. When this library is included on the compile line, the archive is searched to resolve any external symbols. Listing 30.9 shows an example of building and using a library.

LISTING 30.9 BUILDING A LARGE APPLICATION

```
$ gcc -c sine.c
$ gcc -c cosine.c
$ gcc -c tangent.c
$ ar c libtrig.a sine.o cosine.o tangent.o

$ gcc -c mainprog.c
$ gcc -o mainprog mainprog.o libtrig.a
```

Large applications can require hundreds of source code files. Compiling and linking these applications can be a complex and error-prone task of its own. The `make` utility is a tool that helps developers organize the process of building the executable form of complex applications from many source files.

Debugging Tools

Debugging is a science and an art unto itself. Sometimes, the simplest tool—the code listing—is best. At other times, however, you need to use other tools. Three of these tools are `lint`, `gprof`, and `gdb`. Other available tools include `escape`, `cxref`, and `cb`. Many UNIX commands have debugging uses.

`lint` is a command that examines source code for possible problems. The code might meet the standards for C and compile cleanly, but it might not execute correctly. `lint` checks type mismatches and incorrect argument counts on function calls. `lint` also uses the C preprocessor, so you can use command-like options similar to those you would use for `gcc`. The GNU C compiler supports extensive warnings that might eliminate the need for a separate `lint` command.

The `gprof` command is used to study where a program is spending its time. If a program is compiled and linked with `-p` as a flag, a `mon.out` file is created when it executes, with data on how often each function is called and how much time is spent in each function. `gprof` parses and displays this data. An analysis of the output generated by `gprof` helps you determine where performance bottlenecks occur. Whereas optimizing compilers can speed your programs, `gprof`'s analysis will significantly improve program performance.

The third tool is `gdb`—a symbolic debugger. When a program is compiled with `-g`, the symbol tables are retained and a symbolic debugger can be used to track program bugs. The basic technique is to invoke `gdb` after a core dump and get a stack trace. This indicates the source line where the core dump occurred and the functions that were called to reach that line. Often, this is enough to identify the problem. It is not the limit of `gdb`, though.

gdb also provides an environment for debugging programs interactively. Invoking gdb with a program enables you to set breakpoints, examine variable values, and monitor variables. If you suspect a problem near a line of code, you can set a breakpoint at that line and run the program. When the line is reached, execution is interrupted. You can check variable values, examine the stack trace, and observe the program's environment. You can single-step through the program, checking values. You can resume execution at any point. By using breakpoints, you can discover many of the bugs in your code that you've missed.

There is an X Window version of gdb called xxgdb.

cpp is another tool that can be used to debug programs. It performs macro replacements, includes headers, and parses the code. The output is the actual module to be compiled. Normally, though, cpp is never executed by the programmer directly. Instead it is invoked through gcc with either an -E or -P option. -E sends the output directly to the terminal; -P makes a file with an .i suffix.

Introduction to C++

If C is the language most associated with UNIX, C++ is the language that underlies most graphical user interfaces available today.

C++ was originally developed by Dr. Bjarne Stroustrup at the Computer Science Research Center of AT&T's Bell Laboratories (Murray Hill, NJ), also the source of UNIX itself. Dr. Stroustrup's original goal was an object-oriented simulation language. The availability of C compilers for many hardware architectures convinced him to design the language as an extension of C, allowing a preprocessor to translate C++ programs into C for compilation.

After the C language was standardized by a joint committee of the American National Standards Institute and the International Standards Organization (ISO) in 1989, a new joint committee began the effort to formalize C++ as well. This effort has produced several new features and has significantly refined the interpretation of other language features, but it hasn't yet resulted in a formal language standard.

Programming in C++: Basic Concepts

C++ is an object-oriented extension to C. Because C++ is a superset of C, C++ compilers will compile C programs correctly, and it is possible to write non–object-oriented code in C++.

The distinction between an object-oriented language and a procedural one can be subtle and hard to grasp, especially with regard to C++, which retains all of C's characteristics and concepts. One way to describe the difference is to say that when programmers code in a procedural language, they specify actions that process the data, whereas when they write object-oriented code, they create data objects that can be requested to perform actions on or with regard to themselves.

Thus a C function receives one or more values as input, transforms or acts on them in some way, and returns a result. If the values that are passed include pointers, the contents of data variables can be modified by the function. As the standard library routines show, it is likely that the code calling a function won't know, and won't need to know, what steps the function takes when it is invoked. However, such matters as the datatype of the input parameters and the result code are specified when the function is defined and remain invariable throughout program execution.

Functions are associated with C++ objects as well. But as you will see, the actions performed when an object's function is invoked can automatically differ, perhaps substantially, depending on the specific type of the data structure with which it is associated. This is known as *overloading* function names. Overloading is related to a second characteristic of C++—the fact that functions can be defined as belonging to C++ data structures, an aspect of the wider language feature known as *encapsulation*.

In addition to overloading and encapsulation, object-oriented languages allow programmers to define new abstract datatypes (including associated functions) and then derive subsequent datatypes from them. The notion of a new class of data objects, in addition to the built-in classes such as integer, floating-point number, and character, goes beyond the familiar capability to define complex data objects in C. Just as a C data structure that includes, for example, an integer element inherits the properties and functions applicable to integers, so too a C++ class that is derived from another class *inherits* the parent class's functions and properties. When a specific variable or structure (instance) of that class's type is defined, the class (parent or child) is said to be *instantiated*.

In the remainder of this chapter, you will look at some of the basic features of C++ in more detail, along with code listings that provide concrete examples of these concepts. To learn more about the rich capabilities of C++, see the additional resources listed at the end of the chapter.

File Naming

Most C programs will compile with a C++ compiler if you follow strict ANSI rules. For example, you can compile the `hello.c` program shown in Listing 30.1 with the GNU C++ compiler. Typically, you will name the file something like `hello.cc`, `hello.C`, or `hello.cxx`. The GNU C++ compiler will accept any of these three names.

Differences Between C and C++

C++ differs from C in some details apart from the more obvious object-oriented features. Some of these are fairly superficial, including the following:

- The capability to define variables anywhere within a code block rather than always at the start of the block
- The addition of an `enum` datatype to facilitate conditional logic based on case values
- The capability to designate functions as `inline`, causing the compiler to generate another copy of the function code at that point in the program rather than a call to shared code

Other differences have to do with advanced concepts such as memory management and the scope of reference for variable and function names. Because the latter features especially are used in object-oriented C++ programs, they are worth examining more closely in this short introduction to the language.

Scope of Reference in C and C++

The phrase *scope of reference* is used to discuss how a name in C, C++, or certain other programming languages is interpreted when the language permits more than one instance of a name to occur within a program. Consider the code in Listing 30.10, which defines and then calls two different functions. Each function has an internal variable called `tmp`. The `tmp` that is defined within `printnum` is *local* to the `printnum` function—that is, it can be accessed only by logic within `printnum`. Similarly, the `tmp` that is defined within `printchar` is local to the `printchar` function. The scope of reference for each `tmp` variable is limited to the `printnum` and `printchar` functions, respectively.

LISTING 30.10 SCOPE OF REFERENCE EXAMPLE 1

```
#include <stdio.h>                /* I/O function declarations */

void printnum  ( int );           /* function declaration      */
void printchar ( char );          /* function declaration      */

main ()
{
   printnum (5);                  /* print the number 5        */
   printchar ('a');               /* print the letter a        */
}
```

```
/* define the functions called above                         */
/* void means the function does not return a value           */

   void printnum (int inputnum)
{
   int tmp;
   tmp = inputnum;
   printf ("%d \n",tmp);
}

void printchar (char inputchar)
{
   char tmp;
   tmp = inputchar;
   printf ("%c \n",tmp);
}
```

When this program is executed after compilation, it creates the following output:

```
5
a
```

Listing 30.11 shows another example of scope of reference. In this listing, there is a `tmp` variable that is *global*—that is, it is known to the entire program because it is defined within the `main` function—in addition to the two `tmp` variables that are local to the `printnum` and `printchar` functions.

LISTING 30.11 SCOPE OF REFERENCE EXAMPLE 2

```
#include <stdio.h>

void printnum  ( int );        /* function declaration            */
void printchar ( char );       /* function declaration            */

main ()
{
   double tmp;                 /* define a global variable        */
   tmp = 1.234;
   printf ("%f\n",tmp);        /* print the value of the global tmp */
   printnum (5);               /* print the number 5              */
   printf ("%f\n",tmp);        /* print the value of the global tmp */
   printchar ('a');            /* print the letter a              */
   printf ("%f\n",tmp);        /* print the value of the global tmp */
}

/* define the functions used above                               */
/* void means the function does not return a value               */
```

continues

LISTING 30.11 CONTINUED

```
void printnum (int inputnum)
{
   int tmp;
   tmp = inputnum;
   printf ("%d \n",tmp);
}

void printchar (char inputchar)
{
   char tmp;
   tmp = inputchar;
   printf ("%c \n",tmp);
}
```

The global `tmp` is not modified when the local `tmp` variables are used within their respective functions, as shown by the output:

```
1.234
5
1.234
a
1.234
```

C++ provides a means to specify a global variable even when a local variable with the same name is in scope. The operator `::` prefixed to a variable name always resolves that name to the global instance. Thus, the global `tmp` variable defined in `main` in Listing 30.11 could be accessed within the `print` functions by using the label `::tmp`.

Why would a language such as C or C++ allow different scopes of reference for the same variable?

The answer to this is that allowing variable scope of reference also allows functions to be placed into public libraries for other programmers to use. Library functions can be invoked merely by knowing their calling sequences, and no one needs to check to be sure the programmers didn't use the same local variable names. This in turn means library functions can be improved, if necessary, without impacting existing code. This is true whether the library contains application code for reuse or is distributed as the runtime library associated with a compiler.

NOTE

A runtime library is a collection of compiled modules that perform common C, C++, and UNIX functions. The code is written carefully, debugged, and highly optimized. For example, the `printf` function requires machine instructions to format the various output fields, send them to the standard output device, and check to see that there were no I/O errors. Because this takes many machine instructions, it would be inefficient to repeat that sequence for every `printf` call in a program. Instead, a single, all-purpose `printf` function is written once and placed in the standard library by the developers of the compiler. When your program is compiled, the compiler generates calls to these prewritten programs rather than re-creating the logic each time a `printf` call occurs in the source code.

Variable scope of reference is the language feature that allows small C and C++ programs to be designed to perform standalone functions, yet also to be combined into larger utilities as needed. This flexibility is characteristic of UNIX, the first operating system to be built on the C language. As you'll see in the rest of the chapter, variable scope of reference also makes object-oriented programming possible in C++.

Overloading Functions and Operators in C++

Overloading is a technique that allows more than one function to have the same name. In at least two circumstances, a programmer might want to define a new function with the same name as an existing one:

- When the existing version of the function doesn't perform the exact desired functionality, but it must otherwise be included with the program (as with a function from the standard library)
- When the same function must operate differently depending on the format of the data passed to it

In C, a function name can be reused as long as the old function name isn't within scope. A function name's scope of reference is determined in the same way as a data name's scope: a function that is defined (not just called) within the definition of another function is local to that other function.

When two similar C functions must coexist within the same scope, however, they cannot bear the same name. Instead, two different names must be assigned, as with the `strcpy` and `strncpy` functions from the standard library, each of which copies strings but does so in a slightly different fashion.

C++ gets around this restriction by allowing overloaded function names. That is, the C++ language allows programmers to reuse function names within the same scope of reference, as long as the parameters for the function differ in number or type.

Listing 30.12 shows an example of overloading functions. This program defines and calls two versions of the printvar function, one equivalent to printnum in Listing 30.11 and the other to printchar.

LISTING 30.12 AN EXAMPLE OF AN OVERLOADED FUNCTION

```
#include <stdio.h>
void printvar (int tmp)
{
   printf ("%d \n",tmp);
}

void printvar (char tmp)
{
   printf ("a \n",tmp);
}

void main ()
{
   int  numvar;
   char charvar;
   numvar = 5;
   printvar (numvar);
   charvar = 'a';
   printvar (charvar);
}
```

The following is the output of this program when it is executed:

```
5
a
```

Overloading is possible because C++ compilers are able to determine the format of the arguments sent to the printvar function each time it is called from within main. The compiler substitutes a call to the correct version of the function based on those formats. If the function being overloaded resides in a library or in another module, the associated header file (such as stdio.h) must be included in this source code module. This header file contains the prototype for the external function, thereby informing the compiler of the parameters and parameter formats used in the external version of the function.

Standard mathematical, logical, and other operators can also be overloaded. This is an advanced and powerful technique that allows the programmer to customize exactly how a standard language feature will operate on a specific data structure or at certain points in the code. Great care must be exercised when overloading standard operators such as +, MOD, and OR to ensure that the resulting operation functions correctly, is restricted to the appropriate occurrences in the code, and is well documented.

Functions Within C++ Data Structures

A second feature of C++ that supports object-oriented programming, in addition to overloading, is the capability to associate a function with a particular data structure or format. Such functions can be *public* (able to be invoked by any code), can be *private* (able to be invoked only by other functions within the data structure), or can allow limited access.

Data structures in C++ must be defined by using the `struct` keyword and become new datatypes added to the language (within the scope of the structure's definition). Listing 30.13 revisits the structure of Listing 30.3 and adds a display function to print out instances of the license structure. Note the alternative way to designate comments in C++, using a double slash. This tells the compiler to ignore everything that follows on the given line only.

Also notice that Listing 30.13 uses the C++ character output function `cout` rather than the C routine `printf`.

LISTING 30.13 ADDING FUNCTIONS TO DATA STRUCTURES

```
#include <iostream.h>
//              structure = new datatype
struct license {
        char name[128];
        char address[3][128];
        int zipcode;
        int height, weight, month, day, year;
        char license_letter;
        int license_number;

        void display(void)
➥// there will be a function to display license type structures
        };

// now define the display function for this datatype

void license::display()
{
   cout << "Name:     "  << name;
   cout << "Address: "  << address[0];
   cout << "          "  << address[1];
   cout << "          " << address[2] << " " << zipcode;
   cout << "Height:   " << height << " inches";
   cout << "Weight:   " << weight << " lbs";
   cout << "Date:     " << month << "/" << day  << "/" << year;
   cout << "License: " <<license_letter <<license_number;
}
```

continues

LISTING 30.13 CONTINUED

```
main()
{
   struct license newlicensee;      // define a variable of type license
   newlicensee.name = "Joe Smith";  //  and initialize it
   newlicensee.address(0) = "123 Elm Street";
   newlicensee.address(1) = "";
   newlicensee.address(2) = "Smalltown, AnyState";
   newlicensee.zipcode = "98765";
   newlicensee.height = 70;
   newlicensee.weight = 165;
   license.month = 1;
   newlicensee.day = 23;
   newlicensee.year = 97;
   newlicensee.license_letter = A;
   newlicensee.license_number = 567890;


   newlicensee.display;   // and display this instance of the structure
}
```

Note that there are three references to the same `display` function in Listing 30.13. First, the `display` function is prototyped as an element within the structure definition. Second, the function is defined. Because the function definition is valid for all instances of the datatype `license`, the structure's data elements are referenced by the `display` function without naming any instance of the structure. Finally, when a specific instance of `license` is created, its associated `display` function is invoked by prefixing the function name with that of the structure instance.

Listing 30.14 shows the output of this program.

LISTING 30.14 OUTPUT OF THE FUNCTION DEFINED WITHIN A STRUCTURE

```
Name:     Joe Smith
Address: 123 Elm Street

         Smalltown, AnyState  98765
Height:  70 inches
Weight:  160 lbs
Date:    1/23/1997
License: A567890
```

Note that the operator << is the bitwise shift-left operator except when it is used with `cout`. With `cout`, << is used to move data to the screen. This is an example of operator overloading, because the operator can have a different meaning depending on the context of its use. The >> operator is used for bitwise shift right except when used with `cin`; with `cin`, >> is used to move data from the keyboard to the specified variable.

Classes in C++

Overloading and associating functions with data structures lay the groundwork for object-oriented code in C++. Full object orientation is available through the use of the C++ class feature.

A C++ class extends the idea of data structures with associated functions by binding (or encapsulating) data descriptions and manipulation algorithms into new abstract datatypes. When a class is defined, the class type and methods are described in the public interface. The class can also have hidden private functions and data members.

Class declaration defines a datatype and format but does not allocate memory or in any other way create an object of the class's type. The wider program must declare an instance, or object, of this type in order to store values in the data elements or invoke the public class functions. A class is often placed into libraries for use by many different programs, each of which then declares objects that instantiate that class for use during program execution.

Declaring a Class in C++

Listing 30.15 contains an example of a typical class declaration in C++.

LISTING 30.15 DECLARING A CLASS IN C++

```
#include <iostream.h>
// declare the Circle class
class Circle   {
private:
   double rad;                      // private data member
public:
   Circle (double);                 // constructor function
   ~Circle ();                      // deconstructor function
   double area (void);              // member function - compute area
};

//  constructor function for objects of this class
Circle::Circle(double radius)
{
   rad = radius;
}
```

continues

LISTING 30.15 CONTINUED

```
//  deconstructor function for objects of this class
Circle::~Circle()
{
   // does nothing
}

// member function to compute the Circle's area
double Circle::area()
{
    return rad * rad * 3.141592654;
}

//        application program that uses a Circle object
main()
{
    Circle mycircle (2);         // declare a circle of radius = 2
    cout << mycircle.area();     // compute & display its area
}
```

The example in Listing 30.15 begins by declaring the `Circle` class. This class has one private member, a floating-point element. The `Circle` class also has several public members, consisting of three functions—`Circle`, `~Circle`, and `area`.

The *constructor function* of a class is a function called by a program to construct or create an object that is an instance of the class. In the case of the `Circle` class, the constructor function (`Circle(double)`) requires a single parameter, namely the radius of the desired circle. If a constructor function is explicitly defined, it has the same name as the class and does not specify a return value, even of type `void`.

> **NOTE**
>
> When a C++ program is compiled, the compiler generates calls to the runtime system, which allocates sufficient memory each time an object of class `Circle` comes into scope. For example, an object that is defined within a function is created (and goes into scope) whenever the function is called. However, the object's data elements are not initialized unless a constructor function has been defined for the class.

The *deconstructor function* of a class is a function called by a program to deconstruct an object of the class type. A deconstructor takes no parameters and returns nothing. In this example, the `Circle` class's deconstructor function is `~Circle`.

NOTE

Under normal circumstances, the memory associated with an object of a given class is released for reuse whenever the object goes out of scope. In such a case, the programmer can omit defining the deconstructor function. However, in advanced applications or where class assignments cause potential pointer conflicts, explicit deallocation of free-store memory might be necessary.

In addition to the constructor and deconstructor functions, the `Circle` class contains a public function called `area`. Programs can call this function to compute the area of `Circle` objects.

The main program (the `main` function) in Listing 30.15 shows how an object can be declared. `mycircle` is declared to be of type `Circle` and is given a radius of 2.

The final statement in this program calls the function to compute the area of `mycircle` and passes it to the output function for display. Note that the area computation function is identified by a composite name, just as with other functions that are members of C++ data structures outside of class definitions. This usage underscores the fact that the object `mycircle`, of type `Circle`, is being asked to execute a function that is a member of itself and with reference to itself. The programmer could define a `Rectangle` class that also contains an `area` function, thereby overloading the `area` function name with the appropriate algorithm for computing the areas of different kinds of geometric entities.

Inheritance and Polymorphism

A final characteristic of object-oriented languages, and of C++, is support for class inheritance and for polymorphism.

New C++ classes (and hence datatypes) can be defined so that they automatically *inherit* the properties and algorithms associated with their parent classes. This is done whenever a new class uses any of the standard C datatypes. The class from which new class definitions are created is called the *base class*. For example, a structure that includes integer members will also inherit all the mathematical functions associated with integers. New classes that are defined in terms of the base classes are called *derived classes*. The `Circle` class in Listing 30.15 is a derived class.

Derived classes can be based on more than one base class, in which case the derived class inherits multiple datatypes and their associated functions. This is called *multiple inheritance*.

Because functions can be overloaded, it is possible that an object declared as a member of a derived class might act differently than an object of the base class type. For example, the class of positive integers might return an error if the program attempts to assign a negative number to a class object, although such an assignment would be legal with regard to an object of the base integer type.

This capability of different objects within the same class hierarchy to act differently under the same circumstances is referred to as *polymorphism*. Polymorphism is the object-oriented concept that many people have the most difficulty grasping; however, it is also the concept that provides much of the power and elegance of object-oriented design and code. A programmer designing an application using predefined graphical user interface (GUI) classes, for instance, is free to ask various window objects to display themselves appropriately without having to concern herself with how the window color, location, or other display characteristics are handled in each case.

Class inheritance and polymorphism are among the most powerful object-oriented features of C++. Together with the other less dramatic extensions to C, these features have made possible many of the newest applications and systems capabilities of UNIX today, including GUIs for user terminals and many of the most advanced Internet and World Wide Web technologies—some of which will be discussed in subsequent chapters of this book.

GNU C/C++ Compiler Command-Line Switches

Many options are available for the GNU C/C++ compiler. Many of them match the C and C++ compilers available on other UNIX systems. Table 30.7 shows the important switches; look at the man page for `gcc` or the info file on the CD-ROM for the full list and description.

TABLE 30.7 GNU C/C++ COMPILER SWITCHES

Switch	*Description*
`-x language`	Specifies the language (C, C++, and assembler are valid values)
`-c`	Compiles and assembles only (does not link)
`-S`	Compiles (does not assemble or link)
`-E`	Preprocesses only (does not compile, assemble, or link)

Switch	Description
-o *file*	Specifies the output filename (a.out is the default)
-l library	Specifies the libraries to use
-I directory	Searches the specified directory for include files
-w	Inhibits warning messages
-pedantic	Strict ANSI compliance required
-Wall	Prints additional warning messages
-g	Produces debugging information (for use with gdb)
-p	Produces information required by proff
-pg	Produces information for use by groff
-O	Optimizes

New Features of the GNU egcs Compiler System

The egcs (pronounced "eggs") program suite is an experimental version of the gcc compiler whose development is hosted by Cygnus Support (http://www.cygnus.com). Starting with Red Hat 5.1 for Intel, egcs is available for installation as part of your Red Hat Linux system. However, egcs is different from gcc in several ways and might prevent you from properly building programs in several instances (see the next section, "egcs Considerations").

According to Cygnus, egcs "is an experimental step in the development of" gcc. Since its first release in late summer 1997, egcs has incorporated many of the latest developments and features from *parallel* development of gcc with many new developments of its own, such as a built-in Fortran 77 front end. At the time of this writing, egcs also now includes a built-in compiler for the Java language. Although some developers feel that development of egcs represents a fork (or split) in gcc compiler development, Cygnus has stated that "cooperation between the developers of gcc and egcs" could prevent this. The hope, according to Cygnus, is that the new compiler architecture and features of egcs will help gcc be "the best compiler in the world."

egcs Considerations

If you choose not to install egcs either during your initial Red Hat Linux installation or later via rpm or glint, your gcc and any legacy (read *older*) C++ Makefile scripts will function as expected. However, beginning with Red Hat Linux 5.1, you must expect at least one or two important changes if you install egcs alongside gcc. Red Hat Software, Inc. has a short notice concerning these differences for its 5.1 Linux distribution at

http://www.redhat.com/support/docs/rhl/RHL-5.1-Installation-Guide/manual/doc012.html

Have you installed gcc and egcs? If so, the traditional gcc compiler and the egcs compiler are installed, but components, such as cc, gcc, g++, c++, egcs, or g77, point to a different compiler. Table 30.8 lists the components, compilers, and locations for Red Hat Linux 5.1 for Intel (a similar table can be found at the URL given earlier for Red Hat).

TABLE 30.8 gcc AND egcs SOFTWARE LINKS AND LOCATIONS

Command	*Compiler*	*Location*
c++	egcs	/usr/bin/c++
cc	gcc	/usr/bin/cc->gcc (symbolic link)
egcs	egcs	/usr/bin/egcs
g++	egcs	/usr/bin/g++
g77	egcs	/usr/bin/g77 (built-in Fortran 77)
gcc	gcc	/usr/bin/gcc

Under Red Hat Linux 5.1, components of both the “traditional” (read *older*) gcc and the newer egcs are located under the /usr/lib/gcc-lib/i386-redhat-linux directory, in the directories named 2.7.2.3 (gcc) and egcs-2.90.27 (egcs). Table 30.8 shows the names and locations of the primary front ends for both versions, but if you have trouble or want to confirm the version of gcc or egcs installed on your system, use the name of the command, followed by the ñversion command-line option, like this

```
$ g77 --version
egcs-2.90.27 980315 (egcs-1.0.2 release)
$ gcc --version
2.7.2.3
$ cc --version
2.7.2.3
$ g++ --version
egcs-2.90.27 980315 (egcs-1.0.2 release)
$ c++ --version
egcs-2.90.27 980315 (egcs-1.0.2 release)
```

Problems might occur when you're using egcs if you try to build a software package written in C++ that references gcc in its Makefile. For example, trying to compile Chris Cannam's wmx X11 window manager (see Chapter 5, "Window Managers," for details about X Window managers) results in an error and a barf on the build like this:

```
$ make
gcc -c -g -O2 Border.C
gcc: installation problem, cannot exec `cc1plus': No such file or
directory
make: *** [Border.o] Error 1
```

The Makefile script contains names and locations of programs and files used during the build process. The wmx Makefile contained the following two definitions:

```
CC      = gcc
CCC     = gcc
```

While this will work if you have only gcc installed, if you install the egcs suite, you'll need to change the name of the designated C++ compiler in your Makefile to g++, like this:

```
CC      = gcc
CCC     = g++
```

Just be aware that if you use egcs to compile C++ source files (files ending in .C, .cc, or .cxx) you might have to fix the software's Makefile first. However, because egcs is new, here are other caveats of which you should be aware:

- Because of certain problems with assembler language constructs, egcs cannot be used to rebuild your Linux kernel; use gcc instead.
- Because of changes in the way the egcs g++ handles the new keyword in array declarations in C++, egcs might not build the K Desktop Environment, or KDE (see Chapter 5 for more information about KDE); this might be fixed by the time you read this.
- egcs does not work with GNU Pascal.

For more information about egcs, see your system's /usr/doc/egcs directory or the egcs man page, or use the command **info egcs**. For the latest updates, versions, or feature news about egcs, browse to http://egcs.cygnus.com. You'll find an egcs FAQ and pointers to the latest stable egcs release, or snapshots of the most recent development version.

Additional Resources

If you are interested in learning more about C and C++, you should look into the following books:

- *Sams Teach Yourself C in 21 Days*, by Peter Aitken and Bradley Jones, Sams Publishing
- *C How to Program* and *C++ How to Program*, by H. M. Deitel and P. J. Deitel
- *The C Programming Language*, by Brian Kernighan and Dennis Ritchie
- *The Annotated C++ Reference Manual*, by Margaret Ellis and Bjarne Stroustrup
- *Programming in ANSI C*, by Stephen G. Kochan

Summary

UNIX was built on the C language. C is a platform-independent, compiled, procedural language based on functions and the capability to derive new, programmer-defined data structures.

C++ extends the capabilities of C by providing the necessary features for object-oriented design and code. C++ compilers correctly compile ANSI C code. C++ also provides some features, such as the capability to associate functions with data structures, that don't require the use of full class-based, object-oriented techniques. For these reasons, the C++ language allows existing UNIX programs to migrate toward the adoption of object orientation over time.

Perl Programming

by David Pitts

In This Chapter

Perl (Practical Extraction and Report Language) was developed in 1986 by Larry Wall. It has grown in popularity and is now one of the most popular scripting languages for UNIX platforms. Version 5.004_04 comes with the current version of Red Hat Linux.

Perl is similar in syntax to C, but also contains much of the style of UNIX shell scripting. And, thrown in with that, Perl contains the best features of every other programming language you have ever used.

Perl is compiled at runtime (although there is a compiler available), which is either an advantage or a disadvantage, depending on how you look at it. Perl has been ported to virtually every operating system out there, and most Perl programs will run without modifications on any system to which you move them. That is certainly an advantage. In addition, using Perl for the small, almost trivial, applications used in everyday server maintenance is easier than going to all the trouble of writing the code in C and compiling it.

Perl is very forgiving about such things as declaring variables, allocating and deallocating memory, and defining variable types, so you can get down to the actual business of writing code. In fact, these concepts really do not exist in Perl. This results in programs that are short and to the point, while similar programs in C, for example, might spend half the code declaring variables.

A Simple Perl Program

To introduce you to the absolute basics of Perl programming, Listing 31.1 illustrates a trivial Perl program.

LISTING 31.1 A TRIVIAL PERL PROGRAM

```
#!/usr/bin/perl
print "Red Hat Linux Unleashed, 3rd edition, by David Pitts\n";
```

That's the whole thing. Type that in, save it to a file called `trivial.pl`, `chmod +x` it, and execute it.

If you are at all familiar with shell scripting languages, this will look very familiar. Perl combines the simplicity of shell scripting with the power of a full-fledged programming language.

The first line of this program indicates to the operating system where to find the Perl interpreter. This is standard procedure with shell scripts, and you have already seen this syntax in Chapter 25, "Shell Programming."

If /usr/bin/perl is not the correct location for Perl on your system, you can find out where it is located by typing **`which perl`** at the command line. If you do not have Perl installed, you might want to skip forward to the section titled "For More Information" to find out where you can obtain the Perl interpreter.

The second line does precisely what you would expect it to do—it prints the text enclosed in quotation marks. The `\n` notation is used for a newline character.

Perl Variables and Data Structures

Although it does not have the concept of datatype (`integer`, `string`, `char`, and so on), Perl has several kinds of variables.

Scalar variables, indicated as `$variable`, are interpreted as number or string, as the context warrants. You can treat a variable as a number one moment and a string the next if the value of the variable makes sense in that context.

A large collection of special variables are available in Perl, such as `$_`, `$$`, and `$<`, which Perl keeps track of and you can use if you like. (`$_` is the default input variable, `$$` is the process ID, and `$<` is the user ID.) As you become more familiar with Perl, you will find yourself using these variables, and people will accuse you of writing "read-only" code.

Arrays, indicated as `@array`, contain one or more elements that can be referred to by index. For example, `$names[12]` gives me the 13th element in the array `@names` (it's important to remember that numbering starts with 0).

Associative arrays, indicated by `%assoc_array`, store values that can be referenced by key. For example, `$days{Feb}` gives me the element in the associative array `%days` that corresponds with `Feb`.

The following line of Perl code lists all of the elements in an associative array (the `foreach` construct is covered later in this chapter):

```
foreach $key (keys %assoc){
    print "$key = $assoc{$key}\n"};
```

NOTE

`$_` is the "default" variable in Perl. In this example, the loop variable is `$_` because none was specified.

Conditional Statements: `if/else`

The syntax of the Perl `if/else` structure is as follows:

```
if (condition) {
     statement(s)
     }
elsif (condition) {
     statement(s)
     }
else {
     statement(s)
     }
```

`condition` can be any statement or comparison. If the statement returns any true value, the *`statement(s)`* will be executed. Here, true is defined as

- Any nonzero number
- Any nonzero string; that is, any string that is not 0 or empty
- Any conditional that returns a true value

For example, the following piece of code uses the `if/else` structure:

```
if ($favorite eq "chocolate") {
      print "I like chocolate too.\n"
     }
elsif ($favorite eq "spinach") {
      print "Oh, I don't like spinach.\n";
     }
else {
     print "Your favorite food is $favorite.\n"
     }
```

Looping

Perl has four looping constructs: `for`, `foreach`, `while`, and `until`.

`for`

The `for` construct performs a statement (or set of statements) for a set of conditions defined as follows:

```
for (start condition; end condition; increment function) {
     statement(s)
     }
```

At the beginning of the loop, the start condition is set. Each time the loop is executed, the increment function is performed until the end condition is achieved. This looks much like the traditional `for/next` loop. The following code is an example of a `for` loop:

```
for ($i=1; $i<=10; $i++) {
      print "$i\n"
     }
```

foreach

The `foreach` construct performs a statement (or set of statements) for each element in a set, such as a list or array:

```
foreach $name (@names) {
     print "$name\n"
     }
```

while

`while` performs a block of statements as long as a particular condition is true:

```
while ($x<10) {
     print "$x\n";
     $x++;
     }
```

until

`until` is the exact opposite of the `while` statement. It performs a block of statements as long as a particular condition is false—or, rather, until it becomes true:

```
until ($x>10) {
     print "$x\n";
     $x++;
     }
```

Regular Expressions

Perl's greatest strength is in text and file manipulation, accomplished by using the regular expression (regex) library. Regexes allow complicated pattern matching and replacement to be done efficiently and easily.

For example, the following one line of code replaces every occurrence of the string `Bob` or the string `Mary` with `Fred` in a line of text:

```
$string =~ s/bob¦mary/fred/gi;
```

Without going into too many of the gory details, Table 31.1 explains what the preceding line says.

TABLE 31.1 EXPLANATION OF `$string =~ s/bob¦mary/fred/gi;`

Element	*Explanation*
`$string =~`	Performs this pattern match on the text found in the variable called `$string`.
`s`	Substitute.
`/`	Begins the text to be matched.
`bob¦mary`	Matches the text `bob` or `mary`. You should remember that it is looking for the text `mary`, not the word `mary`; that is, it will also match the text `mary` in the word `maryland`.
`/`	Ends text to be matched, begins text to replace it.
`fred`	Replaces anything that was matched with the text `fred`.
`/`	Ends replace text.
`g`	Does this substitution globally; that is, replaces the match text wherever in the string you match it (and any number of times).
`i`	The search text is not case-sensitive. It matches `bob`, `Bob`, or `bOB`.
`;`	Indicates the end of the line of code.

If you are interested in the gory details, I recommend the book *Mastering Regular Expressions* by Jeffrey Friedl, which explains regular expressions from the ground up, going into all the theory behind them and explaining the best ways to use them.

Although replacing one string with another might seem to be a rather trivial task, the code required to do the same thing in another language (for example, C) is rather daunting.

Access to the Shell

Perl is useful for administrative functions because, for one thing, it has access to the shell. This means any process you might ordinarily do by typing commands to the shell, Perl can do for you. You do this with the `` ` ` `` syntax; for example, the following code prints a directory listing:

```
$curr_dir = `pwd`;
@listing = `ls -la`;
print "Listing for $curr_dir\n";
foreach $file (@listing) {
```

```
print "$file";
}
```

NOTE

The `` notation uses the backtick found above the Tab key (on most keyboards), not the single quote.

Access to the command line is fairly common in shell scripting languages, but is less common in higher level programming languages.

Command-Line Mode

In addition to writing programs, Perl can be used from the command line like any other shell scripting language. This enables you to cobble together Perl utilities on-the-fly, rather than having to create a file and execute it.

For example, the following command line runs through the file `foo` and replaces every occurrence of the string `Joe` with `Harry`, saving a backup copy of the file at `foo.bak`:

```
perl -p -i.bak -e s/Joe/Harry/g foo
```

The `-p` switch causes Perl to perform the command for all files listed (in this case, just one file).

The `-i` switch indicates that the file specified is to be edited in place and the original backed up with the extension specified. If no extension is supplied, no backup copy is made.

The `-e` switch indicates that what follows is one or more lines of a script.

Automation, Using Perl

Perl is great for automating some of the tasks involved in maintaining and administering a UNIX machine. Because of its text-manipulation capabilities and its access to the shell, Perl can be used to do any of the processes you might ordinarily do by hand.

The following sections present examples of Perl programs you might use in the daily maintenance of your machine.

Moving Files

One aspect of my job is administering a secure FTP site. Incoming files are placed in an "incoming" directory. When they have been checked, they are moved to a "private" directory for retrieval. Permissions are set in such a way that the file is not shown in a directory listing but can be retrieved if the filename is known. The person who placed the file on the server is informed via email that the file is now available for download.

I quickly discovered that people were having difficulty retrieving files because they incorrectly typed the case of filenames. This was solved by making the file available with an all-uppercase name and an all-lowercase name, in addition to the original filename.

I wrote the Perl program in Listing 31.2 to perform all these tasks with a single command. When I have determined that a file is to go onto the FTP site, I simply type **`move filename user`**, where *`filename`* is the name of the file to be moved and *`user`* is the email address of the person to be notified.

LISTING 31.2 MOVING FILES ONTO AN FTP SITE

```
#!/usr/bin/perl
#
#  Move a file from /incoming to /private
$file = @ARGV[0];
$user = @ARGV[1];

if ($user eq "") {&usage}
else {
     if (-e "/home/ftp/incoming/$file")
          {`cp /home/ftp/incoming/$file /home/ftp/private/$file`;
          chmod 0644, "/home/ftp/private/$file";
          `rm -f /home/ftp/incoming/$file`;
          if (uc($file) ne $file)  {
                $ucfile = uc($file);
                `ln /home/ftp/private/$file /home/ftp/private/$ucfile`;
               }
          if (lc($file) ne $file)  {
                $lcfile = lc($file);
                `ln /home/ftp/private/$file
➥/home/ftp/private/$lcfile`;
               }

# Send mail
open (MAIL, "¦ /usr/sbin/sendmail -t  ftpadmin,$user");
print MAIL <<EndMail;
To: ftpadmin,$user
From: ftpadmin
Subject: File ($file) moved

```

```
29: The file $file has been moved
30: The file is now available as
31: ftp://ftp.databeam.com/private/$file
32:
33: ftpadmin\@databeam.com
34: ==================================
35: EndMail
36: close MAIL;
37: }
38:
39:     else {  #  File does not exist
40:          print "File does not exist!\n";
41:          }   #  End else (-e $file)
42:
43: } #  End else ($user eq "")
44:
45: sub usage {
46: print "move <filename> <username>\n";
47: print "where <username> is the user that you are moving this
➥for.\n\n";
48: }
```

Without going through Listing 31.2 line by line, the following paragraphs take a look at some of the high points that demonstrate the power and syntax of Perl.

In lines 4 and 5, the array `@ARGV` contains all command-line arguments. The place where one argument ends and another begins is taken to be every space, unless arguments are given in quotes.

In line 9, the `-e` file tests for the existence of a file. If the file does not exist, perhaps the user gave me the wrong filename, or one of the other server administrators beat me to it.

Perl enables you to open a pipe to some other process and print data to it, enabling Perl to "use" any other program that has an interactive user interface, such as `sendmail` or an FTP session. That's the purpose of line 23.

The << syntax enables you to print multiple lines of text until the `EOF` string is encountered. This eliminates the necessity to have multiple `print` commands following one another—for example,

```
24: print MAIL <<EndMail;
...
35: EndMail
```

The subroutine syntax allows modularization of code into functions. Subroutines are declared with the syntax shown in lines 45–48 and called with the `&` notation, as shown in line 7:

```
... {&usage}
...
sub usage {
...
}
```

Purging Logs

Many programs maintain some variety of logs. Often, much of the information in the logs is redundant or just useless. The program shown in Listing 31.3 removes all lines from a file that contain a particular word or phrase, so lines you know are not important can be purged.

LISTING 31.3 PURGING LOG FILES

```
#!/usr/bin/perl
#
#       Be careful using this program!!
#       This will remove all lines that contain a given word
#
#       Usage:  remove <word> <file>
###########
$word=@ARGV[0];
$file=@ARGV[1];

unless ($file)  {
print "Usage:  remove <word> <file>\n"; }

else    {
open (FILE, "$file");
@lines=<FILE>;
close FILE;

# remove the offending lines
@lines = grep (!/$word/, @lines);

#  Write it back
open (NEWFILE, ">$file");
for (@lines)    { print NEWFILE }
close NEWFILE;
        } #  End else
```

Listing 31.3 is fairly self-explanatory. It reads in the file and then removes the offending lines by using Perl's `grep` command, which is similar to the standard UNIX `grep`. If you save this as a file called `remove` and place it in your path, you will have a swift way to purge server logs of unwanted messages.

Posting to Usenet

If some portion of your job requires periodic postings to Usenet—a FAQ listing, for example—the following Perl program can automate the process for you. In the sample code, the posted text is read in from a text file, but your input can come from anywhere.

The program shown in Listing 31.4 uses the `Net::NNTP` module, which is a standard part of the Perl distribution.

LISTING 31.4 POSTING AN ARTICLE TO USENET

```
#!/usr/bin/perl
open (POST, "post.file");
@post = <POST>;
close POST;
use Net::NNTP;

$NNTPhost = 'news';

$nntp = Net::NNTP->new($NNTPhost)
        or die "Cannot contact $NNTPhost: $!";

# $nntp->debug(1);
$nntp->post()
        or die "Could not post article: $!";
$nntp->datasend("Newsgroups: news.announce\n");
$nntp->datasend("Subject: FAQ - Frequently Asked Questions\n");
$nntp->datasend("From: ADMIN <root\@rcbowen.com>\n");
$nntp->datasend("\n\n");
for (@post)     {
$nntp->datasend($_);
}

$nntp->quit;
```

For More Information

The Perl community is large and growing. Since the advent of the WWW, Perl has become the most popular language for Common Gateway Interface (CGI) programming. There is a wealth of sources of information on Perl, and some of the better ones are listed here. The following books are good resources:

- *Programming Perl*, Second Edition, by Larry Wall, Randall Schwartz, and Tom Christiansen (O'Reilly & Associates)
- *Effective Perl Programming: Writing Better Programs with Perl*, by Joseph Hall (Addison-Wesley Pub Co)

- *Mastering Regular Expressions*, by Jeffrey Friedl (O'Reilly & Associates)
- *CGI Programming with Perl, Visual Basic, and C*, by Rich Bowen et al. *Web Publishing & Programming Resource Kit*, Volume 4. (Sams.net Publishing)

On Usenet, check out the following:

- `comp.lang.perl.misc`

  Discusses various aspects of the Perl programming language. Make sure your questions are Perl-specific, not generic CGI questions, because the regulars tend to flame folks who can't tell the difference.
- `comp.infosystems.www.authoring.cgi`

  Discusses authoring of CGI programs, so much of the discussion is Perl-specific. Make sure your questions are related to CGI, not just Perl. The regulars are very particular about staying on topic.

Check these sites on the World Wide Web:

- `http://www.perl.com/`

  The Perl Language home page, maintained by Tom Christiansen. This is the place to find all sorts of information about Perl, from its history to its culture to helpful tips. This is also the place to download the Perl interpreter for your system.
- `http://www.perl.com/CPAN`

  Yes, this is part of the site just mentioned, but it merits its own mention. CPAN (the Comprehensive Perl Archive Network) is the place for you to find modules and programs in Perl. Also, if you end up writing something in Perl that you think is particularly useful, you can make it available to the Perl community here.
- `http://www.perl.org/`

  The Perl Institute. A nonprofit organization dedicated to the advancement of Perl.
- `http://www.rcbowen.com/`

  Rich Bowen has been working with the Perl community for many years. He has written a number of commercialized programs, including calendaring and scheduling programs. Much of his work is also available on CPAN.

Summary

Perl, in the words of its creator, Larry Wall, "combines the best elements of C, `sed`, `awk`, and `sh`," but it's also a great language for folks who have no experience with these languages.

Perl's powerful `regex` library and ease of use have made it one of the preferred scripting languages in use today, particularly in the realm of CGI programming. Many people even think of Perl as exclusively a CGI language, when, in fact, it is capable of so much more.

Although this book is focused on Red Hat Linux, Perl is also available for many other platforms, and scripts you write in Perl on one platform will run without changes on another.

CHAPTER

Motif Programming

by Bill Ball

In This Chapter

This chapter introduces you to the OSF/Motif programming libraries. You'll learn about the different versions of Motif; how to install Red Hat's Motif 2.0.1 and 2.1 distribution; how Motif programs, or clients, work; how to write and compile a simple Motif client; how to use the programming utilities `imake` and `xmkmf`; and how you might save money by using a Motif clone, LessTif.

You need to have the GNU `gcc` compiler and associated headers, libraries, and utilities installed on your system. You also need to have X and Motif installed on your system if you want to run any Motif clients, including `mwm`. You do not have to run X to program with Motif, although compiling, running, and seeing a program in action is a lot more fun.

What Is Motif?

First of all, you should understand that, unlike the XFree86 distribution of X, Motif is not free—you must pay for a distribution. Motif has distributions for Linux on the Intel, SPARC, or Alpha platforms. If you want to build Motif clients and distribute them, you'll need to purchase a version for your computer and operating system. And if you want other people to run your clients, you can build the clients in either shared library or static versions, for people who either have or don't have Motif (see "Shared and Static Libraries" later in this chapter).

If you're on a budget or object to having to pay for a client license for Motif, don't despair. Later in this chapter, you'll learn about LessTif, a cost-free alternative to Motif.

Motif is a toolkit of source headers, libraries, a window manager, `mwm`, demonstration programs, and manual pages. Originally announced in 1988, designed by the Open Software Foundation (OSF) in 1989, and now owned and updated by The Open Group, Motif provides a rich selection of tools to build cross-platform, graphical interface applications, or clients.

The idea behind Motif is to provide the tools to build consistent, usable, and portable programs for the X Window System. Motif provides functions and system calls to build client interfaces with the following (and almost anything you need so you can craft graphical interface programs):

- Arrow buttons
- Cascade buttons
- Check boxes
- Drawn buttons
- File selection dialogs

- List widgets
- Menu bars
- Push buttons
- Radio boxes
- Scrollbars
- Toggle buttons
- Dialogs
- Icons
- Drop-down menus
- Pull-down menus
- Tear-off menus

In fact, more than 600 man pages are included with each Motif distribution, documenting its clients, function calls, libraries, and window manager. Although you can use X functions to build clients with a Motif look, why not take advantage of all of the work put into Motif?

Where Do I Get Motif?

A number of vendors supply Motif for Linux. This book is about Red Hat Linux, so I'll concentrate on the Red Hat distribution. Because the object, or philosophy, of OSF/Motif is to provide cross-platform, source-code–level compatibility, you should be able to develop Motif clients on your Intel Linux system that will compile and run on any other computer with a Motif distribution installed.

A number of distributors sell Motif for Linux besides Red Hat. These include the following:

- X Inside Corporation (`http://www.xinside.com`)
- Metro Link Incorporated (`http://www.metrolink.com`)
- InfoMagic (`http://www.infomagic.com`)
- Linux Systems Labs (`http://www.lsl.com`)
- Caldera (`http://www.caldera.com`)

What Version of Motif Should I Use?

To make an intelligent decision regarding which version of Motif to get, you should know a little about the history and direction of the standard. In 1996, The Open Group (TOG) acquired the X Window System from the X Consortium, with the aim of integrating X, Motif, and the Common Desktop Environment (CDE). CDE represents the future of Motif, according to TOG, and offers graphical interface improvements, support for multiuser applications, and new networking features (see Chapter 5, "Window Managers," for more information).

The X Consortium acquired the X Window System from the MIT X Consortium in 1993 and was responsible for the past several releases, the most recent of which is X11R6.4. Broadway, which was the code name for X11R6.3 (the last release of the X Window System), has improvements in network communications to support graphics and audio for use in World Wide Web browsers. Fortunately, TOG revised X11R6.4's license (the latest version of X11) to fall under the same terms as X11R6.3—you're allowed to freely distribute X11R6.4 in source or code form. This move helped avoid a major rift, or fork, in the development tree of the X Window System (see Chapter 4, "X Window," for details).

The current version of Motif is 2.1, but it is not used with the current version of Red Hat's distribution of CDE, which is also 2.1. An earlier version of Motif, 1.2.5, was released to support CDE (and contains fixes made to Motif 1.2 in Motif 2.0). Confused yet? Remember that TOG's aim is to merge X, Motif, and CDE, but what does this mean to the user and what does this mean to the programmer?

For the user, especially the Red Hat Linux user, the choice is up to you. If you want the Motif 1.2.5 libraries, a drag-and-drop, industry-standard interface, and many other improvements, Red Hat's distribution of TriTeal's CDE is the way to go. You should know that the Motif window manager, `mwm`, goes away in the CDE release, replaced by new terminal managers (based on a window manager called `dtwm`).

But for the programmer, the choice might not be as clear, because Red Hat markets CDE and three versions of Motif: 2.01, 2.1, and 2.1-multiuser (a developer version of CDE marketed by Red Hat is no longer available). According to The Open Group, although Motif 2.0 and CDE can be used together and Motif 2.0 is binary-compatible with Motif 1.2, "All of the important Motif 2.0 developer features… will be available in CDEnext Motif" (the latest version of CDE, 2.1, based on Motif 2.1). This means TOG recommends programmers use Motif 2.1 to get the latest programming features. However, you should know that support for C++ programmers was dropped with Motif 2.1 (see Chapter 30, "C and C++ Programming," for details about this language).

One bonus of the Motif 2.1 release is that you get eight critical TOG Motif documents on CD-ROM. These documents, in PostScript format and compressed, include:

- Motif Programmer's Guide
- Motif Programmer's Reference

- Motif and CDE Style Guide
- Motif and CDE Style Guide Reference
- Motif and CDE Style Guide Certification Checklist
- Motif Widget Writer's Guide
- Motif User's Guide (also provided in paperback form with your CD-ROM)
- Motif Glossary

This is a bargain, considering that Motif 2.01 only comes with a User's Guide, and the original Motif Style Guide cost nearly $24 (for a 120-page paperback).

Red Hat Motif Installation

As mentioned before, because this is *Red Hat Linux Unleashed*, this chapter concentrates on the specifics of Red Hat's Motif distribution. Installing Red Hat Motif 2.0.1 or 2.1 is easy. First, make sure you have enough room on your hard drive. You'll need about 20MB for a full installation. If you want to run just the Motif window manager, `mwm`, and other Motif clients, you can save about 15MB by installing just the Motif libraries and `mwm`.

You can install Motif from the Red Hat CD-ROM in two ways, but both require you to mount the disk to a convenient directory with

```
#mount /dev/cdrom
```

or

```
# mount -t iso9660 /dev/cdrom /mnt/cdrom
```

Next, navigate to your CD-ROM's directory with

```
# cd /mnt/cdrom
```

You can then launch the installation script with

```
# ./install-motif
```

The installation script automatically determines what version of Red Hat Linux is installed on your computer and then installs the correct rpm files (for more details about rpm, see Chapter 19, "Getting Started with Red Hat Linux"). Another way to install the software is to use the `rpm` command. The Red Hat folks have assembled the Motif software into the RPM (Red Hat Package Manager) packages discussed in the following sections.

Motif 2.01 and 2.1 Development rpms

These packages contain the static libraries and `#include` files, or headers, needed to build Motif clients. You'll also find the Motif User Interface Language compiler, `uil`, and the Motif function-call manual pages.

Motif 2.01 and 2.1 rpms

If you just want to run `mwm` or the Motif Workspace Manager, `Wsm`, you'll need the shared libraries in this package. More than 800 icons are also installed from this file under the /usr/X11R6/include/X11/icons directory.

Motif 2.01 and 2.1 Mwm rpms

Here's where you'll find not only the window manager, `mwm`, but also `Wsm`, which demonstrates just some of the features of Motif 2.0. Also included are `panner`, `pixmap`, and a handy bitmap browser, `xbmbrowser`, which transverses directories and shows what `.xpm` or `.xbm` graphics look like, a directory at a time.

Motif Demonstration Source rpms

If you're interested in exploring features of Motif 2.0 or 2.1, need source-code examples to help you learn about Motif programming, or want to read the source to the example clients, install this package. You'll also need to install the development libraries before you can build the examples. Some of the concepts these programs demonstrate are discussed later in this chapter, but here's a list of the examples included:

- `Exm`—A sample program that shows how to write a Motif widget (Motif 2.1 only)
- `airport`—Demonstrates Motif drag-and-drop
- `animate`—Animates pixel maps in an X window
- `drag_and_drop`—A thorough demonstration of drag-and-drop features
- `draw`—A simple graphics application
- `earth`—The classic rotating earth
- `filemanager`—A simple, graphical file manager
- `fileview`—A Motif "more" program
- `getsubres`—A Motif widget resources viewer
- `hellomotif`—The classic "Hello, world!"
- `hellomotifi18n`—A better "Hello, world!" in different languages
- `i18ninput`—Shows how to handle text input in different languages

- panner—Shows how Motif clients can use virtual screen support (Motif 2.01 only)
- periodic—Demonstrates displayable Motif widgets
- piano—A simple Motif MIDI application (you'll need MIDI support)
- popups—Shows pop-up menu improvements in Motif 2.0
- sampler2_0—A fairly complete demonstration of Motif 2.0 features
- setdate—Sets the system's date and demonstrates the Motif SpinBox widget
- texteditor—A simple editor with split panes, but no Undo, Print, and so on (Motif 2.01 only)
- transfer—Demonstrates data transfer between Motif clients (Motif 2.01 only)
- workspace—Source to Wsm (Motif 2.01 only)

Along with these programs, you'll find ten other examples in a separate directory.

Motif Demos rpms

If you don't want to spend the time building the sample clients from the source code and just want to try some of the features of Motif, install this package. You'll also need to install the shared libraries before you can run these clients.

A Simple Example of Motif Programming Concepts

This section presents an extremely simple example of a Motif program—just enough to get you started. But before getting into the details, I'll cover the basic concepts in an overview of programming for Motif.

Although writing programs for the Linux command line in C is fairly simple, if you're familiar with programming for X, you know there's a lot more involved in writing a windowing program. You have to consider labels, dialogs, windows, scrolling, colors, buttons, and many other features of how a program works, besides the internal algorithms that make a program unique. Along with this unique functionality, when you program for X, you should consider consistency and ease of use for the user.

This is where Motif can help you. By providing a rich variety of functions, Motif can help programmers build attractive and easy-to-use programs. In Motif programming, a lot of the program code, especially for smaller programs, is devoted to the graphical interface.

When you write C programs for the Linux command line, you'll generally use the `libc` libraries. If you write programs for X, you'll generally use the `Xlib` libraries. When you program for Motif, you'll use X as the window system and the X Toolkit or `Xt` libraries (and others) for the interface.

After you install either Motif 2.01 or 2.1, you'll find a number of libraries under the /usr/X11R6/lib directory (the Motif 2.1 installation includes libraries with names ending in "2.1"):

```
/usr/X11R6/lib/libMrm.a
/usr/X11R6/lib/libUil.a
/usr/X11R6/lib/libXm.a
/usr/X11R6/lib/libXmCxx.a
/usr/X11R6/lib/libMrm.so
/usr/X11R6/lib/libMrm.so.2
/usr/X11R6/lib/libMrm.so.2.0
/usr/X11R6/lib/libXm.so
/usr/X11R6/lib/libXm.so.2
/usr/X11R6/lib/libXm.so.2.0
```

The Motif `#include` files are located under the /usr/X11R6/include/Mrm, /usr/X11R6/include/Xm, and /usr/X11R6/include/uil directories. The location of these libraries and headers is pretty much standard across all computer systems, but if they are located in a different place, this difference will be documented in configuration files and rules files for `imake` and `xmkmf`. (See "Using `imake` and `xmkmf`," later in this chapter, for more on these utilities.)

Widgets and Event-Driven Programming

An important concept to consider when programming for X and Motif is that these programs usually do not just run and quit; these programs are driven by events such as mouse clicks, button pushes, mouse drags, other programs, and keystrokes. Apple Macintosh programmers will feel right at home in programming for Motif. Some of the interface elements that intercept these events are built with Motif routines called "widgets," and as you become more proficient, you'll even write some of your own.

If you're just starting off with Motif programming, don't be put off by the new terms and concepts about this subject. You'll learn about callbacks, children, classes, composites, coupled resources, gadgets, hierarchies, initiators, instantiation, modality, properties, receivers, and subclasses. Although we don't have enough room in this book to cover all of these subjects, Listing 31.1 contains a simple example to get you started.

The Simple Motif Program

Listing 31.1 creates a small window with File, Edit, and Help menus. The application window is resizable, can be minimized or maximized, and—in general—responds like any Motif application. This program demonstrates how to create a window, a menu bar, a pull-down menu, buttons, and a pop-up dialog.

It's not a perfect example, because the interface is in the `main()` part of the program, it doesn't use resources, and it really doesn't do anything. I'll leave the internals of how the program might work up to you.

LISTING 31.1 `motif_skeleton.c`

```
/* a simple skeleton Motif program */
#include <Xm/RowColumn.h>
#include <Xm/MainW.h>
#include <Xm/CascadeB.h>
#include <Xm/MessageB.h>
#include <Xm/SeparatoG.h>
#include <Xm/PushBG.h>

Widget skeleton;    /* our application */
/* what happens when user selects Exit */
void skel_exit_action() {
exit(0);
    }

/* destroy a dialog */
void skel_dialog_handler(skel_dialog)
Widget skel_dialog;
{
XtUnmanageChild(skel_dialog);
}

/* create a Help action dialog*/
void skel_help_action()
{
    Arg       args[10];
    Widget    skel_dialog;
XmString skel_string;

    /* store help string */
    skel_string =
XmStringCreateLocalized("This is Skeleton v0.1, a simple Motif client.");

/* build dialog */
skel_dialog = XmCreateMessageDialog (skeleton, "dialog", args, 0);
XtVaSetValues(skel_dialog, XmNmessageString, skel_string, NULL, NULL);
```

continues

LISTING 31.1 CONTINUED

```
/* call skel_dialog_handler() after OK button is pushed */
XtAddCallback(skel_dialog, XmNokCallback, skel_dialog_handler, NULL);

    /* free storage */
    XmStringFree(skel_string);

    /* display the dialog */
    XtManageChild(skel_dialog);
};

/* main program begins here */
main (argc, argv)
int argc;
char *argv[];
{
    /* declare our widgets, including menu actions */
    Widget    skel_window,              /* main window */
              skel_menubar,             /* main window menu bar */
              skel_filepulldown,        /* File menu */
                  skel_new,
                  skel_open,
                  skel_close,
                  skel_save,
                  skel_exit,
              skel_editpulldown,        /* Edit menu */
                  skel_cut,
                  skel_copy,
                  skel_paste,
              skel_helppulldown,        /* Help menu */
                  skel_version;
    XmString  skel_string;              /* temporary storage */
    XtAppContext skel_app;

XtSetLanguageProc (NULL, NULL, NULL);

/* give the app a name and initial size */
skeleton = XtVaAppInitialize(&skel_app, "Skeleton", NULL, 0, &argc, argv,
NULL, XmNwidth, 320, XmNheight, 240, NULL);

/* create the main window */
skel_window = XtVaCreateManagedWidget("skel", xmMainWindowWidgetClass,
skeleton,
XmNscrollingPolicy, XmAUTOMATIC, NULL);

/* build a menu bar across main window */
skel_menubar = XmCreateMenuBar(skel_window, "skel_menubar", NULL, 0);

/* build the File pull-down menu */
skel_filepulldown = XmCreatePulldownMenu (skel_menubar, "File", NULL, 0);
```

```
➥skel_string = XmStringCreateLocalized ("File");

/* create the menu, assign ALT+F as mnemonic key */
XtVaCreateManagedWidget ("File", xmCascadeButtonWidgetClass, skel_menubar,
XmNlabelString, skel_string, XmNmnemonic, 'F', XmNsubMenuId,
➥skel_filepulldown, NULL);

    /* release storage */
    XmStringFree(skel_string);

/* now add File pull-down menu elements */
skel_new = XtVaCreateManagedWidget("New", xmPushButtonGadgetClass,
skel_filepulldown, NULL);
skel_open = XtVaCreateManagedWidget("Open", xmPushButtonGadgetClass,
skel_filepulldown, NULL);
XtVaCreateManagedWidget("separator", xmSeparatorGadgetClass,
skel_filepulldown,
        NULL);
skel_close = XtVaCreateManagedWidget("Close", xmPushButtonGadgetClass,
skel_filepulldown, NULL);
skel_save = XtVaCreateManagedWidget("Save", xmPushButtonGadgetClass,
skel_filepulldown, NULL);
XtVaCreateManagedWidget("separator", xmSeparatorGadgetClass,
skel_filepulldown,
        NULL);
skel_exit = XtVaCreateManagedWidget("Exit", xmPushButtonGadgetClass,
skel_filepulldown, NULL);

/* add what to do when user selects Exit */
XtAddCallback(skel_exit, XmNactivateCallback, skel_exit_action, NULL);

/* build Edit menu */
skel_editpulldown = XmCreatePulldownMenu(skel_menubar, "Edit", NULL, 0);
skel_string = XmStringCreateLocalized ("Edit");
XtVaCreateManagedWidget ("Edit", xmCascadeButtonWidgetClass, skel_menubar,
XmNlabelString, skel_string, XmNmnemonic, 'E', XmNsubMenuId,
➥skel_editpulldown, NULL);

    /* release storage */
    XmStringFree(skel_string);

/* add Edit pull-down menu elements */
skel_cut = XtVaCreateManagedWidget("Cut", xmPushButtonGadgetClass,
skel_editpulldown, NULL);
skel_copy = XtVaCreateManagedWidget("Copy", xmPushButtonGadgetClass,
skel_editpulldown, NULL);
skel_paste = XtVaCreateManagedWidget("Paste", xmPushButtonGadgetClass,
skel_editpulldown, NULL);

/* build Help menu */
```

continues

LISTING 31.1 CONTINUED

```
skel_helppulldown = XmCreatePulldownMenu(skel_menubar, "Help", NULL, 0);
➥skel_string = XmStringCreateLocalized ("Help");
XtVaCreateManagedWidget ("Help", xmCascadeButtonWidgetClass, skel_menubar,
XmNlabelString, skel_string, XmNmnemonic, 'H', XmNsubMenuId,
➥skel_helppulldown, NULL);

    /* release storage */
    XmStringFree(skel_string);

/* now move the Help pull-down to right side - thanks, Motif FAQ! */
XtVaSetValues(skel_menubar, XmNmenuHelpWidget,
XtNameToWidget(skel_menubar,
"Help"), NULL);

/* now label, create, and assign action to Help menu */
skel_version = XtVaCreateManagedWidget ("Version",
xmPushButtonGadgetClass,
skel_helppulldown, NULL);
XtAddCallback(skel_version, XmNactivateCallback, skel_help_action, NULL);

    XtManageChild(skel_menubar);
    XtRealizeWidget(skeleton);
    XtAppMainLoop (skel_app);
    return (0);
}
```

To compile this program for Motif 2.01, you can use the following command line:

```
# gcc -o skel skeleton.c -L/usr/X11R6/lib -lXm -lXpm -lXt -lXext -lX11
```

To compile this program for Motif 2.1, you need to add a new library and linker directive, like this:

```
# gcc -o skel skeleton.c -L/usr/X11R6/lib -lXp -lXm -lXpm -lXt -lXext -
lX11
```

These lines direct the GNU linker to look in the /usr/X11/lib directories for needed libraries. The program is then linked, using the shared `Xp`, `Xm`, `Xpm`, `Xt`, `Xext`, and `X11` libraries. The final size of the program is fewer than 13,000 characters.

You must run this Motif client during an X Window session. From the command line of terminal window, type

```
# skel
```

and press the Enter key. If you select the Help menu item after the program starts, a small dialog appears, as shown in Figure 32.1.

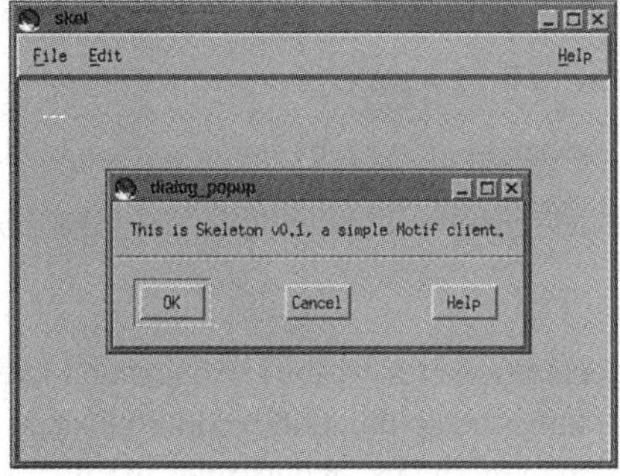

FIGURE 32.1
The sample Motif client also provides a small Help dialog.

How the Program Works

If you've programmed in C to build Linux command-line or X programs, you know that if you use certain routines or functions, you must tell the compiler which `#include` files contain definitions needed by the functions in your program. Our sample program starts out by listing the needed `#include` files for the Motif functions used in `skeleton.c`.

Next, the declaration of skeleton as a top-level widget makes information about our program available outside `main()`. This is because `skel_help_action()`, which creates a Motif dialog, needs to know who the dialog belongs to. The next two routines, `skel_exit_action()` and `skel_dialog_handler()`, are known as *callback* routines.

Callback routines make your program work. These routines are called when you push buttons or select menu items and when your program receives information from other programs or the operating system. If you look at `skel_dialog_handler()`, you see the following line:

```
XtAddCallback(skel_dialog, XmNokCallback, skel_dialog_handler, NULL);
```

This function tells the program what to do after the dialog appears and when you either click on the OK button or press the Return key—all without a lot of extra code.

`skel_help_action()` is also a callback routine, called in response to the `main()` program line:

```
XtAddCallback(skel_version, XmNactivateCallback, skel_help_action, NULL);
```

In this instance, `skel_help_action()` is run when you choose Version from the program's Help menu. The routine `skel_exit_action()` is called when you choose Exit from the program's File menu. After creating room for the text string containing the version information to be displayed, the `skel_help_action()` routine then creates the dialog with

```
skel_dialog = XmCreateMessageDialog (skeleton, "dialog", args, 0);
```

and fills in required information with the routine

```
XtVaSetValues(skel_dialog, XmNmessageString, skel_string, NULL, NULL);
```

followed by the callback routine designation. Finally, it displays the dialog with

```
XtManageChild(skel_dialog);
```

The `main()` routine starts with declarations for various widgets and widget elements. The call to `XtVaAppInitialize()` declares the application name, indicates whether the program should read any command-line arguments, and assigns an initial size in pixel width and height.

Sample Program Resources

The initial window size (and many other default actions of all other Motif and many X11 programs) can also be set by using resources. One way to do this is to open your `.Xdefaults` file in your home directory and type

```
Skeleton.height: 480
Skeleton.width:  640
```

Save the file. Next, replace the program's line

```
skeleton = XtVaAppInitialize(&skel_app, "Skeleton", NULL, 0, &argc,
argv, NULL, XmNwidth, 320, XmNheight, 240, NULL);
```

with

```
skeleton = XtAppInitialize(&skel_app, "Skeleton",NULL,0, &argc, argv,
        NULL, NULL,0);
```

Rebuild the program and run it. You should see a much larger window than the earlier version. Finally, yet another way to feed resources to this program is to create a file called Skeleton, type in the resource strings for width and height mentioned earlier, and save the file into the /usr/X11R6/lib/X11/app-defaults directory. This way, the program will start with a default window size for everyone on your system.

Continuing with the example, the client's main window as a managed widget is created next with `XtVaCreateManagedWidget()`; then a menu bar is built across the top of the window with `XmCreateMenubar()`. After that, a pull-down menu is created with `XmCreatePulldownMenu()`, and a File button is built on the menu, which will respond not only to a mouse click, but also to Alt+F.

Building the rest of the File menu is now easy. Note the callback routine to tell the program what to do when the Exit menu item is selected. After the File menu, the Edit menu is created in the same way, along with the Help menu.

NOTE

Thanks are due to Ken Lee's *Motif FAQ* for the tip on moving the Help menu string to the end of the main window's menu bar.

Finally, the menu bar is displayed, along with the application, and the program starts waiting for keystrokes, clicks, and other events in `XtAppMainLoop()`.

As you can see, even a simple Motif program has a lot of code devoted to handling the user interface. Using Motif can save you a lot of time and effort, because a lot of the code required to build, display, and handle the interface is hidden in the Motif routines, freeing you to concentrate on the internals of what your program does and what gives your programs a consistent look and feel.

Shared and Static Libraries

Using shared libraries when you build applications makes sense because program binaries use a lot less space on your hard drive. But what if you want to compile a program for someone who might not have the Motif libraries installed?

In this case, you might want to build the program by using Motif's static libraries. If you do, be prepared to find that a lot of extra code is linked into your program. How much bigger will the program be and how much of a difference will using a static build make, you might ask? You can see by first building a sample program (for Motif 2.01) in two different versions, using the gcc compiler option `-static`:

```
# gcc -static -o skel.static skeleton.c -L/usr/X11/lib
➥-lXm -lXpm -lXaw -lXt -lXext -lX11
# gcc -o skel.shared skeleton.c -L/usr/X11/lib
➥-lXm -lXpm -lXaw -lXt -lSM -lICE -lXext -lX11
```

Now look at the size of the files `skel.static` and `skel.shared`:

```
# ls -l skel.*
-rwxr-xr-x   1 root     root        12708 Sep 12 05:12 skel.shared
-rwxr-xr-x   1 root     root      1978564 Sep 12 05:11 skel.static
```

How about nearly a 2MB difference? If you're going to build Motif clients, you'll want to use the shared libraries (usually a default) because, as you can see, you'd quickly run out of room on your hard drive.

Interestingly, the shared-library version of the Motif 2.1 version of this program is even smaller than that generated by Motif 2.01:

```
-rwxr-xr-x   1 root     root         7574 Aug  6 11:11 skel
```

The UIL Compiler

Although I don't have enough room to discuss the User Interface Language (UIL), if you want to quickly and easily build your program's interface, you might want to learn this language and its compiler, `uil`. For details on using the compiler and language, read the `uil` and UIL man pages. A number of the Motif demonstration programs use UIL, so you can read source code examples.

Many commercial graphical interface builders are available to enable you to draw and design your interface, test it, and then—with the click of a button—write out the Motif source code. See the *Motif FAQ* for more information (pointers for the FAQ are at the end of this chapter in the "For More Information" section).

Tutorials and Examples

If you're serious about learning Motif programming, you'll need to have several good books and lots of program examples. If you want a basic introduction, you can also try some of the online tutorials or peruse code examples. Try one of these sites:

- `http://www.motifzone.com`

  A great place to visit and read *The Motif Developer*, an online magazine for Motif programmers, with loads of tips and articles about Motif.

- `http://www.cen.com/mw3/code.html`

  Contains a number of useful links to Motif programming code examples, lectures, and tutorials.

- `http://devcentral.iftech.com/learning/tutorials`

  Contains a Motif programming tutorial you might find helpful when getting started.

- `ftp://ftp.vse.cz`

  Look under /pub/linux/freeware_for_motif/motif-tutor for a copy of Jan Borchers' `xmtutor`, an interactive tutorial on Motif programming.

Using `imake` and `xmkmf`

You'll be familiar with Todd Brunhoff's `imake` utility and Jim Fulton's `xmkmf` command if you've created or built programs for the X Window System. Like the `make` command, these commands help you save time, prevent errors, and organize your programming tasks by automating the building process.

imake, a C preprocessor interface to make, uses configuration files found under the /usr/X11R6/lib/X11/config directory. These files include linux.cf, lnxLib.rules, lnxLib.tmpl, lnxdoc.rules, and lnxdoc.tmpl.

The xmkmf command, which creates a Makefile from an Imakefile, is a simple shell script that runs imake, telling it where to find the specifics about your system and which command-line parameters need to be passed to your compiler, assembler, linker, and even man-page formatter. Note that you should never run imake by itself; always use the xmkmf script instead.

Typically, after unpacking the source for an X or Motif program, you use the xmkmf command and then the make command to build your program. Another of the reasons many programmers use imake is to ensure portability. Assuming the imake file is written properly, the xmkmf command will work on nearly any UNIX system, and that includes Linux.

imake works by reading an Imakefile. In turn, the Imakefile contains directions for the cpp compiler preprocessor, whose output is then fed back into imake, which in turn generates the Makefile for your program. The magic of imake is that it simplifies the job of creating Makefiles for every possible computer or operating system your program could be built on or run under.

For example, here's a simple Imakefile for our sample program, skeleton.c:

```
        INCLUDES = -I.
DEPLIBS = XmClientDepLibs
LOCAL_LIBRARIES = XmClientLibs
SRCS= skeleton.c
OBJS= skeleton.o
PROGRAMS = skel
NormalLibraryObjectRule()
MComplexProgramTarget(skeleton,$(LOCAL_LIBRARIES),$(SYSLIBS))
```

To use this listing, type it in your favorite text editor (such as nedit) and save the text as Imakefile. Then, use the two commands

```
# xmkmf
# make
```

to build the program. This will also save you a lot of time if you use the edit-compile-run-edit cycle of programming, because you won't have to retype the compiler command line shown earlier in this chapter (# gcc -o skel skeleton.c -L/usr/X11R6/lib -lXm -lXpm -lXt -lXext -lX11).

LessTif—An Alternative Motif Clone

Much of the success of Linux is a direct result of the generosity of the thousands of programmers who chose to distribute their software either for free or under the GNU General Public License. Motif, as you already know, is not freeware, nor is it distributed under the GPL. As Red Hat Linux users, we're spoiled by the ability to examine program source or make changes as we see fit.

Want the source to Motif 2.1 for your computer's operating system? It will cost you $17,000 at the time of this writing. If you're interested in building a distribution of Motif for Linux, you can get the price list by browsing to `http://www.opengroup.org/tech/desktop/ordering/ motif.price.list.htm`.

For those of us who like source code or want to build Motif-compliant clients without paying for a distribution, the alternative is LessTif, a Motif clone designed to be compatible with Motif 1.2. Distributed under the terms of the GNU GPL, LessTif currently builds more than 50 different Motif clients (probably many more by the time you read this).

You can find a copy of the current LessTif distribution for Linux at `http://www.lesstif.org`.

The current distribution doesn't require that you use `imake` or `xmkmf`, and it comes with shared and static libraries. If you're a real Motif hacker and you're interested in the internals of graphical interface construction and widget programming, you should read the details of how LessTif is constructed. You can get a free copy of Harold Albrecht's book, *Inside LessTif*, at `http://www.igpm.rwth-aachen.de/ ~albrecht/hungry.html`.

For More Information

If you're interested in finding answers to common questions about Motif, read Ken Lee's *Motif FAQ*, which is posted regularly to the newsgroup `comp.windows.x.motif`. Without a doubt, this is the best source of information on getting started with Motif, but it won't replace a good book on Motif programming. You can find the FAQ on the newsgroup or at `ftp://ftp.rahul.net/pub/kenton/faqs/Motif-FAQ`. An HTML version can be found at `http://www.rahul.net/kenton/faqs/Motif-FAQ.html`.

For information on how to use `imake`, read Paul DuBois' *Software Portability with* `imake` from O'Reilly & Associates.

For Motif 1.2 programming and reference material, read Dan Heller and Paula M. Ferguson's *Motif Programming Manual* and Paula M. Ferguson and David Brennan's *Motif Reference Manual*, both from O'Reilly & Associates.

For the latest news about Motif or CDE, check The Open Group's site at `http://www.opengroup.org`.

For the latest information, installation, or programming errata about Red Hat's Motif distribution, see `http://www.redhat.com`.

For the latest binaries of LessTif, programming hints, and a list of Motif 1.2-compatible functions and Motif clients that build under the latest LessTif distribution, see `http://www.lesstif.org`.

For official information on Motif 1.2 from OSF, the following titles (from Prentice-Hall) might help (not needed if you've purchased Motif 2.1):

- *OSF/Motif Programmers Guide*
- *OSF/Motif Programmers Reference Manual*
- *OSF/Motif Style Guide*

For learning about `Xt`, you should look at Adrian Nye and Tim O'Reilly's *X Toolkit Intrinsics Programming Manual, Motif Edition*, and David Flanagan's *X Toolkit Intrinsics Reference Manual*, both from O'Reilly.

Other books about Motif include the following:

- *Motif Programming: The Essentials… and More*, by Marshall Brain, Digital Press
- *The X Toolkit Cookbook*, by Paul E. Kimball, Prentice-Hall, 1995
- *Building OSF/Motif Applications: A Practical Introduction*, by Mark Sebern, Prentice-Hall, 1994

Summary

In this chapter, you've learned about Motif, a commercial software library add-on for Linux that is available from a number of vendors, including Red Hat Software. Although you'll have to decide which version of Motif is best for you, I hope you'll agree about some of the benefits of using Motif to write programs for the X Window System. By following the sample program in Listing 31.1, you've learned a little about how Motif programs work and how to incorporate some of Motif's features into your programs. By using two programming tools included in your Red Hat Linux distribution, `imake` and `xmkmf`, you've also seen how to save time and effort when writing your own programs for Motif or X11. Finally, I've given you some tips on a Motif alternative, LessTif. I hope you'll explore more topics concerning graphical interface programming for X.

tcl and tk Programming

by David Pitts

In This Chapter

The tcl (pronounced "tickle") scripting language and the tk toolkit are programming environments for creating graphical user interfaces for the X Window system. tcl and tk are easy to learn and use, and with them, you can construct user interfaces much faster than with traditional X Window programming methods.

tcl/tk was written by John K. Ousterhout while he was a professor of electrical engineering and computer science at the University of California, Berkeley. It was originally designed to provide a reusable command language for interactive tools, but it has expanded far beyond that and is used in a wide range of software products.

The true power of tcl/tk is that complex graphical applications can be written almost entirely in the tcl scripting language, thus hiding many of the complexities of interface programming encountered in writing interfaces using the C language.

The official tcl/tk Web site is located at http://www.scriptics.com/.

According to their Web site, Scriptics Corporation is the tcl platform company. Formed by John Ousterhout, tcl creator and industry visionary, Scriptics is focused on bringing the tcl scripting language into the corporate mainstream. Scriptics will provide development tools, technology extensions, and commercial support services for tcl while continuing to develop the open source tcl and tk packages.

The site also has links for downloading and installing the latest versions of tcl/tk. Presently, the newest available version of tcl/tk is 8.03.

The programs discussed in this chapter are compatible with most versions of tcl and tk and should work fine for the current version.

tcl Basics

tcl is an interpreted language similar to Perl or the UNIX shell, which means tcl commands are first read and then evaluated. tk is a windowing toolkit that uses the tcl syntax for creating GUI components such as buttons, scrollbars, dialogs, and windows.

To run tcl, the tcl shell (tclsh) or the windowing shell (wish) is required. Both tclsh and wish are similar to standard UNIX shells such as sh or csh, in that they allow commands to be executed interactively or read in from a file. In practice, these shells are seldom used interactively because their interactive capabilities are quite limited.

The main difference between tclsh and wish is that tclsh only understands tcl commands, while wish understands both tcl and tk commands.

Interactive Use of tcl

This section briefly covers the interactive use of the tcl shells to illustrate one of its hazards.

To start using tcl interactively, just type **tclsh** (or **wish**) at the UNIX shell's prompt. The following prompt should appear:

```
%
```

In this chapter, interactive commands start with the percent character (%). At the prompt, type

```
% echo "hello world"
```

The words hello world should appear, followed by a new prompt. Now try

```
% puts "hello world"
```

The same output should appear, but there is a big difference between the two. The first command ran the echo binary to echo the string "hello world", whereas the second command uses the puts (put string) tcl command. The echo version of "hello world" works only when tclsh is run interactively, which is one of the hazards of using tclsh and wish interactively. For example, if you put the command

```
echo "hello world"
```

into the file helloworld.tcl and then source that file from tclsh, as in

```
% source helloworld.tcl
```

you get the following error:

```
invalid command name "echo"
```

To properly use UNIX commands in tcl, use the tcl command exec:

```
% exec echo "hello world"
```

This executes the command with its arguments in a UNIX shell. This is only one example of things that work differently in the interactive mode of the tcl shells.

Noninteractive Use of tcl

Commonly, tclsh and wish are used noninteractively, which means they are invoked on scripts from the UNIX prompt ($) such as

```
$ tclsh myprog.tcl
$ wish myprog.tcl
```

or are called from within a script that has as its first line something like the following:

```
#!/usr/bin/wish
```

Usually this first line must be changed for each installation of the script, because `wish` or `tclsh` will be in different places. To avoid the need to edit the script for each installation, the man page for `tclsh` recommends that the following three lines be used as the first three lines of all `tcl/tk` scripts:

```
#!/bin/sh
# the next line restarts using wish \
exec wish "$0" "$@"
```

This means users only need to have `wish` in their path to use the script. Individual results with this approach could vary, depending on the version of `sh` on the system.

The real advantage of noninteractive use of `tcl` is the same as for noninteractive use of the UNIX shell. Noninteractive use allows for many commands to be grouped together and executed by simply typing the name of the script and allows for faster development and debugging of large programs.

The `tcl` Language

This section contains an introduction to the `tcl` language syntax and its use in scripts. The code in the following section can be run interactively or from a script. The spacing of the output will vary slightly in interactive mode.

Command Structure

The basic structure of a `tcl` command is

```
commandname arguments
```

where *`commandname`* is the command that `tcl` is to execute, and *`arguments`* is the optional arguments to give to that command. The entire line (*`commandname`* and *`arguments`*) is called the command. Commands are separated by newlines (`\n`) or by a semicolon (`;`). If only one command is given on a line, the semicolon is not required. As an illustration, the two commands can be written one per line:

```
set foo 0
set bar 1
```

or on the same line:

```
set foo 0; set bar 1;
```

Comments

Other than commands, the only other lines in a tcl script are comments. As in UNIX shells and Perl, a comment line is a line that begins with a pound symbol (#):

```
# this is a comment
```

but unlike in a shell, the following is not a comment

```
set foo 0 # initialize foo
```

This will result in an error, because the tcl parser thinks a command is terminated either by a newline or a semicolon. To include comments on the same line as a command, the command needs to be terminated by a semicolon, like this:

```
set foo 0;# initialize foo
```

It is probably a good idea to terminate all commands with a semicolon, although it is not required.

Datatypes

tcl doesn't support variable types such as int, float, double, or char. This means a variable can be set to a number, a character, or a string at different times in the same program.

Internally, however, tcl treats all variables as strings. When a variable needs to be manipulated, tcl allows numbers (real and integer) to be given in all the forms that are understood by ANSI C. The following are examples of valid numeric values for variables:

74	Integer
0112	Octal, starts with a 0
0x4a	Hexadecimal, starts with 0x
74.	Real
74.0	Real
7.4e1	Real
7.4e+1	Real

Other values are treated as strings and will generate errors if used in mathematical expressions.

Variables

`tcl` defines two types of variables, *scalars* and *arrays*. To create a scalar variable and assign it a value, use the `set` command. For example,

```
set banana 1;
```

creates the variable `banana` and gives it a value of `1`. To set the value of `banana` to something different, simply use `set` again:

```
set banana "Fresh from Brazil";
```

Now the variable `banana` has the value `"Fresh from Brazil"`. The double quotes tell `tcl` that all the characters including the spaces make up the value of the variable. (Quoting and substitution are covered later in this chapter in the section "Quoting and Substitution.")

To print out the value of `banana`, use the `puts` command:

```
puts $banana;
```

This prints the value of the variable `banana` to the standard output (sometimes referred to as `STDOUT`). Putting `$` before the name of the variable tells `tcl` to access the value assigned to that variable. This convention, known as variable substitution, is similar to conventions used in UNIX shells.

To create a one-dimensional array, enter the following:

```
set fruit(0) banana;
set fruit(1) orange;
```

This creates the array `fruit` and assigns the values `banana` and `orange` to the first and second elements, `0` and `1`.

NOTE

Remember, computers start counting with the number zero (0), not one (1).

The assignments to array indexes need not be in order. The commands

```
set fruit(100) peach;
set fruit(2) kiwi;
set fruit(87) pear;
```

create only three items in the array `fruit`. Arrays in `tcl` are like associative arrays, which associate a "key" with a value. Arrays in `tcl` associate a given string with another string. This makes it possible to have array indexes that are not numbers. The command

```
set fruit(banana) 100
```

sets the value of item banana in the array fruit to 100. The assigned values need not be numeric:

```
set food(koala) eucalyptus;
set food(chipmunk) acorn;
```

To access the value stored in a one-dimensional array variable, use the $ convention:

```
puts $food(koala);
```

This prints out the value stored in the array food at index koala. The array index can also be a variable:

```
set animal chipmunk;
puts $food($animal);
```

These commands will output acorn, given the previous assignments.

Multidimensional arrays are a simple extension of one-dimensional arrays and are set as follows:

```
set myarray(1,1) 0;
```

This sets the value of the item at 1,1 in the array myarray to be 0. By separating the indexes by commas, you can make arrays of three, four, or more dimensions:

```
set array(1,1,1,1,1,1) "foo";
```

In addition to setting array values, tcl provides the array command for getting information about arrays and the parray command for printing out information about arrays. First, take a look at the parray command. Given the declarations

```
set food(koala) eucalyptus;
set food(chipmunk) acorn;
set food(panda) bamboo;
```

the command

```
parray food
```

produces the following output:

```
food(chipmunk) = acorn
food(koala)    = eucalyptus
food(panda)    = bamboo
```

Now look at the array command and its arguments, which are used to get information about an array and its elements. The basic syntax for an array command is as follows:

```
array option arrayname
```

The supported options are discussed later in this section.

One of the most frequently used pieces of information about an array is its size. Given the declarations

```
set fruit(0) banana;
set fruit(1) peach;
set fruit(2) pear;
set fruit(3) apple;
```

The command

```
array size fruit;
```

returns `4`. This number is often useful in loops.

Because arrays can have nonsequential or nonnumeric indexes, the `array` command provides an option for getting elements from an array. Assuming that the `food` array has been defined as presented earlier, the first thing you need to do to start getting elements is to use `startsearch` through the array. This is accomplished by first getting a search ID for the array:

```
set food_sid [array startsearch food];
```

The command

```
array startsearch food
```

returns a string, which is the name of the search (see the section "Quoting and Substitution"). You will need this for future reference, so set its value to that of a variable, in this case, `food_sid`.

To get the first element (and every subsequent element) of the `food` array, use the following:

```
array nextelement food $food_sid;
```

When the array search is done, terminate the search for the array by using

```
array donesearch food $food_sid;
```

One other option to the `array` command that is frequently in use while iterating through an array is the `anymore` option. It returns true (a value of `1`) if there are any more items in the search. For example,

```
array anymore food $food_sid;
```

returns `1` the first two times it is used with the `food` array declared earlier.

To dispose of a variable (scalar or array), use the `unset` command:

```
unset banana;
```

This unsets the variable banana. If you use unset $banana (assuming that banana was set to the value shown earlier) instead of just banana, you get an error like this:

```
can't unset "0": no such variable
```

This occurs because when $ precedes a variable's name, the value of the variable is substituted in before the command is executed.

Manipulating String Values

The simplest form of string manipulation is the append command, which concatenates multiple strings and variables together. As an illustration, the following commands

```
set str1 "Begin";
append str1 " a String";
set str2 " even more text";
append str1 " with some text" " and add" $str2 " to it.";
puts $str1;
```

give this output:

```
Begin a String with some text and add even more text to it.
```

You can achieve the same results by using the following commands:

```
set str1 "Begin";
set str1 "$str1 a String";
set str2 " even more text";
set str1 "$str1 with some text and add$str2 to it.";
```

But this will be slower than using append, because append does not do character copying as set does.

For more advanced string manipulation, tcl provides the string command, which understands a whole host of options. The basic syntax of the string command is

```
string option string1 string2
```

where *string1* and *string2* can either be literal strings ("this is a string") or variables, and *option* is one of the following:

compare	Returns -1, 0, or 1, depending on whether *string1* is lexographically less than, equal to, or greater than *string2* (similar to the C library function strcmp).
first	Returns the index of the first occurrence of *string1* in *string2*, or -1 if *string1* does not occur in *string2*.
last	Returns the index of the last occurrence of *string1* in *string2*, or -1 if *string1* does not occur in *string2*.

The following options to the `string` command interpret *`string2`* as a list of characters to trim from *`string1`*:

`trim`	Removes any leading and trailing characters present in *`string2`* from *`string1`*.
`trimleft`	Removes any leading characters present in *`string2`* from *`string1`*.
`trimright`	Removes any trailing characters present in *`string2`* from *`string1`*.

The following options to the `string` command only take *`string1`* as an argument:

`length`	Returns the number of characters in *`string1`*.
`tolower`	Returns a new string with all of the characters in *`string1`* converted to lowercase.
`toupper`	Returns a new string with all of the characters in *`string1`* converted to uppercase.

Now look at a few examples. First, make a string and get its length:

```
set str " Here Is A Test String ";
string length $str;
```

This gives a length of `23` (the `length` option counts whitespace characters). Now get the location of the first and last occurrences of the string `"st"` in `$str`:

```
string first "st" $str;
string last "st" $str
```

This gives a value of `13` for the first occurrence of `"st"` (corresponding to the occurrence in `Test`) and a value of `13` for the last occurrence of `"st"` (`Test` again). What about the `"st"` in `String`? Well, most of the string comparison functions are case- and whitespace-sensitive, so temporarily convert `$str` to lowercase and try again:

```
string last "st" [string tolower $str];
```

This gives a value of `16`, which corresponds to the `"st"` in `String`. Finally, strip off the leading and trailing spaces and get a length for the string:

```
string length [string trim $str " "];
```

The value `21` is returned, which means the first and last spaces were stripped off.

Manipulating Numeric Values

`tcl` provides two commands for manipulating numeric variables and constants: `incr` and `expr`.

The incr command gives tcl an equivalent to the C language operators +=, -=, ++, and —. The basic syntax is

```
incr variable integer
```

where *variable* must be an integer. The incr command adds the given *integer* to the *variable*; thus, decrementing is handled by giving negative integers. We can demonstrate its usage. First, create a variable and do an incr on it:

```
set a 81;
incr a;
puts $a;
```

$a has a value of 82. By default, incr is the same as ++; if it is not given an integer argument, it adds one to the named variable. Now decrement $a by 3:

```
incr a -3
puts $a
```

Note that $a has a value of 79. One last point is that the integer can be the value of a variable:

```
set a 6;
set b 9;
incr a $b;
puts $a;
```

$a has a value of 15.

For more complex mathematical operations, tcl provides the expr command, which works with all standard ANSI C operators. Operator precedence is mostly the same as in ANSI C.

When any mathematical operations are required, they must be preceded by the expr command. For example, the commands

```
set a 20;
set b 4;
set c $a/$b;
puts $c;
```

result in the output

```
20/4
```

rather than 5, the desired result. To get the right answer, use the expr command:

```
set c [expr $a / $b];
```

In addition to the standard operators +, -, *, and /, the expr command can be given several options that enable it to perform mathematical operations. The basic syntax is

```
expr function number
```

Some of the functions `expr` understands, along with the values they return, are the following:

`abs(x)`	Absolute value of x
`round(x)`	The integer value resulting from rounding x
`cos(x)`	Cosine of x (x in radians)
`cosh(x)`	Hyperbolic cosine of x
`acos(x)`	Arccosine of x (0 to pi)
`sin(x)`	Sine of x (x in radians)
`sinh(x)`	Hyperbolic sine of x
`asin(x)`	Arcsine of x (-pi/2 to pi/2)
`tan(x)`	Tangent of x (x in radians)
`tanh(x)`	Hyperbolic tangent of x
`atan(x)`	Arctangent of x (-pi/2 to pi/2)
`exp(x)`	e raised to the power of x
`log(x)`	Natural log of x
`log10(x)`	Log base 10 of x
`sqrt(x)`	The square root of x

The following math function takes two number arguments:

`pow(x,y)`	x raised to the power of y

This is used as follows:

```
set a 2;
set b [expr pow($a,3)];
puts $b;
```

The output will be `8.0`, the value of 2 raised to the third power.

Quoting and Substitution

Quoting and substitution are both used heavily in relation to variables. You saw the most basic version of quoting (using double quotes to make strings) and substitution earlier in this chapter. `tcl` supports one more type of quoting, brace quoting, and one more type of substitution, command substitution.

To review, the most common use of double quotes is to create strings with embedded whitespace:

```
set kiwi "Fresh from New Zealand";
```

Double quotes can also be used to make multiline strings:

```
set kiwi "Fresh from
New Zealand 3 for a dollar";
```

In addition to making multiline strings, the standard ANSI C language escape sequences can be used in `tcl` strings:

```
set kiwi "Fresh from New Zealand\n\t3 for a dollar."
```

This outputs the following:

```
Fresh from New Zealand
3 for a dollar.
```

The two types of substitution can also be applied within double-quoted strings. The first type of substitution, variable substitution, is explained in the "Variables" section earlier in this chapter. In a double-quoted string, you can access the value of a variable by preceding the variable's name with `$`. Thus the following commands

```
set fruit kiwi;
set place "New Zealand";
set how_many 3;
puts "$fruit, fresh from $place, $how_many for a dollar";
```

output this:

```
kiwi, fresh from New Zealand, 3 for a dollar
```

The other type of substitution is command substitution. A command substitution block begins with a left bracket (`[`) and ends with a right bracket (`]`). For example,

```
set len_in 2;     puts "$len_in inches is [expr $len_in*2.54] cm";
```

outputs

```
2 inches is 5.08 cm
```

The `5.08` is the result of the command

```
expr $len_in*2.54
```

Because this command is in brackets, the value it returns is substituted in. In this case, the `tcl` command `expr` is used, but any `tcl` command can be placed between brackets. Command substitution can be used in most commands and is not limited to double-quoted commands. For example, the commands

```
set len_in 2;
set len_cm [expr $len_in*2.54];
puts "$len_in inches is $len_cm cm";
```

produce the same output as

```
set len_in 2;     puts "$len_in inches is [expr $len_in*2.54] cm";
```

The other type of quoting available in `tcl` is brace quoting, which is similar to using single quotes in UNIX shells. Brace quoting creates a string with the given characters, no substitution (command or variable) takes place, and the C language escape sequences are not interpreted. For example, the command

```
puts "This\nis a\nmulti-line\nstring"
```

produces the following output:

```
This
is a
multi-line
string
```

The command

```
puts {This\nis a\nmulti-line\nstring}
```

produces the following output:

```
This\nis a\nmulti-line\nstring
```

To get tabs, newlines, and other special characters in a brace-quoted string, they must be entered physically, like this:

```
puts {This
is a
multi-line
string}
```

This will produce the desired output. The real use for brace-quoted strings comes when certain characters with special meanings need to be given as values for variables. For example, the commands

```
set price 1.00;
puts "Pears, $$price per pound";
```

give this output:

```
Pears, $1.00 per pound
```

Because the `$$price` has the potential to be confusing, it would be better if the variable `price` had the value `$1.00`. You could use brace quoting to achieve the following:

```
set price {$1.00};
puts "Pears, $price per pound";
```

Brace quoting is also used to defer evaluation in control structures and procedure definitions. In such cases, the values of variables are substituted in after the entire block is read.

Flow Control—if and switch

tcl provides several commands for flow control and supports all the standard ANSI C comparison operators for both string and numeric data.

This section starts with the if/elseif/else commands. The simplest if statement is one like the following:

```
if {$x < 0} {
set x 10;
}
```

This example has only one line in the body of the if clause, but any number of lines and subblocks can be added. If additional tests need to be performed, each test is given in parentheses as follows:

```
if { ($x == "SJ") || ($x == "LA") } {
puts "You Live in California!";
}
```

Tests can be nested as in the following example:

```
if { ( ($arch == "ppc") || ($arch == "intel") ) && ($os != "Linux") } {
puts "Get Linux!";
}
```

Adding an else clause to an if statement is done like this:

```
if {$x <= 0} {
set x 10;
} else {
set x 0;
}
```

You can also add as many elseif statements as desired:

```
if {$x == 0} {
set x 10;
} elseif {$x == 10} {
incr x -1;
} elseif {$x == 100} {
set x 50;
} else {
set x 0;
}
```

In many cases, adding extra elseif statements becomes cumbersome and difficult to understand. To provide a more compact way of expressing the same logic, tcl implements the switch command. switch works by associating a value (string or number) with a block. The preceding if statement, when written as a switch statement, becomes

```
switch $x {
0 {set x 10;}
10 {incr x -1;}
100 {set x 50;}
}
```

By default, only the block corresponding to the matched value is executed, but a `switch` statement can implement "fallthrough" if the block is designated as a single minus sign (-). The `switch` statement

```
switch $x {
0 -
10 -
100 {incr x -1}
}
```

is equivalent to the following `if` statement:

```
if { ($x == 0) || ($x == 10) || ($x == 100) } {
incr x -1;
}
```

Loops

`tcl` provides three loop commands:

- `for`
- `foreach`
- `while`

`tcl` also provides two loop control commands:

- `break`
- `continue`

The `while` loop executes its body while its test condition is true. The structure can be thought of as

```
while {condition} {block}
```

The following is a simple `while` loop that counts to ten:

```
set x 0;
while {$x < 10} {
incr x;
puts $x;
}
```

The `foreach` loop iterates over a set of arguments and executes its body each time. The `foreach` loop has the following structure:

```
foreach variable {items} {block}
```

variable is the name of the variable to which each item in the set *items* is assigned in turn. Here is an example:

```
foreach element {o c n p li} {
switch $element {
o -
n {puts gas;}
c -
p -
li {puts solid;}
}
}
```

In this case, the list of items to check is specified, but a variable can be used also:

```
set elements "o c n p li";
foreach element $elements {
switch $element {
o -
n {puts gas;}
c -
p -
li {puts solid;}
}
}
```

If a variable instead of a list of items is given, braces should not be used, because the braces would be treated as if used for quoting.

The `for` loop allows the most control while looping. It can be broken down as

```
for {initialization} {condition} {increment} {body}
```

A simple `for` loop example that counts to 10 is

```
for {set i 0} {$i <= 10} {incr i} { puts $i; }
```

You have seen simple initialization statements, but the initialization and increment parts of the `for` loop can be as complicated as required.

Now for a look at the loop control commands, `break` and `continue`. The `break` command breaks out of loop and executes the next line of code after the loop's block; the `continue` command skips to the next iteration of the loop.

The `continue` command is handy for reading in initialization files where comments lines need to be allowed. If the following statement is included in a loop that reads in a file, all lines that start with a pound sign (#) will be skipped.

```
if { [regexp {^#} [string trim $line] ]} {continue;}
```

File I/O and File Info

tcl provides a simple and effective method for file input and output similar to the methods in the C standard I/O library. The first step in file I/O is to open a file and get a file handle or file ID. As an example, the command

```
set f [ open /etc/passwd r];
```

opens the file /etc/passwd with mode r and returns a file handle assigned to the variable f. tcl supports the following file open modes:

r	Open for reading only; the file must exist.
r+	Open for reading and writing; the file must exist.
w	Open for writing. The file will be created if it does not exist; otherwise, it is truncated.
w+	Same as w, except the file is opened for reading also.
a	Open the file for appending text; the file will be created if it does not exist.
a+	Same as a, except the file is opened for reading also.

The open command can also be overloaded to run subprocesses with more control than the exec command provides. To open a process instead of a file, replace the filename with a brace-quoted string beginning with a pipe character (¦) and containing the command to run. For example, the following command opens a ps for reading:

```
set f [ open {¦ ps } r ];
```

For processes opened in this manner, the tcl command pid returns the process ID of the file handle associated with a process. For the preceding example,

```
pid $f
```

returns the pid associated with $f, the file handle for the ps command that was opened.

If a file (or process) is opened in a mode that supports reading, you can read from the file by using the gets command. To process all the lines of a file, the following while command is often used:

```
while { [ gets $f line ] >= 0 }
```

This works because the gets command returns -1 when EOF is reached. In this case, the gets command reads in a line from the file handle $f and assigns the value to the variable line. In the body of the loop, $line can be accessed and manipulated.

If a file is opened for writing, the puts command can be used to write output to the file. If the file handle $f corresponds to a file opened for writing, the command

```
puts $f "This is a line of text";
```

writes the string `"This is a line of text"` to the open file.

The only other file I/O command is the `close` command, which takes as its argument a file handle. To close the file you opened earlier, you would simply use

```
close $f;
```

It is probably a good idea to close any file handles that are open at the end of a program. Also, if the same file handle variable is to be reused several times in a program, it is a good idea to close it before the next `open`.

In addition to reading and writing from files, it is sometimes necessary to obtain information about files. `tcl` provides the `file` command to accomplish this. The `file` command's syntax is

```
file option filename
```

where *`filename`* is the name of the file to run the tests on and *`option`* is one of the following options.

The following options return true (`1`) or false (`0`) information about files:

`executable`	True if the file is executable by the current user
`exists`	True if the file exists
`isdirectory`	True if the file is a directory
`isfile`	True if the file is a regular file
`owned`	True if the current user owns the file
`readable`	True if the file is readable by the current user
`writable`	True if the file is writable by the current user

The following options return additional information about a file:

`atime`	Returns the time the file was last accessed in seconds since Jan. 1, 1970
`mtime`	Returns the time the file was last modified in seconds since Jan. 1, 1970
`size`	Returns the size of the file in bytes
`readlink`	Returns the value of a symbolic link if the given file is a symbolic link
`type`	Returns a string giving the type of the file

Procedures

Procedures are the `tcl` equivalent of functions in the C language. To create a procedure, the `proc` command is used, which has the following syntax:

```
proc procedure_name {arguments} {body}
```

The number of arguments is variable, and an empty argument list is specified by `{}`. *`body`* can contain any valid `tcl` statement and can be as long as required.

A simple procedure that takes no arguments is as follows:

```
proc test_proc {} { puts "procedure test"; }
```

To invoke this procedure, simply give its name

```
test_proc;
```

to get the output

```
procedure test
```

A more realistic example is a file output procedure, which takes in as an argument a filename:

```
proc cat {filename} {
set f [open $filename r];
while { [ gets $f line ] >= 0 } {
puts $line;
}
close $f;
}
```

To invoke this procedure with `/etc/passwd` as its argument, use the following:

```
cat /etc/passwd
```

This prints out the contents of /etc/passwd.

Three important commands for use in procedures are `return`, `global`, and `catch`. The `global` command is used to give a procedure access to global variables, and the `return` command is used to return a value from a procedure. The `catch` command is useful for detecting errors and returning a failure value.

You can rewrite the `cat` procedure to be a little more robust by doing the following:

```
proc cat {filename} {
set ret_code 0;
catch {
set f [open $filename r];
while { [ gets $f line ] >= 0 } {
puts $line;
```

```
}
close $f;
set ret_code 1;
}
return $ret_code;
}
```

This code demonstrates the use of both `catch` and `return`. If any parts of the procedure fail, it returns `0` (false), but if the `cat` is successful, it returns `1` (true). This information will be useful if `cat` is called with a process to execute as its argument.

The tk Toolkit

The `tk` toolkit enables X Window graphical user interfaces (GUIs) to be written using the `tcl` scripting language. The `tk` toolkit adds to the `tcl` language by enabling the creation of GUI components called *widgets*. This section looks briefly at the available `tk` widgets and shows how to create them.

Introduction to Widgets

The basic method for creating a widget is

`widget_type path option`

where *`widget_type`* is one of the widget types given in the following list, *`path`* is a window pathname (usually starting with a dot, which is the name of the root window), and *`option`* is any option the widget understands.

The `tk` toolkit defines the following widget types:

`canvas`	Allows for drawing objects
`entry`	Allows for the input of a single line of text
`frame`	Used to contain other widgets
`listbox`	Displays a set of strings and allows for choosing one or more of them
`menu`	Displays a menu bar and menu items
`text`	Displays multiple lines of text
`label`	Displays a single line of static text
`button`	A widget that displays a clickable button
`checkbutton`	Displays a checkable box
`radiobutton`	Displays several mutually exclusive checkable boxes
`scale`	Similar to a slider that sets a value

To create and manipulate widgets, the windowing shell, `wish`, must be used. To invoke `wish` interactively, type **`wish`** at the UNIX prompt. The following `wish` prompt appears:

```
%
```

Along with this, an empty window pops up on the screen. This window is the `wish` root window (called `.`) and all the widgets that are created will appear with it.

Creating Widgets

This section shows how to create a widget and manipulate it. First, create a button, like this:

```
button .button;
```

So what did that do?

Well, the widget type is specified as `button`, so `tk` created a button. The path is `.button`, so `tk` created the button in the root window (`.` is the root `tk` window) and named it `button`.

So where is the button, anyway?

The button isn't displayed right now; `tk` simply created it. To display the button, you need to tell `tk` how to display the widget. For this, use the `pack` command and give it the `path` to the widget you want to display:

```
pack .button;
```

Now the button is showing, but it's blank (see Figure 33.1). This is where widget's options come into play.

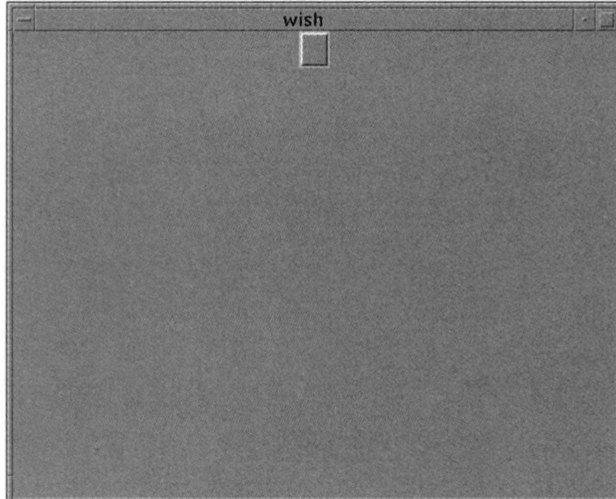

FIGURE 33.1
The widget starts as a plain button.

Widget Options

All tk widgets use standard options that control appearance and function. Most widgets understand the following options:

Option	Description
`-background color`, `-bg color`	The background color of the widget. Valid values are of the form `#RRGGBB`, `#RRRGGGBBB`, or one of the names defined in /usr/lib/X11/rgb.txt.
`-foreground color`, `-fg color`	The foreground color of the widget. Valid values are of the form `#RRGGBB`, `#RRRGGGBBB`, or one of the names defined in /usr/lib/X11/rgb.txt.
`-height pixels`	The widget's height in pixels.
`-width pixels`	The widget's width in pixels.
`-borderwidth pixels`, `-db pixels`	The width of the widget's border in pixels.
`-padx pixels`	Extra space required by the widget in the `x` direction.
`-pady pixels`	Extra space required by the widget in the `y` direction.
`-relief type`	The 3D effect of the widget, where `type` is one of these strings: `flat`, `raised`, `grove`, `ridge`, `sunken`.
`-text string`	The string to display in the widget.
`-font font`	The font to be used for the text displayed in a widget; valid font definitions are given by the command `xlsfonts`.
`-command command`	The `tcl` command to execute when the widget is used; usually this is the name of a procedure or an `exec` statement.

In addition to these options, the `pack` command understands the following options of its own:

Option	Description
`-side type`	Controls the order in which widgets are placed. Valid types are `left`, `right`, `top`, or `bottom`. For example, `left` indicates that new widgets should be placed to the left of existing widgets.
`-fill type`	Controls whether or not widgets are stretched to fill up open space in the window. Valid values are `none`, `x`, `y`, or `both`. For example, `both` indicates that widgets should fill up all open space.

`-expand value` Controls whether or not widgets expand if the window's size increases. `value` is either `0` or `1`, with `1` indicating true.

A `tcl/tk` Widget Programming Example

Now that you know about the options for widgets and for `pack`, you can start using them. One of the interesting features of widgets is their `reliefs`, the widgets' 3D look. To get an idea of how each `relief` looks, make some labels, using the following:

```
foreach i {raised sunken flat groove ridge} {
label .$i -relief $i -text $i;
pack .$i
}
```

This example iterates through the set of relief types, creating one `label` for each type, along with setting each label's `text` to be the `relief` type. The layout will look similar to Figure 33.2.

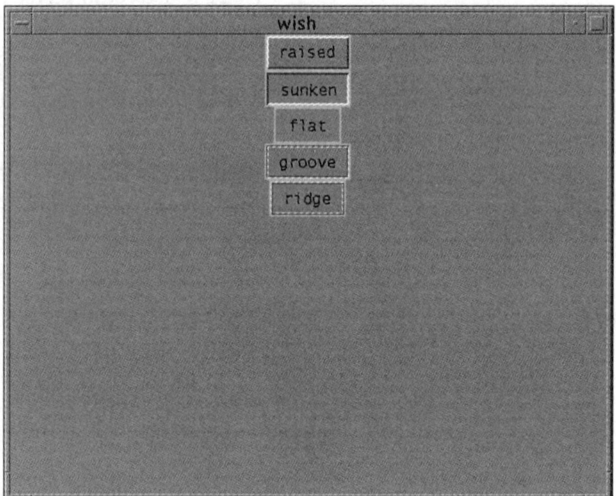

FIGURE 33.2
Labels of varying `relief`.

There are two things to notice here. First, the labels are not all the same size. Second, the labels are stacked one on top of the other. This is an example of the `pack` command's default behavior; it determines the size of each widget automatically and then places each widget below the preceding widget that was placed.

Now make all the labels the same size and pack them next to each other, instead of one on top of the other. There are two ways to do this. The first is to rewrite the loop:

```
foreach i {raised sunken flat groove ridge} {
label .$i -relief $i -text $i -height 10 -width 10;
pack .$i -side left
}
```

The second way is to reconfigure the labels by using the `configure` option, which has the following syntax:

```
widget configure option
```

In this case, you could use the following loop (after the labels are created):

```
foreach i {raised sunken flat groove ridge} {
.$i configure -height 10 -width 10;
pack .$i -side left;
}
```

So why use `configure`?

If `wish` is run interactively and one version of the loop is given, modifying it and running it again produces the following error:

```
window name "raised" already exists in parent
```

This is how `wish` tells the programmer that the program has attempted to re-create an existing widget (this time, with the label raised). So you need to use `configure`; in fact, `configure` is required any time an existing widget needs to be changed.

In this case, the only way to use the new version of the loop is to destroy the existing labels, using the `destroy` command:

```
foreach i {raised sunken flat groove ridge} { destroy .$i }
```

The new result will be similar to Figure 33.3.

Now back to the example. Two things in Figure 33.3 need to be fixed. First, it is difficult to tell the labels apart. Second, most of the window is blank.

You can make the labels easier to distinguish by padding them when they are packed and by increasing their `borderwidths`. To make the labels take up all of the available space, give `pack` the `fill` option for both `x` and `y` and set the `expand` option to true:

```
foreach i {raised sunken flat groove ridge} {
label .$i -relief $i -text $i;
.$i configure -height 5 -width 5 -borderwidth 5;
pack .$i -side left -padx 5 -pady 5 -fill both -expand 1;
}
```

The result will be similar to Figure 33.4.

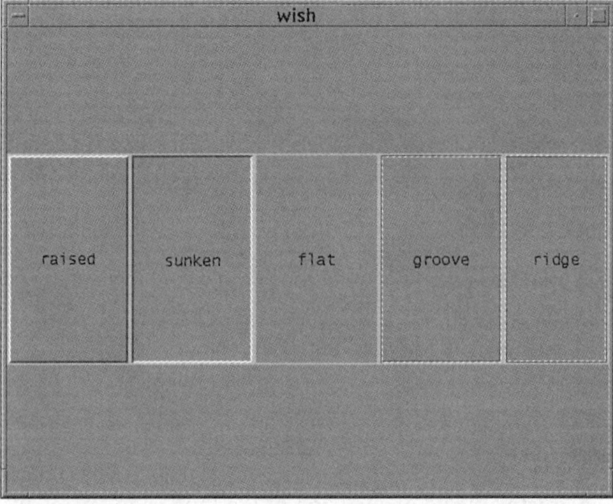

FIGURE 33.3
Labels of varying `relief`, packed next to each other.

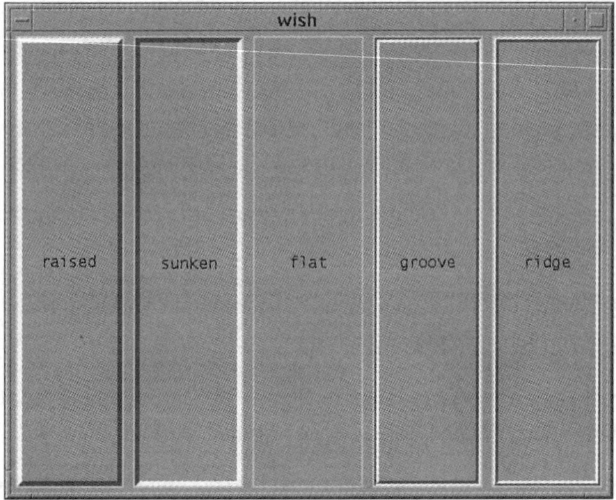

FIGURE 33.4
The labels now fill the space.

This example can be easily changed to use any of the widget types by replacing `label` with a different type of widget.

A `tcl/tk` Interface to `xsetroot`

This section introduces some of the other capabilities of the `tk` toolkit by applying them to the development of a GUI front end for the X Window program `xsetroot`.

Most X Window users will be familiar with the X Window program `xsetroot` that can be used to set the background color of the root window, under X11. The actual command is

```
xsetroot -solid color
```

where *`color`* can be given in the form `#RRGGBB`. The front end will allow for colors to be previewed and then applied.

You can get started now. The first thing you need is a variable that holds the color. Then you need to create two basic frames, one for the main area of the application and another in which to put messages. You will also need a third frame for the controls.

Frames are handy because they can be used to pack items of a particular type or function together. Also, they are useful in partitioning a window into sections that don't change.

Create the frames and the color globally:

```
set color "#000000";
frame .main_frame;
frame .message_frame;
frame .control_frame;
```

Now pack the frames:

```
pack .control_frame -in .main_frame -expand 1 -fill both;
pack .main_frame -anchor c -expand 1;
pack .message_frame -anchor s -padx 2 -pady 2 \
-fill x -expand 1;
```

You also need to create a label to handle messages. I'll do this as a procedure, so it will be easy to modify and execute:

```
proc make_message_label {} {
label .message_label -relief sunken;
pack .message_label -anchor c \
-in .message_frame -padx 2 \
-pady 2 -fill both -expand 1;
}
```

Pack the message label into the `.message_frame` so it is at the bottom of the window at all times.

Now make the scales. You need three scales, one each for red, blue, and green, with each one going from 0 to 255. You also need to pack the scales and their corresponding labels in their own frame:

```
proc make_scales {} {
frame .scale_frame;
foreach i {red green blue} {
```

```
frame .scale_frame_$i -bg $i;
label .label_$i -text $i -bg $i \
-fg white;
scale .scale_$i -from 0 -to 255 \
-command setColor;
pack .label_$i .scale_$i \
-in .scale_frame_$i;
pack .scale_frame_$i -in .scale_frame \
-side left -padx 2 -pady 2;
}
pack .scale_frame -in .control_frame \
-side left -expand 1;
}
```

This procedure is a good example of using frames. In all, this example creates four frames, one for each slider and label pair and overall frame. Adding the labels and sliders to their own frames simplifies the overall layout strategy.

Another example in this procedure is the use of the `-command` option for a widget. Each time the scales change, the command specified by the `-command` option is executed. In this case, the `setColor` command, which sets the global variable `color`, is executed:

```
proc setColor {value} {
global color;
foreach i {red green blue} {
set $i [format %02x [.scale_$i get]];
}
set color "#$red$green$blue";
.preview_label configure -bg $color;
.message_label configure -text "$color";
}
```

You can preview the color change by setting the background color of the widget, `.preview_label`. To create `.preview label`, use the following procedure:

```
proc make_preview {} {
global color;

frame .preview_frame;
label .preview_label -bg $color \
-height 5 -width 5;
pack .preview_label -in .preview_frame \
-padx 2 -pady 2 -fill both \
-anchor c -expand 1;
pack .preview_frame -in .control_frame \
-side bottom -fill both -expand 1 \
-padx 2 -pady 2;
}
```

Now you need to add a few buttons—one to apply the changes and another to quit the program. Use the following procedure:

```
proc make_buttons {} {
frame .button_frame;
button .apply -text "apply" \
-command setRootColor;
button .quit -text "quit" -command exit;
pack .apply .quit -in .button_frame \
-fill both -expand 1 -padx 2 \
-pady 2 -side left;
pack .button_frame -in .main_frame \
-fill both;
}
```

You also need the following procedure, which sets the root color:

```
proc setRootColor {} {
global color;

catch {
exec xsetroot -solid $color;
} msg;

if {$msg != {}} {
set msg "An error occurred";
} else {
set msg "$color";
}

.message_label configure -text $msg;
}
```


Now that you are done with the procedures, invoke them:

```
make_message_label;
make_scales;
make_preview;
make_buttons;
```

You are now ready to test your little `tcl` application. When the application is run, the resulting window should look like Figure 33.5.

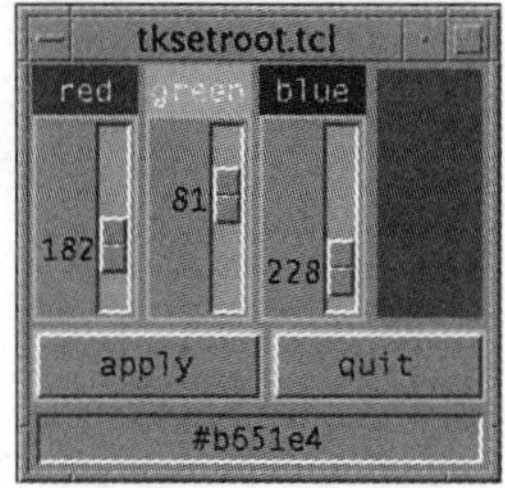

FIGURE 33.5
The `tksetroot` *application window with buttons and colors.*

Listing 33.1 contains the complete source code of the `tksetroot` application.

LISTING 33.1 `tksetroot`

```
set color "#000000";
frame .main_frame;
frame .message_frame;
frame .control_frame;

pack .control_frame -in .main_frame -expand 1 -fill both;
pack .main_frame -anchor c -expand 1;
pack .message_frame -anchor s -padx 2 -pady 2 \
-fill x -expand 1;

proc make_message_label {} {
label .message_label -relief sunken;
pack .message_label -anchor c -in .message_frame \
-padx 2 -pady 2 -fill both -expand 1;
}

proc make_scales {} {
frame .scale_frame;
foreach i {red green blue} {
frame .scale_frame_$i -bg $i;
label .label_$i -text $i -bg $i -fg white;
scale .scale_$i -from 0 -to 255 \
-command setColor;
pack .label_$i .scale_$i -in .scale_frame_$i;
pack .scale_frame_$i -in .scale_frame -side left \
-padx 2 -pady 2;
}
pack .scale_frame -in .control_frame -side left -expand 1;
}

proc setColor {value} {
global color;
foreach i {red green blue} {
set $i [format %02x [.scale_$i get]];
}
set color "#$red$green$blue";
.preview_label configure -bg $color;
.message_label configure -text "$color";
}

proc make_preview {} {
global color;

frame .preview_frame;
label .preview_label -bg $color \
-height 5 -width 5;
```

```
pack .preview_label -in .preview_frame \
-padx 2 -pady 2 -fill both -anchor c \
-expand 1;
pack .preview_frame -in .control_frame \
-side top -fill both -expand 1 \
-padx 2 -pady 2;
}

proc make_buttons {} {
frame .button_frame;
button .apply -text "apply" -command setRootColor;
button .quit -text "quit" -command exit;
pack .apply .quit -in .button_frame -fill both \
-expand 1 -padx 2 -pady 2 -side left;
pack .button_frame -in .main_frame -fill both;
}

proc setRootColor {} {
global color;

catch {
exec xsetroot -solid $color;
} msg;

if {$msg != {}} {
set msg "An error occurred";
} else {
set msg "$color";
}

.message_label configure -text $msg;
}

make_message_label;
make_scales;
make_preview;
make_buttons;
```

Summary

This chapter is an introduction to programming in `tcl/tk`. The examples demonstrate the power of `tcl/tk`, which lies in its capability to make user interfaces within a short amount of time and with little code. Although this chapter covers many of the features of `tcl/tk`, many more were not discussed. I hope that with this chapter as a stepping stone, you will enjoy many years of developing `tcl/tk` applications.

Programming with Python

by Tim Parker

In This Chapter

Python is a public domain, object-oriented, dynamic language. Developed in 1990 by Guido van Rossum and named after the Monty Python troop, Python has become popular as both a scripting language and a rapid-development tool. Python is truly freeware because there are no rules about copying the software or distributing any applications developed with it. When you obtain a copy of Python, you get all of the source code, a debugger, a code profiler, and a set of interfaces for most GUIs in use today. Python runs on practically any operating system platform, including Linux.

Python, which has quickly become one of the most popular languages in use, is often referred to as a bridging language between high-level languages such as C and scripting languages such as Perl and Tcl/Tk. What makes Python so popular? The language lends itself to scripting, but several aspects of Python make it much more than a simple scripting tool. For example, Python is extensible, allowing the language to adapt and expand to meet your requirements. Python code is simple to read and maintain. Python is also object-oriented, although you do not need to use OO features as part of your developments. Sounds powerful, doesn't it? Yet Python is remarkably easy to use, with no type declarations to worry about and no compile-link cycles to go through. As you will see in this chapter, you can quickly learn to use Python, and the language will grow with you as your programming abilities increase.

NOTE

The Python Software Activity (PSA) group was formed to provide a development center for Python. A Web site is devoted to Python at `http://www.python.org`. To support the Python language, the Usenet newsgroup `comp.lang.python` sees lots of traffic. Distributions of Python are available from many Web and FTP sites, and Red Hat offers Python as part of their CD-ROM bundle.

Getting Ready to Run Python

If you want to play with Python as we go through the programming language in more detail, you'll need to install the Python programming tools on your Linux system if they aren't installed already. You also need to set up your environment so it knows about Python and the directories to search for Python files.

Installing Python

Python is supplied on the Red Hat Linux CD-ROM provided with this book, so you don't have to go too far to find it. If for some reason you don't have the CD-ROM, or you want to check for more recent versions, the easiest place to find the code is through the Python FTP site, `ftp://ftp.python.org/pub/python/src`. You can use anonymous FTP to obtain the source code.

Python source files are usually supplied as C source code, which you need to compile and link, using any C compiler on your system. The FTP site also contains precompiled binaries for many target hardware and operating system combinations, making compilation unnecessary. Make sure you download the binary that's appropriate for your machine.

NOTE

To make obtaining the proper binaries or source code even simpler, the Python Web site has been updated to allow you to choose the proper platform and operating system. The appropriate binaries are then transferred for you. Even if you have the binaries, you might want to obtain the source code. This is especially true if you plan to add any C extensions to Python. Any time Python is extended, the entire binary has to be recompiled and relinked, so the source code is necessary.

At the time of writing, the 1.5 release of Python was available on the FTP and Web sites. Versions of Python for several UNIX versions, Linux, Windows, and Macintosh are all available.

If you download just the source code, Python is usually supplied as a gzipped file that requires `gunzip` to unpack. The packed file usually shows the version number as part of the name, such as python1.3, which means version 1.3 of the system. One or more README files are usually included with the Python distribution, often containing the compilation process and hints for your operating system. To begin the installation process, use the command

```
gzip -d python1.X.tar.gz
```

to unpack the gzipped file (you will have to substitute your filename for python1.X.tar.gz in the command, of course). Then, to untar the file, use the command

```
tar xvf python1.X.tar
```

again using the proper filename. The Python files will be untarred in the current directory. The next step is to run the auto-configuration routine by issuing the command

```
./configure
```

and then start the compilation of the executables with the command

```
make
```

This will compile and link the Python files. You can also run a self-test program to ensure everything is completed properly and all files are accounted for by issuing the command

```
make test
```

Finally, complete the installation process by copying the compiled executables and all support files to the proper Linux directories with the command

```
make install
```

Following that, Python is ready to roll. Of course, all these steps are unnecessary if you use the precompiled RPM version of Python.

NOTE

The Python FAQ is posted at regular intervals to the Usenet `comp.lang.python` newsgroup and is available through several FTP and Web sites, including `http://www.python.org`. The FAQ contains up-to-date information about the language and its versions, as well as hints on building the Python executables on many platforms.

Setting Python Environment Variables

You will most likely have to set up several shell environment variables to allow Python to work properly. This doesn't take very long and you don't need to be a Linux guru. Python needs two environment variables, called PATH and PYTHONPATH. The PATH variable already exists for you, set when you log into a shell. If you use the included RPM package to install Python, you won't have to modify the PATH variable at all, as the Python file will be placed in /usr/bin, which is in your path by default.

A quick way of making sure Python is installed in your path is to execute the `python` command

```
python
```

and watch the output. If you get an error message, the PATH environment variable might not be properly set. If Python launches properly, you will see three right-angle brackets. This means the executable is in your search path. You can exit Python with a Ctrl-d. You can confirm your current path with the command

```
echo $PATH
```

which displays your default search path like this:

```
/bin:/usr/bin:$HOME/bin:.
```

If the Python executables are in the /usr/bin directory, this path will find them without a problem. If your path does not have the Python executable location in it, you will need to modify the startup file for your shell (.cshrc, .login, .profile, or .kshrc, depending on the shell). Simply add the executable location to the existing PATH setting, using colons to separate entries. If there is no PATH statement in your startup files, add one, using the existing default path $PATH as one of the directory names.

The PYTHONPATH environment variable needs to be set for each user who will use Python. This path is used to locate files during runtime, and because many of the files are not kept in the default path, you will need to set this variable in your startup files in most cases. The PYTHONPATH variable is usually set to include the current directory, the library location for the Python files (set during installation and usually /usr/lib), and any other directories Python needs, such as Tcl/Tk directories.

Finally, you can create an initialization file for Python to read when it launches (like the shell startup files). The name of the file is given in an environment variable called PYTHONSTARTUP and should be set to the absolute pathname of the startup file. The startup file can contain any valid Python commands you want running.

If you are using Tcl/Tk to integrate GUIs with Python, you will also need to make sure environment variables such as TK_LIBRARY and TCL_LIBRARY are set. Python uses these variables to find the Tcl/Tk files it needs.

Python Command-Line Interpreter

The Python executable can be used as both a line-by-line and a command-line interpreter (just as the Linux shells can be). To use the command-line interpreter, you need to start the Python program, called `python` (lowercase). When you do, you'll see a line of three right angle brackets that represent the Python prompt:

```
$ python
>>>
```

You can exit the python program by using Ctrl-d.

Typing any valid Python command line at the prompt results in carrying out of the action (if there is one):

```
>>> print "Python and Linux are great!"
Python and Linux are great!
```

As you can see, the print command acts like the UNIX echo statement. Double quotation marks help prevent interpretation of the string and should be used with all print statements. Single quotation marks can also be used to enclose a string, but do not use the single back quotes. By default, the print statement sends output to the standard output (usually the screen).

You can use the command-line interpreter as a calculator. If you use variables, they are set automatically to the proper type and can be used later in the program. To generate output from Python, don't use an assignment operator:

```
>>> a = 2
>>> b = 5
>>> a * b
10
>>> bigvar = 37465
>>> smallvar = a / 2
>>> bigvar / smallvar
37465
>>>
```

In the above example, I set variables by using the equals sign. Spaces on either side of the equals sign are ignored, so you can adopt whichever style you want. The statements

```
A = 2
A=2
```

are identical. Case is important to Python, as it is to most UNIX-based languages, so the variables "A" and "a" are different. You can use long variable names to help differentiate variables and their purposes, with mixed case if you want. To display the current value of a variable, type its name at the prompt and any assigned value is shown. If the variable has no value set, an error message is displayed.

Standard mathematical order of precedence applies, so the statement

```
>>> 4 + 8 / 2
```

results in 8 (4 + 4) and not 6 (4 + 8 divided by 2). Division and multiplication are carried out before addition and subtraction.

You can assign numeric and string values to variables and print them both out at the same time, like this:

```
>>> a = "Python"
>>> b = "1"
>>> c = "statements"
>>> print b, a, c
1 Python statements
```

You can also set multiple values at once like this:

```
>>> a = b = c = 19
```

which sets all three variables to 19. You could, of course, do them separately, but setting multiple values often saves time during coding.

NOTE

In Python, the type of a variable is set by the operations performed on it. In any mathematical operation, if any of the variables are floating point, all are converted to floating point automatically.

If you are typing a compound expression, such as an `if` or `for` loop, the command-line interpreter switches the prompt to a set of three dots, allowing you to complete the expression:

```
>>> if b < 10:
...
```

After the three dots, you can complete the compound expression.

To start Python executing a file, supply the name as an argument. If the program needs any arguments, they can be specified on the command line too. For example, the command:

```
python big_prog 12 24 36
```

starts the Python executable running the program `big_prog`, using the three arguments following the program name in the program. You'll see how these arguments are read later in this chapter.

Python supports unlimited precision numbers. By default, numbers are tracked only to a considerable number of significant digits, but appending an `L` to the number switches to unlimited precision mode, as the following example shows:

```
>>> 123456789 * 123456789
```

```
Traceback (innermost last):
  File "<interactive input>", line 0, in ?
OverflowError: integer multiplication
>>> 123456789L * 123456789L
15241578750190521L
>>>
```

The first multiplication overflowed the allowed number of digits and generated an error message. By appending the `L` to the end of the numbers (with no spaces between the number and the `L`) you can impose unlimited precision.

Python Programs

A Python program is a straightforward ASCII file that can be created with any text editor. You can also use any word processor, if it can save files in ASCII format. By convention, Python files end in the extension .py (such as primes.py and sort.py). This filetype convention is not strictly necessary, because Python can open any type of file and execute it, but it does help identify the files.

Each Python script file is called a module. A module is the largest program unit in Python and can be thought of as the main or master file. A module can import other modules. Lines of a Python module can contain comments, statements, and objects.

As with any programming language, Python has a number of statements. The majority of Python statements will be familiar to programmers, such as `if` and `for` loops and the equals sign for assignments. Python does add a few statements for functions and object-oriented tasks, but these are not difficult to learn (especially if you have programmed in other languages). If you do not feel comfortable with these more advanced statements, you have the option to code without them. After all, not all programs are suited to object-oriented approaches.

Python objects are handled by statements and define the types of data being handled. If you have done any OO programming before, you will be familiar with Python's use of objects. For non-object-oriented programmers, objects define simple things such as the type of variable (`string`, `integer`, and so on) as well as other entities such as module and filenames.

If you have never seen a Python module before, you'll be surprised to see how simple it is. Python is similar to the UNIX languages `awk` and Perl in that you don't have to define variable types before assigning them. When you assign a value to a variable, the variable is dynamically created, removing the need for declaration and typing statements at the top of the module and making Python an ideal language for quick-and-dirty programming. It also makes Python programs much shorter and easier to read.

The first line in a Python program usually looks like this:

```
#!/usr/bin/python
```

which tells the shell to use the `python` executable to run the script. The full path might be different on your system, depending on where you installed your Python files. Following this line can come any number of valid Python commands. Python ignores whitespace, so you can use blank lines to separate sections of the program, making your code much more readable.

Python comment lines start with a # sign. You can embed as many comments as you want in your code, because the Python interpreter ignores any line with a pound sign at the beginning. A comment can also be placed anywhere on a line, with everything after the comment symbol ignored by Python:

```
Var1 = 6    # sets Var1
```

At the top of most Python programs, you will see `import` statements. The `import` statement is used to read in another module (similar to an include in C). The most-used module for Python code is called `sys`. The `sys` module contains a set of system-level components. If you don't use any of these components in your code, you don't need to have the following statement at the top of your program, but it also doesn't cause any harm:

```
import sys
```

Control Statements

Like many programming languages, Python has the usual assortment of control statements. The most commonly used statements are the `if` conditional test and the `for` and `while` loops. If you have programmed any other language before, or if you are familiar with shell scripts, you'll find little new about these statements. If you are new to programming, you will probably find the use of these statements a little confusing at first (that's not Python's fault; all languages are like this), but a little practice quickly makes their usage clear.

The `if` Statement

The Python `if` statement syntax uses the condition to be tested on the `if` line, followed by any statements to be executed if the test is true. An `else` can be used to execute statements if the test is negative. The syntax for the Python `if` loop looks like this:

```
if <condition>:
   statements
else:
   statements
```

The `else` section and its following statements are optional. Notice the use of colons at the end of the `if` and `else` lines, indicating to Python that there is a continuation of the section on the next line. There is no termination statement for the `if` statement, such as an `endif` or `fi`.

NOTE

Python tells where the blocks of code to be executed start and end by the statement's indents (when executing a script) or blank lines (when running interactively). This is different from most programming languages that use brackets or some special statement or symbol to terminate each block. The number of spaces or tabs you use to indent statements in a block doesn't matter, as long as you are consistent.

Here's a simple `if` loop:

```
if var1 < 10:
  var2 = 0
  print "the value is less than ten"
else:
  var2 = 1
  print "the value is ten or more"
```

The condition allows all the usual mathematical comparisons (==, !=, > >=, <, <=). Note that you can't use the single equals sign in the `if` loop for a condition test. The single equals sign is used for assignment, not comparison. The double equals sign is used for "exactly equal to."

As with the C programming language, the Python `if` statement doesn't test for actual values but determines a simple true or false. If the condition is true, it has a return code of non-zero, while a false has a return code of zero. The value of the return code dictates whether the statements below the `if` or the `else` are executed. You can show this with a simple Python program, using the command-line interpreter:

```
>>> X = 4
>>> Y = 5
>>> A = X > Y
>>> A
0
```

The zero result shows that the test of X being greater than Y was false, assigning the return value of zero to the variable A.

Python also allows the `elif` (else if) structure in the `if` statement. There can be many nested `elifs`, which might be necessary for multiple branching tests because Python does not offer a switch or case statement. An example of using `elifs` is:

```
if var2 >= 10:
  print "The value is greater than or equal to ten"
elif var2 <= 5:
  print "The value is less than or equal to five"
else:
  print "The value is between five and ten"
```

Python allows a virtually unlimited number of nests in its `if` statements, although your code will start to bog down after too many nests. If you need to nest more than three or four levels deep, you should probably try to find a better way to code the section.

When any section of the `if` statement has been completed as the result of a condition's being true or false, the Python interpreter jumps to the end of the `if` statement. This means the second part of a nested `if` might never be executed. For example, in the program below, when the first test proves true, the first print is executed.

```
x = 6
if x > 5:
  print "X is greater than 5"
elif x > 2:
  print "X is greater than 2"
else:
print "X is less than 2"
```

Even though the second test (where the `elif` is) is also true, it does not get executed, because the Python interpreter jumps to the statements after the end of the `else` section.

The `if` statement can contain Booleans, as you might expect; however, you should write out Booleans in Python instead of using symbols as in C and shell scripts. The Boolean statements are "and", "or", and "not." The following are all legal statements in Python:

```
if a < 5 and b > 6:
if a < b or c > d:
if not a < b:
if a < b or ( a > 5 and b < 10):
```

The use of `not` negates the test, so the third example shown above is the same as testing a >= b. The last example uses parentheses to add another layer of testing, at which Python excels. As long as the conditions and Booleans are used properly, you can construct very long, complex statements in Python that would be almost impossible to construct in a few lines with other programming languages.

If you are reading Python programs written by others, you will often see the `if` condition and statement compressed onto a single line, like this:

```
if x < 5: print "X is less than five"
```

which is perfectly legal. Another common sight in code is comparisons run together, like this:

```
if 3 < X < 5: print "X is four"
```

which is the same as writing:

```
if x > 3 and x < 5: print "X is four"
```

The `for` Loop

The `for` loop is used to perform some iterative process, usually with a defined starting or ending point. The syntax for the `for` loop under Python is:

```
for var in <condition>:
  statements
```

As with the `if` statement, Python knows where the body of the `for` loop is by the indentation. The colon at the end of the `for` statement also indicates a continuation to the interpreter. The var in the above syntax can be any variable name and the condition can be anything that is evaluated to a `true` or `false` statement or a list of values.

A simple `for` loop shows the use of mathematical testing for true or false:

```
y = 1
for x in y < 10:
  print "the value of y is ", y
  y = y + 1
```

When executed, this program counts y from 1 up to 9 and then terminates the loop.

The `for` loop can be used with lists instead of a simple comparison. Because you haven't looked at lists yet, I'll delay showing examples of a list-based `for` until the section "Lists and Ranges."

The `while` Loop

The Python `while` loop is like the `for` loop, continuing to loop as long as some condition is true. The general syntax for the `while` loop is:

```
while <condition>:
  statements
```

As you can guess by now, the block of statements to be executed when the condition is true is indicated by indenting. Here is a simple `while` loop to show its use:

```
a = 0
while a < 10:
  print "a is currently set at ", a
  a = a + 1
print "all done!"
```

The last `print` statement is executed after the `while` loop condition tests false, or even if the `while` loop is not executed at all. This happens because it is not indented to match the rest of the statements in the while block.

NOTE

You can use C-like formatting operations in print functions to produce the results you want, like this:

```
>>> print "The result of %d times %d is %d. %s!" % (2, 3, 2*3,
➥"Yippee")
The result of 2 times 3 is 6. Yippee!
```

The condition is always tested and assigned a return code, and the `while` loop executes as long as the return code is non-zero. You could use this fact to abort the loop when a value hits zero:

```
a = 10
while a:
  print "a is currently set at ", a
  a = a - 1
print "all done!"
```

This starts counting with a set to ten, and because ten is non-zero, the `while` loop is true. When the decrement results in a value of zero for a, the `while` loop stops. This type of syntax might look confusing but is quite common.

Python allows a `break` statement to be used to exit from a `while` statement at any time. Whenever a `break` is encountered, the interpreter immediately assumes the `while` condition is false and carries on execution after the last line of the while block. In the following program:

```
a = 10
while a:
  print "a is currently set at ", a
  a = a - 1
  if a == 4:
     break
print "all done!"
```

the countdown proceeds as you would expect until the value of a is set to four, at which point the `if` condition is true and the break executed. The `all done!` message is printed right after the break is reached, because it is the first statement after the while block. Usually a break is used in an else block as a way of escaping the `while` loop if certain conditions are met. By using the break, we can save a lot of coding in the while condition.

Lists and Ranges

A list is any sequence of zero or more items. You can specify a list in Python by using brackets. A simple list using numbers looks like this:

```
A = [1, 2, 3, 4, 5]
```

This list, called A, has five elements. You can recall the entire list by using the variable name, as this example from the command-line interpreter shows:

```
>>> A = [1, 2, 3, 4, 5]
>>> A
[1, 2, 3, 4, 5]
```

To recall any single element from the list, use the variable name and the subscript of the element number in brackets. Remember that Python is a zero-origin subscripting language, meaning the counting of elements starts at zero:

```
>>> A[2]
3
>>> A[0]
1
```

If you try to access an element that doesn't exist, you usually get an error message from the interpreter.

NOTE

Even though Python performs some bounds checking for elements in a list, you should not expect Python to ensure that your code uses list elements correctly. For example, while Python will reject a reference to A[10] if the list A has only five elements, Python will allow a reference to the same list using A[-4]. We won't discuss the uses of negative list elements here, but you should be careful when using list elements in your code.

You can create lists with strings just as easily, separating each string with a comma and using quotation marks to surround each string:

```
>>> A = ["Python", " powerful", "is", "language", "a"]
>>> A
['Python', ' powerful', 'is', 'language', 'a']
>>> print A[0], A[2], A[4], A[1], A[3]
Python is a  powerful language
```

Lists can be mixed between strings and numeric values just as easily. If you define each element properly, Python lets you manipulate them however you wish:

```
>>> Z = [ 5, "good", "is", 6, "This", 2]
>>> print Z[4], Z[2], Z[1]
This is good
>>> Z[0] + Z[3] / Z[5]
8
```

Note that the order of precedence in the last statement resulted in the value 8 and not 5.5.

The `for` loop is ideal for stepping through a list. In the following code, a list is displayed one element at a time:

```
A = [1, 2, 3, 4, 5, 6, 7, 8, 9, 10]
for x in A:
   print x
```

This program creates a new variable x that holds the value of the indexes in A, one after another. You can do exactly the same with string lists, as the following example typed at the command-line interface shows:

```
>>> A = ["a", "b", "c", "d", "e", "f", "g"]
>>> A
['a', 'b', 'c', 'd', 'e', 'f', 'g']
>>> for x in A:
... print x
...
a
b
c
d
e
f
g
```

To print all the elements one after another on a single line instead of in a column, you need to place a comma after the print statement, like this:

```
... print x,
...
a b c d e f g
```

With a single long string, the same element expansion happens. In the following code, I set the string right at the `for` loop statement:

```
>>> for x in "Python is great":
... print x,
...
P y t h o n   i s   g r e a t
```

A space is placed between each character in the result because that's the way the comma formats output. I could have set the string value before the `for` loop, instead, with exactly the same results.

You can test for the inclusion of a particular value as an element, which yields a return code of zero (false) or non-zero (true). For example, look at the following code:

```
>>> A = [1, 2, 3, 4, 5]
>>> 3 in A
1
>>> 8 in A
0
```

The tests performed cause a search of all the elements to check for a match, and the proper return code is then displayed. This could be handy for some `if` or `for` loops when you need to make sure particular elements exist before continuing processing.

Individual elements in a list can be changed by using the element subscript, as the following example shows:

```
>>> A = [1, 2, 3, 4, 5]
>>> A
[1, 2, 3, 4, 5]
>>> A[3] = 7
>>> A
[1, 2, 3, 7, 5]
```

Ranges, as you would expect, include a set of numbers inclusive of a starting and ending point. With Python, you can set up a range using the "range" keyword followed by two numbers, the lower and upper limits. To display a range from 1 to 10, use the following command:

```
>>> range (1,11)
[1, 2, 3, 4, 5, 6, 7, 8, 9, 10]
```

You might be wondering why you have to specify eleven instead of ten in the range command. Python, like C, stops generating at one less than the upper limit. If you don't specify the lower limit, a list is generated starting at zero:

```
>>> range(10)
[0, 1, 2, 3, 4, 5, 6, 7, 8, 9]
```

This produces ten elements in the list (remember that Python, like C, is a zero-origin language). Upper and lower limits may be positive or negative:

```
>>> range(-10, -5)
[-10, -9, -8, -7, -6]
>>> range(-5,5)
[-5, -4, -3, -2, -1, 0, 1, 2, 3, 4]
>>> range(-5, -10)
[]
```

Notice the last range in the code above. It's perfectly legal to specify a lower limit higher than the upper limit (although it is a little silly). The result is a list with no elements. You can use ranges anywhere in a valid Python program, and they can be assigned to variables or used as part of a command structure:

```
for x in range(5,15):
print x,
5 6 7 8 9 10 11 12 13 14
```

This brings us to the slightly more complicated issue of *tuples*. A tuple is a Python data structure that works like a list but is more efficiently stored and managed. A tuple's elements cannot be moved around and extracted with the same ease as a list's elements. Despite the name, a tuple does not have to have three elements.

The difference between lists and tuples, at least as far as Python's interpreter is concerned, is that a list is a variable-sized array of elements that might need to grow in size. A tuple has a fixed size and doesn't change, and hence is more efficiently stored and managed by the interpreter. A tuple's element values can't be changed without redefining the entire tuple, but a list's elements can be easily changed. This leads to the use of tuples for defining invariant constants in Python, much as the #define statement does in C.

To define a tuple, you set it up much the same as a list, but with parentheses instead of brackets. Python isn't all that fussy about the parentheses as long as there is no ambiguity. Still, it is advisable to always use parentheses when defining a tuple as it helps make clear in your mind that you are working with a tuple. Examples of defining tuples and displaying their values at the command-line interpreter are:

```
>>> a = (1,2,3,4)
>>> a
(1, 2, 3, 4)
>>> a = ("This", "is", "a", "tuple", "of", "strings")
>>> a
('This', 'is', 'a', 'tuple', 'of', 'strings')
```

As the second example shows, you can make a tuple of strings as well as numbers.

Why bother with tuples? They are useful when you want to use either the full tuple value or specific elements out of a tuple as a complete set of information. Each element in a tuple can be assigned to a specific variable, as long as the number of variables matches the number of elements in the tuple:

```
>>> w, x, y, z = (1, 2, 3, 4)
>>> w
1
>>> y
3
>>> x, y
(2, 3)
>>> x, y, z
(2, 3, 4)
```

In a couple of situations, the characteristics of tuples can be especially handy. Consider a case where you need to switch the values of two variables. Suppose you have variables `var1` and `var2`, and you need to move the values of each to the other variable. Normally you would have to do this with a placeholder variable, like this:

```
>>> temp = var1
>>> var1 = var2
>>> var2 = temp
```

With tuples, you can do the swap on a single line:

```
>>> var1, var2 = (var2, var1)
```

As mentioned earlier, you will often see tuples that are written without the parentheses, so the example might look like this in some existing code:

```
>>> var1, var2 = var2, var1
```

The real trick with this kind of shortcut is to remember you are dealing with tuples and not lists.

To convert between lists and tuples, you need to do a little coding that assembles each structure from the other. Often, the easier way is to simply redefine the variable as either a list or a tuple instead of performing a conversion in your program code.

Dictionaries

Python is a high-level language and, as such, has some special data types designed to take advantage of some aspect of the language's features. One of these special data types is the dictionary. Dictionaries are associative arrays. In plainer English, it means data is referred to by a key, similar to a variable. Dictionaries can be thought of as similar to C's pointers. To Python, a dictionary is a simple hash table that can grow at any time.

To create a dictionary, you need to specify both a key and the value to which that key refers. These "key:value" pairs (in Python-speak) are enclosed in braces, with the key and value separated by a colon. Python allows almost any kind of data to be used as a key or a value. Any number of key:value pairs can be in a dictionary. An example of setting up a dictionary is a good place to start. This code creates a dictionary called "a" that uses the key "python" to refer to a value "language" (two strings for key and value in this case):

```
a = {"python": "language"}
```

Brackets are used to refer to the value, either in whole or in part. Using the above definition, you can recall the whole value with this command-line sequence:

```
>>> a = {"python": "language"}
>>> a
{'python': 'language'}
>>> a["python"]
'language'
```

As you can see, referring to the element "python" in the dictionary "a" brings up the value assigned to "python," which is "language." So far this is rather unexciting and it is hard to see why you would want to use dictionaries. The advantage of dictionaries comes when you start using multiple values. Here's an example of a dictionary set up to hold different error messages, keyed by a number:

```
>>> x = {1: "bad file", 2: "server crash", 3: "too many variables"}
>>> x[2]
'server crash'
>>> x[3]
'too many variables'
>>> x[1]
'bad file'
```

Note that when defining multiple key-value pairs, they are separated in the braces by commas. This lets you set the message definitions high up in the Python code, in a single dictionary, and then recall the relevant messages by using an element subscript later in the code when errors occur.

You can use dictionaries in `for` loops to call up multiple element values, as the following code extract shows:

```
>>> y = {1: "This", 2: "is", 3: "really", 4: "handy"}
>>> for a in range(1,5):
... print y[a],
...
This is really handy
```

Still not convinced of the value of dictionaries? It is hard to see how you would want to use them when you are writing only simple scripting code, but as you become more proficient in Python you will start to realize the utility of these data types. It's much like the C language's pointer; you can always code programs without using pointers, but you will reach a level of coding at which using pointers makes programs much more flexible and more efficient.

Functions and Modules

Like many high-level languages, Python uses functions to break large programs into smaller functional blocks. The use of functions also leads directly to code reuse, allowing you to write functions for specific tasks that can be incorporated with little or no change into any future programs you write. To define a function is straightforward. Here's an example of a simple function with a single input:

```
def simplefunction(name):
   print name
```

The keyword `def` identified the code as a function to Python, followed by the name of the function and the variable names to be assigned to any incoming data (in this case, a single object). Indenting indicates the body of the function.

When called, the function executes, using whatever data object is passed, as the following command-line interpreter output shows:

```
>>> def simplefunction(name):
...print name
...
>>> simplefunction("Python")
Python
>>> simplefunction("This is a string")
This is a string
>>> simplefunction(5)
5
```

You can use local variables in a function, as you can with most other languages. A local variable is valid only inside the function and has no meaning when tried outside that function. Here's a function that computes the average of any numbers passed to it:

```
def average(array):
  numvars = 0
  total = 0
  for a in array:
    numvars = numvars + 1
    total = total + a
  print "There are ", numvars, " numbers"
```

```
  print "The total is ", total
  print "The average is ", total/numvars
```

The variables `numvars` and `total` are valid only inside the function average. When this function is called, the following output is generated:

```
>>> average([1, 2, 3, 4, 5])
There are 5 numbers
The total is 15
The average is 3
```

If you want to pass a result back to the calling function (which will often be the case), the `return` statement is used. The following modification of the `average` function returns a numeric average value because of the `return` statement:

```
def average(array):
  numvars = 0
  total = 0
  for a in array:
    numvars = numvars + 1
    total = total + a
  return total/numvars
```

Modules, as we mentioned at the beginning of this chapter, are files or scripts of Python code, usually ending with .py. Again, modules are designed to allow code reuse, so you can write self-contained modules that can be dropped into future applications. Modules are written with any ASCII editor and are called from another module with the `import` statement. The main module in Python (and the module into which all your command-line interpreter statements are entered) is called __main__.

To show how modules work, put the `average` function demonstrated above into a module called average.py. This is saved to disk and must be in the search path of the Python interpreter, defined by the environment variable PYTHONPATH. To use the average.py file in either the command-line interpreter or another module, embed the line:

```
import average
```

near the top of the file (or at least before you call the module). After the import, you can call any function inside the module as though it were in your current module. This is the same as C's `#include` statements.

If several functions are defined in a module and you need to call a specific function, you do so by using the module name and the function name separated by a period. For example, if you have a file called mymath.py that includes functions called `average`, `mean`, and `deviation`, you would call each from another module (after the `import` statement) as `mymath.average`, `mymath.mean`, and `mymath.deviation`. This prevents conflicts with function names that are identical in different modules.

Classes

Python is an object-oriented language and, as such, has features such as classes. If you are not familiar with OO programming, this might all seem confusing and you can skip the use of classes without reducing the utility of Python one bit. However, classes do add OO capabilities to Python that, when properly used, extend the language considerably. Python treats classes much as C++ does. To define a class, you use a modification of the function syntax, defining the class that holds the functions:

```
>>> class myclass:
... def printout(self, string):
...   print string
...
>>> my = myclass()
>>> my.printout("This is a string")
This is a string
```

The first line defines a class called `myclass`. The `myclass` class contains a single function, called `printout`. In OO terms, `myclass` is the class and `printout` is the method. After the function is defined and the command-line interpreter reappears, an instance of `myclass` called `my` is created. Using the class and function format seen for modules and functions, you invoke the `printout` function in the `my` class. In OO terms again, the class name becomes the constructor of the class, which can be used to create any number of instances of that class.

You might wonder why the function definition has two imported variables, `self` and `string`. The variable `string` is whatever is being passed in to the function. The `self` keyword is required for classes because when an instance's method is called, the instance passes itself as the first argument. The use of the word "self" takes care of this method pass. If you were calling a function that had no input, you would have only the single self name in the function definition (the word self is used by convention, but it could be anything):

```
class yourclass:
def printit(self):
   print "This is a function string!"
```

Classes can inherit other classes, allowing overrides and extensions of existing functions. Producing that type of code gets much more complicated and is beyond the scope of an overview chapter like this.

Summary

In this chapter, you've seen the primary programming features of the Python language. When taken in small doses, the language is quite easy to learn and you will soon find yourself gaining confidence, even if you have never programmed before. Python includes a lot more than we have covered here—indeed, we've only scratched the surface. For more information about Python's more advanced features, look for programming guidelines in the Python distributions, on the `http://www.python.org` Web site, or in a dedicated Python book.

Appendixes

PART VI

IN THIS PART

The Linux Documentation Project

by David Pitts

In This Appendix

This appendix describes the goals and current status of the Linux Documentation Project, including the names of projects, volunteers, FTP sites, and so on.

Overview

The Linux Documentation Project (LDP) is working on developing reliable docs for the Linux operating system. The overall goal of the LDP is to collaborate in taking care of all of the issues of Linux documentation, ranging from online docs (man pages, `texinfo` docs, and so on) to printed manuals covering topics such as installing, using, and running Linux. The LDP is essentially a loose team of volunteers with no central organization; anyone who is interested in helping is welcome to join in the effort. We feel that working together and agreeing on the direction and scope of Linux documentation is the best way to reduce problems with conflicting efforts. Two people writing two books on the same aspect of Linux wastes someone's time along the way.

The LDP has set out to produce the canonical set of Linux online and printed documentation. Because our docs will be freely available (according to the GNU GPL) and distributed on the Net, we are able to easily update the documentation to stay on top of the many changes in the Linux world. We're also talking with a few companies about possibly publishing the LDP manuals after more of them become available. (A few smaller companies are printing and distributing LDP manuals even now.) If you're interested in publishing any of the LDP manuals, see the section "Publishing LDP Manuals" in Appendix C, "The Linux Documentation Project Copyright License."

Getting Involved

To get involved with the LDP, join the linux-doc activists mailing list. Send mail to `majordomo@vger.rutgers.edu` with the line `subscribe linux-doc` in the message body (not the subject).

Of course, you'll also need to get in touch with the coordinator of whatever LDP projects you're interested in working on.

Current Projects

For a list of current projects, visit the LDP home page at `http://sunsite.unc.edu/LDP/`. The best way to get involved with one of these projects is to pick up the current version of the manual and send revisions, additions, or suggestions to the coordinator.

Glossary and Global Index

The LDP plans to write a glossary of terms and an index for the entire set of LDP manuals. This comprehensive document should serve as a reference. FTP sites for LDP works are listed at `sunsite.unc.edu` in the directory `/pub/Linux/docs`. LDP manuals appear in `/pub/Linux/docs/LDP`, and how-tos and other documentation appear in `/pub/Linux/docs/HOWTO`.

Documentation Conventions

This section outlines the conventions that are currently used by LDP manuals. If you are interested in writing another manual using different conventions, please notify us of your plans first. We'd like the LDP manuals to have a common look and feel, which is implemented with a LaTeX style file.

The set of printed manuals (that is, everything but the man pages) is formatted using LaTeX. The primary objective is to have printed, not online, manuals. You can use the LaTeX tool (currently under development by Olaf Kirch) to generate plain ASCII (and later, `texinfo`) from the LaTeX source.

Don't suggest that we shouldn't use LaTeX for the LDP manuals; more than 500 pages of material are already written in LaTeX, and we're not about to convert. Many a flame war has been sparked over this issue, but it's a done deal. You don't have to write new manuals using LaTeX, but you should use the same conventions and design we have implemented with the current manuals.

The printed manuals should use Michael K. Johnson's `linuxdoc.sty` style sheet and documentation conventions, which appear in the file `linuxdoc.tar.z` in the `alpha` directory. We want to achieve a unified look in the manuals for the sake of both consistency and portability so that all of the authors and editors are on common ground, using the same style sheet. We can easily change the look and feel of all of the manuals by changing `linuxdoc.sty`.

The LDP license/copyright should be used to copyright all works. It's a liberal copyleft that resembles the GPL but applies to printed documents and protects the LDP manuals from publication without our permission. The license is printed in Appendix C.

The copyright for each manual should be in the name of the head writer or coordinator for the project. The Linux Documentation Project isn't a formal entity and shouldn't be used to copyright the docs.

Important Linux Commands and Shell Operators

by Bill Ball

In This Appendix

This appendix is not meant to replace the man pages and does not detail all of the options for each command. You'll find most of the information you need in the man pages for these programs or, in the case of a shell operator such as > or <, in the man pages for the shell commands. This appendix is designed to give you a feel for the commands and a brief description of what they do. In most cases, more parameters are available than are shown here.

Many descriptions also have examples. If these examples aren't self-evident, an explanation is provided. This is not an exhaustive list—Red Hat Linux comes with many more commands—but these are the most common, and you will find yourself using them over and over again.

To keep things simple, the commands are listed in alphabetical order; however, I do want to summarize by listing what are, at least for me, the ten most common commands—also alphabetically. This list of essential commands could be compared to a list of the top ten words spoken by the cavemen when searching for food and a mate:

1. `cat`
2. `cd`
3. `cp`
4. `find`
5. `grep`
6. `ls`
7. `more`
8. `rm`
9. `vi`
10. `who`

General Guidelines

Many of the programs distributed with Red Hat Linux descended from counterparts in the UNIX world and have inherited the terse, sometimes cryptic naming style. In general, if you want to change something that already exists, the command to do that usually begins with `ch`. If you want to do something for the first time, the command to do that usually begins with `mk`. If you want to undo something completely, the command usually begins with `rm`. For example, to make a new directory, you use the `mkdir` command, and to remove a directory, you use the `rmdir` command.

The List

The commands listed in this appendix are some of the most common commands used in Red Hat Linux. In cases where the command seems ambiguous, an example is provided. With each of these commands, the man pages can provide additional information, as well as more examples.

.

The . shell command tells the shell to execute all of the commands in the file that are passed an argument. This works in bash or pdksh. The equivalent in tcsh is the source command. The following example executes the command adobe:

```
. adobe
```

&

The & shell operator after any other command tells the computer to run the command in the background. By placing a job in the background, the user can then continue using that shell to process other commands. If the command is run in the foreground, the user cannot continue using that shell until the process finishes.

¦

The ¦ (pipe) shell operator is used between separate programs on the command line to "pipe" the output of one command to another. This type of operation is one of the principal strengths of Linux and the shell and can be used to construct complex commands from a series of simple programs. For example, to sort the contents of a file, you can pipe the output of the cat command through the sort command like this:

```
# cat long_list.txt ¦ sort
```

>

The > (standard output) shell operator is used to send the output of a program to a file or other device. Use this operator with caution, as it will overwrite an existing file! To save a listing of the current directory to a text file, use the > operator like this:

```
# ls > dir.txt
```

Note that if the file dir.txt exists, it will be erased and overwritten with the new contents! Also, because Linux works much like other versions of UNIX, you can also send the contents of programs directly to a device, like this:

```
# cat welcome.au >/dev/audio
```

which plays a sound file by sending it directly to a Linux audio device.

<

The < (standard input) shell operator is used to feed a program the contents of a file or input from another device or source. For example, you can use this operator like the `cat` command to sort a file and save the results:

```
# sort < unsorted.txt > sorted.txt
```

>>

The >> (append) shell operator will not replace a designated file, but appends the output of a program onto the end of a specified file. This can be used, for example, to build log files:

```
# cat newfile.txt >> oldfile.txt
```

The contents of newfile.txt will not overwrite oldfile.txt, but will append to the end of it.

<<

The << (here) shell operator is used to tell a program when end-of-input is reached. For example, to use the shell as a text editor, tell the shell to stop accepting input when the word "end" is used like this:

```
# > document.txt << end
This is a line of text.
end
```

After you type the word end, the shell saves your text into the file document text, because you've told the shell that the word end terminates input.

adduser

The `adduser` command is used by root (or someone else who has the authority) to create a new user. The `adduser` command is followed by the account name to be created; for example,

```
# adduser dpitts
```

alias

The `alias` command is used to make aliases or alternative names for commands.

Typically, these aliases are abbreviations of the actual commands. In the following example, the user (probably a DOS user) is adding an alias of `dir` for a directory listing:

```
alias dir=ls
```

Typing `alias` by itself gives you a list of all of your current aliases. Such a list might look like this:

```
svr01:/home/dpitts$ alias
alias d='dir'
alias dir='/bin/ls $LS_OPTIONS --format=vertical'
alias ls='/bin/ls $LS_OPTIONS'
alias v='vdir'
alias vdir='/bin/ls $LS_OPTIONS --format=long'
```


apropos *<parameter>*

The `apropos` command literally means appropriate or regarding (others). When followed by a parameter, `apropos` searches the man pages for entries that include the parameter, performing a keyword search on all of the man pages. This is the equivalent of the `man -k` *<parameter>* command.

ash

`ash` is a simple shell with features much like the `sh`, or Bourne shell. The `ash` shell is run by the symbolic link `bsh`, found under the /bin directory.

at

`at` runs a program at a specified time. You can use the `at` command to schedule a task or job to run at a time you specify on the command line or in a file.

atq

Use `atq` to list the queue of waiting jobs. The `atq` command prints a list of waiting jobs or events for the `at` command (usually found under the /var/spool/at directory).

atrm

Use `atrm` to remove a specified job. The `atrm` command removes one or several jobs waiting in the `at` queue. The `atrm` command can be used by users or the root operator to delete pending events (stop `at` commands from running).

banner

banner prints a large, high-quality banner to the standard output. If the message is omitted, banner prompts for and reads one line from the standard input. For example, enter $ banner hi to create the following banner:

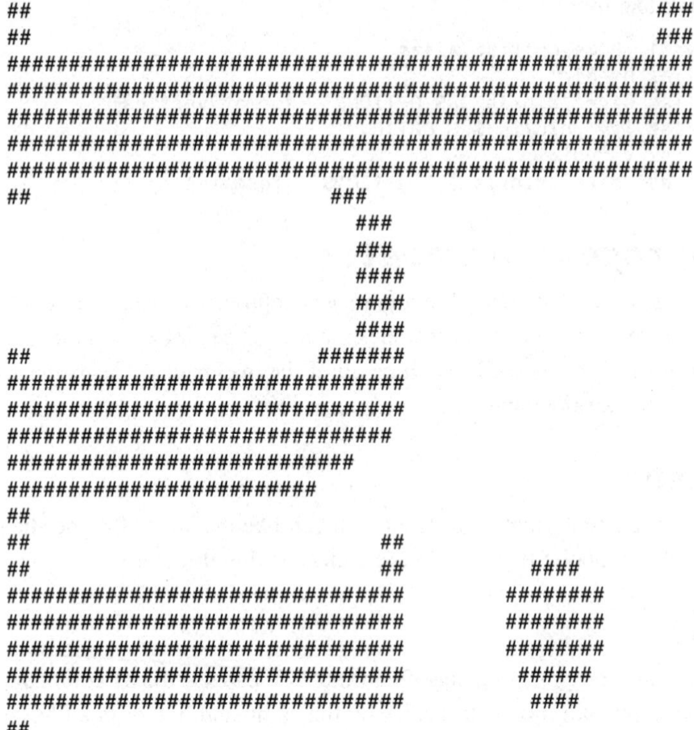

bash

bash is the GNU Bourne Again Shell. The default shell for Red Hat Linux, bash has many features, such as command-line editing, built-in help, and command history. The bash shell is run by the symbolic link sh, found under the /bin directory.

batch

The batch command runs jobs according to load average. This program is used to run events when the computer reaches a certain load average, as determined by real-time values found in the loadavg file in the /proc directory. batch also has other options; read the at command manual pages for details.

bc

A calculator language, `bc` is an interpreter and language for building calculator programs and tools. You can use this interpreter and language to program custom calculators.

bg

The `bg` command is used to force a suspended process to run in the background. For example, say you have started a command in the foreground (without using the `&` after the command) and realize it is going to take a while, but you still need your shell. You can use Ctrl+Z to place the current process on hold. Then you can either leave it on hold—just as if you called your telephone company—or you can type **bg** to place that process in the background and free up your shell to allow you to execute other commands.

bind

Used in `pdksh`, the `bind` command enables the user to change the behavior of key combinations for the purpose of command-line editing. Many times people bind the up, down, left, and right arrow keys so they work the way they would in the Bourne Again Shell (`bsh`). The syntax used for the command is

```
bind <key sequence> <command>
```

The following examples are the `bind` commands to create bindings for scrolling up and down the history list and for moving left and right along the command line:

```
bind `^[[`=prefix-2
bind `^XA`=up-history
bind `^XB`=down-history
bind `^XC`=forward-char
bind `^XD`=backward-char
```

cat

`cat` does not call your favorite feline; instead, it tells the contents of (typically) the file to scroll its contents across the screen. If that file happens to be binary, the cat gets a hairball and shows it to you on the screen. Typically, this is a noisy process as well. What is actually happening is that the `cat` command is scrolling the characters of the file, and the terminal is doing all it can to interpret and display the data in the file. This interpretation can include the character used to create the bell signal, which is where the noise comes from. As you might have surmised, the `cat` command requires something to display and has the following format:

```
cat <filename>
```

cd

cd stands for "change directory." You will find this command extremely useful. The three typical ways of using this command are

`cd ..`	Moves one directory up the directory tree.
`cd ~`	Moves to your home directory from wherever you currently are. This is the same as issuing cd by itself.
`cd` *directory name*	Changes to a specific directory. This can be a directory relative to your current location or can be based on the root directory by placing a forward slash (/) before the directory name.

These examples can be combined. For example, suppose you are in the directory /home/dsp1234 and you wish to go to tng4321's home account. You can perform the following command to move back up the directory one level and then down into the tng4321 directory:

```
cd ../tng4321
```

chfn

The chfn command changes finger information. You can use this command to enter or update information used by the finger networking tool from the /etc/passwd entry for your Linux system. You can enter full names, offices, and office and home phone numbers. Follow chfn with a user's name, like this:

```
# chfn willie
```

chgrp

The chgrp command is used to change the group associated with the permissions of the file or directory. The owner of the file (and, of course, root) has the authority to change the group associated with the file. The format for the command is simply

```
chgrp <new group> <file>
```

chmod

The chmod command is used to change the permissions associated with the object (typically a file or directory). What you are really doing is changing the file mode. You can specify the permissions of the object in two ways: by the numeric coding system or the letter coding system. If you recall, three sets of users are associated with every object: the owner of the object, the group for the object, and everybody else. Using the letter coding system, they are referred to as u for user, g for group, o for other, and a for all.

The three basic types of permissions you can change are `r` for read, `w` for write, and `x` for execute. These three permissions can be changed by using the plus (+) and minus (-) signs. For example, to add read and execute to owner and group of the file `test1`, you would issue the following command:

```
chmod ug+rx test1
```

To remove the read and execute permissions from the user and group of the `test1` file, you would change the plus (+) sign to a minus (-) sign:

```
chmod ug-rx test1
```

This is called making relative changes to the mode of the file.

When using the numeric coding system, you always have to give the absolute value of the permissions, regardless of their previous permissions. The numeric system is based on three sets of base 2 numbers—one set for each category of user, group, and other. The values are `4`, `2`, and `1`, where `4` equals *read*, `2` equals *write*, and `1` equals *execute*. These values are added together to give the set of permissions for that category. With numeric coding, you always specify all three categories. Therefore, to give read, write, and execute permissions to the owner of the file test1, and no permissions to anyone else, you would use the value `700`, like this:

```
chmod 700 test1
```

To make the same file readable and writable by the user, and readable by both the group and others, you would use the following mathematical logic. For the first set of permissions—the user—the value for readable is `4` and the value for writable is `2`. The sum of these two is `6`. The next set of permissions—the group—only gets readable, so that is `4`. The setting for others, as for the group, is `4`. Therefore, the command would be

```
chmod 644 test1
```

The format for the command, using either method, is the same. You issue the `chmod` command followed by the permissions, either absolute or relative, followed by the objects for which you want the mode changed:

```
chmod <permissions> <file>
```

chown

This command is used to change the user ID (owner) associated with the permissions of the file or directory. The owner of the file (and, of course, root) has the authority to change the user associated with the file. The format for the command is simply

```
chown <new user id> <file>
```

chroot

The `chroot` command makes the `/` directory (called the root directory) be something other than `/` on the filesystem. For example, when working with an Internet server, you can set the root directory to equal /usr/ftp. Then, anyone who logs on using FTP (which goes to the root directory by default) will actually go to the directory /usr/ftp. This protects the rest of your directory structure from being seen or even changed by this anonymous guest to your machine. If someone were to enter `cd /etc`, the `ftp` program would try to put her in the root directory and then in the etc directory off of that. Because the root directory is /usr/ftp, the `ftp` program will actually put the user in the /usr/ftp/etc directory (assuming there is one).

The syntax for the command is

```
chroot <original filesystem location> <new filesystem location>
```

chsh

You can use this program to change the type of shell you use when you log in to your Linux system. The shell must be available on the system and must be allowed by the root operator by having its name listed in the /etc/shells file. Type the name of a shell, following the `chsh` command, like this:

```
# chsh zsh
```

control-panel

The `control-panel` command is one of several Red Hat Linux system administration tools. This command is an X11 client (actually a Python language script) used to display several system administration tools, such as `timetool`, `netcfg`, or `modemtool`.

cp

The `cp` command, an abbreviation for copy, enables you to copy objects. For example, to copy the file `file1` to `file2`, issue the following command:

```
cp file1 file2
```

As the example shows, the syntax is very simple:

```
cp <original object name> <new object name>
```

cpio

The `cpio` command copies files in and out of file archives. `cpio` works much like the `tar` (tape archive) command, but with a slightly different syntax. Many Red Hat Linux users are more familiar with the `tar` command.

crond

This is the `cron` daemon. This program, started when you first boot Linux, scans the /etc/crontab file and the /var/spool/cron directory, looking for regularly scheduled jobs entered by the root operator or other system users. It is started when you first boot Linux.

crontab

The `crontab` command, not to be confused with the /etc/crontab file, is used by your system's users to schedule personal cron events. The cron files are stored under the /var/spool/cron directory. System administrators can control whether or not this facility exists on the system through the /etc/cron.allow and /etc/cron.deny files. All current jobs are listed when the `crontab` command is used with the `-l` option. Use the `-e` option to create or edit a job, and the `-r` option to delete a job.

cu

`cu` is a communications program used to call up other computers. This program is text-based and is not as user-friendly as the `minicom` or `seyon` communications programs for Linux.

cut

This program cuts specified columns or fields from input text. The `cut` command, a text filter, can be used to manipulate the output of other text utilities or contents of your files by selectively displaying fields of text.

dc

`dc` is a command-line desk calculator. This calculator, which does not have a graphical interface, uses reverse-polish notation to perform calculations entered from the command line or a file.

dd

The `dd` command converts file formats. For example, to copy a boot image to a disk (assuming the device name for the disk is `/dev/fd0`), you issue the command

```
dd if=<filename> of-/dev/fd0 obs=18k
```

where *filename* might be `BOOT0001.img`, `of` is the object format (what you are copying to), and `obs` is the output block size.

df

Use the `df` *command* to show the amount of free disk space on any currently mounted filesystem. This information is useful in determining whether you have available storage for programs or data.

dir

`dir` lists the contents of directories. This command has many of the same command-line options as the `ls` command.

display

This program requires X11 and is part of the ImageMagick package. This is a menu-driven application you can use to create, edit, change, print, and save graphics during your X11 session. ImageMagick is typically started in the background from the command line of a terminal window like this:

```
# display &
```

dmesg

The `dmesg` command prints a system boot log, dmesg, found in the /var/log directory. This program is handy to diagnose system problems, listing software services and hardware devices found while your system is starting.

du

The `du` command shows how much disk space is used by various files or directories, and can show where the most or least disk space is used on your system.

dump

The `dump` command, usually used by the root operator, creates a backup of either the whole filesystem or selected directories. The companion program to the `dump` command is the `restore` command, which extracts files and directories from a dump backup.

echo

`echo` echoes a string to the display. The `echo` command is generally used to print lines of text to your display console or—through redirection—to files, devices, programs, or the standard output of your shell. The `-e` option lets you use certain control characters in your output string.

ed

`ed` is a bare-bones line editor.

edquota

The `edquota` program, meant to be used by the root operator, is used to change the amount of disk space a user can use. It is used in conjunction with the `quota`, `quotaon`, or `quotaoff` commands.

efax

This is a communications program for sending and receiving faxes under Linux. This command is part of the efax software package and does the actual sending and receiving when called by the shell script `fax`.

efix

`efix` is used to convert files between text and fax graphics formats. The `efix` program is called by the shell script `fax` to convert sent or received fax documents.

elm

`elm` is a mail-handling program you can use to create, compose, edit, and send mail. You can organize your mail into different folders and also organize how your want your incoming mail to be filed. This program is similar to the Pine mail program.

emacs

`emacs` (edit macros) is the GNU text editor. It can be used not only to edit text files but also as a calendar, diary, and appointment scheduler (and much more). `emacs` is also a complete environment to support programming and electronic mail.

emacs-nox

`emacs-nox` is the non-X11 version of the `emacs` editor.

env

The env command is used to see exported environment variables. The result of the command is a two-column list in which the variable's name is on the left and the value associated with that variable is on the right. The command is issued without any parameters. Hence, typing **env** might get you a list similar to this one:

```
svr01:/home/dpitts$ env
HOSTNAME=svr01.mk.net
LOGNAME=dpitts
MAIL=/var/spool/mail/dpitts
TERM=vt100
HOSTTYPE=i386
PATH=/usr/local/bin:/usr/bin:/bin:.:/usr/local/java/bin
HOME=/home2/dpitts
SHELL=/bin/bash
LS_OPTIONS=--8bit --color=tty -F -b -T 0
PS1=\h:\w\$
PS2=>
MANPATH=/usr/local/man:/usr/man/preformat:/usr/man:/usr/lib/perl5/man
LESS=-MM
OSTYPE=Linux
SHLVL=1
```

ex

ex is a symbolic link to the vim editor. In this mode, the vim editor emulates the ex line editor.

fax

Use fax to create, transmit, receive, display, or print a fax. This complex shell script is the driver program for the efax software package and provides an easy-to-use way to send or receive fax documents under Linux.

faxq

Use faxq to list faxes in the fax sending queue. This program is part of the mgetty+sendfax software package for allowing Linux logins and fax transmission and reception.

faxrm

Use faxrm to delete faxes in the sending queue. You can use this program, part of mgetty+sendfax, to delete faxes waiting to be sent.

faxrunq

`faxrunq` sends spooled faxes from the fax queue. This program, run by the root operator or process, sends faxes waiting in the fax queue, usually the /var/spool/fax directory.

faxspool

`faxspool` prepares and sends fax documents to the fax queue. This shell script is a driver program for the mgetty+sendfax program and recognizes nine different file formats when converting and sending documents.

fc

The `fc` command is used to edit the history file. The parameters passed to it, if there are any, can be used to select a range of commands from the history file. This list is then placed in an editing shell. Which editor `fc` uses is based on the value of the variable `FCEDIT`. If no value is present for this variable, the command looks at the `EDITOR` variable. If it is not there, the default is used, which is `vi`.

fdformat

This command only performs a low-level format of a floppy disk. You must then use the `mkfs` command to place a specified filesystem on the disk.

fetchmail

This program gets your mail from your Internet Service Provider, or ISP, and can handle a number of electronic mail protocols besides the Post Office Protocol, or POP. You use this program by itself or in a shell script to get your mail after you've established a Point-to-Point, or PPP connection.

fg

Processes can be run in either the background or the foreground. The `fg` command enables you to take a suspended process and run it in the foreground. This is typically used when you have a process running in the foreground and need to suspend it for some reason (thus allowing you to run other commands). The process will continue until you either place it in the background or bring it to the foreground.

file

The `file` command checks each argument passed to it for one of three things: the filesystem test, the magic number test, or the language test. The first test to succeed causes the file type to be printed. If the file is text (an ASCII file), it then attempts to guess which language. The following example identifies the file nquota as a text file that contains Perl commands. A magic number file is a file that has data in particular fixed formats. Here is an example for checking the file nquota to see what kind of file it is:

```
file nquota
nquota: perl commands text
```

find

Did you ever say to yourself, "Self, where did I put that file?" Well now, instead of talking to yourself and causing those near by to wonder about you, you can ask the computer. You can say, "Computer, where did I put that file?" Okay, it is not that simple, but it is close. All you have to do is ask the computer to find the file.

The find command looks in whatever directory you tell it, as well as all subdirectories under that directory, for the file you specify. After it finds this list, it follows your instructions about what to do with the list. Typically, you just want to know where it is, so you ask it nicely to print out the list. The syntax of the command is the command itself, followed by the directory you want to start searching in, followed by the filename (metacharacters are acceptable), and then what you want done with the list. In the following example, the find command searches for files ending with .pl in the current directory (and all subdirectories). It then prints the results to standard output.

```
find . -name *.pl -print
./public_html/scripts/gant.pl
./public_html/scripts/edit_gant.pl
./public_html/scripts/httools.pl
./public_html/scripts/chart.no.comments.pl
```

finger

Use the finger command to look up user information (usually found in the /etc/passwd file) on your computer or other computer systems.

fmt

The fmt program formats input text into page and line sizes you specify on the command line.

free

The free commands shows how memory is being used on your system.

ftp

This is the File Transfer Protocol program. You can use the `ftp` command to send and receive files interactively from your computer's hard drive or other remote computer systems. The `ftp` command features built-in help. To see the latest offerings from Macmillan Publishing, try:

```
# ftp ftp.mcp.com
```

glint

This X11 client can be called from the command line or the control panel and uses the `rpm` command, or Red Hat package manager, to control the software installed on your system. `glint` presents a graphical interface for software installation, maintenance, or removal. It is usually started in the background, like this:

```
# glint &
```

gnuplot

The `gnuplot` program, which can generate graphic displays of mathematical formulas or other data under the X Window System, supports a variety of displays and printers. You can use this program to see equations and other data.

grep

The `grep` (global regular expression parse) command searches the object you specify for the text you specify. The syntax of the command is `grep <text> <file>`. In the following example, I am searching for instances of the text `httools` in all files in the current directory:

```
grep httools *
edit_gant.cgi:require 'httools.pl';
edit_gant.pl:require 'httools.pl';
gant.cgi:   require 'httools.pl';  # Library containing reusable code
gant.cgi:       &date;      # Calls the todays date subroutine from
httools.pl
gant.cgi:        &date;   #  Calls the todays date subroutine from
httools.pl
gant.cgi:   &header;  # from httools.pl
```

Although this is valuable, the `grep` command can also be used in conjunction with the results of other commands. For example, the following command

```
ps -ef ¦grep -v root
```

IMPORTANT LINUX COMMANDS AND SHELL OPERATORS

calls for the `grep` command to take the output of the `ps` command and take out all instances of the word "root" (the `-v` means everything but the text that follows). The same command without the `-v` (`ps -ef |grep root`) returns all instances that contain the word "root" from the process listing.

groff

`groff` is the front end to the `groff` document-formatting program. This program, by default, calls the `troff` program.

gs

This is the Ghostscript interpreter. This program can interpret and prepare PostScript documents and print on more than three dozen displays and printers.

gunzip

Use this program to decompress files compressed with the `gzip` command back to their original form.

gv

A PostScript and PDF document previewer, this X11 client previews and prints PostScript and portable document files and is handy for reading documentation or previewing graphics or documents before printing. Start the `gv` client by itself in the background, or specify a file on the command line like this:

```
# gv myPostScriptdoc.ps &
```

gvim

This program is a graphical version of the `vim` editor and is used under the X Window System.

gzip

`gzip` is GNU's version of the zip compression software. The syntax can be as simple as

```
gzip <filename>
```

but many times also contains some parameters between the command and the filename to be compressed.

halt

The halt command tells the kernel to shut down. This is a superuser-only command (you must "be root").

head

The head command is a text filter, similar to the tail command, but prints only the number of lines you specify from the beginnings of files.

hostname

hostname is used to either display the current host or domain name of the system or to set the hostname of the system—for example,

```
svr01:/home/dpitts$ hostname
svr01
```

ical

This is an X11 calendar program. The ical client can be used to create and maintain personal or group calendars and to schedule alarms or reminders of important dates or appointments. The calendar files can be printed, along with custom versions of multiday calendars.

ifconfig

This is one of several programs you can use to configure network interfaces. Although usually used by the root operator, the ifconfig command can be handy to use as a check on currently used network interfaces and lists a snapshot of the interfaces and traffic on the interface at the time the program is run.

irc

The Internet Relay Chat program. You can use irc to communicate interactively with other persons on the Internet. The irc program has built-in help and features a split-window display so you can read ongoing discussions and type in your own messages to other people.

ispell

This flexible, interactive spelling checker is used by emacs and other text editors under Linux to check the spelling of text documents. You can also use ispell like the traditional UNIX spell command by using the -l command line option like this

```
# ispell -l < document.txt
```

jed

This editor can emulate the `emacs`, Wordstar, and Brief editors. The X11 version is called `xjed`.

jmacs

This `jmacs` version of the `joe` editor emulates the `emacs` editor and uses its keyboard commands.

joe

The `joe` editor.

jpico

This version of the `joe` editor emulates the `pico` editor included in the Pine mail program distribution.

jstar

A Wordstar-compatible version of the `joe` editor. This editor uses keyboard commands, such as the famous control-key diamond (e,s,d,x) for cursor movement, and emulates most other keyboard commands.

kill

`kill` sends the specified signal to the specified process. If no signal is specified, the `TERM` (15) signal is sent. The `TERM` signal kills processes that do not process it. For processes that do process the `TERM` signal, you might need to use the `KILL` (9) signal because it cannot be caught. The syntax for the `kill` command is `kill` *<option>* *<pid>*, and an example is as follows:

```
svr01:/home/dpitts$kill -9 1438
```

less

`less` is a program similar to `more`, but allows backward movement in the file as well as forward movement. `less` also doesn't have to read the entire input file before starting, so with large input files it starts up faster than text editors such as `vi`.

ln

The `ln` command is used to make a copy of a file that is either a shortcut (symbolic link) or a duplicate file (hard link) to a file. Use the `ls` command's `-l` option to see which files in a directory are symbolic links.

locate

The `locate` program prints locations of files. You can use this command to quickly find files on your system, because it uses a single database of file locations in the locatedb database under the /var/lib directory.

login

`login` is used when signing on to a system. It can also be used to switch from one user to another at any time.

logout

`logout` is used to sign off of a system as the current user. If it is the only user you are logged in as, you are logged off the system.

look

The `look` command is used to search text files for matching lines for a given string. You can also use this command to quickly look up the spelling of a word, as the default file it searches is the system dictionary, words, found under the /usr/dict directory.

lpc

`lpc` is used by the system administrator to control the operation of the line printer system. `lpc` can be used to disable or enable a printer or a printer's spooling queue, to rearrange the order of jobs in a spooling queue, to find out the status of printers, to find out the status of the spooling queues, and to find out the status of the printer daemons. The `lpc` command can be used for any of the printers configured in /etc/printcap.

lpd

`lpd` is the line printer daemon and is normally invoked at boot time from the `rc` file. `lpd` makes a single pass through the /etc/printcap file to find out about the existing printers and prints any files left after a crash. It then uses the system calls `listen` and `accept` to receive requests to print files in the queue, transfer files to the spooling area, display the queue, or remove jobs from the queue.

lpq

lpq examines the spooling area used by lpd for printing files on the line printer and reports the status of the specified jobs or all jobs associated with a user. If invoked without any arguments, lpq reports on any jobs currently in the print queue.

lpr

The line printer command uses a spooling daemon to print the named files when facilities become available. If no names appear, the standard input is assumed. The following is an example of the lpr command:

```
lpr /etc/hosts
```

lprm

The lprm command removes a print job from the document queue. This program is used to stop a print job by specifying its job number on the command line. The example

```
# lprm 28
```

stops print job 28 (which was shown by the lpq command).

ls

The ls command lists the contents of a directory. The format of the output is manipulated with options. The ls command with no options lists all nonhidden files (a file that begins with a dot is a hidden file) in alphabetical order, filling as many columns as fit in the window. Probably the most common set of options used with this command is the -la option. The a means list all (including hidden files) files, and the l means make the output a long listing. Here is an example of this command:

```
svr01:~$ ls -la
total 35
drwxr-xr-x   7 dpitts   users        1024 Jul 21 00:19 ./
drwxr-xr-x 140 root     root         3072 Jul 23 14:38 ../
-rw-r--r--   1 dpitts   users        4541 Jul 23 23:33 .bash_history
-rw-r--r--   1 dpitts   users          18 Sep 16  1996 .forward
-rw-r--r--   2 dpitts   users         136 May 10 01:46 .htaccess
-rw-r--r--   1 dpitts   users         164 Dec 30  1995 .kermrc
-rw-r--r--   1 dpitts   users          34 Jun  6  1993 .less
-rw-r--r--   1 dpitts   users         114 Nov 23  1993 .lessrc
-rw-r--r--   1 dpitts   users          10 Jul 20 22:32 .profile
drwxr-xr-x   2 dpitts   users        1024 Dec 20  1995 .term/
drwx------   2 dpitts   users        1024 Jul 16 02:04 Mail/
drwxr-xr-x   2 dpitts   users        1024 Feb  1  1996 cgi-src/
-rw-r--r--   1 dpitts   users        1643 Jul 21 00:23 hi
```

```
-rwxr-xr-x   1 dpitts   users         496 Jan  3  1997 nquota*
drwxr-xr-x   2 dpitts   users        1024 Jan  3  1997 passwd/
drwxrwxrwx   5 dpitts   users        1024 May 14 20:29 public_html/
```

lynx

The lynx browser is a fast, compact, and efficient text-only Web browser with nearly all the capabilities of other Web browsers. Start lynx from the command line of your console or an X11 terminal window, specifying a Web address like this:

```
# lynx http://www.mcp.com
```

mail

This program provides a bare-bones interface to sending, handling, or reading mail, but can be very handy to send one-line mail messages from the command line. You'll probably prefer to use the Pine mail program instead.

make

The purpose of the make utility is to automatically determine which pieces of a large program need to be recompiled and then to issue the commands necessary to recompile them.

makewhatis

The makewhatis command builds the whatis command database, located in the /usr/man directory.

man

The man command is used to format and display the online manual pages. The manual pages are the text that describes, in detail, how to use a specified command. In the following example, I have called the man page that describes the man pages:

```
svr01:~$ man man
man(1)                                                    man(1)


NAME
       man - format and display the on-line manual pages
       manpath - determine user's search path for man pages
SYNOPSIS
       man  [-adfhktwW]  [-m system] [-p string] [-C config_file]
       [-M path] [-P pager] [-S section_list] [section] name  ...
```

```
DESCRIPTION
       man  formats  and displays the on-line manual pages.  This
       version knows about  the  MANPATH  and  PAGER  environment
       variables, so you can have your own set(s) of personal man
       pages and choose whatever program you like to display  the
       formatted  pages.  If section is specified, man only looks
       in that section of the manual.  You may also  specify  the
       order to search the sections for entries and which prepro-
       cessors to run  on  the  source  files  via  command  line
       options  or  environment  variables.  If name contains a /
       then it is first tried as a filename, so that you  can  do
```

mcopy

The `mcopy` command is part of the mtools software package and copies file to and from DOS-formatted disks without having to mount the disk drive first.

mdel

This command, part of the `mtools` package, deletes files from a DOS disk without mounting the disk drive.

mdir

The `mdir` command lists files on a DOS disk and is part of the mtools disk drive support package.

mesg

The `mesg` utility is run by a user to control the write access others have to the terminal device associated with the standard error output. If write access is allowed, programs such as `talk` and `write` have permission to display messages on the terminal. Write access is allowed by default.

mformat

The `mformat` command performs a low-level format of a floppy disk with a DOS filesystem. This command is part of the mtools software package.

mgetty

Use the `mgetty` program to monitor incoming logins to set terminal speed, type, and other parameters. This command is part of the mgetty+sendfax package.

minicom

`minicom` is a serial communications program. The `minicom` program provides an easy-to-use interface with menus and custom colors and is a capable, flexible communications program used to dial out and connect with other computers.

mkdir

The `mkdir` command is used to make a new directory.

mke2fs

The `mke2fs` command is used to make a second extended Linux filesystem on a specified hard drive or other device, such as a floppy disk. This command does not format the new filesystem, just makes it available for use. `mke2fs` can also be used to label a partition and to specify a mount point or directory where the partition can be accessed after it's mounted.

mkfs

`mkfs` is used to build a Linux filesystem on a device, usually a hard disk partition. The syntax for the command is `mkfs` *`<filesystem>`*, where *`<filesystem>`* is either the device name (such as `/dev/hda1`) or the mount point (for example, `/`, `/usr`, `/home`) for the filesystem.

mkswap

`mkswap` sets up a Linux swap area on a device (usually a disk partition).

The device is usually of the following form:

```
/dev/hda[1-8]
/dev/hdb[1-8]
/dev/sda[1-8]
/dev/sdb[1-8]
```

mlabel

The `mlabel` command, part of the mtools package, is used to label (name) a DOS floppy disk.

more

`more` is a filter for paging through text one screen at a time. This command can only page down through the text, as opposed to `less`, which can page both up and down though the text.

mount

mount attaches the filesystem specified by specialfile (which is often a device name) to the directory specified as the parameter. Only the superuser can mount files. If the mount command is run without parameters, it lists all currently mounted filesystems. The following is an example of the mount command:

```
svr01:/home/dpitts$ mount
/dev/hda1 on / type ext2 (rw)
/dev/hda2 on /var/spool/mail type ext2 (rw,usrquota)
/dev/hda3 on /logs type ext2 (rw,usrquota)
/dev/hdc1 on /home type ext2 (rw,usrquota)
none on /proc type proc (rw)
```

mpage

The mpage command formats multiple pages on a single sheet, saving money and a number of trees your printer would otherwise eat. After you've installed your printer, try printing a document with two sheets per page like this

```
# mpage -2 myfile.txt ¦ lpr
```

mt

mt is a magnetic tape command. You can use this command to erase, rewind, or retension tapes in your tape drive. You can perform nearly 40 different actions with this command.

mv

The mv command is used to move an object from one location to another location. If the last argument names an existing directory, the command moves the rest of the list into that directory. If two files are given, the command moves the first into the second. It is an error to have more than two arguments with this command unless the last argument is a directory.

netcfg

This is a Red Hat Linux network configuration tool. The netcfg command is an X11 client used to configure Linux networking hardware, interfaces, and services.

netstat

netstat displays the status of network connections on either TCP, UDP, RAW, or UNIX sockets to the system. The -r option is used to obtain information about the routing table. The following is an example of the netstat command:

```
svr01:/home/dpitts$ netstat
Active Internet connections
Proto Recv-Q Send-Q Local Address           Foreign Address        (State)
User
tcp        0  16501 www.mk.net:www          sdlb12119.sannet.:3148 FIN_WAIT1
root
tcp        0  16501 auth02.mk.net:www       sdlb12119.sannet.:3188 FIN_WAIT1
root
tcp        0      1 www.anglernet.com:www   ts88.cctrap.com:1070   SYN_RECV
root
tcp        0      1 www.anglernet.com:www   ts88.cctrap.com:1071   SYN_RECV
root
udp        0      0 localhost:domain        *:*
udp        0      0 svr01.mk.net:domain     *:*
udp        0      0 poto.mk.net:domain      *:*
udp        0      0 stats.mk.net:domain     *:*
udp        0      0 home.mk.net:domain      *:*
udp        0      0 www.cmf.net:domain      *:*
Active UNIX domain sockets
Proto RefCnt Flags      Type            State           Path
unix  2      [ ]        SOCK_STREAM     UNCONNECTED     1605182
unix  2      [ ]        SOCK_STREAM     UNCONNECTED     1627039
unix  2      [ ]        SOCK_STREAM     CONNECTED       1652605
```

newgrp

newgrp is used to enter a new group. You can use this command to temporarily become a member of a different group so you can access or work on different files or directories.

nxterm

nxterm is a color-capable xterm terminal emulator for X11. This client is used as a console window during X sessions, and can change features on-the-fly through pop-up menus.

passwd

For the normal user (non-superuser), no arguments are used with the passwd command. The command asks the user for the old password. Following this, the command asks for the new password twice, to make sure it was typed correctly. The new password must be at least six characters long and must contain at least one character that is either uppercase or a nonletter. Also, the new password cannot be the same password as the one being replaced, nor can it match the user's ID (account name).

If the command is run by the superuser, it can be followed by either one or two arguments. If the command is followed by a single user's ID, the superuser can change that user's password. The superuser is not bound by any of the restrictions imposed on the user. If there is an argument after the single user's ID, that argument becomes that user's new password.

pdksh

This public domain Korn shell is a workalike shell with nearly compatible features to the commercial Korn shell, and is found on your Linux system with the name `ksh`.

pico

The `pico` command is a handy, virtually crash-proof text editor that is part of the Pine mail program's software distribution. One handy command line option is `-w`, which disables line wrapping (useful when you're manually configuring system files). `pico` performs spell-checking of text files, but does not print.

pine

Pine is the program for Internet news and email. The Pine program, though normally thought of as a mail-handling program, can also be used to read USENET news. This mail program also comes with a handy editor, called `pico`. You can organize your incoming mail and file messages into different folders.

ping

This command requests packet echos from network hosts. The `ping` command sends out a request for an echo of an information packet from a specific computer on a network. It can be used to check communication links or to check whether the specific host exists or is running. `ping` is used from the command line, followed by an Internet Protocol (IP) number or domain name, like this

```
# ping staffnet.com
```

`ping` continues to send requests until you stop the program with Ctrl+C.

pppd

The Point-to-Point Protocol, or PPP daemon. This program runs in the background in your Linux system while you have a PPP connection with your Internet Service Provider (ISP) and handles the transmission and format of data into and out of your computer.

pppstats

pppstats prints Point-to-Point Protocol network statistics. This program prints a variety of information about a current PPP network connection. It can be useful for determining if the PPP connection is active and how much information is being transferred.

pr

The pr command performs basic formatting of text documents for printing and can also be used to convert input text into different formats through 19 command line options. One is the -h, or header option, which puts specified text at the top of each page. Try this

```
# ls ¦ pr -h "TOP SECRET DOCUMENT" ¦ lpr
```

printtool

The Red Hat Linux printer configuration tool. This X11 client can be run from the command line of a terminal window or through the control panel, and is used to install, set up, and configure printers for Linux.

procmail

The procmail command processes incoming mail by searching messages for specified strings and either discards, files, or replies to messages according to filters or recipes you specify. This is a handy way to handle unwanted incoming mail or organize vast amounts of incoming mail.

ps

ps gives a snapshot of the current processes. An example follows:

```
svr01:/home/dpitts$ ps -ef

PID TTY STAT  TIME COMMAND
10916  p3 S    0:00 -bash TERM=vt100 HOME=/home2/dpitts PATH=/usr/local/bin:/us
10973  p3 R    0:00  \_ ps -ef LESSOPEN=¦lesspipe.sh %s ignoreeof=10 HOSTNAME=s
10974  p3 S    0:00  \_ more LESSOPEN=¦lesspipe.sh %s ignoreeof=10 HOSTNAME=svr
```

pwd

pwd prints the current working directory. It tells you what directory you are in currently.

quota

The `quota` command reports on disk quota settings. This command, usually used by the root operator, shows how much disk space users can use by user or group.

quotacheck

Gives a report on disk-quota usage. This command, usually used by the root operator, scans a specified or current filesystem, reporting on disk usage if disk quotas for users are turned on.

quotaoff

Turns off disk quotas. This command is used by the root operator to disable disk-quota checking for users.

quotaon

Turns on disk quotas. This command is used by the root operator to enable or enforce disk quotas for users and can be helpful in limiting how much disk space a user can take up with programs or data.

rclock

An X11 clock client and appointment reminder. The `rclock` program, besides displaying a variety of clock faces in different colors, can also be used as an appointment or reminder system and features pop-up notes.

red

The restricted `ed` editor. With this version of the `ed` command, you can only edit files in the current directory. `red` does not have a shell escape command.

repquota

Gives a report on disk usage. This command scans different filesystems and reports on usage and quotas if disk quotas are enabled.

restore

Restore a dump backup. The `restore` command features built-in help and an interactive mode to restore files and directories of a backup created by the dump command.

rjoe

Restricted `joe` editor. With this version of the `joe` editor, you can only edit files specified on the command line.

rm

`rm` is used to delete specified files. With the `-r` option (warning: this can be dangerous!), `rm` recursively removes files. Therefore if, as root, you type the command `rm -r /`, you had better have a good backup, because all of your files are now gone. This is a good command to use in conjunction with the `find` command to find files owned by a certain user or in a certain group and delete them. By default, the `rm` command does not remove directories.

rmdir

`rmdir` removes a given *empty* directory; the word *empty* is the key word. The syntax is simply `rmdir <directory name>`.

route

Use `route` to show or configure the Internet Protocol routing table. This is another network utility you can use to monitor communication through interfaces on your computer. Although normally used by system administrators, you can use this command to monitor your PPP connection while you're online.

rxvt

`rxvt` is a color-capable, memory-efficient terminal emulator for X11 with nearly all of the features of the `xterm` client. This client is usually started in the background like this:

```
# rxvt &
```

sed

This is the stream editor, a noninteractive text editor designed to change or manipulate streams of text. The `sed` command can be used to quickly perform global search-and-replace operations on streams of text (for example, through pipes), like this

```
# cat employees.txt ¦ sed 's/Bill/William/g' >newemployees.txt
```

which changes all instances of Bill to William in the original file and creates a new file.

sendfax

Use this to send fax documents. The `sendfax` program, part of the mgetty+sendfax software package, dials out and sends prepared fax-format graphics documents. This program is usually run by the `faxspool` shell script.

set

The `set` command is used to temporarily change an environment variable. In some shells, the `set -o vi` command allows you to bring back previous commands you have in your history file. It is common to place the `set` command in your `.profile`. Some environment variables require an equals sign, and some, as in the example `set -o vi`, do not.

setfdprm

Set floppy drive parameters. This command, usually run by the root operator, is used to set the current floppy device, usually in preparation for a low-level format.

setserial

The `setserial` command is used to configure or fine-tune specific serial ports in your computer. This command can also be used to report on a serial port's status or identity.

seyon

An X11 serial communications program. The `seyon` program only runs under X11, but offers a scripting language and point-and-click set-up of communications parameters.

shutdown

One time during *Star Trek: The Next Generation*, Data commands the computer to "Shut down the holodeck!" Unfortunately, most systems don't have voice controls, but systems can still be shut down. This command happens to be the one to do just that. Technically, the `shutdown` call

```
int shutdown(int s, int how));
```

causes all or part of a full-duplex connection on a socket associated with `s` to be shut down, but who's being technical? The `shutdown` command can also be used to issue a "Vulcan Neck Pinch" (Ctrl+Alt+Del) and restart the system.

slrn

A news reading program, the `slrn` newsreader provides an easy-to-use interface for reading USENET news. It has some advantages over the `tin` newsreader by providing custom colors for different parts of messages and support for mouse clicks and function keys.

sort

The `sort` command comes in handy whenever you need to generate alphabetical lists of the information from your files. Information can also be listed in reverse order. See the `sort` manual page for more information.

stat

Use this to print file information. The `stat` command prints a variety of information about a specified file and can also be used to check for the validity of symbolic links.

statserial

Use the `statserial` command to print serial port statistics. This command, run only by the root operator, shows the current condition of a specified serial port and can be helpful in diagnosing serial port problems.

strings

The `strings` command outputs all text strings found inside binary programs. This can be useful to view the contents of files when you don't have a viewer program for a file's format or for looking at the contents of a binary program (such as to search for help text). For example, to look at all strings inside the `pico` editor, try this

```
# strings /usr/bin/pico | less
```

su

`su` enables a user to temporarily become another user. If a user ID is not given, the computer thinks you want to be the superuser, or root. In either case, a shell is spawned that makes you the new user, complete with that user ID, group ID, and any supplemental groups of that new user. If you are not root and the user has a password (and the user should!), `su` prompts for a password. Root can become any user at any time without knowing passwords. Technically, the user just needs to have a user ID of 0 (which makes a user a superuser) to log on as anyone else without a password.

swapoff

No, `swapoff` is not a move from *Karate Kid*. Instead, it is a command that stops swapping to a file or block device.

swapon

Also not from the movie *Karate Kid*, `swapon` sets the swap area to the file or block device by path. `swapoff` stops swapping to the file and is normally done during system boot.

tail

`tail` prints to standard output the last ten lines of a given file. If no file is given, it reads from standard input. If more than one file is given, it prints a header consisting of the file's name enclosed in left and right arrows (==> <==) before the output of each file. The default value of ten lines can be changed by placing a `-###` in the command. The syntax for the command is

```
tail [-<# of lines to see>] [<filename(s)>]
```

talk

The `talk` command is used to have a "visual" discussion with someone else over a terminal. The basic idea behind this visual discussion is that your input is copied to the other person's terminal, and the other person's input is copied to your terminal. Thus, both people involved in the discussion see the input from both themselves and the other person.

taper

A tape archiving and backup program, the `taper` command features a friendly interface to the `tar` and `gzip` programs to provide archive backups and compression.

tar

`tar` is an archiving program designed to store and extract files from an archive file. A tarred file (called a tar file) can be archived to any medium, including a tape drive or a hard drive. The syntax of a `tar` command is `tar <action> <optional functions> <file(s)/directory(ies)>`. If the last parameter is a directory, all subdirectories under the directory are also tarred.

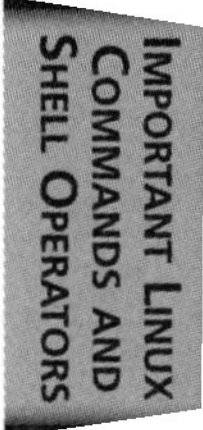

tcsh

This enhanced `csh` shell has all of the features of the `csh` shell with many improvements, such as command-line editing, job control, and command history. This shell is run by the symbolic link `csh` that is found under the /bin directory.

telnet

Start and run a telnet session. You can use the `telnet` command to log in to remote computer systems and run programs or retrieve data.

tin

This is a Usenet news reading program. The tin newsreader, like the `slrn` newsreader, provides a menu system for reading Usenet news, allowing you to quickly browse, save, post, or reply to messages found in a specific Usenet newsgroup. The tin reader looks for a list of desired newsgroups in the file .newsrc in your home directory and can be started like this from the command line of your console or terminal window:

```
# tin -nqr
```

top

You can display CPU processes with the `top` command. This command can be used to print the most active or system resource-intensive processes or programs.

touch

You can use the `touch` command to quickly create a file or update its timestamp.

tput

Change or reset terminal settings. The `tput` command, found under the /usr/bin directory, uses terminal capabilities found in the terminfo database under the /usr/lib directory. This database contains character sequences recognized by different terminals. You can use `tput` in a variety of ways. One handy feature is the `reset` option, which can help you clear up a terminal window if your display becomes munged because of spurious control codes echoed to the screen.

tr

Transliterate characters. The `tr` command, a text filter, translates sets of characters you specify on the command line. The classic example is to translate a text file from all uppercase to lowercase, like this:

```
# cat uppercase.txt ¦ tr A-Z a-z > lowercase.txt
```

tree

Use `tree` to print a visual directory. If you'd like to see how your directories are organized, you can use this command to print a graphic tree.

twm

This is the Tab window manager for X11, from which the `fvwm` window manager, and others, are descended. Although this window manager does not support virtual desktops, you can customize its menus and windows. The `twm` window manager is usually started from the contents of your .xinitrc in your home directory.

ulimit

Show resource limit settings with `ulimit`. This is a built-in command for the `bash` or `ksh` shell and can be used to set limits on a number of system resources. This command is similar to the limit command of the `tcsh` or `csh` shells.

umount

Just as the cavalry unmounts from their horses, filesystems unmount from their locations. The `umount` command is used to perform this action. The syntax of the command is

```
umount <filesystem>
```

unalias

`unalias` is the command to undo an alias. In the `alias` command section earlier in this appendix, I aliased `dir` to be the `ls` command. To unalias this command, you would simply type **`unalias dir`**.

unzip

The `unzip` command lists, tests, or extracts files from a zipped archive. The default is to extract files from the archive. The basic syntax is `unzip <filename>`.

updatedb

This command builds `locate` command's database, called locatedb, in the /var/lib directory.

uptime

You can show how long your system has been running (in case you want to brag to your NT friends). The `uptime` command shows how long your Linux system has been running, who is currently logged on, and what the average system load has been for the last 5, 10, and 15 minutes. Linux system uptimes are generally measured in years (and almost always end due to hardware failure)!

uugetty

Set login parameters, such as terminal type, speed, and protocol. You can use `uugetty` to monitor incoming connections to your Linux system. This program can display login messages or run programs when you log in.

vdir

List the contents of directories with `vdir`. This command is the same as using the `ls` command with the `-l` option to get a detailed directory listing.

vi

Normally known as the `vi` (visual) editor under Red Hat Linux, `vi` is a symbolic link to the `vim` editor. In this mode, the `vim` editor closely emulates the classic `vi` editor, originally distributed with the Berkely Software Distribution.

view

A symbolic link to the `vim` editor.

vim

VIsual editor iMproved. This editor is an improvement of the `vi` editor and can also emulate the `ex` line-oriented editor. The X11 version of this editor is called `gvim`.

vimx

A symbolic link to the `gvim` X11 editor.

vmstat

`vmstat` prints virtual memory statistics. This command shows how much disk space has been used by your system, usually on the swap file partition.

w

Show who is logged on by using the `w` command, which shows not only who is currently logged in to your system but also the same information as the `uptime` command.

wall

`wall` displays the contents of standard input on all terminals of all currently logged-in users. Basically, the command writes to all terminals; hence, its name. The contents of files can also be displayed. The superuser, or root, can write to the terminals of those who have chosen to deny messages or are using a program that automatically denies messages.

wc

This is a word-count program. The `wc` command counts the number of characters, words, and lines in your file and prints a small report to your display. The default is to show all three, but you can limit the report by using the `-c`, `-w`, or `-l` options.

whatis

This command searches the whatis database (located under the /usr/man directory) for command names and prints a one-line synopsis of what each command does. Use the `whatis` command, followed by the name of another command like this:

```
# whatis emacs
```

whereis

Use `whereis` to find commands, command sources, and manual pages. This program searches a built-in list of directories to find and then print matches of the command name you specify.

who

Either the `who` command calls an owl (which it doesn't) or it prints the login name, terminal type, login time, and remote hostname of each user currently logged on. The following is an example of the `who` command:

```
svr01:/home/dpitts$ who
root      ttyp0    Jul 27 11:44 (www01.mk.net)
dpitts    ttyp2    Jul 27 19:32 (d12.dialup.seane)
ehooban   ttyp3    Jul 27 11:47 (205.177.146.78)
dpitts    ttyp4    Jul 27 19:34 (d12.dialup.seane)
```

If two nonoption arguments are passed to the who command, the command prints the entry for the user running it. Typically, this is run with the command `who am I`, but any two arguments will work; for example, the following gives information on my session:

```
svr01:/home/dpitts$ who who who
svr01!dpitts   ttyp2    Jul 27 19:32 (d12.dialup.seane)
```

The `-u` option is nice if you want to see how long it has been since that session has been used, such as in the following:

```
svr01:/home/dpitts$ who -u
root      ttyp0     Jul 27 11:44 08:07 (www01.mk.net)
dpitts    ttyp2     Jul 27 19:32   .   (d12.dialup.seane)
ehooban   ttyp3     Jul 27 11:47 00:09 (205.177.146.78)
dpitts    ttyp4     Jul 27 19:34 00:06 (d12.dialup.seane)
```


whoami

To show your current user identity, the `whoami` command prints the username of who you currently are. It is useful for checking who you are if you're running as the root operator.

xclock

An X11 clock client that can be run with a standard clock face or as a digital clock.

xcutsel

An X11 client that provides a buffer for copy and paste operations. This program is handy for copying and pasting information between programs which may not support direct copying and pasting.

xdaliclock

An X11 digital clock client that features melting digits, transparent backgrounds, and extensive customized features and keyboard commands.

xdm

This X11 Display Manager provides a login interface, called the chooser, that—when properly configured on your system—can manage several X displays.

xfig

An X11 drawing program. The `xfig` client is an interactive drawing program that uses objects rather than pixel images to display figures. You can use this program to develop blueprints or other technical drawings.

xhost +

The `xhost +` command allows xterms to be displayed on a system. Probably the most common reason a remote terminal cannot be opened is that the `xhost +` command has not been run. To turn off the capability to allow xterms, use the `xhost -` command.

xjed

The X11 version of the `jed` editor. This version of the `jed` editor runs under the X Window System and offers keyboard menus.

xload

The X11 system load reporting client. This X11 command is used to show a graphic of the system load average, a combination of memory, CPU, and swap-file space usage. This program, like may X11 clients, is started in the background like this:

```
# xload &
```

xloadimage

An X11 client that can load, translate, and display graphic images or window dumps created by the `xwd` client on your display or desktop. You can also use the `xloadimage` command to provide slide shows of graphics.

xlock

`xlock` is an X11 terminal-locking program that provides password protection and more than 50 screensavers.

xlsfonts

This X11 client displays and searches for fonts recognized by the current X11 server and is useful for finding a specific font or for getting detailed font reports.

xmessage

An X11 client that displays messages on your display. You can also program your own custom messages with labels, buttons, and other information. Although this client is often used with other programs to provide appointment reminders, an `xmessage` can also be used as a sticky-note reminder.

xminicom

Runs the minicom program in an X11 terminal window. This is the preferred way to run the minicom communications program under the X Window System.

xmkmf

The xmkmf command (a shell script) is used to create the Imakefiles for X sources. It actually runs the imake command with a set of arguments.

xmodmap

A utility for modifying keyboards or mouse buttons during an X session. You can use xmodmap to remap your keyboard or rearrange your mouse buttons.

xscreensaver

A screensaver for X11, this client is usually run in the background to blank your screen and run a screensaver program after a preselected time. The xscreensaver client is usually controlled with the xscreensaver-command client.

xscreensaver-command

This X11 client is used to control the xscreensaver program to turn screensaving on or off or to cycle through various screensaving displays.

xset

The xset command sets some of the options in an X Window session. You can use this option to set your bell (xset b *<volume>* *<frequency>* *<duration in milliseconds>*), your mouse speed (xset m *<acceleration>* *<threshold>*), and many others.

xsetroot

An X11 client to change how the root window or background of your display appears, as well as how the cursor looks. You can use this client to add background patterns, colors, or pictures, or to change your root window cursor. Want a blue background for your X11 desktop? Try this

```
# xsetroot -solid blue
```

xv

You can display images in X11 with xv. This X11 client provides many controls for capturing, changing, saving, and printing images and comes with extensive documentation.

xwd

An X11 window-dumping client. You can use this client to take pictures of windows or the entire display. Don't forget to specify an output file like this:

```
# xwd >myscreendump.xwd
```

xwininfo

This X11 information client gathers available information about a window and prints a short report. You can use the xwininfo utility to determine a window's size and placement.

xwud

An X11 graphics utility client that displays window dumps created by the xwd X11 client.

zip

The zip command lists, tests, or adds files to a zipped archive. The default is to add files to an archive.

zsh

The z shell is the largest shell for Linux, with many, many features and lots of documentation. This shell has features derived from the csh and tcsh shells and can emulate the ksh (Korn) shell and sh (Bourne) shells.

Summary

If you read this entire appendix, I congratulate you, because it contains more than 200 commands. You have way too much time on your hands—go out and program some new Linux drivers or something!

I hope this appendix has helped you gain an understanding of some of the commands available for your use, whether you are a user, a systems administrator, or just someone who wants to learn more about Red Hat Linux. I encourage you to use the man pages to learn about the many details left out of this appendix. Most of the commands have arguments that can be passed to them and, although this appendix attempts to point out a few of them, an entire book would be needed just to go into the detail provided in the man pages.

The Linux Documentation Project Copyright License

by David Pitts

IN THIS APPENDIX

Last modified: 6 January 1997

The following copyright license applies to all works by the Linux Documentation Project.

Read the license carefully; it is somewhat like the GNU General Public License, but several conditions in it differ from what you might be used to. If you have any questions, email the LDP coordinator at `mdw@sunsite.unc.edu`.

Copyright License

The Linux Documentation Project manuals may be reproduced and distributed in whole or in part, subject to the following conditions:

All Linux Documentation Project manuals are copyrighted by their respective authors. They are not in the public domain.

- The copyright notice and this permission notice must be preserved completely on all complete or partial copies.
- Any translation or derivative work of *Linux Installation and Getting Started* must be approved by the author in writing before distribution.
- If you distribute *Linux Installation and Getting Started* in part, instructions for obtaining the complete version of this manual must be included and a means for obtaining a complete version provided.
- Small portions may be reproduced as illustrations for reviews or quotes in other works without this permission notice if proper citation is given.
- The GNU General Public License may be reproduced under the conditions given within it.

Exceptions to these rules may be granted for academic purposes: Write to the author and ask. These restrictions are here to protect us as authors, not to restrict you as educators and learners. All source code in *Linux Installation and Getting Started* is placed under the GNU General Public License, available via anonymous FTP from `ftp://prep.ai.mit.edu/pub/gnu/COPYING`.

Publishing LDP Manuals

This section is addressed to publishing companies interested in distributing any of the LDP manuals.

By the license given in the previous section, anyone is allowed to publish and distribute verbatim copies of the Linux Documentation Project manuals. You don't need our explicit permission for this. However, if you want to distribute a translation or derivative work based on any of the LDP manuals, you must obtain permission from the author in writing.

All translations and derivative works of LDP manuals must be placed under the Linux Documentation License in the preceding section. That is, if you plan to release a translation of one of the manuals, it must be freely distributable by the terms stated in that license.

You may, of course, sell the LDP manuals for profit. We encourage you to do so. Keep in mind, however, that because the LDP manuals are freely distributable, anyone may photocopy or distribute printed copies free of charge, if they want to do so.

We do not expect to be paid royalties for any profit earned from selling LDP manuals. However, we would like to suggest that if you do sell LDP manuals for profit, you either offer the author royalties or donate a portion of your earnings to the author, the LDP as a whole, or to the Linux development community. You might also want to send one or more free copies of the LDP manual that you are distributing to the author. Your show of support for the LDP and the Linux community will be appreciated.

We want to be informed of any plans to publish or distribute LDP manuals so that we know how they're becoming available. If you are publishing or planning to publish any LDP manuals, send email to Matt Welsh at `mdw@sunsite.unc.edu`.

We encourage Linux software distributors to distribute the LDP manuals (such as the *Installation and Getting Started Guide*) with their software. The LDP manuals are intended to be used as the "official" Linux documentation, and we'd like to see mail-order distributors bundle the LDP manuals with the software. As the LDP manuals mature, we hope they will fulfill our goal more adequately.

APPENDIX D

Samba Options

Compiled by Jack Tackett, Jr.

IN THIS APPENDIX

Samba is a suite of programs (listed in table D.1) with a variety of command line options. This appendix covers all of the options for the smb.conf file. It also provides a command line reference based on the various man pages for most of the commands you might use for Samba activities.

TABLE D.1 PROGRAMS COMPRISING THE SAMBA SUITE

Program	*Description*
smbd	The daemon that provides the file and print services to SMB clients, such as Windows for Workgroups, Windows NT, or LanManager.(The configuration file for this daemon is described in smb.conf.)
nmbd	The daemon that provides NetBIOS nameserving and browsing support.
smbclient	This program implements an FTP-like client that is useful for accessing SMB shares on other compatible servers.
testparm	This utility enables you to test the /etc/smb.conf configuration file.
smbstatus	This utility enables you to tell who is currently using the `smbd` server.
smbpasswd	This utility changes a user's SMB password in the smb-passwd file.
smbrun	This is an interface program between `smbd` and external programs.
testprns	This program checks a printer's name for validity.
smbtar	This is a shell script for backing up SMB shares directly to a UNIX-based tape drive.
smbmnt/smbmount	Use this utility to mount an SMB filesystem.
smbumount	A utility to unmount an SMB filesystem.

smbd

The command line for the samba daemon is

```
smbd [ -D ] [ -a ] [ -d debuglevel ] [ -l log file ] [ -p port number ]
[ -O socket options ] [ -s configuration file ]
```

The options mean:

-D If specified, this parameter causes the server to operate as a daemon. That is, the server detaches itself and runs in the background, fielding requests on the appropriate port. By default, the server will not operate as a daemon.

-a If this parameter is specified, the log files will be overwritten with each new connection. By default, the log files will be appended to.

-d debuglevel `debuglevel` is an integer from 0 to 10. The default value if this parameter is not specified is zero. The higher the value, the more detail will be logged to the log files about the activities of the server. At level 0, only critical errors and serious warnings will be logged. Level 1 is a reasonable level for day-to-day running—it generates a small amount of information about operations carried out. Levels above 1 will generate considerable amounts of log data and should be used only when you're investigating a problem. Levels above 3 are designed for use only by developers and generate huge amounts of log data, most of which is extremely cryptic.

-l log file If specified, `logfile` specifies a base filename into which operational data from the running server will be logged. The default base name is specified at compile time. The base name is used to generate actual log filenames. For example, if the name specified is "log," the following files will be used for log data:

log.debug (containing debugging information)

log.in (containing inbound transaction data)

log.out (containing outbound transaction data)

The log files generated are never removed by the server.

-O socket options This option, typically specified in the smb.conf files, enables you to set socket options to be used when talking with the client.

Socket options are controls on the networking layer of the operating systems that allow the connection to be tuned. This option will typically be used to tune your Samba server for optimal performance for your local network. Samba has no way to know the optimal parameters for your net, so you must experiment and choose them yourself. I strongly suggest you read the appropriate documentation for your operating system first (perhaps "man setsockopt" will help).

On some systems, Samba might say `Unknown socket option` when you supply an option. This means you either mistyped it or you need to add an include file to includes.h for your OS. If the latter is the case, please send the patch to `samba-bugs@samba.anu.edu.au`.

Any of the supported socket options can be combined in any way you like, as long as your OS allows it. This is the list of socket options currently settable with this option:

```
SO_KEEPALIVE
SO_REUSEADDR
SO_BROADCAST
TCP_NODELAY
IPTOS_LOWDELAY
IPTOS_THROUGHPUT
SO_SNDBUF *
SO_RCVBUF *
SO_SNDLOWAT *
SO_RCVLOWAT *
```

Those marked with an asterisk (*) take an integer argument. The others can optionally take a 1 or 0 argument to enable or disable the option (they will be enabled by default if you don't specify 1 or 0).

To specify an argument, use the syntax SOME_OPTION=VALUE (for example, SO_SNDBUF=8192). Note that you must not have any spaces before or after the equals sign.

If you are on a local network, a sensible option might be socket options=IPTOS_LOWDELAY.

If you have an almost unloaded local network and you don't mind a lot of extra CPU usage in the server, you could try socket options=IPTOS_LOWDELAY TCP_ NODELAY.

If you are on a wide area network, perhaps try setting IPTOS_THROUGHPUT.

Note that several of the options might cause your Samba server to fail completely, so use them with caution.

The default is

```
no socket options-p port number
port number is a positive integer value.
```

The default value if this parameter is not specified is 139.

This number is the port number that will be used when making connections to the server from client software. The standard (well-known) port number for the server is 139, hence the default. If you wish to run the server as an ordinary user rather than as root, most systems will require you to use a port number greater than 1024. Ask your system administrator for help if you are in this situation.

For the server to be useful by most clients if you configure it on a port other than 139, you will require port redirection services on port 139, details of which are outlined in RFC1002.txt section 4.3.5. This parameter is not normally specified except in the above situation.

-s configuration file The default configuration filename is determined at compile time (for Red Hat, this is /etc/smb.conf). The file specified contains the configuration details required by the server. The information in this file includes such server-specific information as what printcap file to use, as well as descriptions of all the services the server is to provide. See the smb.conf man page for more information.

nmbd

The command line for the nmbd demon is:

```
nmbd [ -D ] [ -H netbios hosts file ] [ -d debuglevel ] [ -l log basename
] [ -n netbios name ] [ -p port number ] [ -s configuration file ]
```

The options mean:

-D If specified, this parameter causes the server to operate as a daemon. That is, it detaches itself and runs in the background, fielding requests on the appropriate port. By default, the server will not operate as a daemon.

-H netbios hosts file It might be useful in some situations to be able to specify a list of NetBIOS names for which the server should send a reply if queried. This option enables you to specify a file containing such a list. The syntax of the hosts file is similar to the standard /etc/hosts file format, but has some extensions.

The file contains three columns. Lines beginning with a # are ignored as comments. The first column is an IP address or a hostname. If it is a hostname, it is interpreted as the IP address returned by `gethostbyname()` when read. An IP address of `0.0.0.0` will be interpreted as the server's own IP address.

The second column is a NetBIOS name. This is the name to which the server will respond. It must be less than 20 characters long. The third column is optional and is intended for flags. Currently the only flag supported is `M`, which means this name is the default NetBIOS name for this machine. This has the same effect as specifying the `-n` option to `nmbd`. The default hosts filename is set at compile time, typically as /etc/lmhosts, but this can be changed in the Samba `makefile`.

After startup, the server waits for queries and answers queries for any name known to it. This includes all names in the NetBIOS hosts file, its own name, and any other names it might have learned about from other browsers on the network.

The primary intention of the `-H` option is to allow a mapping from NetBIOS names to Internet domain names.

Example:

```
# This is a sample netbios hosts file

# DO NOT USE THIS FILE AS-IS
# YOU MAY INCONVENIENCE THE OWNERS OF THESE IPs
# if you want to include a name with a space in it then
# use double quotes.

# next add a netbios alias for a faraway host
arvidsjaur.anu.edu.au ARVIDSJAUR

# finally put in an IP for a hard to find host
130.45.3.213 FREDDY
```

`-d` debuglevel This option sets the debug level.

`-l` log file The `log file` parameter specifies a path and base filename into which operational data from the running `nmbd` server will be logged. The actual log filename is generated by appending the extension .nmb to the specified base name. For example, if the name specified is "log," the file log.nmb will contain the debugging data. The default log file is specified at compile time, typically as /var/log/log.nmb.

`-n` netbios name This option enables you to override the NetBIOS name Samba uses for itself.

`-a` If this parameter is specified, the log files will be appended to with each new connection. By default, the log files will be overwritten.

`-p` port number `port number` is a positive integer value. Don't use this option unless you are an expert, in which case you won't need help.

`-s` configuration file The default configuration filename is set at compile time, typically as /etc/smb.conf, but this can be changed in the Samba `makefile`. The file specified contains the configuration details required by the server. See the "smb.conf" section for more information.

smbclient

The command line for the `smbclient` program is:

```
smbclient servicename [ password ] [ -A ] [ -E ] [ -L host ] [ -M host ] [
-I IP number ] [ -N ] [ -P ] [ -U username ] [ -d debuglevel ] [ -l log
basename ] [ -n netbios name ] [ -W workgroup ] [ -O socket options ] [ -p
```

```
port number ] [ -c command string ] [ -T tar options ] [ -D initial
directory ]
```

The options mean:

servicename `servicename` is the name of the service you want to use on the server. A service name takes the form \\server\service, where server is the NetBIOS name of the Lan Manager server offering the desired service, and service is the name of the service offered. Thus, to connect to the service "printer" on the Lan Manager server "lanman," you use the service name \\lanman\printer

Note that the server name required is note necessarily the hostname of the server. The name required is a Lan Manager server name, which might not be the same as the hostname of the machine running the server.

password `password` is the password required to access the specified service on the specified server. If supplied, the `-N` option (suppress password prompt) is assumed. There is no default password. If no password is supplied on the command line (either here or by using the `-U` option (defined later) and `-N` is not specified, the client will prompt for a password, even if the desired service does not require one. (If no password is required, simply press Enter to provide a null password.)

NOTE

Some servers (including OS/2 and Windows for Workgroups) insist on an uppercase password. Lowercase or mixed-case passwords might be rejected by these servers. Be cautious about including passwords in scripts.

`-A` This parameter, if specified, causes the maximum debug level to be selected. Be warned that this generates prodigious amounts of debug data. A security issue is also involved, because cleartext passwords might be written to some log files at the maximum debug level.

`-L` This option enables you to look at what services are available on a server. If you use it as `smbclient -L host`, a list should appear. The `-I` option might be useful if your NetBIOS names don't match your tcp/ip hostnames or if you are trying to reach a host on another network. For example,

```
smbclient -L ftp -I ftp.microsoft.com
```

will list the shares available on Microsoft's public server.

-M This option enables you to send messages to another computer by using the WinPopup protocol. After a connection is established, you type your message, pressing Ctrl-D to end.

If the receiving computer is running WinPopup, the user will receive the message and probably a beep. If they are not running WinPopup, the message will be lost and no error message will occur. The message is also automatically truncated if the message is over 1600 bytes (the limit of the protocol).

One useful trick is to `cat` the message through `smbclient`. For example,

```
cat mymessage.txt ¦ smbclient -M FRED
```

will send the message in the file mymessage.txt to the machine FRED. You might also find the `-U` and `-I` options useful, which enables you to control the `FROM:` and `TO:` parts of the message. See the message command section of smb.conf for a description of how to handle incoming WinPopup messages in Samba. NOTE: Copy WinPopup into the startup group on your WfWg PCs if you want them to always be able to receive messages.

-E This parameter, if specified, causes the client to write messages to the standard error stream (stderr) rather than to the standard output stream. By default, the client writes messages to standard output—typically, the user's TTY.

-I IP number `IP number` represents the IP number of the server to which to connect. It should be specified in standard a.b.c.d notation.

Normally the client will attempt to locate the specified Lan Manager server by looking it up—that is, by broadcasting a request for the given server to identify itself. Using this parameter will force the client to assume the server is on the machine with the specified IP number. This parameter has no default. If a number is not supplied, it will be determined automatically by the client, as described.

-N If specified, this parameter suppresses the normal password prompt from the client to the user. This is useful when accessing a service that does not require a password.

Unless a password is specified on the command line, or this parameter is specified, the client will request a password.

-O socket options See the *socket options* section of smb.conf for details.

-P If specified, the service requested will be connected to as a printer service rather than as a normal filespace service. Operations such as `put` and `get` will not be applicable for such a connection. By default, services will be connected to as non-printer services.

-U username `username` is used by the client to make a connection, assuming your server is running a protocol that allows for usernames. Some servers are fussy about the case of this name, and some insist it must be a valid NetBIOS name. If no username is supplied, it will default to an uppercase version of the environment variable USER or LOGNAME, in that order. If no username is supplied and neither environment variable exists, the username will be empty.

If the USER environment variable contains a "%" character, everything after that will be treated as a password. This allows you to set the environment variable to be `USER=username%password` so a password is not passed on the command line (where it might be seen by the `ps` command). If the service you are connecting to requires a password, it can be supplied by using the `-U` option, by appending a percent symbol (`%`) and then the password to username. For example, to attach to a service as user "fred" with password "secret," you would specify **`-U fred%secret`** on the command line. Note that there are no spaces around the percent symbol.

If you specify the password as part of username, the `-N` option (suppress password prompt) is assumed. If you specify the password as a parameter and as part of username, the password as part of username will take precedence. Putting nothing before or nothing after the percent symbol will cause an empty username or an empty password to be used. NOTE: Some servers (including OS/2 and Windows for Workgroups) insist on an uppercase password. Lowercase or mixed-case passwords might be rejected by these servers. Be cautious about including passwords in scripts.

-d debuglevel `debuglevel` is an integer from 0 to 5.

The default value if this parameter is not specified is zero. The higher this value, the more detail will be logged to the log files about the activities of the client. At level 0, only critical errors and serious warnings will be logged. Level 1 is a reasonable level for day-to day-running—it generates a small amount of information about operations carried out.

Levels above 1 will generate considerable amounts of log data and should only be used when you're investigating a problem. Levels above 3 are designed for use only by developers and generate huge amounts of log data, most of which is extremely cryptic.

-l log basename If specified, `log basename` specifies a base filename into which operational data from the running client will be logged. The default base name is specified at compile time. The base name is used to generate actual log filenames. For example, if the name specified is "log," the following files will be used for log data:

log.client.debug (containing debugging information)

log.client.in (containing inbound transaction data)

log.client.out (containing outbound transaction data)

The log files generated are never removed by the client.

`-n` **netbios name** By default, the client will use the local machine's hostname (in uppercase) as its NetBIOS name. This parameter enables you to override the hostname and use whatever NetBIOS name you wish.

`-W` **workgroup** Override what workgroup is used for the connection. This may be needed to connect to some servers.

`-p` **port number** `port number` is a positive integer value. The default value if this parameter is not specified is 139. This number is the port number that will be used when making connections to the server. The standard (well-known) port number for the server is 139, hence the default. This parameter is not normally specified.

`-T` **tar options** `tar options` consists of one or more of `c`, `x`, `I`, `X`, `b`, `g`, `N`, or `a`, used as:

```
smbclient \\server\share -TcxIXbgNa [ blocksize ] [ newer-file ] tarfile
[ filenames.... ]
```

> `c` **Create a tar file on UNIX** Must be followed by the name of a tar file, tape device, or "-" for standard output. It can be useful to set debugging low (-d0) to avoid corrupting your tar file if using "-". Mutually exclusive with the `x` flag.
>
> `x` **Extract (restore) a local tar file back to a share** Unless the `-D` option is given, the tar files will be restored from the top level of the share. Must be followed by the name of the tar file, device, or "-" for standard input. Mutually exclusive with the `c` flag.
>
> `I` **Include files and directories** Is the default behavior when filenames are specified above. Causes tar files to be included in an extract or create—and therefore everything else to be excluded (see example). Filename globbing does not work for included files for extractions (yet).
>
> `X` **Exclude files and directories** Causes tar files to be excluded from an extract or create (see example). Filename globbing does not work for excluded files (yet).
>
> `b` **Blocksize** Must be followed by a valid (greater than zero) blocksize. Causes tar file to be written out in blocksize*TBLOCK (usually 512 byte) blocks.
>
> `g` **Incremental** Only backs up files that have the archive bit set. Useful only with the `c` flag.
>
> `N` **Newer than** Must be followed by the name of a file whose date is compared against files found on the share during a create. Only files newer than the file specified are backed up to the tar file. Useful only with the `c` flag.
>
> `a` **Set archive bit**—Causes the archive bit to be reset when a file is backed up. Useful with the `g` (and `c`) flags.

Examples

```
smbclient \\mypc\myshare "" -N -Tx backup.tar
```

Restore from tar file backup.tar into myshare on mypc (no password on share).

```
smbclient \\mypc\myshare "" -N -TXx backup.tar users/docs
```

Restore everything except users/docs

```
smbclient \\mypc\myshare "" -N -Tc backup.tar users/docs
```

Create a tar file of the files beneath users/docs.

-D initial directory Change to initial directory before starting. Probably only of any use with the tar (`-T`) option.

-c command string Command string is a semicolon-separated list of commands to be executed instead of prompting from `stdin`. `-N` is implied by `-c`. This is particularly useful in scripts and for printing `stdin` to the server, that is, `-c 'print -'`.

testparm

The command line for the `testparm` program is:

```
testparm [ configfilename [ hostname hostIP ] ]
```

The options mean:

configfilename This is the name of the configuration file to check.

hostname This is the name of the host on which to check access. If this parameter is supplied, the `hostIP` parameter must also be supplied, or strange things might happen.

hostIP This is the IP number of the host specified in the previous parameter. This number must be supplied if the `hostname` parameter is supplied, or strange things might happen.

smbstatus

The command line for the `smbstatus` program is:

```
smbstatus [ -b ] [ -d ] [ -p ] [ -s configuration file ]
```

The options mean:

-b Gives brief output.

-d Gives verbose output.

-p Prints a list of smbd processes and exits. Useful for scripting.

-s configuration file The default configuration filename is determined at compile time. The file specified contains the configuration details required by the server.

smbpasswd

The command line for the smbpasswd utility is:

```
smbpasswd [ -add ] [ username ]
```

The options mean:

-add Specifies that the username following should be added to the smbpasswd file, with the new password typed (press Enter for the old password). This option is ignored if the username following already exists in the smbpasswd file, and it is treated like a regular change password command. Note that the user to be added must already exist in the system password file (usually /etc/passwd) or the request to add the user will fail.

username You may only specify a username to the smbpasswd command if you are running as root. Only root should have the permission to modify other users' SMB passwords.

smbrun

The command line for the smbrun utility is:

```
smbrun shell-command
```

The option means:

shell-command The shell command to execute. The command should have a fully qualified path.

testprns

The command line for the testprns utility is:

```
testprns printername [ printcapname ]
```

The options mean:

printername This is the printer name to validate. Printer names are taken from the first field in each record in the printcap file. Single printer names and sets of aliases separated by vertical bars (|) are recognized. Note that no validation or checking of the printcap syntax is done beyond that required to extract the printer name.

The print spooling system might be more forgiving or less forgiving than `testprns`. However, if `testprns` finds the printer, `smbd` should do so as well.

printcapname This is the name of the printcap file in which to search for the given printer name. If no printcap name is specified, `testprns` will attempt to scan the printcap file specified at compile time (PRINTCAP_NAME).

smbtar

The command line for the `smbtar` program is:

```
smbtar -s server [ -p password ] [ -x service ] [ -X ] [ -d directory ]
[ -u user ] [ -t tape ] [ -b blocksize ] [ -N filename ] [ -i ] [ -r ]
[ -llog level ] [ -v ] filenames...
```

The options mean:

`-s` server The PC where the share resides.

`-x` service The share name on the PC to connect to. Default: backup.

`-X` Exclude mode Exclude filenames from tar create or restore.

`-d` directory Change to initial directory before restoring / backing up files

`-v` Verbose mode

`-p` password The password to use to access a share. There is no default.

`-u` user The user id for connecting. Default: UNIX login name.

`-t` tape Tape device. Can be regular file or tape device. Default: Tape environmental variable; if not set, a file called tar.out.

`-b` blocksize Blocking factor. Defaults to 20. See tar(1) for a fuller explanation.

`-N` filename Back up only files newer than filename. Could be used (for example) on a log file to implement incremental backups.

`-i` Incremental mode tar files are only backed up if they have the archive bit set. The archive bit is reset after each file is read.

-r Restore Files are restored to the share from the tar file.

-l log level Log (debug) level. Corresponds to `-d` flag of smbclient(1).

smbmnt

The command line for the `smbmnt` program is:

```
smbmnt mount-point [ -u uid ] [ -g gid ] [ -f file mode ] [ -d dir mode ]
```

The options mean:

-u uid, -g gid A Lan Manager server does not tell us anything about the owner of a file, but UNIX requires each file to have an owner and belong to a group. With `-u` and `-g`, you can tell `smbmount` which ids it should assign to the files in the mounted directory. The defaults for these values are the current `uid` and `gid`.

-f file mode, -d dir mode Like `-u` and `-g`, these options are also used to bridge differences in concepts between Lan Manager and UNIX. Lan Manager does not know anything about file permissions, so `smbmnt` must be told which permissions it should assign to the mounted files and directories. The values must be given as octal numbers. The default values are taken from the current umask, where the file mode is the current umask. The dir mode adds execute permissions wherever the file mode gives read permissions.

Note that these permissions can differ from the rights the server gives. If you do not have write permissions on the server, you should choose a file mode that matches your actual permissions. This certainly cannot override the restrictions imposed by the server.

In addition to specifying the file mode, the `-f` argument can be used to specify certain bug-fix workarounds. This allows bug fixes to be enabled on a per mount-point basis, rather than being compiled into the kernel. The required bug fixes are specified by prepending an (octal) value to the file mode. For information on the available bug workarounds, refer to the smbfs.txt file in the Linux kernel documentation directory.

smbumount

The command line for the `smbumount` program is:

```
smbumount mount-point
```

where

mount-point indicates the directory on which an SMB filesystem has been previously mounted.

smb.conf

The smb.conf file is the configuration file for the Samba suite and contains runtime configuration information. Parameters define the specific attributes of services. Some parameters are specific to the [global] section (that is, security). Some parameters are usable in all sections (that is, create mode). All others are permissible only in normal sections. For the purposes of the following descriptions, the [homes] and [printers] sections will be considered normal. The letter `G` in parentheses indicates a parameter specific to the [global] section. The letter `S` indicates a parameter can be specified in a service-specific section. Note that all `S` parameters can also be specified in the [global] section—in which case they will define the default behavior for all services.

Parameters are arranged here in alphabetical order—this may not create the best bedfellows, but at least you can find them. Where there are synonyms, the preferred term is defined, others refer you to the preferred term.

Variable Substitutions

Many of the strings that are settable in the config file can take substitutions. For example, the option `path = /tmp/%u` will be interpreted as `path = /tmp/john` if the user connects with the username john. These substitutions are mostly noted in this list of descriptions, some general substitutions apply whenever they might be relevant. These are:

%S The name of the current service, if any.

%P The root directory of the current service, if any.

%u User name of the current service, if any.

%g Primary group name of %u.

%U Session user name (the user name the client wanted, not necessarily the one they received).

%G Primary group name of %U.

%H Home directory of the user given by %U.

%v The Samba version.

%h Hostname Samba is running on.

%m NetBIOS name of the client machine (very useful).

%L NetBIOS name of the server. This enables you to change your config based on what the client calls you. Your server can have a "dual personality."

%M Internet name of the client machine

%N Name of your NIS home directory server, obtained from your NIS auto.map entry. If you have not compiled Samba with `-DAUTOMOUNT`, this value will be the same as `%L`.

%R The selected protocol level after protocol negotiation. As of Samba 1.9.18, it can be CORE, COREPLUS, LANMAN1, LANMAN2, or NT1.

%d Process id of the current server process.

%a Architecture of the remote machine. Only some are recognized, and these might not be 100% reliable. It currently recognizes Samba, WfWg, WinNT, and Win95. Anything else is "UNKNOWN."

%I The IP address of the client machine.

%T Current date and time.

Some quite creative things can be done with these substitutions and other smb.conf options.

Name Mangling

Samba supports "name mangling" so DOS and Windows clients can use files that don't conform to the 8.3 format. It can also be set to adjust the case of 8.3 format filenames. Several options control the way mangling is performed, and they are grouped here rather than listed separately. For the defaults, look at the output of the `testparm` program.

All of these options can be set separately for each service (or globally, of course). The options are:

mangle case = yes/no Controls if names that have characters not of the default case are mangled. For example, if this is Yes, a name such as Mail would be mangled. Default is No.

case sensitive = yes/no Controls whether filenames are case sensitive. If they aren't, Samba must do a filename search and match on passed names. Default is No.

default case = upper/lower Controls the default case for new filenames. Default is lower.

preserve case = yes/no Controls if new files are created with the case the client passes or if they are forced to be the default case. Default is No.

short preserve case = yes/no Controls if new files conforming to 8.3 syntax—that is, all in uppercase and of suitable length—are created uppercase or forced to be the default case. This option can be used with **preserve case = yes** to permit long filenames to retain their case while short names are lowered. Default is No.

Complete List of Parameters

In the list below, (S) denotes a service parameter and (G) denotes a global parameter.

admin users (S) This is a list of users who will be granted administrative privileges on the share. This means they will do all file operations as the superuser (root). You should use this option very carefully, as any user in this list will be able to do anything they like on the share, irrespective of file permissions.

announce as (G) This specifies what type of server `nmbd` will announce itself as in browse lists. By default, this is set to Windows NT. The valid options are NT, Win95, or WfW, meaning Windows NT, Windows 95, and Windows for Workgroups, respectively. Do not change this parameter unless you have a specific need to stop Samba from appearing as an NT server This parameter can prevent Samba servers from participating as browser servers correctly.

announce version (G) This specifies the major and minor version numbers `nmbd` will use when announcing itself as a server. The default is 4.2. Do not change this parameter unless you have a specific need to set a Samba server to be a downlevel server.

auto services (G) This is a list of services you want automatically added to the browse lists. This is most useful for homes and printer services that would otherwise not be visible. Note that if you just want all printers in your printcap file loaded, the `load printers` option is easier.

allow hosts (S) A synonym for this parameter is . This parameter is a comma-delimited set of hosts that are permitted to access a service. If specified in the [global] section, it will apply to all services, regardless of whether the individual service has a different setting. You can specify the hosts by name or IP number; for example, you could restrict access to only the hosts on a Class C subnet with something like `allow hosts = 150.203.5`. The full syntax of the list is described in the man page hosts_access(5).

You can also specify hosts by network/netmask pairs and by netgroup names if your system supports netgroups. The EXCEPT keyword can also be used to limit a wildcard list. The following examples might provide some help:

Example 1: allow all IPs in 150.203.*.* except one:

```
hosts allow = 150.203. EXCEPT 150.203.6.66
```

Example 2: allow hosts that match the given network/netmask:

```
hosts allow = 150.203.15.0/255.255.255.0
```

Example 3: allow a couple of hosts:

```
hosts allow = lapland, arvidsjaur
```

Example 4: allow only hosts in netgroup "foonet" or localhost, but deny access from one particular host:

```
hosts allow = @foonet, localhost
hosts deny = pirate
```

Note that access still requires suitable user-level passwords. See testparm(1) for a way of testing your host access to see if it does what you expect.

alternate permissions (S) This option affects the way the "read only" DOS attribute is produced for UNIX files. If this is False, the read-only bit is set for files on writable shares to which the user cannot write. If this is True, it is set for files for which user write bit is not set. The latter behavior is useful when users copy files from each other's directories and use a file manager that preserves permissions. Without this option, users might get annoyed, because all copied files will have the read only bit set.

available (S) This parameter enables you to turn off a service. If available = no, all attempts to connect to the service will fail. Such failures are logged.

bind interfaces only (G) This global parameter (new for 1.9.18) enables the Samba administrator to limit the interfaces on a machine that will serve `SMB` requests. It affects file service (`smbd`) and name service (`nmbd`) in slightly different ways. For name service, it causes `nmbd` to bind to ports 137 and 138 on the interfaces listed in the `interfaces` parameter. `nmbd` also binds to the "all addresses" interface (`0.0.0.0`) on ports 137 and 138 for the purpose of reading broadcast messages. If this option is not set, `nmbd` will service name requests on all of these sockets. If `bind interfaces only` is set, `nmbd` will check the source address of any packets coming in on the broadcast sockets and discard any that don't match the broadcast addresses of the interfaces in the Interfaces parameter list. As unicast packets are received on the other sockets, it allows `nmbd` to refuse to serve names to machines sending packets that arrive through any interfaces not listed in the Interfaces list. IP Source address spoofing does defeat this simple check, however, so it must not be used seriously as a security feature for `nmbd`.

For file service, this parameter causes `smbd` to bind only to the Interface list given in the `interfaces` parameter. This restricts the networks `smbd` will serve to packets coming in those interfaces. Note that you should not use this parameter for machines serving PPP or other intermittent or non-broadcast network interfaces, because it will not cope with non-permanent interfaces.

browsable (S) Controls whether this share is seen in the list of available shares in a net view and in the browse list.

browse list (G) Controls whether the `smbd` will serve a browse list to a client doing a NetServerEnum call. Normally set to True. You should never need to change this.

case sensitive (G) See the section, "Name Mangling."

case sig names (G) See the section, "Name Mangling."

character set (G) This enables smbd to map incoming characters from a DOS 850 code page to either a Western European (ISO8859-1) or Easter European (ISO8859-2) code page. Normally not set, meaning no filename translation is done.

client code page (G) Currently (Samba 1.9.17 and above) this may be set to one of two values, 850 or 437. It specifies the base DOS code page used by the clients accessing Samba. To determine this, open a DOS command prompt and type the command **`chcp`** to output the code page. The default for USA MS-DOS, Windows 95, and Windows NT releases is code page 437. The default for Western European releases of these operating systems is code page 850. This parameter cooperates with the `valid chars` parameter in determining what characters are valid in filenames and how capitalization is done. It has been added as a convenience for clients whose code page is either 437 or 850, so a convoluted "valid chars" string does not have to be determined. If you set both this parameter and the `valid chars` parameter, the `client code page` parameter MUST be set before `valid chars` in the smb.conf file. The `valid chars` string will then augment the character settings in the `client code page` parameter.

If `client code page` is set to a value other than 850 or 437, it will default to 850. See also *valid chars*.

comment (S) This text field is seen next to a share when a client does a net view to list what shares are available. If you want to set the string displayed next to the machine name, see the *server string* command.

config file (G) This enables you to override the config file to use, instead of the default (usually smb.conf). There is a chicken-and-egg problem here, because this option is set in the config file. For this reason, if the name of the config file changed when the parameters were loaded, it will reload them from the new config file. This option takes the usual substitutions, which can be very useful. If the config file doesn't exist, it won't be loaded (enabling you to special-case the config files of just a few clients). Example:

```
config file = /usr/local/samba/lib/smb.conf.%m
```

copy (S) This parameter enables you to "clone" service entries. The specified service is simply duplicated under the current service's name. Any parameters specified in the current section will override those in the section being copied. This feature enables you to set up a "template" service and create similar services easily. Note that the service being copied must occur earlier in the configuration file than the service doing the copying.

create mask (S) A synonym for this parameter is `create mode`. When a file is created, the necessary permissions are calculated according to the mapping from DOS modes to UNIX permissions, and the resulting UNIX mode is then bit-wise ANDed with this parameter. The `create mask` parameter can be thought of as a bit-wise mask for the UNIX modes of a file. Any bit *not* set here will be removed from the modes set on a file when it is created. The default value of this parameter removes the `group` and `other` write and execute bits from the UNIX modes. Following this, Samba will bit-wise OR the UNIX mode created from this parameter with the value of the `force create mode` parameter, which is set to `000` by default.

For Samba 1.9.17 and above, the `create mask` parameter no longer affects directory modes. See the parameter *directory mode* for details. See also the *force create mode* parameter for forcing particular mode bits to be set on created files. See also the *directory mode* parameter for masking mode bits on created directories.

create mode (S) See *create mask.*

dead time (G) The value of this parameter (a decimal integer) represents the number of minutes of inactivity before a connection is considered dead and is disconnected. The dead time only takes effect if the number of open files is zero. This is useful to prevent a server's resources being exhausted by a large number of inactive connections. Most clients have an auto-reconnect feature when a connection is broken so in most cases this parameter should be transparent to users. Using this parameter with a timeout of a few minutes is recommended for most systems. A dead time of zero indicates that no auto-disconnection should be performed.

debug level (G) The value of this parameter (an integer) allows the debug level (logging level) to be specified in the smb.conf file. This is to give greater flexibility in the configuration of the system. The default will be the debug level specified on the command line.

default (G) See *default service.*

default case (S) See the section on "Name Mangling." Also see *short preserve case.*

default service (G) A synonym for this parameter is *default*. This parameter specifies the name of a service to which you will be connected if the service actually requested cannot be found. Note that the brackets are not given in the parameter value. There is no default value for this parameter. If this parameter is not given, attempting to connect to a nonexistent service will result in an error. Typically the default service would be a public, read-only service. Also note that as of 1.9.14, the apparent service name will be changed to equal that of the requested service. This is very useful because it enables you to use macros such as %S to make a wildcard service. Note also that any _ characters in the name of the service used in the default service will get mapped to a /. This allows for interesting things.

delete readonly (S) This parameter allows read-only files to be deleted. This is not normal DOS semantics but is allowed by UNIX. This option might be useful for running applications such as `rcs`, where UNIX file ownership prevents changing file permissions and DOS semantics prevent deletion of a read-only file.

deny hosts (S) A synonym for this parameter is *hosts deny* and its opposite is *allow hosts*. Hosts listed here are not permitted access to services unless the specific services have their own lists to override this one. If the lists conflict, the Allow list takes precedence.

delete veto files (S) This option is used when Samba is attempting to delete a directory that contains one or more vetoed directories (see the *veto files* option). If this option is set to False (the default) and a vetoed directory contains any non-vetoed files or directories, the directory delete will fail. This is usually what you want. If this option is set to True, Samba will attempt to recursively delete any files and directories within the vetoed directory. This can be useful for integration with file-serving systems, such as NetaTalk, that create metafiles within directories you might normally veto DOS/Windows users from seeing (for example, .AppleDouble). Setting `delete veto files = True` allows these directories to be transparently deleted when the parent directory is deleted (so long as the user has permissions to do so).

`dfree` command (G) The `dfree` command setting should only be used on systems where a problem occurs with the internal disk space calculations. This has been known to happen with Ultrix, but might occur with other operating systems. The symptom seen was an error of `Abort Retry Ignore` at the end of each directory listing.

The `dfree` command setting enables you to substitute an external routine for the internal routines used for calculating the total disk space and amount available. The external program will be passed a single parameter indicating a directory in the filesystem being queried. This will typically consist of the string `./`. The script should return two integers in ASCII. The first should be the total disk space in blocks, and the second should be the number of available blocks. An optional third return value can give the block size in bytes. The default blocksize is 1024 bytes. NOTE: Your script should not be `setuid` or `setgid` and should be owned by (and writable only by) root.

directory (S) See *path*.

directory mask (S) A synonym for this parameter is *directory mode*. This parameter is the octal modes used for converting DOS modes to UNIX modes when creating UNIX directories. When a directory is created, the necessary permissions are calculated according to the mapping from DOS modes to UNIX permissions, and the resulting UNIX mode is then bit-wise ANDed with this parameter. This parameter can be thought of as a bit-wise mask for the UNIX modes of a directory. Any bit not set here will be removed from the modes set on a directory when it is created. The default value of this parameter removes the `group` and `other` write bits from the UNIX mode, allowing only the user who owns the directory to modify it.

Following this, Samba will bit-wise OR the UNIX mode created from this parameter with the value of the `force directory mode` parameter. This parameter is set to `000` by default (that is, no extra mode bits are added). See the *force directory mode* parameter to cause particular mode bits to always be set on created directories. See the `create mode` parameter for masking mode bits on created files.

directory mode (S) See *directory mask*.

dns proxy (G) Specifies that `nmbd` should (as a WINS server), on finding that a NetBIOS name has not been registered, treat the NetBIOS name word-for-word as a DNS name. Note that the maximum length for a NetBIOS name is 15 characters, so the DNS name (or DNS alias) can likewise only be 15 characters, maximum.

Note also that `nmbd` will block completely until the DNS name is resolved. This will result in temporary loss of browsing and WINS services. Enable this option only if you are certain DNS resolution is fast, or you can live with the consequences of periodic pauses in `nmbd` service.

domain controller (G) Specifies the DNS name or IP address of the machine to which to refer domain logons from Win95 machines. You should never need to set this parameter.

domain logons (G) If set to True, the Samba server will serve Windows 95 domain logons for the workgroup it is in. For more details on setting up this feature, see the file DOMAINS.txt in the Samba source documentation directory.

domain master (G) Enable WAN-wide browse list collation. Local master browsers on broadcast-isolated subnets will give Samba their local browse lists and ask for a complete copy of the browse list for the whole Wide Area Network. Browser clients will then contact their local master browser and will receive the domain-wide browse list, instead of just the list for their broadcast-isolated subnet.

dont descend (S) Certain directories on some systems (for example, the /proc tree under Linux) are either not of interest to clients or are infinitely deep (recursive). This parameter allows you to specify a comma-delimited list of directories the server should always show as empty. Note that Samba can be very fussy about the exact format of the `dont descend` entries. For example, you might need ./proc instead of just /proc. Experimentation is the best policy.

dos filetimes (S) Under DOS and Windows, if users can write to a file, they can change the timestamp on it. Under POSIX semantics, only the owner of the file or root may change the timestamp. By default, Samba runs with POSIX semantics and refuses to change the timestamp on a file if `smbd` is acting on behalf of a user who is not the file owner. Setting this option to True allows DOS semantics, and `smbd` will change the file timestamp as DOS requires. This is a correct implementation of a previous compile-time option (UTIME_WORKAROUND) that was broken and is now removed.

encrypt passwords (G) This Boolean controls whether encrypted passwords will be negotiated with the client. Note that this option has no effect if you haven't compiled in the necessary des libraries and encryption code. It defaults to No.

exec (S) This is an alias for *preexec*.

fake oplocks (S) Oplocks are the way SMB clients get permission from a server to locally cache file operations. If a server grants an oplock (opportunistic lock), the client is free to assume it is the only one accessing the file and it will aggressively cache file data. With some oplock types, the client may even cache file open/close operations. This can give enormous performance benefits.

When you set `fake oplocks = yes`, Samba will always grant oplock requests, no matter how many clients are using the file. By enabling this option on all read-only shares or on shares you know will only be accessed from one client at a time, you will see a big performance improvement on many operations. If you enable this option on shares where multiple clients may be accessing the files read-write at the same time, you can get data corruption. Use this option carefully. It is generally much better to use the real oplock support except for physically read-only media such as CD-ROMs. This option is disabled by default.

follow symlinks (S) This parameter allows the Samba administrator to stop `smbd` from following symbolic links in a particular share. Setting this parameter to No prevents any file or directory that is a symbolic link from being followed (the user will get an error). This option is very useful to stop users from adding a symbolic link to /etc/pasword in their home directory, for instance; however, it will slow filename lookups slightly. This option is enabled by default (that is, `smbd` will follow symbolic links).

force create mode (S) This parameter specifies a set of UNIX mode bit permissions that will always be set on a file created by Samba. This is done by bit-wise ORing these bits onto the mode bits of a file being created. The default for this parameter is (in octal) 000. The modes in this parameter are bit-wise ORed onto the file mode after the mask set in the `create mask` parameter is applied. See also the parameter `create mask` for details on masking mode bits on created files.

force directory mode (S) This parameter specifies a set of UNIX mode bit permissions that will always be set on a directory created by Samba. This is done by bit-wise ORing these bits onto the mode bits of a directory being created. The default for this parameter is (in octal) 0000, which will not add any extra permission bits to a created directory. This operation is done after the mode mask in the parameter `directory mask` is applied. See the parameter *directory mask* for details on masking mode bits on created directories.

force group (S) This specifies a group name for all connections to this service. This may be useful for sharing files.

force user (S) This specifies a user name for all connections to this service. This may be useful for sharing files. You should use this parameter carefully, because using it incorrectly can cause security problems. This user name only gets used after a connection is established. Thus a client still needs to connect as a valid user and supply a valid password. When connected, all file operations will be performed as the "forced user," no matter what username the client connected as.

getwd cache (G) This is a tuning option. When `getwd cache` is enabled, a caching algorithm will be used to reduce the time taken for `getwd()` calls. This can have a significant impact on performance, especially when `widelinks` is False.

group (S) This is an alias for `force group` and is kept only for compatibility with old versions of Samba. It might be removed in future versions.

guest account (S) This is a username that will be used for access to services specified as *guest ok* (see definition). Whatever privileges of this user will be available to any client connecting to the guest service. Typically this user will exist in the password file but will not have a valid login. If a username is specified in a given service, the specified username overrides this one.

On some systems, the account "nobody" might not print. In this case, use another account. You should test this by trying to log in as your guest user (perhaps by using the `su -` command) and trying to print by using `lpr`. Note that as of version 1.9 of Samba, this option might be set differently for each service.

guest ok (S) See *public*.

guest only (S) If this parameter is Yes for a service, only guest connections to the service will be permitted. This parameter will have no effect if `guest ok` or `public` is not set for the service.

hide dot files (S) This is a Boolean parameter that controls whether files starting with a dot appear as hidden files.

hide files (S) This is a list of files or directories that are not visible but are accessible. The DOS "hidden" attribute is applied to any files or directories that match. Each entry in the list must be separated by a `/`, which allows spaces to be included in the entry. The `*` and `?` can be used to specify multiple files or directories as in DOS wildcards. Each entry must be a UNIX path, not a DOS path, and must not include the UNIX directory separator `/`. Note that the `case sensitive` option is applicable in hiding files. Setting the `hide files` parameter will affect the performance of Samba, which will check all files and directories for a match as they are scanned. See also *hide dot files*, *veto files*, and the section, "Name Mangling."

homedir map (G) If `nis homedir` is True, this parameter specifies the NIS (or YP) map from which the server for the user's home directory should be extracted. At present, only the Sun auto.home map format is understood. The form of the map is:

```
username server:/some/file/system
```

and the program will extract the servername from before the first :. There should probably be a better parsing system that copes with different map formats and also `Amd` (another automounter) maps.

Note: The -DNETGROUP option is required in the `makefile` for this option to work, and on some architectures, the line `-lrpcsvc` needs to be added to the `LIBSM` variable. This is required for Solaris 2, FreeBSD, and HPUX. See also *nis homedir*.

hosts allow (S) See *allow hosts*.

hosts deny (S) See *deny hosts*.

hosts equiv (G) If this global parameter is a non-null string, it specifies the name of a file to read for the names of hosts and users who will be allowed access without specifying a password. This is not be confused with `allow hosts`, which is about hosts' access to services. The `hosts equiv` parameter is more useful for guest services. `hosts equiv` might be useful for NT clients that will not supply passwords to Samba.

Note: The use of `hosts.equiv` can be a major security hole, because you are trusting the PC to supply the correct username. It is very easy to get a PC to supply a false username. I recommend you use the `hosts.equiv` option only if you know what you are doing.

include (G) This allows you to include one config file inside another. The file is included literally, as though typed in place. It takes the standard substitutions, except `%u`, `%P`, and `%S`.

interfaces (G) This option enables you to set up multiple network interfaces so Samba can properly handle browsing on all interfaces. The option takes a list of ip/netmask pairs. The netmask may be either a bitmask or a bitlength. For example, the following line:

```
interfaces = 192.168.2.10/24 192.168.3.10/24
```

would configure two network interfaces with IP addresses 192.168.2.10 and 192.168.3.10. The netmasks of both interfaces would be set to 255.255.255.0. You could produce an equivalent result by using:

```
interfaces = 192.168.2.10/255.255.255.0 192.168.3.10/255.255.255.0
```

if you prefer that format. If the `interfaces` option is not set, Samba will attempt to find a primary interface but won't attempt to configure more than one interface.

invalid users (S) This is a list of users that should not be allowed to log in to this service. This is really a "paranoid" check to absolutely ensure an improper setting does not breach your security. A name starting with `@` is interpreted as a UNIX group. The current servicename is substituted for `%S`. This is useful in the [homes] section. See also *valid users*.

keep alive (G) The value of this parameter (an integer) represents the number of seconds between "keepalive" packets. If this parameter is zero, no keepalive packets will be sent. Keepalive packets, if sent, allow the server to tell whether a client is still present and responding. Keepalives should, in general, not be needed if the socket being used has the SO_KEEPALIVE attribute set on it (see *socket options*). You should use this option only if you encounter difficulties.

lm announce (G) This parameter determines whether Samba will produce Lanman announce broadcasts needed by OS/2 clients for them to see the Samba server in their browse list. This parameter can have three values: True, False, or Auto. The default is Auto. If set to False, Samba will never produce these broadcasts. If set to True, Samba will produce Lanman announce broadcasts at a frequency set by the parameter `lm interval`. If set to Auto, Samba will not send Lanman announce broadcasts by default but will listen for them. If it hears such a broadcast on the wire, it will then start sending them at a frequency set by the parameter See also *lm interval*.

lm interval (G) If Samba is set to produce Lanman announce broadcasts needed by OS/2 clients (see the `lm announce` parameter), this parameter defines the frequency in seconds with which they will be made. If this is set to zero, no Lanman announcements will be made despite the setting of the `lm announce` parameter. See also *lm announce.*

load printers (G) A Boolean variable that controls whether all printers in the printcap will be loaded for browsing by default.

local master (G) This option allows the nmbd to become a local master browser on a subnet. If set to False then nmbd will not attempt to become a local master browser on a subnet and will also lose in all browsing elections. By default this value is set to True. Setting this value to True doesn't mean that Samba will become the local master browser on a subnet, just that the nmbd will participate in elections for local master browser.

locking (S) This controls whether locking will be performed by the server in response to lock requests from the client. If "locking = no", all lock and unlock requests will appear to succeed and all lock queries will indicate that the queried lock is clear. If `locking = yes`, real locking will be performed by the server. This option may be particularly useful for read-only filesystems which do not need locking (such as CD-ROM drives). Be careful about disabling locking either globally or in a specific service, as lack of locking may result in data corruption.

log file (G) This options allows you to override the name of the Samba log file (also known as the debug file). This option takes the standard substitutions, allowing you to have separate log files for each user or machine. Example:

```
log file = /usr/local/samba/var/log.%m
```

log level (G) See *debug level.*

logon drive (G) This parameter specifies the local path to which the home directory will be connected (see *logon home*) and is used only by NT Workstations.

logon home (G) This parameter specifies the home directory location when a Win95 or NT Workstation logs into a Samba PDC. It enables you to do `NET USE H: /HOME` from a command prompt, for example. This option takes the standard substitutions, allowing you to have separate logon scripts for each user or machine.

logon path (G) This parameter specifies the home directory where roaming profiles (USER.DAT / USER.MAN files for Windows 95) are stored. This option takes the standard substitutions, enables you to have separate logon scripts for each user or machine. It also specifies the directory from which the Desktop, Start menu, Nethood, and Programs folders, and their contents, are loaded and displayed on your Windows 95 client. The share and the path must be readable by the user for the preferences and directories to be loaded onto the Windows 95 client. The share must be writable when the user logs in for the first time, so the Windows 95 client can create the user.dat and other directories. Thereafter, the directories and any contents can, if required, be made read-only. It is not advisable for the USER.DAT file to be made read-only—rename it USER.MAN to achieve the desired effect (a mandatory profile).

Windows clients can sometimes maintain a connection to the [homes] share, even though there is no user logged in. Therefore, it is vital that the logon path does not include a reference to the [homes] share (\\%N\HOMES\profile_path will cause problems). The `logon path` option takes the standard substitutions, enabling you to have separate logon scripts for each user or machine.

logon script (G) This parameter specifies the batch file (.bat) or NT command file (.cmd) to be downloaded and run on a machine when a user successfully logs in. The file must contain the DOS style cr/lf line endings. Using a DOS-style editor to create the file is recommended. The script must be a relative path to the [netlogon] service. If the [netlogon] service specifies a path of /usr/local/samba/netlogon, and logon script = STARTUP.BAT, the file that will be downloaded is

```
/usr/local/samba/netlogon/STARTUP.BAT
```

The contents of the batch file are entirely your choice. A suggested command would be to add NET TIME \\SERVER /SET /YES, to force every machine to synchronize clocks with the same timeserver. Another use would be to add NET USE U: \\SERVER\UTILS for commonly used utilities, or NET USE Q: \\SERVER\ISO9001_QA. Note that it is particularly important not to allow write access to the [netlogon] share or to grant users write permission on the batch files in a secure environment; this would allow the batch files to be arbitrarily modified. The `logon script` option takes the standard substitutions, enabling you to have separate logon scripts for each user or machine.

`lppause` command (S) This parameter specifies the command to be executed on the server host to stop printing or spooling a specific print job. This command should be a program or script that takes a printer name and job number to pause the print job. Currently I don't know of any print spooler system that can do this with a simple option except for the PPR system from Trinity College (ppr-dist.trincoll.edu/pub/ppr). One way of implementing this is by using job priorities, where jobs having a too low priority won't be sent to the printer.

If a `%p` is given, the printer name is put in its place. A `%j` is replaced with the job number (an integer). On HPUX, if the `-p%p` option is added to the `lpq` command, the job will show up with the correct status; that is, if the `job` priority is lower than the `set fence` priority, it will have the PAUSED status, whereas if the priority is equal or higher, it will have the SPOOLED or PRINTING status. It is good practice to include the absolute path in the `lppause` command, because the PATH might not be available to the server.

lpq cache time (G) This controls how long `lpq` info will be cached to prevent calling the `lpq` command too often. A separate cache is kept for each variation of the `lpq` command used by the system, so if you use different `lpq` commands for different users, they won't share cache information. The cache files are stored in /tmp/lpq.xxxx, where xxxx is a hash of the `lpq` command in use. The default is 10 seconds, meaning that the cached results of a previous identical `lpq` command will be used if the cached data is less than 10 seconds old. A large value might be advisable if your `lpq` command is very slow. A value of 0 will disable caching completely.

lpq command (S) This parameter specifies the command to be executed on the server host to obtain `lpq`-style printer status information. This command should be a program or script that takes a printer name as its only parameter and outputs printer status information. Currently, six styles of printer status information are supported—BSD, SYSV, AIX, HPUX, QNX, LPRNG, and PLP—which covers most UNIX systems. You control which type is expected by using the `printing =` option. Some clients (notably Windows for Workgroups) might not correctly send the connection number for the printer about which they are requesting status information. To get around this, the server will report on the first printer service to which the client connects. This only happens if the connection number sent is invalid. If a %p is given, the printer name is put in its place; otherwise, it is placed at the end of the command. Note that it is good practice to include the absolute path in the `lpq` command, because the PATH might not be available to the server.

`lpresume` command (S) This parameter specifies the command to be executed on the server host to restart or continue printing or spooling a specific print job. This command should be a program or script that takes a printer name and job number to resume the print job. See also the *lppause command.*

If a `%p` is given, the printer name is put in its place. A `%j` is replaced with the job number (an integer). Note that it is good practice to include the absolute path in the `lpresume` command, because the PATH might not be available to the server.

`lprm` command (S) This parameter specifies the command to be executed on the server host to delete a print job. This command should be a program or script that takes a printer name and job number and deletes the print job. Currently seven styles of printer control are supported—BSD, SYSV, AIX HPUX, QNX, LPRNG and PLP—which covers most UNIX systems. You control which type is expected by using the `printing =` option. If a `%p` is given, the printer name is put in its place. A `%j` is replaced with the job number (an integer). Note that it is good practice to include the absolute path in the `lprm` command as the PATH might not be available to the server.

magic output (S) This parameter specifies the name of a file that will contain output created by a magic script (see *magic script*). Warning: If two clients use the same magic script in the same directory, the output file content is undefined.

magic script (S) This parameter specifies the name of a file that, if opened, will be executed by the server when the file is closed. This allows a UNIX script to be sent to the Samba host and executed on behalf of the connected user. Scripts executed in this way will be deleted upon completion, permissions permitting. If the script generates output, output will be sent to the file specified by the `magic output` parameter (see *magic output*). Note that some shells are unable to interpret scripts containing carriage-return linefeed instead of linefeed as the end-of-line marker. Magic scripts must be executable "as is" on the host, which for some hosts and some shells will require filtering at the DOS end. Magic scripts are experimental and you should not rely on them.

mangle case (S) See the section on "Name Mangling."

mangled map (S) This is for those who want to directly map UNIX filenames that are not representable on DOS. The mangling of names is not always what is needed. In particular, you might have documents with file extensions that differ between DOS and UNIX. For example, under UNIX, it is common to use .html for HTML files, but .htm is more commonly used under DOS. To map .html to .htm, you put

```
mangled map = (*.html *.htm)
```

One very useful case is to remove the annoying ;1 off the ends of filenames on some CD-ROMS (only visible under some UNIXes). To do this, use a map of `(*;1 *)`.

mangled names (S) This controls whether non-DOS names under UNIX should be mapped to DOS-compatible names ("mangled") and made visible, or whether non-DOS names should simply be ignored. See the section on "Name Mangling" for details on how to control the mangling process. If mangling is used, the mangling algorithm is as follows:

- The first (up to) five alphanumeric characters before the right-most dot of the filename are preserved and forced to uppercase, and they appear as the first (up to) five characters of the mangled name.
- A tilde (~) is appended to the first part of the mangled name, followed by a two-character unique sequence based on the original root name (that is, the original filename minus its final extension). The final extension is included in the hash calculation only if it contains any uppercase characters or is longer than three characters. Note that the character to use can be specified by using the `mangling char` option if you don't like ~.

- The first three alphanumeric characters of the final extension are preserved and forced to uppercase, and they appear as the extension of the mangled name. The final extension is defined as that part of the original filename after the right-most dot. If there are no dots in the filename, the mangled name will have no extension (except in the case of hidden files).
- A file whose UNIX name begins with a dot will be presented as a DOS hidden file. The mangled name will be created as for other filenames, but with the leading dot removed and "___" as its extension, regardless of the actual original extension (that's three underscores). The two-digit hash value consists of uppercase alphanumeric characters.

This algorithm can cause name collisions only if files in a directory share the same first five alphanumeric characters. The probability of such a clash is 1/1300. The name mangling (if enabled) allows a file to be copied between UNIX directories from DOS while retaining its long UNIX filename. UNIX files can be renamed to a new extension from DOS and will retain the same basename. Mangled names do not change between sessions.

mangling char (S) This controls what character is used as the "magic" character in name mangling. The default tilde (~) might interfere with some software. Use this option to set it to whatever you prefer.

mangled stack (G) This parameter controls the number of mangled names that should be cached in the Samba server. This stack is a list of recently mangled base names (extensions are only maintained if they are longer than three characters or contain uppercase characters). The larger this value, the more likely it is that mangled names can be successfully converted to correct long UNIX names; however, large stack sizes will slow most directory access. Smaller stacks save memory in the server (each stack element costs 256 bytes). It is not possible to absolutely guarantee correct long filenames, so be prepared for some surprises.

map archive (S) This controls whether the DOS archive attribute should be mapped to the UNIX owner execute bit. The DOS archive bit is set when a file has been modified since its last backup. One motivation for this option it to keep Samba or your PC from making any file it touches executable under UNIX. This can be quite annoying for shared source code, documents, and so on. Note that this parameter requires the `create mask` to be set such that the owner execute bit is not masked out (that is, it must include 100). See the parameter *create mask* for details.

map hidden (S) This controls whether DOS-style hidden files should be mapped to the UNIX world execute bit. Note that this requires the `create mask` to be set such that the world execute bit is not masked out (that is, it must include 001). See the parameter *create mask* for details.

map system (S) This controls whether DOS-style system files should be mapped to the UNIX group execute bit. Note that this requires the *create mask* to be set such that the group execute bit is not masked out (that is, it must include 010). See the parameter *create mask* for details.

max connections (S) This option allows the number of simultaneous connections to a service to be limited. If `max connections` is greater than 0, connections will be refused if the same number of connections to the service are already open. A value of zero means an unlimited number of connections may be made. Record lock files are used to implement this feature. The lock files will be stored in the directory specified by the `lock directory` option.

max disk size (G) This option enables you to put an upper limit on the apparent size of disks. If you set this option to 100, all shares will appear to be not larger than 100MB in size. Note that this option does not limit the amount of data you can put on the disk. In such a case, you could still store much more than 100MB on the disk, but if a client ever asks for the amount of free disk space or the total disk size, the result will be bounded by the amount specified in `max disk size`. This option is primarily useful to work around bugs in some pieces of software that can't handle very large disks, particularly disks over 1GB in size. A `max disk size` of 0 means no limit.

max log size (G) This option (an integer in kilobytes) specifies the max size to which the log file should grow. Samba periodically checks the size; if it is exceeded, it will rename the file, adding an .old extension. A size of 0 means no limit.

max mux (G) This option controls the maximum number of outstanding simultaneous SMB operations Samba tells the client it will allow. You should never need to set this parameter.

max packet (G) A synonym for this parameter is *packet size*.

max ttl (G) This option tells `nmbd` what the default "time to live" of NetBIOS names should be (in seconds) when `nmbd` is requesting a name either by using a broadcast or from a WINS server. You should never need to change this parameter.

max wins ttl (G) This option tells `nmbd`, when it's acting as a WINS server (`wins support = true`), the maximum "time to live" of NetBIOS names `nmbd` will grant (in seconds). You should never need to change this parameter. The default is three days (259,200 seconds).

max xmit (G) This option controls the maximum packet size that will be negotiated by Samba. The default is 65535, which is the maximum. In some cases, you might get better performance with a smaller value. A value below 2048 is likely to cause problems.

`message` command (G) This specifies what command to run when the server receives a WinPopup-style message. This would normally be a command that would deliver the message somehow. How this is to be done is up to your imagination. Andrew Tridgel uses this:

```
message command = csh -c 'xedit %s;rm %s' &
```

This delivers the message by using `xedit` and removes it afterwards. NOTE: It is very important that this command return immediately—that's why I have the `&` on the end. If it doesn't return immediately, your PCs might freeze when sending messages (but they should recover after 30 seconds). All messages are delivered as the global guest user. The command takes the standard substitutions, although `%u` won't work (`%U` may be better in this case). Apart from the standard substitutions, some additional ones apply; in particular:

`%s` = the filename containing the message

`%t` = the destination that message was sent to (probably the server name)

`%f` = who the message is from

You could make this command send mail or whatever else takes your fancy. Here's a way of sending the messages as mail to root:

```
message command = /bin/mail -s 'message from %f on %m' root < %s; rm %s
```

If you don't have a message command, the message won't be delivered and Samba will tell the sender there was an error. Unfortunately, WfWg totally ignores the error code and carries on regardless, saying the message was delivered. If you want to silently delete it, try `message command = rm %s`. For the really adventurous, try something like this:

```
message command = csh -c 'csh < %s ¦& /usr/local/samba/bin/smbclient -M
%m; rm %s' &
```

This would execute the command as a script on the server and then give them the result in a WinPopup message. Note that you could cause a loop if you send a message from the server by using smbclient—you'd better wrap the command in a script that checks for this.

min print space (S) This sets the minimum amount of free disk space that must be available before a user will be able to spool a print job. It is specified in kilobytes. The default is 0, which means no limit.

min wins ttl (G) This option tells `nmbd`, when it's acting as a WINS server (`wins support = true`), the minimum "time to live" of NetBIOS names `nmbd` will grant (in seconds). You should never need to change this parameter. The default is 6 hours (21,600 seconds).

netbios aliases (G) This is a list of names `nmbd` will advertise as additional names by which the Samba server is known. This allows one machine to appear in browse lists under multiple names. If a machine is acting as a browse server or logon server, none of these names will be advertised as either browse server or logon server; only the primary name of the machine will be advertised with these capabilities. See also *netbios name*.

netbios name (G) This sets the NetBIOS name by which a Samba server is known. By default, it is the same as the first component of the host's DNS name. If a machine is a browse server or logon server, this name (or the first component of the host's DNS name) will be the name under which these services are advertised. See *netbios aliases*.

nis homedir (G) Use this option to get the home share server from a NIS (or YP) map. For UNIX systems that use an automounter, the user's home directory will often be mounted on a workstation on demand from a remote server. When the Samba logon server is not the actual home directory server, two network hops are required to access the home directory. This can be very slow, especially with writing via Samba to an NFS mounted directory. The `nis homedir` option allows Samba to return the home share as being on a different server than the logon server. As long as a Samba daemon is running on the home directory server, it will be mounted on the Samba client directly from the directory server. When Samba is returning the home share to the client, it will consult the NIS (or YP) map specified in `homedir map` and return the server listed there.

null passwords (G) Allow or disallow access to accounts that have null passwords.

only guest (S) A synonym for this command is *guest only*.

only user (S) This is a Boolean option that controls whether connections with usernames not in the user= list will be allowed. By default, this option is disabled so a client can supply a username to be used by the server. Note that this also means Samba won't try to deduce usernames from the service name, which can be annoying for the [homes] section. To get around this, you could use `user = %S`, which means your "user" list will be just the service name (for home directories, this is the name of the user).

oplocks (S) This Boolean option tells `smbd` whether to issue oplocks (opportunistic locks) to file open requests on this share. The oplock code was introduced in Samba 1.9.18 and can dramatically (approximately 30% or more) improve the speed of access to files on Samba servers. It enables the clients to aggressively cache files locally, and you might want to disable this option for unreliable network environments (it is turned on by default in Windows NT Servers). For more information, see the file Speed.txt in the Samba docs/ directory. Oplocks can be selectively turned off on certain files on a per-share basis. See *veto oplock files*.

os level (G) This integer value controls what level Samba advertises itself as for browse elections.

packet size (G) The maximum transmit packet size during a raw read. This option is no longer implemented, as of version 1.7.00, and is kept only so old configuration files do not become invalid.

passwd chat (G) This string controls the "chat" conversation that takes place between `smbd` and the local password-changing program to change the user's password. The string describes a sequence of response/receive pairs that `smbd` uses to determine what to send to the password program and what to expect back. If the expected output is not received, the password is not changed. This chat sequence is often quite site-specific, depending on the local methods used for password control (such as NIS+). The string can contain the macros `%o` and `%n`, which are substituted for the old and new passwords, respectively. It can also contain the standard macros `\n`, `\r`, `\t`, and `\s` to give line-feed, carriage-return, tab, and space.

The string can also contain an `*` to match any sequence of characters. Double quotes can be used to collect strings with spaces in them into a single string. If the send string in any part of the chat sequence is a fullstop (.), then no string will be sent. Similarly, if the expect string is a fullstop, no string is expected.

Example:

```
passwd chat = "*Enter OLD password*" %o\n "*Enter NEW password*" %n\n \

               "*Reenter NEW password*" %n\n "*Password changed*"
```

passwd program (G) This gives the name of a program that can be used to set user passwords. This is only necessary if you have enabled remote password changing at compile time. Any occurrences of `%u` will be replaced with the user name. Also note that many password programs insist on "reasonable" passwords, such as a minimum length or the inclusion of mixed case characters and digits. This can pose a problem because some clients (such as Windows for Workgroups) uppercase the password before sending it.

password level (G) Some client/server combinations have difficulty with mixed-case passwords. One offending client is Windows for Workgroups, which for some reason forces passwords to uppercase when using the LANMAN1 protocol, but leaves them alone when using COREPLUS. This parameter defines the maximum number of characters that may be uppercase in passwords. For example, suppose the password given was FRED. If password level is set to 1 (one), the following combinations would be tried if "FRED" failed: "Fred," "fred," "fRed," "frEd," "freD." If password level was set to 2 (two), the following combinations would also be tried: "Fred," "FrEd," "FreD," "fREd," "fReD," "frED." And so on.

The higher the value of this parameter, the more likely it is that a mixed-case password will be matched against a single-case password. However, you should be aware that use of this parameter reduces security and increases the time taken to process a new connection. A value of zero will cause only two attempts to be made—the password as is and the password in all lowercase. If you find the connections are taking too long with this option, you probably have a slow `crypt()` routine. Samba now comes with a fast `ufc crypt` you can select in the `makefile`. You should also make sure the PASSWORD_LENGTH option is correct for your system in local.h and includes.h. On most systems, only the first eight characters of a password are significant, so PASSWORD_LENGTH should be 8, but on some, longer passwords are significant. The includes.h file tries to select the right length for your system.

password server (G) By specifying the name of another SMB server (such as a Windows NT box) with this option and using `security = server`, you can get Samba to do all of its username/password validation via a remote server. This option sets the name of the password server to use. It must be a NetBIOS name, so if the machine's NetBIOS name is different from its Internet name, you might have to add its NetBIOS name to /etc/hosts. The password server must be a machine capable of using the LM1.2X002 or LM NT 0.12 protocol, and it must be in user level security mode. Note: Using a password server means your UNIX box (running Samba) is only as secure as your password server. Do not choose a password server you don't completely trust. Never point a Samba server at itself for password serving—this will cause a loop and could lock up your Samba server. The name of the password server takes the standard substitutions, but probably the only useful one is `%m`, which means the Samba server will use the incoming client as the password server. If you use this, you'd better trust your clients, and you'd better restrict them with `hosts allow`. If you list several hosts in the `password server` option, `smbd` will try each in turn until it finds one that responds. This is useful in case your primary server goes down. If you are using a WindowsNT server as your password server, you will have to ensure that your users are able to log in from the Samba server because the network logon will appear to come from there rather than from the user's workstation.

path (S) A synonym for this parameter is `directory`. This parameter specifies a directory to which the user of the service is to be given access. In the case of printable services, this is where print data will spool prior to being submitted to the host for printing. For a printable service offering guest access, the service should be read-only and the path should be world-writable and have the sticky bit set. This is not mandatory, of course, but you probably won't get the results you expect if you do otherwise. Any occurrences of `%u` in the path will be replaced with the username the client is using for connecting. Any occurrences of `%m` will be replaced by the name of the machine from which they are connecting. These replacements are very useful for setting up pseudo home directories for users. Note that this path will be based on `root dir`, if one was specified.

postexec (S) This option specifies a command to be run whenever the service is disconnected. It takes the usual substitutions. The command might be run as the root on some systems. An interesting example might be to unmount server resources:

```
postexec = /etc/umount /cdrom
```

See also *preexec*.

postscript (S) This parameter forces a printer to interpret the print files as postscript. This is done by adding a `%!` to the start of print output and is most useful when you have lots of PCs that persist in putting a Ctrl-D at the start of print jobs, which confuses your printer.

preexec (S) This option specifies a command to be run whenever users are connecting to the service. It takes the usual substitutions. An interesting example is to send the users a welcome message every time they log in. Maybe a message of the day? Here is an example:

```
preexec = csh -c 'echo \"Welcome to %S!\" ¦ /usr/local/samba/bin/smbclient
-M %m -I %I' &
```

Of course, this could get annoying after a while. See also *postexec*.

preferred master (G) This Boolean parameter determines if Samba is a preferred master browser for its workgroup. If this is set to True, Samba will force an election on startup, and it will have a slight advantage in winning the election. It is recommended to use this parameter in conjunction with `domain master = yes`, so Samba can guarantee becoming a domain master. Use this option with caution, because if several hosts (whether Samba servers, Windows 95, or NT) are preferred master browsers on the same subnet, they will each periodically and continuously attempt to become the local master browser. This will result in unnecessary broadcast traffic and reduced browsing capabilities.

preserve case (S) This determines if new filenames are created with the case the client passes, or if they are forced to be the "default" case.

`print` command (S) After a print job has finished spooling to a service, this command will be used via a `system()` call to process the spool file. Typically, the command specified will submit the spool file to the host's printing subsystem, but there is no requirement that this be the case. The server will not remove the spool file, so whatever command you specify should remove the spool file when it has been processed; otherwise, you will need to manually remove old spool files. The print command is simply a text string. It will be used verbatim, with two exceptions: all occurrences of `%s` will be replaced by the appropriate spool filename, and all occurrences of `%p` will be replaced by the appropriate printer name. The spool filename is generated automatically by the server; the printer name is discussed shortly.

The full path name will be used for the filename if `%s` is not preceded by a `/`. If you don't like this (it can stuff up some `lpq` output), use `%f` instead. Any occurrences of `%f` get replaced by the spool filename without the full path at the front. The print command MUST contain at least one occurrence of `%s` or `%f`—the `%p` is optional. At the time a job is submitted, if no printer name is supplied, the `%p` will be silently removed from the printer command. If specified in the [global] section, the print command given will be used for any printable service that does not have its own print command specified.

If there is neither a specified print command for a printable service nor a global print command, spool files will be created but not processed and (most importantly) not removed. Note that printing may fail on some UNIXes from the "nobody" account. If this happens, create an alternative guest account that can print and set the "guest account" in the [global] section. You can form quite complex print commands by realizing they are just passed to a shell. For example, the following will log a print job, print the file, and then remove it. Note that ; is the usual separator for commands in shell scripts.

```
print command = echo Printing %s >> /tmp/print.log; lpr -P %p %s; rm %s
```

You might have to vary this command considerably, depending on how you normally print files on your system.

print ok (S) See *printable*.

printable (S) A synonym for this parameter is `print ok`. If this parameter is Yes, clients may open, write to, and submit spool files on the directory specified for the service. Note that a printable service will always allow writing to the service path (user privileges permitting) via the spooling of print data. The read-only parameter controls only nonprinting access to the resource.

printcap name (G) This parameter may be used to override the compiled-in default printcap name used by the server (usually /etc/printcap). On SystemV systems that use `lpstat` to list available printers, you can use `printcap name = lpstat` to automatically obtain lists of available printers. This is the default for systems that define SYSV at compile time in Samba (this includes most SystemV-based systems). If `printcap name` is set to `lpstat` on these systems, Samba will launch `lpstat -v` and attempt to parse the output to obtain a printer list. A minimal printcap file would look something like this:

```
print1¦My Printer 1
print2¦My Printer 2
print3¦My Printer 3
print4¦My Printer 4
print5¦My Printer 5
```

where the | separates aliases of a printer. The fact that the second alias has a space in it gives a hint to Samba that it's a comment. NOTE: Under AIX, the default printcap name is /etc/qconfig. Samba will assume the file is in AIX qconfig format if the string /qconfig appears in the printcap filename.

printer (S) A synonym for this parameter is `printer name`. This parameter specifies the name of the printer to which print jobs spooled through a printable service will be sent. If specified in the [global] section, the printer name given will be used for any printable service that does not have its own printer name specified.

printer driver (S) This option enables you to control the string clients receive when they ask the server for the printer driver associated with a printer. If you are using Windows 95 or Windows NT, you can use this to automate the setup of printers on your system. You need to set this parameter to the exact string (case-sensitive) that describes the appropriate printer driver for your system. If you don't know the exact string to use, you should first try with no `printer driver` option set and the client will give you a list of printer drivers. The appropriate strings are shown in a scrollbox after you have chosen the printer manufacturer.

printer name (S) See *printer*.

printer driver file (G) This parameter tells Samba where the printer driver definition file, used when serving drivers to Windows 95 clients, is to be found. If this is not set, the default is :

```
SAMBA_INSTALL_DIRECTORY/lib/printers.def
```

This file is created from Windows 95 msprint.def files found on the Windows 95 client system.

printer driver location (S) This parameter tells clients of a particular printer share where to find the printer driver files for the automatic installation of drivers for Windows 95 machines. If Samba is set up to serve printer drivers to Windows 95 machines, this should be set to

```
\\MACHINE\PRINTER$
```

Where MACHINE is the NetBIOS name of your Samba server, and PRINTER$ is a share you set up for serving printer driver files.

printing (S) This parameter controls how printer status information is interpreted on your system. It also affects the default values for the `print` command, `lpq` command, and `lprm` command. Currently, six printing styles are supported. They are `printing = bsd`, `printing = sysv`, `printing = hpux`, `printing = aix`, `printing = qnx` and `printing = plp`. To see what the defaults are for the other print commands when using these three options, use the `testparm` program. As of version 1.9.18 of Samba, this option can be set on a per-printer basis

protocol (G) The value of the parameter (a string) is the highest protocol level that will be supported by the server. Possible values are CORE, COREPLUS, LANMAN1, LANMAN2, and NT1. The relative merits of each are discussed in the README file. Normally this option should not be set as the automatic negotiation phase in the SMB protocol.

public (S) A synonym for this parameter is `guest ok`. If this parameter is Yes for a service, no password is required to connect to the service. Privileges will be those of the guest account.

read list (S) This is a list of users given read-only access to a service. If the connecting user is in this list, the user will not be given write access, no matter how the `read-only` option is set. The list can include group names by using the `@group` syntax. See also the `write list` option.

read only (S) See *writable*, for which this is an inverted synonym.

read prediction (G) This option enables or disables the read prediction code used to speed up reads from the server. When `read prediction` is enabled, the server will try to pre-read data from the last accessed file that was opened read-only while waiting for packets.

read raw (G) This parameter determines whether the server will support raw reads when transferring data to clients. If enabled, raw reads allow reads of 65,535 bytes in one packet. This typically provides a major performance benefit. However, some clients either negotiate the allowable block size incorrectly or are incapable of supporting larger block sizes, and for these clients you might need to disable raw reads. In general, this parameter should be viewed as a system-tuning tool and left severely alone. See also *write raw*.

read size (G) The option `read size` affects the overlap of disk reads and writes with network reads and writes. If the amount of data being transferred in several of the SMB commands (currently `SMBwrite`, `SMBwriteX`, and `SMBreadbraw`), is larger than this value, the server begins writing the data before it has received the whole packet from the network. In the case of `SMBreadbraw`, it begins writing to the network before all data has been read from disk. This overlapping works best when the speeds of disk and network access are similar, having very little effect when the speed of one is much greater than the other. The default value is 2,048, but very little experimentation has been done yet to determine the optimal value. It is likely that the best value will vary greatly between systems, anyway. A value over 65,536 is pointless and will cause you to allocate memory unnecessarily.

remote announce (G) This option enables you to set up `nmbd` to periodically announce itself to arbitrary IP addresses with an arbitrary workgroup name. This is useful if you want your Samba server to appear in a remote workgroup for which the normal browse propagation rules don't work. The remote workgroup can be anywhere to which you can send IP packets. Here's an example:

```
remote announce = 192.168.2.255/SERVERS 192.168.4.255/STAFF
```

This line would cause `nmbd` to announce itself to the two given IP addresses, using the given workgroup names. If you leave out the workgroup name, the one given in the `workgroup` option is used instead. The IP addresses you choose would normally be the broadcast addresses of the remote networks, but can also be the IP addresses of known browse masters if your network config is that stable. This option replaces similar functionality from the `nmbd` lmhosts file.

remote browse sync (G) This option enables you to set up `nmbd` to periodically request synchronization of browse lists with the master browser of a Samba server on a remote segment. This option enables you to gain browse lists for multiple workgroups across routed networks in a manner that does not work with any non-Samba servers. This is useful if you want your Samba server and all local clients to appear in a remote workgroup for which the normal browse propagation rules don't work. The remote workgroup can be anywhere to which you can send IP packets. For example:

```
remote browse sync = 192.168.2.255 192.168.4.255
```

The above line would cause `nmbd` to request the master browser on the specified subnets or addresses to synchronize their browse lists with the local server. The IP addresses you choose would normally be the broadcast addresses of the remote networks, but can also be the IP addresses of known browse masters if your network config is that stable. If a machine IP address is given, Samba makes no attempt to validate that the remote machine is available, is listening, or is in fact the browse master on its segment.

revalidate (S) This option determines whether Samba will allow a previously validated username/password pair to be used to attach to a share. Thus, if you connect to \\server\share1 and then to \\server\share2, `revalidate` won't automatically allow the client to request connection to the second share as the same username as the first without a password. If `revalidate` is True, the client will be denied automatic access as the same username.

root (G) See *root directory*.

root dir (G) See *root directory*.

root directory (G) Synonyms for this parameter are `root dir` and `root`. The server will `chroot()` to this directory on startup. This is not strictly necessary for secure operation. Even without it, the server will deny access to files not in one of the service entries. It might also check for, and deny access to, soft links to other parts of the filesystem or attempts to use .. in filenames to access other directories (depending on the setting of the `wide links` parameter).

Adding a `root dir` entry other than `/` adds an extra level of security, but at a price. It absolutely ensures that no access is given to files not in the subtree specified in the `root dir` option, including some files needed for complete operation of the server. To maintain full operability of the server, you will need to mirror some system files into the `root dir` tree. In particular, you will need to mirror /etc/passwd (or a subset of it) and any binaries or configuration files needed for printing (if required). The set of files that must be mirrored is operating system dependent.

root postexec (S) This is the same as `postexec` except the command is run as root. This is useful for unmounting filesystems (such as CD-ROMs) after a connection is closed.

root preexec (S) This is the same as `preexec` except the command is run as root. This is useful for mounting filesystems (such as CD-ROMs) before a connection is finalized.

security (G) This option affects how clients respond to Samba. The option sets the security mode bit in replies to protocol negotiations to turn share level security on or off. Clients decide, based on this bit, whether (and how) to transfer user and password information to the server. The default is `security=SHARE`, mainly because that was the only option at one stage. The alternatives are `security = user` or `security = server`. If your PCs use usernames that are the same as their usernames on the UNIX machine, you will want to use `security = user`. If you mostly use usernames that don't exist on the UNIX box, use `security = share`. There is a bug in WfWg that might affect your decision. When in user level security, a WfWg client will totally ignore the password you type in the Connect Drive dialog box. This makes it very difficult (if not impossible) to connect to a Samba service as anyone except the username with which you are logged into WfWg. If you use `security = server`, Samba will try to validate the username/password by passing it to another SMB server, such as an NT box. If this fails, it will revert to `security = USER`. See the `password server` option for more details.

server string (G) This controls what string will show up in the printer comment box in print manager and next to the IPC connection in Net view. It can be any string you wish to show to your users. It also sets what will appear in browse lists next to the machine name. A `%v` will be replaced with the Samba version number. A `%h` will be replaced with the hostname.

set directory (S) If `set directory = no`, users of the service may not use the `setdir` command to change directories. The `setdir` command is only implemented in the Digital Pathworks client.

shared file entries (G) This parameter is only useful when Samba has been compiled with FAST_SHARE_MODES. It specifies the number of hash bucket entries used for share-file locking. You should never change this parameter unless you have studied the source and know what you are doing.

shared mem size (G) This parameter is only useful when Samba has been compiled with FAST_SHARE_MODES. It specifies the size of the shared memory (in bytes) to use between `smbd` processes. You should never change this parameter unless you have studied the source and know what you are doing.

smb passwd file (G) This option sets the path to the encrypted smbpasswd file. This is a very dangerous option if the smb.conf is user-writable. By default, the path to the `smbpasswd` file is compiled into Samba.

smbrun (G) This sets the full path to the smbrun binary. This defaults to the value in the `makefile`. You must get this path right for many services to work correctly.

share modes (S) This enables or disables the honoring of the share modes during a file open. These modes are used by clients to gain exclusive read or write access to a file. These open modes are not directly supported by UNIX, so they are simulated by using lock files in the lock directory. The lock directory specified in smb.conf must be readable by all users. The share modes enabled by this option are DENY_DOS, DENY_ALL, DENY_READ, DENY_WRITE, DENY_NONE, and DENY_FCB. Enabling this option gives full share compatibility, but might cost a bit of processing time on the UNIX server. They are enabled by default.

short preserve case (S) This determines if new short filenames are created with the case the client passes, or if they are forced to be the default case. See the section on "Name Mangling" for a fuller discussion.

socket address (G) This option enables you to control at what address Samba will listen for connections. This is used to support multiple virtual interfaces on one server, each with a different configuration. By default, Samba will accept connections on any address.

socket options (G) This option (which can also be invoked with the `-O` command line option) enables you to set socket options to be used when talking with the client. Socket options are controls on the networking layer of the operating systems that allow the connection to be tuned.

Typically, you'll use this option to tune your Samba server for optimal performance for your local network. There is no way Samba can know what the optimal parameters are for your net, so you must experiment and choose them yourself. I strongly suggest you read the appropriate documentation for your operating system first (perhaps "man setsockopt" will help). On some systems, Samba might say `Unknown socket option` when you supply an option. This means you either mistyped it or you need to add an include file to includes.h for your OS. If the latter is the case please send the patch to (samba-bugs@samba.anu.edu.au).

Any of the supported socket options may be combined in any way you like, as long as your OS allows it. This is the list of socket options currently settable using this option:

```
SO_KEEPALIVE
SO_REUSEADDR
SO_BROADCAST
TCP_NODELAY
IPTOS_LOWDELAY
IPTOS_THROUGHPUT
SO_SNDBUF *
SO_RCVBUF *
SO_SNDLOWAT *
SO_RCVLOWAT *
```

Those marked with a. `*` take an integer argument. The others can optionally take a 1 or 0 argument to enable or disable the option. They will be enabled by default if you don't specify 1 or 0.

To specify an argument, use the syntax SOME_OPTION=VALUE (for example, SO_SNDBUF=8192). Note that you must not have any spaces before or after the equals sign. If you are on a local network, a sensible option might be `socket options = IPTOS_LOWDELAY`.If you have an almost unloaded local network and you don't mind a lot of extra CPU usage in the server, you could try `socket options = IPTOS_LOWDELAY TCP_NODELAY`. If you are on a wide area network, perhaps try setting `IPTOS_THROUGHPUT`.

Note that several of the options might cause your Samba server to fail completely. Use these options with caution.

status (G) This enables or disables logging of connections to a status file that `smbstatus` can read. With this disabled, `smbstatus` won't be able to tell you what connections are active.

strict locking (S) This is a Boolean that controls the handling of file-locking in the server. When this is set to Yes, the server will check every read and write access for file locks and deny access if locks exist. This can be slow on some systems. When strict locking is No, the server does file-lock checks only when the client explicitly asks for them. Well-behaved clients always ask for lock checks when it is important, so in the vast majority of cases, `strict locking = no` is preferable.

strip dot (G) This is a Boolean that controls whether to strip trailing dots off of UNIX filenames. This helps with some CD-ROMs that have filenames ending in a single dot.

syslog (G) This parameter maps how Samba debug messages are logged onto the system syslog logging levels. Samba debug level 0 maps onto syslog LOG_ERR, debug level 1 maps onto LOG_WARNING, debug level 2 maps to LOG_NOTICE, debug level 3 maps onto LOG_INFO. The parameter sets the threshold for doing the mapping; all Samba debug messages above this threshold are mapped to syslogLOG_DEBUG messages.

syslog only (G) If this parameter is set, Samba debug messages are logged into the system syslog only and not to the debug log files.

sync always (S) This is a Boolean parameter that controls whether writes will always be written to stable storage before the write call returns. If this is False, the server will be guided by the client's request in each write call (clients can set a bit indicating a particular write should be synchronous). If this is True, every write will be followed by a `fsync()` call to ensure the data is written to disk.

time offset (G) This parameter is a setting in minutes to add to the normal GMT to local time conversion. This is useful if you are serving a lot of PCs that have incorrect handling of daylight saving time.

time server (G) This parameter determines whether `nmbd` advertises itself as a time server to Windows clients. The default is False.

unix realname (G) When set, this Boolean parameter causes Samba to supply the real name field from the UNIX password file to the client. This is useful for setting up mail clients and WWW browsers on systems used by more than one person.

user (S) See *username.*

username (S) A synonym for this parameter is *user*. Multiple users can be specified in a comma-delimited list, in which case, the supplied password will be tested against each username in turn (left to right). The `username=` line is needed only when the PC is unable to supply its own username. This is the case for the COREPLUS protocol or when your users have WfWg usernames different from their UNIX usernames. In both cases, you might better use the \\server\share%user syntax instead. The `username=` line is not a great solution in many cases, because Samba will try to validate the supplied password against each of the usernames in the `username=` line in turn. This is slow and a bad idea for lots of users in case of duplicate passwords. You might get timeouts or security breaches by using this parameter unwisely.

Samba relies on the underlying UNIX security. The `username` parameter does not restrict who can log in; it just offers hints to the Samba server as to what usernames might correspond to the supplied password. Users can log in as whomever they please, and they will be able to do no more damage than if they started a Telnet session. The daemon runs as for the username they used, so they cannot do anything that user cannot do. To restrict a service to a particular set of users, you can use the `valid users=` line.

If any of the usernames begin with a `@`, the name will be looked up in the groups file and will expand to a list of all users in the group of that name. Note that searching though a groups file can take quite some time, and some clients might time out during the search.

username level (G) This option helps Samba try to "guess" the real UNIX username, because many DOS clients send an all-uppercase username. By default, Samba tries all-lowercase, followed by the username with the first letter capitalized, and fails if the username is not found on the UNIX machine. If this parameter is set to non-zero, the behavior changes. This parameter is a number that specifies the number of uppercase combinations to try while trying to determine the UNIX user name. The higher the number, the more combinations will be tried, but the slower the discovery of usernames will be. Use this parameter when you have strange usernames on your UNIX machine, such as "AstrangeUser."

username map (G) This option enables you to specify a file containing a mapping of usernames from the clients to the server. This can be used for several purposes. The most common is to map usernames users use on DOS or Windows machines to those the UNIX box uses. The other is to map multiple users to a single username so they can more easily share files. The map file is parsed line by line. Each line should contain a single UNIX username on the left, and then an equals sign (=), followed by a list of usernames on the right. The list of usernames on the right might contain names of the form `@group`, in which case they will match any UNIX username in that group. The special client name `*` is a wildcard and matches any name. The file is processed on each line by taking the supplied username and comparing it with each username on the right side of the equals signs. If the supplied name matches any of the names on the right side, it is replaced with the name on the left. Processing then continues with the next line. If any line begins with a pound sign (#) or a semicolon (;), it is ignored. If any line begins with an exclamation point (!, the processing stops after that line if a mapping was done by the line. Otherwise, mapping continues, with every line being processed. An exclamation point is most useful when you have a wildcard mapping line later in the file.

For example, to map from the name "admin" or "administrator" to the UNIX name "root," you would use

```
root = admin administrator
```

Or to map anyone in the UNIX group "system" to the UNIX name "sys," you would use

```
sys = @system
```

You can have as many mappings as you like in a username map file. You can map Windows usernames that have spaces in them by using double quotes around the name. For example,

```
tridge = "Andrew Tridgell"
```

would map the Windows username "Andrew Tridgell" to the UNIX username "tridge." The following example would map "mary" and "fred" to the UNIX user "sys" and map the rest to "guest." Note the use of the ! to tell Samba to stop processing if it gets a match on that line.

```
!sys = mary fred
guest = *
```

The remapping is applied to all occurrences of usernames. Thus, if you connect to "\\server\fred," and "fred" is remapped to "mary," you will actually be connecting to "\\server\mary" and will need to supply a password suitable for "mary," not "fred." The only exception to this is the username passed to the "password server" (if you have one). The password server will receive whatever username the client supplies, without modification. Also note that no reverse mapping is done. The main effect this has is with printing. Users who have been mapped might have trouble deleting print jobs, because PrintManager under WfWg will think they don't own the print job.

valid chars (S) This option enables you to specify additional characters that should be considered valid by the server in filenames. This is particularly useful for national character sets, such as adding `u-umlaut` or `a-ring`. The option will take a list of characters in integer or character form, with spaces between them. If you give two characters with a colon between them, it will be taken as a lowercase:uppercase pair. If you have an editor capable of entering the characters into the config file, it is probably easiest to use this method. Otherwise, you can specify the characters in octal, decimal, or hexadecimal form, using the usual C notation. For example, to add the single character *Z* to the charset (which is a pointless thing to do, because it's already there), you could do one of the following:

```
valid chars = Z valid chars = z:Z valid chars = 0132:0172
```

The last two examples actually add two characters and alter the uppercase and lowercase mappings appropriately. Note that you MUST specify this parameter after the `client code page` parameter if you have both set. If `client code page` is set after the `valid chars` parameter, the `valid chars` settings will be overwritten. See also the `client code page` parameter.

valid users (S) This is a list of users who should be allowed to log in to this service. A name starting with `@` is interpreted as a UNIX group. If this parameter is empty (the default), any user can log in. If a username is in both this list and the `invalid users` list, access will be denied for that user. The current servicename is substituted for `%S`. This is useful in the [homes] section. See also *invalid users*.

veto files(S) This is a list of files and directories that are neither visible nor accessible. Entries in the list must be separated by a `/`, which allows spaces to be included in the entry. The `*` and `?` can be used to specify multiple files or directories, as in DOS wildcards. Each entry must be a UNIX path, not a DOS path, and must not include the UNIX directory separator `/`. Note that the case sensitivity option is applicable in vetoing files. Here's one feature of the veto files parameter you should be aware of: If a directory containing nothing but files that match the `veto files` parameter (which means Windows/DOS clients cannot ever see them) is deleted, the veto files within that directory are automatically deleted along with it, if the user has UNIX permissions to do so.

Setting this parameter will affect the performance of Samba, which will be forced to check all files and directories for a match as they are scanned. See also *hide files* and *case sensitive*.

veto oplock files (S) This parameter is only valid when the `oplocks` parameter is turned on for a share. It enables the Samba administrator to selectively turn off the granting of oplocks on selected files that match a wildcarded list, similar to the wildcarded list used in the `veto files` parameter.

volume (S) This enables you to override the volume label returned for a share. It's useful for CD-ROMs with installation programs that insist on a particular volume label.

wide links (S) This parameter controls whether links in the UNIX filesystem can be followed by the server. Links that point to areas within the directory tree exported by the server are always allowed; this parameter controls access only to areas that are outside the directory tree being exported.

wins proxy (G) This is a Boolean that controls if `nmbd` will respond to broadcast name queries on behalf of other hosts. You might need to set this to No for some older clients.

wins server (G) This specifies the DNS name (or IP address) of the WINS server with which Samba should register. If you have a WINS server on your network, you should set this to the WINS server's name. You should point this at your WINS server if you have a multi-subnetted network.

wins support (G) This Boolean controls whether Samba will act as a WINS server. You should not set this to True unless you have a multi-subnetted network and wish a particular `nmbd` to be your WINS server. NOTE: You should never set this to True on more than one machine in your network.

workgroup (G) This controls what workgroup your server will appear to be in when queried by clients.

writable (S) A synonym for this parameter is `write ok`. An inverted synonym is `read only`. If this parameter is No, users of a service cannot create or modify files in the service's directory. Note that a printable service (`printable = yes`) will always allow writing to the directory (user privileges permitting), but only via spooling operations.

write list (S) This is a list of users who are given read-write access to a service. If the connecting user is in this list, the user will be given write access, no matter how the `read only` option is set. The list can include group names, using the `@group` syntax. Note that if a user in both the read list and the write list will be given write access. See also the *read list* option.

write ok (S) See *writable*.

write raw (G) This parameter controls whether the server will support raw writes when transferring data from clients.

Glossary

by Bill Ball

GLOSSARY

This is a fairly extensive glossary of terms that are related to the UNIX environment and their definitions. All the authors of this book contributed to this section.

NOTE

The language of the computer field is constantly expanding. If you cannot find a word in this glossary, it is because it is newer than anything the authors knew about or the authors decided is was so obvious that "everyone should already know it."

#—Octothorpe.

$HOME—Environment variable that points to your login directory.

$PATH—Pathname environment variable.

$PATH—The shell environment variable that contains a set of directories to be searched for UNIX commands.

.1—Files with this extension contain manual page entries. The actual extension can be any value between `1` and `9` and can have an alphabetic suffix (`.3x`, `.7`, and so on).

.ag—Applixware graphics file.

.as—Applixware spreadsheet file.

.aw—Applixware word processing file.

.bmp—Bitmap graphics file.

.c—C source file.

.C—C++ source file.

.cc—C++ source file.

.conf—Configuration file.

.cxx—C++ source file.

.db—Database file.

.dvi—Device-independent TeX output.

.gif—GIF graphics file.

.gz—File compressed using the GNU `gzip` utility.

.h—C header file.

.html—HTML document.

.jpg—JPEG graphics file.

.m—Objective C source file.

.o—Compiled object file.

.p—Pascal language source file.

.pbm—Portable bitmap graphics file.

.pdf—Adobe Acrobat file.

.ps—PostScript file

.s—Assembler language file.

.tar—`tar` file.

.tgz—Gzipped `tar` file.

.tif—TIFF graphics file.

.txt—Text document.

.Z—File compressed using the `compress` command.

/—Root directory.

/dev—Device directory.

/dev/null file—The place to send output that you are not interested in seeing; also the place to get input from when you have none (but the program or command requires something). This is also known as the *bit bucket* (where old bits go to die).

/dev/printer—Socket for local print requests.

/etc/cshrc file—The file containing shell environment characteristics common to all users that use the C Shell.

/etc/group file—This file contains information about groups, the users they contain, and passwords required for access by other users. The password might actually be in another file, the shadow group file, to protect it from attacks.

/etc/inittab file—The file that contains a list of active terminal ports for which UNIX will issue the login prompt. This also contains a list of background processes for UNIX to initialize. Some versions of UNIX use other files, such as `/etc/tty`.

/etc/motd file—Message of the day file; usually contains information the system administrator feels is important for you to know. This file is displayed when the user signs on the system.

/etc/passwd file—Contains user information and password. The password might actually be in another file, the shadow password file, to protect it from attacks.

`/etc/profile`—The file containing shell environment characteristics common to all users of the Bourne and Korn shells.

`/usr/local`—Locally developed public executables directory.

`/var/spool`—Various spool directories.

`[]`—Brackets.

`{}`—Braces.

ANSI—American National Standards Institute.

API—Application Program Interface. The specific method prescribed by a computer operating system, application, or third-party tool by which a programmer writing an application program can make requests of the operating system. Also known as Application Programmer's Interface.

`ar`—Archive utility.

arguments—See *parameters*.

ARPA—See *DARPA*.

ASCII—American Standard Code for Information Interchange. Used to represent characters in memory for most computers.

AT&T UNIX—Original version of UNIX developed at AT&T Bell Labs, later known as UNIX Systems Laboratories. Many current versions of UNIX are descendants; even BSD UNIX was derived from early AT&T UNIX.

attribute—The means of describing objects. The attributes for a ball might be rubber, red, 3 cm in diameter. The behavior of the ball might be how high it bounces when thrown. Attribute is another name for the data contained within an object (class).

`awk`—Programming language developed by A.V. Aho, P.J. Weinberger, and Brian W. Kernighan. The language is built on C syntax, includes the regular expression search facilities of `grep`, and adds in the advanced string and array handling features that are missing from the C language. `nawk`, `gawk`, and POSIX `awk` are versions of this language.

background—Processes usually running at a lower priority and with their input disconnected from the interactive session. Any input and output are usually directed to a file or other process.

background process—An autonomous process that runs under UNIX without requiring user interaction.

backup—The process of storing the UNIX system, applications, and data files on removable media for future retrieval.

`bash`—Stands for GNU Bourne Again Shell and is based on the Bourne shell, `sh`, the original command interpreter.

`biff`—Background mail notification utility.

`bison`—GNU parser generator (`yacc` replacement).

block-special—A device file that is used to communicate with a block-oriented I/O device. Disk and tape drives are examples of block devices. The block-special file refers to the entire device. You should not use this file unless you want to ignore the directory structure of the device (that is, if you are coding a device driver).

boot or boot up—The process of starting the operating system (UNIX).

Bourne shell—The original standard user interface to UNIX that supported limited programming capability.

BSD—Berkeley Software Distribution.

BSD UNIX—Version of UNIX developed by Berkeley Software Distribution and written at University of California, Berkeley.

bug—An undocumented program feature.

C—Programming language developed by Brian W. Kernighan and Dennis M. Ritchie. The C language is highly portable and available on many platforms including mainframes, PCs, and, of course, UNIX systems.

C shell—A user interface for UNIX written by Bill Joy at Berkeley. It features C programming-like syntax.

CAD—Computer-aided design.

cast—Programming construct to force type conversion.

`cat`—Concatenate files command.

CD-ROM—Compact Disk-Read Only Memory. Computer-readable data stored on the same physical form as a musical CD. Large capacity, inexpensive, slower than a hard disk, and limited to reading. There are versions that are writable (CD-R, CD Recordable) and other formats that can be written to once or many times.

CGI—Common Gateway Interface. A means of transmitting data between Web pages and programs or scripts executing on the server. Those programs can then process the data and send the results back to the user's browser through dynamically creating HTML.

character special—A device file that is used to communicate with character-oriented I/O devices like terminals, printers, or network communications lines. All I/O access is treated as a series of bytes (characters).

characters, **alphabetic**—The letters A through Z and a through z.

characters, alphanumeric—The letters A through Z and a through z, and the numbers 0 through 9.

characters, control—Any nonprintable characters. The characters are used to control devices, separate records, and eject pages on printers.

characters, numeric—The numbers 0 through 9.

characters, special—Any of the punctuation characters or printable characters that are not alphanumeric. Include the space, comma, period, and many others.

child process—See *subprocess*.

child shell—See *subshell*.

class—A model of objects that have attributes (data) and behavior (code or functions). It is also viewed as a collection of objects in their abstracted form.

command-line editing—UNIX shells support the ability to recall a previously entered command, modify it, and then execute the new version. The command history can remain between sessions (the commands you did yesterday can be available for you when you log in today). Some shells support a command-line editing mode that uses a subset of the `vi`, `emacs`, or `gmacs` editor commands for command recall and modification.

command-line history—See *command-line editing*.

command-line parameters—Used to specify parameters to pass to the execute program or procedure. Also known as *command-line arguments*.

configuration files—Collections of information used to initialize and set up the environment for specific commands and programs. Shell configuration files set up the user's environment.

configuration files, shell—For Bourne shell: `/etc/profile` and `$HOME/.profile`.

For Korn and `pdksh` shells: `/etc/profile`, `$HOME/.profile`, and `ENV= file`.

For C and `tcsh` shells: `/etc/.login`, `/etc/cshrc`, `$HOME/.login`, `$HOME/.cshrc`, and `$HOME/.logout`. Older versions might not support the first two files listed.

For `bash`: `/etc/profile/`, `$HOME/.bash_profile`, `$HOME/.bash_login`, `$HOME/.profile`, `$HOME/.bashrc`, and `~/.bash_logout`.

CPU—Central Processing Unit. The primary "brain" of the computer—the calculation engine and logic controller.

daemon—A system-related background process that often runs with the permissions of root and services requests from other processes.

DARPA—(U.S. Department of) Defense Advanced Research Projects Agency. Funded development of TCP/IP and ARPAnet (predecessor of the Internet).

database server—See *server, database*.

device file—File used to implement access to a physical device. This provides a consistent approach to access of storage media under UNIX; data files and devices (like tapes and communication facilities) are implemented as files. To the programmer, there is no real difference.

directory—A means of organizing and collecting files together. The directory itself is a file that consists of a list of files contained within it. The root (`/`) directory is the top level and every other directory is contained in it (directly or indirectly). A directory might contain other directories, known as *subdirectories*.

directory navigation—The process of moving through directories is known as navigation. Your current directory is known as the current working directory. Your login directory is known as the default or home directory. Using the `cd` command, you can move up and down through the tree structure of directories.

DNS—Domain Name Server. Used to convert between the name of a machine on the Internet (`name.domain.com`) to the numeric address (`123.45.111.123`).

DOS—Disk Operating System. Operating system that is based on the use of disks for the storage of commands. It is also a generic name for MS-DOS and PC-DOS on the personal computer. MS-DOS is the version Microsoft sells; PC-DOS is the version IBM sells. Both are based on Microsoft code.

`double`—Double-precision floating point.

dpi—Dots per inch.

EBCDIC—Extended Binary Coded Decimal Interchange Code. The code used to represent characters in memory for mainframe computers.

`ed`—A common tool used for line-oriented text editing.

`elm`—Interactive mail program.

`emacs`—A freely available editor now part of the GNU software distribution. Originally written by Richard M. Stallman at MIT in the late 1970s, it is available for many platforms. It is extremely extensible and has its own programming language; the name stands for editing with macros.

email—Messages sent through an electronic medium instead of through the local postal service. There are many proprietary e-mail systems that are designed to handle mail within a LAN environment; most of these are also able to send over the Internet. Most Internet (open) e-mail systems make use of MIME to handle attached data (which can be binary).

encapsulation—The process of combining data (attributes) and functions (behavior in the form of code) into an object. The data and functions are closely coupled within an object. Instead of all programmers being able to access the data in a structure their own way, they have to use the code connected with that data. This promotes code reuse and standardized methods of working with the data.

environment variables—See *variables, environmental.*

Ethernet—A networking method where the systems are connected to a single shared bus and all traffic is available to every machine. The data packets contain an identifier of the recipient, and that is the only machine that should process that packet.

expression—A constant, variable, or operands and operators combined. Used to set a value, perform a calculation, or set the pattern for a comparison (regular expressions).

FIFO—First In, First Out. See *pipe, named.*

file—Collection of bytes stored on a device (typically a disk or tape). Can be source code, executable binaries or scripts, or data.

file compression—The process of applying mathematical formulas to data, typically resulting in a form of the data that occupies less space. A compressed file can be uncompressed, resulting in the original file. When the compress/uncompress process results in exactly the same file as was originally compressed, it is known as lossless. If information about the original file is lost, the compression method is known as lossy. Data and programs need lossless compression; images and sounds can stand lossy compression.

file, indexed—A file based on a file structure where data can be retrieved based on specific keys (name, employee number, and so on) or sequentially. The keys are stored in an index. This is not directly supported by the UNIX operating system; usually implemented by the programmer or by using tools from an ISV. A typical form is known as *ISAM.*

file, line sequential—See *file, text.*

file, sequential—This phrase can mean either a file that can only be accessed sequentially (not randomly), or a file without record separators (typically fixed length, but UNIX does not know what that length is and does not care).

file, text—A file with record separators. Can be fixed or variable length; UNIX tools can handle these files because the tools can tell when the record ends (by the separator).

filename—The name used to identify a collection of data (a file). Without a pathname, it is assumed to be in the current directory.

filename generation—The process of the shell interpreting metacharacters (wildcards) to produce a list of matching files. This is referred to as filename expansion or globbing.

filename, fully qualified—The name used to identify a collection of data (a file) and its location. It includes both the path and name of the file; typically, the pathname is fully specified (absolute). See also *pathname* and *pathname, absolute.*

filesystem—A collection of disk storage that is connected (mounted) to the directory structure at some point (sometimes at the root). Filesystems are stored in a disk partition and are sometimes referred to as being the disk partition.

`finger`—User information lookup program.

firewall—A system used to provide a controlled entry point to the internal network from the outside (usually the Internet). This is used to prevent outside or unauthorized systems from accessing systems on your internal network. The capability depends on the individual software package, but the features typically include filter packets and filter datagrams, system (name or IP address) aliasing, and rejecting packets from certain IP addresses. In theory, it provides protection from malicious programs or people on the outside. It can also prevent internal systems from accessing the Internet on the outside. The name comes from the physical barrier between connected buildings or within a single building that is supposed to prevent fire from spreading from one to another.

flags—See *options*.

`float`—Single-precision floating point.

foreground—Programs running while connected to the interactive session.

`fseek`—Internal function used by UNIX to locate data inside a file or filesystem. ANSI standard `fseek` accepts a parameter that can hold a value of +2 to -2 billion. This function, used by the operating system, system tools, and application programs, is the cause of the 2GB file and filesystem size limitation on most systems. With 64-bit operating systems, this limit is going away.

FSF—Free Software Foundation.

FTP—File Transfer Protocol or File Transfer Program. A system-independent means of transferring files between systems connected via TCP/IP. Ensures that the file is transferred correctly, even if there are errors during transmission. Can usually handle character set conversions (ASCII/EBCDIC) and record terminator resolution (linefeed for UNIX, carriage return and linefeed for MS/PC-DOS).

gateway—A combination of hardware, software, and network connections that provides a link between one architecture and another. Typically, a gateway is used to connect a LAN or UNIX server with a mainframe (that uses SNA for networking, resulting in the name SNA gateway). A gateway can also be the connection between the internal and external network (often referred to as a firewall). See also *firewall*.

GID—Group ID number.

globbing—See *filename generation*.

GNU—GNU stands for GNU's Not UNIX, and is the name of free useful software packages commonly found in UNIX environments that are being distributed by the GNU project at MIT, largely through the efforts of Richard Stallman. The circular acronym name ("GNU" containing the acronym GNU as one of the words it stands for) is a joke on Richard Stallman's part. One of the textbooks on operating system design is titled *XINU: XINU Is Not UNIX*, and GNU follows in that path.

GPL—GNU General Public License.

grep—A common tool used to search a file for a pattern. egrep and fgrep are newer versions. egrep allows the use of extended (hence the *e* prefix) regular expressions; fgrep uses limited expressions for faster (hence the *f* prefix) searches.

GUI—Graphical user interface.

here document—The << redirection operator, known as *here document*, allows keyboard input (stdin) for the program to be included in the script.

HTML—Hypertext Markup Language. Describes World Wide Web pages. It is the document language that is used to define the pages available on the Internet through the use of tags. A browser interprets the HTML to display the desired information.

i-node—Used to describe a file and its storage. The directory contains a cross-reference between the i-node and pathname/filename combination. Also known as *inode*. A file's entry in disk data structure (ls -i).

I-Phone—Internet Phone. This is a method of transmitting speech long distances over the Internet in near real-time. Participants avoid paying long distance telephone charges. They still pay for the call to their ISP and the ISP's service charges.

ICCCM—Inter-Client Communications Conventions Manual.

ICMP—Internet Control Message Protocol. Part of TCP/IP that provides network layer management and control.

imake—C preprocessor interface to make utility.

inheritance—A method of object-oriented software reuse in which new classes are developed based on existing ones by using the existing attributes and behavior and adding on to them. If the base object is automobiles (with attributes of engine and four wheels and tires; behavior of acceleration, turning, deceleration), a sports car would modify the attributes: engine might be larger or have more horsepower than the default, the four wheels might include alloy wheels and high-speed–rated tires; the behavior would also be modified: faster acceleration, tighter turning radius, faster deceleration.

inode—See *i-node*.

int—Integer.

Internet—A collection of different networks that provide the ability to move data between them. It is built on the TCP/IP communications protocol. Originally developed by DARPA, it was taken over by NSF, and has now been released from governmental control.

Internet Service Provider—The people that connect you to the Internet.

IRC—Internet relay chat. A server-based application that allows groups of people to communicate simultaneously through text-based conversations. IRC is similar to Citizen Band radio or the chat rooms on some bulletin boards. Some chats can be private (between invited people only) or public (where anyone can join in). IRC now also supports sound files as well as text; it can also be useful for file exchange.

ISAM—Indexed Sequential Access Method. On UNIX and other systems, ISAM refers to a method for accessing data in a keyed or sequential way. The UNIX operating system does not directly support ISAM files; they are typically add-on products.

ISO—International Standards Organization.

ISP—See *Internet Service Provider.*

ISV—Independent Software Vendor. Generic name for software vendors other than your hardware vendor.

K&R—Kernighan and Ritchie.

kernel—The core of the operating system that handles tasks like memory allocation, device input and output, process allocation, security, and user access. UNIX tends to have a small kernel when compared to other operating systems.

keys, control—These are keys that cause some function to be performed instead of displaying a character. These functions have names: The end-of-file key tells UNIX that there is no more input; it is usually Ctrl+D.

keys, special—See *keys, control.*

Korn shell—A user interface for UNIX with extensive scripting (programming) support. Written by David G. Korn. The shell features command-line editing and will also accept scripts written for the Bourne shell.

LAN—Local Area Network. A collection of networking hardware, software, desktop computers, servers, and hosts all connected together within a defined local area. A LAN could be an entire college campus.

limits—See *quota.*

link file—File used to implement a symbolic link producing an alias on one filesystem for a file on another. The file contains only the fully qualified filename of the original (linked-to) file.

link, hard—Directory entry that provides an alias to another file within the same filesystem. Multiple entries appear in the directory (or other directories) for one physical file without replication of the contents.

link, soft—See *link, symbolic.*

link, symbolic—Directory entry that provides an alias to another file that can be in another filesystem. Multiple entries appear in the directory for one physical file without replication of the contents. Implemented through link files; see also *link file.*

LISP—List Processing Language.

login—The process with which a user gains access to a UNIX system. This can also refer to the user ID that is typed at the login prompt.

lp—Line printer.

`lpc`—Line printer control program.

`lpd`—Line printer daemon.

`lpq`—Printer spool queue examination program.

`lprm`—Printer spool queue job removal program.

`ls`—List directory(s) command.

man page—Online reference tool under UNIX that contains the documentation for the system—the actual pages from the printed manuals. It is stored in a searchable form for improved ability to locate information.

manual page—See *man page*.

memory, real—The amount of storage that is being used within the system (silicon; it used to be magnetic cores).

memory, virtual—Memory that exists but you cannot see. Secondary storage (disk) is used to allow the operating system to enable programs to use more memory than is physically available.

Part of a disk is used as a paging file and portions of programs and their data are moved between it and real memory. To the program, it is in real memory. The hardware and operating system performs translation between the memory address the program thinks it is using and where it is actually stored.

metacharacter—A printing character that has special meaning to the shell or another command. It is converted into something else by the shell or command; the asterisk (`*`) is converted by the shell to a list of all files in the current directory.

MIME—Multipurpose Internet Mail Extensions. A set of protocols or methods of attaching binary data (executable programs, images, sound files, and so on) or additional text to email messages.

`motd`—Message of the day.

MPTN—MultiProtocol Transport Network. IBM networking protocol to connect mainframe to TCP/IP network.

Mrm—Motif resource manager.

mtu—Maximum transmission unit.

`mwm`—Motif window manager.

Netnews—This is a loosely controlled collection of discussion groups. A message (similar to an email) is posted in a specific area, and then people can comment on it, publicly replying to the same place (posting a response) for others to see. A collection of messages along the same theme is referred to as a thread. Some of the groups are moderated, which means that nothing is posted without the approval of the owner. Most are not, and the title of the group is no guarantee that the discussion will be related. The official term for this is Usenet news.

NFS—Network File System. Means of connecting disks that are mounted to a remote system to the local system as if they were physically connected.

NIS—Network Information Service. A service that provides information necessary to all machines on a network, such as NFS support for hosts and clients, password verification, and so on.

NNTP—Netnews Transport Protocol. Used to transmit Netnews or Usenet messages over top of TCP/IP. See *Netnews* for more information on the messages transmitted.

Null Statement—A program step that performs no operation but to hold space and fulfill syntactical requirements of the programming language. Also known as a *NO-OP* for no-operation performed.

object—An object in the truest sense of the word is something that has physical properties, like automobiles, rubber balls, and clouds. These things have attributes and behavior. They can be abstracted into data (attribute) and code (behavior). Instead of just writing functions to work on data, they are encapsulated into a package that is known as an object.

operator—Metacharacter that performs a function on values or variables. The plus sign (+) is an operator that adds two integers.

options—Program- or command-specific indicators that control behavior of that program. Sometimes called *flags*. The `-a` option to the `ls` command shows the files that begin with . (such as `.profile`, `.kshrc`, and so on). Without it, these files would not be shown, no matter what wildcards were used. These are used on the command line. See also *parameters*.

OSF—Open Software Foundation.

parameters—Data passed to a command or program through the command line. These can be options (see *options*) that control the command or arguments that the command works on. Some have special meaning based on their position on the command line.

parent process—Process that controls another often referred to as the child process or subprocess. See also *process*.

parent process identifier—Shown in the heading of the `ps` command as PPID. The process identifier of the parent process. See also *parent process*.

parent shell—Shell (typically the login shell) that controls another, often referred to as the child shell or subshell. See also *shell.*

password—The secure code that is used in combination with a user ID to gain access to a UNIX system.

pathname—The means used to represent the location of a file in the directory structure. If you do not specify a pathname, it defaults to the current directory.

pathname, absolute—The means used to represent the location of a file in a directory by specifying the exact location, including all directories in the chain including the root.

pathname, relative—The means used to represent the location of a file in a directory other than the current by navigating up and down through other directories using the current directory as a base.

PDP—Personal Data Processor. Computers manufactured by Digital Equipment Corporation. UNIX was originally written for a PDP-7 and gained popularity on the PDP-11. The entire series were inexpensive minicomputers popular with educational institutions and small businesses.

Perl—Programming language developed by Larry Wall. (Perl stands for "Practical Extraction and Report Language" or "Pathologically Eclectic Rubbish Language"; both are equally valid.) The language provides all of the capabilities of `awk` and `sed`, plus many of the features of the shells and C.

permissions—When applied to files, they are the attributes that control access to a file. There are three levels of access: Owner (the file creator), Group (people belonging to a related group as determined by the system administrator), and Other (everyone else). The permissions are usually `r` for read, `w` for write, and `x` for execute. The execute permissions flag is also used to control who may search a directory.

PGP—Pretty Good Privacy encryption system.

`pine`—Interactive mail program.

pipe—A method of sending the output of one program (redirecting) to become the input of another. The pipe character (`¦`) tells the shell to perform the redirection.

pipe file—See *pipe, named.*

pipe, named—An expanded function of a regular pipe (redirecting the output of one program to become the input of another). Instead of connecting `stdout` to `stdin`, the output of one program is sent to the named pipe and another program reads data from the same file. This is implemented through a special file known as a pipe file or FIFO. The operating system ensures the proper sequencing of the data. Little or no data is actually stored in the pipe file; it just acts as a connection between the two.

polymorphism—Allows code to be written in a general fashion to handle existing and future related classes. Properly developed, the same behavior can act differently depending on the derived object it acts on. With an automobile, the acceleration behavior might be different for a station wagon and a dragster, which are subclasses of the superclass automobile. The function would still be `accelerate()`, but the version would vary (this might sound confusing, but the compiler keeps track and figures it all out).

POSIX—Portable Operating System Interface, UNIX. POSIX is the name for a family of open system standards based on UNIX. The name has been credited to Richard Stallman. The POSIX Shell and Utilities standard developed by IEEE Working Group 1003.2 (POSIX.2) concentrates on the command interpreter interface and utility programs.

PostScript—Adobe Systems, Inc. printer language.

PPP—Point-to-Point Protocol. Internet protocol over serial link (modem).

`pppd`—Point-to-Point-Protocol daemon.

`printcap`—Printer capability database.

process—A discrete running program under UNIX. The user's interactive session is a process. A process can invoke (run) and control another program that is then referred to as a subprocess. Ultimately, everything a user does is a subprocess of the operating system.

process identifier—Shown in the heading of the `ps` command as `PID`. The unique number assigned to every process running in the system.

`pwd`—Print working directory command.

quota—General description of a system-imposed limitation on a user or process. It can apply to disk space, memory usage, CPU usage, maximum number of open files, and many other resources.

quoting—The use of single and double quotes to negate the normal command interpretation and concatenate all words and whitespace within the quotes as a single piece of text.

RCS—Revision Control System.

redirection—The process of directing a data flow from the default. Input can be redirected to get data from a file or the output of another program. Normal output can be sent to another program or a file. Errors can be sent to another program or a file.

regular expression—A way of specifying and matching strings for shells (filename wildcarding), `grep` (file searches), `sed`, and `awk`.

reserved word—A set of characters that are recognized by UNIX and related to a specific program, function, or command.

RFC—Request For Comment. Document used for creation of Internet- and TCP/IP-related standards.

`rlogin`—Remote Login. Gives the same functionality as `telnet`, with the added functionality of not requiring a password from trusted clients, which can also create security concerns (see also *`telnet`*).

root—The user that owns the operating system and controls the computer. The processes of the operating system run as though a user, root, signed on and started them. Root users are all-powerful and can do anything they want. For this reason, they are often referred to as superusers. Root is also the very top of the directory tree structure.

routing—The process of moving network traffic between two different physical networks; also decides which path to take when there are multiple connections between the two machines. It might also send traffic around transmission interruptions.

RPC—Remote Procedural Call. Provides the ability to call functions or subroutines that run on a remote system from the local one.

RPM—Red Hat Package Manager.

script—A program written for a UNIX utility including shells, `awk`, Perl, `sed`, and others. See also *shell scripts*.

SCSI—Small Computer System Interface.

`sed`—A common tool used for stream text editing, having `ed`-like syntax.

server, database—A system designated to run database software (typically a relational database like Oracle, SQL Server, Sybase, or others). Other systems connect to this one to get the data (client applications).

SGID—Set group ID.

shell—The part of UNIX that handles user input and invokes other programs to run commands. Includes a programming language. See also Bourne shell, C shell, Korn shell, `tcsh`, and `bash`.

shell environment—The shell program (Bourne, Korn, C, `tcsh`, or `bash`), invocation options and preset variables that define the characteristics, features, and functionality of the UNIX command-line and program execution interface.

shell or command prompt—The single character or set of characters that the UNIX shell displays for which a user can enter a command or set of commands.

shell scripts—A program written using a shell programming language like those supported by Bourne, Korn, or C shells.

signal—A special flag or interrupt that is used to communicate special events to programs by the operating system and other programs.

SLIP—Serial Line Internet Protocol. Internet over a serial line (modem). The protocol frames and controls the transmission of TCP/IP packets of the line.

SNA—System Network Architecture. IBM networking architecture.

stderr—The normal error output for a program that is sent to the screen by default. Can be redirected to a file.

stdin—The normal input for a program, taken from the keyboard by default. Can be redirected to get input from a file or the output of another program.

stdout—The normal output for a program that is sent to the screen by default. Can be redirected to a file or to the input of another program.

sticky bit—One of the status flags on a file that tells UNIX to load a copy of the file into the page file the first time it is executed. This is done for programs that are commonly used so the bytes are available quickly. When the sticky bit is used on frequently used directories, it is cached in memory.

stream—A sequential collection of data. All files are streams to the UNIX operating system. To it, there is no structure to a file; that is something imposed by application programs or special tools (ISAM packages or relational databases).

subdirectory—See *directory*.

subnet—A portion of a network that shares a common IP address component. Used for security and performance reasons.

subprocess—Process running under the control of another, often referred to as the parent process. See also *process*.

subshell—Shell running under the control of another, often referred to as the parent shell (typically the login shell). See also *shell*.

SUID—Set user ID.

superuser—Usually the root operator.

sysadmin—Burnt-out root operator (system administrator).

system administrator—The person who takes care of the operating system and user administrative issues on UNIX systems. Also called a *system manager*, although that term is much more common in DEC VAX installations.

system manager—See *system administrator*.

system programmer—See *system administrator*.

tar—Tape archiving utility.

TCP—Transmission Control Protocol.

TCP/IP—Transport Control Protocol/Internet Protocol. The pair of protocols and also generic name for suite of tools and protocols that forms the basis for the Internet. Originally developed to connect systems to the ARPAnet.

tcsh—A C shell-like user interface featuring command-line editing.

telnet—Remote login program.

Telnet—Protocol for interactive (character user interface) terminal access to remote systems. The terminal emulator that uses the Telnet protocol is often known as `telnet` or `tnvt100`.

termcap—Terminal capability database.

terminal—A hardware device, normally containing a cathode ray tube (screen) and keyboard for human interaction with a computer system.

text processing languages—A way of developing documents in text editors with embedded commands that handle formatting. The file is fed through a processor that executes the embedded commands, producing a formatted document. These include `roff`, `nroff`, `troff`, `RUNOFF`, TeX, LaTeX, and even the mainframe `SCRIPT`.

TFTP—Trivial File Transfer Protocol or Trivial File Transfer Program. A system-independent means of transferring files between systems connected via TCP/IP. It is different from FTP in that it does not ensure that the file is transferred correctly, does not authenticate users, and is missing a lot of functionality (like the `ls` command).

tin—Interactive news reader.

top—A common tool used to display information about the top processes on the system.

UDP—User Datagram Protocol. Part of TCP/IP used for control messages and data transmission where the delivery acknowledgment is not needed. The application program must ensure data transmission in this case.

UID—User ID number.

UIL—Motif User Interface Language.

URL—Uniform Resource Locator. The method of specifying the protocol, format, login (usually omitted), and location of materials on the Internet.

Usenet—See *Netnews*.

UUCP—UNIX-to-UNIX copy program. Used to build an early, informal network for the transmission of files, email, and Netnews.

variables, attributes—The modifiers that set the variable type. A variable can be string or integer, left- or right-justified, read-only or changeable, and other attributes.

variables, environmental—A place to store data and values (strings and integers) in the area controlled by the shell so they are available to the current and subprocesses. They can just be local to the current shell or available to a subshell (exported).

variables, substitution—The process of interpreting an environmental variable to get its value.

WAN—Wide Area Network.

Web—See *World Wide Web.*

whitespace—Blanks, spaces, and tabs that are normally interpreted to delineate commands and filenames unless quoted.

wildcard—Means of specifying filename(s) whereby the operating system determines some of the characters. Multiple files might match and will be available to the tool.

World Wide Web—A collection of servers and services on the Internet that run software and communicate using a common protocol (HTTP). Instead of the users' having to remember the location of these resources, links are provided from one Web page to another through the use of URLs.

WWW—See *World Wide Web.*

WYSIWYG—What You See Is What You Get.

X—See *X Window System.*

X Window System—A windowing and graphics system developed by MIT, to be used in client/server environments.

X11—See *X Window System.*

X-windows—The wrong term for the X Window System. See *X Window System.*

yacc—Yet another compiler compiler.

INDEX

SYMBOLS

A

C

D

G

H

I

J

K

L

N

Q

R

S

U

Y–Z

GNU GENERAL PUBLIC LICENSE

Version 2, June 1991

Preamble

The licenses for most software are designed to take away your freedom to share and change it. By contrast, the GNU General Public License is intended to guarantee your freedom to share and change free software—to make sure the software is free for all its users. This General Public License applies to most of the Free Software Foundation's software and to any other program whose authors commit to using it. (Some other Free Software Foundation software is covered by the GNU Library General Public License instead.) You can apply it to your programs, too.

When we speak of free software, we are referring to freedom, not price. Our General Public Licenses are designed to make sure that you have the freedom to distribute copies of free software (and charge for this service if you wish), that you receive source code or can get it if you want it, that you can change the software or use pieces of it in new free programs; and that you know you can do these things.

To protect your rights, we need to make restrictions that forbid anyone to deny you these rights or to ask you to surrender the rights. These restrictions translate to certain responsibilities for you if you distribute copies of the software, or if you modify it.

For example, if you distribute copies of such a program, whether gratis or for a fee, you must give the recipients all the rights that you have. You must make sure that they, too, receive or can get the source code. And you must show them these terms so they know their rights.

We protect your rights with two steps: (1) copyright the software, and (2) offer you this license which gives you legal permission to copy, distribute and/or modify the software.

Also, for each author's protection and ours, we want to make certain that everyone understands that there is no warranty for this free software. If the software is modified by someone else and passed on, we want its recipients to know that what they have is not the original, so that any problems introduced by others will not reflect on the original authors' reputations.

Finally, any free program is threatened constantly by software patents. We wish to avoid the danger that redistributors of a free program will individually obtain patent licenses, in effect making the program proprietary. To prevent this, we have made it clear that any patent must be licensed for everyone's free use or not licensed at all.

The precise terms and conditions for copying, distribution and modification follow.

GNU GENERAL PUBLIC LICENSE

TERMS AND CONDITIONS FOR COPYING, DISTRIBUTION AND MODIFICATION

0. This License applies to any program or other work which contains a notice placed by the copyright holder saying it may be distributed under the terms of this General Public License. The "Program", below, refers to any such program or work, and a "work based on the Program" means either the Program or any derivative work under copyright law: that is to say, a work containing the Program or a portion of it, either verbatim or with modifications and/or translated into another language. (Hereinafter, translation is included without limitation in the term "modification".) Each licensee is addressed as "you".

   Activities other than copying, distribution and modification are not covered by this License; they are outside its scope. The act of running the Program is not restricted, and the output from the Program is covered only if its contents constitute a work based on the Program (independent of having been made by running the Program). Whether that is true depends on what the Program does.

1. You may copy and distribute verbatim copies of the Program's source code as you receive it, in any medium, provided that you conspicuously and appropriately publish on each copy an appropriate copyright notice and disclaimer of warranty; keep intact all the notices that refer to this License and to the absence of any warranty; and give any other recipients of the Program a copy of this License along with the Program.

   You may charge a fee for the physical act of transferring a copy, and you may at your option offer warranty protection in exchange for a fee.

2. You may modify your copy or copies of the Program or any portion of it, thus forming a work based on the Program, and copy and distribute such modifications or work under the terms of Section 1 above, provided that you also meet all of these conditions:

   a) You must cause the modified files to carry prominent notices stating that you changed the files and the date of any change.

   b) You must cause any work that you distribute or publish, that in whole or in part contains or is derived from the Program or any part thereof, to be licensed as a whole at no charge to all third parties under the terms of this License.

   c) If the modified program normally reads commands interactively when run, you must cause it, when started running for such interactive use in the most ordinary way, to print or display an announcement including an appropriate copyright notice and a notice that there is no warranty (or else, saying that you provide a warranty) and that users may redistribute the program under these conditions, and telling the user how to view a copy of this License. (Exception: if the Program itself is interactive but does not normally print such an announcement, your work based on the Program is not required to print an announcement.)

   These requirements apply to the modified work as a whole. If identifiable sections of that work are not derived from the Program, and can be reasonably considered independent and separate works in themselves, then this License, and its terms, do not apply to those sections when you distribute them as separate works. But when you distribute the same sections as part of a whole which is a work based on the Program, the distribution of the whole must be on the terms of this License, whose permissions for other licensees extend to the entire whole, and thus to each and every part regardless of who wrote it.

   Thus, it is not the intent of this section to claim rights or contest your rights to work written entirely by you; rather, the intent is to exercise the right to control the distribution of derivative or collective works based on the Program.

   In addition, mere aggregation of another work not based on the Program with the Program (or with a work based on the Program) on a volume of a storage or distribution medium does not bring the other work under the scope of this License.

3. You may copy and distribute the Program (or a work based on it, under Section 2) in object code or executable form under the terms of Sections 1 and 2 above provided that you also do one of the following:

   a) Accompany it with the complete corresponding machine-readable source code, which must be distributed under the terms of Sections 1 and 2 above on a medium customarily used for software interchange; or,

   b) Accompany it with a written offer, valid for at least three years, to give any third party, for a charge no more than your cost of physically performing source distribution, a complete machine-readable copy of the corresponding source code, to be distributed under the terms of Sections 1 and 2 above on a medium customarily used for software interchange; or,

   c) Accompany it with the information you received as to the offer to distribute corresponding source code. (This alternative is allowed only for noncommercial distribution and only if you received the program in object code or executable form with such an offer, in accord with Subsection b above.)

   The source code for a work means the preferred form of the work for making modifications to it. For an executable work, complete source code means all the source code for all modules it contains, plus any associated interface definition files, plus the scripts used to control compilation and installation of the executable. However, as a special exception, the source code distributed need not include anything that is normally distributed (in either source or binary form) with the major components (compiler, kernel, and so on) of the operating system on which the executable runs, unless that component itself accompanies the executable.

   If distribution of executable or object code is made by offering access to copy from a designated place, then offering equivalent access to copy the source code from the same place counts as distribution of the source code, even though third parties are not compelled to copy the source along with the object code.

4. You may not copy, modify, sublicense, or distribute the Program except as expressly provided under this License. Any attempt otherwise to copy, modify, sublicense or distribute the Program is void, and will automatically terminate your rights under this License. However, parties who have received copies, or rights, from you under this License will not have their licenses terminated so long as such parties remain in full compliance.

5. You are not required to accept this License, since you have not signed it. However, nothing else grants you permission to modify or distribute the Program or its derivative works. These actions are prohibited by law if you do not accept this License. Therefore, by modifying or distributing the Program (or any work based on the Program), you indicate your acceptance of this License to do so, and all its terms and conditions for copying, distributing or modifying the Program or works based on it.

6. Each time you redistribute the Program (or any work based on the Program), the recipient automatically receives a license from the original licensor to copy, distribute or modify the Program subject to these terms and conditions. You may not impose any further restrictions on the recipients' exercise of the rights granted herein. You are not responsible for enforcing compliance by third parties to this License.

7. If, as a consequence of a court judgment or allegation of patent infringement or for any other reason (not limited to patent issues), conditions are imposed on you (whether by court order, agreement or otherwise) that contradict the conditions of this License, they do not excuse you from the conditions of this License. If you cannot distribute so as to satisfy simultaneously your obligations under this License and any other pertinent obligations, then as a consequence you may not distribute the Program at all. For example, if a patent license would not permit royalty-free redistribution of the Program by all those who receive copies directly or indirectly through you, then the only way you could satisfy both it and this License would be to refrain entirely from distribution of the Program.

If any portion of this section is held invalid or unenforceable under any particular circumstance, the balance of the section is intended to apply and the section as a whole is intended to apply in other circumstances.

It is not the purpose of this section to induce you to infringe any patents or other property right claims or to contest validity of any such claims; this section has the sole purpose of protecting the integrity of the free software distribution system, which is implemented by public license practices. Many people have made generous contributions to the wide range of software distributed through that system in reliance on consistent application of that system; it is up to the author/donor to decide if he or she is willing to distribute software through any other system and a licensee cannot impose that choice.

This section is intended to make thoroughly clear what is believed to be a consequence of the rest of this License.

8. If the distribution and/or use of the Program is restricted in certain countries either by patents or by copyrighted interfaces, the original copyright holder who places the Program under this License may add an explicit geographical distribution limitation excluding those countries, so that distribution is permitted only in or among countries not thus excluded. In such case, this License incorporates the limitation as if written in the body of this License.

9. The Free Software Foundation may publish revised and/or new versions of the General Public License from time to time. Such new versions will be similar in spirit to the present version, but may differ in detail to address new problems or concerns.

   Each version is given a distinguishing version number. If the Program specifies a version number of this License which applies to it and "any later version", you have the option of following the terms and conditions either of that version or of any later version published by the Free Software Foundation. If the Program does not specify a version number of this License, you may choose any version ever published by the Free Software Foundation.

10. If you wish to incorporate parts of the Program into other free programs whose distribution conditions are different, write to the author to ask for permission. For software which is copyrighted by the Free Software Foundation, write to the Free Software Foundation; we sometimes make exceptions for this. Our decision will be guided by the two goals of preserving the free status of all derivatives of our free software and of promoting the sharing and reuse of software generally.

NO WARRANTY

11. BECAUSE THE PROGRAM IS LICENSED FREE OF CHARGE, THERE IS NO WARRANTY FOR THE PROGRAM, TO THE EXTENT PERMITTED BY APPLICABLE LAW. EXCEPT WHEN OTHERWISE STATED IN WRITING THE COPYRIGHT HOLDERS AND/OR OTHER PARTIES PROVIDE THE PROGRAM "AS IS" WITHOUT WARRANTY OF ANY KIND, EITHER EXPRESSED OR IMPLIED, INCLUDING, BUT NOT LIMITED TO, THE IMPLIED WARRANTIES OF MERCHANTABILITY AND FITNESS FOR A PARTICULAR PURPOSE. THE ENTIRE RISK AS TO THE QUALITY AND PERFORMANCE OF THE PROGRAM IS WITH YOU. SHOULD THE PROGRAM PROVE DEFECTIVE, YOU ASSUME THE COST OF ALL NECESSARY SERVICING, REPAIR OR CORRECTION.

12. IN NO EVENT UNLESS REQUIRED BY APPLICABLE LAW OR AGREED TO IN WRITING WILL ANY COPYRIGHT HOLDER, OR ANY OTHER PARTY WHO MAY MODIFY AND/OR REDISTRIBUTE THE PROGRAM AS PERMITTED ABOVE, BE LIABLE TO YOU FOR DAMAGES, INCLUDING ANY GENERAL, SPECIAL, INCIDENTAL OR CONSEQUENTIAL DAMAGES ARISING OUT OF THE USE OR INABILITY TO USE THE PROGRAM (INCLUDING BUT NOT LIMITED TO LOSS OF DATA OR DATA BEING RENDERED INACCURATE OR LOSSES SUSTAINED BY YOU OR THIRD PARTIES OR A FAILURE OF THE PROGRAM TO OPERATE WITH ANY OTHER PROGRAMS), EVEN IF SUCH HOLDER OR OTHER PARTY HAS BEEN ADVISED OF THE POSSIBILITY OF SUCH DAMAGES.

END OF TERMS AND CONDITIONS

Linux and the GNU system

The GNU project started 12 years ago with the goal of developing a complete free Unix-like operating system. "Free" refers to freedom, not price; it means you are free to run, copy, distribute, study, change, and improve the software.

A Unix-like system consists of many different programs. We found somecomponents already available as free software—for example, X Windows and TeX. We obtained other components by helping to convince their developers to make them free—for example, the Berkeley network utilities. Other components we wrote specifically for GNU—for example, GNU Emacs, the GNU C compiler, the GNU C library, Bash, and Ghostscript. The components in this last category are "GNU software". The GNU system consists of all three categories together.

The GNU project is not just about developing and distributing free software. The heart of the GNU project is an idea: that software should be free, and that the users' freedom is worth defending. For if people have freedom but do not value it, they will not keep it for long. In order to make freedom last, we have to teach people to value it.

The GNU project's method is that free software and the idea of users' freedom support each other. We develop GNU software, and as people encounter GNU programs or the GNU system and start to use them, they also think about the GNU idea. The software shows that the idea can work in practice. People who come to agree with the idea are likely to write additional free software. Thus, the software embodies the idea, spreads the idea, and grows from the idea.

This method was working well—until someone combined the Linux kernel with the GNU system (which still lacked a kernel), and called the combination a "Linux system."

The Linux kernel is a free Unix-compatible kernel written by Linus Torvalds. It was not written specifically for the GNU project, but the Linux kernel and the GNU system work together well. In fact, adding Linux to the GNU system brought the system to completion: it made a free Unix-compatible operating system available for use.

But ironically, the practice of calling it a "Linux system" undermines our method of communicating the GNU idea. At first impression, a "Linux system" sounds like something completely distinct from the "GNU system." And that is what most users think it is.

Most introductions to the "Linux system" acknowledge the role played by the GNU software components. But they don't say that the system as a whole is more or less the same GNU system that the GNU project has been compiling for a decade. They don't say that the idea of a free Unix-like system originates from the GNU project. So most users don't know these things.

This leads many of those users to identify themselves as a separate community of "Linux users", distinct from the GNU user community. They use all of the GNU software; in fact, they use almost all of the GNU system; but they don't think of themselves as GNU users, and they may not think about the GNU idea.

It leads to other problems as well—even hampering cooperation on software maintenance. Normally when users change a GNU program to make it work better on a particular system, they send the change to the maintainer of that program; then they work with the maintainer, explaining the change, arguing for it and sometimes rewriting it, to get it installed.

But people who think of themselves as "Linux users" are more likely to release a forked "Linux-only" version of the GNU program, and consider the job done. We want each and every GNU program to work "out of the box" on Linux-based systems; but if the users do not help, that goal becomes much harder to achieve.

So how should the GNU project respond? What should we do now to spread the idea that freedom for computer users is important? We should continue to talk about the freedom to share and change software—and to teach other users to value these freedoms. If we enjoy having a free operating system, it makes sense for us to think about preserving those freedoms for the long term. If we enjoy having a variety of free software, it makes sense for to think about encouraging others to write additional free software, instead of additional proprietary software.

We should not accept the splitting of the community in two. Instead we should spread the word that "Linux systems" are variant GNU systems—that users of these systems are GNU users, and that they ought to consider the GNU philosophy which brought these systems into existence.

This article is one way of doing that. Another way is to use the terms "Linux-based GNU system" (or "GNU/Linux system" or "Lignux" for short) to refer to the combination of the Linux kernel and the GNU system.

The Linux kernel is Copyright © 1991, 1992, 1993, 1994 Linus Torvaldis (others hold copyrights on some of the drivers, file systems, and other parts of the kernel) and and is licensed under the terms of the GNU General Public License.

The FreeBSD Copyright

All of the documentation and software included in the 4.4BSD and 4.4BSD-Lite Releases is copyrighted by The Regents of the University of California.

Redistribution and use in source and binary forms, with or without modification, are permitted provided that the following conditions are met:

1. Redistributions of source code must retain the above copyright notice, this list of conditions and the following disclaimer.
2. Redistributions in binary form must reproduce the above copyright notice, this list of conditions and the following disclaimer in the documentation and/or other materials provided with the distribution.
3. All advertising materials mentioning features or use of this software must display the following acknowledgement:

   This product includes software developed by the University of California, Berkeley and its contributors.
4. Neither the name of the University nor the names of its contributors may be used to endorse or promote products derived from this software without specific prior written permission.

THIS SOFTWARE IS PROVIDED BY THE REGENTS AND CONTRIBUTORS "AS IS" AND ANY EXPRESS OR IMPLIED WARRANTIES, INCLUDING, BUT NOT LIMITED TO, THE IMPLIED WARRANTIES OF MERCHANTABILITY AND FITNESS FOR A PARTICULAR PURPOSE ARE DISCLAIMED. IN NO EVENT SHALL THE REGENTS OR CONTRIBUTORS BE LIABLE FOR ANY DIRECT, INDIRECT, INCIDENTAL, SPECIAL, EXEMPLARY, OR CONSEQUENTIAL DAMAGES (INCLUDING, BUT NOT LIMITED TO, PROCUREMENT OF SUBSTITUTE GOODS OR SERVICES; LOSS OF USE, DATA, OR PROFITS; OR BUSINESS INTERRUPTION) HOWEVER CAUSED AND ON ANY THEORY OF LIABILITY, WHETHER IN CONTRACT, STRICT LIABILITY, OR TORT (INCLUDING NEGLIGENCE OR OTHERWISE) ARISING IN ANY WAY OUT OF THE USE OF THIS SOFTWARE, EVEN IF ADVISED OF THE POSSIBILITY OF SUCH DAMAGE.

The Institute of Electrical and Electronics Engineers and the American National Standards Committee X3, on Information Processing Systems have given us permission to reprint portions of their documentation.

In the following statement, the phrase "this text" refers to portions of the system documentation.

Portions of this text are reprinted and reproduced in electronic form in the second BSD Networking Software Release, from IEEE Std 1003.1-1988, IEEE Standard Portable Operating System Interface for Computer Environments (POSIX), copyright C 1988 by the Institute of Electrical and Electronics Engineers, Inc. In the event of any discrepancy between these versions and the original IEEE Standard, the original IEEE Standard is the referee document.

In the following statement, the phrase "This material" refers to portions of the system documentation.

This material is reproduced with permission from American National Standards Committee X3, on Information Processing Systems. Computer and Business Equipment Manufacturers Association (CBEMA), 311 First St., NW, Suite 500, Washington, DC 20001-2178. The developmental work of Programming Language C was completed by the X3J11 Technical Committee.

The views and conclusions contained in the software and documentation are those of the authors and should not be interpreted as representing official policies, either expressed or implied, of the Regents of the University of California.

www@FreeBSD.ORG

What's on the CD-ROM

Disclaimer

By opening this package, you are agreeing to be bound by the following agreement:

Some of the programs included with this product are governed by the GNU General Public License, which allows redistribution; see the license information for each product for more information. Other programs are included on the CD-ROM by special permission from their authors.

You may not copy or redistribute the entire CD-ROM as a whole. Copying and redistribution of individual software programs on the CD-ROM is governed by terms set by individual copyright holders. The installer and code from the author(s) is copyrighted by the publisher and the author. Individual programs and other items on the CD-ROM are copyrighted by their various authors or other copyright holders. This software is sold as-is without warranty of any kind, either expressed or implied, including but not limited to the implied warranties of merchantability and fitness for a particular purpose. Neither the publisher nor its dealers or distributors assumes any liability for any alleged or actual damages arising from the use of this program. (Some states do not allow for the exclusion of implied warranties, so the exclusion may not apply to you.)

NOTE: This CD-ROM uses long and mixed-case filenames requiring the use of a protected-mode CD-ROM Driver.